Class struggles in the USSR

Class struggles in the USSR
by Charles Bettelheim

Translated by Brian Pearce

Second period: 1923–1930

Monthly Review Press
New York and London

NOTE: *The translation of this book into English has given the author the opportunity to check a number of his references and, as a result, to revise parts of the text.*

Originally published as *Les Luttes de classes en URSS*, copyright © 1977 by Maspero/Seuil, Paris, France.

Library of Congress Cataloging in Publication Data
Bettelheim, Charles.
  Class struggles in the USSR.
  Translation of Les Luttes de classes en URSS.
  CONTENTS: [1] First period, 1917–1923.—
[2] Second period, 1923–1930.
  Bibliography: v. 1, p. 531–537; v. 2, p.: 595.
  Includes indexes.
  1. Russia—Politics and government—1917–
2. Russia—Social conditions—1917–
3. Kommunisticheskaia Partiia Sovetskogo Soiuza.
4. Russia—History—Revolution, 1917–1921.
I. Title.
DK266.B4413   320.9′47′084   76-28986
ISBN   0–85345–396-9 (v.1) ISBN   0–85345–437-X(v.2)

Monthly Review Press
62 West 14th Street, New York, N.Y. 10011
47 Red Lion Street, London WC1R 4PF

Manufactured in the United States of America

10 9 8 7 6 5 4 3 2 1

Contents

Preface 11

Introduction to the "second period" 21

Part 1. The development of commodity and money relations and of planning in the NEP period 49

1. The reconstitution of a monetary and financial system 53

2. The development of the machinery and procedures of economic planning 73

Part 2. The village during the NEP period. Differentiation and class struggles. Agricultural policy and transformation of social relations in agriculture 83

1. The social conditions of immediate production during the NEP period 85

2. The economic and social conditions governing the reproduction and transformation of production relations in agriculture during the NEP 135

3. The reproduction and transformation of ideological and political relations in the rural areas 163

6   *Contents*

Part 3. *The contradictions and class struggles in the industrial and urban sectors*   187

1. The direct manifestations of the contradictions in the industrial and urban sectors   189

2. The contradictions between the private sector and the state sector in industry and trade   197

3. The forms of ownership in the state sector and the structure of the immediate production process   209

4. The integration of state-owned industry in the overall process of reproduction of the conditions of production   266

5. The categories of price, wages, and profit, and their class significance   285

6. The forms of organization of the working class   330

Part 4. *The changes in ideological and political relations within the Bolshevik Party*   355

1. The fight for the worker-peasant alliance   361

2. The fight for rapid industrialization and for priority for heavy industry   398

3. The Bolshevik ideological formation and its transformations   500

Part 5. *The "great change" and the emergence of new contradictions*   589

Bibliography   595

Index   607

Key to abbreviations, initials, and Russian words used in the text

Artel	A particular form of producers' cooperative
Batrak	Agricultural laborer
Bednyak	Poor peasant
CC	Central Committee of the Party
CCC	Central Control Commission of the Party
CCTU	Central Council of the Trade Unions
Chervonets	A coin equivalent to ten gold roubles or 7.7423 grams of refined gold, issued from 1923 on
CLD	Council for Labor and Defense
CLI	Central Labor Institute
CPR(B)	Communist Party of Russia (Bolsheviks)
CPSU(B)	Communist Party of the Soviet Union (Bolsheviks)
EC	Executive Committee (of a soviet)
Elektrobank	Bank for financing electrification
Glavk	Chief Administration (usually under the direction of a People's Commissariat or of the VSNKh)
Goselro	State Commission for the Electrification of Russia
Gosbank	State bank
Gosplan	State Planning Commission
GPU	State Political Administration (political police)
Khozraschet	Financial autonomy (literally "business accounting")

7

Kolkhoz	Collective farm (usually organized as an *artel*)
Kommuna	Collective farm with joint ownership of means of production carried farther than in an *artel*, and with sharing of the proceeds on the basis of members' needs
Komsomol	Young Communist League
Kontraktatsiya	System of contracts between the peasants and the state purchasing agencies
Kulak	Rich peasant
Mir	Village community
Narkomfin	People's Commissariat of Finance
Narkomtrud	People's Commissariat of Labor
NEP	New Economic Policy
NOT	"Scientific organization of work"
OGPU	Unified State Political Administration (successor to GPU)
Orgraspred	Department for organization and allocation of Party cadres
Osvok	Special commission of the VSNKh for the reconstruction of fixed capital (involved in economic planning)
PB	Political Bureau
Perekachka	Literally, "pumping"; used for the transference of resources from agriculture to industry; equivalent to the concept of "tribute" exacted from agriculture
Podkulachnik	"Abettor of kulaks"
RSDLP	Russian Social Democratic Labor Party
RSDLP(B)	Russian Social Democratic Labor Party (Bolsheviks)
Proletkult	"Proletarian culture"; name of the organization devoted to promoting this concept
Prombank	Bank for financing industry
Promfinplan	Industrial and financial plan

Rabkrin	Workers' and Peasants' Inspectorate
RKK	Commission for settling labor disputes
RSFSR	Russian Socialist Federal Soviet Republic
Serednyak	Middle peasant
Skhod	Village assembly
Sokha	Wooden plough
Sovkhoz	State farm
Sovnarkom	Council of People's Commissars
Sovznak	"Settlement note"; the currency issued under war communism
Splochnaya	"Complete" collectivization of a given area
Supryaga	Traditional form of mutual aid among peasants
Toz	Elementary form of collective farm ("association for joint cultivation of the soil")
Tsekombank	Bank responsible for financing municipal undertakings
TsGAOR	Central Archives of the October Revolution
TsIK	Central Executive Committee of the Congress of Soviets
Uchraspred	Section for listing and allocation of Party cadres (replaced by Orgraspred)
Udarnik	Shock-worker
VLKSM	All-Union Leninist Communist League of Youth, i.e., Young Communist League, or Komsomol
VSNKh	Supreme Council of the National Economy
VTsIK	All-Union Central Executive Committee (of the Congress of Soviets)
WPI	Workers' and Peasants' Inspectorate

Preface

My purpose in the present volume is to continue my analysis of the process of transformation of the Soviet social formation through the years 1923–1930, defining the way in which successes and failures were intermingled in that period, and so prepared the subsequent victories and defeats experienced by the working class and the masses of the people in the USSR.

In order to accomplish this task it is necessary to establish what the social relations were in which the agents of production were integrated, and to reconstitute as clearly as possible the fundamental class struggles of the period being considered.[1] One must also take into account the diverse forms in which actual social relations were perceived by the masses and also by the members and leaders of the Party. Finally, we have to establish the significance and social implications of the theoretical notions and political platforms around which a series of conflicts took place.

This analysis must therefore deal with a complex objective process developing on several different levels, and entailing changes each of which proceeded at its own pace, even though all were interlinked and affected each other. This compels us to renounce any sort of idealistic approach claiming to "expound" the history of the USSR as the "realization" of a certain set of "ideas"—whether those of Marx, of Lenin, or of Stalin.

In other words, only a materialist treatment of the process of transformation of the Soviet social formation will enable us really to understand this process and draw lessons from it.

Such a treatment is all the more essential today because a series of writings filled with open hostility to Marxism, and

11

mainly inspired by the works of Solzhenitsyn, are directed to presenting the history of the USSR as the "outcome" of the ideas of Marx, Engels, Lenin, and Stalin. This idealist approach is, moreover, the "counterpart" of another one, similar though with different "aims," expressed in writings of predominantly apologetic character which present the history of the USSR as the "outcome" of the decisions of the Bolshevik Party and the Soviet state, and which furthermore assume that, generally speaking (that is, leaving aside a few "mistakes" which are considered to have been more or less rapidly corrected), these decisions were directly dictated by "Marxist principles," resulting from analyses carried out in light of these principles.

A feature common to these idealist treatments of the history of the Soviet formation is that they relegate to the background (when they do not purely and simply ignore them) the movement of the objective contradictions, the various forms assumed by class struggles, and the role played by ways of seeing reality that were inherited from the past and affected the aspirations of the masses and the views of the leaders alike. For a materialist analysis of the transformation process of the Soviet formation all these factors need to be reckoned with.[2]

A materialist analysis also requires that we refuse to compare the history of the USSR with any ideal "model" from which it is supposed to have "deviated" at a certain moment, so that *from that moment* everything "took the wrong turning."

It is therefore indispensable to analyze the Soviet social formation *in its originality,* so as to understand the *unique* character of the gigantic upheavals that it has experienced. Reckoning with the *specific features* of the history of the USSR does not debar us (quite the contrary) from *drawing lessons from it for other countries and other periods,* since this history, in its singularity, possesses a universal bearing for the simple reason that the universal *does not exist* otherwise than in the form of the particular. But this universal bearing can be grasped only by means of a *concrete analysis* of the movement of the contradictions, especially of those that developed on the plane of ideology.

The pages that follow will not "present chronologically" the development of the contradictions of the period 1923–1930. *Attention will be focused on the moment when these contradictions converged,* giving rise, in 1928–1930, to a crisis which appeared as a *"general crisis of the NEP."* We shall see, moreover, that some vital aspects of this crisis were connected with the way in which the New Economic Policy was implemented, and with the ambiguous forms assumed by its gradual abandonment. In any case, analyzing this crisis will enable us to perceive a series of contradictions as they manifested themselves in their most acute form, and to trace the way that they had developed and become intermingled in the course of the preceding years, so that light is thrown upon both the *conditions that brought the crisis of 1920–1930 to a head* and also the *class consequences* of this crisis.

The contradictions analyzed in this volume concern, in the first place, the working class. We have to see how the conditions under which this class produced (that is, the characteristics of the processes of production and reproduction) were changed, but have also to describe the forms taken by the rise in the level of consumption by the industrial workers, by the various relations of distribution, and by the way in which the workers were organized. Special attention has been given to the ways whereby the workers (and other social classes, too, especially the bourgeoisie—both the old one and that which was in process of formation) made their presence felt in the ideological and political "machinery" through which the working class could either develop its own initiative, or find its activities being oriented in one direction or another. The successes won during the years under consideration, no less than the setbacks suffered, had a considerable influence on the form taken by the crisis of 1928–1930 and its outcome.

Likewise analyzed in this volume are the social relations in which the peasantry and its various strata were integrated, the struggles that developed within the peasantry, and the contradictions that set the peasant masses against certain decisions of the Soviet government.

The contradictions analyzed often present themselves as economic ones. It is therefore appropriate to bring to light the social relations which both manifested and concealed themselves in the form of prices, wages, and profits, and the class significance of the movements of industrial and agricultural prices, movements which involved, to some extent at least, the fate of the *alliance between the workers and the peasants.*

Our analysis deals fundamentally with political contradictions, but these cannot be reduced (as is too often attempted) merely to the conflicts between the various oppositions and the majority in the Political Bureau. Actually, these contradictions were also internal to the political line laid down by the Party leadership, a line that included contradictory elements which played a far from negligible role in the development of the crisis of 1928–1930. Moreover, this political line frequently contradicted the *actual practice* of the cadres of Party and State, and the *consequences* of this practice reacted, sooner or later, upon the political line, leading to its transformation.

Special attention must be given here to the limited means at the disposal of the Bolshevik Party for putting many of its decisions into effect. This limitation was a product of history. It was connected with the Party's inadequate presence among the peasantry (who formed the overwhelming majority of the Soviet people), and with the hardly proletarian character of many parts of the state machine,[3] and so with the type of relations established between these parts of the state machine and the working people.

However, the limits restricting the activity of the Bolshevik Party and also the possibilities for mass initiative were due not only to political factors, but were also determined by the development of a certain number of *ideological relations*. We must therefore analyze quite closely the *Bolshevik ideological formation and its transformations* (which were themselves inseparable from those taking place in the social formation as a whole). We shall see that some of the conceptions which played an increasing role in the Bolshevik Party, and which were also present among the masses, often led to the existence of some of the developing contradictions being hidden from view, to incorrect interpretation[4] of those contradictions whose existence was recognized, or to the adoption of decisions that were more or less inadequate, in the sense that they failed in their purpose and weakened the positions of the Soviet proletariat.

The characteristic features of the Bolshevik ideological formation reflected, in the first place, the limited experience which the Bolshevik Party and the Soviet proletariat could then draw upon. They were connected also with the conflicts that developed in the Party before October and during the years 1917–1923, and so with the *contradictions in the ideological formation of that period.* Finally, and above all, they resulted from the changes undergone by that ideological formation in face of the *new problems* that arose and the changes in *class relations* within the Soviet formation itself.

The process of change in the Bolshevik ideological formation produced contradictory effects. On the one hand, it led to an enrichment of Marxism, to a clearer perception of the political and economic tasks that the Soviet government had to tackle. On the other, and at the same time, it contributed— owing, especially, to the weakness of the Party's ties with the peasant masses—to the strengthening of conceptions that departed from revolutionary Marxism. It should be noted, too, that these conceptions could in some cases be given illusory "title-deeds of legitimacy" through a mechanistic interpretation of some formulation or other employed by Marx himself.

As we shall see, a significant example of this was the role that the Bolshevik Party gave to the formulations used by Marx in his writings of 1846, in which "society" appears as an "expressive totality" where the aggregate of social relations seems to be determined by the technological conditions of production. This happened with the well-known phrase: "The hand-mill gives you society with the feudal lord: the steam mill, society with the industrial capitalist,"[5] which can be interpreted in a narrowly economist-technicist sense.

A relatively large amount of space is given at the end of this volume to the problems posed by the changes in the Bolshevik ideological formation. These problems have, indeed, a considerable bearing. Analysis of them enables us to understand better how and why a certain number of contradictions that developed in the Soviet social formation were imperfectly grasped, so that the inadequate treatment they received resulted in a series of unsought consequences that were increasingly difficult to control.

What is said on this subject implies in the most direct fashion a lesson that is of universal application. Some of the conceptions alien to revolutionary Marxism that were present in the Bolshevik ideological formation became, during the 1930s, "established truths" which influenced a number of the parties belonging to the Communist International. These parties were thus induced, in historical conditions differing from those of the USSR, to commit mistakes that were *similar* to those committed by the Bolshevik Party.[6]

Analysis of the contradictions and transformations of the Bolshevik ideological formation is still relevant to present-day concerns. Even now, some of those who with justification claim to be Marxist-Leninists have not clearly recognized what may be mistakes in certain formulations adopted by the Bolshevik Party which played a negative role, in the transformation process of the Soviet social formation, by weakening the leading role of the working class.

The identification of revolutionary Marxism with some of the formulations or theses which, though accepted by the Bolshevik Party, were alien to Marxism, continues to do harm to the cause of socialism in another way. Thus, what the Bolshevik Party said, especially from the end of the 1920s on, about the "socialist" significance of state ownership and about the decisive role of the development of the productive forces as the "driving force of social changes" is repeated today by the Soviet revisionists. By reiterating these formulas they

claim to prove their "loyalty" to Marxism-Leninism. Other
opponents of socialism employ similar identifications, and the
results ensuing from the theses to which they relate, in order
to reject what the Soviet revolution has accomplished and
reject, also, the teachings of revolutionary Marxism, without
which it is impossible to carry forward to victory the struggle
for socialism.

At the heart of the analyses that follow, therefore, lies the
question of the relation between the process of change affecting the Soviet social formation and that which affected the
Bolshevik ideological formation. This is a question of capital
importance which I have been able only to begin to deal with
here. Perhaps my essay may serve as the starting point for
"setting right-way-up" the problem referred to by means of
the mistaken expression "the personality cult." What is meant
thereby really took shape only in the 1930s and can therefore
by analyzed only in my next volume. Nevertheless, it is not
without value to make a few methodological observations on
the subject straightaway.

In the first place, it must be said that, in order to deal
rigorously with this question, on the basis of historical materialism, one needs to analyze *first of all* the transformation
process of the *Soviet social formation* and its articulation with
that of the *Bolshevik ideological formation.* The question of
Stalin cannot be presented correctly unless it is situated in
relation to this *dual process.* Historically, Stalin was the product of this process, not its *"author."* To be sure, his role was
considerable, but the line followed by his acts and decisions
cannot be separated either from the *relations of strength between classes,* or from the *means* available to the Bolshevik
Party, or from *the ideas that were predominant in the Party
and among the masses.* It is by taking strict account of all these
objective determining factors that one can *analyze* the activity
of the Bolshevik Party, and so of Stalin, and *understand* how
this activity contributed to maintaining some of the conquests
of October, consolidating Soviet power, and, *at the same time,*
undermining some of these conquests by allowing the development of practices and social relations which greatly

weakened the leading role of the Soviet proletariat and profoundly shook the alliance between the workers and the peasants. But only *concrete analysis* applied to the *specific forms
of the changes undergone by the Soviet social formation* can
enable us to tackle these questions correctly.

Such a concrete analysis shows also to what extent Stalin
was, above all, in most cases, the man who concentrated systematically the views of the leading circles of the Party and
some of the aspirations of a section of the Soviet masses. The
nature of these views and these aspirations was not the same at
all moments in the history of the Soviet formation, and therefore the "question of Stalin" can be tackled correctly only by
"periodizing" it.

In any case, in the following pages I am not concerned with
these problems, since treatment of them is necessarily *subordinate* to a preliminary analysis of the process of change
through which the Soviet formation has passed.

Notes

1. Our knowledge of these struggles can, alas, only be very incomplete. The most significant factors can, of course, be grasped by
   reference to the published documents, by interpreting the
   speeches of the Soviet leaders and the decisions adopted by the
   Party. But a more thorough knowledge of the struggles and of the
   state of mind of the masses, and especially of the different strata
   composing them, will not be achieved until later, when archives
   which are at present closed to researchers are opened to them,
   and, *above all,* when, through a mighty mass movement of concern
   to know their past, the Soviet people themselves come to participate in the reconstitution of their own history. Meanwhile, only
   the most outstanding developments can be appreciated—which is
   already a great deal.
2. In J. Elleinstein's book, *Histoire du phénomène stalinien*
   (English-language translation, *The Stalin Phenomenon*), we find
   an idealist approach and positions characteristic of mechanical
   materialism intermingled. The developments experienced by the

USSR are shown as the result of a certain conception of socialism "adapted" to the specific historical conditions of Russia—to the low level of the productive forces in that country at the start of the Revolution and to the initial situation of its masses. Elleinstein writes of "a people in rags and without education" (English translation, p. 32) and the burden of "Tsarist tradition and Orthodox ritual" (ibid., p. 56). It is on this "historical terrain, very different from that of France" that a specific "type of socialism" is said to have developed (French edition, p. 247; not included in the English translation). A "myth of origin" thus does duty for analysis of a complex process of transformation. Rejection of this myth does not mean, of course, denying that the effects produced upon the Soviet social formation by a number of *contradictions that were not brought under control* (effects the bearing of which is universal, and therefore capable of appearing elsewhere than in the Soviet Union) did take on *forms that were specifically Russian.* However, what matters when we are trying *to draw lessons from the history of the Soviet Union is the content of universal implication to be found in the changes that that country has undergone:* this is why we need to grasp them in their *specific forms* (which are to be "associated" with the specific Russian "terrain"), but also *to go beyond the particularity of these forms.*

3. We need only recall what Lenin had to say on the matter: "The apparatus we call ours is, in fact, still quite alien to us; it is a bourgeois and tsarist hotchpotch . . . " (Lenin, *CW*, vol. 36, p. 606). On this point see volume I of the present work, p. 329. For lack of mass action to revolutionize this "apparatus," its characteristic features could not be radically altered.

4. The most telling example of a mistaken interpretation is provided by the attempt made to account for the "bureaucratic distortions" of the state machinery by attributing these exclusively to the predominance of small-scale production. Actually, these distortions were also connected with the development of centralistic political relations (which was why they got worse during the 1930s, when small-scale peasant production was tending to disappear), a development that was not combated by the Bolshevik Party since it considered that the forms of centralization characteristic of capitalism corresponded to the requirements for domination by society over the processes of production and reproduction.

5. Marx, *The Poverty of Philosophy,* in Marx and Engels, *Collected Works,* vol. 6, p. 166.

6. Of course, if a particular Communist Party *was influenced* by some of the mistaken theses upheld by the Bolshevik Party and the Comintern, *the reason for this must be sought in the social practice of this Party,* in its *relations with the various classes of society,* in its *internal structure,* and in its greater or lesser capacity to generate criticism and self-criticism, drawing up the balance sheet of its own experience and learning lessons therefrom.

Introduction to the "second period"

The purpose of this volume is to show the movement of the contradictions leading to the economic and political crisis that opened at the beginning of 1928 and culminated, from the end of 1929, in the complete abandonment of the New Economic Policy (NEP) which had been inaugurated in 1921.[1] This abandonment corresponded to a radical alteration of political line. The decisive moment of this alteration was called by Stalin himself the "great turn" or "great change."[2]

The analyses that follow relate to the contradictions that led to this abandonment, to the NEP itself, and to the "great change" that marked the real ending of it.

Only as clear a view as can be obtained of the interweaving and transformation of the contradictions characteristic of the Soviet formation between 1923 and 1929 can enable us to appreciate the concrete conditions under which the USSR entered, in 1930, a *new period* of collectivization and industrialization, that of the Five-Year Plans. That new period will be studied in a subsequent volume.

I. The NEP as a policy of alliance between the workers and the peasants

The NEP is often discussed as though it were a mere "economic policy." The very name given to it ("New Economic Policy") suggests such an interpretation, and the measures taken initially in order to implement it seem to have aimed mainly at restoring a certain amount of "freedom of trade" and leaving the peasants a margin of initiative much wider than they had enjoyed during "war communism."

At the beginning of 1922, at the time of the Eleventh Congress of the Bolshevik Party, Lenin was still saying: "The chief thing the people, all the working people, want today is nothing but help in their desperate hunger and need."[3]

Nevertheless, over and above immediate appearances (which were also a reality), and the confusion caused by the expression "New Economic Policy," The NEP was *very much more* than an "economic policy."[4] It was also very much more than a policy of "concessions" made to the peasantry and to some Russian and foreign capitalists.

Actually, the NEP was something other than *a mere "retreat,"* the metaphor that was first used to define it. It was an *active alliance between the working class and the peasantry:* an alliance that was more and more clearly defined by Lenin as intended not just to ensure "restoration of the economy" but also to make it possible to *lead the peasant masses along the road to socialism,* through the aid—economic, ideological, and political—brought to them by the proletariat.[5]

The NEP as an active alliance between the peasantry and the proletariat in power was a special form of the dictatorship of the proletariat, a form corresponding to the specific conditions prevailing in Soviet Russia in the 1920s.

The special features of the class alliance which the NEP aimed to establish should not cause us to forget that this alliance was in strict conformity with the fundamental principles of Marxism. Marx opposed Lassalle, for whom, in relation to the working class, the other social classes constituted "one reactionary mass." In a passage written in June 1919—long before the formulation of the NEP—Lenin stressed that the dictatorship of the proletariat does not mean a dictatorship of the working class over the masses in general, but is an alliance between classes. He declared that whoever "has not understood this from reading Marx's *Capital* has understood nothing in Marx, understood nothing in Socialism . . ."[6]

After recalling that the dictatorship of the proletariat is *the continuation of the class struggle in new forms,* Lenin added:

The dictatorship of the proletariat is a specific form of class alliance between the proletariat, the vanguard of the working people, and the numerous non-proletarian strata of the working people (petty bourgeoisie, small proprietors, the peasantry, the intelligentsia, etc.) or the majority of these strata, an alliance against capital, an alliance whose aim is the complete overthrow of capital, complete suppression of the resistance offered by the bourgeoisie as well as of attempts at restoration on its part, an alliance *for the final establishment and consolidation of socialism* [my emphasis—C. B.].[7]

For Lenin the NEP was thus neither a mere "economic policy" nor a mere "retreat": it was *a special form of the dictatorship of the proletariat,* requiring respect for a certain number of political orientations and fundamental principles.

The *necessity of this form* under the conditions of Soviet Russia was one of the lessons that Lenin drew from "war communism." That experience had shown that it was imperative to replace the attempted "frontal attack" characteristic of the years 1918–1920 by a *war of position.* This "war" could lead to the triumph of socialism provided that the ruling party clearly perceived that the terrain it stood upon at the outset was one of real social relations which were still capitalist, and provided that it set itself the task of helping to bring about *the conditions needed if these relations were to be controlled and transformed, by drawing the peasant masses into this new struggle, which was a struggle for socialism.*

In his closing speech at the Eleventh Congress of the Bolshevik Party, delivered on April 2, 1922, Lenin was particularly explicit on this point. On the one hand, he showed that the phase of "retreat" which had at first characterized the NEP (and which had opened at the beginning of 1921) was at an end, that a stop must be put to that "retreat," though not to the NEP itself. On the other hand, he emphasized two principles: first, the *new advance* must be cautious (in conformity with the requirements of positional warfare), and, secondly and especially, this advance must be made *together with the peasantry.*

The following formulation is particularly significant: "The

main thing now is to advance as an immeasurably wider and larger mass, and *only together with the peasantry,* proving to them by deeds, in practice, by experience, that we are learning and that we shall learn *to assist them, to lead them forward.*"[8]

The two key expressions in this formulation are: (1) "to advance," which shows that in 1922, as Lenin saw it, the NEP must make it possible to *go forward* (and not merely to "restore the productive forces"); and (2) "only together with the peasantry," which implies that the advance (the march toward socialism) must be made *together with the peasant masses,* whom the Party must "learn to assist."

In January 1923 Lenin gave concrete definition to one of the forms that this advance toward socialism should assume so far as the peasantry was concerned: "If the whole of the peasantry had been organised in co-operatives, we would by now have been standing with both feet on the soil of socialism." In the same passage Lenin stressed again that, under the dictatorship of the proletariat, a general development of cooperatives could lead to socialism provided that it resulted not from economic and political coercion, but from the will of the peasant masses themselves, which accounts for this remark: "The organisation of the entire peasantry in co-operative societies presupposes a standard of culture among the peasants . . . that cannot, in fact, be achieved without a cultural revolution."[9]

The phrase quoted is of decisive importance, even though in this particular passage the content of the expression "cultural revolution" remains rather vague.

However, the way in which the NEP actually developed did not depend exclusively on the Party's rallying to the principles proclaimed. What was essential was the *concrete content* of this "rallying," the mode of intervention in the class struggles which it determined, and the Party's practical capacity to *put into deeds* the measures it resolved upon. It was all that which constituted the *reality* of the policy followed during the NEP, and which had an influence—greater or less, from case to case—on the process of reproduction and tranformation of social relations that took place between 1923 and 1928, and culminated in the general crisis of the years 1928 and 1929.

The analysis of the requirements and the limitations of the NEP made by the majority of the Bolshevik Party leadership was far from stable and consistent. It varied from time to time and was not the same for all members of the CC.

Each interpretation appeared as the result of the combining of two fundamental tendencies concerning the significance to be accorded to the NEP. At different moments, *one* of these tendencies was more or less predominant; and this applied both to the Party majority itself and to the positions taken up by one and the same Party leader.

One of these tendencies led to the NEP being reduced to a mere "economic policy," a "retreat," to which one had to resign oneself for the time being, until the situation should make it possible to "get rid of the NEP"[10] and resume the offensive. This tendency implicitly assumed that no *real offensive* could be undertaken until the NEP had been abandoned.

The other tendency—the one that was in closer conformity to Lenin's own line of thought[11]—declared that the NEP was above all a *specific form of the alliance between the workers and the peasants,* and that this form was capable of modification, especially in response to the rallying of the peasant masses to the cooperatives and to collective production. The interpretations in which this attitude was dominant did not consider that it was necessary to "get rid of" the NEP in the near future, but merely to *transform* it.

Predominance of the first of these two tendencies meant, if taken to extremes, looking on the NEP as a capitalist road of development, from which followed the conclusion that it would have to be abandoned as soon as conditions made this possible.

Predominance of the second tendency meant, on the contrary, agreeing that the NEP made development along the *socialist road possible,* provided that the Party took the appropriate measures. This interpretation thus did not present as mutually irreconcilable pursuit of the NEP and advance toward socialism. It did not, however, deny that this advance might include elements of *subordinated capitalist development,* the effects of which must be gradually subjected to control and then transformed by the class struggle.

Over and above all hesitations and temporary fluctuations, the way the NEP was predominantly interpreted by the leadership of the Bolshevik Party was governed by an historical development. The interpretation that prevailed in the first historical period (until 1925) saw in the NEP *essentially a policy of class alliances that was relatively lasting.* It tended, however, to ascribe to this alliance a content that was *mainly economic.* One must emphasize that this was only a *tendency,* and did not rule out the introduction of measures aiming directly to change the political relations between the Bolshevik Party and the peasantry—such as the policy of "revitalizing" the rural soviets.

In a second phase—beginning at the end of 1925, when it was proclaimed that the "restoration period" had been completed (this was not true, since at that time the productive forces of agriculture had not yet been fully "restored")—the idea developed to an increasing extent that the NEP was essentially provisional in character. In practice this idea found expression in a *growing gap* between *statements of principle,* which affirmed positions that were basically unchanged, and the *measures concretely adopted and implemented.* Actually, these measures represented to an ever greater degree a violation, *on the plane of political practice,* of some of the requirements of the NEP, especially as regards relations with the peasant masses. What was going on, therefore, was a *gradual abandonment of all that the NEP stood for as a policy of active alliance between the proletariat and the peasantry.* Thus, what appeared in 1928–1929 to be a "crisis of the NEP" was, in reality, a crisis caused by nonapplication of the NEP—a crisis of the worker-peasant alliance.

The changes affecting the predominant interpretation of the NEP by the Bolshevik Party enable us to understand the nature of certain decisions taken by the Party during the years

1923–1929, but they are far from supplying an adequate explanation of them. On the one hand, a considerable number of decisions were taken (especially from 1928 on) under the pressure of immediate difficulties. They were more or less improvised, and the changes in the way that the NEP was interpreted were then brought in, more in order to furnish retrospective justification for decisions already taken than as a factor determining these decisions.

On the other hand, and especially, these changes in the predominant interpretation of the NEP need to be explained themselves. This explanation can be found only by analyzing the changes that took place in the Bolshevik ideological formation and by relating these changes to their material basis; the successes and failures of the policy followed, the changes in relations of strength between the classes, and the general movement of the economic and social contradictions that were subject to control to a greater or lesser degree.

II. The NEP as an "economic policy" and its results down to 1927

The most immediate aim of the NEP was to rescue the country from the famine and economic chaos in which it was sunk after four years of imperialist war followed by three years of civil war and foreign intervention. At the beginning, these economic tasks were also directly political tasks.

What mattered for the Soviet government was, first and foremost, to take the measures needed if the essential branches of production were quickly to recover their prewar levels, and then to surpass these levels, taking account of the new social and political conditions resulting from the October Revolution. By achieving this aim the Soviet government scored a political victory. It showed its power to save the country from the tremendous difficulties into which it was plunged at the end of the civil war. Thanks to the measures taken, and, above all, to the immense effort and labor put in by the workers and peasants, the results obtained were exceptionally great.

(a) Agricultural production

In 1926–1927 agricultural production took a leap forward. Its value, in prewar prices, reached 11.17 milliard roubles, which meant an advance of over 100 percent on 1921–1922 and 6 percent on 1913—in comparison with 1925–1926, the previous year, when the advance was 5 percent.[12] In 1926–1927 the gross yield of grain was more than 25 percent in excess of that in 1922–1923: it came to about 76.4 million metric tons, as against 74.5 in 1925–1926.[13] At that moment, however, the level of the prewar grain harvest (82.6 million metric tons was the average for the years 1909 to 1913[14]) had not been fully attained; but a number of other branches of agricultural production were progressing, despite the inadequacy and obsolescence of the equipment available on most farms.

The years between 1921–1922 and 1926–1927 thus saw a remarkable advance in agriculture. However, this advance was very uneven between one region and another and between different branches of agriculture. Furthermore, after 1925–1926, agricultural production tended to stagnate. This slowing-down was to have important political consequences.

(b) Industrial production

During the NEP, industrial production, too, made remarkable progress. Production in 1926–1927 was, in terms of volume, three times that of 1921–1922. However, the progress achieved made up mainly for the previous decline; and industrial production in 1926–1927 was only 4 percent more than prewar, whereas it was 15.6 percent more than in the preceding year.[15]

If we take the *processing industry* alone, the progress made was very substantial. In 1927 the index for this branch of production (with 1913 as 100) stood at 114.5. This progress continued, moreover, during the two subsequent years. In 1929 the index for this branch stood at 181.4, which *put the USSR at the head of all the countries of Europe for growth in production by manufacturing industry as compared with prewar.*[16]

If we compare the progress made by the different branches of industry (manufacturing and extractive), we find that the rates of progress were highly uneven. In 1926–1927 production of coal and oil surpassed the prewar level to a marked degree. Iron and steel lagged behind. As for production of cotton goods, it exceeded the prewar figure by 70 percent.[17]

The progress in industrial production of consumer goods did not show the same signs of slowing down as became apparent in agriculture. When we compare it with the increase in population, we see that, taken as a whole, it had progressed at a faster rate: between 1913 and 1926 the population grew by 7 percent, reaching the figure of 147 million, 18 million of whom lived in towns; whereas the index of industrial production of consumer goods reached 120 in 1928 (100 being, in this case, 1914).[18]

(c) The development of exchange

One of the immediate aims of the NEP was a rapid development of exchange between town and country (a development which formed the material basis for the alliance between the workers and the peasants). It was an aim to be attained not only through increased production but also through the establishment of economic relations satisfactory to the peasants—who, under "war communism," had furnished supplies to the towns while receiving hardly any products in return.

The NEP was, in fact, marked by an extensive development of commodity exchange, by restoration of the role of money, by the existence of a vast "free market," and by the influence of price movements upon the supply of and demand for goods and by then influence on the orientation of some investments. Nevertheless, the years beginning in 1921 also saw the developing activity of a group of state organs whose operations aimed at safeguarding expanded reproduction, to some extent, from the *direct influence* of commodity relations, through the increasing role played by *planning*, centralization of fiscal revenue, and the carrying out of *investment programs*.

The figures available do not enable us to estimate precisely how exchange evolved in comparison with 1913. It is certain, however, that the amount of agricultural produce supplied to the towns and urban trade by the peasants, in order to obtain the money that they needed to pay their taxes, was much less in 1926 than in 1913. Thereafter, the bulk of the selling done by the peasants was intended to *pay for their purchases of industrial goods*.

Taken as a whole, the trade turnover in 1926–1927 was 2.5 times what it had been in 1923–1924. Even if we allow for the fact that during this period prices increased by about 50 percent, the overall volume of exchange increased by more than 60 percent in three years. Besides, these figures do not include the very big increase in sales made by the peasants in the urban markets, sales which between 1922–1923 and 1924–1925 multiplied by 3.3 (at current prices) and constituted at the later date more than one-third of the retail trade turnover.[19]

Another proof of the substantial increase in the volume of exchange is provided by the rapid advance in the tonnage carried by the railways, which was multiplied more than threefold between 1922 and 1927, the year when it exceeded the level of 1913 by 5 percent.

These few pointers serve to demonstrate the extent of the economic recovery accomplished between 1922 and 1927. The progress in most branches of production and exchange continued, moreover, after 1927, so that the contrast between this advance and the crisis experienced in the sphere of "procurement" of grain stands out all the more strikingly.

To account for this crisis and the way it developed we shall need to study the contradictory forms assumed by the worker-peasant alliance. This study is all the more necessary because the importance and the role of these contradictions are usually much underestimated.

III. The consolidation of the worker-peasant alliance and the contradictions in the Soviet social formation in 1923–1929

The consolidation of the worker-peasant alliance between 1923 and 1927 was based primarily upon the constructive work carried out under the leadership of the Bolshevik Party. This work was done in the main, as we have seen, in the sphere of production and exchange, but it was a great deal wider in scope than that.

In the sphere of education, there was an unprecedented increase in the numbers of people attending school. The figure for pupils in primary and secondary schools increased, in round figures, from 7.9 million in 1914–1915 to 11.5 million in 1927–1928.[20] As compared with 1922–1923, the increase in numbers was 1.4 million in the towns and 2.8 million in the countryside.[21] True—and I shall come back to this point—the content and methods of the teaching given were far from corresponding fully to what was needed for the building of socialism and to what was implicit in the role that the workers and peasants were supposed to play in that task. Nevertheless, the quantitative progress achieved was remarkable, and real efforts were made to establish a system of education linked with practical work in production.

In the sphere of reading by the masses, great progress was realized. Thus, the number of books in the public libraries, in 1927, was 43.5 million in the towns (as against 4.7 million in 1913), and 25.7 million in the country areas (as against 4.2 million in 1913).[22] This progress was all the more significant because, on the whole, what was published after the October Revolution was marked by a new, revolutionary spirit, and because the controversies of that period were wide-ranging enough to permit the expression of such diverse trends of thought, dogmatic tendencies and a stereotyped style were largely avoided. All the same, we must not lose sight of the fact that, despite what had been achieved, only a little over one-half of the inhabitants between nine and forty-nine years of age could read and write when the census of 1926 was taken.

In the sphere of health, the number of doctors increased from 20,000 in 1913 to 63,000 in 1928,[23] despite the substantial emigration of doctors between 1918 and 1923. The number of practitioners present in the rural districts increased rapidly, but in proportion to the number of inhabitants, still remained much lower than in the towns. Improvements in material and sanitary conditions brought about a fall in the death rate from 21.7 percent in 1924 to 18.8 percent in 1927.

The consolidation of Soviet power and of the worker-peasant alliance had, of course, a *political basis*—in particular, the special attention that the Bolshevik Party gave to the peasant question (in spite of the serious limitations imposed upon its activity by the Party's weak presence among the rural masses). This consolidation was bound up with the development of the mass organizations of the working class (mainly, the trade unions) and of the peasantry (mainly, the rural soviets and the agricultural cooperatives).[24]

The consolidation of Soviet power and of the worker-peasant alliance took place, inevitably, under contradictory conditions. It is the way in which these contradictions developed, became interconnected, and were dealt with that provides the explanation for what the NEP was, how it was transformed, and why it culminated in a "crisis" expressing its abandonment.

The basic contradiction was one that opposed the proletariat to the bourgeoisie. During the NEP this contradiction presented itself particularly in the form of the contradiction between the private sector and the state and cooperative sector, for the latter was, in the main, directed by the Soviet state, itself directed by the Bolshevik Party, the instrument of the dictatorship of the proletariat. In 1928 this sector contributed 44 percent of the national income, 82.4 percent of the gross value of industrial production, and accounted for 76.4 percent of the turnover of the retail trade enterprises. On the other hand, only 3.3 percent of the gross value of agricultural production came from this sector.[25] As we shall see, the decisive role played by the private sector in agriculture, and the considerable one played by private trade (combined with the growing contradictions in the policy followed by the Bolshevik Party from 1926 on), partly explain the crisis that marked the years 1928 and 1929, and the distinctive features of that crisis.

However, the contradictions between the proletariat and the bourgeoisie assumed other forms as well, and these we must analyze—especially those which opposed the working class to the managers of enterprises, both "private" and state-owned, in particular when the latter obstructed the workers' initiative. This contradiction became acute during the second half of 1928.

During the years 1923–1929 an important role was played by the contradiction which opposed—more or less sharply at different times—the peasantry to the Soviet government. In 1929 this contradiction became a decisive one, owing to the way with which it was dealt. It became interwoven with other contradictions, principally that which made the peasantry a contradictory unity, divided into *kulaki* (rich peasants), *bednyaki* (poor peasants), and *serednyaki* (middle peasants).

The vital significance of the supplying of grain to the towns meant that the impact which the development of these contradictions had upon "grain procurement"[26] acquired decisive importance. Reciprocally, it was on this plane that a series of measures were taken that might either consolidate or disturb the worker-peasant alliance. Owing to the way in which they were put into effect, under conditions that we must analyze, the measures taken from 1928 on led progressively to complete abandonment of the NEP.

IV. Grain procurement, its fluctuations, and the state of the worker-peasant alliance

The term "procurement" refers to the *operations for purchasing agricultural produce* carried out by the state's economic organs and by the officially recognized network of cooperatives.

The regular functioning of procurement was decisively important. Politically, its smooth progress constituted the outward sign that one of the material foundations of the worker-peasant alliance was being consolidated. Economically, this smooth progress ensured the supplies needed by the towns and by industry. It contributed to a certain degree of price stability, and to the balance of payments in foreign trade. In the last-mentioned connection, indeed, grain procurement played a role of central importance, for exports of grain were one of the principal sources from which the foreign exchange was obtained for financing imports, especially those that could help industry to develop.

During the NEP, procurement was carried on in competition with the purchasing activities of the "private sector." In principle—and this was an essential aspect of the NEP from the standpoint of the worker-peasant alliance—procurement had to be effected on the basis of the prices at which the peasants were willing to sell, and had to involve *only such quantities as the peasants were ready to deliver.* The principles of the NEP implied that procurement must be a form of *marketing* and not a form of requisition or taxation at the expense of the peasantry. And that was, in fact, how procurement worked down to the end of 1927.

Procurement was highly important for the peasantry, to whom it *guaranteed stable outlets* for their produce. It also constituted *one of the bases for economic planning,* since correct realization of economic plans largely depended on satisfactory functioning of the operations for purchase of agricultural produce.

In principle, the intervention of the procurement agencies on a sufficiently large scale enabled these agencies to *exert overall control over the prices* at which this produce was marketed—which meant also controlling the prices that prevailed in "private" trade. This intervention thus constituted, if it was carried out under proper conditions, an *instrument for implementing a price policy in conformity with the needs of the worker-peasant alliance.* During the first years of the NEP, the Soviet government tried to practice such a price policy. It did not always succeed, however, for reasons to which we shall have to return.

Finally, it should be added that the development of procurement was conceived not merely as an instrument to secure increasing control over the market, but also as a means of gradually ousting private trade. The struggle to oust private trade was one of the forms of the class struggle during the NEP: it aimed to strengthen the *direct economic ties* uniting the peasantry with the Soviet government.

At the Eleventh Party Congress, in 1922, Lenin had stressed that, in order to strengthen the worker-peasant alliance, the Communists appointed to head the central state and cooperative trading organs must *beat the capitalists on their own ground.* "Here is something we must do now in the economic field. We must win the competition against the ordinary shop assistant, the ordinary capitalist, the merchant, who will go to the peasant without arguing about communism."[27]

Lenin explained that the task of the industrial and commercial organs of the Soviet government was to ensure *economic linkage with the peasantry by showing that it could satisfy the peasants' needs better than private capital could.* He added: "Here the 'last and decisive battle' is impending; here there are no political or any other flanking movements that we can undertake, because this is a test in competition with private capital. Either we pass this test in competition with private capital, or we fail completely."[28]

These principles ratified by the Eleventh Party Congress, were adhered to in the main until 1927. The increasing role played by the state and cooperative sector in the general sphere of trade therefore testified to its vitality, to its increasing capacity to carry out procurement in the true sense of the word. The reader must be given an idea of this sector's overall development by showing *what its share was in commercial operations as a whole.* Here are some figures.

On the eve of the final crisis of the NEP (1926–1927), *wholesale trade* was already largely concentrated in the state and cooperative sector. The state's organs dealt with 50.2 percent of it, as against 5.1 percent covered by private trade; the balance of 44.7 percent was handled by cooperative trade, which was itself subject to directives from the state's organs.[29]

Concentration of wholesale trade under the direct control of the Soviet government continued to progress after 1927, but this progress was thenceforth increasingly due to the application of regulatory measures—which nevertheless did not suffice to prevent a series of contradictions from developing in the sphere of trade.

In *retail trade* the position held by the state and cooperative agencies was less clearly dominant than in wholesale trade, but in 1926–1927 they were responsible for the greater part of this, too. At that time they contributed 13.3 percent and 49.8 percent, respectively, of the retail trade turnover, leaving 36.9 percent to private traders. In 1928 and 1929 the share held by the latter fell to 22.5 percent and then to 13.5 percent.[30]

Despite the big role played by state and cooperative trade, it did not succeed in accomplishing all the aims assigned to it by the Bolshevik Party and the Soviet government, especially as regards *prices* and the quantities that it was expected to buy or sell. We shall see this in detail when we come to examine how the final crisis of the NEP developed.

Let us note for the moment that a considerable contradiction appeared between private trade and state and cooperative trade in the matter of prices. Private traders resold at prices higher than those charged by the state and cooperative organs, and so were able to offer the peasants better prices for their products; this had a harmful effect on the procurement operations that the state endeavored to carry out on the basis of stable prices. This contradiction stimulated the adoption of administrative measures directed against private trade, but such measures often seemed to the peasants to be reasons why they were losing money, or being deprived of opportunities to make more money.

In any case, in 1926–1927, state and cooperative trade had succeeded in attaining a predominant position without having had recourse, thus far (at any rate, on any large scale), to measures of prohibition.

According to the directives laid down by the Party in a resolution adopted at the end of 1927 by the Fifteenth Congress,[31] state and cooperative trade had to follow the "price policy" decided by the Party, to enable the Soviet state to carry on an active policy in the buying and selling of produce, and to *subordinate commerce to the objectives of the plan*.

In reality, state and cooperative trade did not at that time succeed in gaining the control over commercial operations that was expected of it. This became especially clear in the crucial sphere of grain procurement. Here, difficulties arose in the most striking way and with the most serious consequences—a situation which we must now proceed to examine.

(a) The progress, and then the crisis, of procurement

The "procurement crisis" that began in 1927–1928 concerned, first and foremost, grain—a group of products which played an *essential role* in the feeding of the townspeople and in Soviet exports at that time. It is therefore to the evolution of *grain procurement* that we must pay attention.

It will first be observed that in 1926–1927 procurement involved 10.59 million metric tons. Like the harvest of that year, it was much bigger than that of the previous year (which had been 8.41 million metric tons[32] and had been carried out with some difficulty.

In 1927–1928 the harvest was less abundant than in the previous year, amounting to 73.6 million metric tons,[33] or 2.8 million less than in 1926–1927 and 0.9 million less than in 1925–1926. Procurement on a slightly smaller scale than in 1925–1926 was to be expected: actually, *the reduction was substantial, and it took place in two phases*, a point that deserves attention.

At first there was a *moderate reduction*: between July and October 1927 procurement involved 3.74 million metric tons, as against 3.96 million metric tons in the same months of the previous year, or a reduction of 5.4 percent—less in value when the reduction in the harvest is taken into account. Then, *between November and December, matters took a dramatic turn.* During those two months procurement accounted for no more than 1.39 million metric tons, which meant *a reduction*

of nearly 55 percent on the corresponding period of 1926–
1927.[34]

Actually, the reduction was not surprising, given the shrink-
age in the size of the harvest. Nevertheless, *this shortfall in
procurement jeopardized the supply of food to the towns.* It
also jeopardized—and this was no less important for the Bolshevik Party—realization of the objectives of the *procurement
plan,* which was itself connected with the *export plan. Procurement targets had been increased by 1.7 million metric
tons over the figure for the preceding year,*[35] *despite the reduction in the harvest.* The Party was therefore impelled to
react fast.

(b) The *"emergency measures"* and their immediate consequences

The way in which the Party and the government reacted to
the serious fall in the amount of grain procured resulted from a
relatively simple analysis of the situation—or rather from an
oversimplified analysis which took account of only one aspect
of the contradictions developing in the countryside, an aspect
which (as will be seen) was not, in fact, the principal one.

Generally speaking, the Bolshevik Party considered that the
reduction in procurement was due mainly to holding back of
grain by the rich peasants, to a sort of "kulaks' strike."[36] Having analyzed the situation in this way, the Party leadership
took the view, at the beginning of 1928, that this "strike" must
be answered with restraints and requisitions. These were
what came to be called the "extraordinary" or "emergency
measures," terms intended to emphasize the temporary character of the measures taken.

In themselves the "emergency measures" need not have
done fundamental violence to the principles of the NEP
(which implied that recourse should not be had to requisitions), *for they were supposed to apply exclusively to kulaks
guilty of illegal hoarding and speculation.* Their "legal basis"
was Article 107 of the Penal Code, adopted in 1926. They

were regarded as being one of the forms of the class struggle aimed, as the Fifteenth Congress resolution put it, at "restricting the exploiting tendencies of the rural bourgeoisie."[37]

If the emergency measures had in fact been applied merely to the quantity of grain that could be seized from the kulak farms, they would not have enabled the procurement agencies to realize their plan, which had very high targets.

In practice, therefore, *the emergency measures turned into something quite different from a struggle against speculation by kulaks.* They constituted a measure of "economic policy" aimed at ensuring, at all costs, transference to the state's granaries of a quantity of grain as near as possible to that provided for in the procurement plan. In order that this plan might be realized, the state organs and the local Party cadres were given very strict instructions. The cadres were threatened with penalties in the event that the procurement proved inadequate. As a result of the pressure brought to bear on them, the local officials were led to requisition quantities of grain very much larger than those they could find on the farms of the kulaks alone. Thus, the emergency measures hit not only the kulaks but also, and above all, the middle peasants and even some of the poor peasants.[38] Mikoyan, who was in charge of the administrative apparatus entrusted with procurement (the Commissariat of Trade), actually noted that *the bulk of the wheat "surplus" was held by the middle peasants,* and that the wheat confiscated from them was taken by means of *measures that were officially denounced as "harmful, illegal and inadmissible."*[39] However, the local organs of the Bolshevik Party insisted on the necessity, if the procurement targets were to be attained, of seizing the grain belonging to the middle peasants. A Party circular issued in the North-Caucasian Region *(Krai)* gave the following guidelines:

> While continuing to drain the surplus grain from kulak households, and employing whatever means are necessary to encourage them to sell their surplus to the state, we must bear in mind that the main bulk of the grain reserves is, nevertheless, in the hands of the middle peasants. For this reason, the February

procurements will be made mainly at the expense of the *sered-nyaks* in the villages, that is to say they will be amassed in small quantities.[40]

Adoption of these practices gave rise to a crisis in numerous regions and provoked discontent on the part of wide strata of the peasantry, who thought that a return to the methods of "war communism" was going on.

The Party's General Secretariat received disturbing reports about the way in which the emergency measures were being applied, and the reactions they were arousing among the peasantry. On February 13, 1928, Stalin sent out a circular to all Party organizations summarizing the situation which had led to the emergency measures being adopted and admitting that mistakes had previously been committed by the Party, including the CC.[41] He welcomed the results obtained by the emergency measures, so far as the amount of grain procured was concerned, but denounced "distortions and excesses" that had been committed in the villages and that might "create new difficulties." Stalin gave as examples of such excesses "compulsory subscription to the agricultural loan, organisation of substitutes for the old interception squads, and, lastly, abuse of powers of arrest, unlawful confiscation of grain surpluses, etc." concluding that "a definite stop must be put to all such practices."[42]

These warnings resulted in a certain falling-off in the quantity of grain procured during March. Nevertheless, the CC meeting at the beginning of April adopted a resolution stressing the need for a rapid return to procurement procedures that conformed to the requirements of the NEP.[43]

The pressure on the peasants, then, was lightened still further, but this relaxation was soon accompanied by a *sharp decline in procurement*. For April it amounted to no more than 246,000 metric tons, as compared with a monthly average of 1,446,000 metric tons in the previous three months of 1928 and procurement of 438,000 metric tons in April 1927.[44]

The Bolshevik Party leadership regarded this decline as excessive. During the next two months the emergency measures were applied afresh, and more severely than before. They even affected the poor peasants (*bednyaki*) to an increasing extent. The Party tried to organize these *bednyaki* for a struggle against the kulaks, while at the same time requiring that they surrender their own grain reserves, so as to set an example—otherwise, sanctions would be applied to them as well.

In the spring of 1928 the attempts to organize *bednyaki* and *batraki* (agricultural laborers) came to nothing. At the beginning of the winter a section of the poor peasants and the laborers *had* helped carry out requisitions from the kulaks, but they had then been given an incentive to help in this task and to organize themselves: 25 percent of the produce confiscated was assigned *to them*. When spring came the situation was different: now, *the procurement organizations were to centralize all the grain,* the better to achieve the targets they had been given.

In this new situation it was observed that the influence of the kulaks over the other strata of the peasantry, far from diminishing, increased.[45] From an immediate point of view that was narrowly economic and statistical, the results attained by the application of the emergency measures could nevertheless be regarded as "favorable." The agricultural campaign (July 1, 1927, to June 30, 1928) terminated, indeed, with a total procurement that came close in amount to that of 1926–1927—10.38 million metric tons, as against 10.59 million—despite a markedly smaller harvest. This immediate "statistical" result was of secondary importance, however. Much more important were the middle- and long-term consequences of the procurement crisis and the application of the emergency measures.

Already in 1928 it became evident that these included serious negative aspects, both economic and political: the whole set of *relations between town and country* had been disturbed, and, above all, the *worker-peasant alliance* had been damaged, since it had proved impossible to apply the emergency measures only to kulaks guilty of speculation.

A situation was being created in which it was getting harder and harder for the Party to do without emergency measures. To be able to do without them the Party would have had to analyze thoroughly the developments that were under way, including those connected with the form of the industrialization process then being initiated. It would also have needed to possess political resources enabling it to restore relations of trust with the peasantry, and the political and ideological resources necessary to work out and introduce *a different form of industrialization.*[46]

But these conditions were not present. Far from renouncing the emergency measures, the Party reverted to use of them in 1928–1929. The negative consequences entailed by these measures were repeated in aggravated form. This led to grave tension, both economic and political. In 1929 the tension was such that mere continuation of the emergency measures would have brought matters to a dead end. A situation was developing that led to *complete abandonment of the NEP,*[47] to the *"great change"* at the end of 1929. And that carried the Soviet formation into a new era full of violent contradictions.

During the 1930s there took place an accelerated industrialization, a rapid increase in the numbers of the proletariat, and the accession of many workers to positions of authority and responsibility in the political, economic, and administrative spheres. At the same time, however, the consequences of the rupture of the worker-peasant alliance made themselves felt. This rupture resulted from a collectivization "from above" characterized by the fact that, except for a minority, the entry of the peasants into the *kolkhoz* system did not reflect an enthusiastic conversion to collective farming.

The rupture of the worker-peasant alliance weakened the dictatorship of the proletariat. It entailed a decline in proletarian democracy, with a strengthening of hierarchical relations and an authoritarian style of leadership. It was accompanied by a substantial fall in grain production and stockbreeding and a grave crisis in food supplies.

V. *The process of abandonment of the NEP*

The complete abandonment of the NEP did not reflect (as concrete analysis shows) the carrying through of any preconceived "plan." Nor did this abandonment take place in response to the "mere requirements of the development of the productive forces" or to those of an "economic crisis." If there was indeed such a crisis, it was only the effect of a *political crisis*, a *crisis in class relations*.

The turn that was made in 1929, a turn of immense historical importance, resulted basically from an *objective process* of class struggles and contradictions that were not subjected to control. A certain number of "decisions" taken by the Bolshevik Party were features of this process, but were only *subordinate factors* in it. They were incapable of really directing the course taken by the process, and their social and political "effects" were, generally speaking, very different from those that had been expected.

Only by clarifying the contradictions and conflicts which form the driving force of this historical process can we understand its course and its characteristics, *and draw lessons from it*. Such clarification calls for analysis of the *economic and social relations* that characterized the NEP, together with *the social forces whose action brought about the transforming of these relations*.

This analysis has been attempted in the pages that follow. It deals first with the general conditions of reproduction, and then with the movement of the social contradictions that developed in the countryside and in the towns. This movement was, primarily, the result of *the activity of the masses engaged in class struggle*, but it was based upon the *existing conditions of production and reproduction*. The direction that it took was determined by the way that the different classes *saw* their interests and their role. The role played by the way classes saw themselves was particularly important in the case of the proletariat and its vanguard, the Bolshevik Party, and this is why space has been given to examination of the debates within the Party and the Party's decisions, and to analysis of the Bolshevik ideological formation and the changes it underwent. Nevertheless, the outcome of these debates, the nature and consequences of the decisions taken by the Party, and the changes in its ideology cannot be *explained* if we confine our analysis to developments taking place in the *superstructure* of the social formation. On the contrary, a genuine explanation requires that what happened in the superstructure be *related to the general movement of the class struggles and to the process of reproduction and transformation of social relations as a whole.*

The complexity of the relations and forces which have to be reckoned with is considerable, as is the complexity of the forms under which these relations and forces conditioned each other and acted one upon another. The following analysis is therefore focused upon what seems essential. It aims only to illuminate the most important aspects of *a historical process the significance of which remains topical in the highest degree.*

Notes

1. On the inauguration of the NEP, see volume I of the present work, pp. 477 ff.
2. Stalin, *Works*, vol. 12, p. 124.
3. Lenin, *CW*, vol. 33, p. 304.
4. The expression "economic policy" is equivocal, anyway: any policy that affects the conditions of production and exchange *also affects class relations, and is therefore always an intervention in the class struggle.*
5. See pp. 484–496 of volume I of the present work.
6. Lenin, *CW*, vol. 29, p. 380.
7. Ibid., vol. 29, p. 381.
8. Ibid., vol. 33, p. 326 (my emphasis—C. B.).
9. Ibid., vol. 33, p. 474.
10. The expression "get rid of the N.E.P." was used by Stalin at the end of 1929, in his speech of December 27 to Marxists

specializing in agrarian problems. In this passage Stalin did not say that the NEP had to be abandoned forthwith. He spoke of this as happening in a future which he left indeterminate. Meanwhile, he said, "We adhere to the N.E.P.," explaining that this did not imply any retreat and that "it serves the cause of socialism" (Stalin, *Works*, vol. 12, p. 178). In reality, as we shall see, the measures taken during the winter of 1929–1930 signified abandonment of the NEP.

11. Even in 1929–1930, when the NEP was being abandoned in practice, this conception continued to be the one theoretically upheld by the Bolshevik Party. Hence the paradox that as late as 1931, when nothing was left of the NEP, the Party was still asserting that it had not been abandoned but was being pursued (see below, note 20, p. 480).

12. Figures calculated from E. Zaleski, *Planning for Economic Growth in the Soviet Union, 1918–1932*, p. 386. Zaleski's figures are drawn fron various Soviet sources. They are, of course, only rather approximate estimates.

13. These figures are given in most of the statistical sources for the period: see in particular, S. Grosskopf, *L'Alliance ouvrière et paysanne en URSS (1921–1928): Le Problème du blé*, pp. 113, 346. In 1927–1928 the yield fell to 73.6 million metric tons (ibid., p. 338).

14. Estimate by V. G. Groman, *Entsiklopediya russkogo eksporta*, vol. I, p. 175. The harvest of 1913 was estimated at 96.7 million metric tons by G. M. Krzhizhanovsky, in *Desyat let khozyaistvennogo stroitelstva SSSR 1917–1927*, p. 34, quoted by Grosskopf, p. 113.

15. See *Gosplan SSSR, Pyatiletny Plan*, vol. I, p. 15. These indices relate to industry as a whole, and are calculated on the basis of prewar prices.

16. In 1929, the apogee of the cycle of years preceding the great between-the-wars crisis, the indices for production by manufacturing industry were 142.7 in France, 117.3 in Germany, and 100.3 in the United Kingdom (see *Industrialisation and Foreign Trade*, p. 134).

17. See S. N. Prokopovicz, *Histoire économique de l'URSS*, p. 282.

18. *Narodnoye khozyaistvo SSSR v 1961 g.*, pp. 7, 169.

19. See Prokopovicz, *Histoire économique*, pp. 459–460, and B. Kerblay, *Les Marchés paysans en URSS*, p. 112.

20. See *Narodnoye khozyaistvo 1958 g.*, p. 806.

46   *Charles Bettelheim*

21. Ibid., p. 814.
22. Ibid., p. 851.
23. Ibid., p. 880.
24. These developments will be analyzed in this book.
25. *Narodnoye khozyaistvo 1958 g.* p. 57.
26. On "procurement," see below, p. 91.
27. Lenin, *CW*, vol. 33, p. 275.
28. Ibid., vol. 33, p. 277.
29. See *Kontrolnye tsifry na 1927–1928 gg.*, pp. 77–88.
30. *Sotsialisticheskoye Stroitelstvo SSSR* (1935), pp. 552–553.
31. See *K.P.S.S. v rezolyutsiyakh i resheniyakh*, vol. 2, p. 342.
32. See A. Mendelson, ed., *Pokazateli konyunkturi*, p. 51.
33. See Table 199 on p. 338 of Grosskopf, *L'Alliance ouvrière*.
34. Percentages calculated from the figures given in the work mentioned in note 32.
35. On January 1, 1928, the rural procurement plan for 1927–1928 had been fulfilled only 39.3 percent, whereas on the same date a year previously it had been fulfilled 63.7 percent. (See M. T. Chernov, "Opyt khlebozagotovok 1929–1930 g.," in *Ekonomicheskoye Obozreniye*, no. 1 [1930], p. 30, quoted in Grosskopf, *L'Alliance ouvrière* p. 334).
36. During the winter of 1925–1926, when there had been a momentary decline in procurement despite a good harvest, the same interpretation tended to be given to this phenomenon: at that time, however, it did not lead to the same measures as were introduced in 1927–1928, and the effects of the initial decline in procurement were quickly overcome.
37. See *K.P.S.S. v rezolyutsiyakh*, vol. 2, pp. 250–255.
38. Grosskopf, *L'Alliance ouvrière* p. 336.
39. Mikoyan in *Pravda*, February 10, 1928.
40. Circular from the *Krai* Party office, North Caucasia, taken from the Central Party Archives. See G. A. Konyukhov, *KPSS v borbe s khlebnymi zatrudneniyami v strane (1928–1929)*, p. 152, quoted in M. Lewin, *Russian Peasants and Soviet Power*, p. 222.
41. See Stalin, *Works*, vol. 11, p. 16.
42. Ibid., vol. 11, p. 19.
43. See *K.P.S.S. v rezolyutsiyakh*, vol. 2, pp. 372 ff.
44. True, during the first quarter of 1926, procurement had brought in only 841,000 metric tons (calculated from figures in the work quoted in note 31).
45. Already in February Mikoyan had spoken of "hesitation" on the

part of the *bednyaki*. A few months later it was being admitted that many of them had even turned toward the kulaks (see Bauman's article, "Uroki khlebozagotovok," in *Bolshevik*, nos. 13–14 [1928], p. 74).

46. Meaning a less centralized, less "modern" kind of industrialization, calling for smaller financial resources and fewer imports, and relying to a greater extent on local resources and on the initiative of the worker and peasant masses.

47. On this point, see below, p. 107.

Part 1
The development of commodity and money relations and of planning in the NEP period

Analyzing the phase of boom followed by crisis with which the NEP came to its end requires that we take into account, for the whole of this period, the development of two types of social relations: on the one hand, *commodity and money relations*, and, on the other, the *political relations* resulting from *economic planning* which *modified the conditions* of reproduction of commodity and money relations.

The latter type of relations did not "disappear" during "war communism": their fundamental condition for existence was still present, for social production had not ceased to be the result of "mutually independent acts of labour, performed in isolation," so that its products could "confront each other as commodities,"[1] despite all the "bans" issued against commodity exchange.

More generally, during "war communism" as during the NEP, the length of *immediate labor time* remained the decisive factor in the production of social wealth, social production was still based on *value*, and the *increase of wealth depended on surplus labor:* the producer had therefore not yet appropriated "his own general productive power," as Marx put it in the *Grundrisse.*[2]

Lenin recognized this reality when he called upon the Bolshevik Party to adopt the NEP. What the Bolshevik Party did, in fact, between 1921 and 1923, was to *recognize the existence of commodity, money, and capitalist relations,*[3] and to create the conditions for these relations to reproduce themselves and, thereby, to reveal themselves clearly; for the transforma-

49

tion and destruction of these relations necessarily has to pass through that phase.

Hence the putting into effect of a series of decisions, of which the principal ones concerned the restoration of a limited private sector in industry and trade,[4] and, above all, an effort aimed at reconstituting open commodity and money relations.[5] This made possible accounting in money terms, and required the presence of a currency that should be as stable as possible.

At the same time, the Bolshevik Party was concerned to help birth the political, ideological, and economic conditions for the *transformation* and then the eventual *disappearance* of these same commodity, money, and capitalist relations. A preliminary stage in this direction was the establishment of a *planning apparatus* which should function *so as to subject the reproduction of commodity and money relations to conditions and political relations imposed by the organs of the dictatorship of the proletariat.*

Notes

1. Marx, *Capital* (London), vol. I, p. 132. This point has already been made in volume I of the present work, p. 462.
2. Marx, *Grundrisse der Kritik der Politischen Ökonomie*, p. 705. In this passage Marx shows that the transformation of the system of the productive forces which begins with the automatizing of production brings about a "monstrous disproportion between the labour time applied and its product," and also a "qualitative imbalance between labour, reduced to a pure abstraction, and the power of the production-process it superintends," with the human being coming to

> relate more as watchman and regulator to the production-process itself. . . . He steps to the side of the production-process instead of being its chief actor. . . . In this transformation, it is neither the direct human labour he himself performs, nor the time during which he works, but rather the appropriation of his own general productive power, his

understanding of nature and his mastery over it by virtue of his presence as a social body—it is, in a word, the development of the social individual which appears as the great foundation-stone of production and of wealth. And when this is so, "as soon as labour in the direct form has ceased to be the great wellspring of wealth, labour-time ceases and must cease to be its measure," which puts an end to the role played by exchange value and surplus labor.

We must obviously guard against a "technicist" interpretation of these formulations. When Marx says that the role played by exchange value, surplus labor, and accumulation of the product of the latter must come to an end, he does not say that this role will come to an end by itself. An essential factor in the process of transformation expounded by Marx is man's *understanding of nature and mastery over it "as a social body,"* and this understanding and mastery proceed by way of a *political and ideological revolution* which dictates a different relation between men and their labor, a relation that sees this labor as what it is, namely, directly social labor. Hence the importance, when the workers have taken political power, of the development of *Communist labor,* which is one of the modes of transformation of the forms of appropriation and distribution (see Lenin's remarks on this point, quoted in volume I of the present work, pp. 198–202).

3. See on this point Lenin, *CW,* vol. 33, pp. 97, 312, and volume I of the present work, pp. 500, 508.

4. The private sector of industry and trade which operated at the beginning of the NEP included both individual craft and trading enterprises and capitalist ones. During "war communism," though the activity of all kinds of craftsmen had not been formally prohibited, it had often been paralyzed through lack of raw materials and means of transport. With the improvement in the general economic situation resulting from the adoption of the NEP, craft activity was resumed. The revival of the rural crafts played a big role in the development of agricultural production.

As regards private capitalist enterprises, and those craft enterprises whose activity had been formally suspended, legal measures were taken in the summer and autumn of 1921 with a view to enabling them to expand their production to a certain extent. A decree of July 7, 1921, authorized "free exercise" of craft occupations and the carrying on of small enterprises employing no more than twenty workers, in the case of those without mechanical

power, or ten workers if they used mechanical power. A decree of
December 10, 1921, restored to their former owners some of the
small businesses which had been nationalized but were not actually operating. A decree of May 22, 1922, enlarged the right to set
up private commercial and industrial enterprises. This right was
granted to any person, whether acting alone or in association, as a
company or a cooperative, "so as to develop the productive forces"
(Article 4)—on condition that the right was not "used in a way
contrary to the economic and social aim assigned to it" (Article 1).
Besides this, it was provided from the start of the NEP that certain
state-owned enterprises could be leased out to private capitalists,
or granted as concessions to foreign capital if it seemed that their
production might thereby be increased more quickly. (See E. H.
Carr, *The Bolshevik Revolution,* vol. 2, pp. 299 ff., and Prokopovicz, *Histoire économique,* pp. 274 ff.)

During the first years of the NEP (broadly speaking, until the
Fourteenth Party Congress, in December 1925), the predominant
idea was that private enterprises were bound to disappear eventually, "by themselves," that is, through competition by state-owned
enterprises which, once they were well organized, would provide
goods at lower prices than the private ones.

At the beginning of 1925 an extension of possibilities of development for private industry was still regarded as acceptable. In
May a decree gave official permission, under certain conditions, to
the private sector to employ as many as 100 wage earners per
enterprise, while the leased enterprises could employ several
hundred: an example is the Moscow factory called "Proletarian
Labor," a private firm producing metal goods and employing
over 650 persons in October 1925. (See Y. S. Rozenfeld, *Promyshlennaya Politika SSSR,* p. 494, and the supplement to
Planovoye Khozyaistvo, no. 12 [1925], p. 7, quoted by E. H. Carr,
Socialism in One Country, vol. I, p. 359.)

As will be seen, the economic role of the private capitalist sector
in industry remained on the whole fairly limited, but the situation
was different where trade, especially retail trade, and the crafts
were concerned (see below, pp. 187 ff.).

5. This effort applied also to the production units of the state sector,
where, as we shall see, "business accounting" or "financial autonomy" (*khozraschet*) was introduced (see below, pp. 268 ff.).

1. The reconstitution of a monetary and financial system

Under "war communism" the currency played only a relatively secondary role.[1] A large proportion of those products which were not consumed by their producers were in that period directly allocated to particular uses by the political authority. This applied to what was produced by the factories and also to that part of the production of the individual peasant farms which was requisitioned. However, much buying and selling went on clandestinely, either by way of barter or by exchanging goods for monetary tokens. The state itself did not stop issuing new notes, though their purchasing power fell lower and lower with every passing month.

When the civil war and intervention ended, the constraints of "war communism" were no longer accepted by the peasant masses. They demanded the cessation of requisitioning, establishment of a stable fiscal system, freedom of trade, and the reintroduction of exchange by means of money, which corresponded to the form of production then prevailing in agriculture. Acceptance of these demands by the Soviet government was one of the principal aspects of the NEP.

Initially (at the beginning of 1921), requisitioning was replaced by a *tax-in-kind*, the amount of which was fixed in advance (unlike the amount requisitioned), so that the more the peasants produced the more produce they had at their disposal. The total revenue from this tax-in-kind was to be such that it would meet the needs of the army and the cost of part of the state machine. As for the agricultural products needed by industry and for foreign trade, they were to be supplied in the main through exchanges of products between the peasants and the state institutions. At the beginning of the NEP the favored form of these exchanges was still barter, and only that part of the peasants' production which was not either consumed by themselves or absorbed by the tax or by "products exchange" with state institutions could be *sold* freely by them in their local markets.

It very soon became apparent that the barter transactions between the state organs and the peasants were not going well. In October 1921 the former were given permission to buy agricultural produce, that is, to pay for it with *money*. At the same time the Soviet government increased its cash receipts by introducing new *taxes which were also payable in money*. Finally, in 1923, the agricultural tax was itself changed from a tax-in-kind to a money tax.[2] Thenceforth, *commodity and money relations* formed the essential link between agriculture and the state, between agriculture and industry, and between the different units of industrial production, even when these belonged to the state.

The process of *reconstituting commodity production* thus entailed a parallel process of *reconstituting the circulation of money*, for, as Marx said, money comes into being "spontaneously in the course of exchange."[3] So long as social production takes place in a private form, the social nature of the wealth produced tends to be incarnated in money.[4]

I.   The process of reconstituting the Soviet monetary system

A study of the process whereby the Soviet monetary system was reconstituted is highly instructive. It reveals the subordination of this process to the prevailing social conditions as a whole and to the various forms assumed by the class struggle. It also enables us to perceive the contradictions that governed subsequent changes in the monetary system. Only the most important facts will be mentioned here.

When the NEP began, the monetary tokens in circulation were issued directly by the state, by the Narkomfin (Commissariat of Finance). The illusions of "war communism" required that they be called not "currency notes" but "settlement notes." These notes, for which the everyday name was "*sovznak*," were issued in large quantities (inflation being regarded by some as a means of "doing away with" money). In 1921 it became clear that the *sovznaks*, whose purchasing power was rapidly sinking, could not fulfill functions which must from now on be those of a currency.

On November 3, 1921, the Soviet government decided to substitute new notes for the old ones—the new notes to be regarded as "currency notes" and no longer as "settlement notes." The existence of a currency was thus officially acknowledged, though Soviet citizens went on talking in terms of *svoznaks*.

For lack of sufficient budgetary receipts the state continued to issue large quantities of notes (in 1922 60 percent of budgetary receipts was due to the issue of new notes) and the purchasing power of the new rouble fell so sharply that in March 1922, 200,000 new roubles were needed to pay for (on the average) what had cost only 60,000 in October 1921 (and which corresponded roughly to one prewar rouble).[5]

The budget for 1921–1922 was then drawn up in terms of the "goods-rouble," a unit of account which was supposed to represent a fixed amount of *purchasing power* (as compared with prewar prices). Each month the Narkomfin calculated the purchasing power of the currency in circulation in relation to the goods-rouble. The number of monetary units that a debtor had to pay (e.g., the wages due from enterprises to their workers) was *revalued in accordance with the depreciation of the currency thus recorded* (for the wage earners this measure signified the establishment of a *sliding scale of wages*).

The development of payments in money by state enterprises meant that the latter had to be provided with the monetary resources that they needed for their operations. To this end, a resolution of the VTsIK, dated October 12, 1921, decided that the state bank (*Gosbank*), which had closed in January 1920, should be reopened.[6] The new state bank began functioning on November 16, 1921.[7] It operated on the basis of *khozraschet*, i.e., financial autonomy,[8] and therefore had to cover its expenditure by its receipts. Its capital was provided by the state and its chairman appointed by Narkomfin. The bank's resources were at first slight: 200 milliard roubles of that period. It could grant only very short-term loans, and those at high rates of interest (between 8 and 12 percent a month).

The pace at which the currency continued to depreciate led the Gosbank's experts (among whom there were a number of former bankers, financiers, and industrialists) to prepare a report in which they set out proposals in conformity with the canons of "financial orthodoxy." This report called for extension of "free markets," priority financial aid to light industry (the branch best capable of bringing about a rapid development of internal trade), review of the conditions governing the way that the foreign trade monopoly worked, an attempt to obtain loans from abroad, and a return to the gold standard. If these proposals had been adopted, the Soviet economy would soon have been reintegrated into world economy, occupying a subordinate position as producer of certain raw materials and agricultural products.[9]

These proposals were rejected by the Eleventh Conference of the Bolshevik Party (December 1921), which, however, emphasized the need, in order to strengthen the worker-peasant alliance, to develop exchanges between agriculture and industry by means of a *stable currency*. The conference's resolution on the reestablishment of the national economy stated that it was necessary to undertake "the restoration of a currency based on gold" and that "the first step to be taken in this direction is the firm implementation of a plan aimed at limiting the issue of paper-money."[10]

In March 1922 calculation in goods-roubles[11] was given up. Thereafter, the state's receipts and expenditures were calculated in *gold roubles*. The actual payments were, of course, made in paper money, but the quantity of paper money corresponding to a certain sum in gold roubles was evaluated by reference to the rate at which Gosbank bought gold on the market.[12]

In fact, although it fell relatively in 1922, the budget deficit financed by currency issues continued to be considerable, and the decline in the purchasing power of the old currency went on until this currency was withdrawn in 1924. A new monetary unit was then made legal tender, with a gold backing, and issued from the beginning of 1923 by Gosbank: namely, the *chervonets* rouble.

The *chervonets* rouble enjoyed great stability for several years. Soviet Russia was at that time *the first country in Europe which, after taking part in the First World War, had succeeded in restoring a relatively stable currency,* an achievement that was obviously not due to merely technical reasons.

II. The currency reform

The *chervonets* (which corresponded to ten gold roubles, or 7.7423 grams of refined gold) circulated at first alongside the old paper rouble, which continued to depreciate quickly. Actually, the *chervonets* became the principal medium of payment. In January 1924 the Thirteenth Conference of the Bolshevik Party noted that four-fifths of the currency in circulation consisted of *chervonets* roubles.[13]

The situation had become ripe for the currency reform, which was decided on by a decree dated February 4, 1924—two weeks after Lenin's death.

(a) The decree of February 1924

By virtue of this decree, Gosbank had supreme control over the issue of the currency that was thenceforth to be legal tender and which was secured on the gold held by Gosbank. The former *sovznaks* were withdrawn from circulation at the rate of 50,000 *sovznaks* of 1923 for one new gold rouble. The state treasury, which had up to then issued notes to cover the budget deficit, lost this right of issue and could thenceforth put out only small denominations, to an amount not exceeding one-half of the *chervonets* issue of Gosbank.[14]

In 1924 the new currency enjoyed the confidence of the peasants, at least so far as current transactions were concerned. However, the loans which the Soviet government tried to raise in the rural areas met with only limited success.[15]

(b)   The class consequences of the monetary system established in 1924

From the standpoint of class relations and the effects of the class struggle upon the political line of the Bolshevik Party, one of the essential aspects of the monetary reform of 1924 was the effective linking of the new currency with gold.

This linkage meant that *Gosbank had to intervene in the market to maintain the rouble's rate in relation to gold and to foreign exchange at the official parity,* which entailed a number of consequences.

Thus, Gosbank needed to possess reserves of gold and foreign exchange sufficient to be able to act effectively upon the market. This dictated an *export policy aimed at keeping these reserves at an adequate level* and tended to strengthen the position of the rich peasants, who were regarded as those best able to produce grain for export. On the other hand, efforts at industrialization had to be relatively restricted, in so far as industrial development was not capable of quickly supplying exportable goods, but, on the contrary, necessitated imports of equipment. The interests of the rich peasants thus tended to be favored more than those of the peasantry in general and those of industry and the working class. On an international level, the Soviet Union tended to settle down in the role of a country supplying agricultural products.

Maintaining the exchange rate of the rouble at official parity in relation to gold and foreign currencies also dictated a restrictive policy where credit and budgetary expenditure were concerned. Consequently, financial and credit policies could not be adapted first and foremost to the *internal needs* of the economy as these had been defined politically by the Bol-

shevik Party. Economic, financial, and budgetary policy was to
some extent subject to the pressure of the world market, as
exercised through the "demands" of the functioning of the
gold standard.

The currency reform of 1924 corresponded to a political
orientation which was that of the bourgeois "experts" of Gosbank and Narkomfin. The Bolshevik leaders clearly did not
grasp the full implication of this political orientation. Some of
them even thought it possible to rejoice in the integration of
the Soviet Union into the European market. This was the case
with Sokolnikov, then commissar of finance, who said: "As
members of the European community, despite the special
features of our political position and although a different class
is in power here, we have become integrated into the European mechanism of economic and financial development."[16]

(c) The subsequent changes in the monetary system

From 1925 on the concrete meaning of the currency reform
decided on in the previous year began to become apparent.
Gosbank was now obliged to throw significant quantities of
gold and foreign currency onto the market in order to keep the
exchange stable.[17] This situation was due to the development
of increasing contradictions between the "demands" of the
functioning of the gold standard and those of a rapid development of industrial production.

At the beginning of 1925 the CC of the Bolshevik Party did
in fact take measures aimed at *depriving Gosbank and Narkomfin of supreme control over budgetary policy.* For this
purpose a commission for the USSR budget was set up, under
the chairmanship of Kuibyshev,[18] which upheld a policy of
budgetary and credit expansion directed toward activating the
development of industry.

Implementation of this policy soon became incompatible
with "support" for the rate of exchange of the rouble. In March
1926 *it was decided that Gosbank must stop selling gold and*

foreign currency in order to keep the rouble at par.[19] Without saying so, the government thus *broke with the currency reform of 1924* which had, in practice, tied the rouble to gold.

In July 1926 the export of Soviet currency was forbidden, and in March 1928 its import as well. Thereafter, the rouble was a *purely internal currency* with a rate of exchange fixed by a government commission. The few financial centers which, in 1924, had begun to quote the *chervonets* rouble now ceased to do so.[20]

The rouble functioned as authentic paper money. It was still the embodiment of the social nature of the wealth produced. It was not a "labour voucher" such as Marx had said might exist during the first phase of communism—for what is characteristic of such vouchers is that "they do not circulate." Later on, this currency was to go on functioning under conditions that remained basically the same as during the NEP, which meant that fully socialized production still had not come into being.[21]

(d)   *The political implications of the*
      abandonment of the gold standard and
      the return to a paper currency

The abandonment of a currency secured on gold and the return to a paper currency had important political consequences. It meant that financial and credit policy, and also import and export policy, were no longer *as directly* subject to pressure of the international markets as they had been before. It was now possible to tackle more actively the problem of financing industrialization.

Moreover, abandonment of the gold standard made the stability of the currency depend essentially on the way relations between the political authority and the different social classes evolved. Actually, this stability was not dependent merely on "technical measures" (that is, on adjustment of the quantity of money and its speed of circulation to the requirements of production and distribution), but also on a *political and ideological relation* between those who held the currency and the political authority that issued it. This relation took the form of "confidence in the currency." As we know, the monetary role performed by a *token of value* can be maintained "only if its function as a symbol is guaranteed by the general intention of commodity owners." In the case of paper money, this "general intention" acquires its "legal conventional existence" in the establishment of a "legal rate of exchange."[22]

The existence of a "legal rate of exchange" does not suffice in the least to guarantee the stability of the currency; in order that this stability not be challenged, it is necessary that the "general intention" of those who hold currency and commodities be maintained. In a class-divided society this "intention" can be preserved only if the class which is in power firmly carries out its leading role. When its performance of this role flags, the "legal rate of exchange" cannot save the currency from depreciating, nor, in certain circumstance, can it prevent the emergence of exchanges effected by means other than legal tender.

It was precisely the conjunction, toward the end of the NEP period, of economic and monetary measures that lacked coherence, together with the sharpening of class contradictions (especially in the sphere of relations between the Soviet government and the peasantry) that upset the working of the monetary system. The leadership of the Bolshevik Party did not expect this to happen. They thought that the economic and political conditions obtaining in the Soviet Union constituted a lasting and powerful "guarantee" of the stability of the currency; this was not really the case, as was shown particularly by the evolution of prices and exchanges.[23]

The Bolshevik Party's illusions regarding the capacity of the Soviet government, under the conditions of the NEP, to control production, exchange, and prices by means of economic and administrative measures reflected an underestimation of the economic and social contradictions and of the decisive role of the ideological and political class struggle. From 1928 on, reality came into harsh conflict with these illusions—which nevertheless were destined to reproduce themselves in new forms.

III.   *The budgetary system*

The restoration of a basically balanced budgetary system constitutes another important aspect of the economic reestablishment process of the first years of the NEP. There was a
material basis for the restoration, namely, the remarkable boom
in industrial and agricultural production. There was a political
basis, too, namely the confidence of the worker and peasant
masses in the Soviet government. This confidence was expressed in the way the agricultural tax was paid—with a minimum of coercion. (In any case, at the beginning of the NEP,
the administration was hardly represented in the rural areas.)

The restoration of the budgetary system also had an economic and juridical basis, namely, the consolidation of the
huge state-owned sector of industry and commerce, which
furnished no small proportion of the budget's receipts. The
budget was balanced in 1923–1924,[24] and this was an essential
factor in the stabilization of the currency. In 1924–1925 there
was a budget surplus, and this happened in the following
years as well, during which time budgetary receipts and expenditure increased very rapidly.[25] In 1924–1925 the economic boom was such that the forecasts of budgetary receipts
and expenditure were revised upward several times. The
rapid expansion of budgetary receipts continued, attaining in
1927–1928 the figure of over 4.58 milliard roubles (not including revenue from the transport and postal services), compared
with expenditure of 4.38 milliard. This was 75 percent more
than the figure for receipts in 1925–1926.[26] In the same period,
budget expenditure on industry and electrification increased
even faster, by 173 percent.[27] These sums represented,
moreover, only a fraction of the total amount of capital investment in the two sectors mentioned, which in 1927–1928 came
to nearly two milliard roubles.[28]

IV.   *The banking system*

The rapid recovery in industrial and agricultural production, the development of commercial exchanges, the equally

rapid expansion of the budget and of investment were accompanied by restoration of a banking system. This served to tap and redistribute monetary resources, ensure the availability of funds for enterprises, grant them credits, and manage a substantial share of the investment fund.

(a) The establishment of a new banking system

The banking system thus set up (which was to continue and develop its activity even when the NEP had been replaced by the policy of Five-Year Plans) embraced, besides Gosbank, which was responsible for issuing currency and looking after the current bank accounts of the state enterprises, also a series of specialized banks: Prombank (the bank for industry), Elektrobank (the bank in charge of financing electrification), Tsekombank (the bank which financed municipal enterprises), and the Agricultural Bank. The network of *credit cooperatives* and the *savings bank* completed the system. It was closely linked with the services of the Commissariat of Finance. It constituted a vast state apparatus employing thousands of functionaries and experts, who were usually of bourgeois or petty-bourgeois origin. The weight and influence of these experts made themselves felt more than once during the NEP period: this was an aspect of the class struggle that the Bolshevik Party was especially ill-prepared to deal with.[29]

While budgetary policy was strict, that was not always true of policy relating to credit and the issuing of currency. Thus, there was a rapid expansion in the amount of money in circulation, mainly connected with the size of the bank credits made available to the economy. Part of these credits corresponded to increased economic activity and therefore covered a real need for circulating funds; but another part, especially after 1925, served to cover investments that would be productive only in the middle or long term. The funds paid out increased the amount of money in circulation and incomes, and ended by exerting inflationary pressure. This situation developed contradictions that were to be felt with particular acuteness from the autumn of 1927 on.[30]

(b)   The illusions connected with the functioning of the banking system

To the illusions engendered by the restoration of a monetary system whose functioning was supposed to be completely controllable by the state, there were soon added similar illusions connected with the existence of a powerful banking system which was supposed to play a central role in directing the country's economic development.

During the first years of the NEP, the banking system was essentially conceived as serving to exercise more effective control over the allocation of credit. Thus, a resolution adopted by the CC at the end of April 1924 declared: "It is indispensable to organise a committee of banks, whose task should be the organisation of bank credit and the avoidance of duplication, the preliminary examination of directive plans of credit, the fixing of co-ordinated discount rates, and the appropriate distribution of banking facilities among different regions and branches of industry."[31]

The committee of banks advocated in this resolution was formed in June 1924. It included representatives of the principal Soviet banks of the period.[32] Gosplan also participated in this committee, which was responsible for drawing up credit plans for submission for the government's approval. In a few years the banking network included thousands of branches and managed milliards of roubles of credit.

The idea then took shape that *credit plans* would make it possible to draw up real *economic* plans. Krzhizhanovsky, the chairman of Gosplan, said at the beginning of 1925 that "credit and planning are blood-brothers in a single system of socialisation." As for Kamenev, he hailed the "new commanding height" of the economy, in which he saw a "decisive factor in the regulation of the economy."[33]

Such formulations as these could seem correct so long as the structure of production had undergone no profound changes. They became sources of grave illusions as soon as the size of investments made it necessary to pay special attention to liquid assets and to the use made of different categories of prod-

ucts. In 1927, however, the CC considered that the existence
of a state banking system linked with state-owned industry
(which supplied the bulk of industrial production) and with a
powerful state and cooperative commercial network made
possible genuine economic planning.

These illusions found expression in a resolution adopted by
the plenum of the CC held on February 7–12, 1927, after it
heard a report presented jointly by Mikoyan and Kuibyshev.
This resolution declared that the conditions had now been
created for solving the problems of developing industry and
agriculture, increasing accumulation and real wages, steadily
strengthening the socialist elements in the national economy,
and restricting the role played by private capitalists. *The resolution stressed the idea that the solution of all these questions
revolved around the problem of prices.* Thus, the problem of
prices appeared as the essential factor in the consolidation of
the worker-peasant alliance,[34] while the other aspects of the
class struggle were overlooked.

In the February 1927 issue of the Party's official journal,
Bolshevik, Mikoyan set out the thesis that a new stage of the
NEP had been reached: according to him it was no longer the
market but the "organised sector" that played the decisive
role in determining prices.[35]

In May 1927 the same journal expressed the view that "the
alleged contradiction between industry and agriculture" had
ceased to matter.[36] These claims were carried farther in an
article published in a journal specially concerned with agricultural and peasant questions, which asserted that "the
Soviet state has brought the grain market under control to the
point where no untoward event or mistake in calculation can
henceforth threaten our plans for construction."[37]

To an increasing extent the Party's thinking was thus dominated by the illusion that the system which had been established since 1924 would make possible control of the most
complex economic developments, including those that were
directly connected with class contradictions. This illusion was
all the more remarkable in that its claim to control was
founded upon the working of those economic apparatuses

which were farthest separated from the masses. The masses were kept in ignorance, moreover, even of measures that affected them as directly as the prices fixed by the state. These prices were told only to the administrative and commercial organs and to the merchants; they were not made public.

At the end of 1927 this illusion regarding the possibility of controlling the development of the economy—and even the contradictions between classes—through proper functioning of the administrative and banking system suffered its first blow with the outbreak of the crisis in the state's procurement of grain.[38] The secrecy surrounding decisions directly affecting the masses was then denounced as a hindrance to the exercise of "pressure of organised public opinion in the form of Party Soviet, trade-union and other organizations, and in the press."[39] However, these criticisms of the "excessive secrecy" surrounding the economic and administrative machinery did not put an end either to this secrecy or to the illusions held regarding the powers possessed by this machinery of state.

Actually, these illusions reflected a conception which had matured between 1924 and 1927 and become deeply rooted in the Party. This conception ascribed a decisive role to the *activity of the state's economic organs* and emphasized in a one-sided way a development of industry based mainly upon investments directly controlled by these organs. It was a conception radically alien to the formulations put forward by Lenin in his last writings, especially in those reviewing the lessons of the first five years of Soviet power.

As we know, Lenin saw the NEP as a road which could lead to socialism provided that the Party put in the forefront the ideological and political class struggle and thereby correctly resolved the contradictions.[40] In order to do that, the Party must help the working masses to *transform economic relations* through becoming aware of the demands of socialism and developing economic and political practices that would enable them to build *collective forms of production and distribution* and to exercise a more thorough and effective *control* over the state apparatuses for which the mass organizations must eventually substitute themselves.

The conception of the NEP which became increasingly established from 1925 on was in contradiction with this view. It assumed, in effect, that the NEP could lead to socialism mainly through "good management" of the economy by the economic and administrative apparatuses (possibly subject, if necessary, to a certain amount of "pressure" from below). Here were a set of illusions constituting an aspect of what R. Linhart has called "an ideal N.E.P."[41]

These illusions, which were connected with practices increasingly remote from the requirements of the NEP, and, in the first place, of the worker-peasant alliance, resulted from the class struggle, from shifts of dominance within the Bolshevik ideological formation,[42] and were reinforced by the very nature of the economic relations that prevailed at that time. These relations, which were essentially commodity, money, and capitalist relations, determined the forms in which the real relations were concealed and inverted, those forms which Marx analyzed in *Capital*.[43]

The illusions which thus took shape were reinforced by the way the Soviet economy operated at that time—*presuming* formal subordination of the state-owned enterprises to the political authority, whereas *in fact* this subordination was extremely limited, precisely because of the slight extent to which the masses controlled the working of the economy. All this made economic reality particularly "opaque."[44]

The existence of the illusions just described was to render still more "unexpected" the outbreak of the crisis that began in 1928, accounting for the sudden political turn made in 1929 and the lack of real preparation for the changes then introduced.

V. *The weak degree of control of the monetary and financial system*

Until the beginning of 1925 the Bolshevik Party's control of the monetary and banking system was relatively weak. The integration of the rouble into the European financial system[45] imposed a number of constraints upon monetary policy and also on credit, investment, and foreign trade policies.

The abandonment of the gold standard removed these constraints from without to a fairly large extent, but they were replaced by others. Among these was the need to strengthen the confidence of the masses in the Soviet currency, a confidence that depended especially on the results of the functioning of the Soviet economy for the working people.

In this sphere the changes that took place in the Bolshevik ideological formation, and the practices connected with these changes, played a very negative role.

Down to 1925 relative priority had been given to satisfying the needs of the masses, including the peasants, and this ensured a more or less regular supply of goods for the population and comparatively stable retail prices.

Between January 1, 1924, and January 1, 1925, the price index maintained by the Bureau of Labor Statistics showed a rise that was relatively slight, given the conditions of the time: about 8 percent. In the following year the rise recorded was only 6.6 percent.[46] Between January 1, 1926, and January 1, 1928, the retail price index even fell a little (by 5.8 percent over the two years) as the rise in retail prices in the private sector (6.8 percent) was offset by their fall in the state and cooperative sector (8 percent).[47]

And yet, from July 1927 on, price control slackened. On the one hand, some of the stores were no longer regularly supplied with goods (this was especially the case with the stores situated in country districts, which found themselves receiving fewer and fewer industrial goods), and there occurred what was called a "goods famine," so that the prices quoted for goods which could not actually be bought were meaningless. On the other hand, and as a consequence of this development, retail prices in private trade began to rise. If the level in July 1927 may be taken as 100, these prices stood at 115.3 in July 1928 and at 150.7 in July 1929.[48] The rise in price particularly affected agricultural products of general consumption: thus, between 1926–1927 and 1928–1929, market prices increased by 220 percent for rye, 222 percent for potatoes, 68 percent for milk, etc.[49] In this sphere, too, frequent shortages added to the difficulties encountered by consumers.

After the middle of 1927 the monetary system and the price system were less and less under control. In the last analysis, this loss of control corresponded to a slackening in control of the development of the class struggle. The loss of control (the forms of which will be analyzed in the following chapters) was expressed especially in an increase of money incomes without any adequate counterpart in increased production of consumer goods, so that there was a rapid increase in the fiduciary circulation, which rose from 1,668 million on January 1, 1928, to 2,773 million on January 1, 1930, an increase of 66 percent.[50]

The rising prices, the decline in the supply of goods to the population—especially the peasant masses—the reappearance of inflation, etc., showed that practices were developing which implied *de facto abandonment of the NEP* and the continuance eventually resulted in its complete abandonment. Among these practices was a policy of accumulation and allocation of investments which led to lasting imbalances that bore more and more heavily on the peasantry. A new political line was gradually establishing itself and becoming embodied in the economic plans then being drawn up. We must now consider the planning organs which were concerned in this, but without forgetting that the content of the plans was, ultimately, the result of a *policy*, an effect of the class struggles.

Notes

1. See volume I of the present book, pp. 388, 461.
2. See M. Dobb, *Soviet Economic Development since 1917*, pp. 125–139.
3. Marx, *A Contribution to the Critique of Political Economy*, p. 49.
4. See on this point Marx, *Capital* (Moscow), vol. III, p. 560.
5. See E. H. Carr, *The Bolshevik Revolution*, vol. 2, p. 348.
6. Ibid., pp. 346–347.
7. This was the Gosbank of the RSFSR; two years later it became

the Gosbank of the USSR (see *Sobranie Uzakonenii*, no. 81 [1923], art. 786).

8. See below, pp. 268 ff.
9. See Carr, *The Bolshevik Revolution*, vol. 2, p. 350.
10. *K.P.S.S. v rezolyutsiyakh*, vol. I, p. 589.
11. See above, p. 55.
12. See *Sobranie Uzakonenii*, no. 26 (1922), art. 310; and no. 31, art. 377; see also Carr, *The Bolshevik Revolution*, vol. 2, p. 355.
13. *K.P.S.S. v rezolyutsiyakh*, vol. I, p. 795.
14. See *Sobranie Uzakonenii*, no. 32 (1924), art. 288; no. 34, art. 308; no. 45 art. 433; E. H. Carr, *The Interregnum*, p. 133, and *Socialism*, vol. I, pp. 475–476.
15. The checking of inflation made it possible to reduce interest rates to a substantial degree. The rate for long-term loans granted to peasants was, in 1924, 8 percent per year, and this fell to 6 percent in 1925. The loans raised by the state bore interest at 5 or 6 percent. The subscribers to these were mainly rich or well-to-do peasants (see Carr, *Socialism*, vol. I, pp. 469–474).
16. *Sotsialisticheskoye Khozyaistvo*, no. 5 (1924), p. 6.
17. See Carr, *Socialism*, vol. I, p. 481.
18. See V. Dyachenko, *Sovetskie finansy v pervoy faze razvitiya sovetskogo gosudarstva*, vol. 1, p. 426; *Sobranie Zakonov*, no. 17 (1925), arts. 127, 128; no. 38, art. 282; no. 71, art. 520.
19. See Carr, *Socialism*, vol. 1, p. 487.
20. See A. Baykov, *The Soviet Economic System*, pp. 102–103.
21. In volume II of *Capital* Marx imagines a society in which production has been "socialised," and writes that, this being so,

> society distributes labour-power and means of production to the different branches of production. The producers may, for all it matters, receive paper vouchers entitling them to withdraw from the social supplies of consumer goods a quantity corresponding to their labour-time. These vouchers are not money. They do not circulate." (*Capital* [Moscow], vol. II, p. 358.)

It will be observed that the "socialisation" mentioned here goes far beyond mere ownership by the state. It implies a thoroughgoing transformation of the ideological and political relations, enabling the producers associated on the scale of society to subject production to *a plan which is genuinely the result of their joint activity* (and not that of an administrative instance separated from them and imposing upon them tasks which it has itself determined).

22. Marx, *Contribution to the Critique of Political Economy*, p. 116.
23. See for example, above, pp. 67 ff. and below pp. 150 ff.
24. Until 1930 the financial year ran from October 1 to September 30. Thereafter, the financial year and the ordinary year coincided.
25. On these questions see Carr, *Socialism*, vol. I, pp. 456 ff., and E. H. Carr and R. W. Davies, *Foundations of a Planned Economy (1926–1929)*, vol. I, pt. 2, pp. 974–975.
26. Carr and Davies, *Foundations*, vol. I, pt. 2, p. 975.
27. See Baykov, *The Soviet Economic System*, p. 95.
28. Carr and Davies, *Foundations*, vol. I, pt. 2, p. 979.
29. It must be stressed that, if experts of bourgeois origin were able to influence the running of the monetary and banking system, this was because they were *integrated into structures* which made possible the *reproduction* of the relations and practices of which they were the "carriers." Subsequently, the presence of "specialists" of proletarian origin in the financial and monetary organs was not to prevent the continued reproduction of bourgeois relations and practices, for the political line being applied had not radically transformed the structure of these organs.
30. Between January 1, 1924 and January 1, 1928, the total amount of money in circulation increased fivefold, growing from 322 to 1,668 million roubles (Baykov, *The Soviet Economic System*, p. 104). Between 1925–1926 and 1927–1928 the amount of money in circulation increased by about 42 percent, whereas the national income, in constant prices, increased by only about 14 percent (Carr and Davies, *Foundations*, vol. I, part 2, pp. 976, 977). This contributed to the increase in prices which will be described at the end of the chapter.
31. Quoted from Carr, *Socialism*, vol. I, p. 473.
32. See A. Z. Arnold, *Banks, Credit and Money in Soviet Russia*, pp. 266, 284–285.
33. *Planovoye Khozyaistvo*, no. 1 (1925), pp. 19, 30–31.
34. See *K.P.S.S. v rezolyutsiyakh*, vol. 2, pp. 224–227, especially p. 225.
35. *Bolshevik*, February 15, 1927, pp. 18–27.
36. Ibid., May 1, 1927, p. 9.
37. *Bednota*, May 13, 1927.
38. See above, pp. 37 ff.

39. *Voprosy Torgovli*, nos. 2–3 (November–December 1927), p. 67, quoted in Carr and Davies, *Foundations*, vol. I, pt. 2, p. 679, n. 2.

40. See volume I of the present work.

41. R. Linhart, "La NEP, quelques caractéristiques de la transition soviétique," in *Etudes de planification socialiste*, pp. 156 ff., especially pp. 185–186.

42. See Part 4 of the present volume.

43. Marx, *Capital* (London), vol. I, pp. 165, 180. See also C. Bettelheim, *Economic Calculation and Forms of Property* (London), pp. 51–57.

44. See also, on this point, R. Linhart's remarks in "La NEP," pp. 195–196. We shall see later that, in the sphere of industry, "production conferences" were supposed to ensure a better awareness of reality, but the actual conditions in which these conferences were held seriously restricted their practical effect.

45. See above, pp. 57–59.

46. Figures calculated from Baykov, *The Soviet Economic System*, p. 96.

47. Figures calculated from A. Mendelson, ed., *Pokazateli konyunktury*, quoted in Carr and Davies, *Foundations*, vol. I, pt. 2, pp. 964–965.

48. Ibid. In the case of agricultural products sold in the private sector, the rise was even more acute, with the index moving from 100 to 204.5 in two years.

49. Ibid.

50. Baykov, *The Soviet Economic System*, p. 104.

2. The development of the machinery and procedures of economic planning

As we know, the NEP was not characterized merely by open development of commodity relations, possibilities of activity (within certain limits) granted to individual and private capitalist enterprises, and "financial autonomy" for state-owned enterprises. Together with these orientations and these measures, others were adopted which were aimed at countering the danger that development might take place along an "ordinary capitalist road." To this end, organs were set up to coordinate the different branches of economic activity and to work out plans.

The existence and functioning of these organs was not at all sufficient to eliminate the dangers of *capitalist development*, dangers that could be removed only by the application of an appropriate *political line*, but they did create, within the NEP framework, some of the *preliminary conditions* for progress by the Soviet economy along the *socialist road*, and this was why Lenin ascribed great importance to their establishment.

The principal function of the planning organs was *political*. They prepared and accompanied *the government's interventions* in the process of reproducing and transforming the *material* and *social* conditions of production. These organs served as the fulcrum of a specific form of political practice, namely, *planning*. In a class-divided society like that of the NEP (and the one that succeeded it), *planning has a class content*. It is affected by class struggles and affects the way that these struggles proceed. The interventions determined by planning are of a *juridico-political* nature. They take place amid the contradictions of social reproduction. They mobilize in a concentrated way the political and ideological forces of the ruling power in order to lead the *processes of production* in a certain direction and to alter their distinctive features, and so the *forms of the processes of appropriation and distribution.*

For "planning" to take place it is necessary that the interventions in production and reproduction actually have an effect, and that they be *coordinated as regards their guiding principles.* Such coordination is the *purpose aimed at,* but it is far from always achieved. *In the absence of adequate real coordination,* the direction actually given to the social process of production and reproduction may differ from what is "desired" by the political leadership. From the political standpoint, however, what is decisive is the *real process,* not what is imagined.

The political interventions connected with planning do not directly modify the nature of the immediate production relations, but only the conditions for their expanded reproduction. The place of the agents of production in relation to each other and to the means of production is only *indirectly modified* by planning—for example, when it favors the expansion of a particular *form of production* (to which certain means of production are allocated by right of priority) while paralyzing another form, which it cuts off from some or all of the material means of production (or even the labor power) that it needs for its reproduction. A real upheaval in the relative positions of the agents of production always results, however, from class struggle, from the activity of the producers, and the changing of the actual conditions of production.

The political interventions connected with planning, and which affect the *reproduction* of social relations, may be carried out either *directly* or *indirectly.* One of the forms of *indirect intervention* (which was typical of the NEP but did not disappear along with it) is that which operates in the sphere of money and prices. For example, an evolution of the "terms of trade" to the disadvantage of agriculture (by a fall in the prices of its products relative to those of industrial goods) brings about a *transfer of values* to industry and the state sector, and so accelerates the expanded reproduction of the means of production at the disposal of this sector, and of the *production relations* characteristic of this sector.

Even when the Soviet government intervenes in the reproduction of social relations within the setting of a plan, the fact of these interventions cannot be directly equated with progress along the *socialist road:* it all depends on the type of change in social relations induced by the interventions. Contrary to what has often been stated, *all planning is not necessarily socialist:* it can and often does, accompany various forms of state capitalism. *The socialist character of planning* depends, therefore, primarily on the *class character of the ruling power,* but also on the content of the plans, the intention they express to create the conditions for *increasing control by the working people over social reproduction.*

The planning organs were established at the beginning of the NEP. Their increasing activity in the second half of the 1920s resulted from the actual conditions under which the Soviet economy was functioning at that time. These conditions exerted an especially strong influence when the period of restoration of industry (the reactivation of inherited equipment) drew to a close and the reconstruction period began (at the end of 1925).

From that moment, indeed, the question of the *allocation of accumulated capital* arose in acute form. This allocation would decide which industries would be given priority development and also the *technology* they would employ. It thus had a bearing on the *division of labor.*

When capital circulates "freely" between the various branches of production, the question of "priorities" and of the "technical" forms assumed by economic development is "settled" by the overall and differential action exerted by class struggles on levels and differences of wages, by the striving for the maximum rate of profit, by the tendency for this rate to be equalized between the different branches, and by the relations of strength between the various industrial and financial groups. Under the pressure of these forces, accumulated capital is distributed in a determined way between the different branches, and invested in techniques which are also determined, in accordance with the capital available to the capitalists and with their estimates of future prospects. The nonrealization of these estimates, which is inevitable given the very conditions under which capitalist expanded reproduction then takes place, determines the form assumed by economic crises.

The existence of a state-owned industrial sector constitutes a considerable obstacle to the reproduction of this mode of distribution of capital between the different branches, but it is not an absolute obstacle. The various industries comprising the state sector can be left "free" to borrow, either from one or more investment banks or on a "finance market."[1] Furthermore, they can fix their prices, which to some degree determines their power to finance themselves or to repay loans. This type of accumulation was not entirely ruled out during the first years of the NEP: the *khozraschet* of industrial and banking enterprises facilitated it.

Nevertheless, the centralization of the industrial sector, the substantial size of the principal existing enterprises (and, even more, of those that the Bolshevik Party wished to develop), and fear (lest "market anarchy" and economic crises should return) formed major obstacles, in the 1920s, to this form of accumulation.

Above all, *the political will of the Soviet government to build socialism* was irreconcilable with a form of accumulation that implied "autonomous" development of the various industries and reproduction of capitalist forms of management. The existence of a state-owned industrial sector, together with the intention to build socialism, thus determined the setting-up of planning organs (with the allocation of accumulation funds as one of their tasks) and the extension of the activity of these organs.

In the "war communism" period[2] the Soviet government had tried to guide production in accordance with the priorities dictated by the civil war. At that time the VSNKh functioned mainly as the organ responsible for centralized direction of *current operations*. When the NEP began, a new organ appeared—the state planning commission, or Gosplan, which was responsible primarily for the preparation of *long-term and middle-term plans*. In addition, some other organs were given planning tasks during the NEP.

I. The VSNKh[3]

Though the VSNKh was chiefly concerned with current operational plans under "war communism," a resolution of the Ninth Party Congress (1920) entrusted it with the preparing of a "single production plan for Soviet Russia as a whole and for the Soviet republics allied with Russia." This plan was to cover "the next historical period."[4]

At the start of the NEP the role of the VSNKh tended to diminish, owing partly to the creation of Gosplan,[5] but also to the development of the financial autonomy of enterprises and the role played by Gosbank and Narkomfin.

From 1925 on the problem of industrialization arose ever more sharply, and the role of the VSNKh increased again. This organ now intervened to a substantial degree in the drawing up of various plans, and established an administrative structure aimed at preparing plans for the economy as a whole, including agriculture and transport. Actually, owing to its close links with the leaders of industry, the VSNKh also gave expression to what they wanted—the development of the industrial sectors under their authority. The enlargement of the "planning" activities of the VSNKh is thus to be seen as connected with the increasing role that the leaders of industry tended to play from 1925 on. This enlargement caused conflict with Gosplan and contributed to rendering more confused the discussions that took place concerning problems of industrialization. Something will be said about this later.

II. Gosplan

Gosplan (the State Planning Commission) was, in principle, the organ responsible for drawing up plans. Established on February 22, 1921, it succeeded Goselro, which had worked out a plan for electrification.[6] It was not an organ for taking decisions. Like the VSNKh, its task was merely to prepare *drafts* which were submitted to the *organs of government, which alone had the power to take decisions and put them into effect.* This situation was expressed in the subordination of Gosplan to the Council of People's Commissars (Sovnarkom) and the Council for Labor and Defense.

During the NEP period, Gosplan's activity often followed lines contradictory to that of the VSNKh. Whereas the latter body was closely linked with the leaders of industry, the Gosplan experts were more concerned with the problems of agriculture and of overall economic equilibrium, which meant that they were closer in interest to the financial organs— Gosbank and Narkomfin.

At the outset, Gosplan had only about forty members, mostly economists and statisticians, seven or eight of whom were Party members; the rest were bourgeois specialists.[7] At the beginning of 1927, Gosplan's staff numbered 500, many of whom were former Mensheviks, but decisive responsibility was in the hands of Party members, notably Krzhizhanovsky, who had headed Goselro.[8]

During the second half of 1925, Gosplan worked out the first annual plan for the national economy. This plan had no binding power, as was shown by the name given to it: "control figures." Covering the year 1925–1926, it was actually a modest document of about 100 pages intended to guide the various People's Commissariats in drawing up their own operational programs. The Presidium of Gosplan itself emphasized the approximate nature of the document it had produced: when it was drawn up, a great deal of needed information was lacking.

The control figures for 1926–1927 were already more soundly based than the first set, but, as before, they were not obligatory. However this time, when the CLD (which had supreme oversight of economic decisions) ratified the control figures, it announced that if the operational plans of an administrative organ conformed to the forecasts given in the control figures, there would be no need to obtain the CLD's ratification of these plans.

The control figures for 1927–1928 made up a detailed document of 500 pages. They had been compiled in close collaboration with the sectoral and regional planning organizations. A decree of June 8, 1927, strengthened, in principle, the predominant role of Gosplan in the drawing up of plans, and a decision of the CC in August 1927 provided that thenceforth the control figures, once ratified, were to constitute *actual directives for the elaboration of operational plans and of the state budget.*[9] From that time on, operational plans were drawn up along with the control figures.[10]

These facts show that the NEP, although involving development of commodity and money relations and increased financial autonomy for state enterprises, entailed no renunciation of endeavors to secure centralized and planned direction of the economy. On the contrary, an important aspect of the NEP record was the establishment of planning organs which, in principle, made possible better coordination of the development of the different branches of the economy.

The uncertainties of the political line decided on by the Bolshevik Party at the end of 1925—at the very moment when the problem of the scope of the industrialization process to be launched, and of the forms it should take, was coming on to the agenda—favored a proliferation of these organs. They drew up "draft plans" that were profoundly contradictory—acting, in fact, as "supports" for different social forces and political tendencies which were then dividing the Party. As examples we can take the existence within Gosplan of an industrial section which in 1926 drew up a particularly generous investment plan, and the creation within the VSNKh of a special organ, Osvok, which became, in practice, independent of the VSNKh, and served for a certain period as a support for the "united opposition."[11]

III. Osvok

Osvok (*Osoboye soveshchanie po vosstanovleniyu osnovnogo kapitala*, "special commission for the restoration of fixed capital") was created by the Presidium of the VSNKh in March 1925. At once it set about preparing its own version of a *five-year plan,* and formed sections and committees for the purpose. Under the chairmanship of P.I. Pyatakov (one of the leaders of the "united opposition," who was to be expelled from the Party in 1927 but was readmitted after a few months of exile), Osvok acted quite independently of the VSNKh, and had numerous ex-Menshevik economists, as well as non-Party engineers and scientists working for it.[12]

In the absence, however, of any effective participation by the masses in the working out of the plans, and of a firmly defined *political line* (the lack of which was revealed by the scope assumed by the economic controversies of the period and the *rapid and divergent changes of content in the resolutions adopted by the Party's leading organs),* the documents emanating from Gosplan, the VSNKh, and the other organs responsible for preparing them set targets that were unrealistic and often mutually incompatible. In them were reflected the increasingly contradictory and ill-analyzed tendencies prevailing in the Bolshevik Party.

Under these conditions, the economic plans produced did not enable more effective control to be established over the contradictions: on the contrary, given their mistaken orientations and incoherences, the attempts that were made to "apply" these plans at all costs merely aggravated the contradictions. In this sense, too, as we shall see, the crisis that opened in 1927–1928 was not an economic crisis but a political one— the result of inadequacies and incoherences which were themselves the outcome of extremely complex class struggles.

This situation was especially reflected in the frequent "revision" of the industrial programs, "revision" that was obviously bound up with changes in the economic and political conjuncture and the way in which this was seen by the Party. This aspect will be illustrated by an examination of the forecasts for industrial investment in the year 1926–1927 and the Party's decisions on the matter.[13]

These "revisions" aggravated the economic imbalances, and caused the resulting shortages to fall more and more heavily upon the peasantry. This was one of the forms assumed, in practice, by the increasing abandonment, from 1926 on, of the requirements of the NEP. The "general crisis" of the

NEP was brought about by this abandonment and the resulting aggravated contradictions.

This abandonment and the forms it assumed call for explanation. In order to arrive at such an explanation we need to analyze the entire set of social relations and class contradictions that developed during the 1920s. Given the decisive role played by the peasantry, this analysis must begin with the position in the countryside.

Notes

1. This market is largely constituted by state enterprises which are in a position to grant loans to each other, or to subscribe to bonds issued by one or more of their number. During NEP these possibilities were available to the state enterprises.
2. See volume I of the present work, pp. 152 ff.
3. The book by Friedrich Pollock, *Die planwirtschaftlichen Versuche in der Sowjetunion 1917–1927*, first published in 1929 and republished in 1971 in Frankfurt, gives a very good account of the planning organs of the NEP period and what they did.
4. Ibid., pp. 233–234.
5. See volume I of the present work, p. 153.
6. See volume I of the present work.
7. Pollock, *Die Planwirtschaftlichen Versuche*, p. 236.
8. *Planovoye Khozyaistvo*, no. 10 (1925), p. 9; *Plenum Byudzhetnoy Komissii Ts.I.K. SSSR*, p. 400; and Carr and Davies, *Foundations*, vol. I, p. 2, pp. 802–803.
9. For the control figures for these years see *Planovoye Khozyaistvo*, no. 11 (1929), pp. 167–168; *Sobranie Zakonov*, no. 37 (1927), art. 373; *K.P.S.S. v rezolyutsiyakh*, vol. 2, pp. 252 ff.
10. From 1931 the document prepared in this way became, once it had been ratified, what was called "the annual plan" (see Dobb, *Soviet Economic Development*, p. 324).
11. See below, Part 4 of this volume.
12. Carr and Davies, *Foundations*, vol. I, p. 2, pp. 844–845.
13. See below, p. 386.

Part 2
The village during the NEP period. Differentiation and class struggles. Agricultural policy and transformation of social relations in agriculture

The analyses offered in the following pages relate to the economic and social structure of the Soviet countryside toward the end of the NEP. Their purpose is to throw light on the conditions governing the articulation of class relations and class struggles in the villages with agricultural policy and to show how these relations and struggles led to the final crisis of the NEP.

It was the articulation of class struggles with agricultural policy that determined the changes which the Soviet countryside underwent between 1924 and 1929. These changes cannot be seen as an "autonomous process," dominated exclusively by some ineluctable "internal necessity." They cannot be divorced from the *policy followed* toward the peasantry and its various strata. In its turn, this policy needs to be related to the development of the contradictions within the urban sector and the way with which these were dealt—problems that will be considered later.

1. The social conditions of immediate production during the NEP period

During the NEP[1] the bulk of agricultural production was due essentially to the activity of peasants working on their own *individual farms*. These produced partly for the peasants' own needs and partly in order to exchange the peasants' products on the market. The state farms and *kolkhozes* played only a minor role. The number of peasants and craftsmen engaged in collective forms of production was only 1.3 percent of the total in 1924 and 2.9 percent in 1928.[2]

Commodity production of grain (the branch of production that was of decisive importance for relations between town and country and in connection with the crisis that began at the end of 1927) was contributed mainly by the individual peasant farms: in 1927 they provided 92.4 percent, while the *sovkhozes* provided only 5.7 percent and the *kolkhozes* 1.9 percent.[3]

I. Remarks on the social differentiation of the peasantry

The "individual peasant farms" constituted a heterogeneous "social category." Hidden behind this expression was the great complexity of production relations characteristic of agriculture in the NEP period. To this complexity corresponded the social differentiation of the Soviet peasantry and the class contradictions which resulted.

*(a) The specific features of the
differentiation among the peasantry
during the NEP period*

Social differentiation among the Soviet peasantry was still *relatively* limited toward the end of the NEP period. On the one hand, the division of the land realized thanks to the October Revolution (which was in some cases still going on so late as 1923–1924) had resulted in its more equal distribution. On the other, the process of social differentiation which developed during the NEP period possessed *special features* which have often been pointed out. This process resulted in a reduction in the proportion of poor peasants in the total peasant population and an increase in the proportion of middle peasants, while the economic importance of the kulaks grew only slightly.

The slow transformation of the structure of the Soviet peasantry was based mainly on a *twofold process affecting the poor peasants:* whereas one section of them joined the proletariat, another entered the ranks of the middle peasantry and strengthened this stratum.[4]

From 1925 on the specific character of this differentiation was demonstrated by investigations sponsored by Rabkrin, by the Commissariat of Finance, and by other administrative bodies.[5] These investigations refuted the claims of the Left opposition, which alleged that Soviet agriculture was undergoing a process of capitalist differentiation leading to *polarization,* with the *proletariat* being strengthened at one end, and the *rural bourgeoisie* at the other.

The theses put before the Fifteenth Party Congress explicitly recognized these distinctive features:

The peculiarities of that differentiation are a result of the altered social conditions. These peculiarities consist in the fact that, in contradiction to the capitalist type of development, which is expressed in the weakening of the middle peasantry, while the two extremes (the poor and the rich farmers) grow, in our country it is the reverse. We have a process of strengthening the middle peasant group, accompanied, so far, by a certain growth of the rich peasants from among the more well-to-do middle peasants, and a diminution of the poor groups, of which some become proletarianised while others—the greater part—are gradually transferring to the middle group.[6]

This presentation was, nevertheless, inadequate, since it referred to "social conditions" in general, and lead the reader to suppose that these *sufficed* to account for the type of differentiation noted, whereas this was not the case.

True, the type of differentiation noted was taking place within the general conditions of Soviet power, with nationalization of the land and the functioning of the *mir* given new life by the Agrarian Code of 1922.[7]

However, within the setting of these general conditions, the form taken by the differentiation of the Soviet peasantry was due to the *political line* that was followed (characterized in particular by the tax abatements enjoyed by the poor and middle peasants) and also, and especially, to the *struggles waged by the poor and middle peasants themselves* with a view to better equipping and organizing themselves.[8]

(b) Statistics illustrating class differentiation in the Soviet peasantry in 1927

A great variety of statistics have been produced concerning class differentiation in the Soviet peasantry. Here I shall use the ones calculated by S. G. Strumilin. This Soviet economist and statistician tried to classify peasant farms in accordance with the *criteria proposed by Lenin at the Second Comintern Congress.*[9] By these criteria the poor peasants were those who could get from their farms only what they needed to live on, or who even needed to take on additional paid work in order to survive. The middle peasants were those who had a small surplus which, when the harvest was good, enabled them to accumulate a little. The rich peasants were those whose surplus was sufficiently large and regular to enable them to accumulate and to exploit the other rural strata by employing wage labor, practicing usury, and so on.

These definitions, as applied by Strumilin and the Central Statistical Board, gave the following table[10] showing the social divisions of the Soviet peasantry in 1926–1927:

Social divisions	percent
Poor peasants	29.4
Middle peasants	67.5
Rich peasants	3.1

These figures were necessarily only approximate.[11] Nevertheless, it is clear that the kulaks were few in number, and, especially, that their share in the sale of produce outside the village was a minor one, as is proved by statistics which, though of different origin, agree on this point.

(c) The supply of grain to the market and the class differentiation of the peasantry

According to the statistics quoted by Grosskopf, in 1925 it was the poor and middle peasants who provided most of the grain that came on to the market—over 88 percent, as against 11.8 percent provided by the rich peasants.[12]

The importance of the sales of grain effected by the poor and middle peasants (despite the relatively small size of the harvest calculated *per head*) was due to the fact that they were *obliged to sell their crops* (for lack of liquid assets) in order to pay their debts and their taxes (which fell due in the autumn) and to make indispensable purchases of manufactured goods, including the equipment their farms lacked, and acquisition of which would enable them to reduce their dependence on the kulaks. *The poor and middle peasants played an even bigger role in the provisioning of the towns,* for the greater part of the grain they sold found its way there toward the end of the summer and in the autumn, whereas the rich peasants, in the course of the year, sold part of their surplus on the village market.[13]

These facts show clearly the erroneousness of the oversimplified thesis of a "kulak strike" which Kamenev put forward starting in 1925 to explain the procurement difficulties of 1925–1926.[14] At that time, Kamenev, relying on figures from the Central Statistical Board which were based not on *peasants' incomes* but on *area of land possessed*,[15] declared that kulak farms made up 12 percent of all peasant farms and held 61 percent of the "grain surplus."[16] From these figures Kamenev drew the mistaken conclusion that the rich peasants received most of the money that was made in the countryside, and were the principal buyers of the consumer goods and industrially made means of production bought there. This thesis *tended to give backing to the ideas of Preobrazhensky, who claimed that to fix high prices for industrial products and low prices for agricultural products would not hurt the mass of the peasantry*—since the poor and middle peasants were supposed not to participate to any great extent in commercial exchanges—while it would enable the state to achieve a higher rate of accumulation by levying a "tribute" from the richest peasants.

Contrary to these claims, about three-quarters of the grain *sent to the towns* came at that time from the farms of the poor and middle peasants, and they bought more than 80 percent of the manufactured goods sold in the villages,[17] especially with a view to providing better equipment for their farms, which were gravely lacking in instruments of production.

The proportions given above for the origin of the grain put on the market are confirmed by the figures Stalin mentioned in his speech of May 28, 1928, to the students of the Sverdlov University. He showed that in 1926–1927 the kulaks provided 20 percent of this grain, as against 74 percent provided by the poor and middle peasants and 6 percent by the collective and state farms.[18]

(d) The social and political role of the kulaks

It would, of course, be a grave mistake to deduce from these facts that the social and political role played at that time by the kulaks was negligible. On the contrary, it was very important.

But its importance lay not in the sphere of production but elsewhere: it lay in the sphere of *circulation,* in the commercial relations the kulaks maintained with the poor and middle peasants; in the sphere of ideology, in the illusion they offered of possible future individual enrichment on a substantial scale, an illusion to which a certain number of middle peasants succumbed, consequently turning away from collective forms of production; in the sphere of politics, especially through the influence the rich peasants could exercise in the peasants' assemblies (the *skhod*).[19]

The important role played by the rich peasants was rooted in the nature of the social relations that reproduced themselves under the NEP: wage labor, leasing of land, hiring out of agricultural implements, and capitalist trade. These relations enabled the kulaks to wield great influence—out of all proportion with the number of their farms or their share in production. It was on the basis of these social relations that there developed the struggle of the rich peasants to exert increasing domination over the poor and middle peasants.

However, it was one thing to recognize these facts but quite another to conclude from them that the kulaks possessed decisive economic influence in production and in the provision of supplies for the towns, as the Trotskyist-Zinovievist opposition mistakenly did conclude.[20] Although the conclusions drawn by this opposition were rejected by the Bolshevik Party, its "analyses" left in circulation a distorted picture of the social relations existing in the Soviet countryside. Despite the ultimate political defeat of the opposition, the essential elements of its analyses were present, in barely modified form, in the interpretation that the Party leadership gave in 1928 and 1929 to the procurement crisis (when it tried to explain this crisis by a "kulaks' strike") and in the way that it sought to "deal with" the contradictions among the peasants and the contradictions that opposed the peasantry as a whole to the Soviet power.

We must now examine successively the role of the different strata of the peasantry in the procurement crisis of 1927–1928, and the role that these strata were in a position to play in future increases in agricultrual production, especially grain production.

II. The class foundations of the procurement crisis of 1927–1928

In order to reveal the class foundations of the procurement crisis of 1927–1928 it is necessary to study the way in which this crisis proceeded. This I shall try to do in the following pages, relying again upon the analyses made by S. Grosskopf, who has demolished many of the "accepted ideas" on the matter.

(a) The first phase of the procurement and the sales made by the kulaks

During the first quarter (July to September) of the agricultural campaign of 1927–1928 the *quantities of grain procured* by the state and cooperative organs were, as we have seen,[21] *greater* than those procured in the very good year 1926–1927. This increase was all the more remarkable because the *harvest* of 1927 was *smaller* than that of the previous year,[22] and the distribution of grain production was unfavorable: the regions most affected by the fall in production were those described as "having a surplus," because their production normally served to meet some of the grain needs of the less favored regions (those described as "having a deficit").

Analysis shows that the increase in procurement during July–September 1927 came mainly from the rich peasants. On the one hand, it was they who had priority as regards means of production and transport, since a big proportion of these means belonged to them; on the other, they were in a hurry to sell before the month of October, the time when the poor and middle peasants usually brought their grain to market, thereby lowering the obtainable price. Furthermore, since the policy followed by the Soviet authorities in 1926–1927 had pre-

vented grain prices from rising in the spring of 1927, the rich
peasants had no hope of a price-rise in the spring of 1928, and
this gave them an extra incentive for getting rid of their produce quickly—hence the increase in procurement in July–
September 1927.[23]

The accelerated delivery of grain by the rich peasants during the summer of 1927 does not mean, of course, that they had
not stocked up a certain amount of grain. It does show, however, that in the autumn of 1927 the bulk of the "reserves"
held in the countryside was not concentrated in their hands.[24]

(b) *The second phase of the procurement
     and the struggles of the poor and middle
     peasants*

Thus, from autumn on it was usually the poor and middle
peasants who supplied the grain procured. In the autumn of
1927 these supplies failed to materialize.

Two immediate reasons account for what happened. First,
the fall in the supply of manufactured goods to the rural areas
in the second half of 1927. Part of the selling of grain done by
the poor and middle peasants was intended to secure the cash
they needed to buy manufactured goods, in particular the
small-scale instruments of production which they lacked. In so
far as in the autumn of 1927 there was also a decline in the
supply of these products, there was as well a decline in sales
of grain. The tax reductions which had been granted to the
poor and middle peasants also meant that the "constraint to
sell" imposed on them by their fiscal obligations was now less
acute.

Another immediate reason for the fall in procurement from
the autumn of 1927 on is connected with a certain degree of
negligence on the part of the state and cooperative organs,
which in 1927 showed particular passivity. This was due to the
fact that the official organs were now less afraid of competition
from private traders, who had been subjected to more severe
restrictions than previously. Their passivity also resulted from
the contradictory directives issued by the central authority to

the official procurement agencies: whereas Gosplan called on them *actively to encourage the peasants to sell* their crops, at the same time directives from the Party and the government *warned them against possible competition among themselves.* The Soviet authorities were indeed concerned to prevent such competition among the procurement organs from bringing about a rise in the price of grain. One of the consequences of these directives was that most of *the buyers on behalf of the procurement organs waited for the peasants to come on their own initiative to offer them grain*—which the peasants did not do.[25]

The shortage of industrial goods available in the countryside, the reduction in taxation and the greater passivity of the procurement organs do not, however, furnish more than a partial explanation of the fall in grain sales. To complete the explanation we need to examine more closely the *conditions under which the poor and middle peasants carried out most of their selling of grain.*

It can be seen already from the facts given above (those that show the high proportion of grain sold from farms where the smallest amount was available per head) that *marketing of grain did not correspond, broadly speaking, to the existence of a "surplus" of grain* held by the peasants. Such a "surplus" would imply that the basic needs of the poor and middle peasants for grain (for their own food, for feeding their animals, and for building up reserves adequate to enable them to wait for the next harvest without anxiety) had been largely covered by their production. That was far from being the true situation.

Actually, in 1927–1928, when weather conditions were generally poor, the bulk of the peasants, who lacked adequate means of production, harvested only a poor crop. To be sure, these peasants, taken as a whole, sold large quantities of grain, but they did so only to the extent that they were obliged to, in order to pay their taxes or to buy industrial goods, if these were to be had.[26] When this constraint or this possibility ceased to be present, they sold as little grain as they could, for, in the case of most of the poor and middle peasants, such sales entailed *serious hardship.* They therefore preferred to improve their level of personal consumption, and of consumption by their underfed animals, and also, if possible, to keep at least a minimum of reserve stocks. For the peasants, having such reserves at their disposal meant limiting the risk that they might be compelled to buy grain from the rich peasants before the next harvest became available, and, since such purchases usually had to be made on credit, to become ever more dependent on the rich peasants.

Investigations carried out in 1926–1927, a year of good harvest, showed that *even in the so-called surplus zones, the needs of agriculture itself were not being adequately met, as regards personal consumption by most of the peasants, feeding of their animals, and maintenance of stocks of seed-corn and reserve supplies.*[27] This applied even more in 1927, when the harvest was considerably smaller. And it was just at that moment that the supply of industrial goods to the rural areas declined sharply and that taxes were reduced. Under those conditions for the poor and middle peasants to have brought to the procurement agencies the same amount of grain as in the previous year would have necessitated a *political* willingness on their part which did not exist at that time, and which had hardly been prepared for by the history of the Party's relations with the peasant masses.[28]

III. *The forms of struggle of the poor and middle peasants in the NEP period*

The problem of the procurement crisis cannot be isolated from the low standard of living of the bulk of the peasantry, [29] the inadequacy of the means of production at their disposal, and *the struggle of the poor and middle peasants to avoid falling into increasing dependence on the rich peasants.*

(a) *The struggle to acquire means of production*

For the poor and middle peasants the chief purpose of their sales of produce was to acquire the means needed to increase their production, and thereby to *reduce their dependence on the rich peasants who owned a large proportion of the means of cultivation and of transport.*

On the morrow of the division of the land, which was generally *not* accompanied by a share-out of the other means of production,[30] the poor and middle peasants were the ones worse off in this respect. Subsequently, therefore, it was they who *suffered most from the meagerness of the supply of instruments of labor to agriculture.* In 1927 the *total number of machines and implements possessed by Soviet agriculture was only two-thirds the prewar figure.* A very large proportion of the implements and machines that were available were held by the rich peasants, who hired them out at high rates to the poor and middle peasants.

Investigations carried out in 1924—and in 1927 the situation had hardly begun to change—showed that *scythes were in short supply and most of the peasants had to do their reaping with sickles. Iron ploughs were also lacking.* Industry supplied very few, just as it supplied little steel to the village craftsmen. Most of the peasants had to do their ploughing with a *sokha*—a wooden swing-plough. *The other tools needed for cultivation were also largely unavailable, as were axes and saws.*[31] As for reapers and threshers, these were mostly possessed by the rich peasants.

The inadequate provision of instruments of labor to the poor and middle peasants was the underlying factor in the development of *specific forms of dependence* by the mass of the peasants upon the rich peasants, and the specific forms of *exploitation* to which the latter subjected the working peasants. This inadequacy explains the *extreme fragility of the economy of the poor and middle peasants* and the *close interdependence between the supply of means of production to the rural areas and the amount of produce the poor and middle peasants were able and willing to supply for procurement.* What happened in the *agricultural year 1925–1926* is extremely instructive from this standpoint, as it was a sort of *"dress rehearsal"* for the crisis of *1927–1928, resulting, however, in different solutions.*

In 1925–1926 the harvest was a good one. During the first

quarter of the agricultural year (July to September), off-village sales by the peasants were considerably bigger than in the previous year, but then, as was to happen again in 1927–1928, these sales fell sharply during the second quarter (October–December). It was in this connection that Kamenev spoke of a "kulaks' strike." Now, not only does analysis of the farms which sold grain at different phases of the year show that this formulation of Kamenev's was wrong, but, above all, the *subsequent progress of sales shows clearly that it was not a matter of a "strike" by a minority of peasants but of a mass phenomenon mainly connected with a poor state of supply to the rural areas of the manufactured goods purchased by the poor and middle peasants*. The immediate origin of this crisis lay in a mistake in the Soviet government's policy toward the peasant masses. The situation could then be quickly redressed by a simple conjunctural measure, namely, *improved supply of manufactured goods to the rural areas*. Eventually the government's plan for acquiring grain was fulfilled in 1925–1926 to the extent of 97 percent, without any need to resort to "emergency measures."

It was thus demonstrated that unless there was a very poor harvest *the level of grain "surplus" and of procurement was decided mainly by the policy of the Soviet state itself*—its price policy, the organization of grain purchases, and the supply of manufactured goods to the peasant masses.[32]

The supply of instruments of production to the poor and middle peasants (gravely inadequate in 1927–1928)[33] was, moreover, a decisive factor not only in relation to procurement *but also in connection with the support rendered by the Soviet government to the struggle of the peasant masses to resist the pressure exerted upon them by the kulaks*.

The lack of equipment from which the poor and middle peasants suffered meant that, in many cases, they were *obliged to lease part (or sometimes all) of their land to the rich peasants, to sell them their labor power, or to hire from them the means of labor (including draught animals)*. Thus, in 1926, in more than 72 percent of the cases where land was leased out, this was done by peasants who lacked means of production. Again, more than 52 percent of the *wage earners* employed in agriculture were *poor, or even middle, peasants who were unable to cultivate their land because they had not enough implements.* Very often, too, as we know, poor and middle peasants were compelled *to "employ"* the owner of a horse or of a plough, who preferred to *figure as an "agricultural worker."*

A Rabkrin report dated 1927 acknowledged that "up to now, we have . . . given little attention to the social relations engendered by the practice of lending and borrowing articles used in farming."[34]

Yet these social relations weighed very heavily upon the poor and middle peasants. It was in order to escape from them that these peasants, wanting to buy implements, went so far as to sell part of the grain that they needed in order to feed themselves and create reserves. At the same time, the shortage of implements available on the market led these same peasants to cut down their sales, while it also aggravated their dependence on the kulaks. Similarly, the policy of high prices for manufactured goods, advocated by Preobrazhensky, was liable to reduce the capacity of the poor and middle peasants to equip themselves, and so to increase their dependence on the kulaks and to strengthen the latter.

Two facts will suffice to show the effects on class relations in the countryside of an inadequate supply of agricultural equipment. On the one hand, according to an investigation carried out in 1924–1925 in the province of Penza, this inadequacy meant that *the middle peasants could sow only between 29 and 37 percent of the sowable land which they possessed to grain crops—in the case of the poor peasants this percentage was as little as 18 or 19 percent, whereas for the rich peasants it was nearly 40 percent.* Furthermore, through not being cultivated well enough (especially through not being ploughed and reaped at the proper times, the *yield from the land of those who "employed" the owner of a horse and plough was more than 18 percent below average, whereas the yield from the land of peasants who owned an iron plough was 23 percent above average.*[35]

On the other hand, the poor and middle peasants often had to pay out the equivalent of *nearly one-fifth of the value of their crop in order to hire farm implements and draught animals.*[36]

Thus, the struggle waged by the poor and middle peasants to equip their farms adequately was also a *struggle to free themselves from domination and exploitation by the rich peasants,* and the *delivery of grain by the poor and middle peasants to the procurement agencies was closely bound up with this struggle and with the capacity of the Soviet government to provide material support for the poor and middle peasants in their struggle.* Generally speaking, this support was very inadequate. In 1927 it was largely missing. *The procurement crisis was due to a great extent to this situation.*

The inadequacy of the support given to the efforts of the poor and middle peasants to equip their farms, a neglect which played into the hands of the rich peasants and compromised the expansion both of the harvest and of procurement, is all the more striking in that Lenin had often drawn the Party's attention to both the economic and the political importance of this problem. For instance, in the midst of the civil war he said: "The socialist state must extend the widest possible aid to the peasants, mainly by supplying the middle peasants with products of urban industries and, especially, improved agricultural implements, seed, and various materials. . . ."[37]

At the beginning of the NEP Lenin returned to this problem. He emphasized that the Soviet government must set itself the task of *supplying the poor peasants with more industrial goods than the capitalists had previously supplied to them,* and that what had to be supplied was "not only cotton goods for the farmer and his family, but also badly needed machines and implements, even if they are of the simplest kind."[38]

These passages are of particular importance. They show that, as early as 1921, *Lenin had formulated the idea of an alliance between the workers and the peasants, the material foundation of which was to be the provision of means of labor* ("even of the simplest kind") to the toiling masses of the countryside. This was the concept of an alliance "based on steel" and not merely on textiles.

Yet the policy actually followed over the years had not been that policy: only in 1926–1927 did current supplies of implements to the rural areas slightly exceed their prewar level.

(b) The struggle of the poor and middle peasants to strengthen forms of organization that would consolidate their independence of the rich peasants

The struggle of the poor and middle peasants *to organize themselves* so as to consolidate their independence from the rich peasants calls for special attention. *We find here confirmation of Lenin's analyses pointing to the possibility of a transition to socialism through organizing the working peasants within the framework of the NEP,*[39] a confirmation all the more remarkable because it resulted from a development which, as Molotov acknowledged, had not received systematic and constant support from the Bolshevik Party.[40] (This does not mean that this self-organization took place without any connection to the *ideas of socialism*, which in fact penetrated in a thousand different ways into the midst of the toiling peasantry.)

One of the forms under which the poor and middle peasants *organized themselves* was the associations for joint utilization of means of production. As a rule, these associations brought together only a small number of farms—usually less than ten. They were of particular importance in the grain-growing regions, in the steppes, in the Ukraine, the Ural region, and Siberia. They were important especially for the utilization of seeders and threshers. In the Ural region 32.9 percent and 28.2 percent, respectively, of these machines were used in common in this way, while in Siberia the corresponding percentages were 29.8 and 32.3. In the case of tractors the percentage was even 100.[41]

The poor and middle peasants resorted also to traditional

forms of mutual aid, such as *supryaga,* by which between five and seven farms jointly utilized labor power, draught animals and implements, and organized themselves to obtain credit. In this setting there developed genuine *collective work,* which resulted in many poor and middle peasants being able to cultivate part of the land they held as a result of the agrarian revolution. This movement also engendered tens of thousands of "simple" producers' cooperatives which did not enjoy the status of *kolkhozes* and were, as a rule, not officially registered. Various investigations have revealed the dimensions of this movement.[42] But, in the report already mentioned, Molotov gave no attention to these simple forms: what he hailed was the advantages of "large units" of production, of "the larger enterprise."[43]

In the Ukraine this form of the poor peasants' struggle was especially well developed. It was connected with the activity of the "poor peasants' committees" (*Komnezamy,* or KNS) which had appeared during the civil war. They continued to exist in that republic even after the ending of "war communism," and also developed during the NEP period. In 1925 more than 14 percent of the peasants in the Ukraine belonged to these KNS, which meant a very high percentage of the poor peasants. Research shows that most of the KNS were solidly organized and contributed effectively to raise production and the standard of living of their members. Not only did they arrange for mutual aid among the latter, and start to introduce new methods of cultivation (by modifying the system of rotation of crops), but they also helped the other peasants and took part in the forming of cooperatives and of other forms of association for joint work.

Other facts, too, testify to the importance of "spontaneous" tendencies to create peasant organizations for joint use of the soil. There was the creation of the "communities for opening up remote tracts of land." When they adopted this form of association, the peasants involved decided to go in for collective forms of cultivation (*poselki* and *vyselki*) instead of individual holdings. These collective forms were established especially in certain regions (such as the provinces of Samara, Saratov, and Orel) where substantial tracts of land were situated too far from the old villages to be regularly cultivated by peasants operating from these villages. It is significant that this movement was inspired mainly by poor peasants and that, instead of forming new "land associations" of the traditional type, they adopted collective forms of cultivation, and because of this it was possible to ensure a rotation of crops covering several years, and to avoid the fragmentation resulting from the former *mir*.[44]

True, from the standpoint of the general structure of Soviet agriculture, the existence of these various types of organization of the poor and middle peasants did not alter the massive predominance of individual peasant farming. Nevertheless, their existence, by the very multiplicity of the forms they assumed and the liveliness and depth of the tendencies they manifested (despite the absence of systematic aid from the Soviet government and the hostility of the rich peasants), shows how great were the possibilities for transition to a socialist organization of agriculture.[45]

IV. Agricultural policy and the procurement crisis of 1927–1928

The facts mentioned above show that the procurement crisis of 1927–1928 was not due mainly to a "kulaks' strike," but was the result of a much more complex process in which some mistakes committed by the Soviet government in relation to the poor and middle peasants played their part. As a result of these mistakes, the initiative and independent class action of these peasants suffered restriction. Subsequently, the indiscriminate resort to "emergency measures," by hitting the middle peasants as well as the kulaks, brought about even a shift in the alignment of class forces, and enabled the kulaks to increase their ideological and political influence over an important section of the peasantry. In this connection, the resistance put up by the peasant masses to the measures taken by the Soviet government from 1928 on not only resulted from their immediate reaction to encroachment on their material interests, but also reflected the influence that the kulaks then wielded over them. It was in that sense that a "kulak threat" made its appearance in 1928–1929.[46]

In order to appreciate this process and how it was linked with the Soviet government's peasant policy, we must briefly recall certain facts.

(a) The shortcomings of agricultural policy in the years 1924–1927

The shortcomings of agricultural policy in the years between 1924 and 1927 were due, in the first place, to the inadequate supply of instruments of production to the rural areas, where it was the poor and middle peasants who had most need of them.[47]

It must be observed that the "cost" of supplying machinery and implements to agriculture did not amount at any time during the NEP to a burden that could be thought too heavy for the Soviet economy to bear. Thus, in 1926–1927, the sum involved in these supplies came to 122.1 million prewar roubles, or 0.8 percent of the national income.[48] It will be seen, too, that the supply of agricultural equipment to be bought by the peasants did not, in principle, impose *any "charge" upon the state budget*. As for supplies on credit, these would have called for only limited advances which could be quickly recovered through the increase in production and in money incomes.

The smallness in the amount of equipment supplied was especially detrimental to the poor and middle peasants. They enjoyed, in practice, no priority in receiving this equipment, and the credit system functioned in such a way that they were not the chief beneficiaries of loans either.[49] Moreover, the importance of supplying the rural areas with traditional instruments of production, or *improved* versions of these (which the poor and middle peasants could acquire most easily), was much underestimated.

Thus, Molotov, in his report to the Fifteenth Party Congress on "Work in the Rural Areas" referred dismissively to the supplying of simple means of production to the peasants as a "sorry 'progress.' "[50]

The lack of an economic effort to give priority aid to the poor and middle peasants entailed serious consequences. Such priority aid was *needed from the political standpoint,* because support for the Soviet government from the poor and middle peasants was indispensable if the dictatorship of the proletariat was to be consolidated; and from the economic standpoint as well, because *it was the farms of the poor and middle peasants that held the biggest potentialities for increasing production, since they were underequipped*—a large proportion of their land was not even being cultivated and, because they had no implements of their own, the yield from what was cultivated was lower then anywhere else, and so most susceptible to rapid increase.

(b) *The underestimation of the potentialities of the poor and middle peasants' farms*

Generally speaking, the shortcomings of agricultural policy in 1924–1927 were bound up with a definite underestimation of the potentialities of the poor and middle peasants' farms.[51]

In 1928 and 1929, even within the setting of the NEP, the potentialities of Soviet agriculture were still considerable, provided that the peasants were properly supplied with instruments of labor and helped in their efforts to extend the area under cultivation and increase yields, and to organize themselves more effectively.

The "image" of the Soviet peasant as "routine-minded" and "lazy" is false. To be convinced of this one has only to note that in 1925–1926 *gross agricultural production reached the prewar level, even though there were fewer means of production in the countryside than at an earlier date.*[52]

The underequipment of agriculture was due to old equipment wearing out and the crying inadequacy of supplies of

new equipment. It was not due at all to any so-called indifference or "indolence" on the part of the peasantry. On the
contrary, statistics show that in 1927 expenditures on purchases of equipment were 70 percent greater than they were
before the war.[53]

The economist Oganovsky observed how much greater the
potentialities of agriculture in this period were than they had
been before the Revolution. He wrote: "Neither the economic
and social facts nor the importance and role of the cadres and
the factors of production are comparable. And if the contexts
are incommensurable there cannot, either, be anything in
common between the results obtained then and those obtainable at the present time, as we can observe here and now."[54]

Some estimates made at that time sought to take account,
partly at least, of the potentialities of NEP agriculture, especially with a view to forecasting the agricultural production
and the "net balance."[55] Thus, Osvok estimated the grain
harvest that could be obtained in 1931 at 87.8 million metric
tons—an increase of 14.9 percent on 1926—which should
provide a "net balance" of 14.6 million metric tons—56 percent more than in 1926, which meant a net market availability
of 18.7 percent.

This estimate was actually based on a very low estimate of
the yield to be obtained in 1931. It assumed that this yield
would be the same as in 1928, so that only the area cultivated
would be larger. It was all the more certainly an underestimate in that, already in 1926, the yield per hectare was higher
than the prewar average,[56] despite the underequipment from
which Soviet agriculture still suffered. If sales of means of
production to agriculture had continued at the same rate as in
1925 it would have been reasonable to expect a grain harvest
of about 92 million metric tons, which would have given a
"net balance" in the region of 17 million metric tons.[57]

The actual potentialities of NEP agriculture at the end of the
1920s were all the greater in that *the poor and middle peasants were at that time ready to enter step by step upon the
road of cooperation,* of collective labor and production (provided that they were really helped by the Soviet government,

and not subjected to measures that harmed them and shook the foundations of the worker-peasant alliance). These forms of labor and production implied—if the peasants entered into them voluntarily—great possibilities of increased harvests. They made possible a fuller utilization of the land area, with employment of machinery and carrying out of cultivation work with the minimum loss of time. This was confirmed by experience during that period.

However, the Party leadership tended to underestimate the possibilities of NEP agriculture and not to reckon with the *real requirements* for developing it along the cooperative and collective road.

(c) The small amount of aid given to the development of collective farming and cooperation

From the beginning of the NEP to the Fifteenth Congress (at the end of 1927), the efforts made by the poor and middle peasants to undertake *various forms of collective labor or production* remained without systematic support. Molotov recognized this fact, though omitting to draw any practical conclusions from it, when he declared: "It is now important to realise . . . that we are lagging behind, that we are not keeping pace with the new Socialist elements now developing in the village. What we lack now is courage and perseverance in stimulating the collectivisation of the village, primarily because we do not know enough about it."[58]

At that time, Molotov did not conclude from this observation that a substantial acceleration of development towards collective farming was really possible. He said, on the contrary, that "the development of individual enterprise along the socialist path is a long and tedious process. It will require many years to pass over from individual to communal farming."[59]

This underestimation of the possibilities of collective farming was accompanied by inadequate backing of the cooperative movement.

We know the role that Lenin ascribed to cooperation as a

form leading to socialist organization of production.[60] Yet by 1927, despite the undeniable development of cooperation, the Bolshevik Party had failed to give it all the necessary aid, being influenced in this by the idea that cooperation mainly served the interests of the rich peasants—whereas experience showed how important it was for the poor and middle peasants. Here, too, Molotov, in his report to the Fifteenth Party Congress, noted the insufficiency of the work accomplished. After quoting Lenin on cooperation he said that "this statement made by Lenin has not yet been fully appreciated by us. At any rate, it has not been sufficiently reflected in our practical work."[61]

And yet a number of Party resolutions had already drawn attention to the role that development of the cooperatives should play. I may mention, in particular, a resolution adopted by the Twelfth Conference of the CPR(B), in August 1922, which emphasized the importance of agricultural credit, and a resolution of the Thirteenth Party Congress (May 1924), which pointed out that the development of cooperative trade would enable the poor peasants to increase their production and sales while limiting the power of the kulaks.[62] In April 1925 the Fifteenth Party Conference reaffirmed the need to organize agricultural credit. It called on the cooperatives to take over the processing and marketing of agricultural produce and the supply of means of production to the peasant masses. This resolution also appealed to the cooperatives to encourage the development of all possible forms of collective working of the soil.

In fact, despite these resolutions, and Lenin's statements about the role to be played by the cooperatives (especially in "raising the small economy and in facilitating its transition . . . to large-scale production on the basis of voluntary association"),[63] the development of the cooperatives was not supported by the Soviet state with all the necessary vigor. The cooperatives were not drawn firmly in a direction that would have strengthened within a short time the farms worked by the poor and middle peasants, thereby also ensuring growth and regularity in grain procurement.

On October 1, 1927, nearly 40 percent of the Soviet peasants were, nevertheless, members of state cooperative societies—but these societies were much more concerned with buying agricultural produce from the peasants than with selling them means of production, which meant that the poor and middle peasants took relatively little interest in them.[64] As regards the credit cooperatives, their activity benefited less than 20 percent of the peasants, they charged relatively high rates of interest, and from 1925 on they granted loans only for comparatively large amounts, exceeding the needs and capacities of the poor peasants, so that the latter got almost no advantage from the existence of these cooperatives and had to turn to the usurers.[65]

The situation that existed at the end of the NEP was due both to the inadequate attention paid to the needs of the poor and middle peasants and to the corruption and negligence that reigned very widely in the grassroots administration of the cooperative system. The funds placed at the disposal of the cooperatives by the state for the purpose of making loans to the poor peasants remained practically unused. The local cooperatives did not take the steps needed for these funds to be employed. Moreover, they were too remote in their activities from the conditions in which the peasants lived, and were often held back by the bureaucratic control exercised by the district soviets.[66] This state of affairs was, of course, related to the feebleness of the Party's roots in the countryside, a crucial problem to which I shall return.

V. *The aggravation of the contradictions*
    through the peasant and agricultural
    policy followed in 1928 and 1929.

In the light of the facts which have been mentioned, the procurement crisis of 1927–1928 thus appears as not at all the result of an "inevitable economic crisis" but as the outcome of *political mistakes*. These were due to the feebleness of the

Party's roots in the countryside and also to ideological reasons which led the Party (even while recognizing that agriculture was the basis of economic development) to underestimate in practice the aid that should have been given to the peasant masses, and to concentrate nearly all its efforts on industry.

The procurement crisis of 1927–1928, unlike that of 1925–1926, did not lead to a rectification of agricultural policy. The increasing stress laid on large-scale industrialization blocked the way to any serious and rapid improvement in the supply of manufactured goods to the rural areas. At the same time, fulfilling the industrialization program required that procurement be maintained, at all costs, at a sufficiently high level. The immediate consequence was the imposition of the "emergency measures" at the beginning of 1928, and the impossibility, despite attempts made by the Party, of giving them up. Yet the renewal of these measures did not help to improve the situation in agriculture—quite the contrary. There was something worse, however: the renewal of the emergency measures was felt by a large section of the peasants to signify an abandonment of the worker-peasant alliance as it had existed until then, while the worsening of the economic situation in the countryside also caused them discontent. This determined a realignment of class forces in the village, and increased the ideological and political influence of the kulaks. A crisis of the worker-peasant alliance thus resulted, and during 1929 caused the Party (because of the way it analyzed the situation) to abandon the NEP suddenly and completely. This abandonment took place, as we shall see, in conditions that were unfavorable to the functioning of the *kolkhozes,* from which ensued, among other things, the very grave crisis of agricultural production that marked the first half of the 1930s.

The fact that through 1928 and 1929 the emergency measures continued to be enforced meant that these measures could no longer be regarded as merely "emergency" measures, as they had been described at the beginning of 1928. They became, on the contrary, "ordinary" measures. What was happening, in practice, was *transition to a policy different from the NEP,* a transition which entailed a series of consequences.

(a) *The chief economic effects of the
situation created by the procurement
crisis and the protracted application of
the "emergency measures"*

The procurement crisis and the protracted application of the emergency measures had *negative repercussions on grain production, and then on agricultural production generally.* These consequences proceeded from two types of sequence of cause and effect. On the one hand, the technico-economic: when requisitioning deprived some peasants of even *the grain they needed for sowing,* that led directly to a subsequent fall in production. On the other hand, ideological and political: when the peasants thought the amount of grain that would remain at their disposal depended not on what they produced but on decisions to be taken by the administrative authorities, they were not disposed to increase their production. Reciprocally, the fall in production and the economic consequences of the application of the emergency measures had, in turn, political effects. At this level "economics turned into politics," as Lenin had noted at the time of the peasant revolts in the last phase of "war communism." This transformation of economics into politics was the most serious result of the introduction and then renewal of the "emergency measures."

(1) *The fresh decline in grain production in
1928, the renewal of the emergency
measures in 1928–1929, and the decline
in procurement*

All the tensions provoked in the rural areas by the application of the emergency measures of 1928, and by the way in which they were applied, had a *negative effect on grain production.* In 1928 this production was *down again* as compared with 1927—it came to only 73.3 million metric tons.[67] As compared with 1926, the decline in production was 3.1 million metric tons.

This fall in production entailed a tendency for procurement to fall. The Soviet government dealt with the situation by continuing, as we know, to resort to emergency measures. However, under the combined effects of the decline in the harvest and the exhaustion of the peasants' reserve stocks, the amount of grain procured now suffered a real *collapse. It came to no more than 8.3 million metric tons, or about 78.4 percent of the procurement obtained without emergency measures in 1926–1927.*[68] This had important consequences for the Soviet economy as a whole.

A particularly notable sign of the exhaustion of the peasants' reserve stocks was the sharp drop in the amount procured in the first half of 1929. During those six months, the amount procured came to no more than about 2.6 million metric tons of grain (less than half the procurement achieved in the first half of 1928).[69] At the same time *prices of grain on the private markets* reached new peaks.[70]

The severe fall in the quantity of grain held by the state and cooperative organs threatened more gravely than ever before the supplying of the towns and the regularity of exports.

There was something even worse: the impact of the emergency measures upon the peasantry was such that their *production effort declined again.* Thus 1929 saw a fresh fall in the grain harvest. It came to no more than 71.7 million metric tons.[71] As compared with 1926, the reduction was 4.7 million metric tons. This decline was all the more catastrophic because it occurred at a moment when the struggle for industrialization was in full swing and called, if it was to be carried on without subjecting the economy as a whole to excessive tension, for an increasing supply of agricultural produce, primarily grain.

The emergency measures thus *did not help really to overcome* the initial difficulties. On the contrary, they *contributed to disrupting the working of the NEP* (in fact, they *put an end to it*) and broke the dynamism that Soviet agriculture had shown until 1926–1927.

It was the collapse of the harvest and of the grain procurement in 1928 and 1929 (that is, one of the consequences of the protracted implementation of the emergency measures) that induced the Bolshevik Party to go over to collectivization on a

vast scale at the end of 1929. The immediate aim of the "turn"
thus made was to stop the decline in procurement. The "turn"
took place in conditions where it was no longer possible to
rely on agricultural successes previously obtained, or on persuasion of the peasants, and their enthusiasm. The large-scale
collectivization begun in the autumn of 1929 was thus carried
out essentially "from above," by means of administrative measures. It did indeed make possible imposition on the *kolkhozes* of *relatively high delivery quotas*, even when their
harvest had been poor, which was the case for several years.
On the morrow of collectivization as thus carried out, from
1931 on, the grain harvest *often fell by 12 or 14 percent below
the level of 1926*. The maintenance and increase of the exactions from grain production were thereafter effected *at the
expense of the peasants' own consumption*—but these facts
already belong to another period, that of the so-called revolution from above.[72]

It will be observed that the measures taken in 1928 and 1929
did not effect overall agricultural production as badly as they
affected grain production. The reason for this was that the
emergency measures hardly affected, directly at any rate,
crops other than grain corps.[73]

The primordial importance ascribed by the Bolshevik Party
to the procurement problem was due to the decisive role that
the "net grain balance" of agriculture played in the provisioning of the town population and in maintaining exports.

(2) The problem of the grain balance

The most significant figure in this connection is that for the
"net grain balance" from agriculture, meaning *the net amount
of grain definitively marketed outside the village*.[74] Even in
1926–1927 (that is, before the application of the emergency
measures) this balance came to no more than 10.5 million
metric tons, as compared with about 19 million metric tons
in 1913.[75] The contraction of the net grain balance in comparison with that before the war was *bigger than the decline in
production*, although the peasantry had not quite recovered

their prewar standard consumption of grain (the rural population having increased).[76]

In general, however, 1926–1927 food consumption by the mass of the peasantry had reached a level markedly higher than in the years preceding the Revolution. The distribution of income among the peasants was much less unequal than before, and a certain increase was observed in the intake per head of products rich in protein (meat, milk, and eggs).[77]

In relation to prewar, the decline in the net grain balance of agriculture gave rise to a series of grave problems. While this balance had fallen by about 44 percent between 1909–1913 and 1926–1927,[78] *consumption by the towns and industry had risen by about 28 percent between 1913 and 1927.*[79] The resort to emergency measures did not bring about any improvement in this aspect of the situation, for *the grain balance of agriculture declined in 1927–1928.* It then stood at only 8.33 million metric tons. In 1928–1929 the emergency measures enabled the grain balance to be kept at the same level[80] as in 1927–1928, despite the decline in the harvest, but this result was secured only by *reducing consumption in the villages,* which had to bear the whole brunt of the fall in grain production.

A reduction in their consumption of grain had thus been forced upon the peasants by means of the emergency measures. Already in 1928 the application of these measures had led to the peasant masses being deprived of *some of the grain they needed for subsistence and for sowing for the next season.* Stalin noted this in his report of July 13, 1928, to the plenum of the CC, when he said that it had proved necessary to "press harder" on certain regions and to take from "the peasants' emergency stocks."[81]

In the regions affected by such exactions, many peasants had tried to obtain from the towns the grain that they needed.[82] The distribution of grain in the towns was thereby disorganized. The urban population, fearing that its consumer needs would not be met, tried to hoard, and this made it necessary to introduce rationing in certain towns.[83] The effect of this was to prevent the peasants from supplying themselves from the shops. In some cases the Soviet administration was even obliged to sell part of the grain procurement back to the peasants.

Altogether, after 1927, the supply of food to both town and country worsened, and the amount of grain available for export fell sharply—to such an extent that symptoms of crisis appeared also in the sphere of external trade.

(3) The procurement crisis and foreign trade

The suddenness with which the emergency measures were applied was due above all to the fact that the Bolshevik Party was poorly represented among the peasantry and its concrete knowledge of peasant and agricultural problems was very inadequate. However, the rigidity shown in the application of these measures was due also to the seriousness of the impact which this decline in procurement had on Soviet foreign trade.

The figures are self-explanatory: whereas in 1926–1927 grain exports amounted to 2,160,000 metric tons (which was only 22.4 percent of the 1913 figure),[84] in 1928 they fell to 89,000 metric tons.[85] And it needs to be added that this was the figure for *gross* exports. They were made possible only by drawing on the State's reserves, which fell to a level so low that the Soviet Union had to reconstitute its emergency stocks by importing grain itself in the summer of 1928—to the amount of 250,000 metric tons.[86]

A tremendous effort was therefore required in 1928 to make up for the fall in the exports of grain. The results of this effort were positive: the total value of exports increased, in spite of everything, by about 3.8 percent, reaching the figure of 799.5 million roubles.[87] This increase was achieved through a substantial boosting of exports of oil, butter, eggs, timber, furs, etc.[88] Only the centralization of exports by the Commissariat of Trade made such an effort feasible: and it was paid for by the *appearance of fresh shortages on the domestic market.*

However, the launching of the industrialization program

(which was based on *extensive reliance on imports of industrial goods from abroad*) came up against difficulties as a result of the *poor progress in exports*. The latter were not sufficient to secure the growing amount of imports needed. The Soviet Union, which had a surplus in its foreign trade balance in 1926–1927, in 1928 showed a deficit of 153.1 million. If the emergency measures were renewed in 1929, this was done also in order to redress the foreign trade situation. It was decided, in fact, to *increase grain exports,* regardless of the fall in procurement: hence the aggravated shortages.

The procurement crisis thus came into violent contradiction with the demands of the industrial plan. This is the principal economic aspect of the crisis at the end of the 1920s. It is an aspect which cannot be separated from *the form of industrialization policy* which was developed at that time.

The political consequences of the procurement crisis and of the measures taken to cope with it were closely interwoven with the "economic" consequences. They conditioned each other. For the future of the worker-peasant alliance, and so for the form of the dictatorship of the proletariat, the political consequences were of decisive importance. They were at the heart of the overall process of the class struggles of this period. It is these consequences that we must now study.

(b) *The principal effects on class relations*
    in the countryside of the situation
    created by the procurement crisis and
    the protracted application of the
    emergency measures

The political consequences for the worker-peasant alliance of the situation which developed after January 1928 were, of course, complex and contradictory. The statements made at the time by the Party leaders, and what appeared in the press, reflect these contradictions. At certain moments stress was laid on the increased influence of the Party among the peasant masses which was supposed to have resulted from the operation of the emergency measures. At other moments, mention was made of the negative effect of these measures, which were said to have enabled the kulaks to rally broad sections of the peasantry around them. Stalin's writings also reveal divergent appreciations, reflecting both the contradictions in the objective situation and the effects of the struggles going on within the Party leadership.

(1) Some formulations by Stalin regarding
    the consequences of the application of
    the emergency measures during the first
    half of 1928

During the plenum of April 1928 Stalin emphasized the strengthening of the Party's leading role which was supposed to have resulted from the application of the emergency measures. After declaring that these measures had "enabled us to put an end to the procurement crisis" (which was soon to be proved untrue) and to render the local Party organizations more or less sound by purging them of "blatantly corrupt elements who refuse to recognize the existence of classes in the countryside," he added: "We have improved our work in the countryside, we have brought the poor peasants closer to us and won the allegiance of the overwhelming majority of the middle peasants, we have isolated the kulaks and have somewhat offended the well-to-do top stratum of the middle peasants."[89]

We know, however, that in practice the emergency measures were far from having affected only the kulaks. Indeed, as early as February 1928 Stalin had sent out a circular warning the Party's local organizations against "excesses," affecting strata of the peasantry other than the rich peasants, which might "create new difficulties"[90] with these other strata.

At the beginning of the summer of 1928, while remaining in favor of the emergency measures—which he thought were impossible to renounce—Stalin took a much more pessimistic view of the situation developing in the countryside, from the standpoint of the political and ideological relations between classes. This found expression in his statements of July 1928,

particularly his report to the Leningrad Party organization on
the results of the plenum held at the beginning of that month.
In this report Stalin acknowledged that the procurement crisis
had not ended in March, and that in April–June it had been
necessary to extend the emergency measures to the point of
taking from the *emergency stocks* held by the peasants, with,
as the result, "renewed recourse to emergency measures, the
arbitrary administrative measures, the infringements of revolutionary law, the house-to-house visitations, the unlawful
searches and so on . . ." Having described these measures
and the form they had taken, Stalin added that they had "worsened the political situation in the country and created a threat
to the bond (between the workers and the peasants)."[91] Dealing with the same problem, the resolution adopted by the July
1928 plenum noted the "discontent among certain strata of the
peasantry, expressed in demonstrations against the arbitrary
administrative measures adopted in a number of regions."[92]

Nine months later, to be sure, at the plenum of April 1929,
when Stalin attacked Bukharin for the first time before the
CC,[93] he again spoke of the need to resort to emergency
measures, asserting that these measures were "backed by the
popular support of the middle- and poor-peasant masses,"[94] a
claim that was not confirmed by the actual way in which
procurement was carried out in the months that followed.

Thus, Stalin's appreciations of the class consequences of the
emergency measures varied a great deal. They do not enable
us to discover the answer to the real question: what was the
principal aspect of the contradictory effects of these measures?

In order to answer this question we need to *take an overall
view of the situation in the countryside*.

(2) An overall view of the situation in the countryside in 1928

When we take this overall view we see clearly that what
constitutes the principal aspect of the situation is the worsening in the relations between the Soviet government and the
peasantry during 1928, a worsening that involved a large pro-

portion of the middle peasants and even some of the poor peasants (those who were affected, directly or indirectly, by the emergency measures).

The symptoms of this worsening situation were undeniable: for example, the contraction in the sown area and in the number of cattle. The latter was due not merely to the shortage of fodder (due to the extent of the emergency measures) but also to the fear felt by some of the middle peasants lest they be regarded as rich peasants.[95] More broadly, the confidence of many peasants in the continuance of the NEP was shaken: they no longer believed in a secure future, and were also placed in an objectively difficult position through the less and less adequate supply of means of production. The climate of uncertainty developing among the peasantry was also connected with the *closure by administrative means of thousands of small-scale enterprises, while the production and distribution previously provided by these enterprises was not replaced by state and cooperative industry and trade.*

The reduction in the number of livestock, which led to a crisis in the supply of milk, butter, and meat, added to the grain crisis.[96]

It was especially during the farming season of 1928–1929 that relations between the Soviet government and broad strata of the peasantry deteriorated. On top of the measures taken at the beginning of 1928 came other measures of a fiscal character. Henceforth a section of the peasantry were to be taxed no longer on the basis of norms fixed in advance (according to the principles adopted at the beginning of the NEP) but on "individual bases" estimated by the agents of the revenue authority. In theory, taxes levied in this way were to affect only the richest of the peasants. Actually, they also affected the middle peasants to a large extent, for a number of reasons: lack of a strict definition of the peasants who were to be taxed in this way; lack of familiarity with rural realities on the part of the revenue service; and opportunity (given these conditions) for some of the kulaks to hide themselves, so that the burden of taxation fell upon peasants who ought not to have been taxed in this way; etc.

After November 1928 Stalin mentioned mistakes made in the application of the "individual tax." He said that only 2 or 3 percent of peasant households should have been affected by it, whereas there were several districts "where 10, 12 and even more percent of the households are taxed, with the result that the middle section of the peasantry is affected."[97]

Following a wave of protests from the rural population, some of the peasants who had been wrongly taxed got their money back. Nevertheless, considerable harm had been done to the relations between the Soviet government and the middle peasants. Thereafter, some of the latter tended to line up with the rich peasants for joint resistance to administrative decision. Furthermore, *the economic weakening of the middle peasants increased their dependence on the kulaks.*

In this situation, toward the end of 1928 the TsIK adopted an important decision regarding the "general principles of the possession and distribution of land."[98] This legislative text made serious changes in the Agrarian Code of 1922[99] which were significant from two points of view: they facilitated transition to collective forms of agricultural work and production, and they restricted the possibility of land-grabbing by the kulaks.

However, the arrangements made in it regarding the general peasant assembly in the village (the *skhod*) showed that the Soviet government was obliged to cut down the powers of this assembly and to subject it to control by the administrative organs. Thereafter, decisions taken by the *skhod,* in which the middle peasants held the majority, could be annulled by the rural soviet, in which these peasants were increasingly reduced to minority status.

Politically, this measure meant a decisive break with the NEP, which had accepted the middle peasant as the central figure in the Soviet countryside. It showed that there had been a rupture between the middle peasants and the government, since it took away from these peasants the power of autonomous decision hitherto allowed them within the framework of the *skhod.* This change of direction implied a profound worsening in the relations of confidence which the NEP had begun to establish between the Soviet government and the middle peasantry. It showed that there was a divergence between the orientations of the latter (who had been to some extent thrust into the camp of the rich peasants) and those of the former. And, however justified some of the new orientations of the Soviet government might be, the introduction of means of constraint which were to be used to bend the will of the basic mass of the peasantry could not but result in grave political crises. Let us recall that only a little over two years before the adoption of the decision subjecting the *skhod* to tutelage—and this decision was to be one of the instruments of what has been called the "revolution from above," that is, of a collectivization not decided upon by the peasant masses themselves—Stalin, referring to Lenin, had said: "For carrying out a revolution it is not enough to have a correct Party line. . . . For carrying out a revolution a further circumstance is required, namely, that the masses, the broad mass of the workers, shall have been convinced *through their own experience* that the Party's line is correct."[100]

As Lenin had forecast six years earlier,[101] evoking circumstances similar to those of 1928, the weakening of the worker-peasant alliance was splitting the Party more and more into a tendency which was determined to "go ahead" even if the peasantry was not satisfied, and one which sought to prevent the rupture of the worker-peasant alliance.

The supporters of the first tendency, who were led by Stalin, were convinced that only rapid industrialization and collectivization would enable the difficulties to be overcome by providing the worker-peasant alliance with a new material foundation (one of "steel," that is, of tractors) and unifying the technological conditions of production by introducing machinery into agriculture.

It was, of course, the representatives of the other tendency (described as "the Right" and led by Bukharin) who gave most attention to the weakening of the worker-peasant alliance and to the way in which the fight against the kulaks was being transformed into a fight against the middle peasants.[102] However, representatives of the first tendency were themselves obliged to acknowledge the *increased political and ideological influence* of the kulaks over the middle peasants and the manifestations of discontent on the part of the latter. This was true of Kaganovich, although he advocated a "hard" line as the only way of ensuring the industrialization of the Soviet Union. In a statement made in 1928 he said that "the *serednyak* is sometimes influenced by the kulak and expresses his dissatisfaction. . . . [He has been hit] by rather heavy taxation, and by our inability at the present time to offer him prices for his grain which are commensurate with the prices of manufactured goods." In the process of taking action against the kulaks, he admitted, "we have penalized" the middle peasants.[103]

The procurement campaign of 1928–1929 began badly. From October on, *pressure by the procurement organs* was again brought to bear over a very wide area. *Pravda* of December 2, 1928, denounced the pressure and harsh measures that were being applied to the middle and poor peasants. The attempts made to organize them had had little success, and these two classes did not constitute a force upon which the Party could really rely in the countryside. At the same time, the poor peasants were also becoming more and more discontented because of the increasing gap between the prices paid by the state (even though these had been raised a little after July 1928) and the prices prevailing on the free market (which were now three or four times as high).[104]

Under these conditions, since there was no solid organization or political consciousness of a sufficiently high level among the peasantry, *part of the harvest was marketed outside the official channels, not only by the kulaks but also by the poor and middle peasants (who were able, through these sales, to retain a certain degree of economic strength in relation to the kulaks.)* Although sales on the "free market" were not, as a rule, actually forbidden, the local authorities often *penalized* them, so as to facilitate their own procurement plans. The penalties affected the middle and poor peasants as well as the kulaks, and their discontent consequently increased.

(3) The peasants' resistance in 1929 and the development of coercive measures

At the beginning of 1929 there were many signs that a peasant resistance was developing against procurement measures that were being imposed with ever greater severity. From January 1929 on the Soviet press mentioned more and more often additional "categories" of peasants who were acting as enemies of the Soviet power. The press spoke of "little kulaks" *(kulachniki)*, who "dance to the tune of the kulaks," and "sub-kulaks *(podkulachniki)* who carry out sabotage on their behalf."[105] These expressions did not relate to socioeconomic categories but to ideological ones. Their appearance reflected a reality: *the growing influence of the kulaks over the poor and middle peasants* whose direct interests were being harmed. They reflected also *an attitude of mistrust toward the peasantry in general which was widespread in the Party.*[106]

This attitude toward wide sections of the peasant masses was in line with the way that the local authorities interpreted the directives they received from the center. In any case, it weakened still further the worker-peasant alliance, and helped to cause a growing proportion of the peasantry to fall under the ideological and political influence of the kulaks.

In his speech at the Party's Sixteenth Conference (at the end of April 1929), Syrtsov, chairman of the Sovnarkom of the RSFSR, who supported the line of maintaining and extending the emergency measures, or other similar measures, described how the relation of forces was evolving in the countryside: "We can literally feel, sense, how things are taking a certain shape, how the kulaks are becoming conscious of themselves as a class, how their own class demands are being put forward."[107]

The counteroffensive thus being waged by the kulaks was obviously possible only because they had succeeded (as a result of the situation which had developed after the beginning of 1928) *in drawing behind them a sufficient body of peasant support.* One of the resolutions adopted by the Sixteenth Conference, while not recognizing that the worker-peasant alliance had been gravely shaken, nevertheless raised the problem of maintaining this alliance: "The question whether the peasant masses will remain faithful to the alliance with the working class, or will allow the bourgeoisie to separate them from it, depends on the line of development that agriculture is to take—the socialist road or the capitalist road—and, in conformity with that, on *who is going to direct the way the economy will develop–the kulak or the socialist state.*"[108]

It is significant that the problem thus presented was not expressed in terms of a *mass line* to be carried out among the peasantry, a task of ideological and political work aimed at persuading the peasants of the correctness of the socialist road: that it was expressed *not in political terms (the leading role of the Party and of the proletariat* in relation to the peasantry), but in *"economic" terms,* in terms of the *direction of the economy by the "state."* Actually, this "direction of the economy by the State" was *assumed* to be dependent essentially on the accelerated development of industry. The Sixteenth Party Conference adopted the figures for the First Five-Year Plan which were put before it. *The future industrial results of that plan appeared as the condition required for transforming agrarian relations* through the spread of collective and state farms, so that the spread of this type of farming was still treated very cautiously by the Sixteenth Conference;[109] but the *immediate political* requirements for strengthening the worker-peasant alliance were neglected, owing to the de facto priority accorded to *industrialization seen as the conditon for this strengthening.*

The priority development of industry (and, above all, of heavy industry) at all costs was at that time regarded as the fundamental task of the hour. This resulted from the conjunction of a number of factors which will be examined later. Among them was the shortage of industrial goods (interpreted as the symptom of a "lag" of industry behind agriculture) and an increase in unemployment, for which rapid industrialization seemed the only answer. On the political plane, accelerated industrialization was seen as a means of consolidating the dictatorship of the proletariat through increasing the numbers of the working class, and also through the strengthening of the country's military potential which this industrial development would make possible.

The importance ascribed one-sidedly to the development of industry, and heavy industry in particular, led to little account being taken of the negative consequences of the *postponement* (until industry should be "sufficiently developed") of the solving of the problems involved in the consolidation of the worker-peasant alliance. Within the framework of the prevailing interpretation of the basic task of the hour, the worsened situation in the countryside, far from impelling the Party to rectify the political line which had brought this about, led on the contrary to the adoption of *fresh measures of coercion, applied, in practice, to the peasantry as a whole;* these were considered necessary for the rapid industrialization of the Soviet Union.

The most serious indication of the worsening situation in the countryside was the sharp fall in the procurement of grain during the first half of 1929.[110]

Faced with this fall, the Party and the government tried to apply measures of a new type, so as to have as little recourse as possible to Article 107,[111] since they had promised this to the peasants after the many protests and demonstrations in 1928. One of these measures took the form of a "voluntary undertaking," a sort of "self-fixing" by the *skhod* itself of the amount of grain to be procured.

Actually, the *skhod* (which, moreover, was often called upon to commit itself without regard to whether or not a quorum of members was present) was confronted with the obligation to ratify the procurement figure laid down by the state organs. A decision taken in July 1929 by the CC shows plainly that the quantities which the village assemblies thus "undertook" to deliver were taken in excess of their capacity and had to be reduced. This exposes the fictitious nature of the so-called self-fixing of the amount of the grain procurement. The use of such methods proved a new source of discontent among the

peasantry, including the poor peasants to whom these measures were applied, and who, moreover, were supposed to
have been consulted through "poor peasants' committees"
which actually had no real existence, and often disappeared
almost as soon as they had been formed.[112]

The most serious source of the increased tension between a
large part of the peasantry and the Soviet government was
constituted, however, by the measures taken against peasants
who failed to deliver to the procurement organs the amounts
of grain laid down. These peasants were subjected to various
penalties. One of these penalties was *expulsion from the
cooperative society, which meant that those expelled had to
buy on the private market, where prices were much higher
than in the cooperative shops. The effect of this was to oblige
these peasants also to sell their produce on the private market, thereby risking prosecution as speculators.* Another pen-
alty applied when the amounts laid down were not delivered
was the imposition of *a fine equivalent to five times the
amount not delivered,* known as the *pyatikratka.* In principle,
the application of this fine was to be decided by the *skhod,*
but, in view of its frequent refusal to do so, in April 1929
power to apply the fine was given to the rural soviet—which
meant, in practice, to an organ in which the peasants carried
little weight and which was dominated by officials.

In June 1929 the government of the RSFSR decided, furthermore, to expand the applicability of Article 61 of the Penal
Code. Henceforth, "refusal to deliver grain in fulfillment of
the voluntary undertaking entered into by the village, a joint
refusal by a group of rural households, and offering resistance
to the implementation of the plan for building up reserves of
grain [will be dealt with] in accordance with part three of this
article."

This part of Article 61 provided for *penalties of up to two
years' imprisonment, confiscation of property and, in some
cases, exile.* Exiling and imprisonment, which had already
begun to be employed as penalties, were thus made legal.
During the campaign of 1929–1930, these measures were
applied with increasing frequency.[113] This was also true of

the "hard tax," which meant to impose upon kulaks, or peasants treated as kulaks, a contribution in grain to be paid within twenty-four hours. Since the rate at which this tax was levied often exceeded what the peasants could pay, they could find themselves sent into exile for failure to meet their obligation.

The application of Article 61 did not affect the kulaks alone, but often struck at the middle peasants. This was so also with the decision taken by the CC in July 1929 to *forbid the sale by state shops of "goods in short supply"* (matches, lamp oil, nails, textiles, etc.) *to peasants who had not delivered the amounts of grain laid down for procurement.*[114] A measure already practiced at the local level, and at first condemned as unjustified, was now given legal force.

The local authorities were supposed to apply the various penalties with discrimination, that is, to avoid hurting the middle and poor peasants, except in exceptional cases. In reality, as shown by the many decisions by the CC condemning the abuses committed by local authorities, this was not so.

The Party leadership tried to draw a distinction between the line laid down, the correctness of which they reaffirmed, and its application, which they recognized as often being mistaken. In principle, this distinction would be justified if the formulation of the line and the demands imposed upon the local authorities had not led the latter to multiply decisions which were unacceptable owing to their class consequences (and which were, moreover, condemned post facto). Such decisions became more and more frequent during 1928 and 1929, so that the situation grew increasingly to resemble what Lenin had described and denounced in March 1919, when he said that "blows which were intended for the kulaks very frequently fell on the middle peasants. In this respect we have sinned a great deal."[115]

During 1929 the peasants' resistance to the various coercive and penal measures developed and took many different forms. It was no longer merely a matter of "passive resistance," expressed in reduction of the sown area and slaughtering of some of the cattle, but of "offensive" reactions of one kind or another. One of these forms of resistance, which implied col-

lective action, was called *volynka:* certain villages simply refused to supply anything whatsoever to the procurement organs. These *volynki* were punished severely. In 1929 peasant
revolts were reported in a number of regions (but do not
appear to have spread widely). The most important of them
occurred in the mountains of Georgia (in Adzharia) and in the
Pskov region. There were also attacks on procurement agents
by kulaks or peasants under kulak influence.[116]

When the Party leadership drew up the balance sheet of the
procurement campaign of 1928–1929 at the beginning of July
1929, they came to the conclusion that the measures which
had been taken down to that time were not providing a real
solution to the problem of supplying the towns, and not enabling a sufficient quantity of grain to be centralized for export. From then on, the leading bodies of the Party, especially
the general secretary's office, were led to reformulate the
problem of collectivization.

Previously, this problem had been regarded as one to be
tackled with care—as a task which it was essential to carry out
with wide backing and confidence on the part of the peasant
masses. Thereafter, collectivization tended to appear as the
immediate means of "solving" the problems created by procurement difficulties and by the fall in grain production.

As we shall see,[117] the Party then committed itself to a
policy of accelerated collectivization for which neither it nor
the peasant masses were ideologically or politically prepared.
This policy was carried out in such a way that it proved the
starting point of a serious rupture in the worker-peasant alliance and an unprecedented crisis in agriculture, especially
grain production and stock-breeding. The supply of foodstuffs
to the towns could then be ensured only through a further fall
in consumption by the peasantry.

Notes

1. Let me remind the reader that the expression "during the NEP"
   means the period from 1921 to 1929. I have already pointed out

that the policy actually carried out during the last years of this period amounted increasingly to a negation of the principles of the NEP. The expression "final crisis," or "general crisis," of the NEP therefore does not really mean a crisis of the "New Economic Policy" so much as the development of the contradictions characteristic of the years 1928 and 1929.

2. *Narodnoye khozyaistvo 1961 g.*, p. 27.

3. *Sdvigi v selskom khozyaistve SSSR*, p. 14.

4. The figures for this development will be found in Grosskopf, *L'Alliance ouvrière*, Table 185, p. 310.

5. Ibid., p. 311.

6. *Report of the 15th Congress of the CPSU.*, Communist Party of Great Britain, London, 1928, p. 362.

7. See volume I of the present book, pp. 235 ff.

8. See above, p. 92.

9. "Preliminary draft theses on the agrarian question, for the 2nd Comintern Congress," in Lenin, *CW*, vol. 31, pp. 152–164.

10. S. G. Strumilin, "Rassloeniye sovyetskoy derevni," in *Planovoye Khozyaistvo* no. 3 (1928), p. 56, quoted in Grosskopf, *L'Alliance ouvrière*, p. 141. In general, this chapter will refer frequently to Grosskopf's book, which the reader interested in a detailed analysis of the problems discussed here should consult. Strumilin's article is available in French in *Recherches internationales à la lumière du marxisme*, no. 85 (no. 4 of 1975), pp. 120 ff.

11. The approximate character of the figures is due especially to the fact that the majority of the investigators whose work furnished the basis for these statistics were not peasants themselves and were therefore not always able to grasp precisely the *real situation* of the different forms. Nevertheless, it is to be observed that quite other sources give a social breakdown of the peasantry very similar to Strumilin's, when these sources employ the *same criteria* of categorization as he does (see Strumilin's article in *Recherches internationales*, no. 85 [no. 4 of 1975], p. 149, and Grosskopf, *L'Alliance ouvrière*, tables on pp. 309–310). It is to be observed, too, that Strumilin, who cannot be accused of being "pro-kulak", considers that the farms of the richer peasants were more strictly inspected than the others and their incomes therefore better known (*Recherches internationales*, p. 130).

12. These figures refer to the share contributed by peasant farms (i.e., excluding the *sovkhozes* and *kolkhozes*) in 1925. Even if

we set aside the share of marketed grain furnished by the well-to-do stratum of the middle peasants, the other middle peasants and the poor peasants alone were responsible for 71.5 percent of it (see Grosskopf, *L'Alliance ouvrière*, p. 142). We are concerned here still with comparative quantities, but they are highly significant. These same quantities were mentioned by Stalin in May 1928 (see above, pp. 89–90).

13. Grosskopf, *L'Alliance ouvrière*, pp. 142–144.
14. See above, pp. 95 ff.
15. Figures for the area of land included in a farm do not permit any conclusion to be drawn regarding the wealth of the farmer, as Lenin showed in *The Development of Capitalism in Russia* (*CW*, volume 3). What had been true before the Revolution was even truer under the NEP. At that time an especially large proportion of the land held by the poor and middle peasants could not be cultivated by them, for lack of tools, machinery, and horses (for some figures, see above, pp. 97–98).
16. L. Kamenev, *Nashi dostizheniya, trudnosti i perspektivy*, p. 9. See also L. Kamenev, *Stati i rechi*, vol. XII (Moscow, 1926), pp. 347–371 (quoted in Grosskopf, *L'Alliance ouvrière*, pp. 138–140).
17. Ya. A. Yakovlev, *Ob oshibkakh khlebofurazhnogo balansa TsSU i ego istolkovatelei*, quoted in Grosskopf, *L'Alliance ouvrière*, p. 142.
18. Stalin, "On the grain front," in *Works*, vol. 11, pp. 85 ff. The percentages (given on p. 89) were furnished by Nemchinov, a member of the collegium of the Central Statistical Board.
19. The special influence of the rich peasants in the *skhod*, and their attachment to the "land commune" have been questioned: see D. J. Male, *Russian Peasant Organisation Before Collectivization*, pp. 162 ff.
20. Grosskopf, *L'Alliance ouvrière*, pp. 137 ff.
21. See above, pp. 36–37.
22. Ibid.
23. G. Pistrak, "Zernovoye khozyaistovo i khlebniy rynok S.S.S.R. vosstanovitelnogo perioda," in *Sotsialistichestoye Khozyaistvo*, no. 5–6 (1927), p. 256. Also Ya. A. Yakovlev, ed., *K voprosu o sotsialisticheskom pereustroistve selskogo khozyaistva*, pp. 98–103, 153–155, quoted in Grosskopf, *L'Alliance ouvrière*, pp. 331 ff.
24. This is confirmed by the way that the emergency measures were

applied subsequently. *They made possible the procurement of the required amount of grain only through taking large-scale levies from the reserves held by the middle peasants, and sometimes by the poor peasants.* This fact was admitted more than once by the Party leadership—see above, pp. 39–40 ff.

25. V. Milyutin, "Uroki khlebozagotovok," in *Na Agrarnom Fronte*, no. 4 (1928), p. vi, and A. Lvov, "Itogi khlebozagotovitelnoy kampanii 1927–1928 g.," in ibid., no. 9 (1928), pp. 65–66; quoted in Grosskopf, *L'Alliance ouvrière*, p. 333.

26. In this connection, although grain production increased considerably under NEP, the remark made by Lenin at the Tenth Party Conference in May 1921 (*CW*, vol. 32, p. 406) was still valid for the great majority of the peasants: in the absence of an adequate supply of industrial products to offer to the peasants, then only taxation would ensure the supply of foodstuffs in amounts adequate to meet the needs of the towns, industry, and exports. Most of the peasants were too poor, and their need of grain for their own consumption too poorly satisfied, to be able to sell their produce in order to hoard, or to invest, say, by subscribing to loans.

27. Grosskopf, *L'Alliance ouvrière*, p. 332.

28. It should be recalled that in the summer and autumn of 1918 the Bolshevik Party supported, in principle, the movement and organization of the poor peasants (see volume I, p. 220). Whatever may have been the weaknesses of that movement (which developed during the civil war), it is significant that during the years 1921–1927 the Party offered no *systematic* backing to the various initiatives of the poor peasants.

29. In 1926–1927 average annual income per head (i.e., per member of a family) was estimated at 78.6 roubles for the poor peasants, 113.3 roubles for the middle peasants, and 239.9 roubles for the rich peasants. That of an agricultural worker was estimated at 108.2 roubles and that of an industrial worker at 334.6 roubles (Grosskopf, *L'Alliance ouvrière*, p. 211). It must be stressed that these are only estimates, and that the "purchasing power" of the rouble varied widely from one locality or region to another.

30. See volume I of the present work, p. 239.

31. Grosskopf, *L'Alliance ouvrière*, pp. 239–246.

32. Ibid., p. 177.

33. See below, p. 142.

34. Yakovlev, ed., *K voprosu*, p. 59, quoted in Grosskopf, *L'Alliance ouvrière*, p. 308.
35. N. Rosnitsky, *Litso derevni*, pp. 28–29, quoted in Grosskopf, *L'Alliance ouvrière*, pp. 308–309.
36. Yakovlev, ed., *K voprosu*, pp. 56–57.
37. Lenin, "Resolution on the attitude to the middle peasants" (March 1919), in *CW*, vol. 29, p. 219.
38. Lenin, "On the Tax in Kind" (April 9, 1921), vol. 32, p. 292.
39. Ibid., p. 288.
40. *Report of the 15th Congress*, p. 376.
41. Grosskopf quotes numerous facts concerning the development of these forms of association and mutual aid (*L'Alliance ouvrière*, pp. 311–315).
42. Ibid., pp. 311–312.
43. *Report of the 15th Congress*, pp. 368–369.
44. On these points see Grosskopf, *L'Alliance ouvrière*, pp. 390–395.
45. Ibid., pp. 311 ff., 415 ff.
46. See above, pp. 121 ff.
47. See above, p. 97.
48. Carr and Davies, *Foundations*, vol. I, part 2, p. 977, and Grosskopf, *L'Alliance ouvrière*, Table 141, p. 244.
49. See above, pp. 106–107.
50. *Report of the 15th Congress*, p. 368.
51. A great deal of weight needs to be given to the problem referred to here. It was, in fact, underestimation of the potentialities that the farms of the poor and middle peasants possessed for several years yet that contributed to impelling the Soviet government to undertake a collectivization that was ill-prepared politically and ideologically, and which it saw as the only way of escape from the supposed exhaustion of the possibility of still increasing agricultural production for a certain period without resort to an improvised revolution in agrarian structures. It should be noted that the thesis of "exhaustion of possibilities for growth in agriculture" in the conditions of 1928 was explicitly affirmed at that time (see the resolution adopted on July 10, 1928, by the plenum of the CC, in *K.P.S.S. v rezolyutsiyakh*, vol. 2, pp. 391 ff.), and that it is still defended in the Soviet Union. Chapters IX and X of V. Yakovtsevsky, *Agrarnye otnosheniya v periode stroitelstva sotsializma*. A French translation of these chapters appeared in *Recherches internationales*, no. 85 (no. 4 of 1975),

pp. 55 ff. On the theses of the "exhaustion" of NEP agriculture and the urgent "economic necessity" of collectivization, see pp. 56–59.

52. Grosskopf, *L'Alliance ouvrière*, p. 238 ff., 377.
53. I. B. Messner, "Predposylki planovogo razvitiya mekhanizatsii selskogo khozyaistva," in *Planovoye Khozyaistvo*, no. 8 (1927), p. 54.
54. N. P. Oganovsky, "Maksimalny variant perspektivnogo plana rekonstruktsii selskogo khozyaistva," in *Planovoye Khozyaistvo*, no. 7 (1927), p. 37, quoted in Grosskopf, *L'Alliance ouvrière*, p. 377.
55. The concept of the "net balance" is explained below.
56. Grosskopf, *L'Alliance ouvrière*, pp. 113, 122.
57. Osvok's forecasts are quoted from ibid., p. 351. The cultivated areas, yields and marketable shares have been calculated from the same source. Actually, increases in yield are usually accompanied by a more than proportionate increase in the share of production marketed.
58. *Report of the 15th Congress*, p. 376.
59. Ibid., p. 365.
60. See volume I of the present book, p. 487 ff., especially p. 488. On this point see also Grosskopf, *L'Alliance ouvrière*, pp. 156–159.
61. *Report of the 15th Congress*, p. 372.
62. *K.P.S.S. v rezolyutsiyakh*, vol. I, pp. 666–667, 851.
63. Lenin, "The Tax in Kind" (April 21, 1921), in *CW*, vol. 32, p. 349.
64. Yakovlev, ed., *K voprosu*, pp. 175, 184, 255, 284.
65. Ibid., pp. 212–213, 222–224, 236, 256, and the remarks of Grosskopf, *L'Alliance ouvrière*, pp. 292–295.
66. Yakovlev, ed., *K voprosu*, pp. 59, 236–237; Rosnitsky, *Litso derevni*, pp. 70–74; N. Baryshev, "Novye zavoyenvaniya derevenskoy bednoty," in *Na Agrarnom Fronte*, no. 9 (1928), p. 75.
67. A. Nove, *An Economic History of the U.S.S.R.*, p. 186.
68. A. Mendelson, ed., *Pokazateli konyunkturi narodnogo khozyaistva SSSR za 1923-1924–1928-1929 gg.*, p. 51.
69. Ibid.
70. *Planovoye Khozyaistvo*, no. 5 (1929), pp. 61–65; and no. 10, p. 94.
71. A. Nove, *Economic History*, p. 186.
72. M. Lewin, "Taking Grain: Soviet Policies of Agricultural Pro-

curement before the War," in C. Abramsky and Beryl G. Williams, eds., *Essays in Honour of E. H. Carr.*

73. According to the estimates published by Gosplan in 1929 and 1931, the index of agricultural production (with 1927–1928 as 100) reached its maximum in 1926–1927 (with 101.1, in prices of that year), and fell to 90.3 in 1930 (Zaleski, *Planning,* p. 387). According to *Narodnoye Khozyaistvo 1958 g.,* p. 350, agricultural production touched bottom in 1933 (when it was 18.5 percent lower than in 1928). However, the Gosplan estimates published in *Sotsialisticheskoye Stroitelstvo SSSR* (1936), pp. 232–233, and Zaleski's calculations (*Planning*), show the lowest level of agricultural production as being reached in 1932, when it was 15.6 percent less than in 1926–1927. *The NEP level of agricultural production was not to be regularly surpassed until after the Second World War,* after 1948 (and for products of animal husbandry, not until 1953). See *Narodnoye Khozyaistvo 1958 g.,* p. 350.

74. This net balance might in some cases be less than the amount of the procurement, in particular when part of the grain procured had to be returned to villages or agricultural regions that had a grain deficit. It must not be confused with the total amount of the grain harvest that was marketed, as *this* figure included sales made inside the village. The question of the net agricultural "surplus" is dealt with later (see below, p. 157).

75. See the figures given in *Materialy osobogo soveshchaniya po vosproizvodstvu osnovnogo kapitala pri prezidiume V.S.N.Kh., seriya III, vypusk II: perspektivy razvitiya selskogo khozyaistva,* p. 86, quoted in Grosskopf, *L'Alliance ouvrière,* p. 346.

76. Between 1913 and 1926–1927 the rural population had risen from 114.6 to 120.7 million, an increase of 5.3 percent (*Narodnoye Khozyaistvo 1958 g.,* p. 9).

77. A. E. Lositsky, "Perspektivy potrebleniya prodovolstvennykh produktov v Soyuze," in *Planovoye Khozyaistvo,* no. 4 (1927), pp. 89–90, quoted in Grosskopf, *L'Alliance ouvrière,* pp. 170, 174.

78. Calculated from the source given in note 15.

79. Calculated from figures in Grosskopf, *L'Alliance ouvrière,* p. 351.

80. *Kontrolnye tsifry 1929–1930 gg.,* p. 538.

81. Stalin, *Works,* vol. 11, p. 215.

82. K. Bryukhanov, "Itogi khlebnoy kampanii 1928–1929g.," in *Ekonomicheskoye Obozreniye*, XI, p. 134, quoted in Grosskopf, *L'Alliance ouvrière*, p. 337.
83. Ibid. See also O. Narkiewicz, "Soviet Administration and the Grain Crisis of 1927–1928," in *Soviet Studies* (October 1968), pp. 237 ff.
84. This reduction in exports as compared with prewar was due to the increased standard of consumption of the masses.
85. *Narodnoye Khozyaistvo* (1932), p. xlviii.
86. Mikoyan, in *Bolshevik*, no. 15 (1928), p. 16.
87. Value in current prices (*Narodnoye Khozyaistvo* [1932], p. xlviii).
88. P. G. Timofeyev, *Ekonomicheskaya geografiya SSSR*, p. 263, quoted in Grosskopf, *L'Alliance ouvrière*, p. 340.
89. Stalin, *Works*, vol. 11, p. 51.
90. Ibid., vol. 11, p. 19; see also above, p. 40.
91. Ibid, vol. 11, p. 215.
92. *K.P.S.S. v rezolyutsiyakh*, vol. 2, p. 395.
93. The struggles within the Party will be discussed in Part 4.
94. Stalin, *Works*, vol. 12, p. 65.
95. Wolf in *Planovoye Khozyaistvo*, no. 2 (1929), pp. 99–100; and Vishnesky in *Na Agrarnom Fronte*, no. 10 (1928).
96. Between 1928 and 1929 the number of cattle fell by nearly 1.7 million, to 68 million, and that of pigs by nearly 5 million, to under 21 million (*Kontrolnye tsifry 1929–1930 gg.*, pp. 530–531).
97. Stalin, *Works*, vol. 11, p. 275.
98. "Obshchiye nachala zemlepolzovaniya i zemleustroistva," in *Kollektivizatsiya Sotsialisticheskogo Khozyaistva*, doc. no. 20; quoted in Lewin, *Russian Peasants*, p. 283.
99. See volume I of the present work, pp. 235 ff.
100. Stalin's report, November 1, 1926, to the Fifteenth Party Conference, in *Works*, vol. 8, p. 296.
101. When he wrote: "Our Party relies on two classes and therefore its instability would be possible and its downfall inevitable if there were no agreement between those two classes" (Lenin, *CW*, vol. 36, p. 594; on this point see p. 323 of volume I of the present work).
102. Lewin, *Russian Peasants*, pp. 284, 372 ff.
103. Ibid., pp. 285–286. Lewin quotes from *Bolshevik*, no. 19 (1928), pp. 20, 26.

134   *Charles Bettelheim*

104. Ibid., p. 287.
105. *Pravda*, January 26, 1929; *Na Agrarnom Fronte*, no. 7 (1929). See also Carr and Davies, *Foundations*, vol. I, pt. 1, pp. 258–259.
106. This mistrust went back a long way. It was expressed also in certain statements by Stalin at various periods before the crisis of 1928–1929 (see below, pp. 560–561).
107. *Shestnadtsataya Konferentsiya VKP(b)* (1962), p. 320, quoted in Carr and Davies, *Foundations*, vol. I, pt. 1, pp. 256–257.
108. *K.P.S.S. v rezolyutsiyakh*, vol. 2, pp. 456–457.
109. See below, pp. 455 ff.
110. See above, pp. 109 ff.
111. See above, p. 38.
112. A. L. Angarov, *Klassovaya borba v sovetskoy derevne*, pp. 20 ff., and Lewin, *Russian Peasants* pp. 390 ff.
113. Lewin, *Russian Peasants* pp. 389–390; *The Penal Code of the R.S.F.S.R.* (text of 1926, with amendments up to December 1, 1932).
114. *Kollektivizatsiya Sotsialistcheskogo Khozyaistva*, doc. no. 49.
115. Lenin, *CW*, vol. 29, p. 159.
116. Lewin, *Russian Peasants*, p. 393.
117. See below, p. 458.

2. The economic and social conditions governing the reproduction and transformation of production relations in agriculture during the NEP

Once "war communism" had been abandoned, the transformation into commodities of a large part of agricultural production, together with the peasants' need to buy on the market nearly all their implements and a large proportion of the consumer goods they required, had the effect of causing the reproduction of production relations in agriculture to depend heavily upon the conditions governing the circulation of commodities.

Under the NEP the system of production for the market and the supply of goods to the rural areas, and particularly the relative levels of agricultural and industrial prices, were therefore to exert a far-reaching influence on the reproduction and transformation of production relations in agriculture. They affected the structure of production and brought about a series of *class consequences*, weakening or strengthening differentially the various strata of the peasantry and categories of producers. The systems of production for the market, of sale and purchase, together with industrial and agricultural prices, constituted a totality of social relations the characteristics and transformations of which were, for their part, subject to the overall effects of the class struggles in general and, in particular, to those of the political line adopted by the Bolshevik Party and the way this line was implemented. The line was materialized in the shape of "price policy" and "planning." On these planes, the class struggles developing among the peasantry became linked with the class struggles between the proletariat and the various sections of the bourgeoisie, and this is why it is important to analyze the conditions under which agricultural products entered into circulation, and also the conditions governing the supply of industrial goods to the peasantry.

I. Preliminary remarks

During the NEP period the changes that the class struggles brought about in exchange conditions had a considerable influence on the concrete practice of the worker-peasant alliance and on the differential class effects of this practice, and especially on relations between the poor, middle, and rich peasants.

Analyzing the social conditions of exchange means also revealing the characteristic features of the economic practices in which the various agents of the exchange processes were involved, and the constraints to which they were subject. These constraints were themselves bound up with the totality of class relations and practices. Whether they assumed the appearance of constraints "exercised by the market" or of "regulatory" constraints, they always possessed an ideological dimension, and this usually played a dominant role. Ideological relations subordinated exchange, in a way not always directly "visible," to the effects of the class struggles, including those struggles which were fought out on the ideological level.

(a) The "constraints" upon buying and selling

Later we shall see, in concrete terms, how these various constraints operated. In order, however, to make clear from the start what is meant, it may be useful to give some indications. The reader will recall, for example, that during most of the NEP period the degree to which the majority of the poor and middle peasants participated in exchange, and the ways in which they did this, were determined by a combination of economic, ideological, and political constraints. These were the constraints which "obliged" them to dispose rapidly of the greater part of the products they marketed, thereby receiving prices much less advantageous than those which the rich peasants were able to obtain some months later. The constraints which were thus brought to bear upon the majority of the poor and middle peasants—and which constituted one of the factors in the "information of market prices"—were due not only to the taxes they had to pay and to their indebtedness (repayment of loans obtained from rich peasants) but also to ideological and political relations in which they were integrated.

On the one hand, there was at the beginning of the NEP no apparatus of coercion capable of forcing the poor and middle peasants as a whole to pay their taxes and repay their debts, and, above all, to do so quickly. The "constraint," which at that time weighed upon the peasant masses, was essentially ideological; it was constituted by the peasants' integration into ideological relations which made them see it a duty to settle their tax and debt obligations quickly and forbade them to undertake collective actions to escape from the exigencies of their creditors and of the fiscal authority. On the other hand, these same ideological relations—profoundly different in this respect from those to which the mass of peasants had been subject before the revolution—encouraged them to increase their production to market in order to equip their farms better, even that part of their crops required to satisfy their "physiological needs." Lenin noted this in the autumn of 1922, when he said that:

> the overwhelming majority of the population of Russia are small peasants, who have now thrown themselves into production with extraordinary zeal, and have achieved (partly owing to the assistance the government has given them by way of seed, etc.) enormous, almost incredible success, particularly if we bear in mind the unprecedented devastation caused by the Civil War, the famine and so forth. The small peasants have been so successful that *they delivered the state tax amounting to hundreds of millions of poods of grain with extraordinary ease, and almost without any coercion.*[1]

The ideological relations in which the peasant masses were integrated in the NEP period, and which largely determined the way they participated in exchange, were extremely complex in nature, and changed as the years went by.

At the outset of the NEP an essential element in these ideological relations was the confidence which the peasant masses felt in the Soviet government's will to help them and improve their lot. This confidence accounted for the "ease" with which the peasant masses, though poor, paid their taxes, and the speed with which they sold part of their production so as to meet this kind of obligation. That same confidence, combined with their idea of what was needed in order to improve their lot, also led them to sell even what might have been considered "necessary" for their own consumption, so as to be able to buy new means of production.[2] Indeed, "the poorest peasants sold . . . most of what they produced not so much under the pressure of taxation as for the purpose of acquiring manufactured goods."[3] This was a "constraint to sell" which resulted from class ideological relations, in particular from relations which stimulated the poor and middle peasants not to go on accepting their lot as "fate" but to escape from kulak domination by *equipping* and, to a lesser extent, by *organizing* themselves. This was one of the objective bases of the dynamism of NEP agriculture.[4] It was also one of the forms of the participation of the peasantry in exchange, forms which exercised a certain effect on the actual conditions of exchange, especially as regards the selling prices of agricultural goods and the fluctuation of these prices. These prices were also bound up with class relations, both because those relations determined the conditions of production (what was produced, and the cost of this production in terms of labor) and the conditions of exchange.

Toward the end of the NEP period, especially from 1928 on, the system of "constraints to sell" affecting agricultural produce underwent change. On the one hand, the apparatus of coercion present in the countryside was strengthened. It intervened in a real way, first in order to secure the payment of taxes, and then to secure the deliveries required under the system of "planned contracts" (I shall come back to this point) or the "emergency measures." On the other hand, the frequently experienced shortage of industrial goods in the rural areas caused the poor and middle peasants to become more hesitant about selling their produce, since they were not sure of being able to buy the means of production and the consumer goods they needed. The procurement crisis of 1928 and 1929 can therefore be analyzed only if we take account of the changes in the ideological and political relations to which the different strata of the peasantry were then subject.

(b) The class effects of the "price policy"

During the NEP, as we shall see, prices were in part "free" and in part "fixed administratively." Actually, even "free" prices depended very largely on measures taken by the state—on the magnitude of its purchases and sales, and on the level of costs of production in state-owned industrial enterprises. Thus, prices, which affected the conditions of reproduction in agriculture, were in considerable measure the result of the overall policy followed by the Soviet government. This policy, therefore, produced *class effects:* it was a *particular form of the class struggle,* connected especially with the development of this struggle at the level of the state machine and the ruling Party.

The *actual* class effects of the "price policy" could be very different from those *expected* by the Party leadership. This observation is especially important in relation to the NEP period, when the class effects of the social conditions governing exchange often differed from the effects that had been expected or aimed at. Analysis of the social conditions of exchange must endeavor to discover the *reasons* for such differences.

In the NEP period these differences resulted from the weakness of the ties that linked the ruling Party with broad sections of the masses (mainly the peasant masses). They also resulted from the weakness of the theoretical analyses carried out by the Party, being themselves consequences of *misun-*

derstanding due to ideology—and so, of class ideological relations. This can be seen clearly if we study the way in which relations developed between town and country, and the class contradictions fostered by this development, contradictions which came to a head in the final crisis of the NEP.

II.   *The conversion of agricultural produce into money*

A study of the overall evolution of the exchange of agricultural produce and the conditions under which this exchange took place enables us to perceive the influence exerted by exchange conditions upon class relations and upon the final crisis of the NEP.

(a)   *The overall evolution of the exchange of agricultural produce and the economic and social significance of this exchange*

The way in which the exchange of agricultural produce evolved, compared with the way agricultural production evolved, shows the extent to which the peasant farms were linked with the market—the extent to which these farms had moved from a subsistence economy to one linked with the Soviet, or even the world, market. It is to be noted that in the course of the NEP period the connection between the peasant economy and the market developed rapidly. Even by 1923–1924 this connection had increased as compared with the prerevolutionary period. This fact refutes an opinion which is rather widely held to the effect that the agrarian revolution, by multiplying small farms, had resulted in an increase in subsistence farming.

Already in 1923–1924 the *total marketed share* of agricultural production was 25 percent larger than prewar, and during the following years this progress continued.[5] As regards grain, which possessed decisive importance, the total marketed share came to 36.1 percent in 1924–1925, compared with 32 percent in 1913.[6] From the political and social standpoint, we need to note that, in the chief grain-producing areas, the total marketed share of the grain produced was higher in the case of the poor peasant farms than in that of the farms of the well-to-do or rich peasants, which explains why the fluctuations in agricultural prices, especially grain prices, and the forms of marketing, were so important for the less prosperous sections of the peasantry.

Another noteworthy point is that the net marketed share of agricultural production[7] increase more slowly than the gross marketed share. Thus, in 1924–1925 the net marketing of agricultural produce (corresponding to what was called the "agricultural balance") was, in absolute figures, 46.6 percent less than prewar.[8] *As a whole, the agricultural balance tended to increase a little faster than gross agricultural production;* but this was not so in the case of grain (the prices for which evolved in a way that was not very favorable to the peasants), a fact that had important economic consequences and contributed to the final crisis of the NEP.[9]

(b) The participants in the exchange of agricultural produce

A study of the principal *direct participants* in exchange is necessary if we are to understand some of the contradictions which exploded toward the end of the NEP period.

A fundamental aspect of the exchange of agricultural produce under the NEP was that *an important fraction of those who sold this produce consisted of poor and middle peasants who were obliged to buy later on (in the same farming year) more or less substantial amounts of the same produce that they themselves had sold previously.* Since they were usually obliged to make their purchases at prices higher than those they had received, these operations signified for them *a loss of real income.* Such operations were forced upon them by their need to obtain money as soon as possible after the harvest, so as to repay their debts, buy indispensable manufactured goods, and pay their taxes. Their subsequent purchases of produce similar to what they had themselves previously sold were often effected with money obtained by means of *auxiliary activities*, or by *contracting fresh debts*. At the beginning of the NEP, about one-fifth of the wheat marketed was sold in this way by peasants who had later to buy wheat in order to meet their needs as consumers.

Those who bought agricultural produce directly, and the prices they paid, were also very diverse. A section of the buyers consisted of the peasants themselves: some bought produce for their own consumption, while others (mainly rich peasants) bought produce in order to sell it later at higher prices.[10]

The *nonpeasant* purchasers of agricultural produce were private traders, state and cooperative organizations, and individuals who came to buy in the peasant markets. In 1924–1925 these groups of purchasers absorbed 28, 37.1, and 34.9 percent, respectively, of this part of market production.[11] In the years that followed, the share accounted for by private traders fell rapidly.

Throughout the NEP period the Soviet government strove to develop the activity of the state and cooperative purchasing organs, in particular to ensure so far as possible the regular provision of supplies for the towns, the army, industry, and foreign trade, and to reduce fluctuations in prices for the consumer. The operations carried out by these organs were based mainly on purchasing plans, and their fulfillment constituted what was called "planned procurement" of agricultural produce (though some of the purchases made by the state and cooperative organs might not, in fact, be "planned").

III. The supply of industrial goods to the peasantry

Supplying industrial goods to the peasantry played an essential part in the reproduction of the material and social conditions of agricultural production. In order to ensure the continuity of their production, the peasants had to be able to obtain, at a price compatible with what they received when they sold their own produce, the articles they needed to provide their farms with means of production and to cover that part of their consumption which was not covered by agricultural produce. The circulation thus realized had also to ensure a certain equilibrium between the ebb and flow of cash. To this end it was necessary that the net cash receipts of the country dwellers should, taking one year with another, be convertible into town-made goods, once taxes payable in cash had been discharged and such savings as the peasants were disposed to make had been provided for.

The first problem that arose in this connection was that of ensuring a satisfactory supply of industrial goods for the countryside.

In the NEP period this supply might come from a variety of sources. It could be provided by private industry or by state-owned industry, and it could originate in the towns or in the countryside itself. Indeed, a substantial proportion of private industry was at that time accounted for by rural handicrafts. Their existence was a source of difficulty for the state sector. On the one hand, they enabled the countryside to survive, to some extent, without the towns, whereas the towns could not survive without the countryside. On the other, the prices at which the rural craftsmen could supply consumers' requirements set an upper limit to the prices at which state industry could sell its own products—unless it managed to control the provision of supplies to rural industry so as to keep within strict limits the competition coming from the latter.

(a) Private industry and rural handicrafts

The measures taken at the start of the NEP made possible a relatively large-scale revival of the activity of rural crafts. These crafts (which were destined to disappear during the 1930s) were of great importance to the peasantry. They provided *a large proportion of the peasants' comsumption of manufactured goods:* implements, building materials, consumer goods (textiles, clothing, pottery, footwear, canned food, etc.). Furthermore, *they ensured incomes not to be frowned on to a large number of poor and middle peasants who spent part of their time working as craftsmen, and, through the sale of craft products in the towns, they were a source of cash receipts for the rural sector.*

Toward the end of the NEP period, "small-scale industry" employed 4.4 million people, or about 60 percent of the total number of workers in industry. Nearly 3.6 million of these workers belonged to craft production units in the villages,[12] and *90 percent of them were also peasants.* In 1926 fewer than one-tenth of these rural craftsmen were organized in officially recognized cooperatives. Approximately another tenth were organized in "unofficial" cooperatives. The rest were "independent" craftsmen. Actually, those craftsmen who did not work for a local clientele but for a distant market were often dependent, in this period, upon private traders—the "Nepmen." The Soviet economist Larin estimated that in 1927 one-quarter of the craftsmen's gross production was more or less controlled by private capital,[13] which came on the scene either to buy up part of the craftsmen's production in order to sell it in other localities, or else to sell raw materials to the craftsmen. Though Larin's estimate is doubtless exaggerated, it remains true that a section of those who were classified as rural craftsmen were, in reality, dependent on private capital. This situation was to a large extent the consequence of the *poor functioning of state commercial organs.*

During the NEP the Bolshevik Party was, in principle, in favor of the rural crafts, which it wished to guide to an increasing degree along the path of cooperation. The resolution adopted by the Fifteenth Party Congress (December 1927), laying down directives for the preparation of the Five-Year Plan, still stressed the role to be played by the craftsmen. This resolution stated that the crafts must be developed as a *necessary complement to large-scale industry, as a means of eliminating the shortage of goods and of reducing unemployment.*

This orientation, in principle favorable to the crafts—especially the rural crafts—went on being reaffirmed down to the end of 1929. In that year it was still being emphasized that, in a number of branches of industry, *the crafts made it possible to obtain large quantities of goods while requiring very much smaller investments than large-scale industry.*[14] Thus, for the production of footwear, the crafts needed only one-tenth as much investment for the same volume of production. Actually, the crafts came up against increasing hostility from the heads of large-scale state industry: the latter saw in the craftsmen so many competitors for markets, supplies, and credits, and they often contrived to ensure that supplies to craftsmen provided by the state's commercial organs were kept at the minimum.

Nineteen twenty-nine, the "year of great change," was also the year of the downfall of the crafts and of rural industry. Thereafter, the maximum of material and financial resources were concentrated on large-scale industry, which also drained away the labor force available for the crafts. The rapid decline of rural industry entailed a series of negative consequences for country life, affecting the supply of goods and the incomes of the countryfolk.

Nevertheless, until the end of the NEP, the existence of rural handicrafts and, more broadly, of small-scale private industry, constituted an important aspect of the social conditions governing production and exchange. But this aspect came more and more into contradiction with the policy followed from 1928 on, and this contradiction, too, was to manifest itself in the final crisis of the NEP.[15]

(b) Retail trade in industrial goods in the rural areas

The rural areas were supplied with industrial goods not only by the rural craftsmen but also by state and cooperative trade and by private trade. Down to 1926–1927 the turnover of private trade was increasing in absolute terms, even though declining relatively. In 1928 the closing of a number of shops and stalls and the canceling of many pedlars' licenses brought about its decline, both absolute and relative.[16] In the rural areas this decline was such that it was far from offset by the increased sales of the state and cooperative sector.[17]

In all events, in 1928 state and cooperative trade was far less developed in the countryside than in the towns. The official network of retail trade made less than 34 percent of its turnover in the villages, though that was where more than 80 percent of the Soviet population lived.[18]

Thus, during most of the NEP period (and, to an even greater extent than before, toward the end of the period) the peasants were at a great disadvantage regarding opportunities for obtaining industrial goods of urban origin. Furthermore, the necessity of getting their supplies largely from private traders helped to reduce the peasantry's "purchasing power." While the private traders sometimes paid prices for some of the agricultural produce they bought higher than those paid by the "official" organs, they sold industrial goods at prices that were a great deal higher than those charged by state and cooperative suppliers. In 1927 the prices of cotton goods prevailing in the sphere of private trade exceeded by more than 19 percent those charged by the state organs. The differences amounted to nearly 57 percent for salt, 14 percent for kerosene, and nearly 23 percent for nails.[19] Naturally, if the peasants paid such high prices to private traders, the reason was that the state and cooperative network was unable to meet their demands.

The closing of many private shops from 1928 on did not improve matters for the peasants, given the increasing shortage of industrial goods and the inability of the official trade network to quickly take the place of the private traders who had been eliminated. In November 1928 a Soviet economic journal depicted the situation, pointing out that the shortage of industrial goods was even worse than that of agricultural produce:

> There are enormous queues. . . . The demand being huge, no more than 20–30 percent can be covered by the supply. . . . The

same applies to leather goods and to footwear. . . . There is no roof iron. . . . On the textile market a great tension prevails. The peasants go to the towns for goods, stand in queues. . . . Peasants produce receipts acknowledging deliveries of grain ranging from 50 to 500 poods; they would each of them buy 100–200 roubles' worth of industrial commodities, but all they are given is 20 roubles' worth. . .[20]

From 1928 on the disorganization of the trade network and the "goods famine," as it was called at the time, thus contributed considerably to the procurement crisis, and then to the final crisis of the NEP.

IV. *The conditions governing the fixing of purchase prices for agricultural produce, and the problem of the "scissors"*

The relative movement of agricultural and industrial prices was an essential factor in the changes affecting reproduction in agriculture.

The role played by the problem of the "scissors"[21] in the destiny of the NEP leads us to study the way in which the state intervened, or refrained from intervening, in the determination of agricultural prices.

(a) *The conditions governing the fixing of purchase prices for agricultural produce*

During most of the NEP period the prices at which agricultural produce was purchased were, in principle, "market prices"—in the sense that the peasants were not "legally obliged" to surrender part of their production to the procurement organs at a price fixed one-sidedly by the Soviet government. *In fact*, the conditions under which the purchase prices paid by the procurement organs were established were subject to considerable variation.

Generally speaking, *where the principal agricultural products destined for industrial processing were concerned* (cotton, flax, sugarbeet, etc.), *the state organs were almost the only purchasers.* These organs thus held a sort of monopoly in the purchase of these products.[22] This situation enabled them to buy at prices that were particularly favorable to them. However, *agricultural policy was at that time aimed at developing technical crops,* and so relatively high purchase prices were fixed for them, so as to encourage their development, and this procedure did indeed result in a rapid increase in the production of technical crops. In a number of regions this proved advantageous mainly to the rich peasants, who were in the best position to cultivate these crops.

During the NEP the conditions under which the official trading organizations fixed prices varied a great deal. At first, they were authorized to negotiate "freely" the prices at which they would buy agricultural produce. Nevertheless, these prices had to be between a "ceiling" and a "floor" fixed by the central trade organs. The latter altered their prices each year, and varied them as between different regions. Later, this system was gradually *replaced by a system of contracts (kontraktatsiya)* which were negotiated between the state organs and the peasants at the beginning of the "campaign." These contracts became elements in the purchasing plan of the state organs. They specified the quantities to be supplied by the peasants, the prices, the quality, the delivery dates, and so on. In return, the state organs undertook to grant certain credits and to ensure the supply of certain means of production. The prices paid for purchases made under these conditions were called "convention prices," since they were, in principle, "negotiated" between the peasants and the state organs. However, the latter had to work from a "basic price" which was fixed each year by Narkomtorg for the various products and regions. The "convention prices" actually paid might be between 5 and 10 percent above or below the "basic price."[23] For products other than grain the "basic price" was usually fixed at a high level so as not to discourage production, and to prevent too considerable a share of this production finding its way into the handicraft sector (this applied especially to wool and skins).

The procurement organs had not only to fulfill their plan as regards quantity, they had also to operate in such a way as to contribute to *keeping prices as stable as possible*. This task was especially important where grain was concerned, since grain prices had a serious bearing on the *cost of living* and the level of *real wages*. In the last years of the NEP this task was given greater and greater priority, and the prices paid for grain procured tended to be lower than "market" prices.[24]

The development of this tendency undermined the worker-peasant alliance. It was all the more harmful because it was above all the poor and middle peasants who were affected by the low prices imposed by the procurement organs: generally, indeed, it was the least well-off of the peasants, who, already in the autumn, sold directly to the state organs a large part of the produce they took to market.

The overall effect of this price policy was not only detrimental to the firmness of the worker-peasant alliance, but also *unfavorable to grain production*. Combined with the poor supply of industrial goods to the rural areas, it was to contribute to the explosion of the final crisis of the NEP.

The contradictions in which the "agricultural price policy" was caught were reflected in the frequent changes made in the conditions governing the fixing of the prices at which the state organs bought various products, and in the treatment of the private traders who competed with the procurement organs.

For most products of agriculture the state organs began by fixing mainly "convention"[25] or "negotiated" *(soglasitelnye)* prices which took fairly direct account of the prices prevailing in the private sector. Later, they fixed mainly "firm" *(tvyordy)* prices, which were lower than those paid in the private sector. The role of these "firm" prices increased more and more, and the state sought to lower them, especially in the case of grain in 1926–1927.[26]

Subsequently, partial upward readjustments of procurement

prices were decided on. However, these readjustments were limited, so that *the gap tended to grow, all the same*, between the "market" prices (which increased rapidly) and the procurement prices (which, moreover, lagged behind increases in the costs of production).[27] This was one of the immediate causes of the growing difficulties in procurement and an important factor in triggering off the final crisis of the NEP.

Under these conditions, for want of being able to organize procurement better and reduce the expenditure connected with it, the Soviet government was led—with a view to stabilizing as much as possible the prices at which it supplied the towns, and to having at its disposal quantities of grain that would not shrink castastrophically—to restrict further and further, and eventually to eliminate altogether, all private trade in grain. Along with this move, the contract system *(kontraktatsiya)* was also used to an increasing extent for the procurement of grain.

In the last years of NEP the Soviet government made these "contracts" obligatory in practice. This meant that they were no longer more than nominally "contracts."[28] In fact, thereafter, what the peasants had to deliver largely amounted to *compulsory deliveries*. The NEP, which was supposed to leave it to the peasants to dispose of that part of their production which they did not need for their own subsistence or to pay the agricultural tax, was now virtually abandoned, and under conditions which led to the adoption of measures of constraint from which the peasants tried to escape. Consequently, instead of isolating the rich peasants, these measures helped to ensure that a growing number of peasants tended to unite in order to resist what they saw as measures of requisition.

(b) The "scissors" disparity between agricultural and industrial prices

The policy followed by the Bolshevik Party in the matter of the evolution of agricultural in comparison with industrial prices was, in principle, one aimed at reducing the prices of industrial goods and "closing the scissors."[29] Such a policy was necessary if the worker-peasant alliance was to be consolidated, and if agriculture was to develop on the basis of its own forces. A judicious application of this policy would enable the poor and middle peasants to strengthen their positions in relation to the rich peasants, to equip their farms better, and to organize themselves, with the Party's aid. The following figures show that this policy appears to have achieved considerable positive results between 1923 (a year when the scissors were wide open, in favor of industrial prices[30]) and 1928:

Ratio of agricultural prices
to retail prices of industrial goods [31]

1913	100.0		
1923–24	33.7	1927–1928	79.0
1925–1926	71.8	1928–1929	90.3
1926–1927	71.1	1929–1930	76.9

These figures inspire the following comments:

1. In 1923–1924 the "purchasing power" of agricultural products had been reduced to about one-third of what it was before the war.

2. Between 1923–1924 and 1927–1928 the "purchasing power" of agricultural products appears to have been multiplied by 2.3.

3. The same line of progress seems to have continued in 1928–1929, when the ratio shown by the index was only 10 percent short of what it had been prewar.

4. In 1929–1930 the situation was sharply overturned, with the index falling below the level it had reached in 1927–1928.

Some corrections need to be made to this picture:

1. The way that the situation of the poor and middle peasants evolved cannot be judged from these figures alone. Most of them enjoyed a situation that was definitely better than before the war, since they had more land. After 1923 they improved their situation still further, by increasing the proportion of land they held.

2. While grain production was crucially important, the peasants who produced mainly grain were particularly disfa-

vored by the evolution of the ratio between prices for grain delivered to the procurement organs (the principal buyers of the grain produced by the poor peasants) and the retail prices of industrial products. This evolution proceeded as follows:

Ratio of prices of grain procured by the state
to retail industrial prices[32]

1913[33]	100.0		
1923–1924	29.1	1927–1928	65.2
1925–1926	68.7	1928–1929	76.1
1926–1927	56.6	1929–1930	76.9[34]

3. The unfavorable effects of the high level of industrial prices were felt seriously by those peasants who had to buy from private traders, since the latter charged especially high prices. Thus, in December 1927, the retail prices of industrial products exceeded the 1913 level by 88 percent in the "official" (state and cooperative) sector, but by 140 percent in the private sector.[35]

In order to present a more concrete picture of the relative price levels, here are the quantities of various products obtained by the peasants in 1927 in exchange for the price that the procurement organs paid *for one hundredweight of rye.*[36]

Quantities obtained in 1927			
	In the cooperative sector	*In the private sector*	*In 1913*
Textiles (meters)	12.99	10.91	23.72
Sugar (kilograms)	7.65	7.45	14.60
Kerosene (kilograms)	44.25	38.75	41.53
Salt (kilograms)	135.5	86.5	165.8
Nails (kilograms)	16.90	13.77	24.36

4. For the period from 1928 on it is not sufficient to consider merely the evolution of agricultural and industrial prices. To confine oneself to this means giving a falsely "embellished" picture of the peasants' situation. From that date, in fact, a large proportion of the peasants' cash income could

no longer, in practice, be exchanged for industrial products, owing to the "goods famine" that prevailed at the time, especially in the countryside.[37] This situation, which had already been experienced in the winter of 1925–1926, was severely detrimental to the poorest peasants and those whose holdings were least well equipped, as they could not improve their equipment and so remained dependent on the rich peasants.

To sum up, the policy of closing the scissors enjoyed comparative success down to 1927. Thereafter a "skid" occurred, parallel with the "procurement crisis" and partly accounting for the latter. This "skid" was a consequence of the mistakes made after 1926–1927 in the orientation of industrial policy, as regards both current production and investments. It revealed that, in the concrete conditions in which it was then situated, the Soviet government did not possess that "power to control prices" which it supposed itself to wield. The sudden confrontation with this truth, combined with the increasing predominance of conceptions that were unfavorable to the NEP, led to the development of the "emergency measures," the deepening of crisis phenomena, and, finally, the complete and unprepared-for abandonment of the New Economic Policy.

V.   The problems of accumulation and the evolution of peasant consumption during the NEP period

The preceding analyses have shown that what is meant by the expression "complete abandonment of the NEP" is, in fact, *abandonment of what was left* of the NEP in 1929. Actually, before 1929, the "NEP as it really was" consisted of a combination of contradictory measures, some of which were in conformity with Lenin's conception of the NEP while others were not—it was a sort of combination of the "NEP" and the "non-NEP." In practice, from 1925 on, the "non-NEP" aspect assumed increasing importance, and it became predominant toward the end of 1929.

From 1922 to 1927, however, respect was shown to some fundamental principles of the NEP, in particular the absence of measures of constraint imposed on the peasant masses, the levying of a fixed agricultural tax payable in cash, and the effort to be made to "close the scissors."

(a) The problems of accumulation and the increasing abandonment of the principles of the NEP

Starting in 1925, the magnitude of the problems arising from the need for accumulation on a scale sufficient to ensure the reequipment of the economy, *and the terms in which these problems were conceived,* resulted in the adoption of a series of measures which contradicted the NEP and jeopardized the improvement in the standard of living of the peasant masses. Such improvement was one of the aims of the NEP as a road to socialism, being intended to help reduce the disparity between the living conditions of the workers and the peasants.

Certain measures adopted during 1925 involved the risk of transforming the "NEP as it really was" into a sort of road to private capitalism. These measures resulted from a resolution adopted by the CC which met between April 23 and 30, 1925.[38] They were concerned mainly with extending the right to lease land and extending wage relations in agriculture.

On the first point, the resolution authorized wider use by the peasants of the right to lease land. Contracts of lease could, in certain cases, be made for a period of twelve years.[39] The resolution thus confirmed a decision taken on April 21, 1925, by the presidium of the VTsIK, modifying by "making more flexible" the provisions of Article 28 of the Agrarian Code of 1922. Thereafter, cases of authorized leasing of land grew so numerous that it was possible for this practice to become relatively normal, whereas the 1922 Code had allowed it in only exceptional cases.[40]

On the second point, the resolution of the CC ratified a decree adopted by the Sovnarkom on April 18, 1925, lifting nearly all restrictions on the employment of wage labor by peasants.[41]

These provisions were to remain in force in the following years, but from 1928 on they tended to become increasingly pointless: to lease land or hire wage workers meant defining oneself as a kulak and so attracting special danger from the "emergency measures."

Nevertheless, between 1925 and 1928 these measures contributed to a certain reinforcement of the positions of the rich and well-to-do peasants, as well as to an increase in the accumulation they accomplished—this was, moreover, one of the purposes aimed at, and it was very explicitly shown by some statements that were made on the eve of the adoption of the resolution mentioned above. The clearest passage to this effect is found in Bukharin's speech of April 17, 1925, when he said:

> The well-to-do upper stratum of the peasantry—the kulaks and, to some extent, the middle peasants too—*are at present afraid to accumulate.* . . . If the peasant instals an iron roof, the next day he will be denounced as a kulak, and that will mean the end of him. If he buys a machine, he does it "in such a way that the Communists won't notice." Improvement in agricultural technique has come to be surrounded by an atmosphere of conspiracy.
>
> If we look at the various strata of the peasantry, we see that the kulak is discontented with us because *we are preventing him from accumulating.* At the same time, the poor peasants sometimes grumble against us because we do not let them take employment as agricultural workers in the service of that same kulak . . . .
>
> Our policy towards the rural areas should develop towards a reduction and partial abolition of the many restrictions which hold back the growth of the farms belonging to the well-to-do peasant and the kulak. We ought to say to the peasants, to all the peasants: *get rich,* develop your farms. . . . Paradoxical as it may seem, we must develop the farm of the well-to-do peasant so as to help the poor peasant and the middle peasant.[42]

In this speech Bukharin was obviously preparing the Party to accept the measures that were to be adopted a few days later. What he said shows how at that time the problem of accumulation was linked with a line that relatively favored the well-to-do strata of the peasantry. According to this line, some of the savings accumulated by the well-to-do peasants were also to be drained off by the state through loans, and made to serve accumulation in state-owned industry.

The measures thus taken did strengthen the kulaks to some extent, but their "contribution" to increased accumulation, especially in the state sector, remained negligible, and this caused the turn in policy in 1926 toward promoting growth in state-sector accumulation *through credit expansion, currency inflation, and an evolution of prices which especially affected, as we have seen, the poor and middle peasants.*

Various figures show that the way in which the NEP was implemented had the result that it failed in one of its purposes, which was to *reduce the gap* between town and country, particularly as regards consumption of industrial goods.

(b) The growing gap between rural and urban consumption of industrial goods

Between 1923 and 1927 the rural population's share of the consumption of industrial goods *fell steadily.*[43] In the middle of the NEP period (in 1925–1926 [and the situation got worse in 1928]), consumption per head of population in the rural areas, where almost all industrial goods were concerned, was *lower than prewar,* amounting to *barely one-quarter of consumption per head in the towns.*[44]

The level of consumption of the less well-off strata of the peasantry was, of course, a good deal lower than what is revealed by *average* figures.

This state of affairs expressed the weaknesses of "NEP as it really was." It was due partly to failure to close the scissors, partly to the smallness of the *net marketed share* of agricultural production (the share which enabled the peasants to buy industrial goods), and also to the shortage of goods in the rural areas. This last point calls for clarification, especially because, according to the interpretation of the crisis of the NEP given by Preobrazhensky and the Trotskyists, the crisis was due to "excessive demand" from agriculture—that is, to a situation which dictated priority development for industry, the "financing" of which must be accepted as a burden by the peasantry. Let us see how the overall peasant demand for industrial goods evolved.

(c) The agricultural "surplus" and the demand for industrial goods.[45]

According to S. Grosskopf's estimates, the net balance of peasant sales, after deduction of taxes and other charges, fell from 1,347 million prewar roubles in 1912–1913, to 980 million prewar roubles in 1925–1926.[46] Taking 1912–1913 as 100, the index for this balance stood at 72.7 in 1925–1926. Leaving aside the cash income which the peasants could get from nonagricultural activities (income which we know has diminished), and savings in cash (which do not markedly affect the amounts being considered), *the balance in question represents the peasants' demand for industrial goods.* Between 1912–1913 and 1925–1926 this demand thus declined by 27.3 percent. Moreover, what this shows is the *monetary expression* of demand, not its *volume,* which was affected by the increase in the retail prices of industrial goods.

In 1925–1926 these prices were 2.2 times what they had been before the war.[47] The peasants' demand for industrial goods in terms of volume was proportionately less, so that we must substitute 33 for 72.7.

The subsequent years saw a certain improvement. If we accept that the net balance of agriculture, after deduction of taxes and other charges, grew in proportion to the net sales of agricultural produce, we get the following picture[48]:

Index of peasant demand for industrial goods
(1912–1913 = 100)

1926–1927	75.2	1927–1928	80.2

The volume of peasant demand for industrial goods obviously increased a little more rapidly during those last two years because industrial prices fell. Indeed, in 1928, as we know, the peasants' demand for industrial goods could not be satisfied.[49]

These few facts suffice to show the formal and abstract character[50] of the interpretations of the crisis of the NEP put forward by Preobrazhensky and the Trotskyists, who attributed the "shortage of industrial goods" to the increase in peasant incomes and the "lag of industry behind agriculture."

Actually, peasant demand does not account in the least for the shortage of industrial goods. The respective dynamics of industrial production and of the monetary demand from the rural areas for industrial goods reveal this clearly. Taking 1913 as 100, the index of industrial production reached the following levels[51]:

$$
\begin{array}{ll}
1925\text{--}1926 & 89.9 \\
1926\text{--}1927 & 103.9 \\
1927\text{--}1928 & 119.6
\end{array}
$$

In 1925–1926 the index of industrial production thus surpassed that of peasant demand for industrial goods by 12.2 points. The gap grew larger in the following years, to 28.7 in 1926–1927 and 39.4 in 1927–1928.

If there was a shortage of industrial goods, the reason for it must be sought above all in the conditions of reproduction characteristic of the urban sector, and not in the countryside. The role thus played by the urban sector had consequences that were all the more negative because the links between the Bolshevik Party and the peasant masses were weak, and the ideological and political relations in which the peasantry itself was caught were not, on the whole, favorable to the strengthening of the worker-peasant alliance.

Notes

1. Lenin, *CW*, vol. 33, pp. 407–408. (Interview with Arthur Ransome, correspondent of the *Manchester Guardian*, November 1922 [my emphasis—C. B.]. One pood=16.4 kilograms.)

2. Hence the expressions so often used by Lenin when describing the Soviet peasant: "hard-working" and "zealous."

3. Grosskopf, *L'Alliance ouvrière*, p. 169.

4. See above, pp. 94 ff.

5. The total marketed share means the ratio between total amount sold and gross production. This share must be distinguished from that of net *amount marketed,* which is obtained by deducting the amount of purchases of agricultural produce made by the peasantry from the total amount sold, and relating this figure to that for gross production. The net share marketed does not represent the evolution of the connection between the peasant farms and the market but the *demand for nonagricultural goods* emanating from these farms. The estimate given here is taken from L. N. Litoshenko's article, "Krestyanskoye khozyaistvo i rynok," in *Ekonomicheskoye Obozreniye*, no. 5 (1925); quoted in Grosskopf, *L'Alliance ouvrière,* p. 167.

6. Grosskopf, *L'Alliance ouvrière*, p. 168.

7. For some figures, see above, p. 157.

8. Calculated from *Kontrolnye tsifry*, p. 73.

9. On these points see Grosskopf, *L'Alliance onvrière*, pp. 67 ff., 347 ff., above, p. 157 ff.

10. Down to 1927–1928 the quantity of produce exchanged *between peasants* was of about the same order of magnitude as that of off-village sales (Carr and Davies, *Foundations,* vol. I, pt. 2, p. 916).

11. These percentages are fractions of the total turnover, so that their magnitude is affected by the prices at which the produce was bought, and these prices were higher for buyers on the peasant markets than for the state's purchasing organs. In 1926, for example, a pood (16.4 kilograms) of rye was sold for between 1.03 and 1.44 rouble on the peasant markets, but was bought for 0.94 rouble by the state (see B. Kerblay, *Les Marchés paysans*, pp. 112, 114). In March 1928, in the Ukraine the price of rye on the peasants' market was 126.3 percent of that paid by the procurement organs; in March 1929 it rose to 369.2 percent of that price. (See *Ekonomicheskaya Zhizn,* April 26, and May 1, 1929, and *Torgovo-Promyshlennaya Gazeta,* April 6, 1929, quoted in A. Baykov, *The Soviet Economic System,* p. 70.)

12. The others (about 860,000) were either urban craftsmen or (fewer than 80,000) workers employed in small-scale capitalist industry (Carr and Davies, *Foundations,* vol. I. pt. 1, pp. 390–391).

13. Yu. Larin, *Chastnyi Kapital v SSSR*, pp. 119–120.

160 *Charles Bettelheim*

14. *Torgovo-Promyshlennaya Gazeta*, July 5, 1929.
15. See below, p. 205 ff.
16. See below, p. 203 ff.
17. The protracted incapacity of state and cooperative trade to re-place private trade in the villages was due particularly to the circumstance that the peddlars and shopkeepers were content with installations that were simpler than those required by the managers and officials of the state and cooperative organs. The latter very often insisted on having a proper shop and a van, where their rivals had made do with a mere shed and horses for transport.
18. Baykov, *The Soviet Economic System*, p. 242.
19. Ibid., p. 67.
20. *Ekonomicheskaya Zhizn*, November 14, 1928, quoted in Baykov, *The Soviet Economic System*, p. 70. Peasants who could produce the receipts mentioned were supposed to be given priority in supplies.
21. The term "scissors" was used with reference to the picture pre-sented by the graphs showing the movement of industrial and agricultural prices. It was said that "the scissors are opening," when these prices diverged, whereas when they came closer together, "the scissors are closing." The scissors were regarded as having "closed" when the *relative* level of prices in 1918 was reached.
22. In 1927–1928 planned state purchases corresponded to the fol-lowing fractions of *marketed production:* 100 percent of cotton and sugarbeet; 98 percent of flax and tobacco; 92 percent of furs; 80 percent of skins; and 70 percent of wool (Baykov, *The Soviet Economic System*, p. 62). In the case of some important agricul-tural products, such as hemp and flax, marketed production was less than prewar. (*Ekonomicheskoye Zhizn*, May 3, 1927; see also Richard Lorenz's thesis, *Das Ende der Neuer Okonomischer Politik*, p. 28, and Grosskopf, *L'Alliance ouvrière*, Table 209, p. 352.)
23. Baykov, *The Soviet Economic System*, p. 63.
24. In 1926–1927 the tendency to fix *low procurement prices for grain* was especially marked. In that year the index of procure-ment prices (100 being the 1911–1914 price level) stood at 118.7 for grain, whereas it was 133.9 for state-procured products as a whole, *and the average index of prices for all agricultural pro-duce, including purchases by individuals and private traders, stood at 149.3* (Kerblay, *Les Marchés paysans*, p. 119). Other

examples of substantial differences between procurement prices and "market" prices have been mentioned above, for the years 1926, 1928, and 1929 (see note 11 above, p. 159).

25. See above, p. 148.

26. In 1926–1927 procurement prices were reduced by 20 percent for grain, and then stood at 25 percent less for wheat and 50 percent less for rye than the peasants could get on the private market (Kerblay, *Les Marchés paysans,* p. 118).

27. Grosskopf, *L'Alliance ouvrière,* p. 335.

28. Especially because the procurement organs did not as a rule succeed in providing the peasants with the amounts of fertilizer, selected seed, etc., which they had undertaken to provide when the "contracts" were signed. This aggravated the *one-sided* character of the obligations to which the peasants had to conform.

29. See note 21 above, p. 160.

30. There was talk at that time of a "scissors crisis."

31. These figures have been calculated from the last column in Table 11 on p. 119 of Kerblay, *Les Marchés paysans.* The index shows the evolution of the ratio between agricultural prices as obtained by the producer and *retail* prices of manufactured goods (a weighted index of the public and private sectors). The way that the weighting has been performed obviously affects the way the indices evolve, and the fact that the public sector's share was smaller in the villages than in the towns has not been taken into account in the table given here—so that the peasants' situation was even worse than is shown. For a calculation which takes this factor into account, see Grosskopf, *L'Alliance ouvrière,* pp. 195–196.

32. Calculated from the same source as the table on p. 151.

33. For 1913 the prices recorded were, of course, market prices.

34. Rye only.

35. A. N. Malafeyev, *Istoriya tsenoobrazovaniya SSSR, 1917–1963,* pp. 384–385. Coefficients calculated from indices with 1913-100.

36. Baykov, *The Soviet Economic System,* p. 67, quoting *Inland Trade of the U.S.S.R. During Ten Years,* p. 82. The 1913 figures show, of course, market prices.

37. See above, p. 147.

38. *K.P.S.S. v rezolyutsiykh,* vol. I, pp. 922–932.

39. Ibid., p. 927.

40. On the Agrarian Code of 1922, see volume I of the present work, pp. 235–237. On the reform of 1925, see *Sobranie Uzakonenii* (1925), no. 27, art. 191; and Carr, *Socialism,* vol. I, pp. 257–258.

41. *K.P.S.S. v rezolyutsiyakh*, vol. I, p. 927, and Carr, *Socialism*, vol. I, p. 268.

42. *Pravda*, April 24, 1925. A revised version of this speech of Bukharin's was published in *Bolshevik*, April 30 and June 1 (nos. 8 and 9/10 of 1925). In this version the word "kulak" was in most instances replaced by "well-to-do peasant." There is a French translation in N. Bukharin et al., *La Question paysanne en URSS*, pp. 139 ff.

43. Between 1923–1924 and 1926–1927 it fell from 59.4 percent to 53.2 percent (Grosskopf, *L'Alliance ouvrière*, p. 206).

44. On the other hand, thanks to the division of the land, the peasant population's consumption per head of *food products* was somewhat greater in 1925–1926 than it had been before the war, and had definitely improved so far as the less well-off sections were concerned. Nevertheless, consumption per head of wheaten flour, sugar, meat, bacon, fat, and eggs *was still less in peasant families than in the families of manual and office workers* (Grosskopf, *L'Alliance ouvrière*, Table 92, p. 170, and Table 96, p. 174).

45. See also some other observations on this question, above, pp. 141 ff.

46. Grosskopf, *L'Alliance ouvrière*, p. 197.

47. Calculated from Kerblay, *Les Marchés paysans*, p. 119.

48. These figures take the percentage increase in net agricultural sales as being as shown in the series of control figures for the years under consideration (*Kontrolnye tsifry 1929–1930 gg.*, p. 540), *that is, assuming as constant the rate of taxation and other charges:* this introduces a slight inaccuracy which seems hard to rectify.

49. See above, pp. 146, 152.

50. In March 1922, the CC of the Russian Communist Party had examined Preobrazhensky's theses on work in the rural areas and rejected them after discussing the criticism made by Lenin, who blamed Preobrazhensky for his abstract formalism (see Lenin, *CW*, vol. 33, pp. 237 ff.). The same formalism is found in Preobrazhensky's later writings: see some significant quotations in Grosskopf, *L'Alliance ouvrière*, pp. 188 ff.

51. This series was compiled by Gosplan for production by industry as a whole (E. Zaleski, *Planning*, pp. 380–381).

3. The reproduction and transformation of ideological and political relations in the rural areas

The problems discussed in this chapter are especially large and complex. Furthermore, the information available concerning them is, as a rule, inadequate and unreliable. We shall therefore not deal with these problems in a thorough way here, but merely point out the outlines and main aspects, as these become apparent in the light of the information we possess. It is plain that only far-reaching additional research (which assumes, among other things, access to the Soviet archives, which is not at present possible) will make it conceivable to subject to really systematic treatment questions which we can only touch upon here.

From the standpoint of ideology and politics, the situation of the Soviet countryside during the NEP was characterized by the poor integration of the peasantry into the Soviet system and the feeble penetration of socialist ideas among them. These circumstances were connected with the low level of activity by the Party and the soviets in the villages and the reproduction, in hardly altered form, of the old ideological relations embodied in the *mir*, the family, and the church.

I. The Party's implantation among the peasants

We know that at the end of the civil war relations between the Bolsheviks and the organs of Soviet power on the one hand, and the peasantry, on the other, were extremely strained.[1] One of the immediate aims of the NEP was, precisely, to reduce this tension, and thereby to strengthen the worker-peasant alliance. There can be no doubt that between 1921 and 1927 the NEP was a success as regards strengthening the peasants' confidence in the Soviet government. This applies especially to their confidence in the government's capacity to get the economy back on its feet. Between 1923 and 1927 considerable progress was achieved in this respect—progress that was to a large extent compromised in 1928–1929 by "blind" application of the "emergency measures."

However, there was a big difference between the peasants' having confidence that the new government was capable of managing the economy and their being ready to give active support to this government—or, going even further, to join the Bolshevik Party. Yet, unless a sufficient number of genuine peasants joined the Party, it could neither exert effective ideological influence in the rural areas nor, without real inside knowledge of their problems, effectively take the peasants' interests in hand, and thereby become capable of developing its own conception of the peasantry's place in the economy and politics of the Soviet power.

As regards the number of peasants joining the Bolshevik Party, and the Party's work in the countryside, the situation left a great deal to be desired. During the NEP period, the Party's implantation in the rural areas remained slight. In his report to the Fourteenth Party Congress, Stalin mentioned that the number of Party members belonging to village cells related to the total adult rural population showed that the percentage of Communists in the rural areas had increased from 0.26 at the time of the Thirteenth Congress to 0.37 at the time of the Fourteenth.[2] Such low proportions make a contrast with the importance of the tasks which the Bolshevik Party had to carry out in the countryside, in a mainly rural country. This organizational situation was, in part, a heritage from the past, but it also reflected the weaknesses in the Party line on peasant questions.

Commenting on the figures quoted, Stalin said:

Our Party's growth in the countryside is terribly slow. I do not mean to say that it ought to grow by leaps and bounds, but the percentage of the peasantry that we have in the Party is, after all, very insignificant. Our Party is a workers' party. Workers will always preponderate in it. ⸳ . . . But it is also clear that without an alliance with the peasantry the dictatorship of the proletariat is impossible, that the Party must have a certain percentage of the best people among the peasantry in its ranks. . . . From this aspect, matters are still far from well.[3]

Nor do the figures quoted fully expose the Party's weakness among the peasantry, because not all members of a rural cell were peasants. According to the CC's statistics of January 1927, less than half of the members of rural cells were actual peasants—the others were officials of Soviet institutions, employees of the cooperative societies, teachers, and so on.[4] Among these members some might be of rural origin, *but they were no longer peasants*. We need to reduce the numbers quoted by about one-half if we are to form an estimate of the Party's implantation among the peasantry in the middle years of the NEP period.

It should be added that in 1927 genuine peasants made up only 10 percent of the Party's total membership—in a country where the peasantry made up more than 80 percent of the population.[5]

Throughout the NEP years the Party's implantation in the rural areas remained extremely slight: in 1928 there were only 186,000 Party members in rural cells, and in 1929, 242,000.[6]

However, the scope of the crisis that the country and the Party were then experiencing was such that, in order to tackle the tasks before them, the Sixteenth Party Conference (April 23–29, 1929) considered it necessary to "purge" the membership, especially in the rural cells. This conference declared that only a purge could transform these cells "into points of support for the Communist Party in the countryside, strengthen confidence in the Party, bring into the Party's ranks the best Communist elements . . . and promote the collectivisation of agriculture."[7]

Actually, the purge was already under way, and the rural cells had not been reconstructed, when the Soviet Union entered the period of mass collectivization. On the whole, *collec-*

*tivization was carried out without the local organs of the
Party being in a position to control the way it developed.*

At the end of the NEP period the social composition of the
Party's rural cells was far from satisfactory: the proportion of
rich and well-to-do peasants was actually higher than their
proportion in the rural population as a whole.[8] An inquiry
carried out in 1929 among the rural Communists showed that
in the RSFSR one-quarter of these Party members possessed
assets exceeding 800 roubles, whereas among the peasantry as
a whole such assets were held by only one peasant in six. Of
the peasants who joined the Party, many became officials.
Apart from them, it was mainly middle peasants—perhaps
employers of wage labor—who had the time needed to participate fully in the Party's activity.[9]

The qualitative weakness of the rural cells was partly the
reason for the exceptional sweep of the purge carried out
among the Communists of the countryside. Between 1929 and
1930, 16 percent from rural cells were expelled as against 8
percent from factory cells.[10] However, the magnitude of this
purge was due not only to the circumstance mentioned, but
also to the distrust felt by certain Party cadres toward peasants
in general. Indeed, one is struck by the fact that the purge was
much less severe (10 percent) in the "nonproductive" cells,
although a Party resolution had described these as the ones
where the most serious abuses occurred (misuse of Party
members' authority for self-seeking purposes, embezzlement
of funds, nepotism, careerism, bureaucratic attitude to the
masses),[11] the ones in which "everyday forms of decay" were
to be observed and in which elements alien to the proletariat,
bureaucratized elements, and persons who, having come from
other Parties, retained their old ideological conceptions were
concentrated.

So massive a purge of the rural cells was due also to the
incompetence and routinism of many of the Party members
then working in the countryside. Numerous reports show that
even politically reliable elements, devoted to the Bolshevik
Party, were not up to the tasks that devolved upon them. They
issued more orders than explanations, and, owing to their lack

of roots in peasant life, the explanations they gave remained abstract, remote from reality, often even failing to deal with concrete problems. Frequently they were unable to convince people or made decrees which were inappropriate and caused discontent.[12] However, the major causes of expulsion from the Party were corruption and nepotism, or a way of life and conduct that were incompatible with membership in the Party.[13]

Altogether, the conditions under which the Party operated in the countryside failed to correspond, both quantitatively and qualitatively, with the demands of the situation. From the quantitative angle, toward the end of the NEP the members of rural cells who were really peasants amounted to only about 0.1 percent of the peasantry. Therefore, the Party could fulfill only with difficulty its role as the instrument of the dictatorship of the proletariat in the countryside, as the apparatus for introducing proletarian ideas among the peasantry, the link between the Soviet power and the peasant masses. This weakness of the Party affected the conditions under which the rural soviets operated: they worked badly, and, in turn, their bad work reflected negatively on the Party itself.

II. The rural soviets

At the outset of the NEP period, when the peasant revolts of 1921 were still recent and movements of discontent among the peasantry not uncommon, the rural soviets were hardly linked with the masses at all. Their composition was frequently determined by Party decisions that were confirmed by elections in which only a minority of peasants took part. The rural soviets were not genuine mass organizations.

In 1924 the Bolshevik Party leadership applied itself specially to the problem of the rural soviets. On October 26 Stalin spoke to the CC on "the Party's tasks in the countryside."[14] He drew attention to *the peasants' mistrust of the towns,* the discontent that still prevailed in many rural areas, the fact that

there was still risk of peasant revolts, and the need *to develop
the rural soviets*. He linked this need with the flourishing of
non-Party organizations—peasant committees, cooperatives,
Young Communist organizations—which was a feature of the
period.[15] In his eyes, the flourishing of these organizations
involved a danger that they might escape from the Party's
guidance, whereas development of the rural soviets would
enable the working class to fulfill completely its role of leadership in relation to the peasantry.[16]

A few days earlier, on October 22, Stalin had already discussed these questions before a conference of secretaries of
rural Party units.[17] He emphasized particularly the need for
revitalizing the soviets. Referring to the revolts which had
occurred in several rural localities in Georgia, he said:

> What happened in Georgia may be repeated all over Russia if we
> do not radically change our very approach to the peasantry, if we
> do not create an atmosphere of complete confidence between the
> Party and the non-Party people, if we do not heed the voice of the
> non-Party people, and, lastly, if we do not revitalise the Soviets
> in order to provide an outlet for the political activity of the toiling
> masses of the peasantry.[18]

The revitalizing of the soviets was seen as a means of forming *nuclei of activists*, among whom *the Party would be able
to recruit*, while *the peasants would learn how to manage
their own affairs*.

In order to carry this task through, according to Stalin, a
radical change would have to be made in the way in which
the Party dealt with peasant problems. "There must be no
domineering [by the Party] and an atmosphere of mutual
confidence must be created between Party and non-Party
people." The rural soviets must be given a "material basis" for
their revitalization through "the institution of local budgets,"
with authority to collect taxes.[19]

Although ratified by the CC,[20] and considered now a Party
practice, the orientations expressed in these speeches were in
reality pursued very unevenly. They were to be reiterated
again and again until the end of the NEP period. Thus, after

the Fourteenth Party Conference, Stalin repeated in May 1925 what he had said in 1924; but he put some points more sharply. When presenting a summary of these tasks that the Fourteenth Party Conference had decided upon to an assembly of activists of the Moscow Party organization, he described the position like this: "The second task consists in gradually but steadily pursuing the line of eliminating the old methods of administration and leadership in the countryside, the line of revitalising the soviets, the line of transforming the soviets into genuinely elected bodies, the line of implanting the principles of soviet democracy in the countryside."[21]

The Party's rural cadres put up considerable resistance to the line of extending soviet democracy. This is proved by some phrases in Stalin's report, where he criticizes the style of work of these cadres and at the same time shows how the peasants were awakening to political life. He begins by denouncing the behavior of a certain district secretary, whose attitude he depicts like this: "What do we want newspapers for? It's quieter and better without them. If the peasants begin reading newspapers they will start asking all sorts of questions and we shall have no end of trouble with them."

Then he adds: "And this secretary calls himself a Communist! It scarcely needs proof that he is not a Communist but a calamity."[22]

That these declarations and resolutions had any extensive effect is far from evident, since it was considered necessary to go on restating them right down to the end of the NEP period. Nevertheless, changes did take place. For example, more peasants took part in elections. The proportional voting, which was only 30 percent in 1923, reached 45 percent in 1925, and rose to more than one-half of the peasant electorate during the second half of the 1920s.[23]

We must not, however, overestimate the significance of such figures. The increased proportion of peasants taking part in elections resulted to some extent from a certain pressure that was brought to bear on them. It was not always followed by corresponding increase in the activity of the rural soviets, or in the interest taken in this activity by the peasant masses.

One of the obstacles in the way of the development of genuine soviet power in the countryside was the influence exerted by the kulaks over a section of the peasant masses during the NEP period. Another was the inadequacy of the financial resources at the disposal of the village soviets, which prevented them from undertaking any really useful activity. Meanwhile the traditional forms of peasant organization continued to exist, and were usually endowed with material and financial means[24] that the soviets lacked; so, they often seemed more "effective" than the latter, and they were frequently dominated by the rich peasants.

Finally, the attitude taken up by the local Party cadres and soviet officials, their "authoritarianism," contributed to holding back the activity of the village and district soviets.

This "authoritarianism" did not result from the "psychology" of the officials in question but from their class attitude. Having to a large extent centralized in their own hands the reality of power in the locality, the officials of the soviet apparatus (who were often former officials of the Tsarist administration), occupied a politically dominant position, and, unless they were true revolutionaries, would not spontaneously let go of it, subject themselves to control by the masses, or permit the latter to run their own affairs. Only class struggle by the peasant masses could alter such behavior, but it was hard for such a struggle to develop, owing to the insufficient presence of the Party among the peasantry, and so the latter tended to look after their affairs through their traditional organizations, like the *skhod*.

In his speeches of June 1925 at the Sverdlov University, Stalin noted that the situation in the rural soviets was highly unsatisfactory. He said that

until now, the situation was that quite a number of rural districts were governed by small groups of people, connected more with the *uyezd* and *gubernia* administrations than with the rural population. The result of this was that those who governed the rural districts mostly looked to the top, the *uyezd*, and least of all looked to the bottom, to the rural population: they felt responsible not to the villages, not to their electors, but to the *uyezd* and *gubernia* administration. . . . The result of this was unchecked arbitrariness and tyranny of the rulers, on the one hand, and discontent and murmuring in the countryside, on the other. We are now putting an end to this state of affairs. . . .[25]

Stalin observed that frequently the elections to the rural soviets were not genuine elections, but a bureaucratic procedure which made possible "smuggling in 'deputies' by means of all kinds of trickery and of pressure exercised by the small groups of rulers who were afraid of losing power."[26]

As a result of the situation thus described, fresh elections were organized in 1925 and 1926. So as to combat the electoral practices previously operative, the right to vote was extended to some categories of the rural population which had hitherto been deprived of it.[27]

Actually, given the ideological and political balance of forces that obtained in the countryside at that time, together with the weakness of the Party's rural cells, rich peasants often succeeded in getting into the rural soviets, which obviously did not render the latter more capable of responding to the real needs of the peasant masses. Penetration of the rural soviets by the kulaks was exposed in articles published in the Soviet press. One of these articles noted that

since the Soviets have begun to take a share in village life, the kulaks have increased their efforts to subordinate them and bring them within the sphere of their influence. Though Party organisations have shown more strength in these elections [1926?] than in previous years, yet in some cases the directives not to apply pressure or administrative measures [on the electorate] were interpreted as an order to stop Party interference in the election campaign.[28]

The consequence had been penetration of the soviets by rich peasants, or their "representatives."

This situation was due at that time to the ideological influence wielded over a section of the middle peasantry by the well-to-do peasants. At the beginning of 1925 Stalin noted the existence of such influence in a number of rural districts[29]—at a time when he was warning against the temptation to stir up class struggle against the kulaks.[30]

The infiltration of the kulaks into the rural soviets was also due to the economic pressure that the rich peasants could bring to bear on the poor and middle strata of the peasantry. This pressure was made possible by the position that the kulaks held in the economic life of the village, by the fact that they leased land, hired out means of production (ploughs, horses, etc.), and were creditors of some of the poor and middle peasants. These bonds of dependence on the rich peasants were reflected in both the composition of the rural soviets and their activity.

The slogan of revitalizing the soviets enjoined the Party's rural cells to do everything possible to help the peasant masses emancipate themselves from the influence of the well-to-do strata of the peasantry and take their affairs in hand for themselves. The fact that this slogan remained on the agenda all through the NEP period shows that the task assigned was still unaccomplished. Thus, in November 1926 Kalinin said to the Executive Committee of the Soviets of the RSFSR: "Our chief task is to draw the broad masses into Soviet construction, i.e., to revitalise the Soviets."[31]

Actually, at the beginning of 1929 the activity of the village soviets was still very inadequate. The village soviet was seen by the peasants as "an artificial creation enjoying none of the prestige or efficacy of the traditional indigenous peasant unit, the *mir*."[32] At that time there were upwards of 72,000 rural soviets, each of which covered several (an average of eight) villages or "inhabited localities." Each rural soviet had an average of eighteen members, but their meetings were very irregular and, usually, only between five and seven of the deputies attended. It even happened quite often that there would be only one or two plenary meetings a year, while the soviet's work was carried on by the chairman and secretary elected by the soviet. These men were paid very little—mere pittances to supplement other sources of livelihood—and often gave up their jobs to take better paid ones. It was not uncommon for the chairman of a rural soviet to be barely literate and scarcely capable of reading the documents sent out by the central government or by the district or regional soviets.[33]

To sum up, during the second phase of the NEP period, apart from the role played by the rich peasants, there were a number of obstacles in the way of a real revitalizing of the rural soviets: the Party's weakness in the countryside, the distrustful attitude of many cadres toward the peasantry, and the existence of a contradictory peasant ideology, which could have been changed only by a policy pursued actively by the Party—a policy aimed at strengthening the influence of revolutionary ideas and speeding up the advance along the socialist road, uniting the initiatives of the poor and middle peasants, and transforming the way in which the "land communities" and the *skhod* functioned.

III. The contradictions in "peasant ideology" and the role played by ideological centers outside Bolshevik Party control in the rural areas

Owing to the existence of distinct and conflicting classes among the peasantry, "peasant ideology" was deeply divided. A number of notions that were mutually contradictory together made up the form of ideology to which the peasants were more or less subject and in the name of which they waged their struggles, becoming either receptive or obstructive to the activity of the Bolshevik Party.

(a) Religious ideas

Religious ideas, as reproduced by the Orthodox Church, by the religious sects, and by the peasant family, constituted a tremendous force for social conservatism which the Bolshevik Party was often at a loss to combat. Very often Party members tried to launch frontal attacks on this force for social conservatism, instead of getting around it and preparing the development of its contradictions. Such frontal attacks usually ended in defeat. In his speech of October 1924 on the Party's immediate tasks in the countryside, Stalin spoke of the problem in these terms:

> Occasionally some comrades are inclined to regard the peasants as materialist philosophers and to think that it is enough to deliver a lecture on natural science to convince the peasant of the non-existence of God. Often they fail to realise that the peasant looks on God in a practical way, i.e., he is not averse to turning away from God sometimes, but he is often torn by doubt: 'Who knows, maybe there is a God after all. Would it not be better to please both the Communists and God, as being safer for my affairs?' He who fails to take this peculiar mentality of the peasant into account totally fails to understand what the relations between Party and non-Party people should be, fails to understand that in matters concerning anti-religious propaganda a careful approach is needed even to the peasant's prejudices.[34]

At the beginning of the NEP period frontal attacks on religion were, as a rule, abstained from, and the obstacles that religious ideas were capable of presenting to the Party's activity were avoided. This was not so when the period was reaching its close. The frontal attacks that were launched at that time ended more often than not in a negative result, with many peasants grouping around the rich peasants and the defenders of religion.

(b) The skhod and the mir

The idea of the peasantry being capable of existing independently of the towns and the state was also an element in peasant ideology. This idea was materialized in the *mir* (transformed into the "land community") and the *skhod,* or general assembly of the peasants in each village.

These were ideological centers possessing very great political importance. Their existence contributed to weakening the village soviets, and gave support to a set of practices of resistance to the worker-peasant alliance which brought grist to the kulaks' mill.

It will be recalled that the Soviet Agrarian Code of 1922 recognized the legal existence of the "land community" and "land association." This was, in practice, a continuation of the former village community or *mir*. It was managed, in principle, by the general assembly of the peasants, or *skhod*. Article 54 of the Code granted legal personality to these land communities. Each of them owned communally what had belonged by tradition to the *mir*, which meant that it possessed material and financial resources that the rural soviet lacked. These resources were derived mainly from the dues paid for use of the common lands, woods, and ponds.[35] The land community could also *tax* its members, and it was regarded as the owner of the smithies, sawmills, etc., belonging to the village.

The *skhod*'s authority was accepted by the majority of the peasants, so that the *mir* (or the equivalent institution in the Ukraine and elsewhere) enjoyed much greater power than the village soviet. The *skhod* was often dominated by the kulaks, as was made clear in reports given to the Communist Academy in 1926. Frequently the poor peasants did not even see any point in attending the meetings of the *skhod:* when they did they were hardly listened to and even sometimes were ejected. At the Thirteenth All-Russia Congress of Soviets, in 1927, delegates complained that at that time only between 10 and 15 percent of the peasants who had the right to take part in the *skhod* actually did so, and this minority consisted mainly of the better-off elements in the villages.[36]

In December 1927 the Fifteenth Party Congress tackled the problems presented by the existence of the *skhod* and the other traditional peasant organizations playing a similar role. One of the rapporteurs noted that the total annual revenue of these organizations came to between 80 and 100 million roubles, whereas the village soviets had at their disposal only 16 million roubles.[37] In a document prepared in 1927 for the *Orgburo*, the Communist Academy's Institute for Building, the Soviets arrived at the following conclusion: "The economically independent land community takes the village soviet under its guardianship. The material dependence of the village soviet on the land community puts a brake on the further development and revitalisation of the work of the Soviet and of its sections, and on the other hand is the basis for the taking over of the work of the village soviet by the land community *skhod.*"[38]

At the Fifteenth Party Congress delegates spoke of the presence of "dual power" in the countryside: the power of the rural soviet, and that of the *skhod* (which was an assembly, be it recalled, in which the poor and less well-off peasants carried little weight).[39] A resolution passed by this congress called for "an improvement in relations between the soviets and the land communities, aimed at ensuring that the former play the leading role."[40] In practice, however, this resolution remained ineffective. Thus, a year and a half later, the Fourteenth All-Russia Congress of Soviets, meeting in May 1929, heard an official report which stated that "the village soviet remains . . . dependent on the land communities, receiving very large grants from them."[41]

The fight to strengthen the village soviets, despite the successes it obtained when the village soviet was provided with certain financial resources[42] and obtained material results, remained in general an unequal struggle in which the *skhod* even managed sometimes to add to its power, turning itself into an "electoral commission" which went so far as to draw up the list of electors to the village soviet.[43] (When this happened there was a reversal of the relations between the soviet and the *skhod*, with the latter dominating the former politically, just as it often dominated it economically, by providing, for example, the salary of the secretary to the village soviet.)

The dominant role played by the traditional forms of organization had considerable ideological consequences. The system of practices to which the *skhod* gave support underlay the reproduction of a set of *contradictory ideological and political relations*. In particular, there were the ideas of village autonomy, of equality, and of solidarity within the *mir*.

(c) The idea of village autonomy

The fact that the *mir* and the *skhod* controlled lands, woods, smithies, mills, etc., gave rise to the illusory notion of *village autonomy*, of the village existing as *a world on its own*, sufficient unto itself.[44]

This idea erected serious *obstacles to intervention in village life by organizations outside the mir*. Thus, the tendency to subordination of the village soviet to the *skhod*, though politically overdetermined by the role of the well-to-do peasants in the *skhod*, was inherent in the ideology of the *mir*. It could be combated only by specific forms of class struggle.

At the same time, the idea of village "autonomy" produced *relative* indifference to the disparities in standard of living between town and country. These were seen as "two worlds," between which there was no common yardstick. Putting in the foreground the task of aligning the standards of living—the material conditions of existence—of these "two worlds" could easily be seen as signifying renunciation of the specific character of village life. The inequalities between town and country were looked upon, to a certain extent, as being the inevitable counterpart of village "autonomy."

To be sure, this did not rule out the advancing of "economic demands," but these were not formulated in terms of "reducing gaps." The tendency for the differences between conditions in village and in town to increase did not, *in itself*, give rise during the NEP period to a struggle aimed at countering its effects. This needs to be taken into account when evaluating the factors which explain why this tendency was able to develop in that period without encountering large-scale resistance.

Finally, the idea of the autonomy of each village constituted an obstacle to any "alliance" between the peasants of several villages in order to fight for common aims. This aspect also contributed to creating a situation in which the growth of inequality between townspeople and countrypeople did not spontaneously engender struggles aimed at checking this differentiation.

In these circumstances, the struggle of the poor and middle peasants to improve their conditions by improving the terms of exchange remained weak. Paradoxically, the *relative* autonomy of the village, which was a reality, and the dependence of the towns upon the countryside, which was greater at that time than the dependence of the countryside upon the towns, did not, as a rule, appear as a "weapon" which the villagers could use in order to secure better conditions of exchange and a better supply of industrial goods.

The reproduction of the ideology of village autonomy thus played a negative role in relation to the attempt made by the Bolshevik Party to organize the struggle of the poor and middle peasants for better living conditions. Of course, this role was *only relative, not absolute.* Nevertheless, the idea of autonomy served as a vehicle for the idea of *development by relying on one's own resources*—but the Bolshevik Party did not lay much stress on that.

To conclude discussion of this point, it is perhaps appropriate to justify use of the word "illusion" to characterize the idea of "village autonomy." It was indeed an illusion, for in the NEP period the village did depend on the town and urban activities for survival and economic development: it was dependent in respect to metals, part of its equipment, selected seeds (whose use was beginning to become widespread), and so on. However, this dependence was still fairly secondary in character, so that the illusion in question corresponded to a certain material and social reality, from which it drew its strength. And this illusion, if not effectively combated by the Party's political and ideological work, tended to block the path to a real alliance between the workers and the peasants, an alliance without which the poor and middle sections of the rural masses could not overthrow the dominance of the rich peasants.[45]

(d) The idea of equality within the mir

One of the components of the peasant ideology as it was reproduced by the *skhod* was the idea that all peasants were "equal" within the *mir*. The material basis of this idea—what underlay it—was the periodical redivision of land carried out by the *skhod*.[46]

However, this "equality" was, in fact, more of an illusion than it had ever been before. We have seen already that possession of means of production other than the land, and of financial resources, was a source of real inequalities, the effects of which were intensified by the political inequalities that they engendered. Thus, at the head of the *mir* there usually stood members of rich or well-to-do families, and this was especially true of the headman, the *starosta*, or "elder," who played the leading role in the *skhod*. Given the division of the land without any corresponding redistribution of the instruments of labor, and given the wear and tear suffered by the most rudimentary of these instruments, the social and political power of the rich peasants was maintained and sometimes even increased.[47]

The very way that the commune functioned served to assist the reproduction of egalitarian illusions. While the redistribution of land actually favored the rich peasants, it also enabled the group of middle peasants to grow stronger in accordance with the process of social differentiation characteristic of the NEP period.

Investigations carried out during this period showed that the *skhod* continued, mainly, to function as in prerevolutionary times—its assemblies were usually convened and conducted by the same families as before, with the same men, or their descendants, in the role of *starosta*.[48]

While the idea of equality within the *mir* was an illusion, the presence of this idea among the peasantry could have been used as a weapon by the Bolshevik Party to transform the *mir* and the *skhod* from within, by striving to ensure that the poor and middle peasants did in fact enjoy all the rights that they possessed in theory. Actually, however, examples of struggles along these lines are few and far between. The Party sought above all, and without much success, to breathe life into the rural soviets, for it saw the *mir* as an archaic institution, doomed to wither away and incapable of serving as framework for revolutionary activity. This attitude was due partly to ideological reasons,[49] but mainly to the circumstance that the Party's weak basis among the peasants made it harder for it to operate in the *skhod*, a purely peasant assembly, than in the soviets, where workers, peasants, and office workers were all represented together.

It needs to be added that very early the Bolshevik Party

developed a tendency to treat with suspicion all "egalitarian" notions, doubtless through a one-sided interpretation of Marx's statements emphasizing the limits to the demand for equality and pointing out how the idea of "equal right" belonged within the limited setting of "bourgeois right."[50] This one-sided interpretation was not unconnected with the ideological pressure exercised by the specialists, engineers, etc., who were paid high salaries. In the case under consideration, it led to an inability to draw petty-bourgeois notions into the wake of proletarian ideology and so *to transform them*.

(e) The associated ideas of "independence of the farm" and "solidarity within the mir"

The ideology of the *skhod* and the *mir*, and the practices reproduced by these ideological organizations, nourished two ideas which were both contradictory and interconnected: the idea of the *independence of the farm assigned to a particular family* and that of solidarity within the *mir*.

The first idea was linked with the *division of the land* of the commune among *families*, which implied that a farm was an "independent" economic unit. It constituted the *material basis of the reproduction of the patriarchal family* and of its relations of domination and subordination, of the domination of the young by the old, for it was *to families—and in practice to "heads of families"*—and not to individuals, that the divided-up land was assigned.

The idea of solidarity within the *mir* was materialized in the various obligations imposed upon the members of the land association and in the forms of "mutual aid" which they were expected to provide.

It was on the basis of this second idea, the ultimate expression of which would be a decision not to redivide the land but to form (as had been allowed for by the law of 1922) *agricultural communes*, for *joint cultivation* of the land, that a struggle for socialist forms of labor and production was possible within the *skhod*.

There did exist, in fact, quite a few examples of development of collective forms of labor and production, under the impulsion of the poor and middle peasants, especially through some of the members of a commune *breaking away* in order to establish a *collective farm.*[51]

On the whole, though, this movement took place in only a limited way. It was not until the end of 1927 that the Bolshevik Party really began to give it backing, and even then only hesitantly, because it did not result in the *large farms* which the Party favored, both for reasons of "principle" and because they lent themselves better to *mechanization.*

The Bolshevik Party failed to exploit seriously the contradictions characteristic of peasant ideology in the NEP period. It sought above all to work directly upon the contradiction which set the poor and middle peasants against the rich, but in this way it achieved only limited results. It allowed the traditional forms of organization to survive de facto, and when they broke up it was in only rare cases that this produced new collective forms.

On this basis "traditional' ideological centers continued to exist, in barely altered forms: the patriarchal family, the church, the religious sects. Similarly—and this deserves special attention—the Soviet school was transformed, becoming more and more openly bourgeois.

(f) The Soviet school and the ideology of the school

At the village level it was the primary school that was the main center for reproducing and transforming the ideology of the educational system. In the first years of Soviet power, this school was the subject of ambitious *projects* for revolutionary change.[52] However, owing to lack of means, and also to resistance from the teachers, such projects had practically no impact on reality.

In 1923, two years after the beginning of the NEP, these projects, which had never materialized except in a few "pilot experiments," were put aside. In the words of Kalashnikov, author of a work on the sociology of education published in 1928: "the romanticism of the early years was channelled into the bed of practical achievements."[53]

In other words, the exigencies of *reestablishing the economy* and of carrying out *the bourgeois-democratic revolution in the countryside* prevailed. While in the towns "reform" experiments went on in the kindergartens and the primary and secondary schools,[54] what predominated in the rural areas (under the pressure of the rich and middle peasants, and of a section of the poor ones, too) was the return to "serious education," to a school of "social advancement based on selection and the ideology of competition (marks, examinations) . . . leading to the restoration of the school as reproducer of bourgeois ideology. . . ."[55] This type of school was what was wanted by the "Nepmen" and by most of the *cadres* of the economic and administrative apparatuses, and it also conformed to the ideology of the bulk of the teachers.

In the reproduction of the conservative ideas that dominated the village in the NEP period, the school that was returning to life[56] played its part along with the family, the church, the *mir*, and the *skhod*, and even with the economic organizations that had been penetrated by elements that were carriers of bourgeois ideology.

The ideas that dominated the Soviet village at that time were not, of course, held by all the peasants (for a section of the middle and poor peasants adhered to the ideas of socialism, even if they did not join the Party), but nevertheless they did ensure, broadly, the "authority" of the rich and powerful among the peasants and "respect" for the social hierarchy of the village. The ground was, therefore, relatively favorable for the continued influence of petty-bourgeois ideas,[57] since the Bolshevik Party, through failing to treat correctly the contradictions that existed among the peasantry, developed only very slowly its implantation in the countryside. Finally, from 1928 on, the Soviet government found itself confronted with contradictions which it could not cope with and which became exacerbated as a result of the specific form of industrialization to which the country was increasingly committed.

Thereafter, the conditions were ripe for the explosion of the final crisis of the NEP. However, the factor which acted as the motive force in this crisis was not to be found among the peasantry: it was constituted by the contradictions in the towns and by the way in which these were met.

Notes

1. See volume I of the present work, especially pp. 355 ff.
2. Stalin, *Works*, vol. 7, p. 356.
3. Ibid., vol. 7, pp. 356–357.
4. Carr and Davies, *Foundations*, vol. II, p. 481.
5. Ibid., vol. II, p. 481, and T. H. Rigby, *Communist Party Membership in the USSR, 1917–1967*, pp. 52, 162. Even if, instead of considering actual class situation, we take class origin as the criterion, we find that Party members of peasant origin made up no more than 20 percent of the total (see Rigby).
6. Rigby, *Communist Party Membership*, p. 189.
7. *K.P.S.S. v rezolyutsiyakh*, vol. 2, p. 489.
8. Rigby, *Communist Party Membership*, p. 170.
9. A. Gaister and A. Levin, article on the composition of the Party's rural orgainzations in *Bolshevik*, nos. 9–10 (1929), pp. 75–90, and Rigby, *Communist Party Membership*, pp. 170, 171.
10. Rigby, *Communist Party Membership*, p. 181.
11. *K.P.S.S. v resolyutsiyakh*, vol. 2, pp. 489–490.
12. In the Smolensk archives (which fell into the hands of the German forces and then were taken over by the American army and transferred to the United States, where they were made available to researchers: National Archives Microfilm Publication no. T-87, National Archives, Washington, D.C.), we find much information about the working of the Party in the country and town, and about the various problems that arose in the Smolensk region between 1917 and 1941. In particular, there are results of investigations, and reports, which show what the situation was in the Bolshevik Party during the NEP period. Merle Fainsod reproduces a small part of this documentation in *Smolensk Under Soviet Rule:* on what is said here see pp. 139 ff.
13. Taking the Party as a whole, the statistics of the purges of 1929–1930 show that the most frequent reason given for expulsion,

accounting for 22 percent of cases, was "defects in private life and behaviour," while 17 percent of those expelled suffered this fate owing to their "passivity," and 17 percent because they were "hostile elements or connected with such." "Criminal conduct" was the trouble in 12 percent of cases, and "violation of Party discipline" in another 12 percent. For 22 percent of cases the reasons for expulsion were not specified (Rigby, *Communist Party Membership*, p. 180).

14. Stalin, *Works*, vol. 6, pp. 327 ff.
15. At that time many of these organizations were not led by Party members, and it sometimes happened that they supported views or demands that the Party did not approve of.
16. Stalin, *Works*, vol. 6, pp. 333–334.
17. Ibid., vol. 6, pp. 315 ff.
18. Ibid., vol. 6, p. 322.
19. Ibid., vol. 6, pp. 324–325.
20. See the resolution on "Immediate Tasks of Work in the Rural Areas" adopted by the plenum of October 25–27, 1924, in *K.P.S.S. v rezolyutsiyakh*, vol. I, pp. 906 ff.
21. Stalin, *Works*, vol. 7, p. 127.
22. Ibid., vol. 7, p. 129.
23. "Iz istorii partiinogo stroitelstva," in *Partiinaya Zhizn*, no. 20 (1957), pp. 80–96, quoted by O. Narkiewicz, *The Making of the Soviet State Apparatus*, pp. 69; 76, n. 16.
24. See above, pp. 175 ff.
25. Stalin, *Works*, vol. 7, pp. 185–186.
26. Ibid., vol. 7, p. 186.
27. Narkiewicz, *Making*, p. 72.
28. I. Bogovoi, "Perevybory sovyetov v derevne i rasshirenii demokratii," in *Bolshevik*, nos. 9–10 (1926), pp. 38–44, quoted in Narkiewicz, *Making*, pp. 71–72.
29. Stalin, *Works*, vol. 7, p. 193.
30. Ibid., vol. 7, p. 179.
31. Quoted in Carr and Davies, *Foundations*, vol. 2, p. 220.
32. Carr and Davies, *Foundations*, vol. 2, p. 250. On the *mir*, see volume I of the present work, pp. 78, 85, 213 ff., 236 ff., 440, 517.
33. Carr and Davies, *Foundations*, vol. 2, pp. 250–251.
34. Stalin, *Works*, vol. 6, p. 323.
35. The waters and woods, having been nationalized, belonged legally to the state, but the land associations continued to dispose of them, as they did also of the property of the former landown-

ers. The cultivated lands were assigned by the land associations to the families that worked them. The woods and uncultivated lands were not distributed but made freely available for use, subject to rules laid down by the *skhod*.

36. See notes 3 to 7, p. 244, of Carr and Davies, *Foundations*, vol. 2.
37. Ibid., p. 346.
38. M. Rezunov, *Selskie sovyety i zemelnye obshchestva*, pp. 33–34; Carr and Davies, *Foundations*, vol. 2, p. 247.
39. *XV-y Syezd VKP(b)*, vol. 2 (1962), p. 1281; and Carr and Davies, *Foundations*, vol. 2, p. 255.
40. *K.P.S.S. v rezolyutsiyakh*, vol. 2, pp. 366–367.
41. *XIV-y Vserossiisky Syezd Sovyetov*, no. 15 (1929), p. 14; and Carr and Davies, *Foundations*, vol. 2, p. 247.
42. It will be observed that, four years after Stalin had issued the call, the slogan of strengthening the financial resources of the rural soviets had remained almost without effect. In May 1929 the Fourteenth All-Russia Congress of Soviets was still asking for these rural soviets to be provided with a budgetary system (Carr and Davies, *Foundations*, vol. 2, p. 258).
43. Ibid., p. 247, n. 8, quoting *Sovyetskoye Stroitelstvo*, no. 12 (29) (December 1928), p. 100.
44. The word *mir*, meaning the village community, although its etymology is not the same as that of *mir* meaning "the world," calls the latter to mind, and these two words were frequently confused.
45. Lenin laid stress on this idea, especially in the preparations for the Second Congress of the Communist International (see "Preliminary Draft Theses on the Agrarian Question, for the Second Comintern Congress," in Lenin, *CW*, vol. 31, pp. 152–164).
46. On the legal foundations of the *skhod*'s activity, see volume I of the present work.
47. Y. Taniuchi, *The Village Gathering in Russia in the Mid-1920s*, especially pp. 21–22; and Narkiewicz, *Making*, p. 125.
48. Taniuchi, *Village*, p. 27; and S. Zhdanovich, "Selskiye sovyety: zemelniye obshchestva," in *Bolshevik*, no. 6 (1928).
49. See volume I of the present work, particularly pp. 214–215.
50. Marx, "Critique of the Gotha Programme," in Marx and Engels, *Selected Works in Three Volumes*, vol. 2, p. 18.
51. See Zhdanovich, "Selskiye sovyety," and Narkiewicz, *Making*, p. 127; also above, p. 100.
52. See volume I of the present work, pp. 168–169.

53. Quoted in D. Lindenberg, *L'Internationale communiste et l'école de classe*, p. 293.

54. In those days there was no hesitation in borrowing pedagogical doctrines from Dewey, Decroly, and Kerschensteiner, whose disciples in the Soviet Union were also inspired by the experiments of the Social Democrats in Germany (ibid., p. 295).

55. Ibid., p. 295.

56. In 1928 and 1929, in connection with the offensive against the kulaks and the slogan of "cultural revolution" that was issued at that time, the NEP-period type of school came under vigorous criticism. Resolutions condemning it were even passed. But these condemnations remained on paper: from 1930–1931 on the *tasks of "economic construction"* carried the day, and even the pedagogical experiments were soon abandoned. There was a return to the most traditional of bourgeois forms in the educational sphere.

57. Even as late as 1926, in certain regions, such as Smolensk, posters were clandestinely stuck up which appear to have been inspired by socialist-revolutionary ideas, although the general attitude of the peasants toward the Soviet government was regarded as being "good" (Fainsod, *Smolensk*, p. 123, quoting the Smolensk Archives: VKP 249, p. 203).

Part 3
The contradictions and class struggles in the industrial and urban sectors

The "procurement crisis" may look as though it was an internal crisis of Soviet agriculture. Interpreted in this way, it seems to have been due, fundamentally, to the state of the relations between classes and of the productive forces in the countryside toward the end of the 1920s: the relations between classes were marked by the dominant position held by the kulaks at that time, which enabled them to dictate their conditions for supplying food to the towns, and the productive forces in agriculture which had reached a "ceiling" that could be surpassed only by means of a rapid change in the conditions of production—by mechanization of agricultural work, which, if it was not to benefit mainly the kulaks, required collectivization. According to this way of seeing the problem, the "procurement crisis" necessarily entailed the "emergency measures," followed by a rapid process of collectivization, which one had to be ready to impose on the peasants should they prove unwilling to accept it voluntarily—hence the thesis of the "economic necessity" of a "revolution from above."[1]

This "economistic" interpretation of the procurement crisis assumes that the NEP was not a road that allowed the middle peasants to assume really the central position in the countryside; that it did not enable the Soviet government to help the poor and middle peasants to improve their conditions of production while gradually taking the road of cooperation and collectivization; or else that "economic exigencies" made it impossible to show patience in dealing with the peasantry.

As we have seen, this "economistic" interpretation is false.[2] At the end of the 1920s the kulaks did not hold a dominant economic position in the countryside and production by the

187

poor and middle peasants could have been increased considerably by helping these peasants to organize themselves and by following a different policy with respect to supplies and prices.

The procurement crisis was not a crisis inherent in agriculture, but a *crisis of relations between town and country* due to mistakes committed in the practice of the worker-peasant alliance. This crisis was bound up with the internal contradictions of the industrial and urban sectors, the fashion in which these contradictions were understood, and the way with which they were dealt.

Notes

1. This "economistic" thesis is usually complemented by a thesis regarding the "military necessities" dictated by the international situation, both of these theses being upheld at the present time in the USSR (see, e.g., *Istoriya KPSS v rezolyutsiyakh*, vol. IV, pt. 2, p. 593). The "economistic" thesis is also defended in West Germany by W. Hofmann, in *Die Arbeitsverfassung der Soviet Union,* p. 8, and *Stalinismus und Antikommunismus,* p. 34 (quoted by R. Lorenz, *Sozialgeschichte der Sowjetunion 1917–1945,* p. 348). It coincides with the position of J. Elleinstein, in his *Histoire de l'URSS,* vol. 2: *Le Socialisme dans un seul pays (1922–1939),* p. 118, who adds, however, that: "The whole problem lay in deciding the pace at which this programme was to be carried out, and the methods to be employed."
2. Furthermore, as is known, neither the emergency measures nor collectivization, as it was carried out, enabled the difficulties in agriculture to be quickly overcome: on the contrary, agricultural production declined and stagnated for more than ten years.

1. The direct manifestations of the contradictions in the industrial and urban sectors

The internal contradictions of the industrial and urban sectors manifested themselves directly in the spheres of prices, wages, accumulation, and currency. The phenomena in question were not, of course, due solely to these contradictions, the results of which need to be analyzed, but also resulted from a particular policy that was followed. This in its turn was a consequence of the ways in which reality was perceived—of the class struggles, that is, that were waged around real relations and the ways in which these struggles were perceived. In the present chapter we shall confine ourselves to describing the direct effects of the contradictions and the way with which these were dealt.

I. Selling price and cost of production in industry

One of the immediate purposes of the NEP was to improve the living conditions of the peasant masses and strengthen the conditions under which the poor and middle peasants carried on their farming. By realizing this aim it was hoped to consolidate the worker-peasant alliance, reduce the economic, political, and ideological roles played by the kulaks, and create conditions favorable to the development of cooperatives and of large-scale collectivization.

Among the economic conditions required for the realization of this aim was a closing of the "scissors," by lowering the prices of industrial goods and supplying the countryside with the industrial goods the peasant masses needed. As we have seen, this aim had been attained only partially and provisionally, and toward the end of the NEP period there was even a serious setback to its realization.[1]

An important point needs to be made here: in 1928–1929 the *retail prices of industrial goods,* which until then had been falling, *started to rise.* If the "scissors" still tended to close, this was due to the fact that *agricultural prices were rising faster than industrial prices.*[2]

The rise in industrial prices did not accord with the "aims of the price policy." It resulted, in the first place, from an increase in demand to which no adequate increase in supply corresponded. The "inflationary" nature of the increase in industrial retail prices is clearly shown by the fact that it occurred *despite a fall in industrial wholesale prices.*[3] This fall was dictated to the state-owned industries by a policy still aimed at "closing the scissors" and stabilizing prices.

After 1926–1927 an imbalance began to appear. Already in that year the percentage increase in the cash income of the population exceeded that of the increase in industrial products available for sale by 3.8 points.[4] The process thus begun continued in the following year, which explains why a *new period* then opened in the evolution of prices.

As we know, the imbalance between the supply of and demand for industrial products affected the peasantry more than any other section.

The situation we have described was bound up with the contradictions in the industrial policy pursued by the Bolshevik Party from 1926 on. This accorded increasing priority to growth in accumulation and production by heavy industry, while *at the same time* increasing urban incomes, especially wages. On the one hand, this was a source of increased demand to which there was no adequate material counterpart. On the other hand, for lack of a parallel increase in the productivity of labor, costs of production in industry were swollen, and this prevented the simultaneous realization of two aims which were then being pursued by the Soviet government: an increase in industry's capacity to finance a substantial proportion of investment, which was being increased at a rapid rate, and continued pursuit of the policy of reducing the production costs and the wholesale prices of industrial goods.

The reduction in costs of production in industry was, on the whole, much less than had been provided for by the plans, and much less than was needed to meet the requirements of the policy being followed in the sphere of wholesale prices and the financing of investment in industry. The following table illustrates the problems that arose:

Increase or reduction of industrial costs (percentage of the previous year)[5]

	1925–1926	1926–1927	1927–1928	1928–1929
Planned	– 7	– 5	– 6	– 7
Realized	+ 1.7	– 1.8	– 5.1	– 4 to 4.5

A considerable proportion of the reduction of costs of production in industry was due either to factors external to industry (reduction in costs of raw materials, or in taxes) or to accounting adjustments (calculation of depreciation and overhead charges),[6] so that the share represented by wages in costs of production tended to increase. It should be noted that in 1926–1927 *average cost of production in industry was twice as high as prewar,* whereas the wholesale prices of industrial products had not reached this level.[7] From this followed both industry's low degree of capacity to finance its own investments and the limits bounding the policy of reducing industrial wholesale prices.

The high level of costs of production was due to some extent to the inflation in the members of administrative personnel in charge of production units, enterprises, and trusts. This phenomenon was denounced by the Party, which issued calls for a "struggle against bureaucracy." In practice, however, no such "struggle" was waged by the working masses. It was left to other administrative organs, which were far from effective in carrying out this task. Moreover, the attempts made to strengthen controls, by developing systems of accounting and reporting to the planning organs and establishing departments for studying and analyzing the time taken to produce goods, increased the burden of administration in the state industrial sector, while the result hoped for from these innovations were far from being achieved.

However, the decisive factor in the increase in costs of production in industry during this period was the increase in wages which was not accompanied by comparable increases in output or productivity.

II. Wages and productivity of labor in industry

According to the figures given by Stalin in the political report of the CC to the Fifteenth Party Congress, the average *real wage* (social services included) in 1926–1927 was 128.4 percent that of prewar.[8] In the same period, productivity of labor in industry had not the 1913 level.[9] During the next two years the situation stayed approximately the same, with wages and productivity in industry increasing at roughly the same pace.[10]

The increase in wages, despite the presence of a considerable body of unemployed toward the end of the NEP period, testifies to the political role that the working class now played. But, at the same time, the relation between this increase and the increase in productivity testifies to the contradictions in the economic policy then being followed. At a time when what was being emphasized was the need to increase accumulation mainly from industry's own resources, while narrowing the "scissors" between industrial and agricultural prices, the increase in the cost of wages borne by industrial production prevented either of these aims from being realized.

As regards relations between the working class and the peasantry, the development just described had negative consequences: it helped to widen, to the disadvantage of the peasants (most of whom had a standard of living lower than that of the workers), the disparity between economic conditions in town and country. From 1928 on this disparity was still further widened by the shortage of industrial goods and the priority given to the towns (except for short periods and only very locally) in the distribution of manufactured products.

In this way, contradictions developed which at first manifested themselves in the form of a process of inflation.

III.   The inflationary process and its immediate origins

The immediate origins of the inflationary process are not hard to detect. They lie in the increase in investments and unproductive expenditure which was both rapid and out of proportion with the "financial results" realized by the state sector. This can be illustrated by certain figures.

Between 1925–1926 (the first year of the "reconstruction period") and 1928–1929, the *total amount of budgetary expenditure, in current roubles, more than doubled,*[11] which meant an increase of 30 percent each year.

In the same years, the increase in the volume of industrial production *destined for consumption* and derived from "census industry"[12] *slowed down.* This production, which increased by 38 percent in 1926, increased by only about 18 percent in 1927 and in 1928.[13] It was still a remarkable increase—but not enough to cope with the increase in cash incomes, especially since there was a slowing-down in production by small-scale industry after 1927–1928.[14]

Altogether, in contrast to an increase of 34 percent in wages between 1925–1926 and 1927–1928, a fresh increase of about 14 percent in the following year,[15] and to the increase mentioned in budgetary expenditure, *real national income was increasing at a much slower pace*—a little over 7 percent per year between 1925–1926 and 1928–1929.[16]

Thus, the last years of the NEP period were marked by an increasing gap between the growth in distributed income and the growth in the quantity of goods available for consumption.

The existence of this gap was closely connected with the rapid increase in gross investment in the state sector and with the way in which this investment was financed.

Investments, not all of which passed through the budget, increased 2.75 times between 1925–1926 and 1929.[17] The larger part of these investments would not result in increased production until several years had gone by. They therefore involved outlays of cash which, for the time being, had no counterpart in production. Here was the hub of the inflationary process, for the state and cooperative sector *provided to an ever smaller extent for its own expanded reproduction*—as we can see clearly when we examine the evolution of profits in state industry, and compare the resources which it contributed to the financial system with those it drew from it.

Between 1924–1925 and 1926–1927, *net profits* (i.e., the difference between the profits and the losses of the various industrial enterprises) evolved as follows:

Net balance of profits from state industries[18]
(in millions of roubles)

1924–1925	1925–1926	1926–1927
364	536	539

The increase was substantial in 1925–1926, but minimal in 1926–1927. In any case, these amounts were less and less adequate to meet the needs of financing the industrial sector. Down to 1924–1925 the latter had supplied to the financial system resources (in taxes, payments of profits into the exchequer, subscriptions to state loans, payments into the state bank, etc.) which were almost equivalent to those it obtained from the financial system in order to cover its needs. In that year, the net contribution of the financial system to the needs of the industrial sector came to only 20 million roubles, or 11.6 percent of the amount contributed by industry to the financial system.[19]

After 1925–1926, when the period of reconstruction and the policy of industrialization began, the situation was completely transformed. In 1926–1927 the financial system's contribution to the needs of the industrial sector exceeded the contribution of industry to the financial system by nearly 35 percent, and thereafter the latter furnished even larger resources to industry. Current financial resources proved inadequate, and it was necessary to *issue paper money*. A rapid increase took place in the amount of money in circulation, which rose from 1,157 million roubles on July 1, 1926, to 2,213 million roubles on July 1, 1929.[20] This increase was out of all proportion to the increase in the national income. It meant a real inflation of the currency, which gave rise to important economic imbalances and political contradictions.

What has been described here was due, of course, to deeper underlying social contradictions, and resulted from the way with which these contradictions were dealt. It is these realities which must now be analyzed.

Notes

1. See above, pp. 145 ff., 150 ff.
2. In a single year, the former rose by 17.2 percent and the latter by 2.5 percent.
3. During the years under consideration here the wholesale prices of industrial goods fell regularly, but more and more slowly (in 1928–1929 their index stood at 185.3, with 1913 as 100). The gap between the index of industrial retail prices and wholesale prices tended to close until 1927–1928, but then opened again in 1928–1929, which shows that there was a demand in excess of supply, at the prices then being asked. For the evolution of industrial wholesale prices, see E. Zaleski, *Planning*, p. 398.
4. Calculated from Table 33 in S. Grosskopf, *L'Alliance ouvrière*, p. 201, quoting the figures of G. M. Krzhizhanovsky, *Desyat let*, pp. 76–77.
5. From Carr and Davies, *Foundations*, vol. I, pt. 2, p. 954. These writers quote the Soviet sources from which their table was compiled.
6. See, for example, the evolution of the factors in costs of production in industry shown in ibid., p. 345, n. 8.
7. *Byulleten Konyunkturnogo Instituta*, nos. 11–12 (1927); *Osnov-*

noye Problemy Kontrolnykh Tsifry (1929–1930), p. 158; A. Baykov, *The Soviet Economic System*, pp. 123 ff.

8. Stalin, *Works*, vol. 10, p. 322.
9. I. Lapidus and K. Ostrovityanov, *Outline of Political Economy*, p. 127.
10. *Ekonomicheskoye Obozreniye*, no. 10 (1929), p. 143; no. 12 (1929), p. 204; and Carr and Davies, *Foundations*, vol. I, pt. 2, pp. 957, 958 (and also p. 539). Actually, from January 1928 on the way in which real wages were calculated was less and less relevant to the true conditions of the working class. These calculations were based on the official price level, but, starting in 1928, supplies became irregular, a black market developed, and workers were obliged to buy many of the goods they needed at prices which were higher than in the "socialized" sector. It is to be observed that whereas in January 1927 the disparity between the price indices in the socialized and private sectors was 30 points (1913=100), this disparity spread to 50 points in January 1928 and to 84 in January 1929 (ibid., p. 964).
11. Carr and Davies, *Foundations*, vol. I, pt. 2, p. 974.
12. "Census industry" comprised those industrial production units which employed 16 or more workers, if they used mechanical motive power, and 30 or more workers if they were without such power. Units of production outside this category constituted "small-scale industry." There were, however, some exceptions to this criterion of classification.
13. Baykov, *The Soviet Economic System*, p. 121; Carr and Davies, *Foundations*, vol. I, pt. 2, p. 948.
14. I shall come back to this question in the next chapter.
15. Carr and Davies, *Foundations*, vol. I, pt. 2, p. 978.
16. Calculated from ibid., p. 977, and Bettelheim, *La Planification soviétique*, p. 268.
17. Proportions calculated by Bettelheim, ibid., p. 268.
18. Baykov, *The Soviet Economic System*, p. 118.
19. Ibid., p. 119.
20. Carr and Davies, *Foundations*, vol. I, pt. 2, p. 976.

2. *The contradictions between the private sector and the state sector in industry and trade*

Between 1921 and 1925 the policy of development and accumulation in the state sector of industry laid down limited objectives which this sector was capable of accomplishing mainly from its own resources. During this period the Bolshevik Party managed to cope, without too much difficulty, with the contradictions that opposed the private sector to the state sector in industry and trade. The state sector developed, as a whole, faster than the private sector, and strengthened positions which, by and large, were already dominant. This consolidation was due principally to the dynamism shown by the state sector, which also enjoyed priority support from the banks. In that period the fundamental principles of the NEP were respected, even though in some towns the local authorities introduced regulations which more or less paralyzed the private sector.[1] From the end of 1925 there was a change. The efforts made to develop the state sector of industry were increased, and tended (contrary to the resolutions of the Party's congresses and conferences) to be concentrated in a one-sided way upon *heavy industry* and upon projects which required *long periods of construction* before entering the phase of production. Furthermore, as we have seen, the scale of this effort at development called for financial resources that exceeded what state industry and trade could mobilize from their own resources; therefore, imbalances between supply and demand were created, and inflationary pressure built up. *Under these conditions, the private sector in industry and trade was placed in an exceptionally advantageous position.*

The shortage of goods enabled private traders to increase their selling prices, while the prices they paid for supplies

197

obtained from the state sector fell as a result of the continuing policy of reducing industrial wholesale prices. Thus, private trade was able to increase its profits to a considerable extent by appropriating a growing fraction of the value produced in the state sector.

Private industry also profited from the goods shortage, by increasing its selling prices while continuing to receive some of its means of production relatively cheaply from the state sector of industry.

Thus, at the very moment when the gap was widening seriously between the volume of financial resources directly at the disposal of state-owned industry and what was needed in order to attain the investment aims laid down for it, profits in the private sector of industry and trade were tending to rise sharply. Moreover, this sector was using material resources which were, to an increasing extent, lacking in the state sector. Although the NEP was not officially abandoned, in order to cope with this situation, *from 1926 on ever more numerous measures were taken to cut down the activity and resources of the private sector in industry and trade.*

Some of these measures were financial, taking the form of increased taxes and forced loans exacted from the private industrialists and traders. The amounts taken from them in this way rose from 91 million roubles in 1925–1926 to 191 million in 1926–1927.[2] Other measures assumed the form of regulations—even penal measures, on the ground that many traders and industrialists were violating Soviet law. After 1926 the administrative organs responsible for approving leases and concessions and issuing patents withdrew some of the authorizations they had previously granted.

However, these measures were introduced without any overall plan, and, in particular, without the state and cooperative sector being fully in a position to take the place of the private enterprises whose activity was being brought to a halt. Consequently, there was a worsening of the shortages from which the population suffered, and in the unsatisfactory supply of goods to certain localities and regions. This deterioration affected principally the rural areas. In order to appreciate what it meant we must examine some figures.

I. The different forms of ownership in industry and how they evolved

Soviet industrial statistics of the NEP period distinguished between four "sectors," in accordance with type of ownership of enterprises: state, cooperative, private, or foreign-concession.

In census industry, on the eve of the final crisis of the NEP (1926–1927), the state sector was predominant, followed, a long way behind, by the cooperative sector. In percentages, production by the different sectors of census industry[3] was as follows:

Percentages of gross production, in current prices, furnished by the sectors of census industry in 1926–1927[4]

State industry	91.3
Cooperative industry	6.4
Private industry	1.8
Industry operated as foreign concessions	0.5

In census industry the state and cooperative sectors thus predominated massively. As a result, the Soviet government possessed, up to a certain point, the power to dictate—momentarily, at least—a reduction in the wholesale prices of most industrial products, despite the inflation of costs and of demand. Actually, this power was far from being "absolute": its effect was mainly to *delay increases* in wholesale prices of industrial products. It is to be observed that by 1928–1929, as a result of the measures taken from 1926 on, the place occupied by the nonstate sectors in census industry was reduced to less than 1 percent.

In small-scale industry the nonstate sector played a major role in 1926–1927. Here are the figures:

Percentages of gross production, in current prices,
furnished by the sectors of small-scale industry
in 1926–1927[5]

State industry	2
Cooperative industry	19
Private industry	79

The big place occupied by private industry prevented the Soviet government from exercising sufficient control over the prices of its products. Some additional information is called for here:

1. In 1926–1927 the value of private industry's production was far from negligible. Taking industry as a whole, it amounted to 4,391 million in current roubles, which represented about 19.7 percent of that year's productions.[6]

2. However—and this is a vital point—within private industry, production was mainly handicraft production and thus not based upon the exploitation of wage labor. According to a study by the economist D. Shapiro, 85 percent of the small-scale enterprises employed no wage workers.[7]

3. From the angle of employment, small-scale industry played a considerable role,[8] but the earnings of the craftsmen contributed little to the inflation of demand: their incomes were of the same order as those of the peasants. A large proportion of small-scale industry was not "urban" but "rural": it was *an important complement to the urban sector of industry, but it was also in competition with the latter.*

As we know, the *principle* governing the policy followed during the NEP period was favorable to small-scale industry. This orientation was inspired by what Lenin wrote at the beginning of the NEP, when he emphasized the need for "generating the utmost local initiative in economic development—in the *gubernias,* still more in the *uyezds,* still more in the *volosts* and villages—for the special purpose of immediately improving peasant farming, even if by 'small' means, on a small scale, helping it by developing small local industry." He pointed out that moving on to a further stage would necessitate the fulfillment of a number of conditions, in particular a large-scale development of electric power production, which would itself demand a period of at least ten years to carry out the initial phase of the electrification plan.[9] In 1926, and even in 1928, they were still a very long way from having fulfilled this condition, and small-scale industry was still absolutely indispensable.

The small-scale industry of the NEP period assumed extremely diverse forms: handicraft, private capitalist (within certain limits), or directed by local organizations (the *mir*, or the rural or district soviet). Lenin was, above all, in favor of the last.[10] He also favored "small commodity-producers' cooperatives," which, he said, were "the predominant and typical form in a small-peasant country."[11]

Down to 1926–1927 the development of small-scale industry encountered only relatively limited hindrances, the purpose of which was to prevent the spread of a private industrial sector of a truly capitalist sort. However, the *aid* given to small-scale industry remained slight, and small producers' cooperatives and the initiatives of local organizations developed only slowly—mainly, under the authority of the "land associations".

Actually, small-scale industry, and handicraft industry in particular, had not recovered its prewar level of production.[12] Craft enterprises had difficulty in getting supplies, owing to competition from state-owned industry, which enjoyed a certain priority. In this matter the policy recommended by Lenin was not fully implemented, and the practices which developed from 1926 on departed farther and farther from that policy. This made it increasingly difficult for the peasants to obtain consumer goods and small items of farm equipment.

As principle, however, Lenin's directives remained the order of the day right down to 1927. Thus, in May of that year the Sovnarkom denounced "the unpardonable negligence shown by the public economic services in face of the problems of small-scale industry and the handicrafts."[13] Nevertheless, the "problems" in question were not solved. In fact, the small enterprises found themselves increasingly up against the *will to dominate shown by the heads of state-owned industry.* The latter fought to increase their supplies, their markets, and the profits of the enterprises they directed. In this fight they enjoyed the *support of the economic administrative services,* whose officials were closely linked with the leadership of the state enterprises.

Starting in 1927–1928, regardless of the resolutions officially adopted in favor of small-scale industry and the handicrafts, the organs of the economic administration took a series of measures whose effect would deprive small-scale industry of an increasing proportion of the raw materials it had been receiving until then, and would cause the complete closure of some of the small production units. This slowing-down of production by small-scale industry took place without any preparation, and under conditions which aggravated the difficulties of agriculture, since the activities of the rural craftsmen had helped and stimulated agricultural production and exchange.

In practice, the final phase of the NEP period was increasingly marked by the dominance of a type of industrial development that was centerd on large-scale industry. This development was profoundly different from what Lenin had recommended for decades: it was costlier in terms of the investment required, demanded much longer construction periods, was qualitatively less diversified, and entailed bigger transport costs.

The dominance of this type of industrial development was supported by the trade unions, which saw in it the guarantee of an increase in the number of wage workers and, as has been mentioned, it was also favored by the heads of the large-scale enterprises and the state administration. The pressure exercised in favor of this line of development assumed several ideological forms. The "superiority" of large-scale industry was regularly invoked, together with the idea that an enlargement of the working class would ensure consolidation of the dictatorship of the proletariat. The need for struggle against the petty bourgeoisie was also a favorite theme of the partisans of large-scale industry. Thus, in this period many small producers were doomed to unemployment, while the administrative apparatus was being enlarged and the power of the heads of large-scale industry increased.

Between 1927 and the end of 1929,[14] then, the growing difficulties of small-scale industry resulted mainly from the practices of the state organs and the heads of large-scale enterprises, and not from the policy which had been affirmed by the Soviet government in 1927. These difficulties were connected with a class struggle which set the nascent state bourgeoisie, indifferent to the needs of the masses, against the small producers, and the craftsmen in particular. Thus, the policy *actually followed* was in contradiction with the principles proclaimed, and it enabled large-scale industry to put rural industry in a more and more awkward situation, by reducing the peasants' opportunities for obtaining supplies and by contributing to the gravity of the final crisis of the NEP. Here, too, this crisis is seen to be bound up with the de facto abandonment of some of the principles of the New Economic Policy.

II. *The different forms of ownership in the sphere of trade, and how they evolved*

During the NEP period trade also was shared among several "sectors."

In wholesale trade private enterprises realized only 5.1 percent of the total turnover in 1926–1927, and this share was quickly reduced in the following years. The major part of wholesale trade was in the hands of the state and cooperative organs, which accounted for 50.2 and 44.7 percent, respectively, of the total turnover in 1926–1927.[15]

As for retail trade, the share taken by the private sector was still an important one in 1926–1927. It then stood at 36.9 percent: cooperative trade dominated this sphere, with 49.8

percent of the turnover, while state trading activity played a minor role.[16] In retail trade, moreover, the cooperatives were less subject to control than in the sphere of wholesale trade.

In an inflationary situation the relatively important role played by private retail trade meant that reductions in wholesale prices brought little benefit to consumers. The years 1922–1928 even saw the retail prices of industrial goods rising while wholesale prices were still falling. These practices on the part of private traders explain, to some extent, the administrative decisions to close down a number of private sales points and the decline to 13.5 percent in 1928–1929 of the "private" share of the retail trade turnover.[17]

Here, too, the measures were taken without any preparation—either by withdrawing licenses to trade or by creating difficulties for transport by rail of goods being marketed by private traders. From 1926–1927 on, tens of thousands of "commercial units" disappeared in this way, most of them being pedlars or petty itinerant merchants who mainly served the rural areas. In the RSFSR alone the number of "private commercial units" declined from 226,760 in 1926–1927 to 159,254 in 1927–1928; *but the number of state and cooperative "commercial units" also declined in the same period.*[18] This development contributed to the worsening of relations between town and country and to the procurement crisis. It was also one of the factors in the final crisis of NEP.

The measures taken to close down "sales points" without replacing them were contrary to the policy which had been officially proclaimed. Not only had the Thirteenth Party Congress, in May 1924, already warned against measures taken in relation to private trade which would hinder the development of exchange[19] and perpetuate, or even widen, the "blank spaces,"[20] but these same warnings had been included in a resolution of the CC which met in February 1927.[21] They were repeated by the Fifteenth Congress in December 1927, which stressed that the ousting of private trade by state and cooperative trade must be adapted to the material and organizational capacities of these forms of trade, so as not to cause a break in the exchange network or to interrupt the provision of supplies.[22]

In practice these warnings were ignored, partly for ideological reasons (the elimination of private trade, like that of private industry, even if their services were not replaced, was then regarded as a development of socialist economic forms[23] and partly through the pressure exercised by the heads of the state trading organs. The latter tended to boost the role and importance of the organs in which they worked by arranging for the maximum quantity of goods to be handled by these organs and without concerning themselves with the more or less balanced distribution of these goods, especially between town and country.

Thus, from 1926 on, a de facto retreat from the NEP gradually took place in trade and industry. This retreat proceeded as an objective process that was largely independent of the decisions taken by the highest authorities of the Bolshevik Party. Under these conditions, the process went forward *without preparation,* and resulted in effects prejudicial to the worker-peasant alliance as well as to the supply of industrial goods to the rural areas. All this contributed to increase the dimensions of the procurement crisis which broke out in 1927–1928.

III. The factors determining the abandonment of the NEP in trade and industry from 1926 on

The turn made in 1926 in the Bolshevik Party's practice with regard to private industry and trade corresponded to an accentuation of the social contradictions and the class struggle. This accentuation had a number of aspects.

1. A fundamental aspect was the sharpening of the contradiction between the bourgeoisie and the proletariat, through the growing hostility of wide sections of the working class towards the "Nepmen." This hostility was stimulated by the rise in retail prices which occurred in the private sector and the increases in speculators' profits resulting from these price-rises. In the industrial sector the struggle between the

workers employed in private enterprises and their capitalist employers was a permanent factor, but there is no obvious evidence that the struggle in this sphere was becoming more acute. In any case, only a very small fraction of the Soviet working class worked in the private sector. They numbered between 150,000 and 180,000, and made up only 4.2 percent of the membership of the trade unions, at a time when 88 percent of the working class was organized in trade unions.[24]

2. Another aspect of the accentuation of class struggles was the development of a growing contradiction between the bourgeoisie and the petty bourgeoisie in private industry and trade, on the one hand, and, on the other, the heads of state-owned industry. The latter were obliged to accomplish the tasks assigned to them by the plans for industrial development, and yet the financial and material means put at their disposal were insignificant. The reduction, or complete elimination, of the private sector thus looked to them like a way of enabling the state-owned enterprises to take over the resources possessed by the private industrialists and traders, and also by the craftsmen.

3. From 1926 on an increasingly acute contradiction developed between the content of the industrial plans—their scope, the priorities they laid down, the techniques they favored—and the continuation of the NEP, which would have required the adoption of industrial plans with a different content.

The development of this last contradiction played a decisive role in aggravating those previously mentioned, but it had itself a twofold class significance:

1. On the ideological plane, a conception of industrialization was increasingly emphasized which was influenced by the capitalist forms of industrialization. This was connected with the changes then being undergone by the Bolshevik ideological formation. The orientation proposed by Lenin concerning the role to be played (at least for some decades) by small-scale industry, local organizations, and relatively simple techniques was gradually lost sight of. Also forgotten were Lenin's views regarding the need to *work out plans which*

took account of the needs of the masses and the material assets actually available, especially in the form of agricultural products.[25]

Instead of an industrialization plan in conformity with these indications, the conception which increasingly prevailed gave one-sided priority to large-scale industry, heavy industry, and the "most up-to-date" techniques. It thrust the needs of the masses into the background, giving ever greater priority to accumulation, which the plans sought to "maximize," without really taking account of the demands of the development of agriculture and of the balance of exchange between town and country, the material basis of the worker-peasant alliance and, therefore, of the consolidation of the dictatorship of the proletariat.

2. This process brings us back to consideration of the production relations in the state sector and the class consequences of these relations. Here, we are at the heart of the contradictions that developed during the years preceding the procurement crisis and the complete abandonment of the NEP. The importance of these contradictions (which concerned mainly the industrial sector) and their fundamental character require that they be subjected to specific analysis. This analysis cannot confine itself to an examination of forms of ownership, but must focus upon the structure of the immediate production process itself and the conditions for reproducing the factors in this process, and also upon the ways in which the production relations were perceived, and their effects upon the class struggles.

Notes

1. See N. Valentinov's article, "De la 'NEP' à la collectivisation," in *Le Contrat social*. (March–April 1964), p. 79.
2. Ibid., p. 79.
3. On the concept of "census industry," see note 12, p. 196 above.
4. Carr and Davies, *Foundations,* vol. I, pt. 2, p. 950.
5. A. Baykov, *The Soviet Economic System*, p. 124.

6. Calculated from ibid., p. 124, and Carr and Davies, *Foundations*, vol. I, pt. 2, pp. 947, 950.
7. Shapiro, "Kustarno-remeslennaya promyshlennost," in *Planovoye Khozyaistvo*, no. 6 (1927), p. 70 ff., quoted in Grosskopf, *L'Alliance ouvrière*, p. 334.
8. See above, p. 144.
9. Lenin, *CW*, vol. 32, pp. 350, 352. In *On Co-operation*, Lenin wrote that incorporation of the whole population in cooperatives could be achieved, "at best, . . . in one or two decades" (ibid., vol. 33, p. 470).
10. In the conclusion to the pamphlet quoted, Lenin returns to this theme, calling for "the development of local initiative and independent action in encouraging exchange between agriculture and industry" to be "given the fullest scope at all costs" (ibid., p. 364).
11. Ibid., p. 347.
12. Baykov, *The Soviet Economic System*, p. 122.
13. *Izvestiya VTsIK*, no. 103 (1927), quoted in Grosskopf, *L'Alliance ouvrière*, pp. 366–367.
14. After 1929 the policy of shutting down private production units became quasiofficial, as a prolongation of the policy of "dekulakisation" which prevailed at that time.
15. *Kontrolnye tsifry 1926–1927 gg.*, p. 484, quoted in Carr and Davies, *Foundations*, vol. I, pt. 2, p. 961.
16. Carr and Davies, *Foundations*, vol. I, pt. 2, p. 962.
17. Ibid.
18. *Voprosy Torgovli*, no. 4 (January 1929), pp. 64–65.
19. *KPSS v rezolyutsiyakh*, vol. 1, pp. 840 ff.
20. Meaning the areas where private trade had been eliminated without being replaced by state and cooperative trade.
21. *K.P.S.S. v rezolyutsiyakh*, vol. 2, pp. 224 ff.
22. Ibid., pp. 351 ff.
23. Thus, in his speech to the CC on July 9, 1928, Stalin declared: "We often say that we are promoting socialist forms of economy in the sphere of trade. But what does that imply? It implies that we are squeezing out of trade thousands upon thousands of small and medium traders" (Stalin, *Works*, vol. 11, p. 178).
24. Carr and Davies, *Foundations*, vol. I, pt. 2, p. 938.
25. See Lenin, *CW*, vol. 32, pp. 372–374: "To Comrade Kryzhizhanovsky, the Presidium of the State Planning Commission" (1921).

3. The forms of ownership in the state sector and the structure of the immediate production process

Toward the end of the NEP, state-owned industry consisted mainly of established industrial enterprises which had been nationalized after the October Revolution, together with a small number of new enterprises. It coincided largely with large-scale industry, and was, in the main, directly subject to the central economic organs of the Soviet state—in practice, the VSNKh.[1] Only a few state-owned industrial enterprises were in the hands of the republics or of regional or local organs. Thus, in 1926–1927, industry directly planned by the VSNKh provided 77 percent of the value of all production by large-scale industry.[2]

Sale of the goods produced was largely in the hands of a network of state (and official cooperative) organs that were independent of the industrial enterprises. However, during the NEP period, state-owned industry also developed its own organs for wholesale trade, and sometimes even for retail trade. These were usually organized at the level of the *unions* of enterprises, the Soviet *trusts*, or at the level of the organs formed by agreements between trusts, unions, and enterprises—organs known as "sales syndicates."[3]

Toward the end of the NEP period, industry's sales organs were gradually detached from the industrial enterprises themselves and integrated, in the form of a special administration, in the People's Commissariats to which the enterprises belonged. In particular, the sale of industrial products to the ultimate consumers was to an increasing extent entrusted to *state trading bodies separate from industry* and operating on the levels of wholesale, semiwholesale, and retail trade. This separation made possible, in principle, better supervision of

209

commercial operations by the central state organs. The most important trading bodies came under the People's Commissariat of Trade (Narkomtorg), while others came under the republics of the regions.[4] The fact that these different organs existed, and the conditions under which products circulated among them, reveal the *commodity* character of production and circulation.

As Lenin had often emphasized, especially in his discussion of state capitalism,[5] state ownership is not equivalent to socialist ownership. Under conditions of the dictatorship of the proletariat, statization makes possible a struggle for *socialization* of production, for real socialist transformation of the production relations. Under the dictatorship of the proletariat, state ownership may be a *socialist form of ownership,* but it cannot remain so except in so far as (given the concrete conditions of class relations) a struggle is waged for the socialist transformation of production relations. So long as this transformation has not been completed, state ownership possesses a *twofold* nature: it is both a socialist form of ownership, because of the class nature of the state, and a state-capitalist form, because of the partly capitalist nature of the existing production relations, the limited extent of transformation undergone by the processes of production and reproduction. If this is lost sight of, the concept of ownership is reduced to its juridical aspect and the actual social significance of the juridical form of ownership, which can be grasped only by analyzing the production relations, is overlooked.[6]

The starting point for this analysis has to be clarification of the structure of the immediate production process, which can be perceived at the levels of forms of management, discipline, cooperation, and organization of labor.

I. The forms of management in the state-owned factories

As regards the forms of management in the state enterprises, we need to recall that at the end of the NEP the measures adopted in the spring of 1918 were still in force. We have seen that these measures introduced a system of one-person management of each enterprise, with the manager appointed by the central organs and not subject to workers' control.[7] These measures had been adopted provisionally, in order to combat what Lenin called "the practice of a lily-livered proletarian government."[8]

In 1926 the difficulties initially encountered in the management of enterprises had been overcome, but the forms of management adopted because of these earlier difficulties remained in force. These forms were not socialist forms: they implied the existence of elements of capitalist relations at the level of the immediate production process itself. Lenin had not hesitated, in 1918, to acknowledge this reality quite plainly. He had defined the adoption of the principle of paying high salaries to managers as "a step backward," leading to a strengthening of capital, since, as he put it, "capital is not a sum of money but a definite social relation." This "step backward" reinforced the "state-capitalist" character of the production relations. Speaking of the establishment of "individual dictatorial powers" (which were to take the form of one-person management), he referred to their importance "from the point of view of the specific tasks of the present moment." He stressed the need for discipline and coercion, mentioning that "the form of coercion is determined by the degree of development of the given revolutionary class."[9] The lower the level of development of this class, the more the form assumed by factory discipline tends to resemble capitalist discipline.

We must ask ourselves why the Bolshevik Party maintained high salaries for managers and the form of one-person management adopted a few months after the October Revolution, when the conditions which had originally caused these practices to be adopted had passed away.

The maintenance of this system was clearly connected with the *class struggle,* with the struggle waged by the heads of enterprises to retain and even strengthen their power and their privileges. However, the way in which this struggle developed, and its outcome, cannot be separated from certain features of the Bolshevik ideological formation and the changes which it underwent. These changes led, especially, to decisive importance being accorded to forms of organization and ownership and to less and less attention being given to the development of a real dialectical analysis that could bring out the contradictory nature of reality.

The *Outline of Political Economy* by Lapidus and Ostrovityanov gives especially systematic expression to the non-dialectical perception of social relations which was characteristic of the Soviet formation at the end of the 1920s. We shall have to come back to a number of aspects of this way of perceiving the economic and social reality of the USSR; for the moment, let us confine ourselves to the following formulation: "We were guided mainly by the fact that the relations in the two main branches of Soviet economics, the socialist state relations on the one hand, and the simple commodity relations in agriculture, on the other, are fundamentally not capitalist. . . ."[10]

The writers do not deny that there were at that time (1928) "state capitalist and private capitalist elements in the Soviet system,"[11] but they recognize their presence only in the private capitalist enterprises. They thus renounce attempting any analysis of the internal contradictions of the state sector. Such a simplified conception of the production relations prevented correct treatment of the contradictions and socialist transformation of the production relations in the state enterprises. It was all the more considerable an obstacle in that, toward the end of the NEP period, this simplified conception was generally accepted in the Bolshevik Party. After 1926 the state-owned enterprises, instead of being seen (as had been the case previously) as belonging to a "state sector" whose contradictory nature called for analysis, were all described as forming part of a "socialist sector" in which the production relations were not contradictory.

Here we see one aspect of the changes in the Bolshevik ideological formation. These changes were connected with the struggle of the managers of state enterprises to strengthen their authority and increase their political and social role.

They cannot be separated from the fact that the increasing extent to which the heads of enterprises were of proletarian origin tended to be identified with progress in the leading role played by the proletariat as a class; whereas this class origin of the managers offered no guarantee of their class position and could, of course, in no way alter the class character of the existing social production relations.

The nature of the social relations reproduced at the level of the immediate labor process was manifested not only in the type of management exercized in relation to the workers, but also in the way that work norms were fixed, in factory discipline, and in the contradictions that developed in these connections.

II. *The fixing of work norms from above*

Where work norms are concerned, it is to be noted in the first place that their observance or nonobservance by the workers was to an ever greater extent controlled by variations in the wages paid to them, especially after the *extension of piecework* approved by a CC resolution of August 19, 1924.[12]

Large-scale application of this resolution began in 1926, in connection with the demands of the industrial plan, and owing to the tendency for wages to increase faster than productivity. In August 1926 the question of revising the norms was brought up by the heads of enterprises and by the VSNKh, who denounced the increasing spread of the "scissors" between productivity and wages, with the latter rising faster than the former.[13] In October 1926 the Fifteenth Party Conference affirmed the need to revise production norms upward; it also called for a strengthening of labor discipline, so as to deal with the resistance that "certain groups of workers" were putting up against increased norms, and to combat more effectively absenteeism and negligent work.[14]

At the Seventh Congress of the Trade Unions, held in December 1926, several delegates complained that managers were using these resolutions as a pretext for intensifying work to an excessive degree. However, while denouncing abuses which led to "a worsening of the material situation of the workers,"[15] the leaders of the trade unions emphasized mainly the need to raise productivity.

In 1927 the current in favor of increasing the work norms imposed from above became stronger. It was shown especially in the adoption by the CC, on March 24, 1927, of a resolution devoted to "rationalisation."[16] This resolution was used by the managers and by the economic organs in an effort to impose ever higher work norms, determined by research departments and services specializing in time-and-motion study.

This procedure tended to reduce the role of collective political work among the workers and to give greater and greater ascendancy to work norms decided upon by "technicians." The resistance with which this tendency met explains why, during the summer of 1927, Kuibyshev, who then became chairman of the VSNKh, called upon that organ to engage more actively in the revision of norms, and not to hesitate in dismissing "redundant" workers.[17]

At the end of 1927 the revision of work norms was going ahead fast. At the beginning of 1928 the trade unions complained that "in the great majority of cases, the economic organs are demanding complete revision of the norms in all enterprises, which is resulting in wage-cuts."[18]

Closely linked with the question of norms and the way they were fixed was the question of labor discipline and the relations between the workers and the management personnel in the enterprises. From the beginning of the NEP period this question had given rise to a struggle between two paths, a struggle that was especially confused because what was really at issue in it—namely, the nature of production relations in the state enterprises—was not clearly perceived. This confusion explains the contradictory nature of the political line followed in the matter by the Bolshevik Party.

When we analyze this line we observe a crisscrossing of two "paths"—one that could lead to a transformation of production relations through developing the initiative of the masses, and another that tended to *maintain* and strengthen the hierarchical forms of labor discipline in the name of the primacy of production. From 1928 on, the second of these "paths" became stronger, and it triumphed decisively in April 1929, with the adoption of the "maximal" variant of the First Five-Year Plan.

The crisscrossing of these two "paths" demands that, for the sake of greater clarity, we examine each of them separately.

III. The class struggle and the struggle to transform the production relations

At the level of the Party leadership, the first explicit manifestation of a line aimed concretely at modifying the relations between the managements of enterprises and the mass of the workers appeared in a resolution adopted by the Thirteenth Party Conference in January 1924. In order to understand the significance of this resolution, however, we need to go back a little and see in what terms the problems dealt with by this resolution had previously been discussed.

(a) Managements and trade unions

The problems explicitly presented were, in the first place, those of the respective roles to be played in the functioning of enterprises, by the *management* and by the *trade unions*. It was in this form that the Eleventh Party Congress (1922) had adopted certain positions, in particular by passing a resolution which approved Lenin's theses on "The Role and Functions of the Trade Unions."[19]

This document dealt with the role to be played by the trade unions in the running of enterprises and the economy as a whole. In the document we can distinguish between a principal aspect, referring to the "present situation" in Soviet Russia, and a secondary aspect (secondary in the sense that it was not urgent at that time), referring to the future.

As regards the "present," the document stressed the need to cope as quickly as possible with the consequences of "post-war ruin, famine and dislocation." It declared that "the speediest and most enduring success in restoring large-scale industry is a condition without which no success can be achieved in the general cause of emancipating labour from the yoke of capital and securing the victory of socialism." And it went on: "To achieve this success in Russia, *in her present state* [my emphasis—C. B.], it is absolutely essential that all authority in the factories should be concentrated in the hands of management."[20] From this the conclusion was drawn that "Under these circumstances, all direct interference by the trade unions in the management of factories must be regarded as positively harmful and impermissible."[21]

It is clear that Lenin's theses are concerned with "the present state" of Russia, and that the very way in which he deals with it implies that once the country has emerged from this situation the principles set forth as relevant to it will cease to apply. The "present state" he was writing about was dominated by famine and poverty, from which the Party was trying to rescue the country as soon as possible, leaving a certain number of capitalist relations untouched for the time being.

The resolution on the trade unions which was adopted by the Eleventh Congress warned, however, against the notion that, *even in the immediate present,* the trade unions were to be pushed out of the sphere of management altogether. What it condemned was "direct interference," and it made its position clear by saying that "it would be absolutely wrong, however, to interpret this indisputable axiom to mean that the trade unions must play no part in the socialist organization of industry and in the management of state industry."[22]

The resolution outlines the forms that this participation is to take: the trade unions are to participate in all the organs for managing and administering the economy as a whole; there is to be training and advancement of administrators drawn from the working class and the working people generally; the trade unions are to participate in all the state planning organs in the drawing up of economic plans and programs; and so on.[23]

Here, too, the text states clearly that the forms of participation listed are for "the immediate period,"[24] *which implies that other forms may develop later on,* so that it is one of the Party's tasks "deliberately and resolutely to start persevering practical activities calculated to extend over a long period of years and designed to give the workers and all working people generally practical training in the art of managing the economy of the whole country."[25]

(b) The production conferences

The position adopted at the Eleventh Congress makes clear the significance of the resolution passed in January 1924 by the Thirteenth Party Conference. It was a first step taken toward according a bigger role to the workers in the state enterprises in defining production tasks and the conditions for their fulfillment.

This resolution urged that regular "production conferences" be held, at which current problems concerning production and the results obtained should be discussed and experience exchanged. The resolution stated that the conferences should be attended by "representatives of the economic organs and of the trade unions *and also workers both Party and non-Party.*"[26] This decision thus tended to subject the managerial activity of the heads of enterprises to supervision no longer by the higher authorities only, but also by the trade unions and the workers, whether Party members or not.

The Sixth Trades Union Congress (September 1924) and the Fourteenth Party Conference (April 1925) confirmed this line. However, its implementation came up against strong resistance, mainly from the economic organs and the heads of enterprises and trusts.

On May 15, 1925, a resolution adopted by the CC recognized that the production conferences had not developed in a satisfactory way, that they had not succeeded in bringing together "really broad strata of the workers."[27] The CC issued instructions which it was hoped would improve this state of affairs. Actually, 1925 was a year of economic tension during which the power of the trade union organizations was in retreat.

At the Fourteenth Party Congress (December 1925) Tomsky, the chairman of the Central Trades Union Council, described the difficulties encountered by the production conferences because of the hostility of the heads of enterprises. Molotov reported that fewer than 600 conferences had been held in Moscow and Leningrad, bringing together about 70,000 workers. A resolution on trade union matters adopted by the CC in October 1925 had taken an ambiguous line on this problem, reflecting the strong pressure then being exercised by most of the heads of enterprises and those who supported their views within the Party. While confirming the need to develop "production meetings," this resolution warned against a "management deviation," in the sense of interfering "directly and without competence to do so in the management and administration of enterprises."[28] This document refers several times to the resolution adopted by the Eleventh Party Congress, which was then nearly four years old, and which, as we have seen, did not rule out direct intervention by the trade unions and the workers in the management of enterprises except in "the present state" of Soviet Russia; whereas the situation at the end of 1925 was very different from what it had been then.[29]

A resolution passed in December 1925 by the Fourteenth Party Congress remained very cautious regarding production meetings, reminding all concerned that the ultimate aim of such meetings was "to give practical instruction to the workers and all the working people in how to run the economy of the country as a whole."[30]

At the beginning of 1926 a fresh impulse was given to the line, aimed at giving the workers a bigger role in defining the tasks of production. In a report on April 13, (in which he dealt with the work of the CC plenum held at the beginning of the month) Stalin forcefully stressed the need to put a *mass line* into effect in order to solve the tasks of industrialization. The part of his report devoted to this problem emphasized the need to reduce unproductive expenditure to the minimum. It thus went against the ideas of the heads of enterprises, who emphasized above all intensification of labor, raising of norms, reduction of wages, and strengthening of labor discipline imposed from above.

What Stalin said on this subject was organically linked with the will to develop industry by means of its own resources, these being constituted first and foremost by the workers themselves. In this connection certain passages in his report of April 13, 1926, were of great importance. Thus, after examining some of the principal tasks to be accomplished in order to advance industrialization, Stalin asked: "Can these tasks be accomplished without the direct assistance and support of the working class?" And he replied:

> No, they cannot. Advancing our industry, raising its productivity, creating new cadres of builders of industry, . . . establishing a regime of the strictest economy, tightening up the state apparatus, making it operate cheaply and honestly, purging it of the dross and filth which have adhered to it during the period of our work of construction, waging a systematic struggle against stealers and squanderers of state property—all these are tasks which no party can cope with without the direct and systematic support of the vast masses of the working class. Hence the task is to draw the vast masses of non-Party workers into all our constructive work. Every worker, every honest peasant must assist the Party and the Government in putting into effect a regime of economy, in combating the misappropriation and dissipation of state reserves, in getting rid of thieves and swindlers, no matter what disguise they assume, and in making our state apparatus healthier and cheaper. Inestimable service in this respect could be rendered by production conferences. . . . The production conferences must be revived at all costs. . . . Their programme must be made broader and more comprehensive. The principal questions of the building of industry must be placed before them. Only in that way is it possible to raise the activity of the vast masses of the working class and to make them conscious participants in the building of industry.[31]

This speech of Stalin's was followed by a reexamination of the problem of the production conferences by the Central Trades Union Council and by the VSNKh (at that time still headed by Dzerzhinsky). In a note which he signed on June 22, 1926, only a few days before his death, Dzerzhinsky did not shrink from declaring that the lack of success of the production conferences was due to "our managers who have not hitherto shown active goodwill in this matter."[32] As a result of this note, a joint resolution was adopted by the Central Trades Union Council and the VSNKh, calling for the establishment of production commissions in all the factories, with the task of preparing proposals and agenda for the production conferences.[33]

In the second half of 1926 and at the beginning of 1927 the struggle between a line directed toward mass participation in management and a line tending to consolidate the dominant position of the heads of enterprises in matters of management, economy, labor discipline, and so on, seems to have become more intense. Nevertheless, neither of these two lines was ever openly counterposed to the other: the conflict proceeded in terms of shifts of emphasis, with the substitution of one word for another having real political significance. Thus, the Fifteenth Party Conference (October 1926) passed two resolutions which again underlined the importance of the production conferences.[34] These documents looked forward to increased activity by production meetings, with extension of their field of competence alike in general questions and questions of detail, so as to achieve a "form of direct participation by the workers in the organisation of production."[35] For this purpose it was provided that "temporary commissions for workers' control in a given enterprise" could be set up, and that their functions be defined by the Central Trades Union Council and the VSNKh.[36]

The resolution on the country's economic situation condemned the line that had been followed by the economic organs. They were accused of having "distorted the Party's directives," with the result that attempts had been made "to effect economies at the expense of the essential interests of the working class."[37] The resolution demanded that the personnel of the economic organs be decisively reduced in numbers, together with administrative costs, that systems of management and decision-making be rationalized, and that a struggle against bureaucracy be launched.

The Fifteenth Conference dealt with the problem of increasing the productivity of labor by stressing "the immense significance of the production-meetings." The resolution adopted said that "without active participation by the worker masses the fight to strengthen labour discipline cannot fully succeed, just as without broad participation by the worker masses it is not possible to solve successfully any of the tasks or to overcome any of the difficulties that arise on the road of socialist construction."[38]

The adoption of these resolutions was strongly resisted. Some managers feared a reappearance of "workers' control" in the form it had taken in October 1917, while others complained that the controls they already had to put up with constituted an excessive burden.[39]

In the two months following the Fifteenth Conference the heads of enterprises and the VSNKh seem to have strengthened their positions. The Seventh Congress of Trade Unions, held in December, dealt only cautiously with the question of production conferences and control commissions. The principal resolution voted by this Congress even stressed that the organizing of commissions "must in no case be interpreted as a direct interference in the functions of administrative or economic management of the enterprise concerned."[40] In practice, the temporary control commissions elected by the production conferences usually consisted of five or seven skilled workers, who dealt with relatively limited questions: analysis of the reasons for a high cost of production, shortcomings in the utilization of labor power, fight against waste.[41]

Applying the resolutions of the Fifteenth Party Conference, the VSNKh and the Central Trades Union Council jointly decided, on February 2, 1927, to set up temporary control commissions, but subsequent events showed that the commissions thus created did not do very much during 1927. At the Fifteenth Party Congress (December 1927) the negative attitude of the economic leaders and heads of enterprises was mentioned as the reason for this. The plenum of April 1928 also blamed the trade-union cadres for the poor organization of the production conferences, the infrequency of their meetings, and the lack of interest in them shown by many workers.[42]

For whatever reason, in April 1928 the production conferences were still not playing the role that the resolutions adopted up to that time had assigned to them.

(c) The "criticism" movement of 1928

The April 1928 session of the CC returned to these same problems. In his report of the session, given on April 13,[43] Stalin dwelt upon the need to develop criticism and self-criticism of a really mass character.[44] What he said in this connection concerned especially the heads of enterprises, engineers, and technicians:

> We must see to it that the vigilance of the working class is not damped down, but stimulated, that hundreds of thousands and millions of workers are drawn into the general work of socialist construction, that hundreds of thousands and millions of workers and peasants, and not merely a dozen leaders, keep watch over the progress of our construction work, notice our errors and bring them into the light of day. . . . But to bring this about, we must develop criticism of our shortcomings from below, we must make criticism the affair of the masses. . . . If the workers take advantage of the opportunity to criticise shortcomings in our work frankly and bluntly, to improve and advance our work, what does that mean? It means that the workers are becoming active participants in the work of directing the country, economy, industry. And this cannot but enhance in the workers the feeling that they are the masters of the country, cannot but enhance their activity, their vigilance, their culture. . . . That, incidentally, is the reason why the question of a cultural revolution is so acute with us.[45]

This passage thus linked together the theme of the need for *class criticism* coming from the rank and file with the theme of a *cultural revolution* and active participation by the working people in the work of running the economy and the country.

The way in which these themes were expounded by Stalin shows that at the beginning of 1928 the contradiction between the demands of the preceding stage of the NEP (the stage of restoring the economy and of the first steps taken along the path of industrial development) and the demands of the new stage (the stage of accelerated industrialization) had reached objectively a high degree of acuteness. Industry could no longer advance "by its own resources" unless the workers attacked the practices and social relations characteristic of the previous phase. If this attack did not take place, if the workers did not revolt against the existing practices and social relations, and if this revolt was not correctly guided, but dispersed itself over secondary "targets," then the growth in the contradictions that resulted must inevitably obstruct the development of industry by means of its own resources, leading either to a crisis of industrialization or to a type of industrial development very different from that which the Bolshevik Party wished to promote on the morrow of its Fifteenth Congress.

The year was marked by a serious development of the workers' struggle, but also by the dispersal of this struggle over a variety of targets—owing to the Bolshevik Party's inability to concentrate it on the main thing, namely, transformation of production relations. What happened in the spring of that year was particularly significant in this connection.

The beginning of 1928 saw several "affairs" coming to a head, affairs which gravely undermined the authority of the heads of enterprises, engineers, and specialists, and also some local and regional Party cadres. Two of these "affairs" were especially important: those of Shakhty and Smolensk. Stalin alluded to them explicitly in his report of April 13, 1928, mentioned above,[46] and in his speech to the Eighth Komsomol Congress on May 16.[47]

The first of these affairs gave rise to a trial which was held between the beginning of May and the beginning of July 1928.[48] The accused in this trial were a number of specialists of bourgeois origin who held managerial posts in the coal-mines of the Ukraine. They were charged with sabotage and counter-revolutionary activity in conspiracy with foreign powers, and were sentenced to severe penalties.

The second affair was more important politically, for it was provincial Party cadres who were gravely implicated in it. Occurring also at the beginning of 1928, it gave rise to an inquiry by the Party's Central Control Commission, and the conclusions were published in *Pravda* on 18 May 1928. According to these conclusions, a number of Party officials in Smolensk Region had become sunk in corruption and depravity. The results of the investigation were put before a gathering of 1,100 Party members, 40 percent of whom were production workers. The report of the inquiry and the discussion at this meeting show that, at the request of political leaders in the region, 60 persons had been arrested—although there were no criminal charges to be brought against them, and there had been cases of suicide on the part of workers whose urgent applications had been met with indifference by the leadership, and so on. As a result of these revelations, about 60 percent of the cadres (at every level) in the Smolensk Region were relieved of their posts, and were replaced mainly by worker militants. However, the punishment meted out to the former cadres was not very severe, and the rank-and-file workers were unhappy about this.[49]

The Smolensk affair was not the only one involving cadres at a regional level and which presented similar features, but it was mainly in connection with this affair that Stalin expounded important themes which found a wide echo in the working class.

These themes were set forth principally in the speech to the Eighth Komsomol Congress. In this speech Stalin stressed that the class struggle was still going on, and that, in relation to its class enemies, the working class must develop "its vigilance, its revolutionary spirit, its readiness for action."[50] He returned to the need for "organising mass control from below."[51] What was particularly significant in this speech was that he called for control from below to be developed in relation not only to specialists and engineers of bourgeois origin but also to *the Party cadres themselves and the engineers of working-class origin*. He denounced the idea that only the *old* bureaucracy constituted a danger. If that were so, he said, everything would be easy. He emphasized that "it is a matter of the new bureaucrats, bureaucrats who sympathise with the Soviet Government, and, finally, Communist bureaucrats."[52]

Stalin then referred to the Smolensk "affair" and some others, asking how it was that such shameful cases of corruption and moral degradation could have occurred in certain Party organizations. This was the explanation he gave: "The fact that Party monopoly was carried to absurd lengths, that the voice of the rank-and-file was stifled, that inner-Party democracy was abolished and bureaucracy became rife. . . ." And he added: "I think that *there is not and cannot be any other way of combating this evil* than by organising control from below by the Party masses, by implanting inner-Party democracy."[53]

Later, Stalin explained that this control must be exercised not only by the masses who had joined the Party but by the working masses as a whole, and by the working class first and foremost:

> We have production conferences in the factories. We have temporary control commissions in the trade unions. It is the task of these organisations to rouse the masses, to bring our shortcomings to light and to indicate ways and means of improving our constructive work. . . . Is it not obvious that it is bureaucracy in the trade unions, coupled with bureaucracy in the Party organisations, that is preventing these highly important organisations of the working class from developing?
>
> Lastly, our economic organisations. Who will deny that our economic bodies suffer from bureaucracy? . . .
>
> There is only one sole way [of putting an end to bureaucracy in all these organizations] and that is to organise control from below, to organise criticism of the bureaucracy in our institutions, of their shortcomings and their mistakes, by the vast masses of the working class. . . .
>
> Only by organising twofold pressure—from above and from below—and only by shifting the principal stress to criticism from below, can we count on waging a successful struggle against bureaucracy and on rooting it out. . . .
>
> The vast masses of the workers who are engaged in building

our industry are day by day accumulating vast experience in construction. . . . Mass criticism from below, control from below, is needed by us in order that . . . this experience of the vast masses should not be wasted, but be reckoned with and translated into practice.

From this follows the immediate task of the Party: *to wage a ruthless struggle against bureaucracy, to organise mass criticism from below, and to take this criticism into account when adopting practical decisions for eliminating our* shortcomings.[54]

While continuing appeals that had been issued earlier, these declarations in the spring of 1928 signified an important step forward as compared with what had been said previously (in particular at the Fifteenth Party Congress). They revealed a shift of emphasis[55] which was of considerable significance, indicating a new stage in the class struggle and in its effects on the Party line.

(d) The challenge to the existing forms of management and way of training engineers and technicians

Comparison of these declarations with some others shows that new conclusions were then in process of emerging with regard to the existing social relations, their nature, and the forms of struggle needed in order to transform them—although the question of transforming social relations was not posed *explicitly*.

In his report of April 13, 1928, Stalin questioned the existing regulations concerning managerial functions, in particular Circular No. 33 dated March 29, 1926, on "The Organisation of the Management of Industrial Establishments."[56] He said of this circular that "these model regulations. . . . confer practically all the rights on the technical director," and that it had become an obstacle to the management of enterprises by Communist leaders risen from the working class.[57]

In the same report, Stalin also raised the question of economic leaders who were Party members of working-class origin but who had begun, he said, "to deteriorate and degenerate and come to *identify themselves in their way of living with the bourgeois experts,"* to whom they were becoming mere "appendages."[58]

Here we see formulations appearing which suggest that within the Party itself there might emerge a new bourgeoisie, taking over from the old one and forming a "Communist bureaucracy." However, these formulations were not developed, and even those quoted were not to be subsequently repeated with the same sharpness. It is clear, nevertheless, that the expressions used reflected the development of acute contradictions in the economic apparatuses and also in those of the Party and the State.

It will also be noted that in this same report of April 13 Stalin raised the question of the training of "Red experts." He observed that this training was bad, poorly adapted to industry's needs, bookish, divorced from production and practical experience. He said that an expert trained in this way "does not want to soil his hands in a factory." According to him, such experts were often badly received by the workers and were unable to get the upper hand over the bourgeois experts. In order to change this situation, Stalin advocated that the training of young experts be carried out differently, that it involve "continuous contact with production, with factory, mine and so forth."[59]

Here, too, a step forward was being made, as compared with the way with which these same problems had been dealt up to that time: we see taking shape a critique of the bourgeois way of training technicians and engineers and a search for something different.

When we analyze this passage, and some others, we can deduce that in the spring of 1928 some new and important formulations were emerging. Today, in the light of the experience of China, and, especially of the proletarian cultural revolution, we find ourselves thinking that if these reflections had been deepened and systematized, they might have led to a more profound challenge to the existing organization of industry; to the relations between the heads of enterprises, engineers, and cadres, on the one hand, and the mass of the workers, on the other; to the relation between education and production practice; and, finally, to the practice of the class struggle. Actually, this deepening and systematization did not take place in the Soviet Union, owing to the turn taken by the class struggle in the second half of 1928.

During that year there was a turn in the conditions of the class struggle. The first half of the year saw a rising tide of initiatives and criticisms coming from below and denouncing the authoritarian way in which many persons in leading positions were performing their tasks. Toward the end of 1928, on the contrary, these initiatives ebbed away. Let us look more closely at what happened.

(e) The rise of the mass movement

In the first months of 1928 a growing number of workers began to criticize managers and engineers, blaming them for their attitude, their decisions, and the way they tried to speed up production—even going so far as to violate the labor laws and safety regulations.[60] Before 1928 such criticism had not been made openly, for fear of punishment. The call for mass criticism helped to alter this situation.

Here something needs to be said about the reasons for increased discontent in the working class at the beginning of 1928. To be specially noted are the continued pressure brought to bear to impose higher work norms from above, the serious difficulties affecting the supply of food, and the way in which the managements carried out the transition to three-shift working. This last point calls for some remarks.

It should be recalled that on October 16, 1927, a Party manifesto was published[61] which provided for a gradual change over from the eight-hour day to the seven-hour day, without any reduction in wages, on condition that productivity per workday was maintained or increased. This decision prepared the way for the change to *three-shift working,* a measure which the VSNKh had been advocating for some time on the grounds that it would make possible more intensive use of plant, and consequently, more employment.

The practical implementation of this measure was to be carried out on the basis of agreements made between the trade unions and the economic organizations. Actually, the heads of enterprises had taken steps already in order to arrange matters in the way that suited them. Thus, despite protests from the trade unions, in most textile mills the workers had been obliged to work two half-shifts a day, each of three and a half hours, which disrupted their lives. We find in the press of the time many protests against the way that shiftwork was being introduced,[62] and against the consequences of nightwork for young persons and pregnant women.[63]

A new source of discontent among the workers was thus created which made them readier even than before to challenge some of the decisions taken by the heads of enterprises. Faced with this questioning of their authority, many of the latter, and many engineers, refused to accept that the workers over whom they had hitherto exercised power should dare to criticize their decisions and their behavior. They tried to take reprisals, individual or collective, which only aggravated the tension.

From May 1928 on the heads of enterprises complained increasingly of a "slackening of labour discipline." These complaints arose mainly in heavy industry and the coal mines. The points most often mentioned were: lower productivity and production, increased costs, poor maintenance of equipment, excessive absenteeism.[64]

Between April and June the number of stoppages (some of which might, of course, have been due to technical causes) was greater than during the corresponding period of the previous year, but it is hard to say what the real reasons were for this phenomenon. The managers and engineers may have been responsible, either because they failed to organize the supply of raw materials to the factories, or because they were trying to "prove" that anything that threatened their authority was also a threat to production. Stoppages brought about in that way may have been comparatively numerous. The managers' reports certainly exaggerated the effects upon production of the tension that was developing. Production was still rising rapidly, all the same.[65] Moreover, this period saw the advance of a movement of *socialist emulation,* which was most probably stimulated by the development of mass initiative which accompanied the multiplication of production conferences and the open voicing of grievances and criticism.

However that may have been, the heads of the economic organs reacted aggressively to the development of the mass movement which called their "authority" in question. Those journals which expressed the views of the managers and the economic organizations developed a veritable antiworker campaign, writing of the "cultural and technical backwardness" of the workers in general and of the "low cultural level" of the workers of peasant origin in particular—which signified that criticisms or proposals coming from the workers were not worth considering.

The managers' journal invoked the principle of one-person management, as if this were a principle not to be touched, instead of a measure adopted at a particular moment in order to deal with conditions specific to that moment. It wrote: "Soviet principles of management of enterprises and production are being replaced by the principle of election, and, in practice, by the responsibility of those who elect."[66]

In the press of the VSNKh and the economic organs many articles appeared accusing the workers not only of indiscipline and absenteeism but also of plundering, larcency, drunkenness at work, and insulting or assaulting the specialists and administrators. Such things certainly did happen. They expressed the exasperation of part of the working class against the resistance offered by the managers to changes in the organization of production proposed by the workers, and also the workers' resentment of increased work norms imposed from above.

In face of the rising tide of criticism by the working class and the reactions thereto of the managers and the middle cadres of the Party, more and more hesitation was shown as to the line to be followed. Stalin's article "Against Vulgarising the Slogan of Self-Criticism"[67] gives clear expression to this hesitation.

The principal aspect of this article was an appeal for mass criticism to continue. Several passages say this, for instance: "With all the more persistence must we rouse the vast masses of the workers and peasants to the task of criticism *from below,* of control *from below,* as the principal antidote to bureaucracy."[68]

Or, again:

Nor can it be denied that, as a result of self-criticism, our business executives are beginning to smarten up, to become more vigilant, to approach questions of economic leadership more seriously, while our Party, Soviet, trade-union and all other personnel are becoming more sensitive and responsive to the requirements of the masses.

True, it cannot be said that inner-Party democracy and working-class democracy generally are already fully established in the mass organisations of the working class. But there is no reason to doubt that further advances will be made in this field as the campaign unfolds.[69]

This formulation thus called for criticism from below to continue. Yet the aims of the movement remained ambiguous. On the problems of discipline Stalin had this to say: "Self-criticism is needed not in order to shatter labour discipline but to *strengthen* it, in order that labour discipline may become *conscious* discipline, capable of withstanding petty-bourgeois slackness."[70]

In a way, this formulation replied to the complaints of the managers about "slackening of discipline," but it did not reply completely, for it did not say in so many words that the conscious discipline mentioned implied, above all, *new forms of discipline*. This lack of precision left a gap affecting the orientation of the mass movement.

Similarly, where problems of management were concerned, the formulations remained ambiguous, as here: "Self-criticism is needed not in order to relax leadership, but to *strengthen* it, in order to convert it from leadership on paper and of little authority into *vigorous* and really *authoritative* leadership."[71] This formulation does not say whether the *forms of leadership* had to be changed or not, nor does it say who is to lead, or the basis on which the authority of the leadership is to be founded.

As well as these ambiguities, this document of June 1928 contained a certain number of remarks which were to be seized on by the opponents of the mass movement, remarks which reflect hesitation and fear inspired by the scope that the movement was attaining. One of these remarks warned against certain "destructive" criticisms the aim of which was not to improve the work of construction.[72] The local cadres and managers were not slow to make use of such a remark to condemn as "destructive" any criticism or proposal that they wished to brush aside.

Another remark entailed more immediate consequences for the future development of the movement, namely:

> It must be observed . . . that there is a definite tendency on the part of a number of our organisations to turn self-criticism into a *witch-hunt* against our business executives. . . . It is a fact that certain local organisations in the Ukraine and Central Russia have started a regular *witch-hunt* against some of our *best* business executives. . . . How else are we to understand the decisions of the local organisations to remove these executives from their posts, decisions which have no binding force whatever and which are obviously designed to discredit them?[73]

This remark shows the wide scope the movement had attained, and also the *limits* within which it was considered to be acceptable. Since these limits were being transcended, what was ultimately at issue was whether support would continue to be given to it, or whether brakes were to be applied to its development.

Actually, during part of the second half of 1928 the movement still went forward, and even assumed dimensions that worried the Party leadership more and more. Thus, in November 1928, Kuibyshev, addressing the plenum of the VSNKh, denounced the situation which had been created by saying: "The formula: 'public opinion is against him' has already become typical." He went on to explain that when the head of an enterprise or a trust found himself in this position, "he has no alternative but to depart, to abandon his post."[74]

This statement constituted a warning against the continuance of a movement which, while becoming widespread, nevertheless threw up no new forms of organization, discipline, and leadership. For lack of proper guidance, the movement of criticism from below failed to organize itself or to bring about a real transformation of social practices and relations.

(f) The ebbing of the mass movement

Under these conditions, the mass movement began to weaken toward the end of 1928. The accounts we have of it (mostly unfavorable to real change) give the impression that the workers' discontent found dispersed expression in individual acts: attacks by a few workers (usually youngsters, and sometimes Komsomols) on particular engineers, technicians, managers, etc. The situation was, however, one in which these more or less isolated acts were not looked on with disapproval by those workers who knew about them, including some Party members.

Through failing to rise to a new stage and through ceasing to be supported, the movement ran out of steam. True, at the end of 1928 the Eighth Congress of the Trade Unions voted a resolution providing for extension of the production conferences and temporary control commissions.[75] But these commissions played no great role, and even tended to disappear in 1929. As for the production conferences, while they were held more or less regularly, they performed only routine tasks.

In 1929, then, it was the struggle to consolidate existing relations that triumphed.

The speed with which the movement of criticism from below began to ebb may seem surprising. It is perhaps to be explained by the conjunction of a number of factors. First, the movement ceased to be supported by the Party's basic organizations, since emphasis had been laid once more upon the importance of factory discipline, and the basic trade-union organizations hesitated more and more to give their backing to initiatives which no longer enjoyed the Party's approval. Secondly, as we shall see, fresh powers were granted to the heads of enterprises, so that they now possessed more effective means to "restore discipline," and were encouraged to make use of them. Finally, the movement, which developed very unevenly, became divided and weakened when it no longer had support from the Bolshevik Party.

IV.   The struggle to consolidate existing relations and for a labor discipline imposed from above

What has been said already about the way with which the problem of fixing work norms was dealt has shown that, along with the struggle to transform existing relations, a struggle was also being waged for the maintenance and consolidation of these relations. From February 1929 on it was *this* struggle that played the principal role.

On February 21, 1929, the CC issued an appeal to all Party organizations to *concentrate all their efforts on strengthening labor discipline*.[76] On March 6, 1929, the Council of People's Commissars increased the disciplinary powers of managers.[77] They were called upon to penalize more strictly all breaches of regulations, and to inflict severe punishment on workers who did not conform to the orders of the management. Respect for factory discipline became for the workers a condition necessary if they were to obtain any social advantages—which included securing or retaining a place to live. The authority of the managements was further increased by a ban placed on interference by Party or trade-union organizations in matters connected with the management of enterprises.

The development of the struggle for discipline imposed from above and against any "interference" in the activity of management was closely bound up with the decision to go over to the realization of an accelerated industrialization plan, which was seen as the only answer to the agricultural difficulties which, from then on, the Party sought increasingly to solve through mechanization and collectivization. It was also bound up with the circumstance that this industrialization drive implied entry into the ranks of the working class of workers of peasant origin, toward whom the Bolshevik Party felt the same mistrust as toward the peasants in general.

The terms of the circular of February 21 were very explicit. It said that labor discipline was deteriorating as a result of "the attraction into production of new strata of workers, most of whom have ties with the country. Because of this, in most cases rural attitudes and private economic interests dominate these strata of workers. . . ."[78]

The Sixteenth Party Conference opened on April 26. One of the principal items on the agenda was adoption of the First Five-Year Plan (which the conference did indeed adopt) in its "optimal"—actually, maximal—version. Kuibyshev, one of the three rapporteurs on this item of the agenda, was the spokesman for the Party line. One highly important aspect of his report consisted of very firm declarations regarding reinforcement of labor discipline,[79] about which he repeated statements made by Lenin in 1918 in utterly different circumstances.

The toughening of labor discipline required far-reaching changes among the trade-union cadres, who, in 1928, had often associated themselves with struggles against the omnipotence of management. Such changes were all the more necessary because a number of these trade-union cadres (starting with Tomsky, the chairman of the Central Trades Union Council) had reserves about the targets of the industrialization plan, which, as they saw it, could only be carried through if an unacceptable intensification of labor and a lowering of real wages were imposed on the working class.

During the last months of 1928 the Party leadership attacked the positions of those who opposed increases in output norms imposed from above. In December 1928, at the Eighth Congress of the Trade Unions, these opponents, including Tomsky, found themselves in a minority. Kaganovich, a supporter of the tightening-up of labor discipline, entered the Trades Union Council to represent the Party Secretariat.

Tomsky wanted to resign from the CC at this moment, but his resignation was rejected.[80]

Between January and May 1929 the trades councils of the principal towns were reorganized. In May 1929 Tomsky was removed from the Central Trades Union Council, along with his closest supporters, which meant almost the entire central leadership of the trade unions. In the month that followed the changes of personnel spread to the chief trade-union federations, and then to the basic organizations of the unions.[81]

During 1929 the Party's activity in the sphere of industry was aimed mainly at strengthening labor discipline and restoring the authority of management.

The slogan of self-criticism did not disappear, of course, but hereafter it was linked closely with the slogan of emulation, and acquired an essentially "productionist" significance—a point to which I shall return.

At the beginning of September the CC took a decision aimed at ensuring strict application of the principle of one-person management, condemning tendencies on the part of Party and trade-union organizations to interfere in management matters. The manager and the administration were to be regarded as solely responsible for realizing the industrial and financial plan and fulfilling production tasks, and for this purpose full power was concentrated in their hands. The Party and trade-union organizations were called upon to strengthen the authority of managements. Political discussion during working hours was forbidden: enterprises must not be transformed into "parliaments."[82]

At the beginning of December 1929 changes were introduced into the organization of industry: all commercial and administrative functions were concentrated in large "Industrial Unions," so as to strengthen the system of one-person management at the level of the factories and workshops.[83]

Thus, the circle was closed. An end had been put to the unsettling of the system of one-person management which had accompanied the rise of the movement of criticism and self-criticism in the year 1928. The exigencies of the industrialization plan took precedence over the changing of production relations.

V. *Taylorism and socialist emulation*

During the NEP period the major aspect of the struggle against the reproduction of elements of capitalist production relations at the level of the immediate production process was constituted by the rise of the movement of criticism and self-criticism which developed in 1928 within the framework of the production conferences. As we have seen, however, this movement proved incapable of progressing beyond relatively narrow limits. Similar observations can be made regarding the movement aimed at developing a sort of "Soviet Taylorism."

(a) *The attempt to develop "Soviet Taylorism"*

At the heart of the immediate production process is the carrying out, by each worker who belongs to a production unit, of precise tasks which are linked with the tasks carried out by the other workers. The regular functioning of the production unit depends on the regularity of everyone's work.

With the development of capitalism, various procedures have been perfected by capital in order to subject each worker to a particular task and ensure that he carries out this task in the shortest possible time—procedures which tend increasingly to deprive the workers of all initiative and reduce them to mere cogs in a mechanism dominated by capital.

Marx revealed this inherent tendency in capital to try and subordinate the wage worker completely, intensifying its exploitation of labor power.

In *Capital* he notes:

Not only is the specialised work distributed among the different individuals, but the individual himself is divided up, and trans-

formed into the automatic motor of a detail operation. . . . The
knowledge, judgment and will which even though to a small
extent, are exercised by the independent peasant or handi-
craftsman . . . are faculties now required only for the workshop
as a whole. The possibility of intelligent direction of production
expands in one direction, because it vanishes in many others.
What is lost by the specialised workers is concentrated in the
capital which confronts them.[84]

The "scientific organization of work" conceived by the American engineer Taylor, and named "Taylorism" after him, was
the most highly developed form of the capitalist labor process
at the beginning of the twentieth century.[85] The Soviet government was confronted from the outset—and more so than
ever during the NEP period—with the problem of forms of
organizing work, and of the place that might be given to a
transformed "Taylorism," which would acquire a new significance and become "Soviet Taylorism."[86]

Well before the October Revolution Lenin produced the
notion of a sort of "socialist Taylorism." He wrote (in March
1924):

> The Taylor system—without its initiators knowing or wishing
> it—is preparing the time when the proletariat will take over all
> social production and appoint its own workers' committees for
> the purpose of properly distributing and rationalising all social
> labour. Large-scale production, machinery, railways, the
> telephone—all provide thousands of opportunities to cut by
> three-fourths the working time of the organised workers, and
> make them four times better off than they are today.[87]

Here we see appearing the conception of a *reversal of the
class effects of Taylorism*. Under the domination of capital,
the latter *expropriates* the workers' knowledge and reduces
them to subjection; under the Soviet regime, "Taylorism,"
taken over by the workers, ensures *reappropriation* by the
workers of a body of knowledge which they apply collectively
in order to master the process of production together.[88]

In Lenin's writings about the Taylor system between 1918
and 1922 two ideas constantly recur: that of the workers mastering technique and the "science of work," whereby they

would dominate the production process by learning to "work better," and that of a reduction in the working day, made possible by increased productivity, which would enable the workers to take charge of affairs of state in a concrete way. The attempts made to "transform" the Taylor system into a "Soviet" system failed. Outwardly, this failure was due to the existing forms of labor discipline and the role played by the one-and-only manager and the specialists who kept the direction and organization of the production process in their hands. More profoundly, it was due to the very nature of "Taylorism," which "codifies" the separation of manual from mental work (in conformity with the tendencies of the capitalist mode of production), and is therefore incapable of doing away with this separation, for that implies collective initiative in a continuous process of transforming the production process, and not merely the "appropriation" of "knowledge" formed on the basis of the preliminary separation of manual from mental work.

However, the failure to create "Soviet Taylorism" does not mean that the Soviet Union did not see repeated attempts to implement the Taylor system, or some elements of this system, on the initiative of various organs.

These attempts were often made by the managements of large enterprises, who promoted time-and-motion study and, on the basis of the results obtained, altered the way work was organized in the workshops and laid down norms for the fulfillment of the various tasks. (I shall come back later to this problem of the fixing of work norms, which cannot be identified merely with "Taylorism.")

The idea of a "Soviet Taylorism" to be undertaken by the workers themselves or by their organizations was, nevertheless, not lost sight of during the NEP period. At the end of 1922 the Central Trades Union Council set up a "central labour institute" for the purpose of popularizing "the scientific organisation of work" (NOT, from *Nauchnaya Organizatsiya Truda*). One of the heads of this institute, Gastev, was a former member of *Proletkult*.[89]

Not long after the foundation of this institute, another

former member of Proletkult, Kerzhentsev, denounced its activity, because he saw in it the devising of an instrument to exercise pressure on every worker. Kerzhentsev then formed the "League of Time," which he placed under the aegis of NOT but with the aim of developing *among the workers themselves* a movement for "more rational" use of time. The League blamed the CLI for trying to "civilise" the workers "from above," by "creating an aristocracy of the working class, the high priest of N.O.T."[90]

Eventually, in 1924, at the insistence of the Party leadership, the two movements merged, but, even when thus united, they failed to play much of a role. What they actually did was concerned much more with the introduction of a sort of speeded-up vocational training than with the organization of work and the establishment of work norms. The CLI claimed to be able to train a "skilled" worker in three months, instead of the twelve months required by the factory training schools. Its methods were approved by a resolution of the Party's CC on March 11, 1926.[91] What was actually involved, with a view to rapid industrialization, was the quick training of "detail workers" who were not given any overall view of technology.

At the beginning of 1928 Gastev, who was still the head of the CLI, confirmed this orientation when he said:

> The time has gone beyond recall when one could speak of the freedom of the worker in regard to the machine, and still more in regard to the enterprise as a whole. . . . Manoeuvres and motions at the bench, the concentration of attention, the movement of the hands, the position of the body, these elementary aspects of behaviour become the cornerstone. Here is the key to the new culture of work, the key to the serious cultural revolution.[92]

These conceptions of the CLI[93] were attacked by N. Chaplin, spokesman of the Komsomol, who declared that this institute wanted to turn the worker into a mere "adjunct of the machine, not a creator of socialist production," and that Gastev's ideas were the same as those of Ford, the American motor-car manufacturer.[94]

However, as a result of the pressure of the industrialization process in the form which it then took, the CLI's conceptions prevailed. They were approved, in practice, by the November 1928 meeting of the CC.[95] Finally, after the Sixteenth Party Conference, in April 1929, had approved the Five-Year Plan, criticism of these conceptions was no longer expressed, except episodically.

Actually, the role of the CLI in the organization of work and the fixing of norms remained minimal. Thus, in 1928, the *Outline of Political Economy* by Lapidus and Ostrovityanov mentioned the role which the institute *could* play, in raising output, in a situation when "the very methods used by the workers in their work are frequently out of date. . . . The productivity of labour also suffers by the fact that every worker executes several operations, and in doing so loses time in the changing of instruments and materials and the adaptation of machinery."[96]

On the eve of the abandonment of NEP the idea of a "Soviet Taylorism" had not been given up altogether, but no practical steps had been taken to implement it. What had taken shape was a wages system based on norms laid down by the heads of enterprises and the planning organs, under conditions that varied widely from case to case, and corresponding to a system of piece wages, often accompanied by bonuses.

(b) Piece wages and work norms

The question of piece wages is considered here as a factor in the immediate production process and a form whereby the agents of production are subjected to a certain pace and intensity of work. The general problem of the *wage relationship,* of its integration in a commodity-producing system, and of the effects of this system upon the general conditions of *social reproduction* will be examined in the course of subsequent chapters.

The first decisions establishing the framework regulating piece wages which continued to prevail during most of the

NEP period were taken in the autumn of 1921. On September 10 of that year a decree provided for wages to be fixed *by way of negotiation* between workers and the enterprises that employed them.[97]

This decision was linked with the establishment of the "financial autonomy" of enterprises (*khozraschet*), which will be discussed later. *It was explicitly aimed at relating the wages actually received by each worker to the "value" of what he produced.* It excluded from wages everything in the nature of "social maintenance," which was to be the responsibility of the state's organs and nothing to do with the separate enterprises. The state regulation of wages which existed under "war communism" was thus abolished, with the only regulation left in force being the state's fixing of a *minimum wage*.

Wage negotiations permitted the making of *individual contracts,* but, from November 1921 *collective agreements* were also negotiated between the trade unions, on the one hand, and, on the other, the managements of enterprises or the economic adminstrations.[98]

The arrangements thus made allowed the enterprises and the economic administrations to vary the numbers employed in accordance with the volume of production to be obtained, and to fix wages and work norms which would enable the enterprises to *cover their costs,* taking into account the *prices* at which they bought and sold.[99] Intervention by the trade unions did not always suffice to limit the effects, on wages and norms, of the right thus conferred on enterprises to vary them both.

The pressure brought to bear by the heads of enterprises to revise work norms in an upward direction (and so to reduce the actual earnings of those workers who were less successful in fulfilling the new norms) was felt more than once during the NEP period, even before the problems of achieving a rapid development of industry were faced.

From 1924 on the Bolshevik Party showed itself favorable to a *systematic extension of piece wages.* A resolution adopted by the CC in August of that year emphasized the need to increase the productivity of labor, required that there be *periodical revision of work norms and piece rates,* and called for removal of the existing restrictions on payment of bonuses for exceeding the norms.[100] The trade unions, which, up to that time, had maintained a certain reserve where piece wages were concerned, now declared themselves more and more in favor of an extensive use of material incentives.[101]

During the months that followed, the managements of enterprises carried out a general revision of work norms—without any improvement in equipment or even any serious modification in the way work was organized. In 1924–1925 the productivity of labor per person-day increased by 46 percent.[102]

The pressure for higher productivity of labor (above all, for higher intensity of labor) led to a substantial increase in industrial accidents: in the mines they rose from a rate of 1,095 per 10,000 in 1923–1924 to 1,524 per 10,000 in 1924–1925.[103] The extension of piece wages and the raising of the norms imposed by managements provoked strong resistance from the working class. At the end of 1925 the Fourteenth Party Congress recognized that mass strikes had taken place without the trade unions, the Party organs, or the economic organizations having been informed: "the trade unions' lack of concern for the workers" was condemned, together with the "unnatural bloc between trade unions, the Party and the Red managers."[104]

The workers' resistance to revision of the norms had as its chief consequence an upward revision of wage rates. Workers' earnings increased by between 10 and 30 percent in 1924–1925. In September 1925 the actual average monthly wage was 51 roubles, whereas the average wage provided for by Gosplan for September 1926 was 48 roubles.[105] This is a fact of great importance: it shows clearly that *the actual level of wages depended more directly upon the course of workers' struggles than upon the decisions taken by the planning organs.*

In fact, these increases in wages appear to have been the price that the managements of enterprises had to pay in order to get acceptance of what then seemed the main concern, namely, generalization of the system of norms and piece wages. And this generalization did indeed make progress. In 1925 between 50 and 60 percent of the workers in large-scale industry and mining were paid at piece rates.[106] In 1928 an inquiry carried out in a certain number of large-scale industries showed that between 60 and 90 percent of the workers were on piece rates.[107]

The extension of piece wages also encountered a certain amount of resistance within the Party. This began among the rank and file, with Communists joining in "unofficial strikes" and being threatened with expulsion for doing so,[108] but it was expressed also in leading circles, even among those who supported the line of the majority in the Political Bureau. Thus, at the end of 1925, at the Fourteenth Party Congress, A. Andreyev, while supporting the resolution in favor of piece wages, described this system as a capitalist method which had to be made use of for the time being, "because of the technical inferiority of our equipment."[109]

During the entire NEP period, indeed, resort to payment at piece rates was basically regarded as a transient measure dictated by circumstances. This attitude was still being given clear expression in 1928 by Lapidus and Ostrovityanov, when they wrote that lack of labor discipline among the workers

> forces the Soviet organs (in agreement with the trade unions) to ensure that the very forms of wages should incite them to increased diligence. *This explains the existence of standards of output and piece-work payment in Soviet state industry.* Obviously, in distinction from the capitalist system, these measures are of a temporary character in Soviet Russia; as the socialist consciousness of the worker is developed and as the old individualist outlook is outlived, both piecework and the compulsory minimum standard will become unnecessary.[110]

The implications of the system of norms and piece rates obviously varied in accordance with the concrete conditions under which the norms and rates were determined. From this point of view the year 1926—the first year of the "reconstruction period," which saw the start of a policy of accelerated industrial development—was a *decisive year*.

Until then, the norms and the wage rates corresponding to them had mainly been fixed by collective agreements (at the level of branches of industry, of regions, of trusts or of enterprises) which gave rise to very little argument between the economic organs and the trade unions, and had to take into account the reactions of the workers concerned, who were probably consulted—at production conferences, for instance. The fixing of rates and norms was thus directly influenced, up to a certain point, by the concrete conditions in which the production units functioned and by the attitudes taken up by the workers in these units. In spite of this, the economic organs (which were called upon by the Party to bring down the cost of production) were far from heeding the workers' aspirations, to which the unions (often connected with the managements of enterprises) gave only partial expression, and so it happened that the norms were increased to such an extent that the workers' monthly earnings suffered reduction. This was the case in 1926, when the Party, in a declaration issued on August 16, denounced the "masked wage-reductions" which had been effected in this way.[111]

The Party then decided to take charge of the decisive factors in the fixing of wages, so that the establishment of norms and wage rates became *the result of decisions taken previously at the highest level,* and the role of the collective agreements was considerably reduced.

After September 1926 the procedure followed was formally this. The PB, after discussion with the VSNKh and the trade unions, fixed the growth rates for the coming year so far as productivity and wages were concerned, together with the relations between them, and these rates then became part of the economic plan. Collective agreements came into the picture only in a second phase. They were concluded between the industrial trusts and the corresponding unions, and took account of the planned targets, being concerned not merely with wages, as had been the case up to then, but also with productivity and production norms.

As a result of this procedure, norms came increasingly to be fixed without regard to the concrete conditions under which enterprises functioned, and their actual organization. They tended to become a constraint imposed from above upon the agents of the production process. Collective agreements became mainly a mere means of confirming and specifying the targets which had been laid down as a whole by the planning organs.

During the last months of 1926 the trade-union press published a number of articles expressing fear lest collective agreements be transformed into instruments for imposing on the workers wage rates, norms, and working conditions which had been decided, in practice, by the economic plan, without regard to any negotiations.[112]

What was to be seen, in fact, in 1926, the first year of the period of industrial reconstruction, was *a process of increasing restriction of the role played by the trade unions and the trade-union committees in the enterprises* in the fixing of wages and working conditions. In 1927 there were conflicts over this issue between the unions and the VSNKh, which were settled by the Commissariat of Labor. In October 1927 the VSNKh and the Central Trades Union Council declared their intention to solve by common consent the problems arising from the roles played by the plan and by collective agreements, respectively, in the fixing of wages and norms. Collective agreements continued, in principle, to be discussed in the factories, but at meetings which were held in order to impart information, not to take decisions.

During 1927–1928 these workers' meetings exercised a certain amount of influence upon the content of the collective agreements, but from the autumn of 1928 on, when the principle of one-person management was reinforced, their role was reduced. In autumn 1928 the pre-eminence of the plan over collective agreements was affirmed by Gosplan and the Commissariat of Labor. Thereafter, when collective agreements were concluded, discussion of norms and wage rates played only a secondary role.[113]

Nevertheless, the reduction in the role of the trade unions and the collective agreements in the fixing of norms and wages cannot be equated with "establishment of control" by the planning organs over the movement of wages and of productivity. The workers, though no longer called upon to participate concretely in the fixing of wages and work norms, resisted to some extent such increases in productivity as they considered unacceptable, and often succeeded in securing wages that were higher than had been provided for by the plans. The disparities between the "targets" of the plans and the actual evolution of wages and output enable us to perceive one aspect of the workers' struggles, although these disparities were due not only to such struggles, but also to defects in the way production and the supply of raw materials to enterprises was organized, and the unrealistic character of some of the tasks laid down by the plans, which had not been submitted to genuine mass discussion in the enterprises.

In all events, the way of fixing production norms which became increasingly predominant toward the end of the NEP period—in connection with the aims of a rapid process of industrialization conceived in a centralized way at the level of the state's technical organs—was not favorable either to realism in planning or to support by the mass of the workers for the targets fixed where output and wages were concerned. The bottlenecks resulting from this state of affairs were a cause of internal imbalances in industry and failures to fulfill the plans for reducing industrial costs,[114] and this increased the contradictions between industry and agriculture and between industry's need for finance and its capacity to accumulate. These factors contributed to aggravating the final crisis of NEP. Moreover, the introduction of piece rates, material incentives, and wage differentials brought about splits within working groups. It strengthened individualism and led to demands for wage increases, because the lower-paid workers found their position all the less acceptable when they saw that others were getting much higher wages for the same number of hours' work.

(c) Splits in the working groups and inequality of wages

The inequality of wages that existed under the NEP corresponded not merely to the introduction of piece rates but also, and more profoundly, to the hierarchical structure of the "collective laborer," to *the very form of the labor process and the type of differentiation that existed between the agents of production.*

This differentiation had its orgins in history (in the form of the labor process in the former capitalist enterprises and its effects on the structure of the working class), but it was reproduced and transformed under the impact of class struggles. These either modified or consolidated the historically given structures of the labor process. In view of the inadequacy of the information we possess concerning the changes, or the absence of changes, in the characteristics of the labor processes, a study of the way wage differentials evolved can provide us with valuable pointers in this regard.

The first thing we observe is that the introduction of NEP and resumption of industrial production was accompanied by a widening of the spread of wage levels, which tended to copy the prewar pattern. Thus, whereas in 1920 (a year when industry was almost paralyzed) a skilled worker earned, on the average, only 4 percent more than an unskilled laborer, in 1922 the gap between their respective earnings was 65 percent.[115] In 1924 the first category of wages was, on the average, twice as large as the second.[116] These overall figures can be illustrated from an investigation carried out in a foundry in Moscow in March 1924, which showed that an unskilled laborer earned 16 to 40 roubles a month, whereas a founder earned 31.95. In this same enterprise, a head of a department earned 79.67 roubles, and the manager of the whole enterprise 116.08 roubles.[117] Moreover, the heads of enterprises received special bonuses and percentages and enjoyed various benefits in kind. At that time there were, in general, seventeen levels of wages, and the ratio of the lowest to the highest was 1:5. It could even be 1:8, with the highest rates being paid to the administrative and technical personnel.[118]

Between 1924 and 1926 inequalities in wages tended to increase, being accentuated by the practice of paying piece wages and awarding bonuses. A struggle developed between those who were for reducing these inequalities and those who saw them as corresponding to a "necessity." Thus, in March 1926, at the Seventh Congress of the Komsomol, one of the leaders of this organization declared: "Among the young . . . the tendency toward equalisation is highly developed: to make all workers, skilled and unskilled, equal. The mood is such that young workers come to us and say that we do not have state enterprises, enterprises of a consistently socialist type as defined by Lenin, but that what we have is exploitation."[119]

According to an investigation carried out in March 1926, workers' wages were often between 13 and 20 roubles a month, while a manager could be getting as much as 400 roubles (plus various material privileges in the form of housing, a car, and so on). For technicians and managers who were Party members the level of wages was usually a little lower, but on the average it came to 187.9 roubles for managers.[120]

The Seventh Trades Union Congress (December 1926) echoed the discontent of the less skilled workers. Tomsky, chairman of the Central Trades Union Council, said in this connection: "In future we must work towards reducing the gap between the wages of the skilled worker and those of the ordinary worker."[121]

No clear line on this question emerged at that time. Whereas in 1927 the position of the trade unions and that of the Congress of Soviets tended to favor a reduction in inequality, the Fifth Komsomol Conference condemned the "egalitarian aspirations" of the "backward sections of working-class youth."[122]

Toward the end of the NEP period the differences in wages obtaining in the working class constituted a source of division and discontent, especially among the youth. At the Eighth Komsomol Congress a delegate did not shrink from saying that some workers were "strutting about like peacocks" while others were almost "beggars."[123] At the end of 1928 the Eighth Trades Union Congress tried to deal afresh with the problem, but the Party, which was more and more concerned with encouraging a larger number of workers to learn a trade, condemned the critical attitude to differentials. As we know, the trade-union leadership elected by this Eighth Congress was eliminated in 1929. A few years later, the positions adopted by the Eighth Trades Union Congress were to be stigmatized as the symptom of an "extensive development of petty-bourgeois egalitarianism."[124]

Generally speaking, despite some contrary currents due mainly to pressure exerted by the worst-off strata of the working class, and by the youth, it was the tendency to consolidate inequality in wages that predominated during the NEP period. This tendency was linked with the reproduction of hierarchical forms in the immediate production process, but it was also reinforced by certain ideological notions, two of which were particularly important.

The first of these related to a distinction that was frequently drawn between workers who had been in industry for a long time and had acquired a trade, and those who were more or less "casual workers," laborers recently arrived from the country, often destined to return there, and still impregnated with "peasant mentality." It was essentially the first of these categories that the Party and the trade unions looked upon as the "real proletariat," whose material interests (and so, whose comparatively high wages) had to be defended: they constituted the firmest pillar of Soviet power. The material interests of the other workers often seemed like those of a mere semi-proletariat, which ought, of course, to be safeguarded, but more for reasons of social justice than for strictly political reasons.

The second of these notions tended to cause a relatively large differentiation between wages to lie accepted as "necessary." This differentiation was usually justified by reference to the "technical level," the decisive role of the skilled workers in a production process which was still of a semihandicraft nature, with machines and mechanization entering into it very little. This notion was expressed, for example, in December 1926 by Tomsky at the Seventh Trades Union Congress. After commenting that in the USSR wage differentials were "colossal" and not to be compared with those observable in Western Europe, he added: "One of the causes [of this situation] is that our technical equipment is still very backward. Individual skill, craft tradition and so on still play too big a role: the automatic machines which simplify the worker's task and bring in automatic methods are too little used."[125]

The predominant factor justifying the big differences in wage levels thus seemed to be "technical" in character, and so reduction of these differences seemed to depend mainly on "development of the productive forces."

(d) Socialist emulation

Although what was characteristic of the NEP was a strong tendency to reproduction of the existing forms of the production process, some movements did develop which, to varying degrees, sought to challenge these forms, or seemed capable of doing this. This was one significance of the attempts made to develop a "Soviet Taylorism,"[126] and, even more so, of the struggles in the first months of 1928 directed toward effecting a certain change in production relations.

For a time, the development of *socialist emulation,* too, seemed likely to lead to a challenge to the existing form of the production process. This was mainly true of the period from 1926 until the second half of 1928. The development in question deserves to be examined, even if only cursorily, for it is all the richer in lessons because the defeat suffered by the revolutionary aspects of the movement, and the reasons for this defeat, were closely linked with the final crisis of the NEP.

The movement for socialist emulation was, at the start, an attempt by the advanced elements of the working class to take in hand *certain factors in the production process,* so as to speed up the growth of industrial production. It had, undoubtedly, a "productionist" aspect, but at the same time it indirectly called into question the authority of management and of the technical cadres.[127] It originated as a movement led by a section of the young workers and encouraged by the Komsomol. This was the situation in the autumn of 1926.[128]

During 1927 the leading economic organs, especially the VSNKh, increasingly came to see in this movement a means of raising the productivity of labor while keeping within financially tolerable bounds the investment effort

called for by the two variants of the First Five-Year Plan that
were then being drawn up. It was principally a matter of
encouraging the workers to increase the *intensity* of labor, but
also to "rationalize" the production process: this was, indeed,
a period when the active role of the production conferences
was developing.

In the autumn of 1927, however, the components and characteristics of the movement of socialist emulation tended to
alter: rank-and-file initiatives were gradually pushed into the
background by systematic intervention on the part of the central economic organs, which called for "emulation between
heads of enterprises, trusts, etc."[129] In this way emulation on
the national scale and emulation at the local level were organized as parallel processes. On its part, the Komsomol continued to promote a socialist emulation that mainly took the
form of "Communist Saturdays," when workers worked without pay, and of undertakings to increase production or to carry
out exceptional tasks, these undertakings being adopted by
teams or groups of workers who formed "brigades" of "shockworkers" (*udarniki*).

It is very hard to distinguish, in the movement which developed in 1928, between the element of genuine enthusiasm,
and sometimes of challenge to the authority of the heads of
enterprises, and the element of mere adhesion to a productivity campaign organized from above, which the workers felt
more or less obliged to support.

In any case, in the summer of 1927 the movement was given
a certain institutional character by the creation, through a
decree of July 27, of the title of "Hero of Labor." This was,
moreover, no mere title: attached to it were material advantages such as exemption from taxes, priority in getting somewhere to live, a pension, and so on.[130]

The drift toward a more "managerial" form of emulation is
to be seen in the decree of June 14, 1928, which credited an
enterprise with between 25 and 50 percent of the savings
realized through emulation, and charged the head of the enterprise with responsibility for using this credit in conforming
with certain guidelines relating mainly to "rationalization" of

production and improvement in the conditions of labor.[131]

September 1928 saw the creation of the order of the Red Banner of Labor, which could be awarded not only to individuals but also to enterprises, institutions, and groups of workers.[132]

On the eve of the official adoption of the First Five-Year Plan—and even more so after it had been adopted—the "productionist" character of the socialist emulation campaign was accentuated. The publication in *Pravda* on January 20, 1929, of a previously unpublished article by Lenin (which he had written in January 1918 but had decided not to publish at the time of the Brest-Litovsk negotiations), entitled "How to Organise Competition?"[133] was the starting point of a vast campaign for organizing shock-brigades and signing pledges to exceed work norms. Thereafter, a large number of factories and mines entered the emulation campaign, which became combined with the drive launched since the end of 1928 to tighten up labor discipline.

The dual aspect of this movement for emulation was well reflected in the article by Stalin which *Pravda* published on May 22, 1929. He showed that socialist emulation could be based only on the enthusiasm of the working masses, on the "energy, initiative and independent activity of the masses," and that it must liberate "the colossal reserves latent in the depths of our system";[134] but Stalin also mentioned in this article that the emulation movement was threatened by those who sought to "canalise" it, to "centralise" it, to "deprive it of its most important feature—the *initiative* of the masses."[135]

In actuality, the "centralizing" aspect ultimately triumphed over the "mass initiative" aspect. The latter was held back by the limits imposed upon it by the principle of one-person management, the targets of a plan decided from above, and the "technical regulations" laid down by the engineers.

Gradually, emulation came to have the effect of setting against each other different groups of workers, and even individual workers: the "best performances" were used by the heads of enterprises to revise work norms upward and increase the intensity of labor. The Soviet press of the time mentioned cases of this sort, in order to condemn them,[136] but this did not prevent them from recurring. The warnings put out by the Trades Union Council[137] provided no more serious an obstacle to this tendency, which was encouraged by the fact that the leading economic organs were calling on the enterprises to "overfulfill" the plan.

Production did indeed increase, but the Central Trades Union Council declared that this increase was being achieved at the cost of "violation of the labour laws and collective agreements and worsening of the situation of the working class."[138]

Toward the end of 1929 the distortions undergone by "socialist emulation" caused growing discontent among the workers, for the raising of the norms entailed a reduction in the earnings of those who could not fulfill them, while "production commitments" undertaken without genuine consultation of the masses led managements to cancel the workers' rest days over a period of several weeks.[139]

The reports in the Smolensk archives show that from May 1929 on there were numerous manifestations of workers' dissatisfaction with the "production commitments" and increased work norms decided upon one-sidedly by the managements of their places of work. This dissatisfaction even gave rise to strikes, especially in the mines.[140] A general report "on the position of the working class in the Western Region" shows that, very often, the workers were not even kept informed of "production commitments," or of the "challenges" that their enterprises threw down: they did not know what was expected of them, but they were aware that the norms had been increased without any increase in wages, and they consequently took up a negative attitude.[141] This report concludes:

> Such attitudes can be attributed in the first place to workers who are connected with agriculture and who have recently come to the factories. This category participates least of all in productive life and to some degree influences the backward workers. It is necessary to say that at the present moment, in connexion with the survey of socialist competition *which has been carried out in*

the enterprises by the economic organs and their apparatuses, in
a number of places there is exceptional apathy and sluggish-
ness.[142]

The situation thus described prevailed in most regions toward the end of 1929. This situation was closely connected
with the fact that the fixing of production targets had become
to an ever greater degree a "management concern," and that
managements had become involved in a sort of "targets race"
which developed far away from the reality of the workshops,
building sites, and mines, a circumstance that favored the
flourishing of unrealistic aims. That period saw the "growth"
of a whole series of production targets, with consequent revision of the plans: thus, the target for production of steel,
which, under the original plan, was to have reached 10 million
metric tons at the end of the Five-Year Plan, "grew" to 17
million metric tons.[143] In the eyes of the workers who were
familiar with the realities involved, this target was unlikely to
be achieved—and, in fact, it was not achieved.[144]

The fixing of unrealizable targets had a negative effect on
the enthusiasm of most of the workers. Enthusiasm did not
entirely evaporate, of course, but it became confined to a
minority who were capable of making great efforts which
enabled them to beat production records. This, however, was
not enough to sustain a real emulation campaign developing
on a mass scale.

In the end, the emulation movement which, at the outset,
had seemed the possible starting point of a genuine transformation of the labor process, did not really develop in that
direction. It did not become that *"communist method of
building socialism,* on the basis of the maximum activity of the
vast masses of the working people" which Stalin had spoken
of in his article of May 22, 1929.[145] It did not bring a large-
scale liberation of new productive forces.

The revolutionary aspect of the emulation movement
gradually died out, through not taking as its target a radical
transformation of production relations. Increasingly, it was
directed toward quantitative production targets, and was taken
over by the heads of enterprises and the economic ap-

paratuses. They used it above all as a means to secure revision of work norms. It thus became an instrument for intensifying labor—hence the indifference and even sometimes the hostility of a section of the workers toward a movement which was not in any deep sense their own.[146]

The reasons for the setback to the mass character of the movement were many. Most important was the one-sidedly "productionist" aspect which it came to assume, as a whole, and which led to its subordination, above all, to the existing relations of hierarchy and discipline, which were even strengthened after the end of 1928. The profound split within the working groups—between a minority of skilled workers enjoying prestige, responsibility, and incomes markedly higher than the others, and a majority of unskilled workers, often looked upon with mistrust (because of their peasant origin) and restricted to poorly paid fragmentary tasks—was also an important obstacle to transforming the emulation movement into a genuine mass movement. This split was closely bound up with the hierarchical general structure of the enterprises and the role assigned to the managers and engineers.

The socialist emulation movement failed, therefore, to lead to a socialist transformation of the productive forces. The concept of such a transformation was, indeed, never clearly formulated at that time, even though it was hinted at, for example, by Stalin when he spoke of "the colossal reserves latent in the depths of our system."[147]

Under these conditions, a revolutionary transformation of the production relations and of the productive forces could not take place. The growth of industrial production turned out to be fundamentally dependent on the accumulation of new means of production, the modernizing of equipment, the maintenance and development of material incentives (piece rates, bonuses, etc.). All this led to the adoption of a plan for extremely heavy investment in industry—which industry was incapable of financing from its own resources. In this way the burdens that the Soviet state's economic policy tended to lay upon the peasantry were made heavier, and the contradictions between town and country characteristic of the final crisis of the NEP were intensified.

In order to appreciate more fully the specific forms assumed by the aggravation of contradictions within the industrial sector itself, we need to analyze the way in which state-owned industry was integrated in the general process of reproduction of the conditions of production.

Notes

1. See above, p. 77.
2. Calculated from *Kontrolnye tsifry (1929–1930)*, pp. 422–423.
3. See below, pp. 275 ff.
4. M. Dobb, *Soviet Economic Development*, p. 143.
5. See volume I of the present work, especially pp. 464 ff.
6. See Marx, in *The Poverty of Philosophy*, where he blames Proudhon for putting in the forefront the juridical form of property (Marx and Engels, *Collected Works*, vol. 6, p. 197: "to define bourgeois property is nothing else than to give an exposition of all the social relations of bourgeois production. To try to give a definition of property as of an independent relation . . . can be nothing but an illusion of metaphysics or jurisprudence." See Marx's letter to Annenkov, December 28, 1846: "In the real world, . . . the division of labour and all M. Proudhon's other categories are social relations forming in their entirety what is known today as property; outside these relations, bourgeois property is nothing but a metaphysical or juristic illusion" [Marx and Engels, *Selected Correspondence*, p. 44]).
7. See volume 1 of the present work, pp. 155 ff.
8. Lenin, *CW*, vol. 27, p. 259: "The Immediate Tasks of the Soviet Government."
9. Ibid., pp. 249, 268.
10. Lapidus and K. Ostrovityanov, *Outline*, p. 472.
11. Ibid.
12. *VKP(b) v rezolyutsiyakh* (1941), pp. 626–629, quoted in Carr, *Socialism*, vol. I, p. 387.
13. *Torgovo-Promyshlennaya Gazeta*, August 23–26, 1926.
14. *K.P.S.S. v rezolyutsiyakh*, vol. 2, pp. 316–317, 319–320. The workers' resistance to revision of the norms led at that time to stoppages and strikes which were not authorized by the trade unions.

15. *VII-oy Syezd Professionalnykh Soyuzov SSSR* (1927), pp. 467, 745.

16. *Direktivy K.P.S.S. i Sovyetskogo Pravitelstva po khozyaistven-nym voprosam* (1957), vol. I, pp. 666–672, and Carr and Davies, *Foundations*, vol. I, pt. 1, pp. 341–342, and pt. 2, p. 492.

17. *Torgovo-Promyshelennaya Gazeta*, August 18, 1927.

18. *Trud*, January 6, 1928.

19. Lenin, *CW*, vol. 33, pp. 184 ff.

20. Ibid., vol. 33, p. 189.

21. Ibid.

22. Ibid.

23. Ibid., vol. 33, pp. 190–191.

24. Ibid., vol. 33, p. 190.

25. Ibid., vol. 33, p. 191.

26. *K.P.S.S. v rezolyutsiyakh*, vol. I, p. 792 (my emphasis—C. B.).

27. *V.K.P.(b.) v profsoyuzakh* (1940), pp. 236–240, quoted in Carr, *Socialism*, vol. I, p. 400, n.1.

28. *K.P.S.S. v rezolyutsiyakh*, vol. 2, p. 65. "Management devia-tion" is given as an approximate translation of the Russian expression *khozyaistvenny uklon*.

29. In its issue of July 15, 1926, the journal *Bolshevik* noted that during 1925 the production-conference movement had suffered a decline and had been looked on with disfavor as encouraging a "management deviation" (pp. 45–58).

30. *K.P.S.S. v rezolyutsiyakh*, p. 99.

31. Stalin, *Works*, vol. 8, pp. 147–148. It will be observed that the production conferences are not assigned any managerial functions. Their role was, above all, to give aid and support to the Party and the government.

32. *Istorichesky Arkhiv*, no. 2 (1960), pp. 89–90, quoted in Carr and Davies, *Foundations*, vol. I, pt. 2, p. 569.

33. *Trud*, July 18, 1926.

34. These were the resolution "On the Country's Economic Situa-tion and the Tasks of the Party" (*K.P.S.S. v rezolyutsiyakh*, vol. 2, pp. 173 ff., especially sec. 3, pp. 177–179); and the resolution on the trade unions (ibid., p. 191 ff.), which included fairly detailed passages on the production meetings (ibid., pp. 196–199).

35. Ibid., p. 179. The term "direct participation" is noteworthy, in that it marks a break with the resolution of the Eleventh Con-gress: see above, p. 216 ff.

36. Ibid., p. 198.

37. Ibid., p. 177.

38. Ibid., p. 190.

39. *XV-taya Konferentsiya VKP(b)* (1927), pp. 276–283, 298–299, 317, 346–347, 356, 408–410; quoted in Carr and Davies, *Foundations,* vol. I, pt. 2, p. 570, ns. 1 and 2.

40. *VII-oy Syezd Professionalnykh Soyuzov SSSR* (1927), pp. 58–59.

41. *XVI-taya Konferentsiya VKP(b)* (1962), p. 814, n. 279; quoted in Carr and Davies, *Foundations*, vol. I, pt. 2, p. 570, n.6.

42. *K.P.S.S. v rezolyutsiyakh*, vol. 2, pp. 383–384.

43. Stalin, *Works*, vol. 11, pp. 30 ff.

44. Ibid., p. 37.

45. Ibid., pp. 39–41.

46. Ibid., pp. 57 ff.

47. Ibid., pp. 73 ff.

48. Carr and Davies, *Foundations,* vol. I, pt. 2, pp. 580 ff.

49. The Smolensk archives enable us to obtain an overall view of what was called at the time the "Smolensk scandal." They show that 13.1 percent of all Party members in the region were expelled as a result of scandal. The investigations carried out on behalf of the CCC revealed the corruption prevailing among some of the provincial cadres, while others were convicted of "drunkenness" and "sexual license." The reports of these investigations showed that in one of the most important factories in the region the women workers had "to submit to the foreman's demands," while, in another, seven workers had killed themselves owing to the indifferent attitude of the Party leaders to their complaints. This "affair" gave rise to an inquiry by the CC, which held numerous meetings in various factories in the region (Fainsod, *Smolensk*, pp. 48–52).

50. Stalin, *Works,* vol. 11, p. 74.

51. Ibid., p. 75.

52. Ibid., p. 75.

53. Ibid., pp. 75–76 (my emphasis—C. B.).

54. Ibid., pp. 76–78.

55. This shift of emphasis is clearly apparent if we compare the orientations of spring 1928, regarding the need for criticism of the cadres, engineers, administrators, etc. (not excluding criticism which was "only 5 or 10 percent true" [ibid., p. 36]), with the warnings against a mistrustful attitude to heads of enter-

prises and economic organizations contained in the report of April 13, 1926 in which Stalin appealed for these leaders to be "surrounded by an atmosphere of confidence," and for avoidance of excessive readiness to criticize them—"a bad habit [that] must be dropped once and for all" (Stalin, *Works*, vol. 8, p. 146).

56. Stalin, *Works*, vol. 11, p. 62; p. 376, n. 14.
57. One of the resolutions adopted by the plenum of April 6–11, 1928, provided for changes in the management of enterprises. However, the scope of these changes was limited (*K.P.S.S. v rezolyutsiyakh*, vol. 2, pp. 386–387).
58. Stalin, *Works*, vol. 11, p. 63 (my emphasis—C. B.).
59. Ibid., pp. 63–64.
60. The Smolensk inquiry revealed numerous cases of this sort. At Shakhty the inquiry showed that the limitation of the working day in the mines to six hours was often not respected, any more than were certain safety regulations (ibid., p. 64).
61. This manifesto was read on October 15, 1927, by Rykov, then chairman of the Sovnarkom, to the TsK of the USSR (*Pravda*, October 16 and 18, 1927).
62. The archives of the Smolensk Regional Committee of the Party show that this committee had to deal with workers' discontent when the transition to three-shift work was made. A factory in this region sent a delegation to Moscow to protest, and workers' meetings demanded that the measure be rescinded. It is not known what response was given to these demands, but we do know that they were numerous (Fainsod, *Smolensk*, pp. 51–52).
63. On these points see Carr and Davies, *Foundations*, vol. 1, pt. 2, pp. 500–504.
64. Such complaints are to be found in the journal of the VSNKh (*Torgovo-Promyshlennaya Gazeta*), for example in the issue of October 16, 1928, and in the official economic journal *Ekonomicheskoye obozreniye*. See Carr and Davies, *Foundations*, vol. I, pt. 2, pp. 508–509.
65. Production by VSNKh-planned industry rose by 16.6 percent in 1926–1927, 26.3 percent in 1927–1928, and 23.7 percent in 1928–1929 (*Kontrolnye tsifry 1929–1930 gg.*, pp. 422–423, 503).
66. *Prepriyatiye*, no. 12 (1928), p. 12. The journal refers to the "one-person responsibility" of the manager, alleged to be threatened with replacement by that of "the electors."
67. *Pravda*, June 26, 1928, in Stalin, *Works*, vol. 11, pp. 133 ff.
68. Stalin, *Works*, vol. 11, p. 138.

69. Ibid., pp. 140–141.
70. Ibid., p. 139.
71. Ibid., p. 139.
72. Ibid., pp. 139–140.
73. Ibid., p. 143.
74. *Torgovo-Promyshlennaya gazeta.*, November 30, 1928.
75. *VIII-oy Syezd Professionalnykh Soyuzov SSSR* (1929), pp. 527–528.
76. *Direktivy* (1957), vol. 2, pp. 18–19.
77. *Resheniya partii i pravitelstva*, pp. 125–131, quoted in R. Lorenz, *Das Ende der Neuer Ökonomischer Politik*, p. 213 and p. 274, n. 3. This writer also quotes A. Etchin, *O yedinonachalii.*
78. See note 76 above; also Fainsod, *Smolensk*, p. 309; and the remarks made on this subject by Robert Linhart, in *Lénine, les paysans, Taylor*, pp. 167–168, n. 1.
79. *XVI-taya Konferentsiya VKP(b)*, (1962), pp. 72–73.
80. See also below, pp. 346 ff.
81. *Trud*, March 29; May 16; June 8, 11, and 20, 1929, quoted in S. Schwarz, *Les Ouvriers en Union Soviétique*, pp. 503–505. (This French edition of *Labor in the Soviet Union* contains a new appendix dealing with the purging of the trade unions in 1929.)
82. *Resheniya*, pp. 125–131, quoted in Lorenz, *Das Ende*, p. 214.
83. *Resheniya*, pp. 136–142.
84. Marx, *Capital (London), vol. I*, p. 482.
85. A clear analysis of the "Taylor system" will be found in Harry Braverman, *Labor and Monopoly Capital*, pp. 85 ff.
86. In his *Lénine, les paysans, Taylor*, Robert Linhart deals with a number of aspects of this question; see especially pp. 77 ff.
87. Lenin, *CW*, vol. 20, p. 154.
88. See Linhart, *Lénine*, pp. 102, 110 ff., 134 ff.
89. E. H. Carr, *The Interregnum*, p. 84, n. 4, and *Socialism*, vol. 1, p. 383.
90. *Trud*, February 20 and 22, 1924.
91. *Direktivy*, vol. 1 (1957), pp. 568–569.
92. *Pravda*, February 10, 1928, quoted in Carr and Davies, *Foundations*, vol. I, pt. 2, p. 478.
93. It is to be observed that the supporters of these views could avail themselves of certain formulations by Marx and Engels, especially what Engels wrote, during the winter of 1872–1873, in his article "On Authority": "The automatic machinery of a big factory is much more despotic than the small capitalists who employ workers have ever been. . . . If man, by dint of his

knowledge and inventive genius, has subdued the forces of nature, the latter avenge themselves upon him by subjecting him, in so far as he employs them, to a veritable despotism independent of all social organisation" (*Marx, Engels and Lenin on Anarchism and Anarcho-Syndicalism*, pp. 101–102). In this formulation, which expresses the correct view that "one can command Nature only by obeying it," no account is taken of the *form* under which the production processes give material embodiment to scientific knowledge. As Marx frequently recalls, however, this form, and therefore also the nature of technical changes, is dominated by social relations.

94. Chaplin's speech at the Eighth Komsomol Congress, quoted in Carr and Davies, *Foundations*, vol. I, pt. 2, p. 479.

95. *V.K.P.(b) v rezolyutsiyakh*, vol. 2, p. 305. Subsequent editions of this work do not reprint this resolution. See Carr and Davies, *Foundations*, vol. I, pt. 2, p. 479, n. 5.

96. Lapidus and Ostrovityanov, *Outline*, pp. 129–130.

97. Carr, *The Bolshevik Revolution*, vol. 2, pp. 319–320.

98. Ibid., p. 321.

99. Consequently wages were at that time higher in enterprises which could charge high prices (as was then the case with the textile industry) than in others, such as the iron and steel industry. See A. G. Rashin, *Zarabotnaya plata na vostanovitelny period khozyaistva SSSR*.

100. *K.P.S.S. v rezolyutsiyakh*, vol. I., pp. 902–905.

101. On the attitude of the trade unions, see *Trud*, August 23, and September 17, 1924, and the discussions at the Sixth Congress of the Trade Unions (*IV-oy Syezd Professionalnykh Soyuzov SSSR* 1925). These discussions show that a minority of the delegates were still opposed to unrestricted extension of piece wages. From February 1925 (see *Trud*, February 4, 1925) the trade unions plunged into a campaign for piece wages to be introduced on the widest possible scale (see Carr, *Socialism*, vol. I, p. 390, n. 4).

102. *Planovoye Khozyaistvo*, no. 2 (1926), p. 54; and Y. S. Rozenfeld, *Promyshlennaya Politika SSSR*, p. 361; Carr, *Socialism*, vol. I, pp. 391–392.

103. *Leningradskaya Pravda*, August 2, 1925, quoted in Carr, *Socialism*, vol. I, pp. 392–393.

104. *XIV-y Syezd VKP(b)* (1926), pp. 722–729, 785. The strikes referred to were "unofficial" strikes, not recognized by the unions

and not reflected in statistics. Between 1924 and 1925 the number of workers "officially" on strike hardly increased and remained small: 43,000 in 1925, as against 42,000 in 1924 (*VII-oy Syezd Professionalnykh Soyuzov SSSR* [1927], p. 90). The number of strikes officially recorded was small: 267 in 1924 (151 of which in state-owned enterprises) and 196 in 1925 (of which 99 occurred in state-owned enterprises). We have even less information regarding the actual number and scope of strikes in subsequent years.

105. *Planovoye Khozyaistvo*, no. 1 (1926), p. 40, quoted in Carr, *Socialism*, vol. I, p. 395.

106. *Sotsialisticheskoye Stroitelstvo SSSR* (1934), p. 337. According to another source, the percentage of workers receiving piece wages was as follows (for September of each year): 1923, 45.7; 1924, 51.4; 1925, 601; 1926, 61.3. See A. G. Rashin, *Zarabotnaya*, pp. 33–34, quoted in Carr, *Socialism*, vol. I, p. 392, n. 2.

107. *Ekonomicheskoye Obozreniye*, no. 10 (1929), p. 148, quoted in Carr and Davies, *Foundations*, vol. I, pt. 2, p. 534.

108. See, for example, Uglanov's article in *Pravda*, October 4, 1925.

109. *XIV-y Syezd VKP(b)* (1926), pp. 793 ff.

110. Lapidus and Ostrovityanov, *Outline*, pp. 132–133. Twenty-six years later, in 1954, the same Ostrovityanov, co-author of the official textbook of political economy, was to affirm that "in socialist economy piece rates provide the worker with the maximum interest in his work" (K. V. Ostrovityanov et al., *Political Economy*, p. 604). There was no longer any question of the system of piece wages being only "temporary."

111. Carr and Davies, *Foundations*, vol. I, pt. 2, p. 522.

112. Ibid., pp. 523–524, and *Trud*, October 10 and 12, 1926.

113. *Torgovo-Promyshlennaya Gazeta* and *Trud*, October 30, 1927; *Obzor deyatelnosti NKT SSSR za 1927–1928 gg.*, p. 71; *Kontrolnye tsifry 1928–1929 gg.* (1929), p. 21; Carr and Davies, *Foundations*, vol. I, pt. 2, pp. 494, 526–529.

114. See the table on p. 191.

115. Gert Meyer, *Studien zur Sozialökonomischen Entwicklung Sowjetrusslands 1921–1923*, p. 194, quoting S. G. Strumilin, *Problemy Ekonomiki Truda*, p. 388.

116. Ibid., p. 195, quoting A. Rashin, "K kharakteristike differentsiatsiya zarabotnoy platy v promyshlennosti," *Vestnik Truda*, no. 2 (1925), p. 50.

117. Ibid., p. 51, quoting the same source.

118. Ibid., p. 196, quoting several Soviet sources from this period.
119. *VII Syezd VLKSM* (1926), p. 49, quoted in Carr and Davies, *Foundations*, vol. I, pt. 2, p. 529.
120. Rashin, *Zarabotnaya plata,* pp. 126–127, quoted in Carr, *Socialism*, vol. I, pp. 380–381.
121. *VII-oy Syezd Professionalnykh Soyuzov SSSR* (1927), p. 51.
122. Carr and Davies, *Foundations*, vol. I, pt. 2, pp. 529–531.
123. *VIII-oy Vsesoyuzny Syezd V.L.K.S.M.* (1928), p. 37.
124. *Voprosy Truda,* November–December 1932, p. 29.
125. *VII-oy Syezd Professionalnykh Soyuzov SSSR* (1927), p. 51.
126. See above, p. 237.
127. See above, pp. 215, 219 ff.
128. L. Rogachevskaya, *Iz istorii rabochego klassa SSSR,* pp. 152–154, n. 4; and *Torgovo-Promyshlennaya Gazeta,* September 1, 1927, quoted by Carr and Davies, *Foundations*, vol. I, pt. 2, p. 513.
129. *Torgovo-Promyshlennaya Gazeta,* September 27, 1927, article by Kuibyshev.
130. *Sobranie Zakonov*, no. 45 (1927), art. 456.
131. Ibid., no. 42 (1928), art. 384, and no. 43, art. 387. This signified an extension of what was called the "manager's fund," which later on played an even greater role as a means of stimulating production (see Carr and Davies, *Foundations*, vol. I, pt. 2, pp. 512, 609–610).
132. *Sobranie Zakonov*, no. 59 (1928), arts 523 and 524.
133. Lenin, *CW*, vol. 26, pp. 404–415.
134. Stalin, *Works*, vol. 12, p. 116.
135. Ibid., p. 115.
136. For example *Trud*, May 30; August 2 and 6, 1929, quoted in Schwarz, *Labor in the Soviet Union,* pp. 189, 190.
137. *Trud*, July 25, 1929.
138. Ibid., August 2, 1929.
139. *Voprosy Truda*, no. 12 (1929), p. 47, quoted by Lorenz in his thesis *Das Ende*, p. 230.
140. Fainsod, *Smolensk*, p. 312, quoting VKP 250, pp. 38–47.
141. Ibid., quoting VKP 300, p. 48.
142. Ibid., p. 313, quoting VKP 300, pp. 49–50 (my emphasis—C. B.).
143. See Krzhizhanovsky's declaration at the beginning of 1929: "A time has come which is bringing us achievements no-one had dreamed of" (*Internationale Presse-Korrespondenz*, no. 112 [1929], p. 2648). See also Mezhlauk's speech published in ibid., no. 116 (1929), p. 2728.

144. Initially, the First Five-Year Plan provided for production of 10.4 million metric tons of steel, but actual production in 1932 was only 5.9 million metric tons (Bettelheim, *La Planification,* p. 288). In all the main fields—agricultural equipment, tractors, motor cars, etc.—the end of 1929 was marked by a growing gap between production targets and real production possibilities.
145. Stalin, *Works,* vol. 12, p. 115.
146. What happened generally does not mean that socialist emulation did not continue for some years to play an important role locally. This was the case especially in certain big building sites and new centers of production (e.g., at the iron-and-steel combine at Magnitogorsk) where young workers were especially numerous.
147. Stalin, *Works,* vol. 12, p. 116.

4. The integration of state-owned industry in the overall process of reproduction of the conditions of production

While the socialist form of the enterprises belonging to the Soviet state does not suffice to determine the nature of the relations which are reproduced in the immediate production process, it does not suffice either to determine the nature of the relations formed between these enterprises in the course of the overall process of reproduction. These relations retain a more or less capitalistic character so long as they preserve the separation between the direct producers and their means of production and the separation of production units (or groups of production units) from each other, this separation being both "transcended" and reproduced by the *commodity relations* which are established between the enterprises. The existence of these relations simultaneously manifests and conceals the separation between enterprises. When the economic plan imposes from without "direct relations" between the production units, this is not enough to "do away with" the real separation that exists between them, but merely modifies its form. Only socialist cooperation between the production units, a unification of the various immediate production processes based upon the joint activity of the various working groups, can end this separation and ensure dominance for socialist planning.

The dictatorship of the proletariat can create the political and ideological conditions for transition from the separate existence of the production units to various forms of socialist cooperation and planning. However, this transition, which is one of the features of the transition to socialism, is not at all a "spontaneous" affair. It calls for a protracted class struggle guided by a political line ensuring the victory of the socialist road. In the absence of such a line the capitalist and commodity relations characteristic of the conditions of functioning of the production units and of the circulation of products among them will continue to be reproduced.

We have seen the extent to which this happened, under the NEP, as regards the social relations characteristic of the immediate production process. Let us now see what happened with regard to the forms of circulation of the products, the material basis of the overall process of reproduction of the conditions of production.

In order to concretize our examination of these forms, let us recall, first, what the form of management of the state-owned enterprises was that was established at the beginning of the NEP. It was essentially through this form (and the changes it underwent) that the state-owned enterprises were integrated in the overall process of reproduction of the conditions of production. This form of management was known as the system of "financial autonomy," or "business accounting" (*khozraschet*).

To understand what was meant by the introduction of "financial autonomy" for the state-owned industrial enterprises, we must recall how the latter operated under "war communism." At that time the production program of such industrial enterprises as were still functioning was aimed above all at satisfying the needs of the front, while ensuring a minimum supply of goods to the population. The problems presented by the development of the productive forces, by accumulation, and by diversification of production were thus either "eliminated" or thrust into the background. Similarly, questions concerning costs of production were almost meaningless in a situation in which what mattered was to obtain at any cost the few products that could still be turned out. Under these conditions the maximum degree of centralization of the management of industry was needed, with the state dictating to the enterprises a certain number of *priority targets*.

The functioning of the economy seemed in those days to be

dominated by use value. The industrial sector looked like a "single state trust," within which the labor force had to be used not independently by each enterprise but as *a single labor force*: labor appeared to be "directly social." This was how the illusions of "war communism" arose—"direct transition to communism," immediate disappearance of money and of the wage relation, and so on.

The NEP was based on rejection of these illusions.[1] It led to the introduction of *khozraschet,* which implied that the state-owned enterprises came out openly as one of the spheres in which commodity and money relations were reproduced. However, the NEP offered no "answer" to the question of how these relations were to be transformed and eliminated.

I. The introduction and development of khozraschet

Khozraschet was introduced by a decree of the Sovnarkom dated August 9, 1921. This decree conferred "financial autonomy" on the state-owned enterprises.[2] A resolution of the Council of Labor and Defense (CLD), dated August 12, 1921, specified that *khozraschet* implied separation of the enterprises from the state, which entailed also separation of the enterprises from each other.[3]

After a phase of decentralization, begun in 1921, and then one of temporary recentralization (introduced by a decree of November 12, 1923), the management of enterprises was again decentralized (decision by the Sovnarkom, August 24, 1926). At that time the VSNKh was taking over the general direction of state-owned industry and planning.[4]

The enterprise (that is, the economic unit possessing autonomy of management) coincided only exceptionally with a production unit—a factory, for instance. Most often, "financial autonomy" was accorded to a group of production units (a "union" of production units belonging to the same branch of industry, and, especially, a "Soviet trust"). Each factory, with the exception of the largest of them, which were officially styled "enterprises," depended on a "trust" or a "union." The trusts and unions were usually the only state industrial organs in contact with the market. At the beginning of the NEP they drew up programs of activity for the factories subordinate to them, taking account mainly of production capacities and possibilities for buying and selling. The factories, therefore, functioned as organs for carrying out a program laid down from above. However, the rise in industrial production during the NEP period was accompanied by a growth in the actual powers granted to the managers of individual factories and transition of the most important production units to "enterprise" status.

The principal characteristics of the way the state enterprises functioned on the basis of *khozraschet* were as follows:

1. Each state-owned enterprise was given a fund of its own, which constituted its capital endowment (the word "capital" being explicitly used, e.g., in the reports of the VSNKh).[5]

2. Each state-owned enterprise bought its raw material and fuel, as well as its other means of production, and *sold* its own products; consequently, it was integrated in *commodity and money relations,* in contrast to the situation that prevailed under "war communism."

3. Each enterprise was directly responsible for the employment of its workers: it had to take its own decisions regarding the number of wage earners to be employed and the conditions for the hiring and firing of these wage earners. This principle established new forms of separation between the workers and their means of production.

4. *The financing of the activity of each of the state-owned enterprises was henceforth to depend essentially on its own receipts and on the banking system.*

5. The possibilities for development of the various state-owned enterprises thus depended essentially on their *capacity for self-financing* and on their *capacity to repay* the loans that they obtained either from Gosbank or from the specialist banks which also belonged to the state.[6]

(a) Khozraschet at the beginning of the NEP

The actual change over by the enterprises to operation in accordance with the principles of *Khozraschet* took place only gradually, starting in the autumn of 1921. In the month of October the state enterprises thus found themselves given permission to dispose freely of an increasing proportion of what they produced, whereas previously their products had been assigned in advance to a state organ which took delivery of them by right.

In the autumn of 1922 the Civil Code endowed each enterprise or trust with civil personality. This sometimes came to be called their "juridical division." Thereafter, each enterprise or trust was able to undertake legal commitments, and became responsible for its commitments under civil law. Its circulating capital could be confiscated if it did not honor its obligations or pay its debts. By the end of 1922 nearly all enterprises were subject to *khozraschet* or, as people then still said, to the "commercial regime."

The establishment of *khozraschet* was crowned by the decree of April 10, 1923, which declared in its Article I that "state trusts are state industrial enterprises to which the state accords *independence in the conduct of their operations* in accordance with the statute laid down for each enterprise, and which operate on principles of commercial accounting *with the object of earning a profit.*"[7]

This decree thus specified that the aim of the enterprise must be to *make a profit.* It ascribed a *certain amount of capital* to each trust, and laid down the *rules for the use of profits* by the enterprises placed under the regime of *khozraschet.* One share, the largest, was to be paid into the Treasury. Another share was to be placed in reserve, in order to ensure the development of the enterprise and the renewal of its equipment. A third share was to be used for *paying percentages to the members of the administration and bonuses to the workers.*[8]

At the time, this financial autonomy and this striving for

profit possessed very special significance, for great "freedom of action" was left to the state's industrial enterprises in the matter of their relations with the commercial circuits and the prices at which they sold their products.

During the first half of the 1920s the extension of *khozraschet* resulted in the concentration of the tasks of management and of the buying and selling of products in the hands of the leaders of the *industrial trusts*. Statistics for the summer of 1923 show that there were then 478 trusts created by the VSNKh grouping 3,561 enterprises and employing one million workers (which meant 75 percent of all workers employed in the state-owned industrial sector).

Under the federal constitution of the USSR there were All-Union trusts, Republican trusts, and local trusts, which were subordinate, respectively, to the VSNKh, the Economic Council of the particular republic, and the local economic council. These were the organizations which *appointed the directors of the trusts*.

At the head of each trust was a body of directors organized as a council. This council appointed the managers of the various enterprises dependent upon it.

The organs which appointed the heads of the trusts or of the enterprises did not interfere in the way they were run, but were responsible for supervising their accounts through an auditing commission made up of three members, one of whom represented the trade union of the workers employed by the trust or enterprise.[9]

These enterprises and trusts carried out buying and selling operations on the basis of *prices determined by contract*, except in cases where prices were subject to regulation. The rule of *aiming to make a profit* which had been laid down by the decree of April 10, 1923, applied also to those very large enterprises which came directly under the VSNKh.

In a number of statements from 1921 on Lenin explained that the introduction of *khozraschet* signified that the state sector had been "put on a commercial, capitalist basis." He stressed that this meant not merely that "it is absolutely essential that all authority in the factories should be concentrated in the hands of the management" (a principle already decided in 1918, and which had been gradually put into force), but that each of these managements "must have authority independently to fix and pay out wages . . . ; it must enjoy the utmost freedom to manoeuvre, exercise strict control of the actual successes achieved in increasing production, in making the factory pay its way and in increasing profits, and carefully select the most talented and capable administrative personnel, etc."[10]

(b) The immediate aims being pursued when khozraschet was introduced

At the outset, the establishment of *khozraschet* aimed essentially at ensuring the reactivation of state-owned industry as quickly as possible. To this end it was necessary to allow wide freedom of initiative to the different enterprises, and therefore to break up the ultracentralized system which had prevailed under "war communism" which was no longer adapted to the diversified economic tasks that were now on the agenda.

Under the existing political conditions (the "deproletarianizing" of the working class, penetrated by very many petty-bourgeois elements, the Party's weak position in many factories, etc.), the Bolshevik Party considered that *decentralized initiative* must depend, first and foremost, on *the responsibility exercised by the heads of enterprises.*

Conduct of the enterprises was then subjected to *"control by the rouble."* In principle, the enterprises were no longer to be subsidized. They were to make profits or, at the very least, to balance their expenditure and their receipts. If they should fail to do this then, for the time being, the only thing for them to do was to close down.

Such strict rules corresponded to the situation at the beginning of the NEP. At that time the state's financial resources were drawn mainly from the peasantry and from inflation of the currency. In order that the NEP might "function" there must neither be any increase in the burden of taxes borne by the peasants nor any continuance of inflation through the payment of subsidies to enterprises that showed a loss. Financial resources must serve, first and foremost, *the restoration of the economy*: they could not be devoted to keeping alive enterprises that were incapable of surviving *by their own resources*.

The closing down of some enterprises through the working of "balanced management" also corresponded to another aspect of the situation: at that time, the shortage of raw materials and fuel was such that *it was not materially possible for all enterprises to function*. Therefore it seemed necessary to *concentrate the available material resources* on those production units that would use them most economically and make it possible to produce *at the least cost*.

The criterion of "profitability" thus decided whether enterprises were kept alive or temporarily closed down. *This criterion did not, of course, guarantee that the production units which continued to function were necessarily those which could best produce what was socially most necessary*. Only thoroughgoing investigation could have revealed which enterprises ought, from this standpoint, to be kept active. But the social and political conditions needed for such investigations to be carried out without their conclusions being seriously affected by the various private interests involved (including the divergent interests of the workers in different enterprises or localities) were not present at that time. The recourse to the criterion of profitability thus reflected, in the last analysis, *a certain situation in the class struggle and a certain state of class consciousness*.

Consequently, the *requirements of the reproduction of capital* tended to impose themselves, under the specific forms that these requirements assume when the different "fractions" of capital function separately. These forms, when they are not dealt with critically, from the standpoint of a class policy, *tend to give priority to financial "profitability," which may come into contradiction with the long-term requirements of expanded reproduction*. At the beginning of the NEP this was shown, in rapid reactivation of the enterprises producing consumer goods, whereas the heavy industrial enterprises producing equipment experienced a grave crisis. The former *made big profits and so possessed the means of paying the highest prices for the means of production they needed,* while the latter suffered from great difficulties, and in many cases had to cease production.

In 1921 and 1922 the VSNKh tended to accept this state of affairs as a "necessary" consequence of *khozraschet.*[11]

The conception of the decisiveness of profitability was upheld for a considerable stretch of the NEP period by the People's Commissariat of Finance and by Gosbank. Bourgeois financial experts were especially numerous in these organs. The theoretical weakness of some of the Party's leaders was particularly marked where financial and monetary questions were concerned. For some years Narkomfin and Gosbank were unwilling to give more than very small subsidies to heavy industry, which experienced hard times. Similarly, these organs opposed the financing on credit of purchases by the poor and middle peasants of the tools that they needed.

The attitude of Narkomfin, especially its opposition to the point of view defended by Lenin,[12] was expressed, for example, at the Congress of Soviets in December 1922. It was then that the commissar of finance, Sokolnikov, declared that the crisis being suffered at that time by a section of industry would make it possible to "clean up" the state sector, and that *khozraschet* had the advantage that it made the state no longer directly responsible for the level of employment, while enabling "true prices" to be established, prices corresponding to "market conditions" and "costs."[13]

Consequently, *in the absence of a sufficiently clear conception of the limits within which khozraschet could play a positive role,* financial autonomy of the enterprises could result in an economic development subjected to the conditions of reproduction of the different "fractions" of social capital, a kind of development that would give rise to economic crises.

While uncritical application of *khozraschet* could bring such consequences, it nevertheless remains true that the introduction of financial autonomy was necessary. In general, during a large part of the transition period, *this form of management facilitates (provided that its limits are clearly understood) measuring, to a certain extent, the way that various enterprises are functioning, and their aptitude to respect the principles of economy which must be observed if part of the product of social labor is not to be squandered. Furthermore, at the time when it was introduced,* khozraschet was the only means whereby costs of production could be quickly lowered, so as to create some of the conditions enabling industry *to offer its products to the peasants at prices that were sufficiently low and stable.*

(c) *The functioning of* khozraschet *at the beginning of the NEP*

During the first years of the NEP *khozraschet* did not always bring about a reduction in selling prices, for this period was one of inflation, shortage of goods, and opportunity for state enterprises to make agreements among themselves.

Being at that time relatively free to fix their selling prices, the various state enterprises, or groups of enterprises, tended to *make the biggest possible profits,* appropriating the largest share they could of the surplus value produced in the state sector and of the value produced in the sector of petty-commodity production (chiefly by the peasants). In that period *a number of trusts came together to form sales groupings* (or "syndicates" for selling their goods, and in some cases for making purchases, too), which were organized in the form of joint-stock companies.

The first of these "syndicates" was formed in the textile industry on February 28, 1922. It was a company with a capital of 20 million gold roubles (prewar roubles), corresponding to 10,000 shares allotted among the trusts and autonomous enterprises which had subscribed to it. The purpose of this "syndicate" was to coordinate the purchasing, selling, and stockpiling activities of its members, and also their financial activities, especially in the sphere of credit. A general meeting of the shareholders was held every six months, and appointed a board of directors and a chairman. This meeting could allocate quotas for production and sales: the board was entrusted with the conduct of current business and *fixing of prices*. This "syndicate" also played a role in international trade, especially in the United States and Britain. The factories under its control employed 535,000 workers in 1924–1925.[14]

Dozens of sales syndicates of this sort were formed at that time, covering most industries. They soon united hundreds of enterprises, employing altogether nearly 80 percent of the workers in the state-owned industrial sector.

The creation of a "Council of Syndicates" to take the place of the VSNKh was even contemplated at one stage, but was rejected by the Bolshevik Party. If it had been realized, this project would have concentrated enormous economic (and therefore, ultimately, political) power in the hands of the leaders of industry. However, though the original scheme was dropped, the VSNKh agreed to the appointment by the sales syndicates of a Consultative Council to work with it.[15]

The evolution which has just been surveyed was a significant one. It showed the strength of the current which was then driving toward what was called a "dictatorship of industry."[16]

The "monopolistic competition" which developed in this way, within the state sector, had a negative influence on the worker-peasant alliance and on industrial production itself.

After the end of 1923 the Soviet government opposed, with increasing success, these monopolistic practices. Having ended inflation, it obliged the state enterprises gradually to reduce their selling prices, in accordance with the original aims of the introduction of *khozraschet*.

Nevertheless, when the period of reconstruction ended in 1925, the demands of the restructuring of industry made it necessary to transform the conditions under which *khozraschet* was applied, so as to subordinate the activity of the enterprises to the tasks laid down by the economic plan.

II. *Khozraschet and state planning*

Development of state-owned industry on the basis of *khozraschet* alone would have resulted in its following a road like that of a private capitalist industry placed in similar relations with agriculture and the world market. There would have been priority development of the light industries, the most "profitable" ones, while the basic industries would have developed much more slowly, or would even have regressed (their previous development, in the tsarist period, had indeed been sustained by state aid). From the standpoint of international relations, this type of development *would have placed the Soviet economy in a "semicolonial" situation*: the USSR would have exported mainly agricultural produce, raw materials, and a few manufactured consumer goods, and imported equipment for industry and agriculture from the Western countries which could supply them more cheaply.

Toward the end of 1921 Lenin had criticized the supporters of such a "development," which would emphasize "criteria of profitability" to the exclusion of everything else. Lenin summed up some of these criticisms in the report he gave on November 13, 1922, to the Fourth Congress of the Comintern. In this report he stressed that the Soviet government ought not to take account merely of the profitability of enterprises. He showed that, if they acted on that principle, then heavy industry, the basis for the country's further development, would be doomed, under the conditions of that time, to suffer a very grave crisis. He then presented the problem of *simultaneous development of agriculture, light industry, and heavy industry,* and said:

> The salvation of Russia lies not only in a good harvest on the peasant farms—that is not enough; and not only in the good condition of light industry, which provides the peasants with consumer goods—this, too, is not enough; we also need *heavy* industry . . . . Heavy industry needs state subsidies. If we are not able to provide them, we are doomed as a civilised state, let alone as a socialist state.[17]

Here he expressed in a few words the conflict which was developing at that time between the use of *khozraschet* as a means of current management, which Lenin supported, and a quite different conception, which wanted to *subject the general development of the economy to "criteria of profitability,"* a conception which "put profit in command."

Lenins's interventions set limits to some of the consequences of the latter conception, but it continued to be manifested during subsequent years. On the pretext of "poor profitability" it tended to hinder, to some extent, the development of heavy industry and the equipment of the poor and middle peasants' farms with new means of production, so that these peasants were rendered more dependent upon the kulaks. The class content of this conception comes out clearly in this consequence.

From the end of 1925, when existing industrial capacity had been almost completely brought into use, the question arose in a particularly acute form: should the pace of development of the various industries be determined primarily by their respective rates of profitability, as these resulted from the working of *khozraschet*, or should the state *intervene with a plan*, to ensure the priority development of certain branches of industry, regardless of their "profitability"? This question was, indeed, settled in favor of the plan, but uncertainty still prevailed where some decisive questions were concerned: *what principles* should guide the priority development of this or that industry, what proportion of the investment fund should be allocated to this or that type of development, what limit should be assigned to the investment fund?

These questions possessed *crucial political importance*: the strengthening or weakening of the worker-peasant alliance, the masses' standard of living, and the conditions of production in the factories depended on the way that they were answered. But these questions were not presented in an all-sided way. The practical "answers" given to them were largely determined by a rather schematic notion of the "requirements" of industrialization, of the role of large-scale industry and heavy industry, and also by the growing influence

wielded by the heads of the big enterprises and by the industrial specialists of the VSNKh. This resulted in the adoption of
economic plans the scope and content of which were less and
less compatible with the maintenance of the NEP, while, as a
consequence of putting these plans into effect, the functioning
of *khozraschet* underwent increasingly extensive changes.

These changes acquired decisive importance from 1928–
1929 on. They tended to subordinate the relations between
the different enterprises no longer directly to the criteria of
profitability resulting from the operation of *khozraschet*
(which did not disappear, but was merely put in a "dominated" situation), but *to the demands of the economic plan*.

The very conception of the plan was changed. Until then,
the annual plan, the only one that was directly operational,
had consisted in the "control figures" which were supposed to
reflect, in the main, the "spontaneous tendencies" of the
economy, and therefore helped mainly to reproduce existing
social relations, and which, moreover, had practically no compulsory aspect.

After 1926 the annual plan (and then, later, the Five-Year
Plan) included *obligatory targets determined on the basis of
political decisions aimed at imposing a certain type of industrial development*. It was no longer merely a matter of trying to
"harmonize" certain "tendencies" (corresponding to an ex-
trapolation of past developments, or to the forecasts made by
the heads of the trusts), but of defining and imposing targets of
a "voluntarist" character which might be very remote from
those toward which the proposals of the heads of enterprises
would have led industry.

The idea of a plan that was mainly a "harmonization" of the
spontaneous tendencies of the economy did not merely correspond to the practice of the first annual "control figures," it
also engendered a theoretical conception, called the "geneticist" conception, which was defended by some Soviet
economists, such as V. Bazarov and V. Groman. The contrary
conception, that of a plan which imposed targets which had
been determined by human will, was called the "teleological"
conception. It was this second conception, the only one com-

patible with aims of economic and social change, that had triumphed. Its most resolute supporters were the economists G. Feldman and S. Strumilin. The political leader who defended it most firmly was Kuibyshev, who said: "We can construct plans based not only on foreseeing what will happen but also on a definite will to achieve specific tasks and purposes."[18]

The victory of the "teleological" conception of the plan did not mean that the plans drawn up were "the expression of the planners' subjectivity." In fact, the plans adopted by the political authorities were *the product of a complex social process*: they were the effect of class relations and class struggles, and were subjected to a series of *social constraints* both during their preparation and during their implementation.

The victory of the "teleological" conception of the plan did not mean, either, *that the actual development of the economy and of industry "submitted itself" strictly to the "demands" of the plan.* The history of the Soviet plans shows that this was far from being the case. Nevertheless, this victory *gave a quite different style to industrial development,* and led to the changes in the working of *khozraschet* which were observable mainly at three levels:

1. The investments realized in the various branches of industry and the various state-owned enterprises were less and less determined by the profits that were obtained or which could be expected in these branches or enterprises: they depended increasingly on the *priorities laid down by the plan*. In practice, a growing proportion of these investments were derived from budgetary grants which became integrated in the permanent funds of the enterprises to which they were given; a diminishing proportion were derived from repayable bank loans.[19] This meant a partial transformation of *khozraschet*.

2. The imperative character of the plan implied that production by each enterprise and each trust was less and less determined by the customers' orders received, with the "most profitable" of these being preferred: it was now determined by *administrative instructions* emanating from higher author-

ity. In Soviet practice in the last years of the NEP, this heightened role played by the superior administrative authorities in the orienting of production was exercised in several ways:

(a) First, in the working out of the production program of each trust, which was increasingly subject to decisions handed down from above. In 1925–1926 the VSNKh defined thus the procedure for working out the industrial plan:

> Inasmuch as the work of every trust, and even more of a whole industry, will be almost entirely determined by the state, which will provide it with a specific amount of supplementary resources, the industrial plan can no longer be constructed by adding up the proposals of the trusts. The proposals of the trusts are moving into the background: into the foreground move the proposals and intentions of the state, which is becoming the real master of its industry. Therefore, it is only the state economic agencies which can construct the industrial plan: the industrial plan must be constructed not from below but from above.[20]

This procedure for drawing up the plan reduced to very little the contribution made by proposals coming from the factories themselves.

(b) In the course of carrying out their production plan, the enterprises had less and less to consider the customers' orders which they might receive. In fact, toward the end of the NEP, the sales syndicates, which centralized the commercial operations of the industrial enterprises, vanished from the scene. Their functions were usually integrated in the various People's Commissariats charged with distributing the products of state enterprises in conformity with the plan.

The plan of each enterprise was subject, moreover, to a number of variations in the course of the year, owing to frequent reestimations of the *need* for goods and of the possibilities of their production by industry. The leading organs of the economy required, however, that the enterprises provide the production laid down in the last instructions received—and these instructions were often sent without consulting the enterprises themselves. From this resulted frequent and important discordances between the targets assigned to enterprises and their actual production capacity.[21]

3. The imperative character of the plan and the *dual nature* of its targets (in terms of use value and of exchange value) led to enterprises being more and more deprived of the possibility of fixing their prices for buying and selling for themselves. Prices were thus "planned." One of the aims pursued by this planning was to ensure a sufficient degree of coincidence between the forecasts of *physical flows* and those of *financial flows*. Actually, the coincidence was not very well ensured, in particular because the forecasts regarding productivity of labor, wages, and costs of production were very imperfectly realized. The imbalances between supply and demand resulting from this state of affairs made all the more necessary the *regulation of prices*, so that state enterprises might be prevented from getting around the financial discipline of the *promfinplan* by taking advantage of goods shortages to raise their selling prices, which would have threatened to bring about a rush of price increases.

Altogether, toward the end of the NEP period, production by each enterprise was less and less determined by the commodity and monetary conditions governing its integration, *via khozraschet*, in the overall process of reproduction. Henceforth, it depended more and more upon the tasks and means assigned by the plan. However, the tasks allocated to enterprises and the means granted them by the plan depended also on the results that they obtained, both on the plane of physical quantities produced and on that of their "financial performance" (the actual evolution of their "profitability," of their costs of production, and so on).

The contradictions between the frequently unrealistic provisions of the plan and the actual results obtained affected the overall process of social reproduction. The development of these contradictions contributed largely to the creation of certain specific features of the final crisis of the NEP, in particular the increase in inflation and the shortage of numerous consumer goods produced by industry. We must therefore look into the nature of the social relations that underlay the development of these contradictions. This brings us to consideration of the significance of the categories of price, wages, and profit, and their role in the class struggles.

Notes

1. On these points see volume I of the present work, especially pp. 333 ff. and 404 ff.
2. In the following pages we are mainly concerned with industrial enterprises, but *khozraschet* applied also to the other state-owned enterprises, in agriculture, trade, banking, etc.
3. *Sobranie uzakonenii*, no. 59 (1921), art. 403; and no. 63, art. 462.
4. F. Pollock, *Die Planwirtschaftlichen*, pp. 184–227, especially pp. 211–212; also M. Dobb, *Soviet Economic Development*, p. 126, and E. H. Carr, *The Bolshevik Revolution*, vol. 2, pp. 302 ff.
5. Carr, *The Bolshevik Revolution*, vol. 2, p. 304.
6. See above, p. 63.
7. Carr, *The Bolshevik Revolution*, vol. 2, p. 308 (my emphasis—C. B.). In July 1923 the VSNKh repeated that the *making of a profit* must be the principle guiding the work of the Soviet trusts (Carr, *The Interregnum*, p. 9).
8. See the extracts from the CLD decree of April 10, 1923, quoted in I. Lapidus and K. Ostrovityanov, *Outline*, p. 182.
9. Dobb, *Soviet Economic Development*, pp. 135–137.
10. Lenin, *CW*, vol. 33, p. 189 (decision of the CC on the tasks of the trade unions, January 12, 1922); vol. 42, p. 476.
11. See volume I of the present work, pp. 152 ff.
12. See above, p. 277.
13. *X-y Vserossiisky Syezd Sovyetov* (1923), pp. 102–111.
14. Y. S. Rozenfeld, *Promyshlennaya Politika SSSR*, p. 230; *The All-Union Textile Syndicate*, pp. 4–15, quoted in Dobb, *Soviet Economic Development*, p. 160, n.l.
15. Dobb, *Soviet Economic Development*, pp. 160–161.
16. The expression "dictatorship of industry" was used in *The New Course* (pp. 72–73), Trotsky's pamphlet in which he tried to justify such a dictatorship. He sought to moderate the implications of this expression and to show that a "dictatorship of industry" was not in contradiction with the worker-peasant alliance, on

the grounds that, ultimately, industry would serve the needs of the peasantry.

17. Lenin, *CW*, vol. 33, p. 426.

18. *II-ya Sessiya Ts IK SSSR 4 soyuza (1927?)*, p. 246, quoted in Carr and Davies, *Foundations*, vol. I, pt. 2, p. 792. On the discussion between supporters of the "geneticist" and "teleological" conceptions, see ibid., pp. 790 ff.; also A. Erlich, *The Soviet Industrialization Debate;* N. Spulber, *Soviet Strategy for Economic Growth,* and *The Soviet Economy,* especially pp. 218 ff.

19. At the end of 1928 it appears that industrial investment was still being financed mainly by repayable bank loans (see *Ekonomicheskoye Obozreniye*, no. 12 [1928], p. 38). In 1929 this ceased to be so. A decree of May 23, 1930 decided that investments made from the unified budget would be treated as non-repayable grants (*Sobranie Zakonov*, no. 28 [*1930*], art. 316). On these points, see J. M. Collette, *Politique des investissements et calcul économique,* pp. 51–65.

20. *Perspektivy Promyshlennosti na 1925–1926 operatsionny god* (1925) quoted in Carr and Davies, *Foundations*, vol. 1, p. 2, p. 825.

21. The targets of the plan were formulated both in terms of physical quantities and "in value terms," the whole constituting an "industrial and financial plan" (*promfinplan*). See *Torgovo-Promyshlennaya Gazeta*, April 14–15, 1928, and Carr and Davies, *Foundations,* vol. I, p. 2, pp. 825 ff.

5. The categories of price, wages, and profit and their class significance

The problems considered in this chapter lie at the heart of our analysis of the transition to socialism. An attempt to deal with them here in an all-sided way would divert us too far from the principal object of our inquiry, namely, the characteristics of the social process which led to the brusque abandonment of the NEP and the changeover to the type of collectivization and industrialization that the USSR actually experienced. It is therefore mainly in order to serve the needs of this inquiry that I shall discuss here the social nature of the categories of price, wages, and profit in the Soviet social formation, and more especially in state-owned industry, during the last years of the NEP period.

The analyses that follow are aimed at revealing the role played by these economic categories—actually by these *social relations*—in a concrete historical process. This demonstration requires that account be taken not only of the place actually occupied by prices, wages, and profits but also of the ideological conception of the role played by these categories, for this had a far-reaching influence on the way the concrete historical process developed, especially because it embodied *a contradiction between reality and the awareness of that reality which it was supposed to constitute.*

I. The ideological conception of the role of the categories of price, wages, and profit

A study of the resolutions adopted by the leading bodies of the Bolshevik Party enables us to distinguish various notions of the role of the categories of price, wages, and profit, and various analyses of the nature of the social relations which manifested themselves through these categories. This study also enables us to observe that when the central planning organs began their activity (that is, during the last years of the NEP), the dominant conception tended increasingly to treat these categories as "empty forms," seeing them not as the expression of social relations but as, in the main, mere "bookkeeping magnitudes."

The *Outline of Political Economy* by Lapidus and Os-trovityanov offers one of the most systematic expositions of this type of conception, and so I shall turn to it in order to extract some significant formulations.

(a) The conception of price and wages as "integument," with mainly "quantitative determination"

Where the role of value from and price form is concerned, the *Outline* starts from the fact that, in relations between state-owned enterprises, the circulation of goods takes place in the form of purchases and sales (as was aimed at by the introduction of *khozraschet*) which are effected at determined prices. The *Outline* agrees that these operations of buying and selling are *market* operations, but at the same time it denies that they express (or conceal) the same social relations as value. The authors of the *Outline* recall that the enterprises between which the goods circulate are "different enterprises of one and the same state, and not two independent owners; for them the market is by no means the sole form of connexion, and therefore it is not possible to speak of value here." From this follows the conclusion that what obtains is merely the outward form of value, its "integument," concerning which it is said, at the same time, that *"despite the absence of value in its content*, the superficial form, the 'integument' of value still has a certain real significance. . . ."[1]

As a whole, this exposition shows obvious embarrassment. In substance, it presents price as an "empty form" (the authors write of an "integument"), which in plain words means *that it is not the form of manifestation of social relations*. What is said to matter above all is *"the quantitative determination of the price,"*[2] and they begin by declaring that that determination is "to a certain extent . . . regulated by the state planning organizations,"[3] only to admit later on that there enters into the fixing of this price a whole series of factors and forces, market forces, with which the state institutions have to reckon.[4] However, the reservations thus introduced concern only the quantitative determination of the price, leaving unchanged the conception that this price is an "integument" or "empty form."

What the *Outline* says about price it says likewise about wages, and here again by referring to the notion of state ownership, the state in question being that of the working class. "If we use such terms as wage-labour in connexion with Soviet industry, they characterise only the superficial forms, behind which is concealed a completely new, a socialist relationship."[5]

Here we see repeated the conception that there is a form of distribution (in this case, wages) which is a mere "external form," similar to the form assumed by capitalist relations, but having a different, even contradictory "content." This inevitably raises a fundamental question: *why* do the new social relations which are said to exist manifest themselves *in the same form as their opposite?* Faced with this contradiction, all that the authors of the *Outline* can say is that "there is a contradiction between form and content under capitalism also, and that such contradiction existed during the transition from feudalism to capitalism."[6]

However, this observation tells us nothing about the significance of such a contradiction, especially as regards the *degree to which the production relations are actually changed:* the reality of such a change is simply identified by the *Outline* with the existence of state ownership and the dictatorship of the proletariat. The problem of the *limits* of this change (at the level of immediate production relations and relations of reproduction) is not raised. Yet it is only the existence of these limits that enables us to understand that, if the wages form is present, this is because the actual production relations are a combination of the former relations with new ones, and it is the role still being played by the former capitalist relations which accounts for the existence of the wages form.[7]

In any case, the formulations quoted above from the *Outline* lead its authors to affirm that "we cannot speak of Soviet industry either in terms of exploitation or in terms of surplus value."[8]

As regards the absence of surplus value the argument offered is extremely brief, merely referring to the statements made earlier about value, price, and wages being just matters of "outward form." It leads, moreover, to a conclusion that contradicts a resolution of the Bolshevik Party. The Twelfth Party Congress (April 17–25, 1923) declared, in a resolution that was passed unanimously, that "the question of surplus value in state-owned industry is a question on which depends the fate of the Soviet power, that is, of the proletariat."[9]

In 1928 this resolution seems to have been forgotten, so that the production of surplus value was presented as resulting, in all circumstances, from a process of exploitation, which is not necessarily so.[10]

(b) Remarks on this conception

The difficulties encountered by the authors of the *Outline* were due to the fact that, for them, state ownership and planning signified the "disappearance" of commodity and capitalist relations. As we have seen, these relations were only very partially altered in the immediate production process (the existence of one-person management and *khozraschet* ensured the reproduction of commodity and capitalist relations, as Lenin had shown). Furthermore, planning, in the form it then took, did not make possible the transformation of the production process as a whole into a really unified process, because it was determined without participation by the masses and imposed upon them.

Actually, at the end of the NEP the social reproduction process was still, fundamentally, made up of different production processes which were both *interdependent* (in that they were particular "moments" in the social reproduction process) and, at the same time, *isolated and separated* (in that they were not *dominated collectively* by the workers, associated on the scale of society).

As long as the social production process has this structure, even the objects produced in the state sector are still "products of the labour of private individuals who work independently of each other," to use Marx's expression when describing the conditions under which "objects of utility become commodities."[11] It is precisely the existence of these conditions that accounts for the presence of the value and price forms. These are therefore not at all mere "integuments," but rather the manifestation of production relations about which the *Outline* contents itself with denying that they are still reproducing themselves.

Economic planning as it was practiced in the NEP period—that is, planning from above—does not fundamentally alter the *exteriority* of the different branches of labor in relation to each other, or the conditions under which the *immediate producers* participate in them.

True, the *economic plan* is the form under which it is possible for relations of cooperation to develop among the producers on the scale of society, for it facilitates bringing into a priori relation with each other the various production processes, which may thus cease to be "isolated." But not every economic plan leads inevitably to real coordination and control of the various production processes. Economic planning may thus be more effective or less—it may even be illusory. The effectiveness of planning depends on the development of the socialist elements in the economic basis and superstructure, the social conditions of production and reproduction, and the political and ideological conditions under which the economic plan is worked out and put into operation. *Even under the dictatorship of the proletariat an economic plan which is essentially drawn up by experts, and subject, above all, to the demands of a process of valorization, cannot be socialist in content.* Socialist content is determined by the *place that the producers themselves occupy in the process of compiling and executing the plan* and by the way in which the immediate producers are integrated in the production process; it depends on the way that the producers recognize their integration in the production process as a *directly social activity,* and not as a "private" activity destined merely to secure them a "personal income."

An economic plan may thus possess, in different degrees, a capitalist or a socialist character. The actual character of a plan may change, and this changing is part of the battlefield between the two roads, socialist and capitalist. The triumph of the socialist road implies the elimination of commodity and capitalist relations. It presumes a change, resulting from a class struggle that develops over a long historical period, in the objective and subjective conditions of production.[12]

In the NEP period this change had hardly begun, and the economic plans were only marginally socialist in character. They could be called "socialist" plans only in the sense that the term "implies the determination of the Soviet power to achieve the transition to socialism."[13]

We may recall the remark made by Marx regarding the "collective labourer" under conditions of capitalist production, in which collective labor does not find its *principle of unity* in itself, this unity being imposed from without upon the workers, who combine their efforts under the pressure of a will which is not their own.[14]

Planning develops a socialist character only in so far as its *principle of unity* is the collective will of the workers, with the essentials of the plan *not* being worked out independently of them. This implies that the plan is the outcome of mass activity; and this it can become only through protracted ideological struggle, thanks to which labor becomes directly social, this also being the condition under which the wage form will disappear.

In the *Grundrisse* Marx shows that the existence of wages, of the value form on the plane of distribution, proves "that

production is not *directly* social, is not 'the offspring of association,' which distributes labour internally. Individuals are
subsumed under social production; social production exists
outside them, as their fate; but social production is not subsumed under individuals, manageable by them as their common wealth."[15]

The value form and the wage relation which develops from
it thus imply that social labor is expended as particular labor,
that it is not general labor, and general labor time still cannot
exist except in the form of a universal object—namely, money,
which ensures the socialization of particular labors.[16]

The existence of the forms "value," "money," and "wages"
thus implies that, despite state ownership of the means of
production, the workers remain socially *separated* from their
means of production, that they can set these in motion only
under constraints which are external to themselves. Under
these conditions, productive activity does not have a directly
social character, but retains the character of an activity that is *at
once* "individual" and social.

Only disappearance of the "private," individual, and particular character of labor[17] and of the "independence" of the
various branches of labor (objectively interdependent), makes
it possible to destroy the conditions for the existence of commodity and capitalist relations. This disappearance can be
ensured only through development on the social scale of *relations of cooperation between the producers.*

The ideological and political struggle for this cooperation
(which is the condition for a change in the immediate production process and in the reproduction process) can alone ensure
the transformation of state ownership into *collective appropriation of the means of production.* In so far as this struggle
is not carried on, or has resulted only in partial changes, state
ownership of the means of production functions still as "collective capital,"[18] reproducing in a changed form the laws of
the capitalist mode of production: this form may be that of
state capitalism under the dictatorship of the proletariat.

In this case, as in that of the workers' cooperatives, we see,
indeed, a *partial break* with the capitalist mode of production,

but a *break that needs to be taken further* if the effects of the capitalist relations which continue to be reproduced are to be completely eliminated. In connection with the "co-operative factories of the labourers themselves," Marx noted that they "naturally reproduce, and must reproduce, everywhere in their actual organisation all the shortcomings of the prevailing system. But the antithesis between capital and labour is overcome within them, if at first only by making the associated labourers into their own capitalist, i.e., by enabling them to use the means of production for the *employment* of their own labour."[19]

In the case of the workers in state-owned factories we have production which is production of value and surplus value, which subordinates the agents of this production to specific demands (distinct from the demands of production of mere use-values) and also confers a particular function upon the managers of the enterprises, who may be *at one and the same time* agents of the reproduction of the "collective capital" and proletarian revolutionaries helping to destroy the existing social relations and bring new ones to birth.

By failing to present the problem in these terms, the *Outline of Political Economy* by Lapidus and Ostrovityanov renders incomprehensible the existence of the forms "value," "money," "price," and "wages" in Soviet society. *It cannot point to any road leading to the disappearance of these forms and the development of socialist relations*—which it regards as already fully existent. Finally, it prevents the reader from understanding the significance of the profit made by the state enterprises, the quantitative aspect of which is alone considered.

(c) The ideological conception of the significance of the profit made by state enterprises toward the end of the NEP

Proceeding as it does from the premises mentioned, the *Outline* necessarily arrives at the assertion that the profit made by state enterprises is not profit, and it is therefore unable to allow it any "significance" other than as a bookkeeping device: "Inasmuch as there can be no thought of surplus value in the socialised state enterprises, there cannot be any thought of profit either. . . . That is why, in speaking of the 'profit' of Soviet state enterprises we should continually keep in view the fact that the word is used by us conventionally, while in its essence, in its content, it has nothing in common with capitalist profit."[20]

Such schematic formulations conceal the real role that profit (which is always in the form of definite *social relations*) continues to play in the Soviet economy. In particular, these formulations prevent either raising the problem of *state capitalism* in the NEP period, or understanding *the obstacles set in the path to full use of the powers of labor by the demands of the valorization of capital,* or dealing correctly with the contradictions between these demands and those of a proletarian policy.

II. The wages and profit forms and the evolution of employment and unemployment toward the end of the NEP

The evolution of industrial employment and unemployment toward the end of the NEP shows clearly that it was subject to the *demands of the valorization of capital.* The reproduction of the wages and profit forms, and the uncritical treatment of these forms, imposed capitalist limits upon the growth in the labor force that could have been employed in industry. These limits were those of the profitability of invested capital— taking into account, of course, the level of wages. We need here to take a general view of the fluctuations in employment and unemployment.

(a) A general view of the fluctuations in employment and unemployment

The first years of the NEP were marked by a sharp decline in the numbers employed in industry and a sudden increase in unemployment. The initial decline in the numbers employed in state enterprises was due to the application of the principle of financial autonomy: the enterprises could keep in employment only the number of wage earners corresponding to the money they made which they could spend on wage payments; they were no longer in receipt of subsidies from the state, and very soon, except for *profitable* operations, they were to be deprived of credit. The aim pursued was to put an end to inflation and secure a reduction in industrial costs of production. At that time, indeed, costs of production were partly "swollen" by payments of wages which did not correspond to any productive activity, because the enterprises lacked the raw materials and power needed if they were to operate at full capacity.

The statistics do not enable us to determine the exact extent to which employment declined, but it certainly affected hundreds of thousands of workers. The railways alone saw the number of wage earners on their payroll fall from 1,240,000 to 720,000. In the spinning mills concentration of production in the best-equipped enterprises made it possible to halve the number of workers employed per thousand spindles,[21] and thereby to make a serious cut in the cost of production. However, in 1923 employment began to recover, thanks to a better supply of raw materials.[22]

After 1924 industrial employment increased almost steadily.[23] What calls for attention, however, is that unemployment also increased, steadily and to a considerable extent: the expansion in employment, though rapid, did not suffice to absorb the labor power in search of wage-paid jobs.

Estimates of the number of unemployed are highly approximate. According to the labor exchange figures, 1,340,000 unemployed persons were registered on July 1, 1924, at 70 exchanges.[24] In 1924–1925 the registers kept by the labor ex-

changes were "purged" of a large number of persons—
namely, those who had not already been wage earners (which
meant mostly young people), those who had been unemployed for three years, and so on. As a result of this "purge"
the number of registered unemployed was brought down to
848,000. Even though subjected to operations of this sort from
time to time, the labor exchange statistics nevertheless
showed a steady increase in unemployment. In 1925–1926
there were, officially, more than one million unemployed; in
1927–1928 nearly 1.3 million; and on April 1, 1929, 1.7 million.[25]

Actually, these statistics greatly underestimate the numbers
unemployed. For example, on January 1, 1927, the labor exchanges reckoned that there were only 867,000 trade unionists
out of work—but, on the same date, the trade unions themselves recorded 1,667,000 members unemployed, or more
than double that figure.[26]

The amount of unemployment and its tendency to get worse
constituted a symptom of deep-lying economic contradictions,
of a crisis situation that was more and more acute. In 1926–
1927 the Party leaders acknowledged that unemployment was
more than a mere passing phenomenon, and that it presented a
grave problem. At the beginning of 1927 Kirov went so far as to
speak of it as "an enormous ulcer in our economic or-
ganism."[27]

(b) The way the Bolshevik Party analyzed the causes of unemployment

However, the Bolshevik Party did not undertake an analysis
of *social relations* (and of the *form* in which they manifested
themselves) such as could account for the developing contradiction between the increase in the number of unemployed
and the increase in *unsatisfied demand* (the growth of "shortages"). The way the Bolshevik Party tried, in 1927, to explain
the increase in unemployment, and the political measures
which followed from this type of explanation, deserve our
attention. Analysis of the social relations in industry and of the

way these relations were expressed was practically nowhere
to be found in the explanations prevalent at that time.

These explanations revolved around two notions. Reference
was made, on the one hand, to the "quantitative inadequacy"
of the *material factors* of production, and, on the other, to the
existence of *"rural overpopulation"* which was seen as the
principal "source" of unemployment, owing to the size of
the flood of workers migrating from the country districts into
the towns.[28] Some examples will enable us to see how these
two notions "functioned," and how their "functioning" was
related to the lack of a genuine analysis of the social relations
existing in industry.

Let us take as an example the speech made at the Fourth
Congress of Soviets (April 1927) by Schlichter, commissar of
agriculture in the Ukrainian Republic. Using the notion of
"rural overpopulation," he estimated that in the RSFSR 10
percent of the rural population was "surplus," the corresponding figures for Byelorussia and the Ukraine being 16 and 18
percent.[29] In that period the figure of between 10 and 15
million for the "surplus" rural population was generally accepted.[30]

What the significance of such figures was is obviously far
from clear.[31] In any case, the notion of "rural overpopulation,"
used in this way, easily brought up the idea of "shortage of
land," which led to the recommending of a policy of migration, of "colonisation" of new lands.[32]

The second "material factor" invoked to "explain" unemployment was related to the idea that there were not enough
instruments of labor available to employ all those who were
looking for work, and from this followed the affirmation that
unemployment was due to the country's "poverty" and the
inadequacy of investment.

Thus, in 1927 the economist Strumilin considered that the
figures for investment in industry that were then included in
the draft of the Five-Year Plan would not suffice to banish
unemployment completely,[33] for the total amount of this investment, divided by the investment "necessary" to "create"
one industrial job, showed that an increase of only about
400,000 jobs in industry could be expected.

At the Sixth Congress of the Comintern the economist Varga expounded the same view: "In the Soviet Union unemployment exists only because the economy is poor. If we could provide all the unemployed with means of production there would never need to be unemployment in the Soviet Union."[34]

This way of arguing is, of course, surprising when it comes from "Marxists." It provokes the question why it was that, for centuries, countries even "poorer" than the Soviet Union of 1927 did not know unemployment, and what "economic law" dictates that a certain amount of investment is needed as the condition for "creating" a job.[35]

However, the majority in the CC, no less than the opposition, accepted this way of arguing. In varying forms we see it in operation in several of Stalin's pronouncements. Thus, at the Fourteenth Party Congress (December 1925), he said that the future pace of industrial development would have to be slowed down owing to "a considerable shortage of capital."[36] The link thus proclaimed between the *pace of industrialization* and that of *accumulation* recurs frequently, for example in a speech made by Stalin in March 1927.[37] Finally, as we shall see in more detail later, this conception led, in 1928, to the "justifying" of the theory that a "tribute" must be levied from the peasantry to finance industrial development.[38]

The "explanation" of unemployment by "shortage" of land and inadequate accumulation (which slowed down the pace of industrialization) was dominant but not exclusive in the 1920s. The notion that there was a "shortage" of land was especially disputed, most often by pointing to the opportunities for employment and production which could be opened up by more intensive cultivation (changing the system of rotation of crops and bringing under the plough land lying at a distance from the village). Those agronomists who mentioned these possibilities, however, usually found themselves up against the argument that the "resources" needed to realize these changes were not available.

In face of the rise in unemployment, the practical measures decided on by the Party and the government were very diverse, but they were often intended to deal with the overt expressions of the phenomenon rather than to attack its social roots.

(c) The measures taken by the Bolshevik Party in face of the rise in unemployment during the final years of the NEP

The first of these measures bore a mainly *administrative* character. It was aimed at discouraging peasants from coming to the towns in too large numbers, to seek employment. Thus, the restrictions imposed on the registering of unemployed persons at the labor exchanges[39] aimed not merely at reducing the number of *registered* unemployed but also at *diverting the intentions* of those peasants who were thinking of migrating to the towns. It was supposed that, on leaving the village, if they found it impossible or very difficult to register at a labor exchange, perhaps they would hesitate to make the move. Accordingly, a decree of June 29, 1927, sought to *regulate the arrival in the towns* of workers of rural origin who were looking for seasonal work. By this means the authorities sought to make better appreciated in the rural areas the narrow limits within which extra labor power could be absorbed by the towns.[40]

This type of measure proved not very effective. The peasants who were leaving the countryside either had no work at all there or else earned extremely little,[41] so that they preferred, in any case, to try their luck in town—even if their conditions of existence there should turn out to be wretched, when they failed to find either a job or a place to live.

On several occasions the authorities tried to send back the peasants who came to the big towns, looking for work, as soon as they arrived at the railway station.[42] This "method" was particularly unsuccessful, and gave rise to more or less violent clashes. It was used only in exceptional circumstances, since it was in contradiction with the seasonal requirements of labor of certain industries, especially building.

The trade unions, too, tried to discourage the drift into the towns of peasants in search of work, by not accepting into membership anyone who had not already worked for wages[43] and by striving to reserve priority in employment for their members.[44]

Around this policy a serious struggle was waged, for it was opposed by the managers of enterprises who favored "freedom to hire." In January 1925 they obtained the formal rescinding of the article in the Labor Code which obliged them to hire workers exclusively through the labor exchanges[45]— an article which had, moreover, been only very partially respected. Thereafter, the hiring of workers took place more and more frequently "at the factory gate," and this encouraged many peasants to come to town. Some managers even sent "recruiters" into the countryside: they preferred, whenever they could, to employ peasants, who "are less demanding and have more physical endurance." In their striving to increase the profitability of "their" enterprises, certain managers even dismissed some of their workers so as to recruit fresh ones coming straight from the villages.[46] This helped to increase unemployment in the towns and worked against the efforts being made to reduce rural emigration.

Finally, in 1928, the obligation to engage workers only through the labor exchanges was reintroduced, at least in principle. The increased role thus given to these institutions was connected with the new situation resulting from the projects for industrialization. This situation made it necessary to organize both "struggle against unemployment" and "regulation of the labour-market." A decree of September 26, 1928, modified the statute of Narkomtrud in accordance with these tasks[47] and strengthened the role of the labor exchanges.

The need to regulate the "labor market" resulted from the fact that the massive unemployment of unskilled workers existed, especially after 1928, alongside partial "shortages" in certain skilled trades. Consequently, the State's economic organizations sought to take administrative measures which would enable them to assign certain workers to the activities and localities where there was considered to be a priority need for their employment.

The same concern with *priority assignment* to particular

jobs led to the adoption of the decree of March 26, 1928. This decree provided that persons detained in prison camps could be assigned to work on building sites. Such measures were later on to be adopted on a very large scale.[48]

For a time the carrying out of a policy of *public works* also played a part in the "struggle against unemployment." The form assumed by this policy was not specially socialist. It was a question of giving employment to unskilled workers by devoting part of the state's financial resources to the creation of some large-scale building sites. When the industrialization process got under way, the policy of public works was criticized and abandoned, on the grounds that it tied up too much "capital."[49]

For several years, the idea that unemployment was due to "land shortage" stimulated also a policy of bringing "new" lands under cultivation, or bringing back under the plough lands which had gone out of cultivation. This policy was particularly favored by the People's Commissariat of Agriculture and the agrarian economists. Its advocates stressed the fact that the cultivated area had not increased at the same rate as that of the increase in the rural population.[50] This had happened mainly because many of the small- and medium-sized peasant farms lacked the means needed for more complete cultivation of all the land they possessed: it was basically a problem of the distribution and use of instruments of labor.

Faced with this situation, two political lines emerged. One aimed at helping the peasants to organize themselves (in particular, to form mutual-aid committees[51] and cooperatives for cultivation and production) and to acquire means of production that would enable them to extend the cultivated areas, especially those that were remote from the villages. *This line aimed at solving the problems at village level, relying first and foremost on the peasants' own resources.* We know that this line had only very limited results.[52]

The other line was more "ambitious." It aimed at mobilizing the resources possessed by the *state machine* for undertaking "colonisation" of "virgin lands." This line was put into practice more or less systematically from 1925 on. Thus, a decree issued on September 6, 1926, by the government of the

RSFSR opened the Autonomous Republic of Karelia to workers who would go there to take up permanent residence.[53]

The Fifteenth Conference, and then the Fifteenth Congress of the Party (1927) declared for the extension of measures like this to Siberia and the far east.[54]

In 1928 funds were made available for settling migrants in Turkestan, Kamchatka, Sakhalin, Bashkiria, and Buryat-Mongolia.[55]

A stream of migration was brought into being by these measures. It involved some 700,000 persons. This was a poor result when compared with the scale of the unemployment problem; but the migration thus organized was aimed not only at "solving" that problem—it also served the purpose of settling in Asia a population of European origin.[56]

In fact, the Bolshevik Party considered that the problem of unemployment could not really be solved except by industrializing the country. From its point of view, the various measures taken in other directions, even when economically "useful" (such as the extension of the cultivated areas) could be no more than temporary palliatives.

As we know, the Fifteenth Party Congress (December 1927) and, especially, the Sixteenth Party Conference (April 1929) emphasized more and more the industrialization of the country, so that the question of unemployment could be approached in a new way. We shall see later what political struggles were fought on this subject within the Party. First of all we need to examine how the problem of unemployment as it arose during the NEP was rooted in the very nature of the reproduction process of that period.

III. Unemployment and the contradictory character of the reproduction process under the NEP

On the theoretical plane, the question of unemployment presents itself basically in these terms: was unemployment due to the reproduction of capitalist and commodity relations, inside the state sector as well as outside it? Was it not the reproduction of these relations, under the conditions then prevailing, that made impossible the employment of a larger number of workers, this increased employment being subjected . to *constraints of valorization* (the need to obtain through increased employment an exchange value larger than would have to be expended in order to give work to the unemployed) which could not then be satisfied?

In other words, did the unemployment situation not signify that, despite the existence of socialist social relations, these relations were not sufficiently developed for the production of additional *use values* (obtainable through putting the unemployed to work) to take precedence over the use of the means of production, for preference, in a way that would ensure their self-valorization, *the production of surplus value*? Or, again, was this situation not a symptom showing that the contradiction between the nascent socialist relations and the commodity and capitalist relations which had not disappeared was *not being dealt with in a way that would make it possible to break through the limits imposed on the volume of employment by the reproduction of commodity and capitalist relations*?

We have to see the question of unemployment in these terms, and to answer these questions in the affirmative—which leads us to reject the idea that socialist relations were "absolutely" dominant in the state sector. That, however, was the idea held not only by economists like Lapidus and Ostrovityanov, but also by the Party leadership.

(a) The absence of a dialectical analysis of the system of social realtions

The absence of a dialectical analysis of the production relations prevailing in the state sector is clearly apparent in many documents produced by the Party leadership, and notably in the political report presented by Stalin to the Fourteenth Party Congress (December 1925). In this report the thesis of the socialist character of the state enterprises was asserted in a one-sided way. The argument offered consisted of a series of

questions and answers that dealt with the matter undialectically (that is, along the lines of "either this or that," excluding
the possibility that something may have a dual nature, being
"both this and its opposite").

Speaking of the state-owned enterprises, Stalin asked:

> Are they state-capitalist enterprises? No, they are not. Why?
> Because they involve not two classes, but one class, the working
> class, which through its state owns the instruments and means of
> production and which is not exploited. . . .
>
> It may be said that, after all, this is not complete socialism,
> bearing in mind the survivals of bureaucracy persisting in the
> managing bodies of our enterprises. That is true, but it does not
> contradict the fact that state industry belongs to the socialist type
> of production.[57]

The speech continued with a discussion of the Soviet state
and an argument by analogy in which reference was made to
Lenin's analyses which showed that the Soviet workers' state
suffered from many "bureaucratic survivals."[58]

However, in 1925 the significance actually ascribed to these
"survivals," at enterprise level and at state level, was extremely limited. They were regarded as being, so to speak,
super-added to the socialist and proletarian relations, and
modifying only in a secondary way the effects of these relations and the conditions of their reproduction. Yet the presence of such "survivals" several years after the October Revolution testifies to the existence of a *contradictory combination
of proletarian and bourgeois relations both in the economic
basis and in the superstructure of the Soviet formation.*[59] This
situation calls for analysis of the way in which these relations
were interlinked, and of the forms of domination of some
relations over others, and for the problems to be presented in
terms not of "survivals" but of the reproduction of a system
embracing elements of capitalist relations which could take
the form of *state capitalism.*

Without a concrete analysis of the system of contradictions
and its development, it is impossible to grasp the complexity
of the real situation, or to deal correctly with the contradictions that this situation contains. Under these conditions one

has to operate through ideological conceptions which prevent one from appreciating that the Soviet state is at once proletarian and nonproletarian. These conceptions also prevent one from realizing that even when an enterprise is socialist in form, the production relations reproduced within it may be capitalist (they can thus be "capitalist enterprises with a socialist signboard"), especially when they are not actually managed by the working class and in conformity with the demands of the building of socialism. The forms of development of industrial enterprises, the *type of technology* used in them, and the *number of jobs* that there can be in them are conditioned not directly by the form assumed by the juridical ownership of these enterprises,[60] but by the nature of the production relations that are reproduced in them, or by the dominant elements of these relations and by the form that these relations or these elements impose upon the reproduction process, given the changes that this process may undergo as a result of the intervention of class struggles and of action by the ruling power.

The forms of the division of labor which were characteristic of the industrial enterprises in the NEP period, the ways in which they were integrated in monetary and commodity relations, and also the forms of the class struggle and of intervention by the ruling power, had as their consequence that the production relations reproduced in them were, to a predominant extent, capitalist relations. The unemployment that developed in that period was precisely the effect of the reproduction of these relations, of *the separation of the workers from their means of production.*

In other words, *labor power "functioned" mainly as a commodity* of which wages were the "price": as a commodity which was either embodied in the production process, or thrown out of it, depending on whether or not it could contribute to the *valorization of capital.*

This was not a matter of mere "objective necessity," for the socialist aspect of the production relations and the basically proletarian nature of the state power would have made it possible to "set at naught" the "demands" of the valorization of capital. Actually, there was a *conjunction* between the existence of capitalist relations and the effects of the failure to make a dialectical analysis, a failure which caused to be mistaken for the demands of *socialist* expanded reproduction what were in reality the demands of the *accumulation of capital*.

(b) *The practical effects of the absence of a dialectical analysis of the existing system of social relations and of the correlative failure to deal adequately with the contradictions associated with the reproduction of this system*

Concretely, as we have seen, under the conditions of the NEP, the dominant aim of production in the state-owned enterprises was to make a profit and to increase this profit.[61] This was what determined the use that the state enterprises made of their capital: when they invested they had, in principle, to increase their profits. Thus, the process of accumulation tended to favor the most "profitable" investments, to the detriment of others. As between an investment that would enable production to be increased and more workers employed, but which (given the cost at which this additional production would be obtained) would increase only slightly the profit realized, and another investment that would greatly increase the profit realized, while increasing only slightly, or not at all, production and employment, it was the second investment that tended to be undertaken. In other words, if there was a contradiction between increasing production and employment and increasing profit, this contradiction was usually "resolved" in accordance with the capitalist law of increasing profit.

The same tendencies prevailed when it was a question of replacing "obsolete" equipment. Where such equipment existed it was often possible to *continue to use it* (even if, at the given level of prices and wages, the enterprise using it was not very profitable), provided some repairs were done, the financing of which would reduce, more or less, the accumulation fund serving to create new production capacities of higher "profitability," but it was equally possible to throw this old equipment on the scrap heap and use the entire accumulation fund to replace it with equipment of "high profitability." Although such replacement operations might not increase production (or might even reduce it), the striving to increase profit frequently led to them being favored, to the detriment of increases in production capacity.

This form of the accumulation process played an important part in the USSR during the second phase of the NEP. Thus, between 1926 and 1928 in the iron and steel industry, a large amount of old equipment was scrapped in order to "modernize" this industry and increase its profitability. The same thing happened in the coal and oil industries in 1928–1929. Similarly, most of the investments made in the textile industry between 1926 and 1928 were aimed not at increasing production capacity but at making the industry "more profitable."[62]

This form of the reproduction process subordinated the increase in the number of workers employed and the increase in production to the demands of increasing profit. Capital thus *restricted both production and employment,* not because its "quantity" (and the mass of instruments of production that materialized it) was inadequate but because the *demand of its valorization and accumulation imposed a limit upon production and upon the employment of wage labor.*

Thus, unemployment was not connected with the "inadequacy" of the available means of production but with the form of the reproduction process and the demands to which this process was subject.

IV. *Expanded reproduction and accumulation*

During the NEP the process of expanded reproduction mainly took the form of a process of accumulation, of growth in the value of the means of production, which were themselves subject to the demands of self-valorization. This form was determined by the place occupied by capitalist production relations (in the state sector as well as elsewhere) and by the predominance of a system of thought which tended to identify expanded reproduction with accumulation. The ideas put forward by Preobrazhensky in *The New Economics*, and by Lapidus and Ostrovityanov in the *Outline of Political Economy*, correspond to this identification. It was acknowledged in practice by the Bolshevik Party, and it furnished the inspiration of the Party's economic policy.[63]

This identification had its roots in *confusion between expanded reproduction of the material and human conditions of production and expanded reproduction of capital*, between the process of growth of the quantity of *use values* available and the process of growth of the *value* of the means of production serving a purpose of self-valorization. Under the capitalist mode of production these two processes of growth tend to coincide, without ever doing so completely. (Under that mode of production, growth in the production of use values may also result from changes in the production process which do not require previous accumulation and may even "release" capital.) But *capitalist* growth in the production of use values is always subject to the demands of self-valorization of capital; under the capitalist mode of production the growth of the productive forces is only a secondary effect of the process of accumulation, and the contradictions of this process determine the characteristics of capitalist and the contradictions of this process determine the characteristics of capitalist growth of the productive forces.[64]

The establishment of the dictatorship of the proletariat and the expropriation of the private capitalists create the beginning of the conditions needed for freeing from the constraints of accumulation *both* the process of growth in the production of use values *and* the entry of fresh labor power into the production process. Thus, a process of expanded reproduction can develop which is increasingly "independent" of the process of accumulation. This development assumes that changes take place in the immediate production process, changes thanks to which increases in production can be brought about by the initiatives of the direct producers, who have appropriated their own general productive power[65] and set themselves the aim of increasing the production of use values. This development also assumes that changes take place in the *social reproduction process,* changes thanks to which the different production units establish a cooperation among themselves that takes priority over the striving to increase the profit realized by each of them. Such changes cannot be "spontaneous": the need for them has to be formulated and systematically worked for, and that presupposes the implementing of an appropriate *political line.*

Actually, for reasons to which we shall return later, such a political line did not take shape during the NEP period, even though the resolutions in favor of developing production conferences and mass criticism and self-criticism[66] adumbrated embryonic forms of this line.

And so, during the NEP period, expanded reproduction was fundamentally subject to the demands of accumulation and the valorization of capital, and from this there followed, where the evolution of employment and unemployment was concerned, a series of particularly grave consequences in a situation in which the number of jobless in the towns was tending to increase rapidly owning to migration from the countryside.

V.   The characteristics of the relations between classes and the domination of expanded reproduction by the demands of accumulation

If, in the NEP period, the demands of accumulation imposed their constraint on the principal form assumed by expanded reproduction, especially in industry, this was certainly due to the theoretical conceptions that prevailed, and which tended to *identify* expanded reproduction with accumulation. But the fact that these conceptions were predominant was itself due to a certain *state of class relations* some essential aspects of which need to be recalled.

The maintenance of what had initially been conceived as *temporary measures* (one-person management, the role of specialists and the resultant hierarchical relations, and *khozraschet*) corresponded to the consolidation of certain social relations and relations between classes. These relations subordinated manual labor to mental labor, ensured the reproduction of hierarchical relations within the "collective laborer," and perpetuated relations of exteriority between the different members of the working groups and between the different working groups subject to the constraints of commodity production and to those of a plan constructed "from above downward." These social relations seriously restricted the possibilities of increasing production on the basis of a process of mass innovation. They tended to give predominance to possibilities of increasing production through changes in the production process initiated from above, in which the means of production were separated from the immediate producers and functioned as capital. In other words, the state of social relations, and the corresponding relations between classes, actually *tended* to subject expanded reproduction to the demands of the accumulation of capital. Moreover, in the absence of a critical analysis of the consequences of these demands—an analysis presupposing systematization of a sufficient body of historical experience, drawing the balance sheet of a certain minimum of open struggles against the reproduction of existing relations in their then current form—what was an *objective tendency* was seen as a "necessary law."

The state of social relations and relations between classes which has been described, and the absence of a systematization of open struggles against the reproduction of existing relations such as would have provided the basis for a *concrete criticism* of the consequences of these relations (and not merely a cristicism inspired by abstract principles), were the result of a complex historical process. This process was marked by the "physical" weakening of the Soviet proletariat consequent upon the civil war and the absorption of the best proletarian forces into the Soviet administrative machinery, and then by the entry into the ranks of the proletariat of new forces, which began, though only toward the end of the NEP period (as we see from the events of 1928)[67] to challenge certain forms of the immediate production process.

The initial weakening of the proletariat had as corollary the strengthening of the role and functions of those who occupied the leading position in the process of production and repro- duction. These were either former bourgeois or—and this was more and more the case toward the end of the NEP—officials of proletarian origin. The functions which these officials, whatever their origin, fulfilled in the process of production and reproduction were *bourgeois functions,* associated with management of processes which were those of the reproduc- tion of a "collective capital" (divided, though, into relatively separate fractions). In this way a social stratum came into being which *objectively possessed a dual nature.* It was pro- letarian by class origin and, generally speaking, by its devo- tion to the aims of the socialist revolution. It was bourgeois by the functions it assumed and, sometimes, by the way in which it fulfilled these functions and the way of life it adopted. It thus tended, in some of its objective and subjective features, to *constitute a bourgeois force.* This tendency took shape all the more easily because the working class (which was only in process of reconstitution) did not offer timely opposition to it, and because the Party, lacking experience in this field, and influenced by the conceptions of those of the leading eco- nomic cadres who were members of it, opposed the tendency only feebly. This relative passivity was itself an effect of the process of becoming independent of the masses which had affected the state and the Party apparatus alike[68]—a process the counterpart of which was the too weak development of that socialist *democracy* without which no revolutionary trans- formation of production relations and productive forces can be accomplished. Here, too, politics "commands" economics.

*(a) The development of bourgeois features
by the cadres holding posts of
leadership in the economic apparatuses,
and the form of the reproduction
process*

The development of bourgeois features by the cadres holding posts of leadership in the economic apparatuses affected in
many ways the form taken by the reproduction process. Here I
shall make only a few points.

In the first place, this development hindered the rise of
mass initiatives and criticism from below, and blocked the
development of new production relations which could allow
new, socialist forms of labor and of the productive forces to
assert themselves. Under these conditions, the immense potential of latent productive forces contained within the Soviet
social formation contributed only very little to the actual increase in production. This increase therefore continued basically to depend above all on the process of accumulation.

The scrapping of "obsolete" equipment was due, also, to
both the theoretical notions which have already been mentioned[69] *and* to concrete intervention in the process of production and reproduction by the heads of the large state-owned
enterprises.

In a situation where mass unemployment existed, the "obsolete" equipment which the state enterprises ceased to use
for reasons of "profitability" could, instead of being turned
into scrap iron, have been used by unemployed workers organized in cooperatives and by small local industrial enterprises in the rural areas, for which peasants, perhaps working
part time, could have provided the work force. Use of the
equipment in this way would have enabled its potential for
production and employment to be conserved. If the state factories had handed over their relatively obsolete equipment to
workers' cooperatives or small-scale rural industries, this
would have increased total production capacity, employment,
and resources for future accumulation. Operations of this sort

have been carried out on a large scale in the People's Republic of China.

In the USSR, however, both in the NEP period and subsequently, such handing over of "obsolete" equipment took place but rarely. Furthermore, the heads of the large state-owned enterprises were, as a rule, *hostile* to the workers' coooperatives and local peasant industry, and tried to restrict their field of activity. They often succeeded in doing this, despite the attitude or principle maintained by the Party, which, throughout most of the NEP period, declared itself in favor of local industry.

The feebleness of the help given to workers' cooperatives and peasants' local industry was due, certainly in part, to ideological reasons (to a bourgeois conception of "technical progress") in the name of which a connection was made between "socialism" and the "advanced state" of technology, leading to condemnation of the use of "obsolete" technical means. This was what lay behind a statement like Kuibyshev's in October 1927 that "socialism is a *technically* higher stage of development of society"[70]—a one sided interpretation of certain formulations by Lenin which appear sometimes to ascribe a major role to "the development of technology."

But it was not ideology that was the most important factor in this conflict between large-scale state-owned industry, on the one hand, and the workers' cooperatives and peasants' local industry, on the other, a conflict of which two immediate effects were increased unemployment and the flight from the countryside. The principal factor here was the action taken by the heads of the state enterprises (and those of the state economic organs with which they were connected), aimed at keeping control over all industrial activity. Their action sought to increase the scope of the operations for which they were responsible, and sometimes also the income they derived from them (particularly in the form of percentages).

Such action can be observed at a number of levels.[71] It enabled large-scale state-owned industry to keep at its disposal a more numerous industrial reserve army than would otherwise have been the case, and one which included skilled workers. It made possible a tightening of factory discipline and higher "profitability" for the big enterprises, which also helped to establish the idea that the big enterprises "functioned better" than the small ones.

The measures taken by the central economic organs to the advantage of the big enterprises favored the most highly developed forms of the capitalist division of labor and the subordination of expanded reproduction to the accumulation of capital, thus contributing, in the given conditions, to an increase in unemployment.

This type of development was thus based upon the predominance in industry of expanded reproduction of the social relations and relations between classes that were characteristic of the large-scale enterprises. This predominance was facilitated by the limited nature of the proletarian class actions directed against the existing forms of division of labor and by the absence of a critical analysis.

(b) The level of wages, the "profitability" of different techniques, and the problem of unemployment

Under NEP conditions the development of unemployment seems to have been determined by the very limited size of the accumulation fund, by the will to invest this fund preferably in "profitable" techniques, and by the fact that only those investments appeared "profitable" which made possible the installation of "up-to-date" equipment. Investments like these absorbed a large proportion of the investment fund while not directly engendering more than a limited number of jobs.

But the "profitability" of different types of investment is not a "technical datum": it is bound up with the levels of prices and wages and with the type of discipline prevailing in the production units. Throughout the NEP period, the wage level rose steadily, despite the amount of unemployment and its tendency to increase. This rising wage level created an incentive—in the name of "profitability"—for those techniques to be preferred which were comparatively costly in terms of capital but which "economized" on living labor. This being so, we need to look into the reasons determining the increase in wages which took place regardless of the campaigns that were continually being waged to "stabilize" them and prevent their increase from swelling the costs of production.

To a certain extent, this increase in wages taking place in spite of the presence of unemployment may seem to be linked with the position held by the working class as a result of the establishment of the dictatorship of the proletariat. Such an interpretation is problematical, however, in that *the form assumed by expanded reproduction was such that the increase in the wages of those who had jobs produced a negative effect on the standard of living of the proletariat as a whole,* by stimulating an increase in unemployment.

Actually, concrete analysis shows that, in general, wage-increases were effected contrary to the provisions of the annual plans, and were connected above all with the development of the contradictions within the production units. In so far as the heads of enterprises restricted the workers' initiative and opposed the development of movements of mass criticism, wage increases served as a means of appeasing the discontent of the workers motivated by the conditions in which they lived and worked. The increases granted in 1927 and 1928 had their source, fundamentally, in this system of contradictions. They were the result of a particular form of class struggle, and were the corollary of the absence of changes in the form of the immediate production process. This absence had also some effects on the inequalities in wages.[72]

(c) The predominant form of labor discipline and the type of technological development

The existence of the contradictions just mentioned means that the dominant aspect of *labor discipline* in the state-owned enterprises was at that time a capitalist type of discipline—with which the recourse to piece wages and material incentives was connected. The strengthening of this type of discipline also tended to favor the adoption of those forms of the labor process in which the machine is used as a means of imposing "its own discipline" upon the direct producers.[73]

In other words, the failure to develop a genuine socialist labor discipline combined with the role played by the striving for "profitability" led, under the conditions that prevailed in the NEP period, to *identifying the outlook for technological changes in the Soviet factories with the changes which had taken place in the capitalist countries.* It is particularly significant that the *Outline of Political Economy* by Lapidus and Ostrovityanov, in a section which, since it is entitled "Socialist Technique," leads the reader to expect at least some indication of the distinction between "socialist technique" and capitalist technique, puts the problem like this: "What are the main lines of technical development in the Soviet Union? They follow from the tendencies which we pointed out in analysing capitalist technique."[74]

Which amounts to saying that "socialist technique" has merely to *follow the road of capitalist technique.* To be sure, the *Outline* is able to refer to various passages in Lenin to "justify" this conception[75]—but these passages had been written seven years earlier, before the task of restoring the Soviet economy had been accomplished. The fact that once this task *had* been accomplished, and the tasks of reconstructing industry were being faced, no new prospect appeared in the field of technique, shows that *the existing social relations and relations between classes did not allow the question of a radical transformation of technical development to be put on the agenda.*

Thus, to the dominance of the capitalist form of expanded reproduction there corresponded *predominance of the capitalist forms of technical change,* or, more generally, of the *capitalist form of development of the productive forces.*

VI. The form of the reproduction process and the nature of the relations between classes

Taken as a whole, the form assumed by the reproduction process under the NEP was determined by the historical limits within which the class struggles unfolded in the Soviet Union: it was within these limits that the changes undergone by the process of production and reproduction occurred. The limits themselves were set, on the plane of social forces, by the weakness of the Soviet proletariat. This weakness was not so much "numerical" as ideological. It was a matter of the slight extent to which the proletarian ideology had penetrated the masses,[76] a circumstance itself connected with the poor development of socialist democracy. On the plane of theoretical ideology it was connected with the absence of a rigorous analysis of the nature of the existing production relations and of the need to struggle to change them as as to make decisive progress toward socialism. This "ideological limitation" was rooted in the history of the class struggles and in the effects that these struggles had had upon the changes in the Bolshevik ideological formation. The forms taken by these class struggles did not allow the development of a rigorous analysis of the social relations and relations between classes existing in the NEP period.

It is difficult to analyze production relations and class relations under the NEP because of the extremely contradictory nature of these relations and of the completely new forms that they assumed. Even today, when we possess a much longer and broader historical experience, together with the lessons drawn from it by Mao Tse-tung and the Chinese Communist Party, this analysis can be made on only a certain level of abstraction. But even so limited a type of analysis is indispensable if we are to grasp the movement of the contradictions.

One of the essential points is this: that the existence of what Lenin called "the system of the dictatorship of the proletariat"[77] did not cause the proletariat to "disappear," but *modified* its form of existence and its *relations* with the other classes of society.[78]

In the NEP period, this system retained the essential features it had possessed in 1921, though the expansion of the machinery of state, the development of *khozraschet* (in the form in which this was then practiced) and of the banking and financial apparatuses, together with the strengthening of factory discipline, had changed the forms of *separation of the working class from its means of production*.

It was because of this separation that the working class was *still a proletariat:* the proletariat cannot disappear until all forms of separation between the direct producers and their means of production have disappeared. However, the existence of the system of the dictatorship of the proletariat implies the *destruction of part of the previous relations of separation,* in particular, because, *through the system of its organization* (Party, trade unions and soviets) the proletariat is *united* with its means of production and is able, to some extent, to determine the use that is made of them. In other words, the Soviet working class is *at once a proletariat and not a proletariat*: a proletariat, in so far as it is separated from its means of production and integrated in a system of capitalist relations which have undergone only partial changes; not a proletariat, in so far as it is united with its means of production and dominates them through the development of *new social relations*[79] *in the superstructure and in the economic basis*.

The specific features assumed by this dual nature of the proletariat change as a result of class struggles: the destruction of the relations of separation consolidates the dictatorship of the proletariat and at the same time helps to put an end to the conditions that make the working class a proletariat.

In the NEP period, the Soviet proletariat, at the level of the immediate production relations and of the dominant form of the reproduction process, remained fundamentally separated from its means of production: the domination it exercised over the latter was effected essentially through certain of its organizations—actually, above all, through the Bolshevik Party as the organized vanguard of the proletariat (which it was in so far as its ideology and its ties with the masses enabled it to serve effectively the historical interests of the proletariat and thereby of all mankind).

Since the proletariat had not disappeared, neither had the bourgeoisie, though its form of existence and its relations with the other classes had been *modified*. The chief modification

concerned the agents who played a leading role in the reproduction of capitalist production relations in the state sector.
They constituted *a bourgeoisie which was at the same time
not a bourgeoisie:* a bourgeoisie, in so far as it carried out its
directing task on the basis of the reproduction of (more or less
altered) capitalist relations; but not a bourgeoisie, in so far as it
carried out this task under conditions that were entirely new,
that is, in so far as it was *subordinated ideologically and
politically to the dictatorship of the proletariat.*

Here, too, the specific features assumed by the dual nature
of this bourgeoisie, which is at the same time not a
bourgeoisie, change as a result of class struggles: the destruction or strengthening of the relations of separation depends
above all upon the struggle of the workers themselves and the
correct guidance of this struggle. The successes won in this
struggle affect social relations in their entirety. They contribute to the elimination, stage by stage, of the ideology and
practices which tend to be reproduced on the basis of the
existence of production relations that have as yet been only
partially transformed.

The elimination of bourgeois ideology and practices is a
condition of the changing of the production relations themselves: hence the decisive role played by the ideological class
struggle, especially as regards style of work and leadership,
and socialist democracy. This struggle is of decisive importance not only in the production units but also in all the
ideological apparatuses.

To the dual nature of the proletariat and the bourgeois
which characterizes the socialist transition (and which assumed specific features in the NEP period) there corresponds
the struggle between the two roads which is inherent in this
transition. The socialist road triumphs in proportion as
capitalist social relations and the corresponding social practice are destroyed. Historically, this destruction is indispensable if the dictatorship of the proletariat is to be consolidated:
as Marx noted, "The political rule of the producer cannot
coexist with the perpetuation of his social slavery."[80] The
"perpetuation" of social slavery is bound up with the repro-

duction of capitalist relations on the plane of production and reproduction. If the class struggle of the workers themselves does not put an end to this, it tends necessarily to undermine their political domination and put an end to *that*.

To the dual nature of the classes in the NEP period corresponded the dual nature of the State, of the Party (in which was concentrated the struggle between the proletarian line and the bourgeois line), and of the process of production and reproduction.

On this last point, it must be emphasized once more that the *production of surplus value* (connected with the reproduction of the value and wage forms which ensure the merging of the expenditure of necessary labor with the expenditure of surplus labor) ceases to signify *exploitation* in so far as the use made of the surplus value is no longer dominated exclusively by the laws of the capitalist mode of production, but is *directed* by the system of the dictatorship of the proletariat— for which profit and accumulation, even if they continue to be *means* serving the development of production, *cease to be production's purpose.*

VII. The changing of the form of the reproduction process at the end of the NEP

At the end of the NEP period two decisive factors came into play which modified the form of the reproduction process. These two factors were interconnected, but it was the second that played the *determining role,* because it was directly connected with a change in the relations between classes.

(a) The extension of the domain of planning

The first factor which altered the conditions of reproduction was the the extension of planning. This does not mean that planning became more "precise" and more "coherent" (on the

contrary, the First Five-Year Plan, with the subsequent modifications and the annual plans of that first quinquennium,
were particularly lacking in coherence), but that the imperatives of the plan now extended, in principle, to all aspects of
economic activity, and in particular to the bulk of investments,
which thereafter passed through the state budget. This extension restricted the effects of *khozraschet,* in so far as the latter
had intended to maintain a certain connection between the
profitability of each enterprise and the amount invested in it.
The overall investment plan aimed to break this connection
and to subject the process of accumulation to demands other
than those corresponding to the making of the maximum profit
by each enterprise, or to the equalization of the rates of profit
in the various branches of industry.

Planning sought to realize the largest possible overall accumulation and to ensure the fastest possible growth of industry, on the basis of priority development of heavy industry.
True, the concrete conditions in which the plans were drawn
up, revised, and put into effect did not make it possible to say
that the tasks thus assigned to planning were actually fulfilled,
but the aim that planning pursued did tend to alter radically
some of the effects of the "separation" between state enterprises insituted by *khozraschet.*

In place of a distribution of investments that depended,
more or less, on sectoral "profitability" there was substituted a
distribution dominated by a striving to achieve *acceleration of
the growth of production,* and, in the first place, of production
by heavy industry. In the language of the period, the demands
of "profitability" at the level of enterprises and branches were
superseded, in principle, by the demands of "profitability on
the scale of society as a whole."

This meant a break with the previous form of the reproduction process. To a certain extent, this break took place in the
direction *of a socialist development of the economy,* but it
nevertheless remained *subject to the demands of the valorization process:* it was only the scale of this process that was
enlarged.

Maintenance of the demands of the valorization process was

expressed in the importance still accorded to *economic calculations in terms of prices*, and, even more, in *the overall limits which the amount of accumulation set to increased employment*. These limits implied that "unprofitable techniques" still tended to be eliminated, even when they made possible increases in employment and production.

The existence of these limits was manifested in the various drafts and successive variants of the First Five-Year Plan.[81] *These different drafts all made provision for the retention of a considerable number of unemployed.* It was only with the "great turn" that unemployment vanished: thereafter, indeed, the poor capacity of state industry for *internal accumulation* tended to be made up for by *"primitive accumulation"* connected with levying of "tribute" from the peasantry. Actually, this tribute had already begun to be exacted by means of the "emergency measures," which enabled deliveries of agricultural produce to be obtained without the counterpart of deliveries to the peasants of industrial goods of the same value. The tribute was subsequently increased by the exactions forced out of agriculture through the framework of collectivization.[82]

(b) The recourse to "primitive accumulation" and the change in class relations

Ultimately "the extension of planning" (in the sense given to this expression) was made possible by *a radical change in class relations,* through the elimination of private trade and industry and through collectivization, which put an end to the individual peasant farms of old.

The elimination of private trade and industry and of traditional individual peasant farming signified *a victory of socialist economic forms,* a victory of the proletariat *over the private bourgeoisie.* However, as will be seen in the next volume, *the means employed to achieve this end were not, in the main, proletarian means*—the changes were brought about "from above"—and this *limited the political and social*

*significance of the changes effected, strengthening the
capitalist elements in the production relations that were reproduced in the state and cooperative sectors, and
strengthening the bourgeois aspects of the state machine.*

If the victory of the socialist forms resulted mainly from the
carrying out of measures taken "from above," this was because
it was not the culmination of a broad struggle by the masses. It
was essentailly the result of the *contradictions in the process
of accumulation,* of the fact that, in the absence of a mass
struggle, it had not proved possible to free the process of
reproduction from the *constraints of accumulation,* and so the
limits of accumulation had had to be shifted by bringing into
play *constraint by the state.*

For this reason as well as for others (connected with the
absence of sufficiently thoroughgoing internal changes in the
functioning of state industry), the victory of socialist economic
forms was not accompanied by the disappearance of the limits
that the demands of accumulation imposed upon expanded
reproduction. But though these *limits* did not disappear, they
were shifted through the extension of socialist economic
forms. This shift entailed in its turn *a series of contradictory
effects,* due to the very conditions under which it had been
made. On the one hand it strengthened the dictatorship of the
proletariat, by ensuring a rapid increase in the size of
the working class, abolishing unemployment, and enabling the
Soviet Union to become a great industrial power. On the
other, it weakened the dictatorship of the proletariat by causing a split in the worker-peasant alliance, starting an unprecedented crisis in agriculture, and giving rise to the development of apparatuses of coercion and repression which
extended their activity to the broad masses and set back
socialist democracy.

An upheaval in relations between classes, the historical
implications of which can be estimated only through concrete
analysis of all its consequences, was the ultimate content of
the final crisis of the NEP. This crisis was led up to by the
failure really to consolidate the worker-peasant alliance and
the impossibility of freeing the reproduction process from the

constraints of the process of accumulation. These two factors in the final crisis of the NEP were related also to the ideological and political relations in which the Soviet proletariat and its vanguard, the Bolshevik Party, were integrated, and so to the forms of organization of the working class.

Notes

1. Lapidus and K. Ostrovityanov, *Outline,* p. 176 (my emphasis—C.B.).
2. Ibid., p. 177 (my emphasis—C. B.).
3. Ibid.
4. Ibid.
5. Ibid., p. 98.
6. Ibid., p. 99–100.
7. Without entering upon a discussion of all the problems involved here, let us merely recall these few formulations by Marx:

   > Wages represent also wage-labour, which is examined in a different section; the particular function that labour performs as a factor of production in the one case appears as a function of distribution in the other. If labour did not have the distinct form of wage-labour, then its share in the product would not appear as wages. . . . The structure of distribution is entirely determined by the structure of production. Distribution itself is a product of production, not only with regard to the content . . . but also with regard to the form, since the particular mode of men's participation in production determines the specific form of distribution, the form in which they share in distribution. (*Critique of Political Economy,* p. 200.)

   Again:

   > The wage presupposes wage-labour, and profit—capital. These definite forms of distribution thus presuppose definite social characteristics of production conditions, and definite relations of production-agents. The specific distribution relations are thus merely the expression of the specific historical production-relations. . . . Capitalist distribution differs

from those forms of distribution which arise from other modes of production, and every form of distribution disappears with the specific form of production from which it is descended and to which it corresponds. (*Capital* [Moscow], vol. III, pp. 860–861.)

8. Lapidus and Ostrovityanov, *Outline*, p. 99.
9. *K.P.S.S. v rezolyutsiyakh*, vol. I, p. 689. This resolution also noted that if industrial accumulation was to be achieved by means of subsidies from the budget, this would mean it was being achieved at the expense of the peasantry.
10. See above, pp. 291–292.
11. Marx, *Capital* (London), vol. I, p. 165.
12. See Bettelheim, *Economic Calculation and Forms of Property*, pp. 67–68. However, in this passage there is too one-sided a stress laid upon the objective conditions, resulting in underestimation of the necessary role of the ideological class struggle in the changing of the production relations themselves.
13. These were the terms used by Lenin to describe, in 1921, the nature of the "socialist republic of soviets," an expression which he said did not signify "that the existing economic system is recognized as a socialist order" (Lenin, *CW*, vol. 32, p. 330; see also volume I of the present work, p. 445).
14. On this point see Marx, *Grundrisse*, p. 470.
15. Ibid., p. 158.
16. Ibid., p. 168.
17. The *partial* disappearance of this character (connected with the existence of state ownership of the means of production and actual use thereof in conformity with the economic aims of a state of the dictatorship of the proletariat) does indeed give rise to new, socialist relations, but, so long as it remains partial, it permits the survival, in changed (but nevertheless possibly dominant) form, of commodity and capitalist relations or elements of these relations. This was what Mao Tse-tung meant when he spoke of "socialist relations of production" being "still far from perfect" in China ("On the Correct Solution of Contradictions Among the People," in *Four Essays on Philosophy*, p. 94).
18. The notion of "collective capital," resulting from state ownership, is found in Marx and Engels—e.g., in *Capital* (London), vol. I, p. 779.
19. Marx, *Capital* (Moscow), vol. III, p. 431. I have italicized the word "employment" (in the French version, *"mise en valeur"*)

because it is precisely in the subordination of labor to the production of exchange values, and not to the production of *use
values* for the satisfaction of *collectively calculated social needs,*
that the line of demarcation runs between the situation of these
"co-operators" and that in which all the means of production are
"in the hands of associated producers" (ibid, p. 430).

20. Lapidus and Ostrovityanov, *Outline,* pp. 178–179.
21. On the layoffs at the start of NEP, see S. G. Strumilin, *Na
khozyaistvennom fronte,* p. 86, and *Na novykh putyakh,* III, p.
14, quoted in E. H. Carr, *The Bolshevik Revolution,* vol. 2, p. 321.
22. *Narodnoye Khozyaistvo SSSR: statistichesky spravochnik;* and
A. Baykov, *The Soviet Economic Systems,* p. 147; also *Voprosy
truda v tsifrakh i diagrammakh 1922–1926 gg.*
23. According to a statistical source of 1929 (*Ekonomicheskoye
Obozreniye,* no. 9 [1929], p. 124), the number of workers (including office workers) employed in census industry rose from
2,678,000 (a figure close to that for 1913) in 1925–1926 to
3,366,000 in 1928–1929—an increase of nearly 700,000, or 27
percent, in three years. During the same period the total number
of wage earners, including those employed in the administration,
rose from 10,173,000 to 12,168,000—an increase of about two
million, or nearly 20 percent. The rate of increase in employment
was highest in the building industry, where it more than doubled, reaching the figure of 918,000 (Carr and Davies, *Foundations,* vol. 1, pt. 2, p. 955). Out of more than 12 million wage
earners employed in 1928–1929, 2,500,000 were employed in the
administration and services (education, health, justice, the economic administrations) and two million in agriculture, forestry,
and fisheries. At that time the urban population was 29 million
and the rural population, 125.3 million (ibid., pp. 454, 955).
24. *Sotsialisticheskoye Khozyaistvo,* no. 4 (1925), p. 413.
25. Carr and Davies, *Foundations,* vol. I, pt. 2, p. 456, and *Voprosy
Truda,* July–August 1935, p. 46.
26. *Pravda,* November 29, 1927.
27. *Pravda,* January 29, 1927.
28. The size of this "flood" was certainly substantial. Thus, at the
Fifteenth Party Congress it was admitted that in 1927, 500,000
peasants from Tambov region had been obliged to try and find
work in industry, and that 220,000 peasants from Ryazan region
had had to go to Moscow, Leningrad, and other towns in search of
seasonal employment (*XV-y Syezd VKP[b]* [1962], vol. 2, pp.

1094, 1254, 1256; quoted in Carr and Davies, *Foundations,* vol. I, pt. 2, p. 453, n. 3).

29. *SSSR: IV Syezd Sovyetov* (1927), pp. 428–429.

30. Carr and Davies, *Foundations,* vol. I, pt. 2, p. 927.

31. Those who talked of "rural overpopulation" and of "land short-age" did not deny that the exodus from the countryside was mainly an exodus of landless and poor peasants, and that a fresh division of the land might, therefore, have slowed down the flow of rural migrants, though without stopping it altogether, since, in any case, the average amount of land per peasant was regarded as being "insufficient." However, there was no question, in the 1920s, of carrying out a fresh division of the land, for it was accepted that only peasant farms of a certain size were capable of providing the marketed production that was indispensable for the feeding of the towns.

32. See above, pp. 300–301.

33. Strumilin, *Na Plamovom Fronte,* pp. 448 ff.

34. *Sechster Kongress der Kommunistischen Internationale,* vol. III (1928), p. 519, quoted in Carr and Davies, *Foundations,* vol. 1, pt. 2, p. 466.

35. No less surprisingly (but to be explained likewise by the con-juncture of the class struggle), *the chief obstacle to a substantial increase in the number of wage workers* was only rarely men-tioned in the discussions about unemployment, though it was more or less taken into account in the "control figures" drawn up by Gosplan from 1925 on. This obstacle was constituted by the quantity of goods available on the market. If one was not to allow phenomena of shortage and price increase to develop, it was not possible to allow a mass of incomes to be formed that would be larger than the available counterpart (at the given level of prices) in the form of purchasable commodities. And, given the *differ-ence in income* between the *poor* peasants (who were the peas-ants who were looking for jobs in industry) and the workers, the "conversion" of "too many" of the former into wage workers would risk causing an increase in shortages (unless this conver-sion was carried out under conditions different from those which were then characteristic of state industry and guided its de-velopment).

36. Stalin, *Works,* vol. 7, p. 322.

37. Ibid., vol. 9, p. 177.

38. Ibid., vol. 11, p. 167.

39. See above, p. 194.

40. *Sobranie Zakonov*, no. 41 (1927), art. 410.
41. The *average* wage of an agricultural worker was 313 roubles in 1928, when the *average* wage in industry was 823 roubles (*Trud v SSSR* [1936], statistical handbook, pp. 10, 97, quoted in O. Hoeffding, *Soviet National Income and Product in 1928*, p. 67). From 1926 on there was an increase in the proportion of workers coming from the rural areas who retained their holdings in the villages. In the Donbas mines 37.4 percent of the workers taken on between 1926 and 1929 kept their land, and this was the case with 28.4 percent of the workers in the Moscow metal industry (*Sostav fabrichno-zavodskogo proletariata SSSR* [1930], quoted in Carr and Davies, *Foundations*, vol. 1, pt. 2, p. 455).
42. Carr and Davies, *Foundations*, vol. I, pt. 2, p. 459.
43. *Trud*, October 26, 1926.
44. This contributed to increasing the proportion of young persons among the unemployed. In 1928 43.6 percent of the registered unemployed were aged between 18 and 24, and 30.8 percent aged between 24 and 29 (*VIII-oy Syezd Professionalnykh Soyuzov SSSR* [1928], p. 323).
45. *Izvestiya*, January 14, 1925.
46. *Trud*, December 1, 1926.
47. *Sobranie Zakonov*, no. 62 (1928), art. 563.
48. On the decree of March 26, 1928, see *Yezhenedelnik Sovyetskoy Yustitsii*, nos. 46–47 (1928), quoted in Carr and Davies, *Foundations*, vol. 1, pt. 2, p. 465, n. 5.
49. *Kontrolnye tsifry 1928–1929 gg.*, p. 20.
50. In 1927 the area actually cultivated was 97.4 percent of what it had been in 1913. Between these same years the rural population had grown by 7 percent, and the number of farms by 21 percent (S. Grosskopf, *L'Alliance ouvrière*, p. 381).
51. After the October Revolution there were various types of peasants' mutual-aid committees (*Krestkomy*, or KKOV). In the RSFSR a decree of March 29, 1926, provided for land to be placed free of charge at the disposal of these committees, but they did not come to much. A report presented to Rabkrin in the spring of 1928 pointed to their stagnation (*Pravda*, April 7, 1928).
52. See above, pp. 99 ff. and 105 ff.
53. *Sobranie Uzakonenii*, no. 70 (1926), art. 548.
54. *XV-taya Konferentsiya VKP(b)* (1927), pp. 253–254.
55. Carr and Davies, *Foundations*, vol. I, pt. 2, pp. 927–929, and G. von Mende, *Studien zur Kolonisation der Sowjetunion*.
56. To some extent this "colonization" meant settlement by rich

peasants who had the personal means needed in order to establish themselves on new land (R. Lorenz, *Sozialgeschichte der Sowjetunion 1917–1945*, p. 140).

57. Stalin, *Works*, vol. 7, p. 312.

58. See volume I of the present work, especially pp. 33 ff. and 490 ff.

59. We know that in December 1920 Lenin counterposed to the oversimplified conception put forward by Trotsky, who spoke of the Soviet state as a "workers' state," without analyzing its contradictions, the following observation: "The whole point is that it is not quite a workers' state." He then spoke of the "bureaucratic distortions" of the Soviet state, which made it necessary for the workers to defend themselves against the workers' state (Lenin, *CW*, vol. 32, pp. 24, 48). Soon afterward, opposing the positions then maintained by Trotsky and Bukharin, Lenin made more explicit the content of his own position, by recalling that "Dialectics requires an all-round consideration of relationships in their concrete development but not a patchwork of bits and pieces" (ibid., vol. 32, p. 91). The pertinence of these formulations makes it inadmissible that, after several years' existence of the Soviet state and the state-owned enterprises, anyone should be satisfied to talk, "on the one hand," of their socialist character and, "on the other" of "bureaucratic survivals." It necessitates consideration of these realities in all their aspects and connections, in their development and their contradictions (ibid., vol. 32, p. 94).

60. This form belongs to the political level: it makes *possible* under certain conditions, a certain *transformation of the production relations*, but it does not directly determine such a transformation.

61. The dominance of this aim did not, of course, drop from heaven, but reflected the objective conditions of reproduction: the low level of development of socialist relations effectively subordinated the expanded reproduction of the productive forces to an accumulation which, in the given conditions, depended above all on *the self-valorization of the capital functioning in the state sector*. At the beginning of the 1930s the attempt to increase the "tribute" levied from the peasantry was to "free" (temporarily and partially) from this constraint the expanded reproduction of the productive forces.

62. Carr and Davies, *Foundations*, vol. I, pt. 1, p. 417.

63. This identification led to the assertion that, as regards the internal functioning of the state sector, *increased employment* was determined in the last analysis by *increased profit*.

64. Under the capitalist mode of production the principal aspect of the process of accumulation is that it is a process of exploitation, a process of bourgeois class struggle for increased exploitation of the proletariat (see A. D. Magaline, *Lutte de classes et dévalorisation du capital*).

65. See above, p. 50 ff., the quotation from Marx's *Grundrisse*.

66. See above, p. 290.

67. See above, pp. 222–233.

68. See volume I of the present work, pp. 255, 285, 303, 309, 399, 408.

69. See above, p. 306.

70. *II-ya Sessiya TsIK SSSR 4 Soyuza* (1927?), p. 250, quoted in Carr and Davies, *Foundations*, vol. I, pt. 1, p. 415 (my emphasis— C.B.).

71. See above, pp. 202 ff.

72. See above, pp. 248 ff.

73. On this see H. Braverman, *Labor and Monopoly Capital*, pp. 169 ff.

74. Lapidus and Ostrovityanov, *Outline*, p. 485.

75. Ibid., pp. 485–486.

76. See volume I of the present work, pp. 93–94.

77. See volume I of the present work, p. 97 ff.

78. See also Lenin's "Economics and politics in the era of the dictatorship of the proletariat," in *CW*, vol. 30, p. 115.

79. These new social relations concern also the *political relations*, the forms of *proletarian socialist democracy*. The actual development of these forms (the decisive importance of which Lenin showed in his *The State and Revolution*) determined changes in the relations between the producers and the means of production belonging to the State, and this development helps to change the economic basis and is a condition of the strengthening of the dictatorship of the proletariat.

80. Marx, *The Civil War in France*, in Marx and Engels, *Selected Works in Three Volumes*, vol. 2, p. 223.

81. On the successive drafts of this plan see Carr and Davies, *Foundations*, vol. I, pt. 2, pp. 837 ff.

82. In fact this "tribute" was soon exhausted, and the accumulation fund had to be increased by way of increased prices and the lowering of real wages. This development will be analyzed in volume III of the present work.

6. The forms of organization of the working class

The ideological relations in which the working class was integrated in the NEP period were complex and diverse. There is no lack of "sources" for them, but these are, generally speaking, indirect, and also more or less "controlled," so that there is practically no expression in them of certain ideological currents. These "sources" consist of readers' letters published in the newspapers; novels and short stories in which the workers' lives are "described," with their reactions to everyday problems, to the decisions taken by the Party and the government, and so on; and also reports presented to congresses, conferences, and other meetings of the Party and the trade unions; and internal reports of the Party and the OGPU, some of which have been published. Nevertheless, it is not easy, and is sometimes even impossible, to succeed by means of such sources (the content of which can usually not be dissociated from the ideological or political purposes aimed at by those who composed or published them) in grasping the diversity of the ideological currents running through the different strata of the working class, and the changes these currents underwent in the course of a period so lively as the NEP years.

However, the chief ideological currents running through the working class were reflected, even if only partially and in an inevitably impoverished or simplified form, in the activity and the decisions of the organizations of the working class, and also in the open demonstrations in which the active elements of this class took part. It is at this level, the one most directly linked with the taking of political decisions, that I shall endeavor to define certain aspects of the ideological changes undergone by the Soviet working class in the NEP period, and especially toward the end of it. We therefore need

330

to pay attention here, first and foremost, to the principal forms of working-class organization and to the place occupied by the workers in these organizations.

I. The development of the Bolshevik Party

The Bolshevik Party was the vanguard of the Soviet proletariat by virtue of its class basis, its ideology, and its political line. The last two factors are of vital importance in this context. Theory and practice alike teach us that *the fact that a party is rooted in the working class is not enough to make it a proletarian party.* There are many examples of "labor parties" which, because of their ideology and political line, are actually in the service of the bourgeoisie and therefore constitute what Lenin called "bourgeois labor parties." Conversely, the working-class members of a proletarian party may be relatively few (especially in a country where the working class itself is not large) without that circumstance damaging its proletarian character, which is determined by its ideology and political line. It is very important, all the same, to analyze the class composition of the Bolshevik Party, because the presence in the Party of members who did not belong to the working class exerted constant pressure upon its ideology and its political line.

We shall examine in the last part of this volume the principal aspects of the ideological and political struggles waged in the Bolshevik Party between 1924 and 1929. For the moment, we shall confine ourselves to looking at the ways in which the working class and other classes or social groups were present in the Bolshevik Party.[1]

(a) The increase in Party membership

In 1929 the Bolshevik Party was profoundly different from what it had been before Lenin's death. It had then taken a big step toward becoming transformed from a Party made up of revolutionary militants (which it had been in 1917) into an organization possessing some of the characteristics of a mass party. This transformation, which had begun (but only begun) in Lenin's lifetime, started to take definite shape in 1929: the change was bound up with the new and numerous tasks which the Party had to carry out once the dictatorship of the proletariat had been established.

Two figures enable us to perceive the magnitude of the quantitative change referred to. On January 1, 1923, the Bolshevik Party had 499,000 members; on January 1, 1930, it had 1,680,000.[2] We thus see that in seven years the Party's membership had more than trebled—which means, among other things, that towards the end of the NEP the majority of the members had only a very brief experience of the political life of their organization.

The initial impetus to this rapid expansion was given in 1924, immediately after Lenin's death, with what were called the "Lenin enrollments."[3] As a result of the entry of these recruits, on January 1, 1926, the Party had 1,080,000 members—more than twice as many as in 1923.[4]

The official aim of the recruitment campaign of 1924 and 1925, and also of that of 1927 (the "October enrolment"), was to *proletarianize the Party*—that is, to *strengthen its working-class basis.*

There is reason, however, to question the *actual class consequences* of the mass-scale recruitment carried out between 1924 and 1930, especially in the first years of the NEP. Until about 1925–1926 the persons working in the factories were often far from being genuine, long-established proletarians. Lenin drew the Party's attention more than once to this situation. At the Eleventh Party Congress, on March 27, 1922, he said: "During the war people who were by no means proletarians went into the factories; they went into the factories to dodge the war. Are the social and economic conditions in our country today such as to induce real proletarians to go into the factories? No. . . . Very often those who go into the factories are not proletarians; they are casual elements of every description."[5]

The day before he made this speech, Lenin had sent a letter to the members of the CC in which he warned against the possible effects of mass- recruitment. The reasons for this warning were those he set out in his speech of March 27, but he also mentioned another, of a more permanent order— namely, the danger of infiltration into a "ruling party" of bourgeois and petty-bourgeois elements motivated by careerism, and prepared to disguise themselves as "workers" in order to get into the Party. Lenin wrote: "It must be borne in mind that the temptation to join the ruling party at the present time is very great."[6] And he added that, if the Party achieved fresh successes, then

there will be a big increase in the efforts of petty-bourgeois elements, and of elements positively hostile to all that is proletarian, to penetrate into the Party. Six months' probation for workers will not diminish this pressure in the least, for it is the easiest thing in the world for anyone to qualify for this short probation period. . . . From all this I draw the conclusion that. . . . we must without fail, define the term 'worker' in such a way as to include only those who have acquired a proletarian mentality from their very conditions of life. But this is impossible unless the persons concerned have worked in a factory for many years— not from ulterior motives, but because of the general conditions of their economic and social life.[7]

Lenin proceeded to lay down a number of requirements aimed at ensuring a truly proletarian recruitment, and emphasized the need for *"reducing"* the number of Party members.[8] Actually, the requirements specified by Lenin were not observed, and the Party's membership, instead of being reduced, was very quickly increased. In principle, as has been said, the purpose aimed at was to *broaden the working-class basis of the Party.* It is far from certain that this purpose was attained.

In December 1925, at the Party's Fourteenth Congress, some counsels of caution were drawn from the evolution of the Party's membership since 1924. A resolution declared that

Congress rejects the policy leading to an excessive swelling of the Party's ranks and its becoming filled with semi-proletarian elements which have not been through the school of the trade unions and of the proletarian organisations in general. Congress rejects such temptations, since they have nothing in common with Leninism and are a negation of the correct relationship between the Party, which is the vanguard of the class, and the class itself, and would make Communist leadership impossible.[9]

In practice this resolution had little effect on the actual recruitment policy followed. At the end of 1926 and, especially, in 1927 (with the campaign for the "October enrollment") the Party again began quickly to increase its membership, so as to ensure that 50 percent of the members were workers actually working in industry.[10] This target was reaffirmed in a resolution of November 1928.[11]

(b) The working-class membership of the Bolshevik Party

The changes in the numbers of factory workers, the quick turnover of this personnel, and the tendency for nonproletarian elements to pass themselves off as workers in order to gain entry to the Party make the statistics for the number of workers who were Party members rather unreliable. This unreliability is enhanced by the vague and fluctuating definitions of class which were were used and by the inadequate checking of applicants for membership.[12]

When analyzing statistics dealing with the social composition of the Party it is also necessary to distinguish between "social position," meaning the position a person had occupied for a more or less lengthy period before joining the Party, and his actual occupation at a certain moment. This distinction is important, for a significant proportion of those who joined the Party as "workers" ceased to perform manual work and became office workers and officials.

By the criterion of "social position," the number of worker members of the Party increased from 212,000 in 1923 to 1,100,000 in 1930. It thus increased five times faster than the increase in total membership.[13] From this standpoint there was undoubtedly a broadening of the Party's proletarian basis, although a certain vagueness still prevailed as to the genuinely "working-class" character of some of the members.

Using the criterion of "actual occupation," the relative increase in the number of workers was also very rapid—even more rapid since, after 1924–1925, a smaller proportion of the worker members became office workers.

(c) The Party's social composition

However, the Party's social composition was affected not only by the influx of worker members but also by that of elements from other sections of society, and by the transformation of worker members into office workers. Looked at from this angle, the proletarian character of the Party's social basis, while on the whole becoming stronger during the NEP, was markedly less well defined than if one takes into account only the "social position" of the members.

In 1927, according to the census taken on January 10, the Party was made up as follows: 30 percent workers in industry and transport, 1.5 percent agricultural workers, and 8.4 percent peasants, while "office workers" and "others" represented 60.1 percent of the members.[14]

Thus, the numerically most important social group in the Party consisted of the office workers and "others." In fact, the specific weight of this group in the Party's current activity was much more considerable than is suggested by their mere percentage. To this group belonged the cadres of the Party and the administration, that is, those who held positions of authority and whose activity contributed largely to giving their true significance to the decisions of principle and guidelines adopted by the Party's leading organs. This was a new aspect of the process whereby the Party and the State acquired independence, a process that had begun earlier.[15]

Many discussions, and, especially, the purges to which the adminstrative organs of the Party and the State had to be subjected (the chief posts in the state organs were filled by nomination of Party members to them[16]) show that the group of members who were "office workers" (or officials) consisted not only of revolutionary militants devoted to the cause of socialism but also of petty-bourgeois elements who were, as Lenin put it, "hostile to all that is proletarian."[17]

The number of "scandals" which gave rise to investigations and sanctions shows that these were not merely isolated cases, but constituted a phenomenon of social significance. This was concretized in the presence within the Party of a social stratum which led a life different from that of the workers in the factories and the fields, arrogated privileges to itself, and was unaware of the real problems faced by the masses. Those who belonged to this stratum were actually cut off from the working class, even if they had come from it. They often tended to form cliques whose members covered up for each other—what are called in the USSR, "family circles." At the Party's Fifteenth Congress Stalin said:

> Often we settle questions . . . by the family, domestic-circle method, so to speak. Ivan Ivanovich, a member of the top leadership of such and such an organisation, has, say, made a gross mistake and has messed things up. But Ivan Fyodorovich is reluctant to criticise him, to expose his mistakes and to correct them. He is reluctant to do so because he does not want to 'make enemies.' . . . Today I shall let him, Ivan Fyodorovich, off; tomorrow he will let me, Ivan Ivanovich, off. . . . Is it not obvious that we shall cease to be proletarian revolutionaries, and that we shall certainly perish if we fail to eradicate from our midst this philistinism, this family-circle method of settling highly important questions of our work of construction?[18]

Thus, mainly among the office–worker members of the Party (a group including a high proportion of the cadres), contradictory social forces developed. On the one hand were those who identified themselves with the proletariat, constituted as a ruling class becoming master of its conditions of existence. On the other were those who, by the practices they developed and by their relations with the means of production, formed a bourgeoisie and a petty bourgeoisie in the process of becoming. That bourgeois and petty-bourgeois social forces should exist, and be present in the Party, is inevitable in the transition to socialism: it corresponds to the contradictory nature of the social relations characteristic of that period. It is just this that makes indispensable continued class struggle, the development of the workers' initiatives, socialist democracy, and strengthening the Party's implantation in the proletariat and among the poor peasantry and the less well-off strata of the middle peasantry.

During the NEP such reinforcement of what constituted the firmest foundation of the Party hardly occurred at all, as may be seen from the fact that in 1927 only 30 percent of the Party members were actually workers in industry and transport. Hence the effort constantly being made to increase recruitment from the working class, and hence the target defined for this recruitment, that at least 50 percent of the Party membership be actual workers. In fact, this target was not attained.[19]

The difficulties encountered in broadening the Party's proletarian base bring us to the problem of the Party's concrete relations with the working class.

(d) The Party's relations with the working class

With the information at present available, and keeping within the limits of the problems dealt with in this volume, we can give only partial indications here of what the Bolshevik Party's relations were with the working class. Some of these indications are of a "statistical" order, and so possess an appearance of precision, while others are qualitative, which inevitably means that there is room for a wide margin of interpretation. There is another reason, too, why these indications are very approximate, namely, that relations between the working class and the Bolshevik Party varied considerably from one region or town to another, and from one period to another: consequently it is dangerous to generalize, or to extend to every year and the whole country what may seem true for a particular moment or in a particular locality.

One thing is certain: the social mass basis of the Bolshevik Party and the Soviet state was the proletariat. Without the active support given to the Bolshevik Party and the Soviet government by the live forces of the proletariat by its advance elements and the larger part of its intermediate elements, it would not have been possible to consolidate the changes made by the Revolution, or to bring about the extremely rapid recovery that the Soviet economy experienced under the NEP.

This support does not, of course, imply that the Soviet working class as a whole was constantly in complete agreement with all the decisions taken by the Party and the government. Such unanimity would have been incompatible with the contradictions that existed in the working class itself; the more so because at different times (and, in particular, on the morrow of the civil war) this class contained many elements of petty-bourgeois origin who were not proletarianized ideologically, and who had an attitude that was either passive or hostile toward the Soviet government and the Party. Moreover, even among the genuinely proletarian elements, hesitation or discontent was expressed at certain moments. During the NEP period such phenomena seem to have been connected mainly with the reappearance of private capitalists and merchants and the strengthening of the influence of the kulaks. But they were also connected, especially in the second part of the NEP period, with the appearance of persons in leading positions (in particular, in the enterprises) who developed authoritarian relations with the workers and sought to smother their criticism. The way the production conferences were conducted[20] illustrates this aspect of the matter.

The consolidation of relations of trust between the Party and the working class is determined by the correctness of the Party's political line and by the way in which this is actually applied. It depends on the concrete actions stimulated by the Party and by the direct presence of the Party in the working class—hence the importance of the increase in the worker membership of the Bolshevik Party.

At the Fourteenth Party Congress, in 1925, Stalin said that the proportion of workers who were members of the Party was 8 percent, as compared with 7 percent at the time of the Thirteenth Congress.[21] In 1927 the corresponding figure was estimated at a little under 8 percent.[22]

Altogether, from 1925 on, the increase in the working-class membership of the Party had difficulty in keeping ahead of the rate of growth of the total number of workers: hence the stabilization at around 8 percent of the proportion of the working class who were Party members. However, the "presence" of the Party among the workers varied a great deal as between industries. In the principal industries it averaged out at 10.5 percent, with a maximum figure of 13.5 percent in the oil industry and a minimum figure of 6.2 percent in the textile industry,[23] which was largely staffed by women.[24]

The percentage of Party members was higher in the industries where skilled workers were employed than in those where the work force consisted of unskilled workers. Observable also are big geographical variations: the percentage of Party members in the working class was very high—19 percent, in Leningrad, as against only 9 percent in Moscow and much lower percentages in most of the other cities.

These figures show why the campaigns aimed at ensuring that 50 percent of the Party's membership was made up of actual workers did not succeed. Two reasons were of major importance here. First, the speed with which the number of "office workers" who were members of the Party increased: there were more "office workers" than "workers" in the Party, though the total number of office workers in the population, which was 3.5 million in 1926–1927, was smaller than the number of manual workers (4.6 million). Second, the fact that, despite the efforts made by the Party organizers, most workers hesitated to join the Party. From this resulted the development of practices, condemned by the Party leadership, such as "collective adhesions"—which were followed, moreover, in the months succeeding the campaigns that produced these "adhesions," by a considerable number of the new members dropping out.[25]

The unwillingness of many workers to join the Party seems to have been due mainly to the fact that the bulk of the workers who had entered industry only recently, and had no tradition of organization, did not feel ready to take on the responsibilities of Party membership. In particular, they were not inclined to add to their production tasks those tasks incumbent on Party activists,[26] which they were often called upon to do. We know that in this period such a combination of tasks frequently amounted to a heavy burden which told seriously upon the health of many activists, who suffered from tuberculosis, anemia, or nervous disorders.[27]

The workers' reluctance to respond more positively to the recruitment campaigns was due, also, to yet another factor, especially during the second half of the NEP period. It frequently arose from the fact that the members of the Party's basic organizations were assigned mainly executive tasks, and played only a very minor role in the forming of decisions, not only as regards general problems but even where local affairs were concerned.

The results of an investigation made in 1928 showed that one of the reasons often mentioned by workers to explain their failure to join the Party was that they had the impression that its basic organizations—the ones about which, as workers, they had first-hand knowledge—were incapable of combating the defects in economic work and in the work of the soviets and other organs, or of defending the immediate interests of the workers. On the last point, especially, they noticed that the representatives of the Party apparatus who attended production conferences rarely supported proposals put forward by the workers: this was one aspect of the defective functioning of socialist democracy. They also noticed that relations between the local Party cadres and the workers were bad, with the workers sometimes accusing these cadres of profiting by their position to acquire various personal advantages.[28]

Reluctance to join the Party must not be confused with hostility to it as the organ leading the dictatorship of the proletariat—as may be seen by the positive reaction generally forthcoming from the workers to the Party's slogans, and the fact that many of them were prepared to give active support to its initiatives, even though they would not join it. Thus, only about 30 percent of worker "activists" were members of the Party,[29] and these activists were even sometimes called "non-Party Communists."[30]

It is therefore necessary to distinguish between the membership of the Party and the support given to it, including active support, for this did not necessarily imply a decision to become a Party member.

(e) The Party's relations with the bourgeoisie

The proletarian character of the Bolshevik Party does not mean that it was "guaranteed" against penetration by bourgeois and petty-bourgeois elements. On the contrary, as we have seen, such penetration was inevitable. Already in 1922 Lenin had pointed out that, as "the ruling party," the Bolshevik Party was subjected to a constant threat of infiltration by bourgeois and petty-bourgeois elements.[31] If such infiltration developed, it would affect the Party's relations with the masses, its practices, its political line, and its ideology. It might even result in the Party losing its proletarian character and becoming a bourgeois Party—changing, in fact, into its opposite.[32]

The Party was thus the battlefield of a struggle between the proletariat and the bourgeoise, of a struggle in which *what was at stake was the class character of the Party and the government.*

The presence in the Party of the bourgeoisie or its representatives assumed a variety of forms, corresponding to the defense of interests which were to some extent contradictory. Thus, during the NEP period, the interests of the kulaks and the Nepmen—that is, of the private bourgeoisie—found more or less conscious defenders in the Party, for defense of these interests could be presented as defense of a political line favorable to "faster" development of production, especially agricultural production. But defense of the interests of the bourgeoisie might also show another face. It might take the form of struggle to "strengthen" the state sector and for "sound management" of this sector. This was the reason given for demanding that greater power be granted to the experts and technicians and also to the heads of state enterprise, with subordination of the immediate producers to the orders of the specialists, and so on. This form of struggle tended objectively toward the constituting and strengthening of a state bourgeoisie who had the means of production at their sovereign disposal, and decided what use was to be made of the accumulation fund. This form of struggle was developing already in the NEP period, but it was with the 1930s—when the private bourgeoisie had been practically eliminated—that it acquired decisive importance.

II.   The broadening of the mass basis of the trade unions and the acquisition of independence by the trade-union apparatuses

Unlike the Party, which organized the vanguard of the proletariat, the trade unions were mass organizations, and so their membership was much larger. During 1926 the Soviet trade unions had some 9,300,000 members, and in mid-1928 more than 11,000,000 which meant about 80 percent of all wage earners.[33]

The trade unions were organized in accordance with branches of activity. They could recruit not only the *workers* in a given branch, but also the *technical personnel* and the office workers. About one-third of the trade-union members were nonmanual workers.[34] It was not compulsory to join a union, and those members who did not pay their dues regularly were expelled. The high proportion of trade-union membership testifies to the workers' attachment to this form of organization. Nevertheless, being a member of a union did bring various material advantages (because the unions were in charge of certain social services, and because they tended to give priority to the defense of their members' interests) so that it would be wrong to see the high level of unionization as a sign of mass approval by the workers for all aspects of the activity of their trade unions.

However, direct influence by the rank and file on trade-union activity was relatively limited, for the trade-union cadres formed an apparatus the composition of which was not directly controlled by the mass of the workers. The practice of appointment from above to responsible posts prevailed. It led to the consolidation of a body of trade-union officials who often had been remote from manual work for a long time.[35] This was an aspect of the process whereby the instruments of the dictatorship of the proletariat acquired independence—a process which had begun before the coming of the NEP.[36]

The role played by the trade unions was twofold. On the one hand, they defended the immediate interests of the workers. On the other, they were an agency of proletarian education: they helped to bring the ideas of socialism into the working class and to support the policy of the Bolshevik Party. This dual role, defined by the Party at the close of the "trade-union discussion" in the winter of 1920–1921,[37] was regularly reaffirmed by the Party and by the unions. However, emphasis was placed differently at different times upon one or the other of these roles, and their concrete significance might vary.

In general, it can be said that during the first phase of the NEP, emphasis was fairly widely placed on the unions' role as defenders of the workers' immediate interests, especially when the collective labor agreements were being concluded each year. From 1925–1926 on, when the drive for industrialization was developing, emphasis fell more and more upon the educative role of the trade unions—and this was interpreted as meaning, above all, that they must *give direct backing to increasing production and fulfilling the economic plan.*

The reduced emphasis on the unions' role as defenders of the workers' immediate interests corresponded to explicit political orientations, which were expressed first by the VSNKh and its press (especially the TPG) and then supported more and more by the Party and the Komsomol, in connection with the demands of rapid growth of industrial production. The gradual transition to centralized fixing of wages and work norms also restricted the field in which the unions could operate directly at enterprise level. Along with this there was a fall in the number of workers involved in disputes between unions and managements—from 3,212,300 in 1925–1926 to 2,463,000 in 1926–1927 and 1,874,300 in 1927–1928.[38] The relative fall was, of course, much greater, since the number of wage earners increased rapidly during those years. It was clearly connected with a less demanding attitude on the part of the unions, for those years saw frequent increases in work norms, which provoked demonstrations of discontent on the part of the rank and file of the workers. Disputes between unions and managements were settled by the mediation of a number of organs: the chief of these organs, the commission for settling disputes, RKK, dealt in 1928 with 84.9 percent of the disputes arising. If they were not settled at this level, disputes were referred to a conciliation board, and then, if need be, to an arbitration tribunal. These organs were responsible in 1928 for settling 20 percent and 80 percent, respectively, of the disputes not settled at the lower level.[39]

After 1926 the number of strikes (or, at least, of officially recognized strikes) declined markedly. At the Eighth Congress of the Trade Unions (December 1928) it was mentioned that in 1926, 43,200 workers had participated in strikes (32,900 of these being in state-owned enterprises). The number had fallen in 1927 to 25,400 (of whom 20,000 were in state-owned enterprises) and to 9,700 (of whom 8,900 were in state-owned enterprises) during the first half of 1928. Only about 2 percent of these strikes had taken place with the agreement of the unions[40]—the rest broke out "spontaneously" and without union approval. In January 1927 a secret directive from the chairman of the Central Committee of the Woodworkers' Union specified that "the strike must be sanctioned beforehand by the Central Committe of the Trade Union, without which the calling of a strike is categorically forbidden."[41] This circular noted that "the most important task of the trade union organs is to take preparatory measures in time in order to prevent a strike movement in state enterprises."

Strikes did not disappear altogether, but they became exceptional, and were hardly mentioned anymore in the newspapers. Generally speaking, the trade unions succeeded in conforming to the task indicated in the circular quoted above. They were helped in this by the enthusiasm for production which, at the start of the Five-Year Plan, took possession of a large section of the working class; but also by the repression applied to persons responsible for forbidden strikes. When there were serious reasons for discontent, this expressed itself in either "unofficial strikes" (rarely) or "go-slows" or increased absenteeism (more often).

However, the trade-union leadership which was in office during most of the NEP period, and which was headed by Tomsky, put up a certain amount of resistance to the demand presented to it by the leaders of industry, to play a more active role in raising the productivity of labor and combating absenteeism, together with various forms of indiscipline.[42]

Eventually this resistance was denounced by the Party. On April 23, 1929, the CC accused Tomsky (together with the two other leaders of the "Right" in the Party) of cherishing "trade-unionist" tendencies consisting of giving priority to promotion of the workers' immediate demands over the tasks of economic construction.[43] A little more than a month later, on May 29, 1929, the Central Trades Union Council relieved Tomsky of his post as chairman and appointed Shvernik secretary of the trade unions.[44] Thereafter, it was officially declared that the primary task of the unions was to fight for fulfillment of the targets of industrialization.[45]

Thus, the former trade-union leadership's refusal to accept the demands imposed upon the workers by the policy of rapid industrialization led to great changes in the makeup of the trade-union apparatus. These changes were carried out "from above," without consultation with the rank and file. This method brought serious contradictions with it. Nevertheless, for the moment, it entailed no obvious negative consequences, for, as a whole, the workers were convinced that rapid industrialization was needed, in order to put an end as soon as possible to unemployment, to provide a firm foundation for socialism, and to improve the standard of living. Many of them were therefore ready to let the leadership of the trade unions be taken over by the supporters of a productionist line.

III. The working class and the activity of the soviets

One of the slogans of the October Revolution had been: "All power to the soviets!" In a formal sense, this slogan was realized during the October days; but very soon, with the coming of the civil war, this became true, in the main, for the central soviet organs only, whereas the activity of the local ones was greatly reduced. At the end of the civil war, at the moment when the Kronstadt rebels took as their slogans, "Soviets without Communists!" and then at the very beginning of the NEP, the activity of the Soviet organs was essentially concentrated in the leading organs of the soviets of the republics.[46]

The conditions under which the soviets were operating at the end of the NEP resulted from the efforts made to "revitalize" them,[47] starting from the situation just described, and from the obstacles encountered by these efforts. The successes obtained were uneven, being more definite in the case of the soviets at the top of the pyramid than in that of the soviets at the bottom, the ones which, in principle, should have been most directly linked with the masses.

It is necessary, indeed, to recall that the organization of Soviet power was pyramidal in structure. At the base of the pyramid were the local soviets. The deputies to these local soviets were chosen by direct vote of the majority of the electors in each constituency. The voters were presented with lists drawn up by the Party after consultation (in principle) with meetings of non-Party people. These lists did not consist of only Party members: the policy of "revitalizing" the soviets even called for a broad appeal to candidates who were not members of the Party. The deputies elected to the local soviets then elected deputies to the higher-level soviets (those of subdistricts, districts, and so on, up to the soviets of each republic and of the USSR as a whole, this last having some 2,000 members).

Most power was held by the soviet of the USSR. In the NEP period, this soviet met twice yearly. Between these meetings, its executive committee (the VTsIK) met three or four times. "Permanent" power, however, was vested in the Presidium of the VTsIK. The soviets of the republics, regions, districts, and subdistricts worked in more or less the same way as that of the USSR. The powers of these soviets were smaller, but they, too, were concentrated in the hands of executive committees, or rather, in those of the presidiums of these executive committees.

In practice these soviets were assemblies to which their executive committees and the governments (where the soviets of the USSR and of the Union Republics were concerned) reported on their activities, receiving the comments and criticisms of the deputies.

In 1929 members of working-class origin did not quite constitute the majority in the VTsIK of the USSR,[48] but they did in the VTsIK of the RSFSR (52 percent) and in the urban soviets (53.4 percent).[49] However, we must distinguish between those who were merely of working-class origin and those who were still actually workers. When this distinction is made, we find that the proportion represented by those who were actually workers was markedly less. Thus, an inquiry made in 1928 into a sample of urban soviets in the RSFSR showed that, while 47 percent of the deputies were workers by social origin, only 37.9 percent were still working in production.[50]

In principle, the most direct action affecting everyday conditions of existence (outside workplaces, at any rate) was exercisable by the basic soviets—where the working class was concerned, by the urban soviets.

In fact, already at the end of the NEP period, and despite the decisions taken from July 1926 on,[51] these urban soviets did not always even exist. It was only on February 8, 1928, that a decree of the VTsIK of the Soviet Union called upon the Executive Committees of the republics to establish soviets in all towns of 100,000 inhabitants and upward, and to endow them with real powers, together with a minimum of financial resources.[52] In spite of this decree, relations between the urban soviets and the soviets of the subdistricts and districts continued to be strained, because the latter kept up their tutelage over the former. The urban soviets were not allowed to elect executive committees: they had only a presidium, whose activity was subject to supervision by the Executive Committee of the next-higher soviet.

Despite the obstacles put in the way of their development by the higher level administrations, whenever urban soviets came into being they showed remarkable vitality and gave opportunities to tens of thousands of workers to take part in the management of local affairs.[53] Yet, regardless of the decisions of principle taken by the Party, these urban soviets remained very poor in material and financial resources.

This situation is instructive, for it shows what a struggle was waged by the members of the higher apparatuses to keep hold of as much power and authority as possible, a struggle that caused them frequently to obstruct orientations given out by the central bodies of the Bolshevik Party. One of the matters at stake in this struggle was the control to be exercised over day-to-day conditions of existence *either* by deputies who largely came directly from the working class and still lived in the midst of that class, *or* by a body of functionaries who, although generally members of the Party[54] had become administrators, separated from production and tending to form an independent group that escaped from direct control by the working masses.

The outcome of this struggle, which was one of the aspects of the struggle for Soviet democracy, was not determined merely by the "decisions" of principle taken by the leading organs of the Party regarding the "division of competences" between the different organs which together made up the structure of soviet power. The struggle was decided by the overall process of the class struggles. It was decided, in the last analysis, by the expansion or the decline of the role played by the direct producers in the production units themselves. It was overdetermined by the Party's general political line, and in particular by the place that this line accorded to rank-and-file initiative or to centralized decision-making. And, toward the end of the NEP period, the turn that had been made toward giving priority to modern large-scale industry, and to maximum accumulation, created conditions that were less and less favorable to strengthening the role of the basic soviets. The problem of the forms of participation by the working class in the soviets cannot therefore, in the end, be considered in isolation from the struggles that went on within the Bolshevik Party, struggles through which the Party's political line became defined and transformed.

Notes

1. The question of the peasantry's relations with the Party will be touched on only briefly here, since it has been examined earlier (see above, pp. 163 ff.).
2. T. H. Rigby, *Communist Party Membership*, p. 53. These are round figures. The source quoted by Rigby is *Partiinaya Zhizn*, no. 19 (October 1967), pp. 8–10. Generally speaking, these figures are based on reports sent up from the basic units. They are usually a little higher than those obtained from the censuses of Party membership which were carried out from time to time. There were other official estimates, but the differences are not, as a rule, very large (see ibid. p. 54).
3. There were two of these, in 1924 and in 1925.
4. Rigby, *Communist Party Membership* p. 52. All these figures embrace both full members and "candidates," who had to undergo a period of probation.
5. Lenin, *CW*, vol. 33, p. 229.
6. Ibid., vol. 33, p. 256.
7. Ibid., vol. 33, p. 257.
8. Ibid., vol. 33, p. 258.
9. *K.P.S.S. v rezolyutsiyakh*, vol. 2, p. 81.

10. Molotov's report and the CC's decision at the end of 1926 (*Izvestiya Ts.K.*, nos. 47–48 [December 2, 1926], quoted in Rigby, *Communist Party Membership*, p. 165), and the resolution of October 19, 1927, "on the regulation of the growth of the Party in connexion with the Party census" *Izvestiya Ts.K.*, no. 39 [October 22, 1927]; and Carr and Davies, *Foundations*, vol. II, p. 110).

11. *K.P.S.S. v rezolyutsiyakh*, vol. 2, pp. 545–547.

12. In August 1925 a circular signed by Molotov, as secretary of the CC, noted that the inadequacy of the definitions used made it impossible to regulate the social composition of the Party. This circular laid down the principles that were thereafter to be observed in social classification. It brought some clarity into the statistics, but allowed a degree of vagueness still to prevail, especially as regards the checking of statements made by applicants for membership. The circular distinguished between "workers," mainly employed as wage earners performing manual labor in production, transport, and agriculture: "peasants," working independently or in a family or collective enterprise in the sphere of agriculture (or stockbreeding, fishing, etc.); and "office workers," working in the apparatuses of administration, the economy, cultural activity, etc. The classification included a heading "others," to cover students, individual craftsmen, etc. (*Izvestiya Ts.K.*, no. 34 [September 7, 1925], summarized in Rigby, *Communist Party Membership*, pp. 159–160).

13. Figures calculated from the total membership and the percentages of class composition, according to Rigby, *Communist Party Membership*, pp. 52, 116.

14. Ibid., p. 162. It will be noted that the current figures based on reports from basic units showed a higher percentage of workers (and of peasants) than the census, which was regarded as more precise. According to the current figures, the proportion of members who were workers in industry and transport was 36.8 percent—22.6 percent more than was shown in the census.

15. See volume I of the present work, pp. 307 ff. and 408 ff.

16. The practice of *nomination*, and no longer of *election* (which often continued in a purely "theoretical" way) to very important positions in the Party and the administration came in gradually. It may be regarded as having become consolidated by 1926, when it was in the hands of one of the Party's administrative organs, the *Orgraspred*—in principle under the supervision of

the CC, but in practice controlled by the Secretariat. The *Orgraspred* was the organ which in 1924 replaced the *Uchraspred*. A list of posts which were to be filled only by the *Orgraspred*, or with its consent, was drawn up: this was what was called the *nomenklatura*. (The files on Party members who were eligible to fill posts listed in the *nomenklatura* were held by the *Orgraspred*, and the list of these persons is also sometimes referred to as the *nomenklatura*.) Included were posts which in theory were supposed to be filled by election (see Carr, *Socialism*, vol. 2, pp. 203–212, and Carr and Davies, *Foundations*, vol. 2, p. 122).

17. See above, p. 333, The Quotation from Lenin, *CW*. vol. 33, p. 256.
18. Stalin, *Works*, vol. 10. pp. 338–339.
19. Rigby, *Communist Party Membership*, p. 116.
20. See above, pp. 217–234.
21. Stalin, *Works*, vol. 7, pp. 353–354.
21. Rigby, *Communist Party Membership*, pp. 52, 163 (census figures).
23. Carr and Davies, *Foundations*, vol. 2, p. 108, quoting *Sotsialny i Natsionalny Sostav VKP(b)* (1928), p. 51.
24. In 1927, only 10.5 percent of Party members were women (Carr and Davies, *Foundations*, vol. 2, p. 103).
25. Ibid. p. 114, n. 1.
26. The Party activists ran the Party cells, held meetings for discussion and explanation, and took on responsibilities in the commissions of the soviets (in the cooperative and cultural organizations), and so on—all of which might add up to a considerable number of hours over and above their day's work in the factory. The activists were not Party "functionaries" but continued to get their living by working in production. As a rule, those workers who became Party functionaries, or who were appointed to posts of adminstrative responsibility, were recruited from among the activists.
27. Rigby, *Communist Party Membership*, pp. 117–118.
28. See *Izvestiya Ts.K.*, October 31, 1928, pp. 2–3, quoted in Carr and Davies, *Foundations*, vol. 2, pp. 112–113.
29. Rigby, *Communist Party Membership*, p. 166.
30. Carr and Davies, *Foundations*, vol. 2, p. 128, quoting *Pravda*, February 20, 1927.
31. See above, p. 333.
32. See volume I of the present book, pp. 296 ff.
33. *VII-oy Syezd Professionalnykh Soyuzov SSSR* (1929), p. 57.

34. Ibid., p. 77.
35. Carr and Davies, *Foundations*, vol. 1, pt. 2, 547.
36. See volume I of the present work, pp. 408 ff.
37. See volume I of this work, pp. 289 ff.
38. Carr and Davies, *Foundations*, vol. I, pt. 2, p. 563.
39. Ibid., p. 565.
40. *Professionalnye Soyuzy SSSR, 1926–1928: Otchet k VIII Syezdu* (1928), pp. 358–360.
41. Fainsod, *Smolensk*, p. 318.
42. See, for example, *Torgovo-Promyshlennaya Gazeta*, September 7 and 12, 1928, quoted in Carr and Davies, *Foundations*, vol. 1, pt. 2, p. 554.
43. *K.P.S.S. v rezolyutsiyakh*, vol. 2, pp. 429–447.
44. On these questions see also p. 236 above and pp. 453 ff. below.
45. *Trud*, June 2, 1929; and Carr and Davies, *Foundations*, vol. 1, pt. 2, pp. 562–563.
46. See volume I of the present work, pp. 255 ff., 294 ff., 333 ff., and 447 ff.
47. The slogan of "revitalizing" the soviets applied mainly to the local soviets, whose activity had in many cases become purely formal. The slogan was put forward insistently from October 1924 on. After being featured by *Pravda* on October 11th, it was the subject of decisions by the TsIK of the RSFSR in the form of decrees, corresponding decrees being issued in the other republics of the Soviet Union. The CC meeting of October 25, 1924, treated the question as one of great importance, focusing its attention upon the problems of the rural areas (see *KPSS*, vol. 1, pp. 906 ff.). The same problems were the subject of discussions and decisions in January and April 1925. In July 1926 the Party put the emphasis on reactivating the urban soviets. The question was taken up again in January, April, and July 1927, and then again in February 1928 and January 1929 (Carr and Davies, *Foundations*, vol. 2, pp. 264–266). The need to keep coming back to the question of reactivating the soviets, and the discussions to which this question gave rise, show the strength of the resistance encountered by any attempt on the part of the local soviets to take effective charge of the matters that concerned them (see above, pp. 167 ff).
48. Their percentage was 46.5, as against 20.8 percent for members of peasant origin and 32.7 percent for the "other" social categories, which meant mostly "office workers" (*Bolshaya Sovyetskaya Entsiklopediya*, 1st ed., vol. 11, p. 542).

49. Ibid., p. 542.
50. *Izvestiya,* May 23, 1928, quoted in Carr and Davies, *Foundations,* vol. 2, p. 264, n. 2.
51. See above, p. 352, n.2.
52. *Sobranie Zakonov,* no. 10 (1928), arts. 86, 87.
53. Carr and Davies, *Foundations,* vol. 2, pp. 268 ff., especially p. 269, n. 1.
54. In general, in 1929 at least 70 percent of members of Executive Committees were Party members. The percentage of Party members in the urban soviets in the same year was 46.1 percent (*Bolshaya Sovyetskaya Entsiklopediya,* 1st ed., vol. 11, p. 542).

Part 4
The changes in ideological and political relations within the Bolshevik Party

Under the conditions of the NEP the leadership of the Bolshevik Party (its congresses and conferences, and, still more, the Central Committee, the Political Bureau, and the Party Secretariat) formed the chief foreground of politics, with the government and the VTsIK only secondary. This was where, through a series of conflicts, there took place, in a comparatively open way, the process of working out the political line to be followed and the conceptions on which that line was based.

I have spoken here of a "foreground" so as to emphasize the fact that, in reality, the political line was not worked out "in a test tube," inside some "sovereign" political ruling group. Social conflicts, whether organized or not, actually had their effect, direct or indirect, upon the analyses made by the Party and upon the process whereby it decided its line. The Party (or its leadership) was not a "demiurge" placed somewhere "above" all contradictions and acting somehow "from without" upon these contradictions.

The tasks that the Bolshevik Party undertook were determined by the existence of objective contradictions. However, the way these tasks were precisely defined, and the means that were adopted to fulfill them, resulted from the fashion in which these contradictions were identified by the Party, the type of analysis to which they were subjected, the resources actually available for action upon them, and the estimate made of the possibility of taking action with these resources.

The analyses which the Party developed, and the conclusions to which they pointed, were dependent, therefore, not only on the objective situation but also on the ideological forms through which the struggles fought out inside the Party were conducted. The aggregate of these forms constituted what may be called the *Bolshevik ideological formation*. It was a result of history, produced by systematization of the Party's experience and, more broadly, of the experience of the international labor movement, a systematization effected by applying the concepts of Marxism and Leninism, along with notions regarded as being compatible with these concepts. Like everything else, the Bolshevik ideological formation contained contradictions of its own, and it changed during the NEP period in consequence of the class struggles and of "experience gained"—meaning the Party's interpretation of the successes and failures of the political line followed up to that point.

The *actual* political line was never identical with that which was laid down *in principle*. The more or less extensive gap between the two, which tended to widen toward the end of the NEP, was determined by many different factors, and in particular by the greater or lesser correctness of the conclusions drawn from analysis of the contradictions and of the evaluation made of the means that could be employed to deal correctly with them. The gap between the actual political line and the line of principle depended also on the support or opposition that the various class forces—and the apparatuses through which they operated—offered to the line as it was defined in principle.

Through the struggles which occurred in this Party during the NEP period we can see how the position of certain leaders was strengthened, whereas the authority of those who defended conceptions that were rejected by the Party's leading bodies suffered decline. This process became especially acute toward the end of the NEP period, when, in contrast to what had happened in Lenin's time, leaders whose ideas were rejected found themselves, more and more often, removed from the Party leadership and even expelled from the Party, which meant a narrowing of inner-Party democracy. The working of democratic centralism demands that a variety of opinions be expressed and that Party members be allowed to engage in a genuine debate. In this way the form in which ideological and political struggles were carried on in the Party was altered.

The problems which the Party had to confront on the eve of the "great change" were both many and complicated. Basically, they were the same problems as those the Party had been faced with in 1923–1924 (on this, see volume I of the present work, pp. 506 ff.), but the terms in which they were presented were partly different.

The decisive problem was, and remained all through these years, how to unite the masses of the people so as to develop their active support for the Soviet government. At the heart of this problem lay the task of consolidating the worker-peasant alliance.

On the fulfillment of this task depended the possibility of radically transforming some of the existing social relations, and this transformation was also constantly on the agenda during the NEP period. It concerned, first and foremost, political relations, for what was required was to destroy the state apparatus inherited from Tsardom, to revive the soviets, and to develop democratic centralism, which could not be done without developing mass democracy. The problem of a radical transformation also existed at the level of the immediate production relations: what was required was, in particular, to change labor relations in the state-owned enterprises. The solution of such a problem as this was dependent on the Party's capacity to stimulate real mass actions.

The industrialization of the country and the transformation of its agriculture were problems that were present throughout the NEP period, more or less acutely, but the type of industrialization and of change in agriculture that took place was dictated by the nature of the changes in the immediate production relations, in political relations, and in relations between classes.

All these problems came up, with greater or lesser clarity at different times, during the discussions that went on in the Party during this period. However, the solutions that the Party tried to apply varied from time to time, partly because these problems arose in terms that were to some extent new, and partly because the analysis made of them changed, in connection with the changes undergone by the Bolshevik ideological formation.

When one considers the years 1924 to 1929 as a whole, one is struck by the fact that the Party never clearly defined what *the chief link in the situation* was, the link on which action must be taken first and foremost so as to be able to wield sufficient power over the whole set of contradictions. Nevertheless, it can be said that between 1924 and 1927 the decisions taken by the Party's leading bodies were more or less consistently dominated by the problem of maintaining the worker-peasant alliance. It was on this problem that the Party's efforts were mainly concentrated, even though it did not always deal correctly with it and was unsuccessful in arousing a mass movement among the peasantry.

The worker-peasant alliance was, indeed, the chief link at that time, the factor on which action needed to be taken first and foremost in order to strengthen the dictatorship of the proletariat. The various oppositions which took shape within the Party between 1924 and 1927 all *overlooked or neglected this chief link*. Even when some of their formulations were correct (especially when they demanded that disputed questions be discussed more openly and thoroughly, and that genuine democratic centralism be developed), the general orientation of the political line they advocated was mistaken, because it neglected the main thing—what was needed in order to strengthen the worker-peasant alliance.

From 1928 on (and even earlier, if certain practical decisions are taken into account), however, the Party tended no longer to focus its efforts mainly on the worker-peasant alliance, although this was far from having been consolidated, and its consolidation continued to be the principal problem. The Bolshevik Party then acted increasingly *as though* industrialization of the country was the *sine qua non* for solving all other problems. In this way the conditions accumulated which dictated the "great change" at the end of 1929. The "Right" opposition tried to prevent this turn, for which neither the

Party nor the peasantry were really prepared. But it was incapable of formulating a political line that could have prevented the kulaks from gathering around them an increasing number of middle peasants. It was therefore doomed to defeat when the Party launched itself along the road of a collectivization and an industrialization which it could not control.

In order to get a better grasp of the ideological and political changes that led to the "great change," we need to examine the conditions under which the struggle for the worker-peasant alliance, and then for industrialization, was waged within the Party. This is the indispensable starting point for an analysis of the essential features of the Bolshevik ideological formation and of the process of change that it underwent.

1. The fight for the worker-peasant alliance

When we study the period between the Twelfth and Fifteenth Party Congresses (from 1923 to the end of 1927), we see that, for the Party leadership, the chief political task was, in principle, the strengthening of the worker-peasant alliance. This was so even if the primacy of the task was not always made clearly explicit and the concrete conditions for realizing it often remained vague, both on the plane of formulations and, even more, on that of political and economic practice. In any case, it was around this problem that the sharpest conflicts were fought against the chief opposition trends. These struggles, and the way they unfolded, are of major importance as regards the ideological and political changes that occurred (especially in respect to organizational practice), and so we must briefly recall how they developed between 1924 and 1927, taking as our chronological "reference points" the chief meetings held by the Party's leading bodies.

I. From the Twelfth to the Thirteenth Party Congress

During the period separating the Twelfth Congress from the Thirteenth, which was held on May 23–31, 1924, a little more than four months after Lenin's death, political struggles were waged around problems of the worker-peasant alliance and of inner-Party democracy. They gave rise to a number of discussions and decisions of which we can only summarize here the most important aspects.

The Thirteenth Congress resolved that, "in order to solve

361

the problem of the Party's work in the countryside, it is necessary to start from the principle that the task for the whole of this
historical period is to realize the alliance between the working
class and the peasantry."[1] The resolutions devoted to work in
the rural areas and to cooperation[2] show the importance accorded by the Congress to the worker-peasant alliance and to
the efforts being made to decide how to develop this alliance
so as to lead the peasantry "to socialism through co-operation."[3] These resolutions also show the difficulties encountered by the progress of Party activity in the countryside, and
reveal a tendency to rely upon, for the fulfillment of rural tasks,
mainly the rural intelligentsia and those industrial workers
who had "links with the villages,"[4] rather than upon the peasants themselves. Moreover, in terms of day-to-day practice,
the Party gave only minimal aid to the poor and middle peasants.

While, at the time of the Thirteenth Congress, the Party
seemed united on the need to strengthen the worker-peasant
alliance, the divisions on this matter were actually as deep as
on some others. In 1923–1924 opposition to the worker-
peasant alliance was expressed mainly in the demands put
forward to strengthen the role of Gosplan and to increase
credits to heavy industry (which, under the conditions of the
time, could be done only at the expense of agriculture and
the peasantry).

Open opposition to the economic policy followed by the
Party between the Twelfth and Thirteenth Congresses was
shown when, on October 15, 1923, forty-six members of the
CC sent a letter to the Political Bureau. This letter, which
came to be spoken of as the "platform of the 46" was signed by
Pyatakov, Preobrazhensky, Osinsky, Kaganovich, and Sapronov.[5] It attributed the economic difficulties encountered in
1923 (especially the slump in sales of industrial goods experienced toward the end of the year) to shortcomings in credit
policy, planning, and aid to industry.[6]

The "platform of the 46" declared that if economic difficulties had piled up in this way, it was not due to incapacity on the
part of the leadership but to the fact that the problems con-

cerned had not been widely discussed, discussion of them being confined to "Party functionaries recruited from above," while the mass of the Party members were excluded. The platform therefore proceeded to deal in a severely critical way with the way that the Party functioned:

> This is a fact which is known to every member of the Party. Members of the Party who are dissatisfied with this or that decision of the Central Committee, or even of a provincial committee, who have this or that doubt in their minds, who privately note this or that error, irregularity or disorder, are afraid to speak about it at Party meetings, and are even afraid to talk about it in conversation, unless the partner in the conversation is thoroughly reliable from the point of view of 'discretion'; free discussion within the Party has practically vanished, the public opinion of the Party is stifled.[7]

Although Trotsky, who was a member of the Political Bureau, did not sign this platform, he was thought to share the views expressed in it, on account of the letters he sent, around this same time, to the other members of the PB, letters of similar content.[8]

Thus, in the months preceding the Thirteenth Congress, great tension developed within the CC, centered on problems of "economic policy" (and so, of the worker-peasant alliance) and of the Party's internal regime.

On the first of these points the opposition suffered formal defeat, as may be seen from the resolutions of the Thirteenth Conference (January 16–18, 1924) and the Thirteenth Congress. On the second, matters were more complicated.

On the one hand, the Thirteenth Conference adopted a resolution on "building the Party"[9] which acknowledged that the situation called for a serious change in the Party's orientation, in the sense of effective and systematic application of the principles of "workers' democracy." The resolution specified that "workers' democracy means open discussion by all Party members of the most important questions . . . , freedom of discussion within the Party, and also election from below of leading functionaries and committees."[10] In reality, the adoption of this resolution did little to modify the authoritarian practices which prevailed.

On the other hand, the Thirteenth Conference condemned, as factional activity, the "platform of the 46" and Trotsky's statements, thereby confirming a resolution passed by the plenum of the CC and the CCC at its meeting of October 25–27, 1923.[11]

The Thirteenth Congress strengthened the positions of those who had declared for consolidating the worker-peasant alliance, especially Stalin, who was reelected to the post of general secretary, although he had offered his resignation after Lenin's "Letter to the Congress" had been discussed by the CC and by the senior members of the Congress delegations.[12]

Trotsky's position, on the contrary, was markedly weakened, especially after the very severe criticism made of him by Zinoviev, who called upon him to admit his mistakes publicly.[13] Trotsky refused to do this, while saying that he bowed to the decisions taken, regardless of whether they were right or wrong.[14]

Despite the overt appearance of divergencies in the PB, the Thirteenth Congress seemed to be still dominated by a spirit of unity. The composition of the PB underwent little change: Trotsky continued to be a member, and Bukharin entered it, taking the place of Lenin, who died on January 21, 1924.

II.   From the Thirteenth to the Fourteenth
Party Congress

After the Thirteenth Congress Trotsky's position continued to weaken. On November 6, 1924, he published a book entitled *The Lessons of October,* in which he leveled an attack specifically at Kamenev and Zinoviev for their hesitancy at the moment of the October Revolution. This gave rise to a series of counterattacks on their part, the most important of which, at the time, was the one launched by Kamenev in a speech on November 18.[15] His chief criticism of Trotsky was his alleged "underestimation of the role of the peasantry, masked by revolutionary phraseology."[16] The Party gathering to which Kamenev had spoken passed a motion denouncing "Trotsky's breach of the promises he made at the Thirteenth Congress." Similar resolutions were adopted at other Party meetings.[17] On January 15, 1925, Trotsky sent a letter to the CC in which he said that he had not sought to reopen a discussion in the Party, and offered his resignation from the chairmanship of the Revolutionary Military Council.

(a) The condemnation of "Trotskyism"

On January 17 the plenum of the CC adopted a resolution condemning Trotsky for his attacks on the unity of the Party. It denounced Trotskyism as "a falsification of Communism in the spirit of adaptation to 'European' models of pseudo-Marxism, that is, in the last analysis, to the spirit of 'European' Social-Democracy." Trotsky was relieved of his functions as chairman of the Revolutionary Military Council and warned that any further violation of the Party's decisions would make his continued membership of the PB impossible and put on the agenda the question of expelling him from the CC.[18]

During the discussions preceding the adoption of this resolution, Zinoviev had demanded that Trotsky be expelled from the Party, or at least removed from the CC. This demand was rejected, and Kamenev then called for Trotsky's removal from the PB. These demands were opposed by Stalin, Kalinin, Voroshilov, and Ordzhonikidze.[19] At the Party's Fourteenth Congress Stalin mentioned these demands put forward by Zinoviev and Kamenev, explaining that they had not been accepted because "we knew that the policy of amputation was fraught with great dangers for the Party, that the method of amputation, the method of blood-letting—and they demanded blood—was dangerous, infectious: today you amputate one limb, tomorrow another, the day after tomorrow a third—what will we have left in the Party?"[20]

These discussions were thus among the first occasions on which open dissension occurred between Stalin, on the one hand, and Zinoviev and Kamenev, on the other.

*(b) The worker-peasant alliance and the
building of socialism in one country*

The resolution of the plenum of January 1925 had been preceded by the publication of a series of articles criticizing Trotsky's concept of "permanent revolution." One of these, published by Stalin in *Pravda* and *Izvestiya* of December 20, 1924, was to have considerable importance. It was entitled: "October and Comrade Trotsky's Theory of Permanent Revolution." In this article Stalin counterposed to Trotsky's theory the thesis of building socialism in one country. The Fourteenth Party Conference (April 27–29, 1925) embodied this thesis officially in one of the resolutions it adopted.[21]

In a report on the Fourteenth Conference which he gave in May 1925 Stalin said that this resolution implied that the community of interest between the workers and the peasants was sufficiently strong to outweigh, under the dictatorship of the proletariat, the contradictions setting them against each other: hence, it was possible for the socialist road to triumph in the USSR. It was just this possibility that Trotsky rejected when he declared that "in a backward country" the contradictions between the working class and the peasantry could not be resolved—that they could be resolved only on the international plane. Stalin quoted this passage from Trotsky: "The contradictions in the position of a workers' government in a backward country with an overwhelmingly peasant population can be solved only on an international scale, in the arena of the world proletarian revolution." And Stalin added: "Needless to say, this proposition has nothing in common with Leninism."[22]

We thus see clearly that what was at issue in the conflict between Trotsky's concept of "permanent revolution" and acceptance of the possiblity of building socialism in one country, not excluding a country with a peasant majority, was the *firmness of the worker-peasant alliance,* and therefore, the *significance of the NEP.* Trotsky's thesis reduced the NEP to a measure dictated by circumstances, a "retreat" which must result in capitalism becoming stronger and stronger. According to this thesis, in the conditions prevailing in Russia, the only way to hold back the realization of this threat was to undertake rapid industrialization, and this could be carried through only at the expense of the peasantry, for industry was too weak to have its own source of accumulation. This point of view was developed systematically by Preobrazhensky, in his conception of "primitive socialist accumulation."[23]

In Stalin's report on the Fourteenth Conference he showed that the conference had rejected this view and acknowledged that, within the setting of the NEP, it was possible to deal correctly with the contradictions that inevitably counterposed the proletariat to "the class of private-property-owners, i.e., the peasantry,"[24] and that, under these conditions, the socialist road could triumph over the capitalist road: "The socialist path . . . means development by a continuous improvement in the well-being of the majority of the peasantry. It is in the interest of both the proletariat and the peasantry, particularly of the latter, that development should proceed along . . . the socialist path, for that is the peasantry's only salvation from impoverishment and a semi-starvation existence."[25]

Politically, the Fourteenth Conference stressed the need, if the worker-peasant alliance was to be strengthened, to respect revolutionary legality and to eliminate the survivals from "war communism" in political and administrative work. One of the resolutions adopted mentioned that the achievement of these aims required the entry in larger numbers of agricultural workers and poor and middle peasants into the Party organizations.[26] The Fourteenth Conference also declared that, at the stage which had now been reached, the Party's principal task must be *to revitalize the Soviets and improve the leadership of the peasantry by the proletariat through the organs of Soviet power*, so that it was necessary to go forward to the phase of developing soviet democracy. In his report on the Fourteenth Conference, Stalin said that "the task of implanting Soviet democracy and revitalizing the Soviets in the countryside should make it possible for us to reconstruct our state apparatus, to link it with the masses of the people, to make it sound and honest, simple and inexpensive. . . ."[27]

This task—which was never fully realized—corresponded to what Lenin had called for when he demanded the destruction of the state machine inherited from tsardom and its replacement by one that would be genuinely proletarian.[28]

It was a task that required, too, a change in the style of the leadership given by the Party. Stalin said that an end must be put to incorrect forms of leadership, that the Party must stop giving orders to the peasants: "We must learn to explain to the peasants patiently the questions they do not understand, we must learn to convince the peasants, sparing neither time nor effort for this purpose."[29]

Fundamentally, then, the Fourteenth Conference defined some of the conditions for strengthening the worker-peasant alliance, especially on the political plane, that of the Party's relations with the peasant masses and Soviet democracy.

(c) The Fourteenth Conference and peasant problems

The decisions taken by the Fourteenth Conference and by the CC also concerned economic problems, especially the policy to be followed toward the well-to-do and rich peasants.

On the eve of the conference a number of speeches were made which showed that the Party leadership was taking a less restrictive attitude to the rich peasants, whose possibilities of accumulating and of increasing agricultural production were seen as indispensable to the development of the economy. At the beginning of April, for instance, Kamenev said to the Congress of Soviets of the Moscow region:

> We must also revise our laws relating to the use of land, to the employment of wage-labour [by farmers—C. B.], and to the leasing of land [which] are holding back the development of the productive forces in the countryside and exacerbating class relations instead of guiding them in the proper way. . . . We are for the development of the productive forces, we are against survivals which hinder the development of the productive forces. . . . We are for accumulation by the peasants, but we are for regulating this accumulation.[30]

On April 17, 1925, Bukharin spoke on the same theme at a mass meeting in Moscow, at which he said: "Our policy towards the rural areas must develop in such a way as partly to remove and abolish a number of restrictions which hinder the growth of the farms of the well-to-do peasant and the kulak. To the peasants, to all the peasants, we must say, Get rich, develop your farms, don't be afraid that coercion will be used against you."[31]

Except for the expression, "Get rich," the same themes were expounded at the Fourteenth Conference, and met with open opposition only from one delegate, Yuri Larin.[32]

Meeting on the day after the close of the conference, April 30, the CC adopted a resolution on "the Party's current tasks in economic policy in connexion with the economic needs of the rural areas."[33] This resolution widened the right to lease land, removed restrictions on the employment of wage earners in agriculture, reduced the agricultural tax, and condemned the practice of imposing fixed prices when procuring agricultural produce.[34]

The decisions of the CC of April 30, 1925, were based on the work done at the Fourteenth Conference and marked a drift toward a conception of the NEP whose practical application contradicted the demands of the alliance between the working class *and the mass of the peasantry*. These decisions aimed at finding a solution to the general problem of accumulation in the Soviet economy by favoring *accumulation by the rich and well-to-do peasants*.

(d) The birth of the new opposition and its condemnation by the Fourteenth Congress

This conception of the NEP facilitated fresh attacks on the worker-peasant alliance. At the beginning of the summer of 1925, several leaders of the Party began openly criticizing the decisions taken in April. Some of them, including Zinoviev, secretary of the Leningrad organization, put forward formulations which tended to challenge the NEP itself.

The first public onslaught on the decisions taken in the spring was made in a speech by Zinoviev on June 21, 1925. He said that these decisions demonstrated the determination of the leadership to rely not on "the wretched peasant nag" but on the fat kulak horse.[35] In September Zinoviev published a book entitled *Leninism*,[36] in which, interpreting certain quotations from Lenin, he asserted that in abandoning "war communism" for the NEP the Party had abandoned the socialist economic forms for "state capitalism in a proletarian state," and added: "Let us have no illusions, no self-deception! Let us call state capitalism, state capitalism."[37]

On September 5 Zinoviev, Kamenev, Sokolnikov, and Krupskaya drew up a document which became known as the "platform of the 4." Those who signed it included two members of the Political Bureau and Lenin's widow, while the signature of Sokolnikov, who had hitherto been a resolute supporter of a "rightist" conception of the NEP, made this platform seem the point of convergence of dissenters of differing views.

The "new opposition" thus born attacked the NEP and, echoing some workers' demands, called for increases in wages. It denounced "the practices of the apparatus" and called for freedom of discussion and democracy in the Party.[38]

Some of the points made by the new opposition met with response among part of the working class, especially their call for wage increases, which, in the situation existing then, was demagogic. It led some Party members to take part in unofficial strikes.

On the whole, however, the opposition found little support in the Party. The turnabout made by Zinoviev and Kamenev, who had previously been unconditional defenders of the NEP and of the wages policy followed until then,[39] could evoke nothing but skepticism.

The contradictions in the platform of the new opposition, the contrary positions so recently defended by Zinoviev and Kamenev, and the conditions under which the delegates to the Fourteenth Congress (December 18–31, 1925) were chosen ensured that the representatives of this opposition at the congress were few in number. However, they did succeed in speaking. Zinoviev even presented a "political counter-report," opposed to the one presented by Stalin. Though frequently interrupted, he developed his arguments, calling for respect for democracy in the Party. He declared that the situation of 1921 and 1923, which had justified the restrictions imposed on freedom of discussion in the Party, now belonged to the past. "Today we have different workers, greater activity in the masses, other slogans." And he added: "While permitting no factions, and on the question of factions maintaining our previous positions, we should at the same time instruct the Central Committee to draw into Party work all the forces of all former groups in our Party, and offer them the possibility to work under the leadership of the Central Committee."[40]

As regards the problems of the NEP, Zinoviev reiterated his formulations of the summer and autumn, and concentrated his attack upon Bukharin.

When he replied,[41] Stalin, quoting Lenin, said that the concessions made to the peasantry were above all concessions to the middle peasants, and that they were intended to strengthen the worker-peasant alliance.[42] He reminded his listeners that the

> N.E.P. is a special policy of the proletarian state aimed at permitting capitalism while the commanding positions are held by the proletarian state, aimed at a struggle between the capitalist and socialist elements, aimed at increasing the role of the socialist elements to the detriment of the capitalist elements, aimed at the victory of the socialist elements over the capitalist elements, aimed at the abolition of classes and the building of the foundations of a socialist economy.[43]

His agrument regarding the question of state capitalism[44] was weak. Though he admitted that state capitalism was compatible with the dictatorship of the proletariat, as Lenin had said, he confined the notion of state capitalism to foreign concessions. For him, the predominant role played by the state-owned industrial sector sufficed to dispose of the question of state capitalism. He no more took up the question of the capitalist relations that might prevail in state-owned industry than did the "new opposition."[45]

Stalin ended his speech with an appeal for unity, saying: "The Party wants unity, and it will achieve it *with* Kamenev and Zinoviev, if they are willing, *without them* if they are unwilling."[46]

On December 23 a resolution whose terms were conceived so as to avoid a break with the members of the opposition was tabled. This resolution was passed by 559 votes to the 65 cast by the oppositionists.[47]

On January 1, 1926, a new Political Bureau was elected by a CC whose composition had been partly altered. Zinoviev was still a member of the PB, but Kamenev was reduced to the rank of "alternative member." Bukharin, Rykov, Stalin, Tomsky, and Trotsky were reelected; three new members entered the PB: Voroshilov, Kalinin, and Molotov.

The opposition had suffered a heavy defeat. The Party apparatus in Leningrad was reorganized by a delegation from the central secretariat. Zinoviev was replaced by Kirov as first secretary of the Leningrad organization.

Among the important questions discussed by the Fourteenth Congress were also those of the trade unions and the industrial policy.

(e) The Fourteenth Congress and the trade-union question

The Fourteenth Congress pronounced a judgment that was, on the whole, severe in its strictures on the way that trade-union activity had been carried on in 1925. The resolution adopted said that the unions had more often than not failed to face up to their obligations, allowing "their chief task, defence of the economic interests of the masses," to fall into the background.[48] It noted that a certain remoteness had developed "between the trade-union organs and the masses," which resulted in "a weakening of trade-union discipline, as was shown with particular clarity in a series of economic conflicts in the spring of 1925."[49] It called for wider participation by the masses in the work of the trade-union organizations, and demanded that the unions participate more systematically in the analyzing of economic and production problems, so as to be able to carry out a task of information and explanation.[50] It warned against any tendency to form an "unnatural bloc" between the economic organs, the heads of enterprises, and the trade unions.[51] Consequently, the resolution denounced the numerous cases in which collective agreements were concluded with the economic organs by trade unions ignorant of the actual situation "of the workers and office-workers on whose behalf they sign," so that the agreements in question "enjoyed little authority in the eyes of the workers and offered few guarantees to the economic organs."[52]

In his political report to the Fourteenth Congress Stalin dealt with the problems of industry. He considered that, since it had now attained a level of production close to the prewar level, "further steps in industry mean developing it on a new technical basis, with the utilisation of new equipment and the building of new plants."[53] What was now required was to cross a threshold, and consequently, owing to "a considerable shortage of capital," the future development of industry "will, in all probability, proceed at a less rapid tempo than it has done up to now."[54] Stalin thus forecast that industry would grow more slowly than agriculture. In order to overcome the difficulties resulting from this situation he advocated that efforts at industrialization be not restricted to the large-scale industry directed by the central organs but that industrial development be assisted "in every district, in every *okrug*, in every *gubernia*, region and national republic."[55] This was a prospect very far removed from the policy that was to be put into practice a few months later.

Elsewhere, in the reply he made to the discussion of his political report, Stalin spoke of the need to develop industries to produce equipment and machinery, so that the Soviet Union should not run the risk of becoming "an appendage of the capitalist countries."[56]

One of the resolutions adopted by the Congress expressed the same demand, considering that it was of fundamental importance "to carry on economic construction with a view to converting the U.S.S.R. from a country that imports machinery and equipment into one that produces them for itself."[57]

The Fourteenth Congress thus took up the problem of industrialization while remaining very vague as to the pace at which it should progress and the conditions for financing it.

III.   From the Fourteenth Congress to the eve of the Fifteenth

The "compromise" adopted by the Fourteenth Congress on the question of the "new opposition" did not put a stop to the oppositional activity of Zinoviev and Kamenev and their allies. The continuance of this activity reflected the reservations felt by a fairly large number of Party members regarding the NEP and a peasant policy which they considered to be a hindrance to rapid industrialization. The opposition declared for speeding up the pace of industrial development and persisted in advocating that recourse be had, for this purpose, to "primitive socialist accumulation." In 1926 the discussion on this subject was broadened. It revolved mainly around Preobrazhensky's book *The New Economics*,[58] which Bukharin subjected to a series of critical articles, one of the most important of which appeared in *Pravda* under the title: "The 'Law of Primitive Socialist Accumulation,' or Why We Should Not Replace Lenin by Preobrazhensky."[59]

(a)   The birth of the "united opposition"

At the Fourteenth Congress Zinoviev had prepared the ground for an attempt at bringing together "all the former groups in the Party,"[60] which signified principally an "opening" in the direction of Trotsky.[61]

This "opening" led, at the end of March or the beginning of April, to contact being made between Trotsky, Zinoviev, and Kamenev. About this time they agreed to cease repeating the accusations they had been hurling at each other until then. In this way there began to take shape an opposition which Stalin was to describe as "an unprincipled bloc."[62]

Trotsky now came forward actively after having remained passive for almost two years. He made himself the advocate of a rate of industrial development higher than that officially proposed by Dzerzhinsky. The latter criticized Trotsky and Zinoviev sharply for their statements, accusing them of preparing a "new platform," *to be based on exploitation of the peasants.* Stalin spoke to the same effect. Eventually the resolution on industrialization was adopted unanimously, but the debate revealed how Trotsky, Kamenev and Zinoviev were now aligned together.[63]

This alignment led to the formation, at the beginning of 1926, of what was called the "united opposition," on the basis of the "declaration of the thirteen."[64] This dealt mainly with industrial policy and with the divisions in the Party. Trotsky expounded particularly the idea that the Party's "bureaucracy" threatened the revolution with a sort of "Thermidor."[65] At the plenum of July 14–23, 1926, the "united opposition" acted openly in concert, demanding higher wages for the workers and an increase in the agricultural tax on the rich peasants.[66]

The Party leadership denounced the demagogic character of the opposition's arguments and the very serious threat that they offered *to the worker-peasant alliance.* Dzerzhinsky, as chairman of the VSNKh, made a long, closely reasoned speech on this theme.[67] But the Party leadership also used organizational measures to reply to the opposition. At the plenum of July 1926, Zinoviev was removed from the PB and one of his associates, M. Lashevich, from the CC and also from his post in the Revolutionary Military Council. These measures were taken as punishment for factional activity.[68] On this occasion Rudzutak entered the Political Bureau, and Mikoyan, Andreyev, Ordzhonikidze, Kaganovich, and Kirov became "alternative members." Trotsky retained his membership.

However, the united opposition continued its activity. Trotsky, Zinoviev, and others of its leaders spoke at meetings of factory cells, as the Party rules allowed them to do. At first, their speeches seem to have evoked some response, but very soon the Party organizations in Moscow and Leningrad set themselves to put a stop to the opposition's activity, intervening physically to prevent its spokesmen from getting their message across. They succeeded in doing this, for the rank and file of the Party remained ultimately indifferent to the opposition's theses.

During 1926, finding itself unable to obtain a hearing, the opposition organized itself. Thereby it took the path of factional activity. According to various sources, its active supporters numbered between four and eight thousand. These figures are very small in comparison with the Party's total membership at that time (about a million), but not negligible in relation to the numbers of those who took part actively in political discussions, which meant not more than a few tens of thousands.[69]

In any case, the development of the opposition's organization did not escape the attention of the OGPU. The leaders of the opposition, fearing punishment for factional activity, therefore sought a discussion with the Party secretariat. After this discussion, on October 16 they signed a declaration in which, without renouncing the line of the "declaration of the thirteen," they admitted that they had broken discipline and engaged in factional activity.[70]

By putting their names to this statement the leaders of the opposition hoped to be allowed to present their views in writing to the Fifteenth Party Conference. The CC plenum which met on October 23–26 rejected this demand, however, and took measures against the opposition's leaders. Trotsky was removed from the PB, Kamenev lost his position as an "alternative member" of that body, and Zinoviev ceased to be chairman of the Executive Committee of the Comintern.[71]

(b) The Fifteenth Conference and the first defeat of the "united opposition" in 1926

The Fifteenth Conference, which was held between October 26 and November 3, 1926, saw the united opposition defeated. The debate on this subject was opened by Stalin, who laid before the conference theses on "the opposition bloc in the C.P.S.U.(B.)"[72] and on November 1 presented a report on "the Social-Democratic deviation in our Party."[73]

Stalin's theses denounced the rallying of the "new opposition" to the positions of Trotskyism: his report analyzed the way the opposition had developed, and gave a critique of its positions. He formulated with particular clarity some of the principles of the NEP, especially as regards relations between industry and agriculture. He said: "The opposition bloc . . . fails to realise and refuses to recognise that industry cannot be advanced if the interests of agriculture are ignored or violated. It fails to understand that *while industry is the leading element in the national economy, agriculture in its turn is the base on which our industry can develop.*"[74]

Stalin then showed that the opposition's theses led to peasant farming being treated as a "colony" which the proletarian state had to "exploit," and he quoted Preobrazhensky to this effect: "The more a country that is passing to a socialist organisation is economically backward, petty-bourgeois, and of a peasant character . . . the more it has to rely for socialist accumulation on *the exploitation of pre-socialist forms of economy.*"[75]

Stalin's formulation emphasizing that *agriculture was the basis for the development of industry* was of great importance—it made explicit one of the principles of the NEP which held a preponderant place in the documents approved by the Bolshevik Party's leading organs right down to 1928.

Kamenev, Trotsky, and Zinoviev spoke at the Conference in support of the views they had been advocating jointly since the spring, and declared that they sought to achieve a "common effort" by the Party as a whole. The speeches of Kamenev and Zinoviev were violently interrupted, while Trotsky was listened to in silence. All three were replied to, in particular, by Molotov and Bukharin, who refuted the opposition's arguments, while some of its former supporters—notably Krupskaya—broke with it. Stalin replied to the discussion,[76] going over again the main arguments of his opening report. He concluded by saying to the members of the opposition:

"Either you observe these conditions, which are at the same time the conditions for the complete unity of our Party, or you do not—and then the Party, which gave you a beating yesterday, will proceed to finish you off tomorrow."[77]

The resolution condemning the opposition bloc[78] was passed unanimously by the Fifteenth Conference which thus confirmed the sanctions taken by the preceding plenum against Trotsky, Zinoviev, and Kamenev.

One of the resolutions of the Fifteenth Conference made explicit in a particularly clear way what was implied by the principles of the NEP. It pointed out that in order to strengthen the worker-peasant alliance there must be an improvement in the supply of machines and other goods to the rural areas, better organization of the marketing of agricultural produce, provision of credit for agriculture, and aid to the poor peasants, through special credits and through support for the development of collective farming. The resolution was favorable to the development of *rural industry*, especially for the processing of agricultural produce, and it condemned the opposition's advocacy of raising industrial prices and lowering agricultural prices.[79]

Actually, as we know, the practical measures that this resolution called for were not taken. In the months that followed, the rural areas experienced a grave shortage of manufactured products, while the rural crafts were deprived of a large proportion of their raw material of urban origin, this being reserved to an ever greater extent for the needs of large-scale industry.

(c) *The breakup of the opposition, its attempt to reorganize, and its fresh defeat on the eve of the Fifteenth Congress*

After the defeat it suffered at the Fifteenth Conference, the opposition began to disintegrate. The supporters of the "democratic centralism" group broke away and tried to form a group (the "group of 15") which would operate outside the Party, with a view, as they put it, to constituting "a nucleus for defence of the cause of the proletarian revolution," which they saw as having been betrayed by the Party and by the opposition.[80] This group had no political weight and soon disappeared.

On the morrow of the Fifteenth Conference, Zinoviev and Kamenev were willing to cease maintaining a position different from that of the majority, whereas Trotsky wished to keep up the opposition's fight, even though he realized that it could not alter the balance of forces within the Party. At the end of 1926 Zinoviev and Kamenev rejoined Trotsky, and the opposition, which had suffered numerous defections, once more operated as a clandestine faction.[81]

At the end of March 1927 Trotsky began attacking, in letters addressed to the PB, the line advocated by the Comintern for the Chinese Communist Party, and demanded that a discussion be opened on the "China question."[82] Trotsky believed in "the unconditional predominance, the direct domination of capitalist relations in China," and that "a class of landlords as a separate class does not exist in China. The landowners and the bourgeoisie are one and the same."[83] Consequently, he rejected any policy of a united front with the Chinese bourgeoisie, and was later to declare that "only the predominance of the proletariat in the decisive industrial and political centres of the country creates the necessary basis for the organisation of a Red Army and for the extension of a soviet system into the countryside."[84]

Although they were mistaken as to the real line of the Kuomintang, and gravely underestimated its capacity to turn on the working class (as shown in the repression begun by Chiang Kai-shek on April 12, in Shanghai), the leadership of the Bolshevik Party and the Executive Committee of the Comintern made an analysis that was more correct than the opposition's of the nature of the Chinese revolution. This analysis was set forth by Stalin in a series of theses published in *Pravda* on April 21, 1927.[85]

Having failed to get the China question discussed by the CC, the united opposition appealed to the Executive Committee of the Comintern, supporting its approach with a statement called the "declaration of the 83," from the number of its original signatories.[86] By acting in this way it appeared once more in the role of an organized faction.

On May 24 Trotsky addressed the Executive Committee of the Comintern, presenting his analysis of the situation. Stalin replied, showing the ultraleft character of Trotsky's views and recalling Lenin's theses on the possibility and necessity of farming *peasant soviets* in countries such as China and India.[87] Here, too, the question of alliance with the peasant masses, with the place and role of the latter in an action for revolutionary change led by the proletariat, formed the *line of demarcation* between the positions defended by the majority of the Bolshevik Party and those of the opposition.

After listening to several other speeches, the Executive Committee of the Comintern condemned Trotsky's views and confirmed, though with some corrections, the line which had been followed until then.[88]

The opposition's resumed activity evoked a series of sanctions. Some members of the opposition were arrested, others were posted to the provinces or sent abroad. The opposition then appeared to retreat, by signing, on the occasion of the plenum of August 7 a declaration stating: "We will carry out all the decisions of the Communist Party and of its Central Committee. We are prepared to do everything possible to destroy all factional elements which have formed themselves as a consequence of the fact that on account of the inner-Party regime we were compelled to inform the Party of our opinions, which were falsely reported in the whole press of the country."[89]

This declaration saved the opposition, for the moment, from expulsion from the Party. Nevertheless, though they drew up a "platform" recapitulating their views, they found that they were refused the right to publish the platform and circulate it in the Party in preparation for the Fifteenth Congress. They therefore took steps to print and circulate it clandestinely, and held illegal meetings. Eventually, at the plenum of October 21–23, 1927, Stalin called for sanctions to be taken against

Trotsky and Zinoviev. After a discussion marked by violent incidents, these two were removed from the CC on the grounds that they had broken Party discipline.[90]

The opposition was now nearing its final defeat. Its motions (when they could be presented at meetings of Party members) received only a very small number of votes. The right to speak was almost always denied to its representatives. In a last effort, the opposition tried, during the demonstration commemorating the tenth anniversary of the October Revolution, to organize its own procession of demonstrators. They numbered in the few hundreds, and were quickly dispersed or arrested. On November 14, eighteen days before the Fifteenth Congress, Zinoviev and Trotsky were expelled from the Party. Kamenev and some other supporters of the opposition who were still on the CC were removed from it. The united opposition had practically ceased to exist. The Fifteenth Congress was held without the delegates including any open advocates of the line of accelerated industrialization. The Congress ratified the decisions taken by the CC on November 14. It condemned the opposition for breaking with Leninist ideology, for taking up "Menshevik positions," for having "denied the socialist nature of state-owned industry" and the possibility of "the socialist road of development for the countryside under the conditions of the dictatorship of the proletariat," together with "the policy of alliance between the proletariat and the basic mass of the peasantry on the basis of Socialist construction." The opposition was accused of having "in practice denied that the dictatorship of the proletariat exists in the U.S.S.R." (by its talk of "Thermidor"), thereby making itself a tool of petty-bourgeois democracy and international social democracy. It was also condemned for indiscipline and factional activity.[91]

IV. The Fifteenth Congress

The Fifteenth Congress of the Bolshevik Party was held on the morrow of the political defeat of the supporters of an

opposition which gave the "exigencies" of rapid and centralized industrialization priority over the policy of consolidating the worker-peasant alliance within the framework of the
NEP. The Congress resolutions included some especially
clear formulations regarding this policy.

(a) The resolutions of the Fifteenth
Congress

These resolutions dealt chiefly with agricultural and peasant questions and with problems of industry and planning.[92]
They reaffirmed the need to continue the NEP while stressing
a concrete policy which included certain modifications in this
policy as compared with the previous period. These concerned, especially, measures to restrict "the exploiting tendencies of the kulaks."

This new orientation was put forward for the first time by
Bukharin,[93] in a speech delivered two months before the Congress, on October 12, 1927. In this speech Bukharin said that it
was now possible to exercise "increased pressure on the
kulaks," because, during the last two years, the alliance with
the peasant masses had been strengthened, together with the
State's commanding positions.[94]

The Fifteenth Congress also declared in favor of a policy of
collectivization, but emphasized that this must be *carried
through with caution, by means of persuasion and without
constraint.* There could be observed, however, certain shades
of difference between the way in which, on the one hand,
Bukharin, Rykov (who was then chairman of the Sovnarkom of
the USSR), and Kalinin, and, on the other, Stalin, presented
the question of collectivization. For the former, collectivization was *one of the elements in a policy* aimed at solving the
problems of agriculture. Stalin said of collectivization that
"there is no other way out"—no other solution to the problems
of Soviet agriculture[95] though, during the Congress, he did not
advocate either rapid collectivization or the use of coercion.

As regards the conditions for developing industrialization,
the Congress resolutions repeated, in the main, the formula-

tions to be found in Bukharin's writings following the Fourteenth Congress, calling for more rapid industrialization while
at the same time attacking the "super-industrializers" of the
united opposition, the advocates of maximum accumulation to
be achieved at the expense of the peasantry (especially by
"opening the scissors").[96]

The resolution of the Fifteenth Congress on the drawing up
of the Five-Year Plan counterposed to the striving for
"maximum" accumulation the need for "optimum" accumulation:

> As regards relations between production and consumption, it
> must be clearly seen that we cannot proceed from a simultaneous
> maximising of both, as the opposition now demands. . . . Paying
> attention to the relative contradiction between these two factors,
> their reciprocal action and the connexions between them, and
> appreciating that, from the standpoint of long-term development,
> their interests generally coincide, we must proceed from an op-
> timum combination of these two factors.[97]

The resolution declared that the same requirements must be
observed as regards

> relations between town and country, between socialist industry
> and peasant farming. It is not right to proceed from the demand
> for a maximum transfer [*perekachka:* literally, pumping] of re-
> sources from peasant farming into industry for this would not
> only signify a political breach with the peasantry but also would
> undermine the supply of raw materials to industry itself, disrupt
> both the internal market and exports, and upset the entire eco-
> nomic system.[98]

On the question of rates of development, the resolution also
stressed the idea of an "optimum" rate, declaring: "Here we
must proceed not from the maximum rate of accumulation in
the near future or within a few years, but from a relation
between the factors in the economy such that the highest rate
of development may be ensured over a long period."[99]

In the course of this resolution the opposition's slogan of
raising industrial prices was again condemned, on the grounds
that it would favor bureaucratic degeneration and monopolis-

tic disintegration of industry, harm the consumers (and, in the first place, the working class and the poorer strata in town and industry), give the kulaks a trump card to play, and finally, bring about a sharp decline in the rate of development, by compromising industry's agricultural basis.[100]

The resolution likewise upheld the need to observe an optimum relation between the development of light industry and heavy industry. It emphasized that, when shifting the center of gravity from light to heavy industry, care must be taken that the latter did not tie up too large a share of the state's capital in the construction of very big enterprises whose products would not come on to the market for many years, and, consequently, that account must be taken of the fact that the faster turnover of capital in light industry (producing consumer goods of prime necessity) enabled the capital resulting from it to be subsequently used in heavy industry, while at the same time ensuring the development of light industry itself.[101]

The Fifteenth Party Conference, in November 1926, had already resolved that observance of these principles would make it possible gradually to speed up the pace at which the economy was developing, and to "catch up with and then surpass" the "levels of industrial development of the leading capitalist countries in a relatively short historical period."[102]

From the standpoint of the class struggle and of the relation between class forces, the Fifteenth Congress reaffirmed that the decisions of the Fifteenth Conference and of the Fourteenth Congress had laid down a policy that was basically correct, especially as regards the rural area. The resolution adopted considered that these decisions had helped to strengthen the alliance between the working class and the mass of the peasants, and that this created the possibility of going over, with the help of all the poor and middle peasants, to a systematic curbing of kulak farming and private enterprise generally, so as to bring about "a relative decline . . . in the private capitalist elements in town and country alike."[103]

Finally, the Congress noted that the Five-Year Plan would be drawn up in awareness that there might be some bad harvests.[104] It should therefore not be too "taut," but sufficiently "flexible" to be adapted to the fluctuations of agricultural production.

The theses on "optimum accumulation" and on the need to maintain correct proportions between the development of industry and agriculture, between heavy industry and light industry, between town and country, repeated almost word for word the formulations used by Bukharin in his fight against the united opposition. Bukharin had expressed thus his conception of the relations that should be established between light and heavy industry:

> I think that the formula which calls for maximum investment in heavy industry is not quite correct—or, rather, that it is absolutely incorrect. While we must emphasise mainly the development of heavy industry, we must at the same time combine this with a corresponding development of light industry, in which turnover is faster and profits made sooner, and which repays in a shorter time the outlay devoted to it.[105]

Bukharin claimed that, if proper proportions were observed in the development of the different sectors of the economy, the result would be economic development that would follow "a rising curve."[106] This formulation, aimed at warning against desire to speed up too suddenly the rate of economic growth, was to be interpreted later as expressing belief in the possibility of a sort of "indefinite acceleration" of economic growth.

The resolutions adopted unanimously by the Fifteenth Congress reaffirmed, even more clearly than the Fourteenth Congress and the Fifteenth Conference had done, the need to establish definite relations and proportions between the different sectors of the economy. These resolutions recognized that respect for these relations was essential if the economy was to advance without jolts, if a policy of "closing the scissors" between industrial and agricultural prices was to be carried out, and if there was to be a regular supply of goods to the rural area and to the towns on a basis of prices which would not be subject to inflationary increases.

However, these principles were violated by the adoption of a series of measures that were incompatible with them, and from this followed the development of contradictions which made themselves sharply felt from the end of 1927 on. The procurement crisis was a spectacular consequence of these contradictions, which, because they were not brought under control, found expression in two political lines which came into conflict more and more obviously in 1928 and 1929.

Before examining the content of this conflict and the forms it took, a few words should be said about the contradictions between the policy actually followed and the resolutions passed by the Congress.

(b) The development of the contradictions
between the principles stated in the
resolutions of the Party's congresses
and conferences and the economic
policy actually carried out

These contradictions existed at several levels. Broadly, we can say that they mainly affected the scope and the orientation of the industrial investment plans which constituted the nucleus of the actual economic policy. In a secondary way, they concerned pragmatic measures taken with a view to palliating to some degree certain consequences resulting from the scope and orientation of these investment plans.

(1) The industrial investment plans from
1926–1927 on

We have already seen that the Fourteenth Congress and the Fifteenth Conference warned against too rapid an increase in industrial investment, because of the danger that such an increase would present to the worker-peasant alliance.[107] Nevertheless, the Fifteenth Conference adopted a resolution, on the situation and the economic tasks of the reconstruction period, which fixed at a minimum of 900 million roubles the amount of industrial investment for the year 1926–1927.[108] Yet, a few months previously, an amount of investment close to that had been rejected by Dzerzhinsky on the grounds that such a figure was incompatible with the actual economic situation.[109]

In adopting this figure the conference practically ratified the investment programs already in motion by the industrial organizations. To some extent, these organizations operated with sufficient autonomy for the Party's leading bodies to find themselves (through not having intervened in good time) faced with *faits accomplis* which they were, so to speak, obliged to "confirm."

The same process occurred during the months that followed, for the figure adopted by the Fifteenth Conference was largely *surpassed*. In December 1926 the VSNKh approved a plan for industrial investment which totaled 947 million roubles. Five weeks later, the CC and the Sovnarkom ratified this figure, while making some reservations. Subsequently, 991 million roubles were allocated for industrial investments— but, in the end, these investments absorbed 1,068 million, nearly one-third more than in the previous year,[110] while the absolute amount of investment in industries producing consumer goods *declined*.[111] Thus, all the appeals for "caution" issued previously by the Party's leading bodies, and by Stalin himself, were "forgotten."[112] And yet the political significance of these appeals could not have been clearer: what was needed was to ensure industrial development based on *cooperation* with the peasantry and *not on exploitation* of them.[113]

This "forgetting" of the previously made calls for prudence had political implications. Its immediate basis was the relative autonomy of the industrial organizations, and it reflected the power of that social force which was represented by the heads of these organizations and of the great enterprises. It presupposed the gradual, but not openly admitted, rallying of a section of the Party's leaders to an *actual policy* that accorded major importance to the rapid growth of large-scale industry producing means of production, a policy which was *increasingly remote from* the demands of the worker-peasant alliance, with its implications of relatively preferential supplying of goods to the rural areas, and grain procurement on a noncoercive basis.

This change in policy actually pursued corresponded also to a certain change in the Bolshevik ideological formation—the increased role of conceptions which favored *the most up-to-date industrial techniques* and ascribed a decisive role to *accumulation* in the development of industrial production (even though small and medium rural industry still possessed enormous possibilities for increased production, production that would have greatly helped the peasants to increase their harvests). Little by little, an orientation was gaining ground in the Party which favored industrial investment of a magntiude and nature such as to be incompatible with the maintenance of the NEP. In this sense, the "general crisis of the NEP" was simply the crisis that resulted from the de facto abandonment, in decisive domains, of the New Economic Policy.

Nevertheless, the open change of "line," and the "turn" that went with it, were not to be proclaimed until after a series of struggles had been waged, through 1928 and 1929, inside the Party leadership.

(2) *The rapid growth in budgetary expenditure and its immediate effects*

The appeals for caution issued by the Party's congresses and conferences applied also to the size of budgetary expenditure. It was feared that too rapid an increase in this would undermine the policy of stabilizing prices, and even reducing industrial prices, which was one of the components of the NEP. Here, too, these appeals were gradually "forgotten." In 1926–1927 *the total amount of budgetary expenditure was 41 percent greater than in the previous year,* whereas the national income, in constant prices, had increased by only 6.3 percent.[114] A period was thus entered in which the increase in public expenditure bore no relation to the increase in real resources. This was the point of departure of grave imbalances, shortages in the rural area, price increases, and increased hardships for the poor and middle peasants.

In this situation the prices reigning in the sphere of private trade reflect in a very clear way the inflation that was developing. Between December 1926 and June 1929 the retail prices of agricultural produce in private shops increased by 130 percent.[115]

The relative indifference shown to the inflationary consequence of an increase in budgetary expenditure that had no counterpart in increased real resources reflected the progress of illusions (connected with the changes in the Bolshevik ideological formation) regarding the capacity of the political authority to bring about price changes independently of changes in costs and of shortage of supplies. Thus, Kuibyshev thought it possible to proclaim the "victory of the plan" over market forces.[116] The economist Strumilin went even further when he declared: "We are not bound by any (objective) law. There is no fortress that Bolsheviks cannot storm. The question of tempo is subject to men's will."[117]

These were the earliest expressions of the "voluntarist" illusions which developed rapidly during the years 1928 and 1929. They contributed to the appearance of a series of economic imbalances which had profoundly negative effects on the worker-peasant alliance.

(3) The contradictions entailed by the tax measures taken in favor of the poor and middle peasants

Starting at the end of 1923, price policy aimed at improving the standard of living of the peasant masses. This policy met with success so long as it made possible the closing of the "scissors" between industrial and agricultural prices,[118] and so long as the increased cash incomes of the peasants found a counterpart in a sufficiently increased supply of manufactured goods available in the villages. Generally speaking, despite temporary or local difficulties, this was so until the autumn of 1927.

At that moment the situation worsened seriously, for the supply of goods to the village declined as a result of the industrial investment policy and of the priority given to supplying the towns. With many village shops empty of goods, the

Soviet government decided, on the occasion of the tenth anniversary of the October Revolution, to relieve the poorest section of the peasantry almost completely of their obligation to pay the agricultural tax. This meant that 35 percent of all peasant households were exonerated from paying taxes in October 1927, as against 25 percent in the previous year. Furthermore, it was decided to use less pressure to get in arrears of tax payments,[119] so that at the beginning of 1928 these amounted to 20 percent of the agricultural tax payable during the fiscal year begun in 1927.

These measures would have been in accordance with the line of the NEP if the villages had been properly supplied with goods. As, however, this was not the case, the peasants looked askance at money they could exchange for goods only to a limited extent. This was one of the causes of the decline in agricultural deliveries which was observed from October 1927 on, the decline which led to the adoption of the "emergency measures" and the abandonment of the NEP.

(4) The contradictions in wage policy

Implementation of the policy of "closing the scissors" between industrial and agricultural prices encountered obstacles of several kinds: first and foremost, the high level of costs of production in industry, due to the fact that wages often increased faster than the productivity of labor.[120] This was an effect of the pressure brought to bear by the workers in the factories, pressure to which the heads of enterprises eventually yielded.[121]

At the same time, wage increases unaccompanied by a sufficient increase in the production of consumer goods brought about either pressure for an increase in retail prices or the development of "shortages" of goods. The shortage of industrial products became very serious when, owing to the priority given to investments in heavy industry, there was a slowing down in the rate of growth of the production of manufactured consumer goods, which happened in 1927. Yet, in that same year, the demand for manufactured consumer goods on the part of the wage earners increased sharply, for employment in industry (including building) increased by 12.4 percent[122] and average wages by 10 percent.[123]

Consequently, in the second half of 1927 the Soviet authorities found themselves faced with a rapid and simultaneous growth of purchasing power in the towns and in the villages. Unable to satisfy the whole of the increased demand for goods, they decided to give priority to the urban market. This being so, the shortage of industrial goods hit the rural areas hard just when the procurement of grain was being carried out.

The years 1926–1927 and 1927–1928 were thus marked by aggravation of the contradictions between the policy actually pursued and the political line decided on by the Party's congresses and conferences. Other contradictions also affected various aspects of the policy actually implemented, which were not mutually coherent, resulting as they did from pressures exerted by different classes and social strata. There was the workers' pressure for higher wages and a rapid increase in employment; pressure from the poor and middle peasantry for a reduction in taxes; pressure from the heads of large-scale state-owned industry and the central industrial organs for the rapid launching of an industrialization plan that gave priority to heavy industry. But these contradictions also corresponded to different conceptions that were present in the Bolshevik Party regarding what was demanded for the building of socialism, conceptions which tended to diverge further and further when the effects of the contradictions in the policy followed by the Party up to that point started to develop, and when beginning in early 1928, those effects took the form of an open crisis.

It then became necessary to deal with the contradictions between the line laid down in principle and the policy actually followed. This was an essential aspect of the struggles which, in 1928 and 1929, counterposed within the Party leadership those who thought it possible and necessary to reaffirm the principles accepted by the Fifteenth Congress, and who called for these principles to be put into effect, and those who considered that the time had come for an immediate and rapid industrialization drive (such as was already implicit in the annual plans adopted in and after 1926–1927) and who came out in favor of a political line contradictory to the resolutions of the Fifteenth Congress.

Among the supporters of the first of these "lines," the one that was called the "Right-wing" line, were Bukharin, Rykov, and Tomsky. The second line, which called for the levying of "tribute" from the peasantry, and collectivization carried through with the minimum of delay, was supported by Stalin, Kuibyshev, and Molotov. The demands of this line gradually prevailed, and it triumphed at the end of 1929.

Notes

1. *K.P.S.S. v rezolyutsiyakh*, vol. I, p. 850.
2. Ibid., pp. 842, 850 ff.
3. Ibid., p. 850.
4. Ibid., pp. 857, 858.
5. The text of the "platform of the 46" is given in E. H. Carr *The Interregnum*, pp. 367 ff.
6. Ibid., p. 367–368.
7. Ibid., p. 368.
8. Ibid., pp. 106–107.
9. *K.P.S.S. v rezolyutsiyakh*, vol. I, pp. 771 ff.
10. Ibid., p. 773.
11. Ibid., pp. 767 ff., 778 ff.
12. On this letter of Lenin's see volume I of the present work, pp. 323–324, and Lenin, *CW*, vol. 36, pp. 593–596. On the reelection of Stalin, see P. Broué, *Le Parti bolchévique*, p. 202, and L. Schapiro, *The Communist Party of the Soviet Union*, p. 287.
13. Carr, *The Interregnum*, p. 362.
14. *XIII-y Syezd RKP(b)* (1924), pp. 153–168.
15. L. Kamenev, *Stati i ryechi* (1925), vol. I, pp. 188–243.
16. Ibid., and Carr, *Socialism*, vol. 2, p. 15.
17. See *Pravda*, November 19 and 23, 1924.
18. *K.P.S.S. v rezolyutsiyakh*, vol. I, pp. 913 ff.

19. Carr, *Socialism*, vol. 2, p. 31.
20. Stalin, *Works*, vol. 7, p. 390.
21. *K.P.S.S. v resolyutsiyakh*, vol. 2, pp. 43 ff.
22. Stalin, *Works*, vol. 7, pp. 112–113. The quotation was taken from Trotsky's preface to his book *1905*.
23. E. Preobrazhensky, *The New Economics*, pp. 77 ff. The expression "primitive socialist accumulation" had already been used by Trotsky in 1922: it seems to have been originated by Sapronov, one of the signatories of the platform of the 46 (Broué, *Le Parti bolchévique*, p. 213). Formally, Trotsky's interpretation of the thesis of primitive socialist accumulation differed somewhat from Preobrazhensky's (see I. Deutscher, *The Prophet Unarmed*), but the political implications of accepting this thesis were not affected.

    The article by N. Bukharin entitled "A Critique of the Opposition's Economic Platform," in *Bolshevik*, No. 1 (January 15, 1925), gives a systematic criticism of the economic views expounded by the opposition of the 46 and by Trotsky and Preobrazhensky in 1922–1924. A French translation of this article is included in N. Bukharin et al., *Le Débat soviétique sur la loi de la valeur*, pp. 201 ff.
24. Stalin, *Works*, vol. 7, p. 111.
25. Ibid., p. 112.
26. *K.P.S.S. v rezolyutsiyakh*, vol. 2, pp. 11, 13.
27. Stalin, *Works*, vol. 7, pp. 127–128.
28. See volume I of the present work, especially pp. 329 ff., 446 ff., 522 ff.
29. Stalin, *Works*, vol. 7, p. 128.
30. Kamenev, *Stati i ryechi* (1926), vol. 12, pp. 132–133.
31. *Pravda*, April 24, 1925. This version was described as "abridged." A complete but revised text of the speech was subsequently published in *Bolshevik*, nos. 8 and 9–10 (1925).
32. Carr, *Socialism*, vol. 1, p. 263.
33. *K.P.S.S. v rezolyutsiyakh*, vol. I, pp. 922–932.
34. Carr, *Socialism*, vol. 1, pp. 268–269.
35. *Leningradskaya Pravda*, June 24, 1925, quoted in Carr, *Socialism*, vol. 1, p. 286.
36. G. Zinoviev, *Leninizm*.
37. Ibid., pp. 236–258.
38. Carr, *Socialism*, vol. 2, pp. 66–68, 108 ff.
39. In November 1924, Zinoviev had still been warning against a

"narrowly trade-unionist policy," reminding the unions that they had to pursue "the politics of the working class in a peasant country" (*VI-ox Syezd Professionalnykh Soyuzov SSSR* [1925], p. 29).

40. Carr, *Socialism*, vol. 2, pp. 141–142.
41. Stalin, *Works*, vol. 7, pp. 362 ff.
42. Ibid., pp. 367–368.
43. Ibid., p. 374.
44. Ibid., pp. 375 ff.
45. Stalin also dealt with this question in his political report, where his analysis of it was equally limited (ibid., pp. 312–313).
46. Ibid., p. 401.
47. *XIV-y Syezd VKP(b)* (1926), pp. 521–524; see Carr, *Socialism*, vol. 2, p. 144.
48. *K.P.S.S. v rezolyutsiyakh*, vol. 2, p. 95.
49. Ibid., p. 96.
50. Ibid., p. 98.
51. Ibid., p. 100.
52. Ibid., p. 101.
53. Stalin, *Works*, vol. 7, p. 322.
54. Ibid., p. 322. Here he voiced the doctrine which was later to be known as that of "decreasing tempos," and which Stalin himself was to denounce as "Trotskyist."
55. Ibid., p. 323.
56. Ibid., pp. 364–365.
57. *K.P.S.S. v rezolyutsiyakh*, vol. 2, p. 75.
58. See above, p. 393, n. 23.
59. *Pravda*, no. 153 (1926). There is a French translation in N. Bukharin, *Le Socialisme dans un seul pays*, pp. 67.
60. See above, p. 371.
61. Besides the Trotskyist opposition there still survived at this time a group which called for "democratic centralism," led by Sapronov, and the remains of the "Workers' Opposition," led by Shlyapnikov (on these groups, see volume I of the present work, pp. 368–410). Several members of these groups had been expelled from the Party, and some arrested. In 1923 the GPU had liquidated two other groups, most of whose members were non-Party: the "Workers' Truth" group, inspired by Bogdanov, and the "Workers' Group" founded by Myasnikov (see Schapiro, *The Communist Party*, pp. 300–301).
62. At the Fifteenth Party Conference: Stalin, *Works*, vol. 8, pp. 225 ff.

63. Carr, *Socialism*, vol. 2, pp. 172–173
64. Schapiro, *The Communist Party*, p. 302. The text of the "declaration" is in the Trotsky archives at Harvard University.
65. Carr and Davies, *Foundations*, vol. I, p. 5; Schapiro, *The Communist Party*, p. 303.
66. Deutscher, *The Prophet Unarmed*, pp. 275–276; Carr and Davies, *Foundations*, vol. I, p. 5.
67. *Pravda*, August 1, 1926. It was after making this speech that Dzerzhinsky, who was a sick man, had a fatal heart attack. A week later he was succeeded at the head of the VSNKh by Kuibyshev.
68. *K.P.S.S. v rezolyutsiyakh*, vol. 2, pp. 160 ff., and Schapiro, *The Communist Party*, p. 304.
69. Deutscher, *The Prophet Unarmed*, pp. 273–274.
70. Broué, *Le Parti bolchévique*, pp. 243–244.
71. *K.P.S.S. v rezolyutsiyakh*, vol. 2, pp. 170–171.
72. Stalin, *Works*, vol. 8, p. 225.
73. Ibid., pp. 245 ff.
74. Ibid., p. 301 (my emphasis—C. B.).
75. Quoted in ibid., p. 302. Preobrazhensky's original text was published under the title: "The Fundamental Law of Socialist Accumulation," in *Vestnik Kommunisticheskoy Akademii*, no. 8 (1924). In the corresponding passage in his book *The New Economics*, p. 124, he replaced the expression "exploitation" by "alienating part of the surplus product."
76. Stalin, *Works*, Vol. 8, pp. 311 ff.
77. Ibid., p. 370.
78. *K.P.S.S. v rezolyutsiyakh*, vol. 2, pp. 209 ff.
79. Ibid., vol. 2, pp. 180–181.
80. Broué, *Le Parti bolchévique*, pp. 249–250.
81. Ibid., pp. 250–252, 259.
82. Deutscher, *The Prophet Unarmed*, p. 327, and B. Fabrègues, "La 'Revolution permanente': une absurde théorie gauchiste," pt. 2, "La Revolution chinoise," in *Communisme*, no. 12 (September-October 1974), pp. 33 ff.
83. Trotsky, *The Third International After Lenin*, p. 209, and *Writings, 1930–1931*, p. 21.
84. Trotsky, *Writings, 1930–1931*, p. 19. These lines, written in 1930, express Trotsky's fundamental position as it was in 1927—a position which the history of the Chinese revolution has utterly refuted.
85. Stalin, *Works*, vol. 9, pp. 224 ff.

86. Deutscher, *The Prophet Unarmed*, p. 334.
87. Stalin, *Works*, vol. 9, p. 302.
88. Deutscher, *The Prophet Unarmed*, p. 337.
89. *International Press Correspondence*, vol. 7, no. 48 (August 18, 1927)
90. *K.P.S.S. v rezolyutsiyakh*, vol. 2, p. 311.
91. Ibid., vol. 2, pp. 368 ff.
92. Ibid., vol. 2, pp. 312–371.
93. An analysis of the way Bukharin's ideas evolved is given in Stephen F. Cohen, *Bukharin and the Bolshevik Revolution: A Political Biography, 1888–1938*: for the period leading up to the Fifteenth Congress see especially chapter 7, pp. 213 ff.
94. *International Press Correspondence*, vol. 7, p. 1422. See also an article by Bukharin which appeared a fortnight later (in *V zashchitu proletarskoy diktatury: Sbornik*, pp. 202–211, 215, 224–231).
95. Stalin, *Works*, vol. 10, p. 313.
96. Bukharin, *Le Socialisme*, pp. 67 ff.
97. *K.P.S.S. v rezolyutsiyakh*, vol. 2, p. 333.
98. Ibid.
99. Ibid., p. 334.
100. Ibid.
101. Ibid.
102. Ibid., p. 175. This appears to have been the first time that the formulation "catch up with and then surpass" was used officially (Cohen, *Bukharin*, p. 245).
103. *K.P.S.S. v rezolyutsiyakh*, vol. 2, p. 334.
104. Ibid., p. 332.
105. Bukharin, *V zashchitu*, p. 225.
106. Bukharin, *Building Up Socialsim*, p. 62.
107. See above, pp. 374 ff., 377 ff.
108. *K.P.S.S. v rezolyutsiyakh*, vol. 2, pp. 173 ff., especially p. 185.
109. Carr and Davies, *Foundations*, vol. 1, pt. 2, pp. 278–281.
110. *Torgovo-Promyshlennaya Gazeta* December 30, 1926; Sobranie Zakonov, no. 10 (1927), art. 98; Carr and Davies, *Foundations*, vol. 1, pt. 1, p. 278.
111. Carr and Davies, *Foundations*, vol. 1, pt. 1, p. 294.
112. This "forgetfulness" was repeated in the succeeding years, when industrial investments came to 1,304 million roubles (1927–1928) and 1,679 million roubles (1928–1929): see ibid., pp. 296, 314.

113. See Stalin's speech of November 3, 1926, in *Works,* vol. 8, pp. 368–369.
114. Carr and Davies, *Foundations,* vol. I, pt. 2, p. 742.
115. In the same period the retail prices of foodstuffs in state and cooperative shops increased by only 11 percent. The retail prices of industrial goods increased at about the same rate as in the "private" sector, i.e., 15 percent (ibid., pp. 964–965).
116. *Torgovo-Promyshlennaya Gazeta,* August 14, 1927.
117. *Planovoye Khozyaistvo,* no. 7 (1927), p. 11. The metaphor of the "fortress" which can always be "stormed" was all the more remarkable in that Lenin, faced with the negative political consequences of "war communism," made use precisely of the "fortress" metaphor when he advocated substituting a strategy of siege and advance step by step for futile attempts at frontal assault (see volume 1 of the present work, pp. 457–459).

Four years later, Stalin was again to use this metaphor, saying, "Everything can be achieved, everything can be overcome, if there is a passionate desire for it. . . . There are no fortresses that Bolsheviks cannot capture" (*Works,* vol. 13, pp. 40, 43).
118. See above, pp. 150 ff.
119. *Pravda,* October 16, 1927, report of the decisions of the second session of the TsIK elected by the Fourth Congress of Soviets of the USSR, and various sources quoted in Grosskopf, *L'Alliance ouvrière,* p. 331, n. 25; p. 356.
120. In 1925 the "scissors" between wages and productivity caused an increase of 2 percent in industrial costs, instead of the 6 percent reduction provided for by the plan (A. Baykov, *The Soviet Economic System,* p. 123). In 1926–1927 the rates of increase of productivity and wages were 9 percent and 12 percent, respectively, which went counter to the intention that had been proclaimed to reduce costs of production in industry, so as to reduce the prices at which industrial products were sold while at the same time increasing industry's capacity to accumulate (*K.P.S.S. v rezolyutisyakh,* vol. 2, pp. 181 ff).
121. See above, p. 314.
122. *Trud v SSSR,* p. 10.
123. *Ekonomicheskoye Obozreniye,* no. 12 (1929), p. 204.

2. The fight for rapid industrialization and for priority for heavy industry

From January 1928 on, elements of a political line different from that approved by the Fifteenth Congress began to be formulated explicitly. They made their appearance in the speeches delivered by Stalin in Siberia (at Novosibirsk, Omsk, Barnaul, etc.), where he went in order to call for vigorous application of the emergency measures.[1]

In these speeches, Stalin did not speak only about those measures. He also dwelt upon the *technical superiority* of the collective and state farms. He stressed that these farms produced "marketable surpluses" larger than those produced by the kulak farms. He even mentioned quantitative targets which had not been contemplated by the Fifteenth Congress, saying that it was necessary to ensure that, "in the course of the next three or four years the collective farms and state farms, as deliverers of grain, are in a position to supply the state with at least one-third of the grain required."[2]

I. The clashes in the first months of 1928

The three first months of 1928 were marked by the development of divergences (which were not publicly proclaimed) between, on the one hand, the "three" (Bukharin, Rykov, and Tomsky) and, on the other, Stalin, Molotov, and Kuibyshev. The remaining members of the PB vacillated, more or less, between these two camps.

(a) The plenum of April 1928

During the plenum of April 1928 no direct clash occurred between Stalin and Bukharin. Nevertheless, each of them presented a different picture of the situation.

Stalin denounced those who wanted a policy for the rural areas that would "please everyone" saying that such a policy had "nothing in common with Leninism."[3] On his part, Bukharin denounced the tendency of "certain people" to look upon the emergency measures as something "almost normal," and to "exaggerate the recourse to administrative measures."[4]

In general, however, the April plenum passed off without obvious tension between the members of the PB. Broadly, the resolution which was adopted on the question of procurement and preparations for the agricultural campaign of 1928–1929 repeated the theses of the Fifteenth Congress. *It explained the procurement crisis essentially by mistakes made in the application of economic policy*, referring only in a subordinate way to the "kulaks' offensive": it was the mistakes which had been made, said the resolution, that had been exploited by the kulaks and speculators. The resolution consequently stressed the need to establish "more correct proportions between the different elements in the economy."[5]

(b) The first clashes in the summer of 1928

The resumed application of the emergency measures at the beginning of the summer of 1928 resulted in a sharp increase in the tension between the two tendencies that existed in the PB. From then on they fought each other harder and harder, each of them trying to win the support of those members of the PB who were still hesitant.

However, it was not in the PB that the first systematic criticism of the policy actually being followed by the Party's administrative organs was formulated. This was done by the Communist Frumkin, who was assistant commissar of finance. On June 15, 1928, he declared, in a letter addressed to the PB, that the policy applied since the Fifteenth Congress repre-

sented a "new political line in relation to the countryside." He
said that this line was harmful, having "led to lawless actions
against the entire peasantry" and aroused anti-Soviet feeling
among the peasants, a feeling which was "already beginning
to spread to the working-class centres." According to Frumkin,
the acts of sabotage being committed should be attributed
primarily to the worsening of the internal situation, due to
political mistakes, and only to a secondary extent to influences
from outside.[6]

The PB decided to circulate Frumkin's letter to the members of the CC, following it up with a reply from the PB itself.
This reply was composed by Stalin personally, and was sent
directly to the members of the CC, contrary to the decision
taken by the PB. Bukharin, Tomsky, and Rykov, reacting
against this irregularity, accused Stalin of substituting his individual leadership for the collective leadership of the PB,
and treating the PB not as the Party's highest organ but as a
mere advisory council attached to the general secretary's
office. The other members of the PB did not see Stalin's
initiative in this light, and agreed only to a mild reprimand, in
the form of an admission by the PB that Stalin's reply to
Frumkin had been "incomplete."[7]

This incident was one of the first to indicate, more or less
formally, *a serious departure from the principle that leadership was the prerogative of the PB*. It was the start of a gradual
shifting of political authority, which passed increasingly out of
the hands of the PB and the CC and into those of the general
secretary. At that stage, however, the decisions taken by the
PB and the CC continued to determine, in the main, the
conditions governing application of the political line formally
decided on by the Party's congresses and conferences, or the
modifications introduced into this line.

During the summer of 1928 the divergences that developed
within the PB were not always made explicit to the world
outside (not even to the CC plenum of July 4–12, 1928). Yet
these divergences were becoming sharper and sharper, and
echoes of them even reached the CC. Until the end of the
year, however, the myth of the "unity of the PB" was preserved.[8]

At the meetings which preceded the plenum of July 1928 serious disagreements were expressed *within the PB*.[9] Bukharin and Stalin clashed, coming close to a rupture between them. The former demanded that a general discussion be opened regarding all the problems posed by the procurement crisis, especially in connection with the tempo of industrialization, and Stalin was unwilling to agree to this. Bukharin prepared draft theses for submission to the CC. Stalin said that he accepted them, but the other members of the PB gave only partial approval. To avoid an open rupture, Bukharin accepted the text as amended (which, he said, included "nine-tenths" of his theses).[10] The PB adopted this text unanimously, and submitted it to the CC.

This unanimity was only for show: in fact, the lines advocated by Stalin and Bukharin were more and more divergent. In his speech of July 9 Stalin defended the emergency measures and maintained that rapid industrialization would make it possible to strengthen the alliance with the peasantry. He expounded the idea that "the alliance between the working class and the peasantry cannot be stable and lasting . . . if the bond based on textiles is not supplemented by the bond based on metals."[11]

In this speech Stalin brought up the crucial question of *how industrialization was to be financed*, and said that there could be only "two such sources: firstly, the working class, which creates values and advances our industry; secondly, the peasantry."[12] Thus for the first time he systematically supported an idea very close to that of "primitive accumulation," advocated by Preobrazhensky (whose ideas had previously been condemned by the Party), namely, that the peasantry must of necessity pay relatively high prices for industrial products and be "more or less underpaid" for their own produce. Stalin explained: "It is something in the nature of a 'tribute', of a supertax, which we are compelled to levy for the time being in order to preserve and accelerate our present rate of industrial development, . . . in order to raise further the standard of life of the rural population and then to abolish altogether this additional tax, these 'scissors' between town and country."[13]

In a speech made next day, July 10, Bukharin, while not

openly attacking Stalin's position, took what was practically the opposite view. He stressed the idea that steady industrialization could not be achieved without a prosperous agriculture, whereas the requisition measures were causing agriculture to decline. He asserted that mass discontent was developing in the villages, which constituted a threat to Soviet power and risked uniting the middle peasants around the kulaks. While agreeing that the emergency measures had been needed in the past, he declared that the CC should abolish them for the future. Economically, he said, they no longer made any substantial contribution, and politically they were producing harsh consequences of a deeply negative character, "bringing us into conflict with the broadest strata of the peasantry." He emphasized the need to distinguish clearly between pressure exerted on the *kulak*, in conformity with the Party's decisions, and pressure exerted on the *middle peasant*, which was inadmissible, since it jeopardized the worker-peasant alliance. He warned against the desire to advance simultaneously in all directions: certain balances ought to be maintained, through correct planning, and price policy should be improved so as to strengthen the alliance with the peasantry. Bukharin ended by opposing exaggerated state centralization such as would stifle initiative.[14]

Tomsky supported Bukharin's views, as also did Andreyev, who spoke about peasant riots;[15] Osinsky, who called for an increase in the prices paid to the peasants;[16] and Rykov, who criticized the emergency measures. Molotov and Kaganovich, on the other hand, supported the emergency measures and the price policy which had been followed so far.

The plenum itself learned little of the respective positions of the two opposing tendencies. The resolution put before it by the PB was apparently more favorable to the theses of the "Right," coming down in favor of an upward readjustment of grain prices and repeating most of Bukharin's arguments.[17] The usual formulations regarding the relation between industry and agriculture were repeated, such as this: "While industry itself is a powerful drawing-force for agriculture, making possible its transformation on the basis of socialist industrialization, agriculture constitutes the foundation for the development of industry. . . ."[18]

The resolution emphasized that *collective farms must be formed only on a voluntary basis*[19] and explained the procurement crisis mainly by *economic imbalances and political mistakes*, which capitalist elements in town and country had been able to exploit. It acknowledged that revolutionary legality had been violated, arousing protests among the peasants and enabling "counter-revolutionary elements to spread gossip about N.E.P. being abolished."[20]

Altogether, the voting of the resolution on the economic situation seems to have reflected "victory" for those who were soon to be denounced as representatives of a "Right deviation." The resolution did indeed embody their principal theses. This was how the vote was usually interpreted by persons who were already aware of the existence of a serious conflict of tendencies within the leadership.[21]

In fact, however, during the plenum of July 1928 *the Right suffered a defeat*. It actually lost ground. The resolution adopted merely repeated what had already been set forth in the resolutions of the Fifteenth Congress, while the theory of the "tribute" to be levied from the peasantry *had not aroused real objections* on the part of the majority in the CC. On this essential point, the July plenum marked the implicit triumph of a thesis which the future majority in the Party leadership would strive to put into effect in order to realize the policy of industrialization which was to be adopted a few months later.

II. The deepening of the split in the Party leadership in the late summer and autumn of 1928

Immediately after the closure of the plenum the positions of the Right were attacked in various ways by their opponents, who developed their offensive first of all on the international plane.

(a) The extension of the divergences to international questions

The first of these attacks was launched against Bukharin during the Sixth Congress of the Comintern (July 17–September 1, 1928). As chairman of that organization, Bukharin presented the principal reports. These contained an evaluation of the situation and prospects in international affairs which resulted not from the discussions at the July plenum of the CC but from discussions which had not been published.[22] According to echoes from these, and also to subsequent discussions, the disagreements between Bukharin and the majority in the CC (which did not emerge publicly at this time) related to the tactics to be adopted by the Comintern in a situation when a world capitalist crisis was in the offing.

For Bukharin, the development of an economic crisis in the advanced capitalist countries *would not lead directly to a prospect of revolution*. He thought that the metropolitan centers of imperialism would not experience internal collapse in the years ahead, and that the center of gravity of the world revolution lay in the countries of the East (thereby developing further one of the ideas set forth by Lenin in his last writings[23]).

Bukharin and his supporters therefore condemned as being "radically wrong, harmful and grossly mistaken from the tactical standpoint" the statement that the crisis of Western capitalism would prove to be the eve of a revolutionary upsurge.[24] Bukharin thought that it was necessary to declare in favor of unity in the struggle of the working class, and not to launch into a sectarian line that would result in "isolation" of the Communist Parties, with a tragic outcome. The characterization of Social Democracy as "Social-Fascism"[25] seemed to him extremely dangerous: the ideological struggle against the Social Democratic parties must, of course, lead to their being denounced as bourgeois parties, but *not* to identifying them with Fascist organizations.

Stalin and the majority at the plenum of July 1928 appreciated the situation differently. *As they saw it, the advanced capitalist countries were then on the brink of revolutionary upheavals,*[26] and this dictated three tactical requirements: (1) refusal of any collaboration with the Social Democrats, and the need to create new, revolutionary trade unions, so as to take advantage of the new situation (which corresponded to what was called the "third period"[27]; (2) destruction of reformist influence over the working class, for in this new situation the Social Democratic parties became the main enemy of the working class; (3) purging of the Communist parties of all vacillating elements, and especially of the "Right deviationists," who, in the existing circumstances, became the main danger within the Communist movement.

In his speeches and in the theses he put before the Comintern Congress,[28] Bukharin, taking as his point of departure the fact that the Social Democratic parties and the trade unions under their influence embraced the immense majority of the European workers, refused to draw a line through these organizations, to regard them as "Social-fascist" and denounce them as the main enemy of the labor movement. Taking account, however, of attitudes which had been revealed during the plenum of July 1928, he made use of a cautious formulation: he said that "social-democracy has social-fascist tendencies," but at once added that "it would be foolish to lump social-democracy together with fascism." He opposed the idea that Communists might ally themselves with Fascists against Socialists, saying: "Our tactics do not exclude the possibility of appealing to social-democratic workers and even to some lower social-democratic organizations, but we cannot appeal to fascist organizations."[29]

These formulations were criticized by the delegation of the Soviet Communist Party, which put down a number of amendments,[30] thereby seriously undermining, for the first time, Bukharin's international prestige, and splitting the Congress into two tendencies, one "pro-Bukharin" and the other "pro-Stalin." In fact, Stalin, who was unusually active at this Congress of the Comintern, came out openly against Bukharin.[31] He was elected to the Congress Presidium, to the Program Commission, and to the Political Commissions entrusted with drawing up the theses on the international situation and the tasks of the Comintern.

The adoption of important amendments to his theses meant a grave defeat for Bukharin. It revealed that he was in a minority in the Soviet delegation, so that his standing within his own party was lowered. Furthermore, the content of some of the amendments passed was later to be used against Bukharin and his supporters in the Bolshevik Party.[32]

(b) The denunciation of a "Right danger" and of a "conciliationist mood" in the Bolshevik Party

During the Sixth Congress no mention was made of the existence of a "Right danger" in the Soviet Communist Party—only in the foreign sections of the Comintern. On September 18, 1928, however, *Pravda* denounced a "basically Right-wing mood" alleged to be present in the Soviet Party. A month later, the problem of this "Right danger" was put on the order of the day by Stalin in a speech delivered on October 19, 1928, before the Moscow Party Committee.[33]

In this speech he still spoke only of a "Right danger," not of a deviation in the strict sense. He referred to "a tendency, an inclination that has not yet taken shape, it is true, and is perhaps not yet consciously realised, but nevertheless a tendency of a section of the Communist Party to depart from the general line of our Party in the direction of bourgeois ideology."[34] Stalin went on to define what this Right tendency consisted of, saying that it "*underestimates* the strength of our enemies, the strength of capitalism." This led, he claimed, to a readiness to make concessions to capitalism, to calling for a slowing-down of the pace of development of Soviet industry, to treating the question of collective and state farms as secondary, and so on. He linked the existence of this danger with the fact that "we live in a small-peasant country" and that the roots of capitalism had, therefore, not been torn out, which implied "the *possibility* of the restoration of capitalism in our country."[35]

Stalin said that the danger of a "Left" (Trotskyist) deviation still existed, but that the Right danger was now more important, because less obvious. He therefore called for stress to be laid upon the Right danger, though without relaxing the fight against the "Left." Finally, he said that the danger of a Right deviation was present in the Party at almost all levels, either in the form of representatives of this ideological tendency or in that of a conciliatory mood. The latter, he alleged, had been shown even in the CC at the July plenum. Nevertheless, "in the Political Bureau there are neither Right nor 'Left' deviations nor conciliators towards those deviations. This must be said quite categorically."[36]

Thus, at the end of 1928, public criticism of Bukharin's positions began to take shape, although neither he nor Rykov nor Tomsky was attacked by name. Not considering themselves officially as being the targets aimed at, the three associated themselves with the denunciation of the "Rights" and the "conciliators." Their position was consequently to become practically untenable when they found these epithets applied to themselves.

(c) Bukharin's attempt at a counterattack

All the same, Bukharin did not remain silent at the end of 1928. He even tried to counterattack in a long article[37] published in *Pravda* (which he edited) on September 30, 1928, under the title, "Notes of an Economist."[38]

This article constituted an implicit reply to Kuibyshev's statements in defense of the new program of industrial development put forward by the VSNKh, which included a rate of development higher than had been provided for in June. An increase of 20.1 percent in gross industrial production was proposed for 1928–1929, with one-third of all investment allocated to the building of new factories. These figures, already very high, were regarded as inadequate by the leaders of industry, whose views Kuibyshev supported: they refused to contemplate any reduction in industrial investment, despite the difficult budgetary situation. Kuibyshev accused of "defeatism" those who criticized this program, and he asserted the need, at all costs, to concentrate investment in heavy industry, even if this meant provoking economic imbalances and "discontent and active resistance" on the part of the population.[39]

Bukharin vigorously opposed a conception of an industrialization to be achieved at the expense of the standard of living of the masses and, as he thought, first and foremost, at the expense of agriculture and of the peasants, thereby destroying the foundations of the worker-peasant alliance. Bukharin's article remained on the terrain of theory and principles: he did not openly attack any specifically defined "tendency" still within the Party, but rather the ideas of the Trotskyist "super-industrializers." Indeed, his real "political target" could be recognized only by those, in the leading circles of the Party and of the state machine, who were already aware of the discussions that had been going on. At that period, as has been said, this was practically true, also so far as the "political target" aimed at by the attacks on the "Right deviation" was concerned.

In his "Notes of an Economist" Bukharin developed systematically the principle (laid down by the Fifteenth Congress) that it was necessary to work out a plan which would permit harmonious development of industry and agriculture and of the different sectors of industry themselves. According to him, this plan must respect certain proportions dictated by the demands of expanded reproduction of the different branches of the economy. It must not give one-sided preference to one branch at the expense of the others, leaving these to stagnate, to lag behind or even to regress.

In referring to the demands of expanded reproduction, Bukharin emphasized that if these were not respected, the economic and political consequences could be grave. He said that, in "the society of the transition period," account must be taken of the relations shown in the diagrams of Marx's *Capital*, volume II, so as to ensure "the conditions for exact co-

ordination of the different spheres of production and consumption and of the different branches of production among
themselves, or, in other words, to establish the conditions for a
'dynamic economic equilibrium.' " And he added: "Serious
mistakes in the direction of the economy, violating the fundamental proportions of the economy . . . can cause regroupings
of classes to take place which would be extremely unfavorable
to the proletariat."[40]

Bukharin described refusal to strive for *correct proportions*
in the development of the different sectors of the economy as a
surrender "to petty-bourgeois indecision: 'It will work out all
right, one way or another—something good will come of it.' "[41]

Taking up the problem of transferrring to industry part of
the value created in agriculture, he agreed that this could and
even must take place, but he opposed too large a transfer,
which would hinder expanded reproduction in agriculture.
On this subject he wrote:

> Naively, the ideologists of Trotskyism suppose that by squeezing
> as much as possible each year out of the peasantry so as to invest
> it in industry we could ensure the fastest rate of development for
> industry in general. But, clearly, this is not so. The highest
> permanent rate of development is to be obtained by a combina-
> tion in which industry will grow on the basis of an economy in
> rapid growth. . . . This presupposes that rapid real accumulation
> can take place in agriculture, something which is remote from
> the Trotskyist policy. . . . *The Trotskyists do not understand
> that the development of industry depends on the development of
> agriculture.*

At the same time Bukharin attacked those whom he called
"the petty-bourgeois 'knights' who stand forth to forbid our
imposing any burden at all upon the agriculturists for the
benefit of industry," and whose standpoint was that of "the
survival of petty economy for ever and ever," adding that
these "ideologists of the 'farmer' prepare the way for real
kulak elements."

Bukharin concluded: "While the Trotskyists do not understand that the development of industry depends on the de-

velopment of agriculture, the ideologists of petty-bourgeois conservatism do not understand that the development of agriculture is dependent on industry. . . ."[42]

Concretely, Bukharin accepted the maintenance of investment at the level attained, but not the way this investment was distributed. He declared that the future growth of investment required that the situation of agriculture be improved. For him, refusal to recognize this requirement meant not realizing that *agriculture was the basis for the actual development of industry* (as was still acknowledged to be the case in the resolution of the plenum of July 1928). As he saw it, steps must be taken quickly to overcome the inadequacy of the production of grain and of industrial crops (sugar beet, cotton, flax, oil seeds, etc.), and it must be appreciated that the shortage of industrial products and raw materials was due to the growth in the investment of money running ahead of the growth of production, with the result that *industry was lagging behind the demand engendered by its own rate of expansion*. This being so, to speed up the tempo would merely worsen the shortages and protract the period in which factories were being built, thereby adversely affecting the long-term rate of development of the economy as a whole.[43]

Bukharin therefore wanted an upper limit to be fixed for the expansion of industrial investment, so that the sums allocated to industry could be employed in "real" construction. "It is not possible," he said, "to build today's factories with tomorrow's bricks."[44] In this connection he denounced what he called "a kind of fetishism of money" the effect of which was that "people think that, if they have money, they can automatically have everything else," whereas it *is material shortages* that have to be reckoned with at each moment, so as to overcome them in reality.[45]

The article called for costs of production to be reduced drastically, through an appeal to the masses combined with the use of science. In Bukharin's view, no appeal to the masses could succeed unless "over-centralisation" was renounced, and that meant taking "some steps towards the Commune-State," together with a struggle against "the elements of a bureaucratic degeneration absolutely indifferent to the interests of the masses," so denouncing "functionaries . . . who are ready to draw up any sort of plan"—a phrase aimed directly, though without naming them, at the specialists of the VSNKh.[46]

On the theoretical plane this article amounted, as can be seen, to a systematic onslaught on the increasingly great priority accorded, in a one-sided way, to investment in industry, and on the claim that this priority would make possible the solving of the problems of agriculture, and particularly that of grain procurement. The argument set out showed that, in the immediate future, such a conception could only worsen the economic situation and the tension between the Soviet govenment and the peasantry.

This article of Bukharin's was far from answering all the questions that had arisen at that time in the domains of economics and politics. It had the twofold defect of not showing *how to help the poor and middle peasants to advance along the road to collective forms of production* (failing to show the decisive role that ideological and political struggle must play in doing this), and of not defining what *concrete measures might be taken on the basis of the practical experience* of the peasants themselves. Despite these weaknesses, however, the article had the merit that it stressed (referring, moreover, to the decisions of principle previously taken by the Party) the necessity of *not attacking the standard of living of the masses;* of respecting certain *objective relations* between consumption and accumulation, between industry and agriculture, and between heavy and light industry; and of not setting targets which failed to correspond to the material and human resources available, and which, instead of enabling the economy to operate with *reserves*, actually multiplied shortages.

"Notes of an Economist" also indicated the negative consequences, from the angle of the class struggle, of failure to respect a number of objective requirements. Yet this article made practically no political impact at all: as it attacked, in principle, only certain conceptions which had been condemned long since—those of the Trotskyists—it did not give rise to any real discussion.

(d) The open offensive against the "Right deviation" and the plenum of November 1928

At the meeting (November 16–24, 1928) of the plenum of the CC an offensive was launched against what was thereafter officially called the "Right deviation"—without its principal representatives being named as yet. It was still claimed that there were no adherents of this deviation in the PB, nor any "conciliators" toward it. This statement conformed, moreover, to a request presented by Bukharin, Rykov, and Tomsky, who thereby shut the door on any possibility of discussing, clearly and precisely—at least at the level of the CC—the different conceptions held and the significance of the resulting divergences of view.

From the Trotsky Archives and Kamenev's notes on his talks with Bukharin (their meeting on July 11 had been followed by several others) we know that, during the meeting of the PB which preceded the plenum, Bukharin, Rykov, and Tomsky had asked Stalin to deny the "baseless rumours" about divergences in the PB. They also asked for a general discussion to be opened on the situation in the country. Though given satisfaction on the first point,[47] they were rebuffed on the second.

Following this rebuff, and that given to their demand for a reduction in the proposals for investments, which they considered to be too large and liable to interfere seriously with the regular supply of goods to the population, Rykov (who was then chairman of the Sovnarkom) and Bukharin wished to resign from the responsible posts they held, so as to dissociate themselves from the line which had been adopted and which they saw as running counter to the decisions of the Fifteenth Congress. After a compromise had been reached on some secondary matters, they withdrew their resignations: had they gone through with them, this would have started a crisis of leadership and made it very hard to persist with the policy they criticized.

The plenum of November 1928 was dominated by Stalin's speech on "Industrialisation of the Country and the Right Deviation in the C.P.S.U.(B.)."[48] This speech contained some propositions which, though they did not appear word for word in the draft resolution before the plenum, Stalin considered were implicit in this resolution.[49] They expressed, in fact, the way in which Stalin, from this time on, was to present the problem of industrialization and collectivization. We must therefore examine closely these propositions destined to play such a decisive role, for they constituted the initial formulation of *a new political line which broke with the resolutions previously adopted by the Party Congresses and endorsed the actual practice of the economic and administrative organs*.

(e) The beginning of a break with the Bolshevik Party's previous line

Two of Stalin's propositions call for special attention.

(1) Stalin's view on industrialization and the expansion of industry producing means of production

He considered the key factor in industrialization to be "the development of the production of the means of production, while ensuring *the greatest possible speed of this development*."[50] This contradicted the resolution of the fundamental role of agricultural development in the continuity and maintenance of the balanced character of industrialization. By stressing development "at the greatest possible speed" of the production of means of production (which meant heavy industry), he ignored the need to respect certain *ratios* between the development of the different branches of the economy: hence his assertion that what was needed was "the maximum capital investment in industry."[51]

This assertion also broke with the resolutions previously

adopted by the Party's congresses and plenums.[52] It went even further than what was said in the resolution put before the plenum of November 1928 by the PB, which spoke merely of "the most rapid development possible of the socialist sector of the economy," of an "intense rate of development of industry," with the word "maximum" used only in relation to "the mobilisation of the Party and of the worker and peasant masses."

Subsequently, the idea of the necessity for maximum investment in heavy industry was to be repeated many times, to the point of affirming that "the basic economic law of socialism" was "inseparably linked with the law of priority development of industries producing means of production,"[53] this law having allegedly been propounded by Lenin. It is true that Lenin spoke of the necessity for priority development of the production of means of production, but when he did so he was speaking of capitalism. In his polemic with the Narodniks, Lenin referred to this "priority" as being related to the capitalist forms of uneven development. Under capitalism, he said, "to expand production . . . it is first of all necessary . . . to expand that department of social production which manufactures means of production . . .," adding that "it is well known that the law of development of capital is that constant capital grows faster than variable capital. . . ."[54]

This law of capitalism is a consequence of its contradictions: it tends to develop the productive forces even when this development keeps coming up against the limits to growth in the masses' capacity to consume which are set by the striving for profit.

In Stalin's speech of November 19, 1928, the problems of industrialization and of "development of the production of the means of production at the greatest possible speed" were not yet presented in terms of a "basic law." They were considered from the angle of the conditions, both external and internal, in which the Soviet Union was then placed.[55]

Examination of the external conditions, with which Stalin began, showed that the USSR was "a country whose technical equipment is terribly backward," while being surrounded by many capitalist countries with much more highly developed industrial technique. Hence, said Stalin, there was a contradiction between the extremely backward technique possessed by the Soviet Union and its soviet system, which was "the most advanced type of state power in the world."[56] This contradiction must be resolved if the Soviet Union was not to find itself in a situation with no way out.

Stalin "generalized" the argument by saying that what was at stake was not only the building of socialism but the defense of the country's independence: "economic backwardness," he said, had been "an evil" even before the Revolution—and in this connection he referred to Peter the Great, who "feverishly built mills and factories"[57] in order to defend Russia.

Developing his argument, Stalin quoted from Lenin's article "The Impending Catastrophe And How to Combat It," written in September 1917. But, although this article does indeed say that it is necessary to surpass, as quickly as possible, "the economically advanced countries," it says nothing about *maximum* investment in industry or about *priority* development for the industries producing means of production.

As regards the "internal conditions" invoked to justify the tempo of industrialization proposed, Stalin abandoned the formula according to which agriculture was the *foundation* of the economy, while industry was its *driving force*. He now put forward the idea of "industry as the main foundation of our entire national economy" and of the need to "reconstruct agriculture on a new technical basis,"[58] which would require the provision of the maximum quantity of instruments and means of production. Emphasis was placed here upon *technical changes*, not on changes in production relations.

(2) Stalin's view on the reconstruction of the technical basis of agriculture

Referring to a speech by Lenin at the Eighth Congress of Soviets (in December 1920, well before Lenin's writings on cooperation and material aid to the poor and middle peasants), Stalin expounded the second theme of his speech. This was the affirmation that the rate of development of agriculture was lagging behind that of industry, and that this fact accounted for the grain problem, which could be solved only by reconstructing agriculture *"on a new technical basis."*[59]

Here we observe a constant sliding from consideration of one type of contradiction to consideration of another type, these two types being: (1) the contradictions arising from the existence of *two social forms of production* (state-owned industry, socialist in character, on the one hand, and petty-peasant production, on the other); and (2) the contradictions due to the existence of two "technical bases" of production (the up-to-date, large-scale industrial production units, on the one hand, and on the other, "backward" small-scale production). The argument aimed at justifying development of the industries producing means of production at the greatest possible speed brought forward as the "principal contradiction" in this domain the existence of two technical bases. *Changing the social forms of production seems here to be subordinate to changing technique* and developing heavy industry.

Yet there is no such subordination. Socialist development of collective forms of production is a matter above all of ideological and political class struggle, not of technique.[60] This development makes it possible in a first phase (as was proved by the experience of the "spontaneous" forms of collective labor and production which appeared during the NEP) to increase production without providing "new" technical means on a massive scale. Actually, in 1928 a far from negligible increase in production by the poor and middle peasants could have been achieved merely by supplying simple instruments of labor which would not have necessitated huge investments in heavy industry.

More generally, the idea of eliminating as quickly as possible the diversity of the "technical bases" of production does not correspond to any objective requirement for the building of socialism. This can, on the contrary, be carried out on the basis of a great diversity of techniques, by "walking on both legs," as they say in China nowadays. Such diversity makes it possible to *advance faster*, without any sharp increase in the rate of investment, and to progress steadily, without excessive strain, so that increasing mastery of increasingly advanced means of production is ensured, in agriculture and industry alike.

The possibilities of *technical diversification* opened up by socialism, and the varying forms that can be assumed by mastery of technique on the part of the direct producers, were denied by Stalin in his speech of November 19, 1928. In so doing he went against the Party's earlier resolutions and against Lenin's last writings. We see outlined here a path of economic development dominated by expanded production of means of production. It is upon this that the success of collectivization is made to depend—collectivization being seen not as the outcome of the struggle of the poor and middle peasants to free themselves from production relations that oppress them and make possible their exploitation, but as a *technical change* having the purpose of increasing agricultural production and, in particular, *the marketable part of this production* which the state is allowed to acquire at stable and relatively low prices.[61]

Thus, Stalin's speech of November 19, 1928, opened the way to a certain conception of industrialization and of agricultural development which enjoyed the approval of the VSNKh and of the leaders of industry. It accorded priority to industry and to heavy industry in the first place, and it made agricultural development depend on increased industrial production.

Apparently, however, this path of development was not the only one considered. Stalin's speech also assigns great importance in principle to immediate aid to the farms of the poor and middle peasants, to multiplying the *links* between these farms and the trading apparatuses of the state and the cooperatives (by extending a system of contracts between them, providing for reciprocal obligations) and to increasing forthwith the supply of goods and credits to these farms. From this standpoint, the NEP did not seem to have been abandoned, and transition to collective forms of production remained subject to the explicit wishes of the poor and middle peasants.[62]

In reality, however, the magnitude of the investments provided for heavy industry, and the aggravation of the shortage of industrial products supplied to the rural areas which resulted from this (especially as regards means of production such as the poor and middle peasants could use), increasingly negated, at ground level, the intentions expressed regarding aid to be given to the bulk of the peasant producers. Consequently, the *immediate possibilities* of growth in agricultural production, and, above all, in grain production, continued to be gravely compromised. Also compromised was the strengthening of the worker-peasant alliance, for the policy that was pursued in practice tended to demand more and more produce from the peasant masses without the necessary measures being taken to increase the supply, in exchange, of the industrial products that the poor and middle peasants needed.

The adoption by the plenum of the "control figures" for 1928–1929,[63] and the effort made to put them into effect, giving priority to heavy industry,[64] helped to worsen the discontent which had been gathering in the rural areas since the beginning of 1928. In this way, a basis was created for a real threat to the Soviet power, through the dissatisfied peasants rallying behind the kulaks. At the same time, the possibility of drawing the mass of the poor and middle peasants on to the path of collectivization on *a voluntary basis* was reduced because of the weakening of the Party's leading role among the peasantry.

III.   *The open split in the Party leadership*

During the winter of 1928–1929 the way in which the decisions of the plenum of November 1928 were applied, and in which the targets of the First Five-Year Plan were defined, confirmed that the basic principles of the NEP were being increasingly abandoned. An open split became inevitable, between the positions of Bukharin and his supporters (who wanted to lay down a path of industrialization that would remain within the framework of the NEP) and the positions of those who considered, in fact (if not in words), that rapid industrialization of the country was now incompatible with maintenance of the NEP.

The articles, speeches, and declarations of the supporters of the two contrasting policies of industrialization resembled less and less a discussion aimed at convincing those who held a different view: debate gave way to polemic, and *reciprocal accusations* tended to take the place of arguments and analysis of the concrete situation. It is therefore futile to try to reconstitute a "debate" which was no debate. Instead, we must try to bring out those few facts and arguments which, in spite of everything, were put forward, on one side or the other, during the winter of 1928–1929 and at the beginning of spring 1929, and which enable us to grasp better the political and ideological meaning of the split which was consummated at the plenum of April 1929.

(a) The positions defended by Bukharin during the winter of 1928–1929

It was in the winter of 1928–1929 that Bukharin defended his positions publicly for the last time, while continuing to expound his views before the PB and the CC. He was, of course, repeating many of his earlier formulations, but these were often articulated in a new way and, on certain points, were more fully elaborated.

One argument frequently advanced by the supporters of accelerated industrialization (which was to be carried out "for the time being" at the expense of agriculture) was that an imperialist attack on the Soviet Union was probably imminent. Bukharin did not deny that this danger existed. However, his analyses led him to emphasize especially the revolutionary role of the peoples of Asia and also to declare that *the decisive factor in the defence of the Soviet Union was its internal political situation*—in particular, the firmness of the worker-peasant alliance. To take a road which would compromise this alliance for the sake of promoting a more rapid industrialization program therefore seemed to him extremely dangerous.[65]

Bukharin emphasized the conditions for the strengthening of the worker-peasant alliance, largely repeating the content of Lenin's last articles, which, he said, set out "a vast long-term plan for all our Communist work. . . ." As Bukharin saw it, the future of the revolution depended on a firm and trusting alliance with the peasantry, and it was essential for the Party to seek to strengthen this alliance through organizational and cultural work that took account of the peasants' interests. He warned against the idea of a "third revolution" which would impose collective forms of production from above. He maintained that industrialization and accumulation must be carried out in a way that respected conditions of exchange which were acceptable to the peasants, through efforts aimed at economy and efficiency. These themes were in conformity with the resolutions of the Fifteenth Congress, but when reaffirmed at the beginning of 1929 they looked like a criticism of the political line which had been followed de facto for the past year. They brought many attacks on Bukharin from the supporters of maximizing investment in heavy industry. One of these, Postyshev, described Bukharin as a "vulgar peasant philosopher."[66]

In the same period as Bukharin's articles were published there appeared in *Pravda*, on January 20, 1929, an article by Nadezhda Krupskaya, Lenin's widow, entitled "Lenin and the Building of Collective Farms." Recalling the decisive place given by Lenin to the development of cooperation and the formation of collective farms, she emphasized that he had said that the peasants ought not to be forced to take the path of cooperation and collective farming against their will. She recalled also the importance ascribed by Lenin to Engels' article published in *Die Neue Zeit* in 1894 ("The Peasant Question in France and Germany"), in which he said that socialism would not expropriate the peasant but would *help* him to go over to cooperation and communes by using the power of example, and showing all the patience needed. In conclusion, she said that she thought it stupid to try and upset "from above" the economic relations in which the middle peasant was involved, and to resort to measures of coercion in order to do so.

This article of Krupskaya's came as a reply to those among the supporters of absolute priority for heavy industry who were declaring themselves increasingly in favor of forced collectivization. Krupskaya defended, on this point, the same positions as Bukharin.

The latter's public statements accounted for only part of his writing at that time. He also prepared a "platform" destined for the PB. He read this at the meeting of the PB held on January 30, 1929, and came under violent attack from the advocates of the speediest possible development of heavy industry. His position, which was supported by Rykov and Tomsky, did not apparently give rise to a genuine fundamental discussion. A few days earlier (on January 20, the day when Trotsky was expelled from the Soviet Union), a clandestine Trotskyist sheet had published a report of the talks between Bukharin and Kamenev, and it was essentially Bukharin's conduct—described as "factional"—that was attacked by his opponents.[67]

All that we know of the "platform" presented by Bukharin on January 30 and of the declaration made by the "three" on February 9 are a few quotations—which, nevertheless, enable us to reconstitute the bulk of what they said during that session of the PB.

One of the reproaches addressed by the three to the executive organs related to their failure to observe the decisions taken by the Fifteenth Congress and by the plenums of the CC regarding help to the farms of the poor and middle peasants. The notion of industrialization based on a "tribute" to be levied from the peasantry was also subjected to systematic criticism. The tribute idea entailed, as the three saw it, the risk that it could lead to "military-feudal exploitation of the peasantry." These terms were reproduced and condemned in the PB resolution of February 9.[68] In the report he presented to the plenum of April 1929 Stalin was to defend the idea of the tribute, while maintaining that it was inconceivable for the peasantry to be "exploited" in the Soviet Union.[69]

Bukharin considered it necessary to develop collective farming, but he refused to see this process as dependent on measures of coercion aimed primarily at using it as a means to serve an industrialization policy which assigned very high priority to heavy industry. Bukharin stressed that development of collective farming must be associated with a real *ideological struggle*, and he recalled, in this connection, what Lenin had written on the necessity of a *cultural revolution*.

Bukharin's opposition to the levying of a tribute from the peasantry as the basis for industrialization was bound up, first and foremost, with his conception of the worker-peasant alliance, which, he considered, must be based on a policy of systematically reducing the gap between the standard of living of the peasant masses and that of the working class. This attitude of his was inspired also by his view that important sources for accumulation and industrial development existed elsewhere than in agriculture. What was referred to here was, especially, the possibility of cutting down the size of the administrative machinery of the state, through greater decentralization and the freeing of local initiative that would make possible "real participation by the real masses" (as Lenin put it) in developing the productive forces.[70] Yet Bukharin did not really ask himself *why* what he was advocating had not actually been done, although this same line had long figured in the Party's resolutions. Formulating *this* question would have obliged him also to question himself regarding the social forces and social relations which obstructed the actual execution of some of the Party's decisions, and the forms of struggle that would make it possible to break through these obstacles: but, then, men never pose problems to themselves for which they cannot find solutions.

At the meetings of the PB in March and at the beginning of April 1929, held to prepare the plenum of the CC on April 16–23 and the Sixteenth Party Conference on April 23–29, Bukharin and Rykov put forward counterproposals to the draft of the Five-Year Plan which had been submitted to the PB. This draft provided for investment in the state sector to be multiplied by three or four, depending on the variant, and for 80 percent of this investment to be destined for heavy industry. Their counterproposals were rejected, together with a draft plan submitted by Rykov which aimed at developing agriculture, seen as the basis for industrial development. After this plan had been rejected, Bukharin, Rykov, and Tomsky abstained from taking part in the vote by which the PB gave its approval to the industrial provisions of the Five-Year Plan.

At the same time as they criticized the economic conceptions of the advocates of one-sided priority for the development of heavy industry and of financing this development by a massive transfer of resources from agriculture to industry, the three, and Bukharin in particular, also criticized *the developments that were going on in the superstructure*. Their criticism related to the *distention of the state apparatus* and the increase in it that could be foreseen if collectivization was not carried out voluntarily but so as to serve as a device for extracting a tribute from agriculture.[71]

Bukharin also criticized various aspects of the way the Party functioned. His arguments concerned primarily the content of the discussions that were held in the Party—these, he said, dealt mainly with internal problems of organization, instead of analyzing the concrete situation and systematically consulting the masses:

> Problems of great seriousness are not even discussed. The entire country is deeply concerned about the grain problem, and the problem of food supplies. Yet the conferences of the proletarian party in power remain silent. The whole country feels that all is not well with the peasantry. Yet our Party conferences say nothing. . . . This policy fails to face up to the real difficulties, it's no kind of policy at all. The working class must be told *the truth about the situation*, we must take account of the *needs of the masses*, and in our management of their affairs we must identify ourselves with the masses.[72]

The stress laid on Soviet democracy, on the role of the masses, and on organizing the supervision that the masses should exercise over the various apparatuses, corresponded to a long-standing preoccupation of Bukharin's. This was reaffirmed in an article he published in *Pravda* on December 2, 1928, and in his speech on "Lenin's political testament," in which he called for multiplication of "all possible forms of association by the working people so as at all costs, to avoid bureaucratisation," and to ensure that the Party knew the feeling of the masses and their reasons for discontent. This attitude of Bukharin's was later to be charged against him as showing a tendency to bow before "the backwardness and discontent of the masses."[73]

Bukharin's argument was also aimed at what he regarded as the development of a sort of blind discipline in the Party. He called on Party members "to take not a single word on trust . . . to utter not a single word against their conscience." He appealed to Bolshevism's tradition of critical thought.[74] For Bukharin there was a connection between the tendency to give up critical thought and what he saw as the gradual disappearance of collective leadership by the CC, in favor of the growing concentration of authority in the hands of one man.

This challenge to the type of discipline practiced in the Party was rejected by the majority of the PB, who insisted on the need for "iron discipline" and emphasized the weak points in the positions of the three. The absence of a sufficiently precise statement of *how* they conceived the conditions for transition to collective forms of agricultural production, their tendency to lay special stress on the *economic* forms of the worker-peasant alliance (based on the supply of consumer goods to the villages), their reservations regarding the role of the agricultural tax imposed on the well-to-do peasants—all these features made it easy to identify the positions of the three with defense of the status quo of the NEP, or even with defense of the interests of the kulaks. And the majority in the PB resolved to take that step. They also blamed Bukharin and Sokolnikov for their contacts with Kamenev, and Bukharin for publishing in the press writings which had not been previously discussed by the PB. These actions were considered as amounting to factional activity.

(b) The condemnation of the positions of
Bukharin, Rykov, and Tomsky by the PB
and by the plenum of the CC and the
CCC

All these accusations and reprimands were summed up in a draft resolution for submission to the PB and to the Presidium of the CCC. However, a commission of the CC was given the task of composing a "compromise" document: if the three voted for this, the draft resolution would be withdrawn. Acceptance of this compromise by the three[75] would have implied Bukharin's withdrawal of his resignation from his posts at *Pravda* and in the Comintern. On February 7, the three refused to vote for it and decided to keep their resignations in force until the April plenum (Rykov alone was subsequently to go back on this decision).

This action meant a *complete break* between the three and the majority in the PB. Stalin, in particular, saw the three thenceforth as constituting a "distinct group" whom he accused of opposing the Party line and wanting to "compel the Party . . . to stop fighting against the Right deviation." In his speech to the April plenum, Stalin declared that it was not possible to tolerate "in our own ranks, in our own Party, in the political General Staff of the proletariat . . . the free functioning of the Right deviators, who are trying to demobilise the Party [and] demoralise the working class," for that would "mean that we are ready . . . to betray the revolution."[76]

The PB majority passed a resolution on "the internal affairs of the Party"[77] and ratified a resolution dealing with the same matters which had been voted on February 9 by the PB and the Presidium of the CCC.[78] These documents condemned Bukharin's criticisms in "Notes of an Economist" as being groundless, "eclectic," and calculated to "discredit the line of the CC." They also condemned, for the same reasons, Bukharin's declaration of January 30, 1929, and what was said about his positions in the notes taken by Kamenev. In its conclusions, however, the resolution of the plenum laid special stress upon the *hesitations* of Bukharin and Tomsky in relation to the "new" line, and upon the need to safeguard Party unity. In contrast to the severer criticisms of Bukharin expressed in Stalin's speech,[79] the plenum resolution did not accuse the three of being Right deviationists. It spoke of their "*de facto* solidarity" with the opportunist tendencies in the Comintern and the role of "centre of attraction played *objectively*" by the three where those tendencies were concerned. Later on, the same resolution spoke of a "convergence *on basic questions* between the positions of the 'three' and those of the Right deviation."[80]

These formulations implied that the political positions of the three and those of the Right deviation did not fully coincide. The practical consequence of this was that the three kept their membership in the PB, even though they had not agreed to vote for the compromise document of February 7. The resolution forbade the three to give any public expression to their disagreements, thereby imposing new limits to the ideological struggle, which was being allowed to take place only inside an ever narrower circle.

While refusing to accept the resignation of Bukharin and Tomsky, the plenum relieved them of their posts, at *Pravda* and in the Comintern in the case of Bukharin, and in the trade-union leadership in the case of Tomsky.[81] The three had suffered a heavy defeat, and one that was to prove final.

The resolution of the PB which was ratified by the plenum also included a series of criticisms of the three. In particular, it rejected Bukharin's analysis of the economic situation. It declared that the supply of goods to the rural areas was better than in the previous year, and that procurement was proceeding in a way that could be regarded as satisfactory.[82] This appreciation of the situation had nothing in common with reality. *Except during two months, the procurement of grain in the first half of 1929 fell far below the figure for the previous year: for these six months as a whole it came to 2.6 million metric tons, as against 5.2 in 1928.*[83] Besides, these results had only been obtained by bringing strong administrative pressure to bear on the middle peasants, which had given rise, in a number of regions, to *open expressions of discontent by broad strata of the peasantry.* The grain shortage which then developed brought about a considerable rise in the market price of grain, and there were cases of speculation.[84] The plenum of April 1929 willfully ignored these realities, and that was to have serious effects later on, both economic and political.

(c) Stalin's speech at the plenum of April 1929

The bulk of this speech[85] was devoted to criticizing the positions of the three. In close connection with this critique Stalin put forward certain theses[86] to which we must now turn.[87]

(1) The intensification of the class struggle

The first thesis concerned the intensification of the class struggle *"at the present stage of development and under the present conditions* of the relation of forces."[88] It was thus not a "general thesis" but a formulation aimed at characterizing the conjuncture of a particular moment.

This characterization was correct, yet inadequate, for it was not derived from a many-sided analysis of the conjuncture. Thus, Stalin declined to explain the intensification of the bourgeois class struggle by the mistakes made by the Party in its handling of the problems of the poor and middle peasantry, as a result of the weakening of the machinery of the dictatorship of the proletariat and of its connections with the masses. As he saw it, any analysis of the situation which took account of such factors amounted to trying to attribute the intensification of the class struggle to "causes connected with the character of the apparatus,"[89] or to saying that what had been "good" last year had suddenly become "bad"[90] (for he denied that there had been any change in this matter during the intervening period).

Restricting in this way his analysis of the causes of the intensification of the class struggle amounted to focusing one-sided attention upon the attempts made by the adversaries of the dictatorship of the proletariat, without examining what it was, in the disposition of the latter's forces, that enabled these adversaries to *transform their attempts into effective counteroffensives*. Whether they could do this or not depended on the firmness of the bonds between the working class and its allies, and on the political line of the Party. What the analysis left out was therefore the main thing, the political line and its contradictions: this prevented correct treatment of these contradictions and speedy introduction of the necessary rectifications.

(2) The problem of the "tribute" and of the possibility of the peasantry being exploited by the Soviet state

The second thesis set out in this speech of April 1929 was that of the need to impose upon the peasantry "something in the nature of a tribute," so as to make possible industrialization of the Soviet Union.[91]

In the general way in which it was presented, this thesis was both true and false. It was true in the sense that, in the concrete conditions in which the Soviet Union was placed, no industrialization of any magnitude was possible unless the peasantry made *a certain contribution*[92] to the effort of industrial development.

Formulated, however, in so general a fashion, this thesis could open the way for a wrong policy, one entailing grave consequences, for it was not accompanied by any indication of *the limits which this tribute must not exceed* if it was not to jeopardize the worker-peasant alliance and the requirements for expanded reproduction in agriculture. The facts were not slow in revealing that these limits were being exceeded.

The negative consequences of the "tribute" thesis set forth in these general terms were enhanced decisively by the linking of this thesis with another, false one, namely, the assertion that "the very nature of the Soviet regime precludes any sort of exploitation of the peasantry by the state."[93]

Such a formulation did not allow for either the *contradictory nature of the Soviet state* (a state of the working class but *also* a "bourgeois state," as Lenin put it, in so far as it ensured the reproduction of certain bourgeois relations, particularly on the plane of distribution), or for the presence of bourgeois elements in the Soviet state machine. Yet these factors could constitute the objective conditions for *despoiling and exploiting* the peasants (and the workers, too, for that matter) and drive the peasantry into opposition to the Soviet power. This formulation of Stalin's was therefore a *step backward* as compared with Lenin's.

(3) The "new forms of the bond" and the "technical basis" for increasing agricultural production

Stalin's speech at the plenum of April 1929 set forth a thesis of the necessity for "new forms of the bond between town and country." These new forms were to involve the supplying by industry of *means of production* to agriculture—agricultural machinery, tractors, fertilizers, etc.—for, now, "it is a question of reconstructing agriculture," reorganizing agricultural production "on the basis of new technique and collective labour."[94]

This thesis developed and sharpened the contrast which had been made up to that time between a worker-peasant alliance based on textiles and that based on steel. The prospect which it opened up certainly corresponded to future needs, but the formulations used gave rise to a series of problems, and the following in particular:

(a) Even at the end of the NEP period the "restoration" of agriculture was far from having been completed. Millions of small- and medium-sized farms still lacked the most elementary instruments of production.[95] In practice, this meant that it was still possible to help the poor and middle peasants to bring about a rapid increase in agricultural production in return for *modest investments,* and without having to wait for the building of new steelworks, new tractor factories, and so on. The problem of waiting periods and rates of progress therefore did not really arise in the terms in which it was formulated at the plenum of April 1929.[96]

(b) According to Stalin, the period of "restoration" was one which had to be a period when what predominated was a form of the worker-peasant alliance aimed at satisfying "*mainly* the personal requirements of the peasant, hardly touching the productive requirements of his economy."[97] True, this was how the alliance had been practiced, but that practice had been mistaken: from the very beginning of the NEP, supplying the peasant farms with means of production, even if only rudimentary ones, should have been a priority task, as Lenin had said. The alliance based mainly on textiles had not helped the poor and middle peasants to free themselves from domination by the rich ones.

(4) Mechanization and collectivization

Stalin's speech presented collectivization as having been necessitated by technical changes and by the need for increased marketable production. The development of collective production in agriculture did not appear as a form of class struggle but as a technical and economic necessity.

What was stressed was "the danger of a rift between town and country" due to the inadequate rate of growth in agriculture as compared with industry, from which Stalin drew the conclusion that, "in order to eliminate this danger of a rift, we must begin seriously re-equipping agriculture on the basis of new technique. But in order to re-equip it we must gradually unite the scattered individual peasant farms into large state farms, into collective farms."[98]

In this conception, which was the one that eventually prevailed, the aspirations and needs of the poor and middle peasants were not the main consideration. It was the needs *of the towns and of industry* that dictated the *technical conditions* of agricultural production and these, in turn, that dictated its *social conditions*. We may well wonder why such a conception took shape (I shall return to this question when I deal with the changes in the Bolshevik ideological formation), but what is certain is that its implementing explains why collectivization was carried out in the way it was, and also its "counterproductive" consequences—a setback to agricultural production instead of an advance.

(5) *Mechanization and industrialization*

The thesis of the *urgent need* for a technical transformation of agriculture having been laid down, that of the need for rapid industrialization could be "deduced" therefrom: "it will be impossible to supply the countryside with machines and tractors unless we *accelerate* the development of our industry."[99]

Here Stalin argues in a circle: agriculture must be rapidly supplied with up-to-date equipment so that it does not lag behind industry, and industry's rate of development must be accelerated so that it may rapidly provide the equipment for agriculture. Illusory movement around this circle was what compelled the continual readjustment upward of the targets of the First Five-Year Plan.

(6) *The procurement crisis of 1928–1929 and the relations between classes*

In Stalin's speech at the plenum of April 1929 the difficulties experienced in grain procurement were explained essentially by the alleged "economic strengthening" of the kulaks. Having asked what were the causes of these difficulties, Stalin answered himself with the following formulation: "During these years the kulak and well-to-do elements have grown, the series of good harvests has not been without benefit to them, they have become stronger economically; they have accumulated a little capital and now are in a position to manoeuvre in the market."[100]

Unfortunately, this "economistic" explanation of the procurement crisis begs some questions: (a) When was this "series of good harvests"? The last good harvest had been that of

1926. (b) Starting in early 1928, it had been necessary to employ emergency measures, and the exhaustion of the grain stocks held by the rich peasants had, as the Party leadership admitted, compelled the extension of these measures so that they affected the middle peasants. This being so, how could the "capital" held by the kulaks in 1929 be larger (in the form of grain, at any rate) than it had been in 1927?

In reality, if the position of the kulaks had indeed been strengthened between 1927 and 1929, this was because *their ideological and political influence had grown.*

And this growth in the kulaks' influence was due to the mistakes made by the Party in its peasant policy. Any examination of these mistakes, however, such as would have been necessary if they were to be eliminated, was ruled out from the start in Stalin's speech. When he mentioned the procurement difficulties, he asked: "Perhaps the policy of the Central Committee is responsible for this?" only to answer himself with an unproved assertion: "No, the policy of the Central Committee has nothing to do with it."[101]

This last formulation—which contradicted everything that had been admitted in 1928—made it necessary to "explain" the procurement crisis by an economic strengthening of the kulaks, and prevented any correction of the policy followed, since this was held to "have nothing to do with" the situation.

Stalin's speech at the April plenum was of quite special importance. On the one hand, the theses contained in it, even when they were inadequate, or contradicted reality, were not subjected to any systematic criticism: the ideological campaign waged during the period preceding the plenum was such that any questioning of these theses was immediately repudiated as constituting a "pro-kulak" position, and the development of a real movement of criticism and self-criticism, which would presuppose respect for democratic centralism, was consequently blocked. On the other hand, these theses were the point of departure for a new turn in the Party line, a turn toward the road of an accelerated industrialization the burdens of which were to be borne by the peasantry. This was confirmed (though still in hesitant fashion) by the Sixteenth Party Conference, which led to the "great change" effected at the end of 1929.

IV. *The Sixteenth Party Conference (April 23–29, 1929) and its consequences*

The Sixteenth Party Conference saw a last attempt at strengthening socialist relations *while basically remaining within the framework of the NEP* and *laying the foundations for transition to a higher stage.* The decisions it took are therefore of considerable interest, even if the prospect outlined by this conference failed to materialize. The contradictory character of some of these decisions, and the rapid course taken by the class struggle, meant that, a few months after the Sixteenth Conference, the Party leadership was faced with a choice—either to renounce some of the economic (especially industrial) targets defined in April 1929, or to try and realize these targets by taking *economic and political measures other than those provided for* by that conference (including brusque abandonment of the NEP).

The second of these roads was the one that was followed. It was to take the Soviet Union into a *wholly new era,* before the conditions had matured for mastering many of the new and immense problems it presented.

Analysis of the principal aspects and decisions of the Sixteenth Conference enables us to see more clearly the conditions that made it seem possible, in April 1929, to reconcile maintenance of the NEP with the launching of a process of rapid social and economic changes. This analysis, together with examination of the concrete situation at that time, can also enable us to see the contradictory character of the decisions taken by the Sixteenth Conference, and some of the reasons which explain why these contradictions were "resolved" during the second half of 1929 in the sense which has been mentioned.

(a) The condemnation of the political positions of the "three"

One of the characteristic features of the Sixteenth Conference was the way that the problem of political divergences within the PB was dealt with. These divergences, despite their importance and the seriousness of the questions they raised, were *not gone into in a fundamental way.*

It was only on the eve of the closure of the conference, and "at the request of the delegates," that Molotov gave a report on the work of the plenum which had just been held. He then put down a short resolution which "noted" that "the Bukharin group" had departed from the Party's general line and was pursuing a "Right deviation." This resolution was adopted without discussion. Though it approved the decision taken by the CC regarding "the Bukharin group"[102] it was not included in the report of the Sixteenth Conference published in 1929: nor did this report include those passages in delegates' speeches in which they attacked Bukharin.[103]

For several months yet, the existence of profound divergences within the PB was still kept secret. Rykov was even included among those entrusted with presenting a report to the Sixteenth Conference on the Five-Year Plan, and he continued to serve as chairman of the Sovnarkom.[104]

The lack of a broad discussion dealing with the opposing political positions did not help to clarify the situation, and, in particular, to distinguish between what, in the positions of the three, might properly be called a Right deviation and what might be correct views.

The reasons why no real discussion was ever held have never been given. It may be supposed that desire to demonstrate the "unity" of the PB was the decisive factor, since such a discussion was sought neither by the majority nor by the three. Nobody wanted to risk a split in the Party. While the majority in the PB enjoyed the support of a section of the proletariat in large-scale industry and of many of the leaders of economic and industrial organizations, the positions of the three were backed by a high proportion of the Party members working in the countryside, by many trade-union cadres, and by a section of the workers in the consumer-goods industries, especially in the textile mills.[105] It should be added that, the greater the tension in the rural areas became, the more dangerous it seemed to allow the Party leadership to seem divided, since open resistance to the "emergency measures" might then develop among the peasantry.

At all events, the absence of a genuine discussion made it impossible for the respective positions to be clarified, with identification of what was and what was not correct in the theses of the two sides. This being so, the contradictions in the resolutions of the Sixteenth Conference were not analyzed, either. Thereafter that tendency prevailed which accorded one-sided priority to heavy industry and ignored the demands of the worker-peasant alliance. Significantly, some of the supporters of the former opposition, especially the Trotskyists among them, considered that the line of the Sixteenth Conference was such that they could ask to be readmitted to the Party—though Trotsky, from his exile abroad, condemned this move.[106]

(b) The fight against "bureaucracy"

An important aspect of the Sixteenth Conference was its placing on the agenda "the fight against bureaucracy." The conference linked this question closely with that of the economic and social changes to be brought about, with collectivization and industrialization. *A connection was thus made between radical transformation of the state machine (revolutionizing of the superstructures) and success in socialist transformation of the economic basis.*

The resolution adopted on this subject by the Sixteenth Conference sought to define some of the requirements which must be satisfied if a real breakthrough by the masses into the activity of the soviets and the administrative bodies was to be achieved, and resistance to the revolutionary changes overcome in this way. It denounced the harmful political consequences of the manner in which the state apparatus functioned. Thus, the resolution in question[107] declared:

> The struggle by the Party and the Soviets against bureaucratic perversion of the machinery of state, which often conceals from the broad masses of the working people the actual nature of the proletarian state, constitutes one of the most important forms of the class struggle.
>
> The tremendous tasks laid down by the Five-Year Plan . . . cannot be accomplished without a decisive improvement in the machinery of state, without simplifying it and reducing its cost, without precise execution of their respective tasks by each link in the chain, without decisive overcoming of inertia, red-tape, bureaucratic suppression, mutual 'covering-up' and indifference to the needs of the working people. . . .[108]

The contradiction between the magnitude of the tasks and the agrarian and technological changes laid down by the Five-Year Plan and the way the bureaucratic apparatus functioned was thus clearly appreciated. Nevertheless, the ideological conditions for revolutionary transformation of the machinery of state were left imprecise. The questions raised by such a transformation were approached, mainly from the angle of *organization,* and this was not adequate for showing the path whereby the initiative of the masses could succeed in smashing the tendency of the apparatuses to dominate them and to function in a bourgeois rather than a proletarian way.

On the plane of organization, the resolution of the Sixteenth Conference stressed mainly the following points:[109]

(1) *Checking up* on the execution of the Party's political line. The resolution recalled what Lenin had said about the state machine often working "against us"[110]—which testified to how little improvement had been made in this situation since Lenin's death. It suggested, among other measures, that increased scope be given to rank-and-file control commissions, stating that "these commissions must be elected directly in the factories and workshops and by the Soviets of the corresponding towns."[111]

(2) Improvement in the composition of the personnel of the state machine, and introduction of a system of leadership cor-

responding to the economic system and to the demands of the building of socialism[112]—these were two themes which were also emphasized in this resolution of the Sixteenth Conference. The indications given for realizing these aims were, however, vague and even contradictory. There were a number of considerations regarding "decentralization of leadership functions," "personal leadership," labor discipline, and "active participation by the masses in leadership," without it being made clear which of these were of principal importance and which were secondary. This resulted from the presence of contradictory tendencies: one favoring reinforcement of the existing organs of leadership and the other favoring broader intervention by the masses in the drawing up of plans and the taking of decisions.

Finally, this part of the resolution seems to have been dominated above all by concern to obtain *"economic" results*: rationalization of the production apparatus, increased productivity of labor, cutting down of the unproductive departments and services in the enterprises, reduction in the costs of the state trading apparatus, and so on.

(c) The organization of supervision by the masses

The organization of supervision by the masses occupied a central position in this resolution, which called upon the non-Party workers and peasants to learn to make use of the rights which the Soviet Republic guaranteed them—for, as the resolution said, "any fight against bureaucracy which is not based upon the activity and initiative of the working class, but seeks to substitute for supervision by the workers and peasants themselves the activity of some apparatus or other is doomed, however good its intentions, to produce no serious result as regards real improvement in and fundamental reconstruction of the machinery of state."[113]

The resolution then listed various experiments which had already been made[114] and urged that these be learned from. Nevertheless, it did not analyze why these experiments had produced such limited results, and nothing was said about what should be done to ensure that things would be different in future.

"The tasks of the fight against elements of bureaucracy in the Party and in the state machine" were also dealt with in the resolution.[115] This part of the document was, in principle, one of the most important, for it tried to define the road leading to reversal of the trend which had separated the Party from the masses and caused the latter to hesitate to criticize the Party and Party members, as Stalin had observed in his report to the plenum of April 1928.

In that report Stalin had noted that, because of the growing prestige of the Party leadership, "the masses begin to look up at [the leaders] from below and do not venture to criticize them"—which "cannot but give rise to a certain danger of the leaders losing contact with the masses and the masses getting out of touch with the leaders," so that the latter are in danger of "becoming conceited and regarding themselves as infallible. . . . nothing can come of this but the ruin of the Party."[116]

The resolution spoke of the need for developing *criticism from below, without respect of persons,* so as to eliminate bureaucratized elements and those who were connected with the kulak and capitalist elements still present in the country; of the need to combat *violations of democracy in the Party,* to hold elections in order to remove those who had lost the sympathy of the masses and contact with them, and to resist the tendency of leading bodies to substitute themselves for the organs they were supposed to lead (e.g., usurpation by the presidiums of soviets of the functions of the soviets themselves).[117]

This resolution, the principal terms of which I have summarized, therefore presented as *a condition for the building of socialism a fundamental reorganization of the machinery of state and of the way that this functioned.* It revealed that what had already been said on this subject over several years had remained more or less inoperative. Reading this document, we can see, too, that there was great uncertainty regarding the targets to be aimed at. Were they, *first and foremost,* increased "efficiency" in the machinery of state? Or did they consist in transforming this machinery in revolutionary fashion so that new proletarian political relations might develop? The resolution gave no clear answer to this question—or, rather, this question was hardly raised in it. It could therefore not give a precise answer to the *concrete problems of the road to be followed* in order to transform the machinery of state: hence the juxtaposition in it of various recommendations the relative priority of which was not indicated.

In practice, during the months that followed the adopting of this resolution, the tasks laid down in the sphere of industrialization were amplified, and the pace at which these targets were to be reached was speeded up. Thereafter, most attention was focused upon economic questions, while the priority which had been accorded to the requirements for transforming the machinery of state was lost sight of. The few changes that were carried out, all the same, were carried out *from above,* which did not fail to bring with it some negative consequences, and in particular to reduce, instead of increasing, the place accorded to intervention and supervision by the masses.

(1) The need to purge the Party, and its significance

The Sixteenth Conference formally decided on a Party purge.[118] This operation was bound up with the attempt to recast the state machine, but also with the general crisis of the NEP and the fight against Right deviation. The conference recalled that the purge to be undertaken would be the first *general* purge since the one carried through in 1921, at the outset of the restoration period.[119]

Between 1922 and 1929 there had indeed been only partial purges,[120] connected with the regular activity of the CCC.[121] The decision of the Sixteenth Conference, however, aimed at an operation of an exceptional and general character.

A few days before he placed before the Sixteenth Conference the theses on purging the Party, with the corresponding resolution, Yaroslavsky gave a report on these questions to a conference of the Moscow Party organization. His report was especially severe in what it said about the rural Party organizations. He also criticized those factory workers who had kept their ties with the village, for, he said, these workers looked on their work in industry merely "as a means of enriching their farms." He stressed that the purge must be effected on ideological lines, every member being judged "from the standpoint of the accomplishment of the tasks of the class struggle. At the same time, he warned against "inquisitorial methods," "enquiries among neighbors," etc.[122]

The theses on the purge were examined by the Sixteenth Conference only on the last day of its discussions. The corresponding instructions for the local control commissions were dispatched even before this examination had been undertaken. The resolution on the purge did not give rise, therefore, to any real debate. Nevertheless, the interruptions made by certain delegates show that a section of the conference feared that this purge would serve principally to restrict discussion in the Party. However, the resolution was passed unanimously.[123]

The policy of purging the Party was inspired by the ideas which underlay the resolution on the fight against "bureaucracy." Several paragraphs of that resolution concerned the Party itself, and deserve to be mentioned here. The following paragraph is especially noteworthy.

> The conference draws the attention of the whole Party and of every Party member individually to the need to wage *the most resolute, the most determined, the most persevering struggle against elements of bureaucracy in the Party itself, in the Party apparatus: these elements result from the many ties between the Party apparatus and the soviets, from the involvement of a very large number of Party members in administrative work, and from the influence exerted upon Communists working in the state machine by elements belonging to the bourgeois intelligentsia and to the corps of officials.*[124]

This paragraph is remarkable because of the importance it ascribes to the fight against "bureaucracy" in the Party; but also because of the *limited character of the reasons it gives for the existence of this phenomenon* which restricted the practical significance of the methods recommended for struggle against it. Problems of the division of labor and of participation by the cadres in productive work were thus not put in the center of the analysis of what constituted, in reality, the development of bourgeois political practices.

The measures proposed were difficult to apply. However, the list of the principal measures which was given illustrates the way in which the Party worked on the eve of the "great change," and also the attempts made to modify this way of working so as to reduce the "bureaucratization" of the Party.

Among these measures was reduction in the number of paid Party functionaries and their replacement, wherever possible, by a group of especially active Party members (the Party "activists"). These should form, in every factory, locality, administration, etc., where they were sufficiently numerous, an organization called the Party's *aktiv*. Organizations like this did indeed develop in 1929, but without, apparently, causing a real reduction in the number of functionaries on the Party's payroll.[125] The extent of any such reduction would, in any case, not have been obvious, for a very large proportion of the Party cadres held jobs in the state machine and were paid in that capacity.[126]

The resolution on the Party purge also mentioned the need to fight against violations of democracy within the Party, so as to eliminate "bureaucratized" elements who had lost the confidence of the masses. It linked changing the Party's style of work and its makeup, on the one hand, with correct fulfillment of the tasks arising from the reconstruction of the economy and the industrialization of the country, on the other. It pointed out that during the NEP period, the Party had recruited, not only hundreds of thousands of proletarians, but also petty bourgeois who, by their personal and social example, "bring disorganization into the ranks of the Party, [who] despise the opinions of the workers and the working peasants, . . . [and] are careerist elements . . . whom the Party has got rid of only to an inadequate extent through the systematic, day-to-day work of the control commissions. . . ."[127] Hence the need for a more thoroughgoing purge.

The formulations used in the resolution showed that in 1929 the composition of the Party was even worse than it had been in 1922, when the situation was already far from satisfactory.[128] They also showed the need, if the road to new social changes was to be followed successfully, for a series of measures to be taken which would place the Party under supervision by the masses and remove from it the elements alien to communism.

The resolution made the point that, although the factory and workshop cells were the soundest section of the Party, this did not imply that those cells did not equally need purging, for, there too, "elements have infiltrated which are incapable of playing the role of a Communist vanguard," owing to their thirst for personal enrichment, their failure to participate actively in improving labor discipline, or the fact that they had not broken with religion, or that their antisemitism showed that they had a counter-revolutionary attitude, etc.[129] The resolution declared that, without purging the entire Party it would not be possible "fully to draw into the Party's ranks the best elements from the considerable body of non-Party proletarian activists," and thereby put the Party in a position to fulfill the "great and complex tasks of the new phase."[130]

The resolution was even more severe on the situation prevailing in the rural cells. It stressed the need to show special care in checking the composition of these cells, so as to remove from them elements alien to the ideology and politics of the proletariat. It provided a long list of the characteristics of persons who ought to be expelled from the Party.

Finally, the resolution mentioned the need to purge the cells operating in the "non-productive" sectors, pointing out that the specific role played by these called for particular attention to be given them.[131]

(2) The ways in which the policy of purging was applied, and its limitations

On the plane of *principle*, the resolution emphasized the need to bring the masses into the application of the policy of purging the Party. Thus, dealing with purges to be carried out in the village cells, with the help of "activists" from among the agricultural workers and the poor and middle peasants, it declared that such purges must be effected before the eyes of the broad masses of the peasantry: "only a purge like that can transform the rural cells."[132]

On the plane of *concrete measures*, however, the resolution put the problem mainly in terms of organization, and *not of a mass movement*. It dealt essentially with the part to be played by the CCC and the local control commissions, and merely mentioned participation by the non-Party masses in purging operations. The masses were not called upon to *develop their initiative* so as to remove from the Party the elements that were not genuinely proletarian and Communist, or to insist that those Party members who had made mistakes be placed in conditions which would enable them to turn over a new leaf. The results of the purges would thus depend mainly on the way that the control commissions functioned, their notion of their task and of the requirements for a thorough cleanup in the Party, and the information they could collect (in the absence of a broad mass movement) on the practices and relations engaged in by the Party members whose cases they examined. Given that the members of the control commissions were actually chosen from among the Party cadres, they were unable, in most cases, to act otherwise than in accordance with what those whom they were called upon to "judge" considered proper. Since there was no mass movement, they were therefore led to "punish," in the main, only the most glaring cases of careerism, corruption, contempt for the masses, and bureaucratic and bourgeois behavior, while "ordinary" cases were usually passed over, although it was also upon the treatment of these—especially when they were numerous—that the masses' trust, or lack of it, in the Party and its members depended, and so the Party's own capacity for revolutionary action.

The way in which the question of purging the Party was presented included other aspects, too, for the commissions were required to take into consideration the members' opinions[133] and ensure that "hidden" supporters of various trends—such as the "Democratic Centralism" group, Myasnikov's supporters, and other "anti-Party groups," including the Trotskyists—were "ruthlessly expelled." What was struck at here was not any *activity*, but mere opinions, *including supposed opinions*, since the resolution spoke of "hidden opinions," which were to be the target of a "ruthless" struggle.[134] This made it possible to expel anyone who expressed reservations regarding some of the Party leadership's appreciations of the economic or political state of the country, or who drew different practical conclusions from these appreciations. In the absence of adequate control from below, and of genuine desire for unity, and without clear awareness that it was inevitable for ideological contradictions to arise in the Party, and that these must be dealt with otherwise than by coercion, the terms of the resolution favored resorting to "administrative methods" in the sphere of the ideological struggle. And that entailed grave consequences for the Party itself, for Marxism can develop only in open struggle and discussion: besides which, if the Party is to have *concrete knowledge* of the economic, social, and political situation as it really is, then every Party member must be allowed to express his views.

It was precisely because the resolution on the purge, and the directives sent to the local control commissions by the CCC, emphasized expulsions as the means of uniting the Party ideologically,[135] that Yaroslavsky's speech at the Sixteenth Conference was interrupted by delegates who were unhappy about the content of the resolution, and about the fact that they were not allowed to discuss it. These interruptions were all the more significant because, in his speech, Yaroslavsky avoided dealing with the directly political aspects of the purge. It was also remarkable that the delegates who had interrupted and criticized Yaroslavsky's speech nevertheless eventually adopted the resolution, which was passed unanimously.[136]

(3) Remarks on some immediate effects of the purges

From the quantitative standpoint the purge of 1929–1930 was relatively less important than that of 1921–1922. Whereas in the earlier period the purge eliminated a quarter of the

Party's membership, in 1929–1930 it affected only about 11 percent—and some of these were subsequently readmitted.[137]

The effects of the purge upon relations between the Party and the masses were also very limited. The purge was mainly carried out by internal Party commissions, without active participation by the worker and peasant masses, as the resolution of the Sixteenth Conference had demanded. Actually, that resolution had hardly been adopted when the bulk of the Party's forces found themselves committed to the struggle for industrialization and large-scale collectivization. As a result, the purge carried out in 1929–1930 did not lead to the decisive changes in the functioning and composition of the Party that the Sixteenth Conference had considered necessary: the changes did not enable the Party to become the indispensable instrument for a real socialist transformation of social relations, with authentic knowledge of the situation and aspirations of the broad masses of the peasantry. This knowledge was, instead, darkened thereafter by the fear which members of the Party's basic units might feel regarding the consequences of reporting difficulties which were due to mistaken directives from the higher authorities, since such initiatives could easily be identified with manifestation of "ideological dissent" and punished by expulsion. More generally, the use of such measures as weapons of "ideological struggle" reduced the Party's capacity to enrich itself from the experience and thought of the majority of its members: the latter were often led, through concern not to "make trouble for themselves," to express agreement with every directive, however trivial, and not to reveal any opinion that might differ from that held by the leadership. The development of this attitude had a profoundly negative effect on the functioning of democratic centralism, on Party life, and on the Party's relations with the masses.

In the immediate period, however, the measures taken in 1929–1930 helped to make the Party a more "efficient" *instrument for carrying out decisions* than it had previously been, and this was what the leadership had wanted, so as to be able to cope with increasingly heavy tasks of economic construction.

(d) The plans for industrial development

The Sixteenth Conference was a decisive moment—but only one such moment—in the conflict between the advocates of "maximum" industrial growth and those who advocated "optimum" growth. This moment, in contrast to what had happened at the Fifteenth Congress, saw the victory of the former over the latter. A new, explicit political line of immediate and accelerated industrialization was thus defined, which was to produce a series of effects on class relations, and especially on the worker-peasant alliance. The more this line hardened and developed, the more clearly its class consequences were to emerge; and that was not yet the situation at the time when the Sixteenth Conference was held.

In order to evaluate correctly the implications of the decision taken regarding industrial policy, we must see how the contrasting lines on this matter were reflected—before, during, and after the Sixteenth Conference—in the "plan figures" for industrialization and investment. We must also see how the line that prevailed meant bringing nearer the final break with the NEP: this was a contradiction within the resolutions of the Sixteenth Conference, which actually resolved that the NEP should not be abandoned in the near future.[138]

(1) The evolution of the plans for industry and investment before the Sixteenth Party Conference

We have seen how, after the Fifteenth Congress, two lines on industrialization were in conflict.[139] One line continued to defend the orientation of the Congress, declaring that, while industry was the "driving force" of the economy, agriculture was its "basis," and upholding the need for *allocating investments in such a way as to enable every branch of the economy to develop at a rate that would enable it to meet the needs of the other branches and those of the consumers* (hence the idea of an "optimum" development). The other line asserted that what was required was "maximum" development of industry, with priority given to investment in heavy industry. We have seen that this second line, to which Stalin adhered more and more closely, until he became its defender, tended to win the battle—implicitly, at least, since, until the spring of 1929, no formal resolution decided clearly between these two orientations.

The increased influence of the advocates of "maximum" industrial growth was reflected in the gradual raising of the targets of industrial production and investment proposed by the various organs which participated in the framing of the plans. Thus, in December 1927 Gosplan forecast that, during the First Five-Year Plan (which was then intended to end in 1931–1932), production by large-scale industry would be multiplied by 1.77 (according to the "minimum" version of the plan) or by 2.03 (according to the so-called optimum version).[140] In August 1928 the VSNKh proposed a draft which forecast that at the end of the five-year period (now ending in 1932–1933), production by large-scale industry would be 2.27 times as great. In December 1928 the so-called optimum variant prepared by Gosplan and the VSNKh forecast a coefficient of 2.68. In April 1929 the "optimum" variant adopted by the Sixteenth Conference forecast a coefficient of 2.79. *Thus, between December 1927 and April 1929, the "forecast coefficient of five-year growth" in large-scale industry increased by 37 or 60 percent, depending on the variant.*[141]

Parallel with this increase, the amount forecast for gross investment in plant rose from 16 milliard roubles (March 1927) to 64.6 milliard (April 1929).[142] Thus, within two years, the forecast for investment had increased fourfold. More than 40 percent of this investment was earmarked for industry, and, within that total, heavy industry's share rose from 69.4 percent to 78 percent.[143]

This "growth" in the targets for investment and industrial production was all the more significant because it did not result from a more rigorous analysis of the Soviet economy's potentialities and the prospects opened up by the changing of property relations and production relations. Examination of the successive drafts of the Five-Year Plan shows that the "growth" in the industrial targets reflected, fundamentally, a change in the political line—that is, increased influence by the advocates of rapid industrialization. To convince oneself of this it is enough to look at the resolution on the Five-Year Plan adopted by the Sixteenth Conference and by the Congress of Soviets, together with the decisions and forecasts relating to the industrial targets.

(2) The decisions of the Sixteenth Party Conference and of the Congress of Soviets

The resolution on the Five-Year Plan adopted by the Sixteenth Conference was ratified in May 1929 by the Congresses of Soviets of the RSFSR and the Ukraine and by the Fifth All-Union Congress of Soviets.[144] This resolution adopted the so-called optimum variant of the draft prepared by Gosplan. It declared (thereby rejecting the conclusions of the Fifteenth Party Congress) that the plan must ensure "maximum development of production of means of production as the basis for the industrialization of the country."[145] *The principle according to which agriculture was the basis of the economy was thus no longer stated.*

In the resolution adopted by the Sixteenth Conference, realization of the forecasts for increases in industry and investment presupposed that agricultural production would increase to more than 50 percent over the prewar figure.[146] Yet agricultural production had not increased since 1926, and was even tending to decline, as a result of the application of the "emergency measures." Nothing, therefore, justified such optimism (which facts were, moreover, to refute absolutely) where the progress of agricultural production was concerned. The forecasts for agriculture were also unrealistic in assuming that, throughout the five-year period, there would be only *good* harvests.[147]

By adopting the hypothesis of maximum and uninterrupted growth, the resolution on the Five-Year Plan took no account of a number of points made by Lenin regarding the need, if one was to draw up an economic plan properly, to follow the method of *guiding links,* so as to proceed from the determining of one task to another. Lenin also spoke of the need to define the minimum (not "optimum") conditions that would have to be fulfilled if the various tasks were to be accomplished, and to prepare several variants to be applied in the light of the conditions that actually prevailed—which meant not persisting in the attempt to fulfill certain tasks if the conditions for their fulfillment failed to materialize. Lenin also stressed that, in the actual situation of Soviet Russia, the point of departure, or base factor, for the compiling of the plan must be the actual availability of foodstuffs, which, in practice, meant grain. None of these points made by Lenin was taken into account in 1928–1929, either in the drawing up of the optimum version or in connection with what happened later on, when harvests turned out to be much poorer than had been forecast in the Plan.[148]

The resolution on the Five-Year Plan also forecast that the productivity of labor in industry would increase by 150 percent. This forecast was actually nothing but a *wish.* It was based on no objective facts, and contradicted the actual evolution of productivity—and it was not realized. However, on the basis of these "forecasts" regarding agriculture and the productivity of labor, the Plan provided for real wages to rise by 71 percent, while costs of production would fall by 35 percent in industry and 50 percent in building.[149] These forecasts of reductions in costs were based on the hypothesis (which nothing justified, and which was not fulfilled) of a very great improvement in the use made of raw materials and power.

There were many reasons why forecasts were adopted which were so unrealistic[150] and which were known to be such by a large number of Party members and cadres, though they dared not say this publicly. Among these reasons were the development of *unemployment* during the preceding years, and the *steadily growing difficulties in the sphere of food supplies,* which impelled the Party to seek a way of *escaping from a situation which had become dangerous for the Soviet power.* The worsening of relations with the peasantry as a result of the application of the emergency measures meant that, for many Party members and cadres, this way out of the crisis had to take the form of industrialization at the fastest possible rate, while they looked upon as "defeatists" those (very few) who took upon themselves the risk involved in pointing out what was unrealistic and contradictory in a number of the forecasts. The worsening of the worker-peasant alliance which began early in 1928 thus played a considerable role in the rallying of support for the forecasts of the Five-Year Plan as it was then laid down. This support reflected the illusion that a technological and economic solution could be found for the political problem presented by the deterioration of the alliance. It gave expression to a "technicist-economist" component in the Bolshevik ideological formation (something to which I shall return)—a component which acquired special importance under the impact of a series of factors: the enthusiasm for industrialization with which a section of the working class, especially the youth, was fired; pressure by the heads of the big enterprises and industrial trusts; the influence of a nationalism which was flattered by the idea of "catching up with and surpassing" the industrialized countries within a short period; and so on.

A set of objective and subjective conditions thus favored the elaboration and acceptance of an industrial plan which was extremely ambitious,[151] to the extent that it contained not only unrealistic forecasts but also many internal contradictions.

Even a moderately close study of the forecasts of the Five-Year Plan, and of the way the economy actually functioned, reveals, indeed, that in a certain number of sectors the material resources needed for reaching the set of targets laid down were not available, and would not become available within the five-year period. Thus, in 1928–1929, the quantity of iron and steel products needed for satisfying the needs arising from the Plan's targets was 30 percent larger than the production actually available, which meant that 30 percent of the demand engendered by the Plan could not be met. A similar "deficit," on the order of 25 percent, was observed where nonferrous metals were concerned, and the same was true in relation to many other products.[152]

The incompatibilities between the various targets of the Plan, and the unrealism of some of its forecasts, were not unknown to the economists and technicians who prepared it. However, in the atmosphere of "ruthless struggle" against the Right which reigned at the beginning of 1929, most of them preferred to keep quiet, or to voice their doubts only cryptically, for such warnings might easily be described as expressions of "defeatism" and signs of one's adherence to the "Right tendency."

Strumilin, though himself an advocate of ambitious targets, noted that most of the specialists working on the Plan were no longer prepared to point out its weaknesses, or the adjustments that needed to be made in it. He wrote on this subject: "Unfortunately, it would not be reasonable to put to the test the civil courage of these specialists, who are already saying, in the corridors, that they prefer to stand for higher tempos rather than sit [i.e., in prison] for lower ones."[153]

It was not only fear of repressive measures that led such men to keep their mouths shut about the unrealistic character of certain aspects of the Plan (which called in question the "realism" of the Plan as a whole), but also the ideological and political atmosphere which developed during 1928, in connection with the rupture, already far advanced, of the worker-peasant alliance. Even those Party leaders who favored rapid industrialization, but who were aware of the unrealism of certain forecasts, ceased to voice their doubts in public.

A letter sent by Kuibyshev to his wife at the end of 1928 (and not published until nearly forty years later) testifies to the situation in which some leaders were placed, even though they were far from being suspected of "Rightism": "Here is what worried me yesterday and today: I am unable to tie up the balance, and as I cannot go for contracting the capital outlays—contracting the tempo—there will be no other way but to take upon myself an almost unmanageable task in the realm of lowering costs."[154]

In this situation, the plan was drawn up without even any definition of the concrete conditions that would have to be combined if the forecast increases in production and productivity were to be realized. Essentially, the plan counted on the effects to be brought about by technological changes which had not yet been studied, and on the introduction of "up-to-date techniques" which were to be imported, without allowing for the time needed for these techniques to be mastered on the scale of society as a whole.

It must be noted that the plan, which was conceived as a plan for building socialism, *offered no prospect of change in the social organization of labor and production.* The relations which had become consolidated in the state sector during the NEP period seemed untouchable. Nowhere was there any question of realizing the prospect outlined by Marx, who wrote that *socialism would change labor relations* and bring about "a new organisation of production, or rather the delivery (setting free) of the social forms of production in present organised labour (engendered by present industry) of the trammels of slavery, of their present class character. . . ."[155]

In the absence of development of new forms of the organization of labor, an increase so rapid as was forecast for the productivity of labor in industry was expected to result mainly from the exercise of increased authority over the workers by the managers of enterprises. The resolution on the Five-Year Plan gave precise attention to this point. It called for "determined struggle against unjustified absenteeism and slackness in production" and for strengthening labor discipline.[156]

(3) Labor discipline, material incentives, and the role of the trade unions

At the beginning of 1929, a broad campaign was launched for the strengthening of discipline. On January 17 a CC resolution drew a harsh picture of the situation in the Donbas mines, denouncing "a decline in labor-discipline among the miners and the technical personnel responsible for supervising the lower echelons." It also denounced "inadequate improvement in the productivity of labour."[157] On February 21 the CC called for stricter labor discipline.[158] On March 6 the Sovnarkom adopted a decree imposing severer punishments for absenteeism and unpunctuality. The managers of enterprises were called upon to enforce the strictest penalties, and the labor exchanges to give priority to workers who had not been dismissed for indiscipline. [159] In the same month, the head of the department of "labour economy" in the VSNKh, I. Kraval, complained of the inadequacy of penalties for offences against discipline, and the indulgence shown in such cases by the arbitration commissions, the inspectorate of labor and the courts.[160] Thus at the very moment when the First Five-Year Plan was relying on labor discipline to bring about a rapid increase in productivity, the existing conditions failed to justify this expectation. The Party therefore increasingly called upon the trade unions to help in strengthening discipline. After adopting the resolution on the Five-Year Plan, the Sixteenth Conference addressed an "appeal to all the workers and working peasants of the Soviet Union,"[161] which stressed the gigantic scale of the tasks that had to be accomplished in order to ensure a rapid development of industry. This document emphasized the role that should be played by emulation in the phase that was opening, and the "indissoluble link which binds together *emulation* and the Five-Year Plan." It called for the adoption by the trade unions and by the economic organs of "a system of incentives for those who engage in emulation."[162]

We have seen [163] that a large number of trade-union leaders, including Tomsky, resisted, to some extent, directives which, in their eyes (with the knowledge they possessed of the workers' day-to-day problems) implied the exercise of too strong a pressure upon the workers. They considered that, carried beyond a certain point, this pressure might produce negative effects. Hence their reservations regarding the scale of the tasks projected in the domain of productivity of labor and reducing production costs.

Already in December 1928, at the Eighth Congress of the trade unions, open clashes took place between Tomsky and those who supported his views, on the one hand, and, on the other, the advocates of a "maximum" tempo of industrialization.

Pravda of December 12 uttered a warning to trade unions which gave insufficient attention "to the new tasks of the reconstruction period." At the Congress itself, Kezelev, one of the leaders of the metalworkers' unions, denounced this charge as "a calumny against the trade-union movement," including in his rebuttal also some articles of the same sort which had appeared in *Komsomolskaya Pravda*. In these articles he saw "an attitude of disdain" toward the interests of the working masses and a revival of "Trotskyism" (alluding to the controversy of 1920–1921 about the "statisation" of the trade unions).[164] He declared that taking the road of industrialization required that "increased attention be given to the everyday personal interests and needs of the worker masses."[165]

A large proportion of the trade-union cadres who supported this view were relieved of their posts by a decision of the Party. In 1929–1930, in Moscow, Leningrad, the Ukraine, and the Ural region, between 78 and 86 percent of the members of factory trade-union committees were replaced.[166] These very high percentages show that the overhauling of the factory committees was due to disagreement on the part of the majority of the trade-union officials with demands which they considered could only produce a loss of confidence in the trade unions among the working class.

After this overhaul, the trade-union apparatus was better equipped to act so as to bring about an increase in the productivity of labor, particularly by helping to revise wages and work norms.

A situation thus developed which was marked by a hardening of labor discipline and by the introduction of output norms imposed from above—a situation unfavorable to an increase in initiative on the part of the masses and to their participation in the fight against "bureaucracy" for which the Sixteenth Conference had appealed.

(e) Agrarian policy

While the Sixteenth Conference inaugurated a new political line in the industrial sphere, it reaffirmed existing principles, those of the NEP, so far as relations with the peasantry were concerned.

True, the resolution on agriculture[167] dwelt upon the development of collective and state farms, but it stated that this must be brought about very gradually, in view of the amount of ideological and political work that the Party would first have to undertake in the rural areas. The middle peasant thus continued to be presented as "the central figure"[168] in agriculture, and was due to remain so for a long time yet. Here are some indications of how cautiously the problem of collectivization was still dealt with at that time.

(1) The Sixteenth Conference and the problems of agriculture

According to one of the resolutions adopted by the Sixteenth Conference, the maximum possible development of the "socialised sector" (state and collective farms) would enable the sown areas of this sector to be increased to 26 million hectares in 1933, or 17.5 percent of the entire area to be sown in that year. It was forecast that in 1933 this sector would provide 15.5 percent of the gross production of grain, and 43 percent of the marketed production, or over 8.4 million metric tons.[169]

Individual farming was thus still to play the predominant role in agriculture, providing nearly 90 percent of total gross production.[170]

Furthermore, the resolution on agriculture said that "in the next few years the principal increase in agricultural production will come from the individual farms of the poor and middle peasants," for "small farming is still far from having exhausted its potentialities, and will not exhaust them so soon. . ."[171]

The complete transformation of the agrarian structures was thus situated in a perspective of at least a decade, and kept within the framework of the NEP.[172]

The resolution on agriculture adopted by the Sixteenth Conference dwelt at length on "the systematic aid that the Soviet power must render to the poor and middle peasants in order to increase the productivity of their labour."[173] Consequently, the state farms and the machine-and-tractor stations were being called upon to *help individual peasants*. The contract system (*kontraktatsiya*) was also regarded as a means for increasing the productivity of the farms of the poor and middle peasants, while constituting a form of linkage between agriculture and industry—which was to give priority to supplying means of production to peasants who had entered into contracts for delivery of their produce.[174]

Thus, the Sixteenth Conference stressed, above all, consolidation of the worker-peasant alliance, within the setting of the NEP, this consolidation implying massive aid to individual farms by supplying them with means of production: this was one of the "new forms of the bond." It was to be combined with an increase in direct aid to the peasants by workers going into the countryside to help with the work in the fields, and to develop ideological and political activity there so as to contribute to the struggle of the poor and middle peasants against the kulaks.[175]

The political line drawn by the Sixteenth Conference was meant to be, for several years, appropriate to the requirements for strengthening Soviet power in the rural areas. It was therefore a "cautious" line, which should avoid improvisations and precipitancy.

(2) The reasons for the "caution" shown in the agrarian policy decided on by the Sixteenth Conference

The "cautious" character of the agrarian policy decided on by the Sixteenth Conference makes a striking contrast with its ambitious industrial policy. This "caution" reflected the Party's knowledge of the very great weakness of its rural organizations and its inadequate implantation among the peasantry. It also took account of the weakness of the village soviets, whose authority, still almost entirely formal in 1929, would have to be strengthened if it was desired that the Soviet power should exercise real influence on rural life and stimulate a broad movement for collectivization.[176]

V. The contradiction between industrial and agricultural policy, and the "great change"

The caution which characterized the agrarian policy resolved upon by the Sixteenth Conference soon came into contradiction with the industrial policy it had adopted. Carrying out the latter required that the countryside supply the towns and industry, and also the export trade, with quantities of agricultural produce very much larger than the peasants were prepared to hand over under the conditions of what remained of the NEP. The industrial policy decided on at the beginning of 1929 actually entailed fresh violations of the principles of the NEP, for the increasing resources absorbed by industrialization reduced further and further the possibility of supplying the villages with manufactured goods. Consequently, at a time when the procurement organs were striving to get more produce out of the rural areas, the towns were becoming less and less capable of supplying these areas with products of industry.

In 1929 the peasants found that the system of emergency measures was growing more burdensome, and that it now functioned continuously. The discontent resulting from this led to reductions in the sown area, increased difficulty in getting supplies for the towns, and cuts in food rations. There were even disturbances in some regions.[177]

Thus, the contradiction between the Party's industrial and agricultural policies soon made itself felt. This meant that either one policy or the other, or both together, would have to be revised, so that they could be coordinated.

The predominance of the will to industrialize (which was connected with the worsening of the internal contradictions of the urban sector) and the conviction that any "retreat" in face of peasant discontent would jeopardize industrialization, as that process was conceived, led to the industrial policy being maintained, and measures adopted which were more and more overtly in breach of the NEP, even if the latter was not yet "officially" abandoned.

(a) The attempt to speed up industrialization and the turn toward rapid collectivization

The growing deterioration of the worker-peasant alliance gave, paradoxically, an incentive to accelerating industrialization still further. The Party leadership thought that in this way they could reduce the time during which the shortage of industrial products would be felt. In the immediate period, however, this shortage was aggravated still further.

Similarly, the deterioration of the alliance impelled the Party leadership to turn toward rapid collectivization of farming[178] (the ideological and political conditions for which were still not present), because state and collective farms increasingly appeared to offer the only solution to the difficulties in agriculture and the problems of feeding the towns. Since collectivization and mechanization were seen as being linked, accelerated collectivization led to raising the targets for production of tractors and agricultural machinery, which meant that more steel was needed, and caused the tempos laid down for increases in industrial production to be speeded up still further, becoming ever more unrealistic.

Thus, the plan approved by the Sixteenth Conference forecast an increase of 22 percent in industrial production in one year. A few months later, without anything having happened to justify such a revision, the annual plan for 1929–1930 raised this forecast to the fantastic height of 32 percent. Eventually, the official statistics recorded an actual increase of 20 percent—and that was an optimistic estimate, since it did not fully reckon with the effects of increased prices on the "value" of industrial production.[179]

The replacement of the targets agreed to at the Sixteenth Conference by others which were more and more "radical" meant a new break with the still apparently "NEP" line adopted by that conference.

(b) The break with the line of the Sixteenth Conference and its effects on political relations within the Bolshevik Party

In the history of the Bolshevik Party, the break with the line of the Sixteenth Conference hastened the development of a new style of leadership, a new type of relations between the Secretariat and the Party's highest bodies—the PB, the CC, the conferences and the congresses of the Party. Thus, between April and December 1929, numerous decisions of historic significance—since they led to the complete abandonment of the NEP—were taken without the highest Party bodies being consulted. When these bodies met, all they could do was to ratify decisions which were already being carried out and which had been announced publicly: to question them would have meant opening a crisis of leadership that would be highly dangerous in the situation that the country was in. Consequently, during those months of 1929, the CC did no more than seek (ineffectually) to restrict somewhat the degree of the "turn" away from the decisions of the Sixteenth Conference.

The "Right opposition" suffered its final defeat in this period. In May and June 1929 Bukharin published the last article in which he tried, cautiously, to show disagreement with certain aspects of the economic line which was becoming dominant.[180] Thereafter he was to be deprived of the opportunity to give the slightest public expression to his doubts. On August 21 and 24 *Pravda* launched an open attack on Bukharin. It was the start of a "general offensive" conducted by the entire press and directed against all who were associated in any way, real or supposed, with the positions of the "Right." Nearly all such persons were dismissed from their posts. These measures even affected Lenin's widow and his sister, N. Krupskaya and Maria Ulyanova.[181] In contrast to what had happened in the case of previous oppositions, no chance to reply was allowed to the Right opposition, even for the pur-

pose of refuting baseless charges. Still less was there any
question of letting them express their disagreement with decisions taken which ran counter to the resolutions of the Sixteenth Conference.[182] Under these conditions, the Party
cadres' opportunities for studying the situation as a whole
became extremely restricted.

Worse still, fear of being penalized for "Right deviation"
caused most of the cadres to present a falsely optimistic picture of the situation. In this way, under the impact of the
contradictions between the industrial and agricultural lines,
and of a set of illusions regarding the real situation, the policy
of the "great change" began—the starting point of a process of
collectivization carried out under conditions such that its consequences for the worker-peasant alliance and for agricultural
production were profoundly different from what the Party
leadership expected.

VI. The "great change" at the end of 1929

The principal aspect of the "great change" was the abandonment of the line of the Sixteenth Conference which had
advised a step-by-step approach to collectivization, so that this
might be based on firm foundations, in particular by making
the transition to collective forms of production depend on the
willingness of the peasant masses. It was concern for this that
had guided the fixing of the targets to be reached in the
agrarian sphere by the end of the First Five-Year Plan. A few
points will serve to illustrate the speed and sweep with which
the line of the Sixteenth Conference on agriculture was abandoned.

(a) Accelerated collectivization and
abandonment of the Sixteenth
Conference line

As regards the speeding-up of collectivization, two periods
need to be distinguished clearly: one covering the months

June to October 1929, the other beginning in November 1929 and ending in early March 1930.

The first of these periods was one which saw the development of a collectivisation that was basically voluntary and in accordance with the aspirations of the poor and middle peasants who were then taking the road of collective farming. During this first period, 900,000 peasant households joined the collective farms, which meant an increase in the percentage of collectivized households from 3.9 to 7.6,[183] a considerable leap forward. However, there were some circumstances which limited the implications and significance of what happened at that time.

(1) During this period it was poor peasants who made up the main body of recruits to the collectivized households: they accounted for 78 percent of the members of the "communes," 67 percent of the members of the "artels," and 60 percent of the members of the "tozes,"[184] whereas they made up only 35 percent of the rural population (according to the same statistical sources).[185] It could not be said, therefore, that the *middle* peasant had taken the road to the collective farm, even though, toward October, the proportion of middle peasants did increase a little.[186]

(2) The development of the movement was extremely uneven, and this was still the case at the end of 1929.[187]

(3) Collectivization was only voluntary *on the whole*. Already in September 1929 the collective-farm leadership issued directives regarding the formation of collective farms in which they said that what must be aimed at was the collectivizing of "entire localities" (this was what was called "complete," *sploshnaya,* collectivization), the collectivizing of practically all the means of production, and the forming of *large-scale kolkhozes.*[188] But the collectivizing of an "entire locality" rarely corresponded to the will of the peasants concerned: it was exceptional at that period for *all* the peasants of a locality to be ready at the same time to join the *kolkhoz.* Likewise, it was rare for them to be ready to renounce individual ownership of almost all their means of production and to form large-scale *kolkhozes.*

Already in the summer of 1929 administrative pressure was

being brought to bear on the peasants to get them to enter the *kolkhozes*. This pressure took, first of all, the form of "economic threats." The local authorities said to the peasants, including the poor peasants: "If you don't join the kolkhoz you will be given neither seed nor machinery."[189] In some regions, however, the pressures soon became more direct. Those who declined to join the *kolkhoz* were subjected to fines, given a spell in prison, and threatened with deportation to another part of the country.[190]

The period that began in November 1929 was marked by a considerable increase in the pressure exerted on the peasants, so that the nature of the collectivization movement changed. The article by Stalin entitled "A Year of Great Change"[191] opened this period. In it he announced for the coming year (1930) targets that were a great deal more ambitious than those which had been laid down for 1932–1933. He said that in 1930 the state and collective farms would provide over 50 percent of the marketed production of grain—1.8 and 4.9 million metric tons respectively.[192] The sown areas of these farms taken as a whole were to cover 18.3 million hectares, as against 6 million in 1929. Thus, the tempos which had been forecast only a few months earlier were now to be exceeded, and the line of the Sixteenth Conference abandoned.

But the revision of tempos did not stop there. Less than a month after Stalin's article appeared, the Sovnarkom decided that 30 million hectares must be collectivized in 1930, and that the *sovkhozes* must cover an area of 3.7 million hectares[193]: about a quarter of all peasant households were to be collectivized during 1930.

The close link between the forecasts for collectivization and the targets for procurement shows that the deciding factor in fixing the pace of collectivization was not the transforming in depth of the situation of the peasant masses, but the will to establish as quickly as possible structures that would facilitate securing from the countryside the quantities of grain needed for the *realization of the industrial targets*.

This speeding-up of collectivization was based upon an exaggeratedly optimistic view of the situation in the rural areas—a view that underlay a series of mistakes which were to have the gravest consequences for the subsequent functioning of the *kolkhozes* and for the worker-peasant alliance.

(b) The optimistic view of the situation at the end of 1929

Already in his article of November 1929 Stalin felt able to say that *"the middle peasant is joining the collective farm,"* adding that this was "the basis of that radical change in the development of agriculture that constitutes the most important achievement of the Soviet government during the last year."[194] He went on to say that "the new and decisive feature of the present collective-farm movement is that the peasants are joining the collective farms not in separate groups, as was formerly the case, but by whole villages, *volosts*, districts and even *okrugs*."[195]

These formulations considerably overestimated the progress achieved by the collectivization movement. Actually, at the time when Stalin's article appeared, collectivization embraced only a minority of peasant households, mainly those of poor peasants, and "complete" collectivization was exceptional.[196]

The weeks that followed showed (as we shall see shortly) that accelerated collectivization, in the forms which it assumed, came up against strong resistance from the peasant masses. This was to be admitted in March 1930.

However, in the speech he gave on December 27, 1929, to a conference of Marxists specializing in agrarian problems, Stalin emphasized once more the "ease" with which, according to him, the collective farm movement was developing. One of the reasons he mentioned as explaining this feature of the movement was the fact that "in our country the land is nationalised, and this facilitates the transition of the individual peasant to collectivist lines."[197] Stalin reaffirmed that the conditions existed for "complete" collectivization to be carried out successfully in many regions, adding that this was why it was possible to go over "from the policy of restricting the exploiting tendencies of the kulak to the policy of eliminating the kulaks as a class."[198]

A study of what actually happened in the rural areas during the winter of 1929–1930 shows that the entry of the peasants into the collective farms took place under conditions that were far from being as favorable as might be supposed from the statements just quoted.

(c) The concrete conditions of the "turn" toward collectivization in the autumn of 1929

The "turn" toward collectivization in the autumn of 1929 took place under very contradictory conditions. On the one hand, there was the continuing and broadening movement of many poor peasants, and of a certain proportion of the middle peasants (especially those who had only recently emerged from poverty), into collective farming: this movement was facilitated by the help which, since the Sixteenth Conference, the Party and the state apparatus gave to newly formed *kolkhozes*. On the other hand, though, this turn was due (and to an increasing extent) to the intensification of administrative pressure exerted upon the peasants.

The fixing of "collectivisation targets" which were continually being raised, and which were determined without any preliminary investigation, contributed to the multiplication of these administrative pressures. The local authorities engaged in a kind of "emulation" in scoring high percentages of collectivization. They were moved to act in this way by fear of the penalties that could rain down upon the cadres in places which "lagged behind,"[199] and by the false notion they had that a "general advance" of the movement[200] was in fact going on, so that they were apprehensive of being left behind. Furthermore, increasing intervention by elements from outside the villages, usually very enthusiastic but also very ignorant of the local situation, contributed to the employment of measures which had nothing in common with an effort to *persuade* the peasants—something that would have required more time than was available to the delegates or teams sent from the towns to speed up collectivization. The "delegates for collectivisation" were often assigned tasks to be fulfilled within a very short period, with penalties for nonfulfillment, and this prevented them from engaging in time-consuming mass work.[201]

The forms of pressure brought to bear on the peasants (in order to "encourage" entry into the *kolkhoz* by those who were not ready to join it voluntarily) were very diverse. They could be measures of an administrative, economic, or penal character—the last being usually connected with the operations of "dekulakization" to be described later.

The two "non-penal sanctions" most commonly used against peasants who were unwilling to join the *kolkhoz* were: a ban on the trading organs selling them any goods whatsoever, and depriving them of their land (which was taken by the *kolkhoz*). In other cases, peasants who failed to join the *kolkhoz* found themselves compelled to exchange the land they cultivated for other land, of poor quality, situated far from the village. Sometimes their seed corn, their cattle, and all or some of their instruments of labor were confiscated. They were allowed a few days in which to make up their minds.[202]

To these sanctions others could be added, such as fixing a high level of taxation on an individual peasant, forbidding the children of peasants who were not collective farmers to attend school,[203] and so on. Such measures were "illegal" and were subsequently condemned by the Party leadership. However, between November 1929 and March 1930 they were widely employed by the local authorities.

At the same time, the policy of "dekulakization" was used to get as many peasants as possible into the *kolkhozes*. In principle, this policy should have meant taking severe measures only against a minority of kulaks. Thus, shortly before the end of 1929, a subcommission of the CC proposed that the kulaks be divided into three categories. The first was to consist of the active opponents of Soviet power, guilty of hostile acts. Those belonging to this category were to be sentenced to prison or exile. At the time, the number of heads of families belonging to this category was estimated at about 52,000. The second category of kulaks would consist of nonactive opponents of Soviet power. The village assemblies were to decide their fate. In principle, the subcommission considered that these kulaks should be banished from the village, but not sent to Siberia: their number was estimated at 112,000. Finally, the third category was to be made up of those thought to be "capable of re-education": its members could be allowed to join the *kolkhoz*, but without the right to vote for five years, after which they would become full-fledged members. In the RSFSR alone this category was estimated to include about 650,000 households. The subcommission considered that it was important to make use of the labor power of the kulaks' families, numbering in all some five million persons (this being presumably the figure for the USSR as a whole).[204]

However, the PB rejected this proposal. In their view, it did not answer to the requirements of the policy of "eliminating the kulaks as a class." At the November plenum Molotov had said that it was necessary to "adopt towards the kulak the attitude that has to be adopted towards our worst enemy not yet liquidated."[205]

At the end of 1929 and the beginning of 1930 dekulakization was carried out without any precise political orientation. In principle, it was supposed to be a task for the poor peasants, but, in practice, this group was not organized, and so dekulakization was carried out in most cases by elements from outside the village—workers' "brigades," or the GPU—who, with (or sometimes without) the help of some poor peasants (real or alleged), themselves drew up the list of "kulaks" and divided them into three categories. Those who fell into the first category were arrested by the GPU. Those in the second category were exiled. Those in the third category were allowed to remain where they were, with a minimum of possessions, and were assigned poor-quality land outside the village: if they failed to supply the procurement quota fixed for them, their possessions could be confiscated and themselves exiled. The information available indicated that only a minority were assigned to the third category.[206]

In relation to collectivization as it was carried out at the end of 1929 and the beginning of 1930, dekulakization became a means of forcing the poor and middle peasants to join the *kolkhozes*, since, if they failed to do so, they could easily be labeled "kulaks." Under these conditions, many peasants joined the *kolkhoz* not from conviction but from fear of being "dekulakized" by the local authorities. The numbers sent into exile in 1930 were considerable. Entire trains, called by the peasants "death-trains," carried the exiles off toward the north, the steppes, and the forests. Many of them died on the way, from cold, hunger, or disease. Anna Louise Strong wrote: "Several times during the spring and summer I saw these echelons moving along the railroad: a doleful sight, men, women and children uprooted."[207]

Sometimes only the women and children were exiled, since the head of the family had been arrested; at other times, entire families were exiled; and at yet other times, the children were left behind, to become beggars and tramps (*besprizornyie*).[208]

Such activities (which were denounced in March 1930) played a considerable role in the collectivization campaign of the winter of 1929–1930, and seriously affected the quality of the *kolkhozes* formed under such coercion. Thus, writing of collectivization in the Ural region, the agrarian journal *Na Agrarnom Fronte* said: "The local organisations in the rural areas found in dekulakisation a powerful means for drawing peasants into the kolkhozes and for changing some kolkhozes into communes. The recourse to intimidation, associated with other procedures, was often accompanied by threats of dekulakisation against those who did not let themselves be 'drawn in.' "[209]

In these circumstances, the expression "kulak" no longer meant merely a rich peasant: it now meant any peasant who did not want to join the *kolkhoz*.

Generally speaking, it referred to a certain attitude to collectivization. In 1930 a publication of the Communist Academy wrote: "By 'kulak' we mean the carrier of certain political tendencies which are most frequently discernible in the *podkulachnik*, male or female."[210]

The documents and publications of the time show that there were many cases in which poor or middle peasants were dekulakized in this way. Dekulakization might also result in the possessions of those dekulakized being appropriated, or bought at absurdly low prices, by the persons who carried out the operation: a house was bought for a rouble, a cow for 15 kopecks.[211] The absence of previous implantation of the Party in the countryside, and the intervention of "dekulakization agents" coming from outside and acting in haste, thus resulted in the expropriation, arrest, or exiling even of agricultural laborers and of persons known to be poor peasants.[212]

As the journal *Na Agrarnom Fronte* put it: "The peasant is beginning to associate with this idea [the idea of mass collectivization] the possibility that he too may find himself one day among the dekulakised, falling thus into the camp of the enemies of Soviet power."[213]

(d) Accelerated collectivization halted in March 1930

A situation of insecurity and tension thus developed in the rural areas which was most detrimental to the worker-peasant alliance. In March 1930 an article by Stalin called a halt to the methods which had characterized the "great change" and speeded up the tempo of collectivization. The article appeared in *Pravda* on March 2, 1930, under the title: "Dizzy with Success."[214] A few days later (March 15th) came a decision by the CC entitled: "On the Fight Against Distortions of the Party Line in the Collective-Farm Movement."[215]

An essential feature of Stalin's article "Dizzy with Success" was the warnings which it contained, directed against certain "dangerous and harmful sentiments," of which, however "it cannot be said that [they] are at all widespread in the ranks of our Party."[216]

One of the tendencies which Stalin denounced in this way was that which violated the principle that peasants should join the *kolkhoz* without coercion. Another was shown in allowing insufficiently for the diversity of conditions in the different regions of the USSR.

Stalin deplored the fact that, instead of the preparatory work needed to get the peasants to join the *kolkhozes* of their own free will, there had been "bureaucratic decreeing of the collective-farm movement." He mentioned that in certain regions, and specifically in Turkestan, the local authorities had coerced the peasants who did not want to join the *kolkhoz* "by threatening to use armed force, by threatening that peasants who are not yet ready to join the collective farms will be deprived of irrigation-water and manufactured goods."[217] Stalin said of these methods that they were worthy of Sergeant Prishibeyev. He emphasized that such practices were a violation of the Party line and could only have the effect of "discrediting the idea of the collective-farm movement."[218]

Another tendency denounced in Stalin's article of March 2 was that which failed to respect the *artel* form as the predominant form of collective farm. He mentions attempts to "leap straight away into the agricultural commune," which, he says, can only result in "irritating the collective-farm peasant" and making it harder to deal with "the grain problem," which "is still *unsolved*."[219]

The article then tries to analyze the reasons why these tendencies have appeared. The explanation offered is that the "easiness" of the successes achieved had "gone to the heads" of a certain number of Party members and cadres: they had "become dizzy with success," so that they thought that complete collectivization could be achieved very quickly, even by being forced upon reluctant peasants.

The article included an appeal: *"We must put an end to these sentiments. That is now one of the immediate tasks of the Party."*[220]

The appearance of this article caused much disarray among the local Party cadres, who were wholly committed to the fight for collectivization and had not previously received any serious warnings against the methods to which they were having recourse. At first, some cadres thought that the article must be a forgery, and attempts were made, at the level of the Party's basic units, to prevent its republication in the regional press and stop its diffusion among the masses: some newspapers containing the article were even confiscated from peasants.[221]

The CC's decision published on March 15, 1930, reaffirmed that the practices denounced by Stalin were indeed to be regarded as "deviations from the Party line," and detrimental to the future development of the collective-farm movement.

One month after his article "Dizzy with Success," Stalin returned to the subject of the conditions under which collectivization had proceeded in the winter of 1929–1930. He did this in the form of a "reply" to the numerous letters provoked by his earlier article.[222]

In this "reply" Stalin said that the *root* of the mistakes made lay in "a wrong approach to the middle peasant. Resort to coercion in economic relations with the middle peasant. Forgetfulness of the fact that the economic bond with the masses of the middle peasants must be built not on the basis of coercive measures, but on the basis of agreement with the middle peasant, of alliance with him."[223] He mentioned three "chief errors," namely: violation of the principle that peasants' entry into the collective farms should be voluntary; forgetting the fact that the rate of progress of collectivization could not be the same in every region; and violation of the Leninist principle of "not running ahead of the development of the masses, of not decreeing the movement of the masses, of not becoming divorced from the masses."[224]

The explanation given remained the same as that presented a month previously. It was only a matter of "some of our comrades, intoxicated by the first successes of the collective-farm movement," who "forgot" the instructions of Lenin and of the CC and fell victim to the "dizziness" of "vanity and conceit."[225]

And so, a serious violation of the Party line, affecting the entire country, was "explained" by referring to a mere psychological metaphor—"dizziness from success" which had proved too much for "some of our comrades." Given the scale of what had happened, and the gravity of its consequences, such an "explanation" is obviously inadequate. Mistakes made on such a scale and persisted in for several months could only result from a political line and a style of leadership that engendered certain practices.

This political line was the one based on the proclaimed existence of a "great change" which, in reality, had not occurred. Because of this false estimate of the situation, the local cadres of the Party were given collectivization targets which did not correspond to the state of mind of the peasant masses. The pressure brought to bear on the cadres had caused the local authorities to develop practices which had nothing to do with any "dizziness from success" but were *bourgeois practices*—meaning recourse to threats and coercion against the masses, which was the method used very widely to drive the peasants into the collective farms against their will.

Moreover, it must not be lost sight of that the Party leadership allowed matters to go on like this *for several months*. This means, since the leadership cannot have been wholly out of touch with reality, that it let *these practices continue*, because, from its point of view, attainment of the "targets" of collectivization seemed at that time more important than respect for the will of the peasant masses. The CC called a halt[226] at a moment when these "targets" had been attained and even exceeded, and when continuing to apply such crude coercion risked bringing about extremely dangerous consequences both politically and economically (in particular, compromising the prospects for the spring sowing).

In any case, the stop put to certain methods of dekulakization and collectivization did not prevent some of those who had been labeled "kulaks" from continuing to be sent into exile (for months on end whole trains were devoted to this task, even hindering the transport of goods[227]), nor did it prevent similar methods from reappearing after a few weeks had passed.

(e) The immediate effects of the "great change" and of the halt called in March–April 1930

The magnitude of the operation carried out during the winter of 1929–1930 dealt a decisive blow to the kulaks. They practically ceased to exist as a class. In a few months, the main base of private capitalism in the Soviet Union was smashed, and this meant the beginning of a radical change in the social relations which had prevailed until then in the Soviet countryside.

Nevertheless, the blow struck at the kulaks had been struck, in the main, by forces from outside the village, and using practices which hit hard at broad strata of the peasantry. The result was that serious damage was done to the worker-peasant alliance. Stalin admitted this when he said that, if the mistakes made were "persisted in," and "not eliminated rapidly and completely" (which they were not), they would "lead us straight to the discrediting of the collective-farm movement, to dissension in our relations with the middle peasants, to the disorganization of the poor peasants."[228]

The "discrediting" of the collective-farm movement soon revealed itself in quantitative terms. By February 20, 1930, 50 percent of the peasant farms had been collectivized, which was considered at the time to be a real and serious success, for "we had *overfulfilled* the five-year plan of collectivisation by more than 100 percent."[229] The percentage of collectivization even advanced to 59 percent by March 1, 1930.[230] In his article "Dizzy with Success," Stalin declared that the task of the hour was "to *consolidate* the successes achieved and to *utilize* them systematically for our further advancement."[231]

Instead of a consolidation and a continuation of the advance made, however, what happened was something quite different. The relaxation of constraint was accompanied by a rapid reduction in the percentage of households collectivized, a reduction which continued until October 1930, by which time this percentage had fallen to 21.7 percent.[232] The dimensions of the retreat show how brittle was the "collectivization" accomplished in the winter of 1929–1930. It was all the more so because some of the *kolkhozes* which had been formed in haste and which survived the "halt" of March 1930 functioned very poorly, as is apparent from a number of documents and indices.[233]

A few words must be said here about the *qualitative* aspect of the collectivization of the winter of 1929–1930. This aspect was dominated by a certain number of features which were far from being eliminated later on. On the one hand, some of the collective farmers, who had entered the *kolkhozes* against their will, worked grudgingly: some peasants who had been supporters of Soviet power until then were even turned into more or less hostile elements. This was one aspect of the very grave damage done to the worker-peasant alliance. On the other hand, quite a few peasants who were not hostile to Soviet power had joined the *kolkhozes* without being convinced of the superiority of collective farming. They retained their outlook as individual petty producers, and did not bring to the *kolkhoz* the spirit of collective initiative which was needed if it was to work properly. This circumstance found reflection in the considerable amount of stealing of collective property that went on, and also in the fact that many *kolkhozes* were managed in such a way that some of their marketable production was sold otherwise than through the lawful channels.[234] The Soviet government was soon convinced of the necessity to put the *kolkhozes* under the control of elements alien to the peasantry, so as to impose work norms and standards of management by means of disciplinary measures. New hierarchical relations were established in the countryside, which prevented the collective farmers from running their own affairs.

Furthermore, the peasants who had been made to join the collective farms against their will had often slaughtered some of their cattle,[235] so that the collective farms lacked draft animals and, in general, had very little livestock.

Thus, a series of objective and subjective conditions compromised the success of collectivization from the start. This explains why it was that, for many years, collective farming produced material results that were much inferior to the farming of the NEP period, and why, in order to appease peasant discontent and help to bring about a certain recovery in production, the Soviet government decided in 1930 to permit the collective-farm peasants to cultivate individual holdings which were quite sizable, and to possess livestock of their own. Later, it was even necessary to reestablish a "legal" free market and to allow collective farms and collective farmers to dispose of part of their production therein. These measures, by their scope and because of the conditions in which they had to be taken, produced in their turn a negative effect on the proper functioning of the *kolkhozes*, for the private activities of the collective farmers seriously encroached upon their work in the collective-farm fields.[236] Thus, by setting in motion an immense social transformation without the active participation of the broad masses of the peasantry, and frequently even against their will, serious prejudice was done not only to the worker-peasant alliance but also to collective farming itself and to the role that it might have played in the development of agricultural production. The subsequent political consequences of all this, which had a marked effect on class relations as a whole, were such as to raise the question whether accelerated collectivization, in the form that it took at the end of 1929, was really necessary.

(f) The question of the need for accelerated collectivization and of the forms this took at the end of 1929

What we know about the conditions in which the accelerated process of collectivization that was set going in the last months of 1929 actually developed permits us to conclude that it corresponded to a *political* necessity, and not to an "economic necessity." In 1929 it was materially possible to bring about a rapid increase in industrial and agricultural production without undertaking unprepared "mass collectivization." This increase could have been effected in such a way that the poor and middle peasants strengthened their positions and became organized so as to *take the offensive themselves against the kulaks and go over to collective production*. What was missing that was wanted if matters were to take this course was the *ideological and political* conditions for working out and applying such a line, together with the time needed for these political conditions to be prepared. But if there was no time, that was not because of "economic difficul-

ties" which had to be coped with in a hurry. There "was no
time" because the way in which the *class struggle* had developed since 1927 had created a situation that was increasingly dangerous for Soviet power. The dangers which had
accumulated were largely due to the contradictions in the
political line followed after 1927, the line of speeding up a
certain type of industrialization which increasingly deprived
the rural areas of manufactured goods and led to indiscriminate application of the emergency measures.

In the situation which gave rise to these measures, the
Bolshevik Party leadership presented the problem of the rapid
development of collective farms and state farms first and
foremost *in economic terms*. As they saw it, this development
offered the only means of quickly increasing the production of
grain (the Soviet Union was expected to become "in about
three years' time . . . one of the world's largest grain producers,
if not the largest") and this was to enable the state to achieve
"decisive successes" in grain procurement and the accumulation of emergency reserves.[237] Transformation of social relations and struggle against the kulaks thus appeared as *conditions* to be realized in order to reach the *economic targets*
aimed at. At the outset, the turn toward collectivization was
presented as an integral part of an *economic policy* aimed at
establishing new forms of production, and class struggle was,
as it were, *subordinated* to the purposes of the Party's economic policy. Very soon, however, the actual process took a
quite different course,[238] as a result of the development of the
contradictions. The latter had become extremely acute
through not being correctly dealt with in good time, and engendered a series of pragmatic measures which did not constitute a coherent political line (hence the succession of hasty
"turns" and "halts," made without preparation because they
were not foreseen). It was the interlinking of these contradictions (between classes in the village, between the Party's
industrial and agricultural policies, between the interests of
town and country, etc.) and the interventions to which they
gave rise (interventions not inspired by an overall analysis)
which caused a process of uncontrolled collectivization to

begin. And this, despite the victory won over the private bourgeoisie, led to a split in the worker-peasant alliance and a profound weakening of Soviet agriculture.

The absence of control over the collectivization process resulted in a succession of more or less improvised measures, intended to deal with a series of unforeseen "crises" for which the Party had been unable to prepare itself. If, despite the lack of a coherent political line, the process of collectivization seems to have developed with a certain "logicality," that was because of the "objective logic" of the succession of crises and because the measures taken to deal with them were themselves dictated by a relatively stable ideological conception.

Underlying the collectivization process were the developing and shifting contradictions between classes. The form it took was largely the result of political and ideological determinations. It was due, among other things, to the Bolshevik Party's extremely weak implantation in the countryside and the inadequacy of the help given to the poor and middle peasants—especially the almost complete lack of support for the efforts that some of these peasants had made to follow the path of collectivization. It was due to a conception of industrialization that was oriented increasingly toward modern large-scale industry, requiring large investments and imports of equipment. It was due to a style of leadership which did not allow the true lessons to be drawn from the experience accumulated by the workers and peasants during the first five years of the NEP. It was due, finally, to a style of discussion within the Party which was aimed above all at striking down anyone who expressed views different from those of the majority in the PB or of the Secretariat. When the right and the opportunity to express their views had been taken from such dissenters,[239] and they tried to make their voices heard nevertheless, penal measures were taken against them, and they were treated as enemies.[240] Yet it was necessary, if the questions raised were to be clarified, that democratic centralism should really operate, that genuine discussion should develop, that the refutation of errors should be based on concrete analyses, and not, as increasingly came to be the practice during the last years of the NEP, on the use of a selection of quotations from Lenin, usually torn from the context in which the ideas they contained had been formulated.

The style of discussion which became established in the last years of the NEP did not help to *show up* the mistakes made by the various oppositions, so that as soon as these groups had been eliminated, usually by organizational methods, the substance of some of their theses easily reemerged, in some more or less modified form—the best example of this being the theory of exacting "tribute" from the peasantry, which was, basically, only another version of the theory of "primitive socialist accumulation."[241]

This same style of discussion led, as a rule, to rejection *en bloc* of everything said by the opposition: thus, after the Sixteenth Conference, when the "Right" opposition stressed the need to undertake a form of industrialization compatible with the principle that agriculture was the basis of economic development (a thesis which the majority of the Party had accepted up to that time), this position was denounced as "pro-peasant," "pro-kulak," and hostile to industrialization.

On the plane of ideology, the form taken by the collectivization process—which, in practice, did not put "in command" the task of strengthening the alliance with the poor and middle peasants—was determined by the growing predominance in the Bolshevik Party's ideology of an "economist-technicist" element. This led to the belief that the difficulties that arose during the last years of the NEP would be solved through the development of modern industry and the transformation of the "technological bases" of production, especially in agriculture. The increasing role ascribed to "technological progress" extended even to ideological and political problems. Consequently, recognition of the necessity for ideological and political struggle against the petty-bourgeois and individualist ideas existing among the peasantry tended to be replaced by the thesis according to which it would be by the introduction of machinery into agriculture that the "peasant mentality" would be changed.[242]

This conception could not but favor an accelerated process

of collectivization, carried through even without the peasants
having first been convinced of the correctness of the
collective-farm road. Indeed, it led to a belief that through the
use of machinery the peasants' ideas would change, this use of
machinery being the "essential" means for changing the
"peasant mentality."

From this example it can be seen that changes in the
superstructure were subordinated to technological changes.
In order to understand how such subordination can have appeared "acceptable," we need to take an overall view of the
Bolshevik ideological formation, and of the way in which this
was itself transformed.

Notes

1. Stalin, *Works*, vol. 11, p. 3.
2. Ibid., p. 7.
3. Ibid., p. 52 (Stalin's report to the Moscow Party organization,
   April 13, 1928).
4. N. Bukharin, *Uroki khlebozagotovok, Shakhtinskogo dela, i
   zadachi partii*, pp. 32–33. (Article first published in *Pravda*,
   April 19, 1928).
5. *K.P:S.S. v rezolyutsiyakh*, vol. 2, pp. 372 ff., especially p. 377.
6. Frumkin's letter is known to us only in part, from the quotations
   from it included by Stalin in a reply dated June 20 (*Works*, vol.
   11, p. 121 ff.), and from a speech by Thälmann reported in
   Pravda, August 11, 1929 (M. Lewin, *Russian Peasants*, p. 336, n.
   17).
7. Lewin, *Russian Peasants*, p. 300.
8. These divergences were "publicly" acknowledged by Stalin in
   a speech in February 1929, to a restricted audience—a joint
   meeting of the PB and the Presidium of the CCC. The text of
   this speech was published for the first time in volume 11 of
   Stalin's *Works*, the Russian original of which appeared in 1949
   (see *Works*, vol. 11, p. 335).
9. There had, in fact, been a stormy discussion between Rykov and
   Stalin in February 1928, when the general secretary returned
   from his tour of Siberia and Rykov spoke against the way the

emergency measures were being applied. In the Trotsky Archives there is a letter (T.1106) mentioning this discussion. At the seventeenth Party Congress Rykov himself said that the "Right Opposition" had begun at the time of the application of the emergency measures decided upon in the winter of 1927–1928. See *XVII-y Syezd VKP(b)* (1934), p. 210, quoted in Carr and Davies, *Foundations*, vol. 1, pt. 1, p. 61, n. 5.

10. At the time of the July plenum, Bukharin called on Kamenev, the former leader of the united opposition, who had been expelled from the Party by the Fifteenth Congress but was then in the course of applying for readmission. It is mainly from Kamenev that we know of Bukharin's reactions to the discussions in the PB and the plenum in the summer of 1928. The account of Bukharin's conversation with Kamenev is document T.1897 in the Trotsky Archives (quoted in Carr and Davies, *Foundations*, vol. 1, pt. 1, p. 82, n. 1).

11. Actually, the "bond based on metals" was one of the requirements of the NEP as it had been formulated by Lenin. This requirement, which implied, first and foremost, supplying to the poor and middle peasants adequate quantities of instruments of labor, even if only simple ones, had been very little honored between 1923 and 1928, as was shown by the *under-equipment* of the farms worked by these peasants. In 1928 Stalin gave a different interpretation of the "bond based on metals": for him, it had to mean the *large-scale supply of tractors and machines* to agriculture. His speech, entitled "Industrialization and the Grain Problem," is in *Works*, vol. 11, p. 164 ff. (see especially p. 172).

12. Ibid., p. 167.

13. Ibid. The full text of this speech was not published until twenty years later, doubtless because this declaration signified a break with the resolutions adopted previously on the need to continue a policy of "closing the scissors."

14. What Bukharin said is known to us only indirectly, in particular from document T.1901 in the Trotsky Archives. See also Robert V. Daniels, *The Conscience of the Revolution: Communist Opposition in Soviet Russia*, pp. 331–333; Carr and Davies, *Foundations*, vol. 1, pt. 1, p. 79; and Lewin, *Russian Peasants*, pp. 303–304.

15. Carr and Davies, *Foundations*, vol. 1, pt. 1, p. 65.

16. Ibid., pp. 76–77.

17. *K.P.S.S. v rezolyutsiyakh*, vol. 2, pp. 372–379.
18. Ibid., p. 392. In November 1926, as we saw, Stalin had said something similar: see his report to the Fifteenth Party Conference, in *Works*, vol. 8, p. 301.
19. *K.P.S.S. v rezolyutsiyakh*, vol. 2, p. 393.
20. Ibid., pp. 394, 395. It is to be observed that the position that the NEP was *not* being abandoned was kept up not only through 1928 but for long after, even when nothing was left that corresponded to the principles of the New Economic Policy. Thus, *Pravda* of March 21, 1931, was still saying: "N.E.P. has not yet ended." The persistence of this claim was due not only to the fact that throughout the 1920s the NEP had become the symbol of the worker-peasant alliance, but also to the fact that the economic, political, and ideological conditions Lenin had stated were necessary before it would be possible to proceed to a stage higher than the NEP had not been attained, so that it was difficult to proclaim officially the going over to a different policy.
21. Carr and Davies, *Foundations*, vol. 1, pt. 1, p. 81.
22. See document T.1897 in the Trotsky Archives, quoted by Cohen, *Bukharin*, pp. 291–292.
23. On this see volume I of the present work, pp. 423–424.
24. See the article by E. Goldenberg, a supporter of Bukharin's views, on "The German Problem," in *Bolshevik*, March 15, 1928, p. 35.
25. This characterization of Social Democracy had been given for the first time by Zinoviev in the early 1920s, but was then dropped by him (see Theodore Draper, "The Ghost of Social-Fascism," in *Commentary*, February 1960, pp. 29–42). Stalin took up the idea in 1924, notably in an article published in *Bolshevik*, no. 11 (1924), with the title: "Concerning the International Situation." In this he wrote: "Fascism is not only a military-technical category. Fascism is the bourgeoisie's fighting organization that relies on the active support of Social-Democracy. Social-Democracy is objectively the moderate wing of Fascism. . . . These organizations . . . are not antipodes, they are twins" (*Works*, vol. 6, p. 294). Nevertheless, this conception did not dominate Comintern policy in 1924, and until the Sixth Congress the Communist Parties practiced the "united front" in various forms.
26. At the plenum of April 1929 Stalin was to assert that "the elements of a new revolutionary upsurge are accumulating in the

capitalist countries" (*Works,* vol. 12, p. 17)—an assertion refuted
by events.

27. The "third period" followed that of "relative stabilization,"
between 1923 and 1927, itself having been preceded by the
revolutionary period of 1917–1923 (see F. Claudín, *The Communist Movement: From Comintern to Cominform,* especially
pp. 156–157).

28. In his report to the CC plenum of April 1929 Stalin said that his
first disagreements with Bukharin on international questions
arose at the time of the Sixth Comintern Congress. According to
Stalin, Bukharin there put forward theses which, contrary to the
rules normally observed, had not been previously submitted to
the Soviet Party delegation, so that the latter was obliged to
move twenty amendments, which "created a rather awkward
situation for Bukharin" (*Works,* vol. 12, p. 21).

29. Bukharin's speeches are in *VI Kongressy Kominterna,* vol. III,
pp. 30–31, 137–138, 143–145; and vol. V, p. 130; quoted in
Cohen, *Bukharin,* p. 293. English translations will be found in
International Press Correspondence, vol. 8, nos. 41, 49, 56, 59
(July 30, August 13 and 27, September 4, 1928).

30. See above, note 28.

31. At the plenum of April 1929 Stalin spoke about his disagreements with Bukharin which had been reflected in the
amendments voted by the Sixth Congress. He mentioned four
fundamental points of divergence:

(a) The international situation. The Soviet Party delegation
had moved an amendment declaring that aggravation of the
world economic crisis opened up "the prospect of maturing
conditions for a new revolutionary upsurge."

(b) The fight against Social Democracy. The Soviet Party
delegation criticized Bukharin's theses for saying no more than
that this fight was one of the basic tasks of the sections of the
Comintern, for it considered that this statement did not go far
enough. Its amendments declared that, if the fight against Social
Democracy was to be carried through successfully, "stress must
be laid on the fight against the so-called 'Left-wing of Social
Democracy, that 'Left' wing which, by playing with 'Left'
phrases and thus adroitly deceiving the workers, is retarding
their mass defection from Social-Democracy."

(c) Bukharin's theses spoke of the need to fight against the
Right deviation, but said nothing about the need to fight against
conciliation with the Right deviation.

(d) Party discipline. Another fault found in Bukharin's theses was that "no mention was made of the necessity of maintaining iron discipline in the Communist Parties" (Stalin, *Works,* vol. 12, pp. 23–24).

32. These few points indicate what the lines of cleavage were that separated Bukharin's views from those of the majority of the July 1928 plenum, where international problems were concerned. I do not propose to analyze here the reasons for and significance of these divisions, and still less to discuss the attitudes taken up by the various delegations at the Sixth Comintern Congress. However, it is to be noted that the resolutions adopted by the Sixth Congress committed the Comintern to a particular form of struggle by the working class, since these resolutions failed to show clearly the need for *class alliances.* Noteworthy also is the clash at the Congress between the sharply opposed views expressed by Ercoli (Togliatti) and by Thaelmann. For the former,

> Fascism, as a mass movement, is a movement of the petty and middle bourgeoisie dominated by the big bourgeoisie and the agrarians; moreover, it has no basis in a traditional organization of the working class. On the other hand, Social-Democracy is a movement with a labour and petty-bourgeois basis; it derives its force mainly from an organisation which is recognized by enormous sections of the workers as the traditional organisation of their class.

For Thaelmann, however, "the 'Left-wing' Social-Democratic leaders are the most dangerous enemies of Communism in the labour movement." It was Thaelmann's formulation that was incorporated in the resolution passed by the Sixth Congress on the international situation, (*International Press Correspondence,* vol. 8, no. 50 [August 16, 1928], p. 879; no. 53 [August 23, 1928], p. 941; no. 83 [November 23, 1928], p. 1571).

33. *Pravda,* October 23, 1928, and Stalin, *Works,* vol. 11, p. 231 ff.
34. Stalin, *Works,* vol. 11, pp. 234–235.
35. Ibid., pp. 237, 240.
36. Ibid., pp. 242, 244–245.
37. A French translation of this article is included in Bukharin et al., *La Question paysanne,* pp. 213–240.
38. A resolution of the Political Bureau dated October 8, 1928, reprimanded Bukharin for having published this article without

previous "authorization." The resolution was passed by the majority against the votes of Rykov, Tomsky, and Bukharin himself (F. M. Vaganov, *Pravy Uklon v VKP(b)*, pp. 161–163, 174–175).

39. *Torgovo-Promyshlennaya Gazeta*, September 14, 1928; *Pravda*, September 25, 1928; Robert V. Daniels, *A Documentary History of Communism*, p. 311; Cohen, *Bukharin*, p. 295; Carr and Davies, *Foundations*, vol. 1, pt. 1, pp. 315–317.

40. Bukharin et al, *La Question paysanne*, pp. 218, 220.

41. Ibid., p. 220.

42. Ibid., p. 222.

43. Ibid., p. 231.

44. Ibid., p. 235.

45. Ibid., pp. 235–236.

46. Ibid., pp. 239–240.

47. Besides the sources in the Trotsky Archives, already mentioned, references to these requests by Bukharin are to be found in the *Sotsialistichesky Vestnik* (the organ of the Menshevik émigrés), no. 9 (1929), which reproduced the gist of one of Bukharin's conversations with Kamenev, and in a number of speeches at the Sixteenth Party Congress, especially the speech of Ordzhonikidze (see *XVI-y Syezd VKP*[b] [1930], p. 256, quoted in Lewin, *Russian Peasants*, pp. 315–316).

48. This is the title under which the speech appears in Stalin's *Works*, vol. 11, pp. 255 ff. Delivered on November 19, it was published in *Pravda* on November 24, 1928. Stalin made reference in the speech to Bukharin's article "Notes of an Economist," but without criticizing it, and so without setting out any arguments intended to refute it. A few months later, when the breach with Bukharin had been consummated, this same article was to be presented (though still without any arguments being offered) as evidence of "eclectic confusion inadmissible for a Marxist" (see the resolution adopted on February 9, 1929, by the PB and confirmed by the plenum of April 23, 1929, in *K.P.S.S. v rezolyutsiyakh*, vol. 2, pp. 436 ff., especially pp. 437–438).

49. "It may be asked where this is said in the theses, in what passage of the theses. (*A voice*: 'Yes, where is it said?') Evidence of this in the theses is the sum-total of capital investments in industry for 1928–1929" (Stalin, *Works*, vol. 11, p. 266).

50. Ibid., vol. 11, p. 255 (my emphasis—C. B.).

51. Ibid., p. 256.
52. These resolutions, as we have seen, emphasized the opposite idea of *optimum* accumulation and respect for a *correct proportionality* in investments, as between the different branches of the economy.
53. See the textbook *Political Economy*, edited by Ostrovityanov and others, p. 533.
54. Lenin, *CW*, vol. 2, pp. 155–156. This observation has been developed by E. Poulain in his thesis on *Le Mode d'industrialisation socialiste en Chine*, p. 146. He mentions that the Soviet textbook quoted in the preceding note presents as a victory the fact that between 1925 and 1958 the production of means of production in the USSR was multiplied by 103, whereas that of consumer goods was multiplied only by 15.6, and he adds this comment by Mao Tse-tung: "The problem is to know whether or not this proportion of 103 to 15.6 is advantageous or not to the development of industry" (Hu Chi-hsi, ed., *Mao Tsé-toung et la construction du socialisme*, p. 117).
55. Stalin, *Works*, vol. 11, p. 257.
56. Ibid.
57. Ibid., pp. 258–259.
58. Ibid., pp. 262, 263.
59. Ibid., pp. 255, 263–264 (my emphasis—C. B.).
60. The respective places assigned by Stalin in his speech of November 19, 1928, to technical changes and to ideological changes is shown by the following formulation: ". . . the reconstruction of agriculture on a new technical basis, causing a revolution in the minds of the peasants and helping them to shake off conservatism, routine" (ibid., p. 279). Here what "acts" is technique, with the peasant *acted upon*.
61. One of Stalin's first pronouncements on the role that the state and collective farms could play in increasing the marketable share of production was his speech of May 28, 1928, to the students of the Sverdlov University (*Works*, vol. 11, pp. 85 ff.). In this speech Stalin declared that "the basis of our grain difficulties lies in the fact that the increase in the production of marketable grain is not keeping pace with the increase in the demand for grain. . . . The strength of large-scale farming, irrespective of whether it is landlord, kulak or collective farming, lies in the fact that large farms are able to employ machines, scientific methods, fertilisers, to increase the productivity of

labour, and thus to produce the maximum quantity of marketable grain" (ibid., pp. 86, 88).

These remarks were followed by a table (compiled by Nemchinov) comparing gross production and marketable production of grain in the different types of farm, before and after the Revolution. This table shows that the largest proportion of marketable production (47.2 percent) was that contributed by the collective and state farms (ibid., p. 89).

After July 1928, when Stalin emphasized the need for the "tribute" to be paid by agriculture to industry, the development of collective forms of farming appeared more and more as the most effective means for ensuring that this tribute would be regularly forthcoming. The establishment of this means was itself subordinated to transformation of the technical basis of agriculture, for, as Stalin saw it, the will and initiative of the peasants were not the driving force of new forms of production or of the development of *really new productive forces*.

62. Ibid., pp. 272–279.

63. The resolution on the "control figures" was adopted unanimously by the plenum. Bukharin, Rykov, and Tomsky did not wish to oppose it publicly. The former "Left" opposition (now absent from the Party's leading organs) supported the line of industrialization based on maximum investment in heavy industry. Kamenev, who was now given permission to rejoin the Party, published in *Pravda* on November 16, 1928, an article attacking those who wanted to launch a "struggle to reduce the given rate of industrialization."

64. Two points need to be noted here:

(a) In practice, the sums actually assigned to industrial investment exceeded those laid down in the resolution of the November 1928 plenum, but without the conditions specified by that plenum being honored, so that the "shortages" of industrial products in the branches denied priority were made still more severe (Carr and Davies, *Foundations*, vol. I, pt. 1, p. 314, n. 1).

(b) The principle of giving priority to heavy industry dominated not only the compiling of the plans but also their execution. This meant that, if the material means needed for realizing *all* the targets fixed by the plan proved not to be available in sufficient quantity (as was indeed the case), then the means actually to be had were assigned preferentially to the priority

branches—the others receiving even less than had been provided for in the plan, so that additional distortions ensued. (See,
e.g., Kubyshev's statement in *Torgovo-Promyshlennaya Gazeta*,
December 4, 1928, quoted in Carr and Davies, *Foundations*,
vol. 1, pt. 2, p. 882.)

65. Bukharin expounded these ideas in an article in *Pravda* on
January 20, 1929, and, especially, in a long speech he made on
January 21 on the occasion of the fifth anniversary of Lenin's
death. This speech was published in the principal newspapers
on January 24, and then as a pamphlet with the title: *Lenin's
Political Testament*.

66. Quoted in Vaganov, *Pravy Uklon*, p. 198.

67. The greater part of the resolution passed by the PB on February
9, condemning the positions of Bukharin, Rykov, and Tomsky,
dealt with their demand for a Party discussion of their proposals, their allegedly "factional" activity, Bukharin's contacts
with Kamenev, the relations maintained by the three with
"supporters of an opportunist line in the Comintern," and so on.
The resolution did not examine the basic political positions of
the three, but proceeded by way of assertions. Thus, it declared
that, "in the recent period, the Bukharin group have passed,
where basic questions of our policy are concerned, from oscilla-
tion between the Party line and the line of the Right deviation
to defence of the positions of the Right deviation" (*K.P.S.S. v
rezolyutsiyakh*, vol. 2, p. 432). The three were in this way
charged with placing themselves "objectively on the line . . . of
a weakening of the positions of the proletariat in the struggle
against capitalist economic forms" (ibid.). And yet, in January
1929, the three were in fact merely defending the positions they
had been defending for a year, positions which were those of
the Fifteenth Party Congress.

68. Ibid., p. 435.

69. And yet, during the struggle against the united opposition, Stalin had accused the latter of wanting the Soviet state to exploit
the peasantry (see Stalin, *Works*, vol. 8, pp. 368–369).

70. Lewin, *Russian Peasants*, pp. 333 ff.

71. Ibid., pp. 334–335.

72. Quoted in ibid., p. 321.

73. See the article in *Pravda*, December 11, 1929, entitled:
"Against Opportunism in the Movement of Worker and Peasant
Correspondents," and the collective work entitled: *Za
Marksistsko-leninskoye ucheniye o pechati*.

74. Bukharin, *Politicheskoye zaveshchaniye Lenina*, p. 27, quoted in Cohen, *Bukharin*, p. 304.
75. The document is reproduced in a speech of Stalin's to the April plenum of the CC (*Works*, vol. 12, pp. 7–8).
76. Ibid., p. 111.
77. *K.P.S.S. v rezolyutsiyakh*, vol. 2, pp. 429 ff.
78. Ibid., pp. 436 ff., especially p. 445.
79. This speech of Stalin's is in his *Works*, vol. 12, pp. 1–113. Cohen notes (*Bukharin*, pp. 453–454) that Stalin's speech as it was in fact delivered certainly called for condemnations more severe than those that were adopted and are mentioned in the version of the speech published twenty years later.
80. *K.P.S.S. v rezolyutsiyakh*, vol. 2, pp. 431, 432, 435 (my emphasis—C. B.).
81. Ibid., vol. 2, p. 436. This resolution was not published at the time, but only much later. It was not until June–July 1929 that the measures resolved upon against Bukharin and Tomsky took effect publicly (Lewin, *Russian Peasants*, p. 325).
82. *K.P.S.S. v rezolyutsiyakh*, vol. 2, p. 440.
83. Carr and Davies, *Foundations*, vol. 1, pt. 2, p. 943.
84. Ibid., vol. 1, pt. 1, pp. 101–105.
85. This was the speech published as "The Right Deviation in the CPSU(B)," in *Works*, vol. 12, pp. 1–113. In the version printed at the time, about thirty pages were "cut," presumably because of some of the formulations they contained, and were not made public until 1949.
86. Stalin, *Works*, vol. 12, pp. 37 ff.
87. Only the principal aspects of these theses are considered here. Their implications will be discussed later, in volume III of the present work. It was in the following years, indeed, that they gave rise to fresh developments, and became linked with a form of political practice that concretized their meaning.
88. Stalin, *Works*, vol. 12, p. 38.
89. Ibid., p. 39.
90. Ibid.
91. Ibid., p. 53.
92. Whether it was correct or not to call this contribution a "tribute" is a point of only secondary importance.
93. Stalin, *Works*, vol. 12, p. 53.
94. Ibid., pp. 60–61.
95. See above, pp. 101 ff.
96. Not only did Stalin consider that the period of "restoration" was

completed in agriculture (that is, that the former "technical basis" had been restored), but he alleged that the "old technique" was "now useless, or nearly useless"—a meaningless proposition (ibid., p. 61).

97. Ibid., p. 60.
98. Ibid., p. 62.
99. Ibid., p. 64 (my emphasis—C. B.).
100. Ibid., p. 92.
101. Ibid., p. 91.
102. *K.P.S.S. v rezolyutsiyakh*, vol. 2, pp. 494–495.
103. This resolution was published for the first time in 1933. The criticisms of Bukharin made by some of the delegates to the Sixteenth Conference, together with Molotov's report, are to be found in later editions of the proceedings of this conference: see *XVI-taya Konferentsiya VKP(b)* (1962), in which Molotov's report appears on pp. 58 ff.
104. Carr and Davies, *Foundations*, vol. II, pp. 92–93.
105. Ibid., pp. 94–95.
106. Ibid., pp. 59, 67, 97. Preobrazhensky had already asked for readmission a year before the Sixteenth Conference.
107. *K.P.S.S. v rezolyutsiyakh*, vol. 2, pp. 470 ff.
108. Ibid., p. 470.
109. Ibid., pp. 471–472, 482–483.
110. Ibid., p. 471; see also volume I of the present work, pp. 330–331.
111. Ibid., p. 473.
112. Ibid., pp. 474–475, 477 ff.
113. Ibid., p. 482.
114. It mentioned the work of the sections of Rabkrin, the production conferences, the temporary commissions for "workers' control," the training of worker-correspondents (whose comments and criticisms were sent to the newspapers), discussion by general assemblies of workers and office workers of the results of investigations, and so on.
115. *K.P.S.S v rezolyutsiyakh*, vol. 2, pp. 483 ff.
116. Stalin, *Works*, vol. 11, p. 34.
117. *K.P.S.S. v rezolyutsiyakh*, vol. 2, pp. 483 ff.
118. Ibid., pp. 485 ff.
119. See volume I of the present work, pp. 317 ff.
120. Between 1922 and 1928 about 260,000 members left the Party. In 1927 some 44,000 left, of whom 17,000 were expelled by

decision of the CCC (the total membership at that time being about 1.2 million): Carr and Davies, *Foundations*, vol. 2, pp. 132–133, 474.

121. In 1923 the Party's CCC and Rabkrin were merged. The CCC thus came to operate in the sphere of the state machine as well as supervising the activity of Party members. The role of the CCC became especially important in 1926 and after because of the fight against the oppositions and the application of disciplinary measures. In theory the CCC was independent of the CC (both being directly elected by the Congress), and it sat separately. From 1925 on, however, the CCC more and more often came to sit jointly with the CC, in the form of a "plenum," and it tended to become, in practice, a mere department of the CC (Carr and Davies, *Foundations*, vol. 2, pp. 116–117).

122. Ye. Yaroslavsky, *Chistka Partii,* pp. 29–33.

123. *K.P.S.S. v rezolyutsiyakh*, vol. 2, p. 485, and *XVI-taya Konferentsiya VKP(b)* (1962), pp. 589–611.

124. *K.P.S.S. v rezolyutsiyakh*, vol. 2, p. 483.

125. The Party's financial problems were not then discussed in public. Only in exceptional cases were a few figures given relating to some of the Party's functionaries and their remuneration (Carr and Davies, *Foundations*, vol. 2, p. 121).

126. Nomination to important posts in the state machine was possible only with the agreement of the Party (that is, of the services attached to the Party Secretariat) and, in some cases, of other authorities. The various posts appointment to which was supervised in this way formed part of the *nomenklatura*. Nomination to these posts was not reserved for Party members, but the percentage of Party members nominated to them was, as a rule, higher in proportion to the degree of responsibility of the posts concerned. Thus, in 1927, over 75 percent of the chairmen and members of trusts under the VSNKh were Party members, and 96.9 percent of the managers of major industrial enterprises came directly under VSNKh. In general, it was persons who were already Party members who were appointed to these posts, but it sometimes happened that specialists appointed to them were admitted to the Party at the same time (ibid., pp. 122–125).

127. *K.P.S.S. v rezolyutsiyakh*, vol. 2, p. 487.

128. See volume I of the present work, especially pp. 308–209, 313–314, 321–322, 426–427, 447–448. Let us recall some of the

terms used by Lenin at the beginning of 1922: "Taken as a whole (if we take the level of the overwhelming majority of Party members), our Party is less politically trained than is necessary for real proletarian leadership in the present difficult situation." He expected at that time "a big increase in the efforts of petty-bourgeois elements, and of elements positively hostile to all that is proletarian, to penetrate into the Party" (Lenin, *CW*, vol. 33, pp. 256, 257).

129. *K.P.S.S. v rezolyutsiyakh*, vol. 2, p. 488.
130. Ibid.
131. Ibid., pp. 489–490.
132. Ibid.
133. Ibid., pp. 490–491.
134. It must be pointed out that the resolution on purging the Party which was adopted by the Sixteenth Conference was, in this respect, profoundly different from that which was formulated in June 1921 on Lenin's initiative (see Lenin, *CW*, vol. 42, pp. 315–316; Lenin's proposal was approved by the PB on June 25, 1921: ibid., p. 567). At the time of the purge in 1921 a circular from the CC declared that it was *not permissible to expel a member for ideological differences*, and the case of members of the former "workers' opposition" was quoted as an example. This circular appears to have been honored, on the whole (T. H. Rigby, *Communist Party Membership*, p. 99).
135. Carr and Davies, *Foundations*, vol. 2, pp. 144–145.
136. Ibid., pp. 145–146.
137. Rigby, *Communist Party Membership*, pp. 97, 178–179.
138. This aspect of the decisions of the Sixteenth Conference is analyzed later, under the heading: "The Sixteenth Conference and the problems of agriculture," above, p. 455.
139. See above, pp. 370 ff., and 407 ff.
140. It will be seen that, in reality, what was called the "optimum" version of the plan was a "maximum" version: it presupposed a steady increase in harvests, in productivity of labor, and so on—in other words, "optimum" objective conditions, and that was why it was called the "optimum" version. The same confusion of terms was to apply where the subsequent alternative versions of the Five-Year Plan were concerned. This confusion facilitated the adoption of a "maximum" version described as an "optimum" version, giving the latter term a meaning quite different from the one intended by the advocates of balanced development of the different branches of the economy.

141. The figures for the various drafts of the Five-Year Plan are given in Zaleski, *Planning,* p. 54, with mention of the sources for them.

142. Ibid., p. 57, and *K.P.S.S. v rezolyutsiyakh,* vol. 2, p. 449. It is to be noted that the resolution of the Sixteenth Conference which adopted the figure of 64.6 milliard roubles declared that the "optimum" variant of the plan was approved (*K.P.S.S. v rezolyutsiyakh,* vol. 2, p. 453), although this variant actually forecast the figure of 74.2 milliards for investment (Zaleski, *Planning,* p. 246).

143. Zaleski, *Planning,* p. 57.

144. The meeting of this Congress coincided with the publication of the detailed Five-Year Plan: *Pyatiletny Plan Narodnokhozyaistvennogo stroitelstva SSSR* (1929)—three volumes, with 1,700 pages in all. It included the list of enterprises to be built or enlarged in order that the targets decided on might be reached.

145. *K.P.S.S. v rezolyutsiyakh,* vol. 2, p. 453.

146. Ibid., p. 449.

147. This is only one example of the conditions that were presupposed for the fulfillment of the Plan. These conditions were listed by G. F. Grinko in his article "Plan velikikh rabot," in *Planovoye Khozyaistvo,* no. 2 (1929), pp. 9–10: see M. Lewin, "Disappearance of Planning in the Plan," *Slavic Review,* June 1973, p. 272.

148. These points of Lenin's were set forth in his letter to Krzhizhanovsky, the chairman of Gosplan: *CW,* vol. 32, pp. 371 ff.

149. *K.P.S.S. v rezolyutsiyakh,* vol. 2, pp. 452, 454.

150. The facts exposed this unrealism, for, while it was possible to say that the First Five-Year Plan was "fulfilled in four years," this could be done only by taking certain figures as "indices of fulfillment" and ignoring everything that was *not* fulfilled, in spheres that were vital for the standard of living of the masses (light industry, agriculture, real wages) and for accumulation (productivity of labor, costs of production, etc.).

151. As has been said, while the Plan, as a set of forecasts, was not fulfilled, a circumstance which entailed a series of consequences that were negative in their impact on the worker-peasant alliance and on the working and living conditions of the working class—the "industrial ambition" that it embodied was, partly, satisfied, for under its impetus Soviet industry made

gigantic progress in a certain number of spheres. It is useless to speculate whether a more coherent and more realistic plan, putting industry directly at the service of agriculture, would have enabled the same material results to have been achieved without entailing the same negative consequences: history cannot be "done over again."

152. See Table IX on p. 87 of Zaleski, *Planning*.
153. *Planovoye Khozyaistvo*, no. 1 (1929), p. 109; partly quoted in Lewin, "Disappearance," *Slavic Review*, June 1973, p. 272.
154. G. V. Kuibysheva et al., V. V. *Kuibyshev: Biografiya*, quoted in Lewin, "Disappearance," *Slavic Review*, June 1973, p. 273, n. 6.
155. Marx, first outline of *The Civil War in France*, in Marx and Engels, *On The Paris Commune*, p. 157. (The English is Marx's own.)
156. *K.P.S.S. v rezolyutsiyakh*, vol. 2, p. 454.
157. *Direktivy K.P.S.S. i Sovyetskogo pravitelstva po khozyaistvennym voprosam*, vol. II, p. 7.
158. Ibid., pp. 12–17.
159. *Sobranie Zakonov*, no. 19 (1929), art. 167.
160. *Ekonomicheskaya Zhizn*, March 3, 1929.
161. *K.P.S.S. v rezolyutsiyakh*, vol. 2, pp. 495–499.
162. Ibid., pp. 498–499.
163. See above, pp. 235, 345.
164. See volume I of the present work, pp. 384 ff.
165. *VIII-oy Syezd Professionalnykh Soyuzov, SSSR*, pp. 3–14, 24, 55.
166. S. P. Trapeznikov, *Kommunisticheskaya partiya v periode nastupleniya sotsializma*, pp. 40–41.
167. *K.P.S.S. v rezolyutsiyakh*, vol. 2, pp. 455 ff.
168. Ibid., p. 455.
169. Ibid., pp. 451, 459. The text of the Five-Year Plan gave considerably different figures. Thus, in 1933, the population engaged in the "socialized sector" was to constitute only 9.6 percent of the total rural population (that is, 12.9 million people, instead of the 20 million forecast by the Sixteenth Party Conference) and the arable land included in this sector was to account for only 10.6 percent of the total arable land (*Pyatiletny Plan*, vol. 2, pt. I, pp. 323–329; Zaleski, *Planning*, p. 60; *K.P.S.S. v rezolyutsiyakh*, vol. 2, p. 451).
170. *K.P.S.S. v rezolyutsiyakh*, vol. 2, p. 451.

171. Ibid., p. 459.
172. See the article by Strumilin, an unconditional advocate of rapid planned development, in *Planovoye Khozyaistvo*, no. 3 (1929), especially p. 36; also *Pravda*, June 2 and 16, 1929.
173. *K.P.S.S. v rezolyutsiyakh*, vol. 2, p. 459.
174. Ibid., pp. 459–460, 468.
175. Ibid., pp. 468–469; also a series of articles in *Pravda* at the beginning of 1929.
176. See above, pp. 163 ff.
177. In the Moscow region alone there were over 2,000 peasant demonstrations; some of these were accompanied by acts of violence. The demonstrations were blamed on the kulaks, who may indeed have instigated them, but this does not explain how it was that the kulaks were able to enlist the support of a sufficient number of peasants to justify talk of peasant demonstrations significant enough to be mentioned (see Kozlova, *Moskovskiye Kommunisty*, p. 43, quoted in Cohen, *Bukharin*, p. 330).
178. See above, p. 441.
179. Zaleski, *Planning*, pp. 105, 149; *Narodnoye khozyaistvo 1970 g.*, p. 131.
180. This article was published in two parts, in *Pravda* of May 26 and June 6, 1929, under the titles: "Nekotorye problemy sovremennogo kapitalizma i teoretikov burzhuazii" (pp. 2–3) and "Teoriya 'organizovannoy bezkhozyaistvennosti'" (pp. 3–5). It is interesting to observe that in these writings Bukharin criticized bourgeois theories of the "superiority" of the very large enterprise—theories which obviously influenced the way the Five-Year Plan was conceived and the projects in it.
181. Cohen, *Bukharin*, p. 461, n. 272.
182. At the plenum of November 10–17, 1929, Bukharin, Rykov, and Tomsky made a joint statement in which they gave their analysis of the situation. It was not published, but the majority of the plenum considered it unacceptable. However, no new "organizational measures" were taken, for the time being, against Tomsky and Rykov, whereas Bukharin was removed from the PB (*K.P.S.S. v rezolyutsiyakh*, vol. 2, pp. 542–543). A few days later, on November 25 the three published a "self-criticism" in which they declared that their "views" had "turned out to be mistaken," and pledged themselves "to conduct a decisive struggle against all deviations from the Party's general line and,

above all, against the Right deviation" (Cohen, *Bukharin,* p. 335). This "self-criticism" signified publicly the complete political defeat suffered by the three—but not the end of the attacks upon them. These were aimed chiefly at Bukharin, who was required to make a fuller self-criticism on the occasion of the Sixteenth Party Congress (June 26–July 3, 1930). At that congress Rykov and Tomsky made fresh self-criticisms, but Bukharin refused to follow suit. He was nevertheless reelected to the CC. After some discussion, Bukharin did eventually provide a fresh self-criticism (*Pravda,* November 20, 1930), but this did not put a stop to the attacks upon him. As for Rykov, despite his political attitudes, he remained chairman of the Sovnarkom until December 1930, when he was replaced by Molotov (Cohen, *Bukharin,* pp. 331, 349). The three were now no more than members of the CC, and occupied only secondary posts. However, starting in 1933, Bukharin once again played a role of some importance (Ibid., pp. 354–356). In 1936 the three were accused (but not indicted) during the first of the "great trials," that of Zinoviev and Kamenev. In August 1936 Tomsky killed himself. At the beginning of 1938, Bukharin and Rykov were accused of forming an "anti-Soviet bloc" with the Trotskyists, of having become agents of German and Japanese imperialism, and of a number of other crimes. They were sentenced to death and executed.

183. V. P. Danilov, ed., *Ocherki istorii kollektivizatsii selskogo khozyaistva v soyuznykh respublikakh,* pp. 32–33, 74–75, quoted in Lewin, *Russian Peasants,* p. 428.

184. After the October Revolution, and especially under "war communism," peasant practice had created three basic types of collective production, distinguished from each other by the degree to which labor and means of production were socialized. In ascending order of socialization, these were the three forms:

(a) The *toz,* an acronym of the Russian words meaning "association for tilling the soil." This form of collective made "common" the work required for cultivation (as a rule, only of the principal crops) together with the land and major equipment needed for this work. The rest of the land and equipment, together with some of the animals and buildings, remained with the private farms, which thus did not disappear completely. In general, the share-out of the produce of the work done jointly was effected, mainly, on the basis of the amount of labor time put in by each member.

(b) The *artel* involved a higher degree of socialization. All that remained of the individual farm was a few plots and a little stock, the rest being collectivized. What had been produced jointly was shared out strictly on the basis of each member's contribution in labor.

(c) In the *kommuna* ("commune") there was practically complete socialization of all the means of production. The sharing of what was produced took account not only of the labor contributed by each person but also of the number and age of the members of the different peasant families.

The *artel* was the form preferred by the Soviet government. Subsequently, it was the main form in which collectivization was to develop.

185. *Postroyeniye fundamenta sotsialisticheskoy ekonomiki v SSSR 1926–1932*, p. 291, quoted in Lewin, *Russian Peasants*, p. 444, n. 88.
186. Danilov, *Ocherki istorii*, p. 32.
187. See below, p. 495, n. 196.
188. *Materialy po istorii SSSR*, U.S.S.R. Academy of Sciences, vol. VII, pp. 230–231, 236.
189. Vareikis, "O partiinom rukovodstve kolkhoza," in *Na Agrarnom Fronte*, no. 8 (1929), pp. 64–65.
190. Ibid.
191. *Pravda*, November 7, 1929: Stalin, *Works*, vol. 12, pp. 124 ff.
192. Ibid., p. 132.
193. *Pravda*, December 4, 1929.
194. Stalin, *Works*, vol. 12, p. 138.
195. Ibid. This rallying of the peasants "by whole villages," and so on, was what was meant by "complete" (*sploshnaya*) collectivization. See above, p. 461.
196. On December 15, 1929 (more than a month after the publication of Stalin's article), only between 0.1 and 5 percent of households had been collectivized in 59 percent of the 1,416 *rayons* of the RSFSR (Abramov, in Danilov, *Ocherki istorii*, p. 96, quoted in Lewin, *Russian Peasants*, p. 478, n. 33). At the end of 1929, when very strong pressure was being brought to bear on the peasants, the statistics, even though they tended to "inflate" the results of the campaign, showed only about 10 percent of the *okrugs* as having undergone "complete collectivisation" (N. Ivnitsky, "O nachalnom etape sploshnoy kollektivizatsii," in *Voprosy Istorii KPSS*, no. 4 [1962], p. 62). This shows how very unevenly the movement developed.

197. Stalin, *Works*, vol. 12, p. 159.
198. Ibid., p. 176.
199. The administrative officials who were closest to the peasantry were in a position to appreciate better their resistance to large-scale collectivization effected without preparation. They were opposed to a method which fixed "percentages of collectivisation" without any relation to local realities. They were often punished for this. In some regions, nearly half of the chairmen of village soviets were removed from their posts on various grounds (see the Smolensk archives, *VKP* 61, pp. 98–168, quoted in Fainsod, *Smolensk*, p. 142).
200. The mistaken idea that a general advance of the collectivization movement was going on sprang not only from the statements made by the Party leadership and the way that the press presented the situation, but also from the boastful claims made by many regional Party secretaries (themselves "caught" by the atmosphere of "competition in percentages of collectivisation" which was then developing). Thus, at the plenum of November 10–17, 1929, some regional secretaries talked of mass entry by the middle peasants into the *kolkhozes*, whereas fewer than 5 percent of these peasants had actually joined in the regions for which these men were responsible (Lewin, *Russian Peasants*, p. 478, n. 33).
201. At the end of 1929 and the beginning of 1930 the "delegates for collectivisation" received orders directing them to collectivize certain localities within less than a week. For example, the delegates for the sub-district of Sosnovsky, in the district of Tver, were given in mid-February 1930 the order to carry through in five days the collectivizing of the localities assigned to them. The Party leadership of the subdistrict instructed them to report at 9 A.M. on February 20, at the office of the Party Committee, to give an account of how they had fulfilled their tasks. The order stated: "There can be no excuse for not fulfilling the tasks assigned. Those who have not accomplished their mission will be brought to trial within 24 hours" (Ts.G.A.O.R., collection 374, inventory 9, file 418, sheet 4, quoted in Yakovtsevsky, *Agrarnye otnosheniya*, p. 237; also in *Recherches internationales*, no. 85 [no. 4 of 1975], p. 83).
202. See, e.g., Ts.G.A.O.R., collection 374, inventory 9, file 403, sheets 7–8; and file 418, sheet 61; quoted in Yakovtsevsky, *Agrarnye otnosheniya*, p. 328 (also in *Recherches Internationales*, no. 85 [no. 4 of 1975] p. 84).

203. Ibid.
204. Lewin, *Russian Peasants*, pp. 475–476.
205. *Bolshevik*, no. 22 (1929), p. 19.
206. See, e.g., Fainsod, *Smolensk*, pp. 242 ff.
207. A. L. Strong, *The Soviets Conquer Wheat*, p. 88.
208. Lewin, *Russian Peasants*, p. 505.
209. *Na Agrarnom Fronte*, nos. 7–8 (1930), p. 95.
210. In V. Ulashevich, ed., *Zhenshchina v kolkhoze*, article by Leikin, p. 28, quoted in Lewin, *Russian Peasants*, p. 494. The term *podkulachnik* ("abettor of kulaks") could therefore be applied to a poor peasant.
211. *Na Agrarnom Fronte*, nos. 7–8 (1930), p. 94; *Bolshevik*, no. 6 (1930), p. 21; and also sources quoted in Lewin, *Russian Peasants*, p. 502.
212. Pashukanis, ed., *15 let sovyetskogo stroitelstva*, p. 474.
213. *Na Agrarnom Fronte*, no. 6 (1930), p. 20.
214. Stalin, *Works*, vol. 12, pp. 197–205.
215. *K.P.S.S. v rezolyutsiyakh*, vol. 2, pp. 548–551.
216. Stalin, *Works*, vol. 12, pp. 198–199. The information and analyses subsequently published showed that in fact, these "sentiments" were extremely "widespread" and had seriously affected collectivization.
217. Ibid., p. 201.
218. Ibid. Sergeant Prishibeyev is a dictatorial old soldier in a story by Chekhov (English translation, *Anglo-Soviet, Journal*, vol. XVII, no. 2 [Summer 1956]).
219. Stalin, *Works*, vol. 12, pp. 203–204.
220. Ibid., p. 205.
221. Ts.G.A.O.R., collection 374, inventory 9, file 418, sheets 7 and 72, quoted in Yakovtsevsky, *Agrarnye otnosheniya*, p. 331. (Also in *Recherches Internationales*, no. 85 [no. 4 of 1975], p. 87.)
222. This article was published in *Pravda*, April 3, 1930, under the title: "Reply to Collective–Farm Comrades" (Stalin, *Works*, vol. 12, pp. 207 ff.).
223. Stalin, *Works*, vol. 12, p. 208.
224. Ibid., pp. 209–216.
225. Ibid., pp. 216–217.
226. It should be noted that in some regions the local authorities intervened sooner than the CC did. Thus, on February 12, 1930, the Party Committee of Velikive Luki, an area then attached to Smolensk region, sent a circular to local Party organizations in which the exiling and expropriation of poor and middle peas-

ants was "unconditionally prohibited" (Smolensk Archives, *VKP 53*, pp. 6 ff., quoted in Fainsod, *Smolensk,* pp. 242–243).

227. Lewin, *Russian Peasants*, pp. 505–506.
228. Stalin, *Works*, vol. 12, pp. 217–218.
229. Ibid., p. 197.
230. Lewin, *Russian Peasants*, pp. 427, 515; Zaleski, *Planning*, p. 102; Bettelheim, *La Planification soviétique*, p. 33.
231. Stalin, *Works*, vol. 12, p. 198.
232. Same sources as in note 230. In the Moscow region only 7.2 percent of the households were still collectivized in June 1930, as against 73 percent in March (M. Bogdenko, *Istoricheskie Zapiski,* no. 76, pp. 20 ff., quoted in Nove, *An Economic History,* p. 172).
233. This question must be held over for examination in volume III of the present work, where the whole subject of collectivization will be discussed.
234. Lewin, *Russian Peasants*, pp. 436, 464.
235. The importance of this slaughtering of cattle will be considered in volume III of the present work.
236. These points, too, will be gone into in more detail in volume III of the present work.
237. Stalin, *Works*, vol. 12, p. 138. Actually, the production of grain declined sharply from 1930 on, and this situation continued until 1935.
238. I shall not, for the moment, consider the fact that the *economic targets aimed at* were not reached. Collectivization did not enable the problems of grain production, or even those of "marketable production" to be "solved more effectively." Nor did it, contrary to a widely held view, enable a better solution to be found to the problem of accumulation (i.e., the question of the tribute to be levied from the peasantry). This will also be considered in volume III of the present work. Some interesting points on the subject are made in the article by J. F. Karez, "From Stalin to Brezhnev: Soviet Agricultural Policy in Historical Perspective" (especially pp. 41–51), in James R. Millar, ed., *The Soviet Rural Community*.
239. We know that, while the "resolution on Party unity" passed by the Tenth Congress prohibited the forming of "factions," it did not forbid discussion. On the contrary, it assumed that any disagreements would be "brought publicly before the whole Party," and it provided for the publishing of a *Discussion Bulle-*

tin (see volume I of this work, pp. 399–400). In fact, however, during the NEP period open discussion of differences was increasingly restricted—and the *Discussion Bulletin* never appeared.

240. Mao Tse-tung constantly urged the Chinese Communist Party to avoid such practices, which weaken the Party. In 1937 he said: "If there were no contradictions in the Party and no ideological struggles to resolve them, the Party's life would come to an end" (*Quotations from Chairman Mao Tse-tung*, pp. 260–261). In 1942 he condemned the method of "lashing out at" those who had made mistakes (ibid., p. 262). In 1957 he declared, in connection with discussions taking place outside as well as inside the Party, that even bourgeois and petty-bourgeois ideas should be allowed expression, so that they might be criticized, for it is through struggle that Marxism progresses. He said that, in any case, "inevitably, the bourgeoisie and petty-bourgeoisie will give expression to their own ideologies. . . . We should not use the method of suppression and prevent them from expressing themselves, but should allow them to do so, and at the same time argue with them and direct appropriate criticism at them. . . . However, such criticism should not be dogmatic and the metaphysical method should not be used, but efforts should be made to apply the dialectical method. What is needed is scientific analysis and convincing argument" (ibid., pp. 53–54).

241. See above, p. 367.
242. See below, p. 519.

3. The Bolshevik ideological formation and its transformations

The dominant role played in deciding the outcome of the class struggles by the Bolshevik Party's interventions in the political, economic, and social life of the Soviet formation was due to the integration of the Party in these struggles and to the place it occupied in the system of government—to its role, in fact, as the ruling Party. This means that the Party's interventions helped to impose a certain course of development upon most of the struggles, but not necessarily that this course was the one that the Party intended. The degree to which the course and outcome of these struggles coincided with the Party's aims depended on the adequacy to the real situation of the analysis, or the conception, of this situation on the basis of which the Party acted, and, above all, on the social forces that the Party was able to rally round its policy and to mobilize.

Basically, the nature and the forms of the Party's interventions were dominated by the system of ideas which, at any given moment, constituted, with their distinctive articulation, *the Bolshevik ideological formation*. This did not come from nowhere, but was the historical product of the class struggles and of the lessons (true or false) drawn from them, and of the political relations existing within the Party and between the Party and the various classes of society.

The Bolshevik ideological formation was not something laid down "once for all time." It was a complex social reality, objective and subject to change. It was realized in practices and forms of organization, as well as in the formulations embodied in a set of documents. This reality had definite effects upon those whom it served as an instrument for analyzing and interpreting the world, and also for changing the world. These effects differed in accordance with the internal contradictions of the ideological formation, the diversity of the places occupied in the social formation by those to whom Bolshevism served as a guide, and the different social practices in which these persons were engaged.

Marxism-Leninism was the theoretical basis of Bolshevism, but cannot be identified with the Bolshevik ideological formation. *That* was a contradictory reality within which a constant struggle went on between revolutionary Marxist thinking, Marxism as constituted historically, and various ideological currents which were alien to Marxism—parodying it, because they often borrowed its "terminology."

The distinctions thus made call for some clarification. They imply that the Bolshevik ideological formation cannot, as a whole, be treated as equivalent to Marxism-Leninism. They imply also that revolutionary Marxist thinking cannot be treated as equivalent, at all times, to Marxism as it was historically constituted in each epoch, on the basis of fusion between revolutionary Marxist thinking and the organized movement of the vanguard of the proletariat. Marxism constituted in that way signified a systematized set of ideas and practices which enabled the revolutionary working-class movement claiming to be Marxist to deal, in the concrete conditions in which it found itself, with the problems which it had to confront. These successive systematizations—necessary for action, but including elements that were more or less improvised and corresponding to the demands, real or apparent, of a given conjuncture of the class struggle—were the Marxism of each epoch: that of German Social Democracy, that of the Second International at the end of the nineteenth century, and, in the early twentieth century, that of the Third International, and so on.

At the core of Marxism as historically constituted, a variable place was given to revolutionary principles and conceptions resulting from scientific analysis carried out from the standpoint of the proletariat's class positions and based on the lessons drawn from the proletariat's own struggles. The outcome of this analysis and of these lessons is the scientific nucleus of Marxism. Marxist scientific thought was not "brought from outside" into the working class. It was a scientific systematization of that class's own struggles and initiatives. It resulted from a process of elaboration which started from the masses and returned to the masses, and which involved a conceptual systematization.

Marxist scientific thought is not "given" once and for all: it has to be developed, enriched, and rectified on the basis of new struggles and new initiatives. Substantial rectifications are inevitable, for Marxist scientific thought, which can be called revolutionary Marxism, has to learn from the struggles waged by the working masses as they advance along a road never previously explored.

Revolutionary Marxism is not a system, but it does include elements of the systematic, thanks to which, in the contradictory reality which it constitutes, the scientific knowledge that is its nucleus plays the dominant role, enabling it to grasp objective reality and to act upon this with full awareness of what is involved.

The very development of revolutionary Marxism implies the existence of contradictions within it[1] and the transformation of these contradictions through a process which makes it possible for scientific knowledge to be corrected and completed as regards the element of objectivity which it grasps. Hence Lenin's formulation: "We do not regard Marx's theory as something completed and inviolable: on the contrary, we are convinced that it has only laid the foundation-stone of the science which socialists *must* develop in all directions if they wish to keep pace with life."[2]

Like every other science, therefore, revolutionary Marxism undergoes a process of development. At every stage of this process some of the theoretical formulations or ideological conceptions[3] which formed part of the revolutionary Marxism of the previous epoch are eliminated; they are thenceforth alien to it, which does not mean that they are necessarily eliminated at once and "definitively," either from Marxism as it is constituted historically in the revolutionary working-class involvement, or, still less, from the various ideological currents which, though alien to Marxism, play a role in the revolutionary movement.

The process of transforming revolutionary Marxism and the process of transforming Marxism as historically constituted in each epoch are not "parallel" processes. The former is the development of a science, whereas the latter is the transformation of an ideology which has a scientific basis. Under the impact of the difficulties experienced by the struggles of the working class, Marxism as historically constituted in each epoch experiences not only theoretical enrichment (connected with the development of scientific knowledge, itself due to social practice) but also impoverishment, through the fading, obscuring, or covering-up, to a greater or less degree, of some of the principles or ideas of revolutionary Marxism.[4]

All this helps to make a necessary distinction, and illustrates the meaning of a phrase of Marx's which was no mere witticism: "All I know is that *I* am not a Marxist."[5] By this he meant that he refused to identify his work with the Marxism of the German Social Democrats, or of some other "Marxisms"—as we see from his reaction to the way his ideas were interpreted by some Russian writers. This refusal meant rejecting the reduction of his scientific discoveries to an ideological system such as that which German Social Democracy constructed in its necessary fight against Lassallism, and also in its compromise with the latter. This system doubtless corresponded to some of the needs of the German labor movement of the time, and was the starting point for successive changes (from which, in particular, the Marxism of the Third International emerged); but it excluded part of the heritage of revolutionary Marxism[6] (and sometimes "utilized" passages from Marx which did not correspond to the more mature forms of his work). The Marxism of German Social Democracy tended to "overlook"[7] some of the analyses made by Marx after the Paris Commune, regarding the forms of political authority, the state, the organizations of the working class, the forms of property and appropriation, etc.[8]

We have seen the struggle waged by Lenin to transform the Marxism of his epoch, in order to develop it and to bring back into it a number of fundamental theses of revolutionary Marxism (especially on the problem of the state), so as to combat "economism." We have seen, too, the obstacles and resistances that this struggle encountered even inside the Bolshevik Party.[9]

The presence in the Bolshevik ideological formation of currents alien to Marxism[10] was a necessary consequence of the class struggle. At different times, these currents had a more or less considerable influence on Bolshevism. One of the characteristic features of Lenin's activity was his striving to expose the theoretical roots of the conceptions which he fought against. He applied this method also to the mistakes which he himself made and acknowledged: not restricting himself to a correction or to a self-criticism, he undertook an analysis. This was an essential feature of Lenin's practice, and one that tended to disappear from subsequent Bolshevik practice, which preferred usually to carry out "silent rectifications" that did not contribute to a genuine development of Marxism and left intact the possibility of falling into the same errors again.[11]

However, the currents in Bolshevism that were alien to Marxism did not necessarily disappear just because they had been criticized. Insofar as the social foundations on which they were based continued to exist, they themselves survived, though, as a rule, in modified forms.

The history of the Bolshevik ideological formation appears as a history of the transformation of various currents which composed the contradictory unity of Bolshevism, and of the relations of domination and subordination between them.

This was no "history of ideas," but the history of the effects upon the Bolshevik ideological formation of the changes in class relations and class struggles, and in the way that the Party was involved in these struggles. It included periods when the influence of revolutionary Marxism grew and periods when its influence declined. We cannot trace that history here: it would require a number of analyses which are still to be undertaken. But it is necessary to mention some of the characteristics of the process of transformation of the Bolshevik ideological formation, and to point out that when the influence of currents alien to Marxism grew stronger within it, the capacity of Marxism to develop was reduced, and it tended to "congeal," with ready-made formulas replacing those concrete analyses which are, in Lenin's words, "the soul of Marxism."

The transformations undergone by the Bolshevik ideological formation were due either to the development of new knowledge or to the inhibition of old knowledge. These transformations had as their internal cause the contradictions within the Bolshevik formation itself, but their actual movement was dictated by the class struggles that went on in the Soviet social formation, and by the impact that these struggles had on social relations and practices, especially on the conditions for mass social experiment. The changes undergone by the Bolshevik ideological formation produced, owing to the position held by the Bolshevik Party in the system of ideological apparatuses, reactions which affected the Soviet formation itself, by way of the Party's interventions.

Let it be noted here that in the concrete history of the Bolshevik ideological formation there took place a gradual inhibition of certain concepts which made it possible to analyze the movement of reproduction of commodity and capitalist relations, the existence of which is manifested through the forms "value," "price," "wages," and "profit." Gradually, these forms came to be treated more and more as "empty forms," "integuments," which were used for "practical" (or "technical") purposes (accounting in money terms, "efficiency" of management, etc.); whereas awareness of the social relations which they manifest (and conceal) was inhibited in the Bolshevik ideological formation. This inhibition corresponded to the increasing dominance of the ideological notions of bourgeois political economy: it was still possible to consider the problem of the quantity of value, but no longer to ask *why* such forms still existed. Here let us recall an observation of Marx's: "Political economy . . . has never once asked the question why this content has assumed that particular form. . . ."[12]

Yet it is only by asking such a question that one can go beyond empirical knowledge, covering the apparent relation between forms (reality as it seems to itself [*sich darstellt*]), to real scientific knowledge, knowledge of *the real movement*.

Empirical knowledge can *orient* action in a general way, but only scientific knowledge can give it precise guidance, enabling it actually to achieve its aim, because such knowledge makes possible analysis, foresight, and action with full awareness of what is involved.

The inhibition, during certain periods, of some of the scientific knowledge making up revolutionary Marxism was a result of the class struggle, which engendered a variety of ideological currents. What happened toward the end of the NEP had decisive political significance: it reduced the Bolshevik Party's capacity to analyze, to foresee, and to act in full awareness of what was involved.

Another observation needs to be made. The internal contradictions of Bolshevism, the struggles fought out within it between Marxism-Leninism and various other ideological trends, were not directly due to the different "tendencies" whose conflicts mark the history of the Bolshevik Party. These "tendencies" were themselves contradictory combinations of ideological currents that were present in the Bolshevik ideological formation.

The internal contradictions of Bolshevism made themselves felt in the ideology of the Party majority as well as in that of the various oppositions. The latter were differentiated by their particular ways of combining the ideas of revolutionary Marxism with ideas that were alien to it. As time went by, these combinations underwent variations that also affected the ideology of the Party majority, which was by no means always identical. Furthermore, the changes this ideology underwent did not correspond simply to a deepening of revolutionary Marxism or an extension of its influence within the Bolshevik ideological formation (as is suggested by the idea of a "linear development" which takes no account of the class struggle and its ideological effects). They corresponded also to the setbacks which restored life and prestige (in barely modified forms) to ideological configurations which had previously been recognized as being strongly marked by ideas alien to revolutionary Marxism. This was the case toward the end of the NEP, when the Party majority rallied round the idea of "maximum development of the production of means of production,"[13] to be accomplished through *maximum accumulation* obtained chiefly by exacting "tribute" from the peasantry.[14]

These same ideas had earlier been promoted by Preobrazhensky and the Trotskyist opposition, and had been correctly condemned in the name of defense of the worker-peasant alliance.[15]

If we look at the principal documents approved at various times by the leading organs of the Bolshevik Party, together with the speeches, books, and articles of most of its leaders, we can see that the Bolshevik ideological formation was indeed a battlefield where revolutionary Marxism was constantly in combat with ideas that were alien to it.

During the first half of the 1920s, the principal formulations issued by the Party leaders, and embodied in the resolutions adopted at that time, either reaffirmed the essential theses of revolutionary Marxism or else constituted a certain deepening of basic Marxist positions. This was so as regards the demands of the worker-peasant alliance, the role to be assigned to the organizing of the masses in many different ways, the need to tackle the problems of building socialism, the indispensability of developing soviet democracy. During those years, the dominance of the ideas of revolutionary Marxism tended, on the whole, to grow stronger. However, as we have seen, a number of positions of principle or decisions taken failed to exercise any broad and lasting influence on the practices of the state machine and the Party. This was often the case with regard to democratic centralism, soviet democracy, economic and political relations with the peasant masses, and relations between the Russian Republic and the other Soviet republics.[16]

After 1925–1926, various changes affected the Bolshevik ideological formation, contributing to the reinforcement of ideological elements that were alien to revolutionary Marxism. The party then launched into an industrial policy which aggravated the contradictions within the state industrial sector, and engaged in practices detrimental to the firmness of the worker-peasant alliance. At the same time, it became *blinder* to the negative effects of these practices, which seemed to it to have been dictated as "necessities" inherent in the building of socialism.

In order to make the foregoing more explicit we must survey some of the elements alien to revolutionary Marxism which were present in the Bolshevik ideological formation, and show the place that these elements occupied at different moments, together with some of their political consequences.

I. The internal contradictions of the Bolshevik ideological formation

I am not going to undertake here a systematic examination of the elements alien to revolutionary Marxism which were at work within the Bolshevik ideological formation, or to analyze the historical conditions responsible for their appearance and development. This would form the subject of a specific study which remains to be made. The following remarks are intended mainly to show the presence of certain elements which played an important part in the ideological struggles and the political interventions, and, in certain cases, to indicate some of the conditions in which they appeared. The limited purpose of these remarks means that the order in which they are set out is not intended to reveal the existence of some "central" ideological theme that may have played a dominant role in relation to the elements alien to revolutionary Marxism. The order in which the questions are examined is merely that which seems easiest—starting with themes that are relatively well known and going on to deal with others that are less well known.

(a) The economist-technicist conception of the productive forces and the primacy accorded to the development of technology[17]

For revolutionary Marxism, the class struggle is the driving force of history, and so history, as long as classes exist, is the

history of class struggle.[18] This struggle leads necessarily to
the dictatorship of the proletariat, itself a transition to the
abolition of all classes, to a classless society.[19] Class struggles,
like classes themselves, have as their material basis the forms
and modes of production in which producers and nonprodu-
cers are integrated. They transform the conditions of production, cause new productive forces to emerge, break up old
production relations, and engender new relations. Knowledge
of the inner laws of the process of transformation of the production relations is not a necessary constituent factor in this
process. The latter usually presents itself to the mind in
ideological forms—legal, political, religious, artistic,
philosophical—which result from the contradictions of material life. It is through these ideological forms that the struggles
are usually fought out, and not necessarily on the basis of
knowledge of real relations[20] which result from a materialist
analysis of the movement of history. Characteristic of Bolshevism was its principled application of such an analysis.
Nevertheless, in some Bolshevik documents, the interlinking
of the different factors entering into the analysis (classes, production relations, productive forces) was not what was proper
to revolutionary Marxism. We must pause to consider this
question.[21]

(1) "Development of the productive forces" and "development of society"

A good illustration of what has just been said is to be found
in Stalin's *Dialectical and Historical Materialism*.[22] Although
it is later in date than the period being studied in this book, I
shall refer to it here because it is the most systematic exposition of what gradually became, after the late 1920s, the dominant conception in the Bolshevik Party.[23]

I shall start by indicating how those theses of *Dialectical
and Historical Materialism* to which attention will chiefly be
paid are situated in the general structure of this work. The first
part of it, about which I shall say only a little, is devoted to
expounding dialectical materialism.[24] Here we find recalled
certain propositions of Lenin's regarding the role of *internal*

contradictions in the development of things. References to "struggle of opposite tendencies" and to "the class struggle of the proletariat" illustrate these propositions. Two points call for emphasis:

a. In the second part of the work, devoted to historical materialism,[25] the class struggle as driving force of history barely gets mentioned.

b. The first part contains an explicit critique of Bogdanov's "fideism,"[26] whose incompatibility with Marxism is very briefly mentioned,[27] but in the second part we find no criticism of Bogdanov's "socialogical" conceptions[28] (which were continued by *Proletkult*[29]). This deficiency is not unconnected with the actual content of the second part of the work, which we shall now examine.

The fundamental thesis propounded in the second part of *Dialectical and Historical Materialism* is that "the determining force of social development" is constituted by "the concrete conditions of the material life of society." This thesis is complemented by another statement—that "the party of the proletariat must not base its activity on abstract 'principles of human reason,' but on the concrete conditions of the material life of society, as the determining force of social development: not on the good wishes of 'great men' but on the real needs of development of the material life of society."[30]

These propositions are presented as being in conformity with those formulated by Marx in his 1859 preface to the *Contribution to the Critique of Political Economy*.[31] Actually, they include a number of specific features which give them a *different meaning* from that of Marx's revolutionary theses. To be observed, in particular, are:

a. The use of the formulas "social development" or "development of society," thus presenting "society" as an *entity* developing historically. They take the place held in the 1859 preface by the expression, "process of social, political and intellectual life,"[32] which emphasizes the conception of a social process and does not mention "society" either as "subject" or "object."

b. The use of the expression "concrete conditions of the

material life of society," a vague notion to which Stalin's essay endeavors later on to give a more precise content (as we shall see).

c. The introduction of the notion of "real needs of development of the material life of society." This implies that there are "needs of society," not at the level of the *reproduction* of the production relations (where this notion is used by Marx, when he speaks of "social needs") but at that of some "development of society" on which "the party of the proletariat must base its activity."

This notion of "needs of development" is substituted for the objective contradictions and class conflicts, and also for the *needs of the masses*, on which the party of the proletariat must, in fact, base itself so as to ensure, not the "development of society" but the *revolutionary transformation of the production relations*.

Thus, the formulations present in this part of the essay replace the concepts of revolutionary Marxism with different ones, derived (in spite of apparent "similarities") from a different conception of the movement of history. In this conception, the dominant figure is the "concrete conditions of the material life of society," while knowledge of the "needs of development" replaces analysis of class struggles and contradictions.

As Stalin proceeds, he makes clear the significance of this dominant figure—all the more dominant because it is said to be the "determining force of social development."

Among the "conditions of the material life of society" Stalin mentions, first of all, nature which surrounds society, geographical environment.[33] However, he declines to see this "environment" as "the chief force determining the physiognomy of society" because "the changes and development of society proceed at an incomparably faster rate than the changes and development of geographical environment."[34] After mentioning also "growth of population" as being among the "conditions of material life of society", and after rejecting the idea that it can be "the determining force of social development," Stalin says: "This force, historical materialism holds, is the *method of procuring the means of life* necessary for human existence, *the mode of production of material values. . . .*"[35]

In this formulation, as can be seen from the whole passage, a "technicist" element predominates. It makes the mode of production (*and not the contradictions in it*) the principal force of "social development." The mode of production is not conceived as the contradictory unity of the relations of production and the productive forces, but as an *organized sum* of elements or aspects which the passage enumerates. One of these aspects is constituted by the *"productive forces"* (themselves made up of the following "elements": the instruments of production, the people who operate them thanks to a certain "production experience" and "labour-skill"). The other "aspect" is the *"relations of production."*[36]

This enumeration, which mentions neither classes nor social contradictions, throws no light on what is the "chief force" of "the development of society." The latter is, first, simply affirmed, and then identified with the *development of production*, of which it is said that it "never stays at one point for a long time."[37] In its turn, this "development" is identified with the "development of the productive forces," which thus appears as the deus ex machina, the source of all "development of society": for it is said that the latter always depends on the development of the productive forces which itself depends primarily on the instruments of production.[38]

At this point we find ourselves faced with formulations differing radically from those of revolutionary Marxism, for which the historical process is determined, in the last analysis by class contradictions. The material basis of these is not mere *change* in the instruments of production but the *contradictions* in the economic basis (the contradictory unity of the production relations and the productive forces), and they develop by way of the ideological forms which these contradictions themselves engender. Revolutionary Marxism does not ascribe the development of the productive forces to a spontaneous process, or to "contradictions" external to the mode of production, counterposing "society" to "nature."

However, according to the conception developed in *Dialectical and Historical Materialism*, it is the *instruments of production*, and the changes which these undergo as a result of the ceaseless development of production, that determine changes in society.[39] Social classes and their struggles do not play the role of driving force here—indeed, in this part of Stalin's work they do not figure at all.[40] As for production relations, they appear to lead, somehow, an existence which is *external* to the productive forces: they merely "influence" the development of these forces "accelerating or retarding" it, but this development must, "sooner or later," lead to the transformation of these relations, so that they eventually "come into correspondence with . . . the level of development of the productive forces"—otherwise there occurs "a crisis of production, a destruction of productive forces."[41]

This outline of the conception of "social development" which is given in *Dialectical and Historical Materialism* has been necessary for more than one reason. First, because the systematic form of this work makes it possible to consider what relation the ideas contained in it bear to Marx's analyses. Secondly, because this work poses the problem of the objective basis for the increasing predominance of the conceptions which it contains.

The remarks which follow are an attempt to answer these two questions. They concern also some other contradictory aspects of the Bolshevik ideological formation, which will be dealt with later.

(2) The conception of "social development" as an effect of the development of the "productive forces," and Marx's analyses

The formulations of *Dialectical and Historical Materialism*, summarized and discussed in the foregoing pages undoubtedly bear some relationship to certain writings by Marx. This gives them a sort of "Marxist authenticity," the narrow limits of which need to be recognized, however, if we do not wish to fall into a "talmudistic" notion of Marxism which tends to reduce it to a commentary on, or a rearrangement of, quotations isolated from their context. We need to distinguish in the writings of Marx and Engels between what was radically new, contributing vitally to the formation of revolutionary Marxism, and what was merely repetition of old ideas, or provisional points of transition toward revolutionary positions and analyses.[42] Concretely, as regards the relations between social changes (and more especially changes in production relations) and changes in the material conditions of production, we find in the works of Marx and Engels two major categories of formulation.

The earlier category affirms essentially a materialist view of history, stressing that history is not the outcome of men's ideas but of the conditions of production. This is, very broadly, the position of Marx in his youthful writings, particularly *The German Ideology* and *The Poverty of Philosophy*, which date from 1846 and 1847, respectively.[43] This same position is set forth strikingly in a letter addressed by Marx on December 28, 1846, to one of his Russian correspondents, Pavel Annenkov, who had emigrated to France. In this letter Marx says:

Assume a particular state of development in the productive forces of man and you will get a particular form of commerce and consumption. Assume particular stages of development in production, commerce and consumption, and you will have a corresponding social constitution, a corresponding organization of the family, of orders or of classes, in a word, a corresponding civil society, and you will get particular political conditions which are only the official expression of civil society.[44]

Taken by itself, this formulation makes the totality of social relations and practices the "expression" of the "productive forces." "Society" is here presented as an "expressive totality," which is not contradictory, and the changes in which seem to depend upon "development in production." The central role played by the revolutionary struggle of the masses in the process of social change does not appear here, whereas it is stressed by Marx in those of his writings which develop a revolutionary and dialectical materialist position. The content of *these* writings is incompatible with a conception of "society" forming an "expressive totality," for they show that the driving force of history is the movement of internal contradictions and the class struggles. These formulations are set forth in a particularly striking way in the *Manifesto of the Communist Party*, but they are not absent from earlier writings, including the letter to Annenkov which I have just quoted.

Only gradually do formulations consistently expressing materialist and revolutionary positions become dominant in Marx's writings. And even when this has happened, the earlier type of formulation re-surfaces (which should not surprise us), at least in modified forms. This is what we see, for instance, in the case of the 1859 preface to the *Contribution to the Critique of Political Economy.* This preface presents a dialectic of contradiction between productive forces and production relations which leaves the reader to assume the existence of a "development" of the productive forces that is autonomous, so to speak, with its movement partly unexplained. It nevertheless remains true that, in this work, the transformation of social relations is not related *directly* to the "development of the productive forces," but to the contradictions which this development entails, and to the *ideological forms* in which "men become conscious" of the contradictions and fight out their conflicts.[45]

In volume I of *Capital*, however, some formulations very close to those of 1846 are still present. Certain ones even sometimes accentuate the importance attributed to technology. Thus, Marx writes: "Technology reveals the active relation of man to nature, the direct process of the production of his life, and thereby it also lays bare the process of the production of the social relations of his life, and of the mental conceptions that flow from these relations."[46]

In such passages, social relations and their changes are apparently ascribed to technology, while the social conditions governing the changes in technology are passed over in silence.

The writings which break away from the difficulties bound

up with the juxtaposition of two types of formulation are those
in which Marx ascribes the movement of history, and so, also,
the development of the productive forces and even of
"technology" *to the changing of social relations and the
struggles between classes*. These formulations go much
further than those quoted already: they are at the heart of
revolutionary Marxism.

On this point I shall confine myself to two examples, taken
from writings of 1865 and concerned with the development of
capitalist relations. Dealing with this question, Marx shows
that capitalist relations do not result from a "technological
change" but from class struggle—in this case, bourgeois class
struggle. This change corresponds to what Marx calls "the
formal subsumption of labour under capital," which involves
constraint to perform surplus labor. Marx points out that *when
capital begins to subordinate wage labor and in this way
develops new social relations, it does so on the basis of the
existing technology*. As he says, "*technologically speaking*
[Marx's emphasis—C. B.] the labour-process goes on as before": what is new is "that it is now subordinated to capital."[47]

It is precisely on the basis of these new (or modified) relations that *new productive forces develop*, namely, those that
correspond to the development of machine production. Marx
writes: "On the basis of that change, . . . specific changes in
the mode of production are introduced which create new
forces of production, and these in turn influence the mode of
production so that new real conditions come into being."[48]

Here we see a real dialectical movement, in which *what
changes first* is *not* the "productive forces," or the "instruments of production," but *social relations*, and this as the
result of class struggle, of bourgeois class struggle. We are
therefore *very far away* from the affirmation made in *Dialectical and Historical Materialism* that changes in production
"*always* begin with changes and development of the productive forces, and in the first place, with changes and development of the *instruments of production*."[49]

It is one of the distinctive features of revolutionary Marxism
that it reckons with the possibility and necessity of first of all

changing production relations, in order to ensure, under certain conditions, the development of the productive forces. It was toward the end of the 1920s that this feature of revolutionary Marxism tended to become inhibited from the Bolshevik ideological formation, in favor of a *mechanical materialist* position, which emphasized in a *one-sided* way the changing of the instruments of production.[50]

(3) *The objective basis of the increasing predominance in the Bolshevik ideological formation of a conception of "social development" set in motion by technological changes*

We need to ask the question: what happened toward the end of the 1920s which accounts for the tendency for *mechanical* materialist conceptions to become predominant in the Bolshevik ideological formation? Or, to go further, what was the objective, social basis of this tendency?

Briefly, we can say that this basis was provided by the nature of the relations that developed between the Bolshevik Party and the masses. Toward the end of the 1920s these had become essentially relations of *exteriority*. This is clear where the peasant masses were concerned (and they formed by far the majority of the population), since the Party was almost completely absent from the rural areas. But it is true also, even though to a lesser degree, where a large part of the working class was concerned, for a high proportion of the most politicized elements of that class, once they had joined the Party, were very quickly absorbed into the various apparatuses, so that they left the working class.

During the 1920s, the Party struggled to prevent this state of affairs from becoming established, but the successes achieved were very limited.

The nature of the relations between the Bolshevik Party and the masses was due, in the first place, to the conditions which existed at the beginning of our period, at the start of the NEP; to the chaos and disorganization that prevailed at that time; to the massive predominance in the machinery of state of elements alien to the working class, over whom the Party exercised only formal control; and to the split that had occurred between the Soviet power and the majority of the peasantry at the end of "war communism"; etc.[51]

Subsequently, lack of experience, and the weight of the ideological elements alien to revolutionary Marxism which were present in the Bolshevik ideological formation, prevented decisive successes being achieved in the development of firm relations of interiority between the Party and the masses.

As a result, the Bolshevik Party was able to render only limited aid to the struggle of the masses for a revolutionary transformation of social relations, the struggle which alone could open the way to a socialist development of the productive forces.

This struggle did exist, being carried on by the most advanced elements of the masses in town and country, but, through not being sufficiently united and supported by the Bolshevik Party, it did not lead to revolutionary changes. The Party's lack of attention to and adequate support for the struggles of the poor and middle peasants had particularly serious consequences in this connection. The same applies to the Party's inability to help the production conferences to result in a revolutionizing of the production relations.[52]

Toward the end of the NEP period it was thus difficult to secure a further increase in production through a mass struggle bringing about a change in production relations. Under these conditions, increased production seemed to depend above all upon a rapid "modernization" of technology, realized by means of massive investment, the resources for which would be mobilized by state action, and it was from this "modernization" that the *transformation of social relations* was expected to follow. The stress laid upon the role of technology corresponded, at the same time, to the growing weight in society of the technicians and cadres, separated from the masses—especially the heads of the big enterprises and of the state's central economic organs.

The situation which developed in this way constituted *the*

objective basis for the strengthening, within the Bolshevik ideological formation, of elements alien to revolutionary Marxism. This strengthening not only contributed to decisive importance being accorded to technology and technicians, and to state centralization, but also had the result that Bolshevism reformulated the relations between ideological and technological changes.

(b) Ideological changes and technological changes

One of the tasks that the Bolshevik Party strove to carry out was to ensure that the masses mastered revolutionary ideas, which presupposed rejection by the workers and peasants of the old ideas—religion, superstitions, acceptance of hierarchical relations, etc. However, the way that this task was undertaken by the Party shows that, within the Bolshevik ideological formation, there were increasingly dominant, toward the end of the 1920s, mechanical materialist conceptions which trusted above all in changes in the *conditions of production* to bring about a "change in ideas," or, as it is sometimes put, a "change of mentality."

An especially significant example of this mechanistic conception is provided by the way the problem of the penetration of socialist ideas among the peasantry was treated. Stalin discussed this problem in his speech "Concerning Questions of Agrarian Policy in the U.S.S.R.," on December 27, 1929, when the policy of mass collectivization was being put into effect.

In this speech, Stalin said:

A great deal of work has still to be done to remould the peasant collective farmer, to set right his individualistic mentality and to transform him into a real working member of a socialist society. And the more rapidly the collective farms are provided with machines, the more rapidly will this be achieved. . . . *The great importance of the collective farms lies precisely in that they represent the principal base for the employment of machinery and tractors in agriculture, that they constitute the principal base for remoulding the peasant, for changing his mentality in the spirit of socialism.*[53]

This formulation shows that the transition to collectivization was not regarded as having to result from a process of struggle which, through self-education of the peasant masses, would ensure the development of the ideas of socialism among them. On the contrary, it was *the use of machinery and tractors* that was to be the *means* to "set right" the "individualistic mentality" of the peasants. Similarly, the "great importance of the collective farms" was not that they would entail a change in production relations but that they were "the principal base for the employment of machinery and tractors."

According to this conception, therefore, it was not the peasants who were *to transform themselves* through class struggles and the lessons they drew from their experience, with the Party's help, but the peasants who were to be *transformed* because they were to be *acted upon by means of technology*.[54]

In presenting the problem of the ideological transformation of the peasantry in terms not of class struggle but of preliminary material changes,[55] Stalin was not defending a merely "personal" position. This position was then the one held by almost the entire Party. And it was a position that related not to the peasantry only, but also to the working class. The Party looked forward, as a result of the numerical growth of the working class, its integration in *modern* technology, and the *development of the towns* (that is, as a result of a certain number of material changes), to a transformation of the "ideas" of a working class which was of immediately peasant origin. Hence, for example, a resolution of the plenum of April 1928, which considered as essential for the building of socialism "the rapid growth of large-scale industry on the basis of modern technology . . . , the growth of the towns and industrial centres, the growth, in quantity and quality alike, of the working class."[56]

The nature of the mechanical link thus alleged to exist between ideological changes and technological changes (including those affecting habitat) may be seen as a "particular case" of the thesis which sees in the "development of the productive forces" the driving force of the "development of society." However, this is not entirely correct, for what is involved here is not so much the *ideological superstructure* corresponding to a certain *mode of production* as the "psychology," the "mentality," of the workers and peasants, and the "action" upon this of the environment, and, above all, of the *instruments of production* and the technological characteristics of the *labor process*. Here we are dealing with positions which are remote from revolutionary Marxism, and which lead to the posing of "psychological" problems while a decisive role is accorded not to class struggles but to the technological conditions of the labor-process.[57]

The effects of the growing predominance of "economist-technicist" conceptions were manifold. They helped to give prevalence to the idea that in building socialism what was most important was "building its material basis," and that it was necessary to adopt a policy of accelerated industrialization in which absolute priority must be given to heavy industry. These conceptions favored the decisive role attributed to the development of machine production and "modern" technology: hence the slogan of the 1930s, "technique decides everything,"[58] which opened the way for strengthening the position of the technicians and granting a privileged role to "science" and scientists.

Above all, conceptions such as these inhibited the role of proletarian class struggle and revolutionary mass action, replacing it with the struggle for production and for the development of the productive forces, which were expected to produce the most radical social changes, *including the disappearance in due course of the division between manual and mental labor*.[59]

The growing predominance within the Bolshevik ideological formation of the conceptions mentioned was due *fundamentally* to the contradictions which were developing in the Soviet formation, and the limited means available to the Bolshevik Party for dealing with them through action by the masses. Under these conditions the Party, in order to cope with the problems confronting it, strove to increase production as quickly as possible by means of technological changes, and it expected that these would result in ideological changes that must strengthen the dictatorship of the proletariat.

In this way, oblivion came to be increasingly the fate of

Marx's analyses showing the necessity, if the revolution was to advance, of ideological changes that were not at all the outcome of technological changes, but rather of revolutionary mass struggle, smashing the old social and ideological relations and making possible the building of new relations. Such a struggle was not a "struggle of ideas" but a class struggle, destroying old *practices* and old *social relations*, realized in *ideological apparatuses*, and making possible the building of new relations and new practices.

As regards the formation and development of ideas, that is, of ideological relations and the practices associated with them, we must distinguish between Marx's writings about the *ideas which correspond to a mode of production which is already dominant* and those which deal with the development of *revolutionary ideas*.

The writings in which Marx deals with the "dominant ideas" are the better known—such as the passage where he says that "the ideas of the ruling class are in every epoch the ruling ideas: i.e., the class which is the ruling *material* force of society is at the same time its ruling *intellectual* force."[60] If the writings that Marx devoted to the dominant ideology are the most numerous, this is because it was of decisive importance politically, in the period when he was writing, to combat the idealist prejudice according to which the dominant ideas could be "swept away" without *struggling against the material domination of the class whose dominance was strengthened by these ideas*. The fewness of the writings in which Marx deals with the development of revolutionary ideas is due no doubt, to the very small amount of experience available in his time that was relevant to the conditions for this development, the conditions enabling the proletariat to exercise its ideological *hegemony*.[61]

In any case, the analyses of Marx,[62] and also those of Lenin, devoted to the conditions for the development and appropriation of revolutionary ideas by the masses are relatively few. However, quite apart from the relative frequency or infrequency of a particular kind of writing in Marx's works, what accounts for the pushing into the background, in the Bolshevik ideological formation, of the decisive and indispensable role of action by the masses in the changing of social relations in general, and ideological relations in particular, is the *increasing role played in reality by the State*, which gave rise to the idea of the "revolution from above."

(c) The idea of the "revolution from above"

This idea appeared in fairly clear-cut form for the first time in the resolution of the Sixteenth Party Conference which ratified the First Five-Year Plan. This resolution declared that the building of socialism required the concentration not only of the forces of the Party and of the working class but *also*— what was new—of *the forces of the State*.[63] In this resolution the building of socialism was shown as calling not for the development, first and foremost, of the initiative of the masses, and consequently the withering-away of the state—what Marx meant when he showed that the State is *a power separated from the masses*, appropriating their forces in order to use these against them—but, on the contrary, and contradicting the lessons of the Paris Commune and of *The State and Revolution*, for *strengthening of the State*.[64]

In this way there emerged the thesis of a "revolution from above," to be accomplished not by the masses but by the State, on the "initiative" of the latter, to which the masses were merely to give their "support."

The idea of the "revolution from above" was explicitly present in the official account of the large-scale collectivization carried out from the end of 1929 on. Speaking of this, the *History of the C.P.S.U. (B.)* approved by the CC declared that, "The distinguishing feature of this revolution is that it was accomplished *from above*, on the initiative of the state, and directly supported *from below*. . . ."[65] However, we know from Marx and Engels that a "revolution" accomplished from above, even if it be supported by the masses, is no true revolution.[66]

Thus, at the end of the NEP period, the role of the State became primordial, both in reality (where it was determined by the evolution of class relations, which favored the development of the most up-to-date techniques and the State's centralization of financial resources) and in the Bolshevik ideological formation. At this second level we observe a profound transformation of this ideological formation, which entailed increasing departure from the positions of revolutionary Marxism as these were set out in the works of Marx, Engels, and Lenin (especially in *The State and Revolution*).[67]

It is not possible to review here all the passages in revolutionary Marxism which deal with the question of the State, especially in relation to the dictatorship of the proletariat. However, these passages and the theses they set forth are so important, and they were so thoroughly inhibited from the Bolshevik ideological formation from the end of NEP on, that a few of them must be mentioned.

The first point to be recalled is that "the state of the dictatorship of the proletariat" is only *that* in so far as it is, at one and the same time, a state *and not a state*, with the second aspect more important than the first, and becoming more and more important as proletarian power is strengthened. Hence Engels' remark in March 1875, in a letter to Bebel: "The whole talk about the state should be dropped, especially since the Commune, which was no longer a state in the proper sense of the word. . . . We would therefore propose to replace state everywhere [in the Gotha Programme] by *Gemeinwesen*, a good old German word which can very well convey the meaning of the French word '*commune*.' "[68]

Marx's observations in *The Civil War in France* are also highly significant. They deal with those features of the proletariat's political rule which make it possible for this rule to become increasingly *a non-state*, by causing the *separation* between the machinery of government and the masses to disappear. In the conjuncture of the class struggles at the end of the 1920s these very features (which had not been strongly present in the preceding years) tended themselves to disappear.

In *The Civil War in France*, drawing lessons from the Paris

Commune, Marx contrasted the forms of proletarian rule with state forms which make possible the oppression and exploitation of the working people. He shows how the "centralized state machinery," with its "military, bureaucratic" and other organs, "entoils [enmeshes] the living civil society like a boa constrictor." To this machinery there corresponds "the regulated plan of a state power, with a systematic and hierarchic division of labour." It gives rise to a "state interest" which is administered by a bureaucratic body of "state priests with exactly determined hierarchical functions." Marx sees this bureaucratic body as a "deadening incubus," "a host of state vermin," which "serves as a means of annihilating . . . all aspirations for the emancipation of the popular masses."[69]

Analyzing the Paris Commune, he shows that it not only brought about the elimination of the bourgeoisie's political power but was also a *revolution against the State itself*. He says explicitly: "This was . . . a revolution not against this or that, Legitimate, Constitutional, Republican or Imperialist form of state power. It was a revolution against the *State* itself, of this super-naturalist abortion of society," upon which is based a "centralised and organised governmental power usurping to be the master instead of the servant of society." It was because it was a revolution against the State, "the reabsorption of the state power by society . . . by the popular masses themselves, forming their own force instead of the organised force of their suppression," that the Commune was "the political form of their social emancipation," or "the political form . . . of the liberation of labour from the usurpation [slaveholding] of the monopolists of the means of labour." Marx explains that "the Commune is not the social movement of the working class . . . but the organised means of action." It "does not [do] away with the class struggles through which the working classes strive for the abolition of all classes, and therefore of all [class rule] . . . but it affords the rational medium in which the class struggle can run through its different phases in the most rational and humane way. It could start violent reactions and as violent revolutions. It begins the *emancipation of labour*—its great goal—by doing away with the unproductive and mischievous work of the state parasites. . . ."[70]

We know that, after October 1917, the Soviet political system, which at first reproduced many of the features of the Paris Commune, underwent changes which resulted in the masses becoming more and more separated from the organs of power. Lenin analyzed this evolution at the time and stressed the necessity of *returning to the principles of the Commune*—though, in the complex situation at the end of "war communism" this necessity seemed to him less urgent than the efforts which were indispensable if the country was to be saved from famine and chaos.[71] During the NEP period the need to go back to the principles of the Paris Commune was reasserted, but without this resulting in any definite proposals. It was mainly a question of "restricting" and "checking on" bureaucracy rather than of doing away with it. After 1928–1929, when rapid industrialization together with collectivization taking the form of a "revolution from above" were seen as the first-priority tasks, there was no more talk of the Paris Commune. On the contrary, emphasis was laid upon strengthening the State and on the authority of its functionaries, integrated in a highly hierarchical system of relations. This was a change in the Bolshevik ideological formation which inhibited an essential component of revolutionary Marxism.

This inhibition did not take place in the "realm of ideas," it was the result of *real changes* and, above all, of *uncontrolled contradictions* which led to *increasing use of coercion in dealing with the masses*. The strengthening of state forms of rule which accompanied this process, together with the support given by a section of the masses to the policy of collectivization and industrialization, did indeed make it possible to obtain a certain number of *remarkable material results*. This contributed to the development of *voluntarist illusions*, which we have already noted were characteristic of the period which saw the end of the NEP and the beginning of the implementation of the First Five-Year Plan.

(d) Juridical form of ownership and production relations

Identification of juridical forms of ownership with production relations, against which Lenin had warned the Party,[72] and which was related to the "illusions of jurisprudence" spoken of by Marx,[73] was, as we know, one of the essential features of the "simplified Marxism" which was tending to become dominant in the Bolshevik ideological formation. After the end of the 1920s the significance of a certain number of theses of revolutionary Marxism concerning the problems of forms of ownership and forms of appropriation was increasingly obscured. The development of Marx's views on this subject, therefore, could not but be "forgotten." This circumstance makes it necessary for me to recall what the nature of that development actually was.

Fundamentally, until the beginning of 1850, Marx and Engels stressed the role to be played by *state ownership* in the expropriation of the bourgeoisie. This was their position in the *Manifesto*. After 1850, however, formulations concerning state ownership became less and less frequent, and what Marx and Engels put in the forefront was the concept of *social appropriation*. Thus, in his 1895 introduction to *The Class Struggles in France*, Engels pointed out that it was in this book, and in *The 18th Brumaire* that Marx first declared himself for "the appropriation of the means of production by society."[74] Considering the role previously assigned by Marx to state ownership, and the contrast later so firmly made by him (especially after the Paris Commune) between "state" and "society," this formulation is highly significant.

However, the Bolshevik ideological formation as it was at the end of the 1920s "overlooked" this distinction, for practical purposes. The twofold result was that production relations were identified with ownership, and state ownership with social appropriation.

In fact, these identifications had seemed "obvious" to many Party members since the period of "war communism." This "obviousness" acquired new, decisive importance from the end of 1925 on, in connection with the increasing role of state intervention in the economic basis (the first annual plans, in the form of "control figures," the increase in investment by way of the state budget, etc.). Numerous undialectical formulations regarding the working of the state-owned enterprises made their appearance.

This happened, for example, in Stalin's political report of December 1925 to the Party's Fourteenth Congress. In this report, as we know, the problem of the socialist character of the state-owned enterprises was approached in an undialectical way, in the form of questions and answers, along the lines of "either this or that," and not of "this and also its opposite."[75]

Yet the problem lay precisely in the fact that, under conditions of the dictatorship of the proletariat, the state-owned enterprises could be *both socialist enterprises* (because of the leading role that the working class could play in them) and *state-capitalist enterprises*, in so far as the specific form of working-class rule is not a state form, and in so far as the bourgeoisie had not disappeared but only changed its form of existence. The bourgeoisie was also present in the state-owned enterprises because of the reproduction in them of the capitalist division of labor and the distribution relations corresponding thereto, and so, likewise, of "bourgeois right."[76]

Actually, the identification, purely and simply, of state ownership with social appropriation, and the failure to distinguish between form of ownership and production relations, prevented the making of analyses that were essential if a clear-eyed struggle was to be waged against the development of a new bourgeoisie within the enterprises and in the machinery of the State and the Party. This bourgeoisie was one of a new type, in that it did not possess *juridical private property*—a circumstance, which did not hinder it, however, from disposing, de facto, of the means of production.[77] And it is *facts* that count, not *juridical categories*.

(e) The contradictory forms of existence of commodity relations and the illusory "treatment" of the contradictions connected with these forms

During the struggle waged by the Bolshevik Party from 1926–1927 on in order to subject the development of the productive forces to an overall plan, a conception became strengthened which tended to *counterpose the "plan" to the market in an undialectical way*.

The consolidation in the Party's thinking of this ideological pair of terms, "plan" and "market," contributed to an increase in the internal contradictions of the Bolshevik ideological formation and blunted the capacity to analyze the real contradictions.

To grasp the nature of the problems involved here, we need to begin by reminding ourselves what the system of relations was that was formed between enterprises during the NEP period, and which was to be reproduced later in a new form. Basically, these were *commodity relations,* and that was true as well of the relations between the enterprises and their workers. The first set of relations took the form of *price* and the second the form of *wages*. These forms were engendered by the contradiction between the private and independent character ("working for oneself") of the work performed and the social character of production.

However, as a result of the development of Gosplan's activity and the framing of the economic plans, *commodity relations assumed two contradictory forms*. On the one hand, a form with prices and wages which seemed to proceed from the "free" functioning of the "market" and the forces which come into conflict therein; on the other, a form corresponding to the fixing "by the plan" of prices, wages, and (in principle) quantities of goods to be produced.

In so far as commodity relations survived, with the conditions ensuring their reproduction, these were *two forms of existence of commodity relations*. One of these forms implied that the economic basis was operating in comparative independence; the other, that the operation of the economic basis was subjected, more or less completely and really, to *political imperatives*. These were two forms of motion developing on the basis of one and the same contradiction—that which was expressed in the existence of prices and wages. One of these forms tended to "resolve" the contradiction a posteriori (*ex post*), the other to "resolve" it a priori (*ex ante*). These forms of motion, based upon the same contradiction, were therefore, although contradictory, not mutually exclusive. What tended to separate them was that the first form ensured *its own reproduction* whereas the second *could* help to prepare (given conditions going beyond "planning" and involving transformation of the production processes themselves) *its own disappearance*, by helping to make production a *directly political activity: direct production for society, which implies a plan that is no longer based upon commodity relations but results from cooperation between the producers on the scale of society*.[78]

Correct treatment of the *contradictory unity of two forms of commodity relations* requires that the existence of this unity and of these contradictions be acknowledged, and, consequently, that the "plan" (in the conditions in which it is formulated and put into effect) *not* be presented formally as a category "external" to commodity relations, as the realization of "the essence of organization."

In the conditions of the fierce struggle that was waged from the end of the 1920s on to ensure "domination by the plan," however, an ideological slippage took place which tended to present this "domination," even when prices and wages still existed, as *equivalent to the "abolition" of commodity relations*. This ideological slippage was also connected with the strengthening of the state bourgeoisie in process of formation (constituted within the apparatuses of the State and the Party) through practices which gave priority to *accumulation* over *the initiatives of the direct producers,* to dead labor over *living labor.* This ideological slippage was conditioned theoretically by inhibition of the primacy of contradiction over unity.[79]

The idea of economic planning as "abolition" of commodity relations "obliterates" one of the essential conclusions to be drawn from Marx's analyses, namely, that commodity and money relations can disappear only as the result of a long struggle culminating in an overturn of production relations, political relations, and ideological relations, and "the appropriation [by man] of his own general productive power."[80]

This "obliteration" implies that the contradictory unity of the two forms of existence of commodity relations is now thought of as signifying opposition between two "objects," the "plan" and the "market," and that decisive significance is attributed to this opposition. By seeing the "contradiction between plan and market" in this way one loses sight of the primary importance of class contradictions as well as of the conditions, objective and subjective, necessary for the disappearance of commodity and money relations and the development of production which is directly social, and therefore dominated by politics.

The ideological forms which developed under these conditions tended to identify the struggle between the capitalist road and the socialist road with the struggle between the "anarchy" of the market and "harmonious development" ensured by planning. These ideological elements are seen explicitly at work in the writings of Preobrazhensky, who contrasted "the law of value" (associated with "private economy") and "the socialist planning principle" (associated with the "state sector" of the Soviet economy).[81]

According to this economist, the extension of planning is bound up with the struggle "to increase the means of production belonging to the proletarian state," so that, under the conditions of the NEP, when a non-state economy existed, it was necessary to struggle "for the maximum primitive socialist accumulation."[82]

Thus, instead of the real problem of the struggle between

the capitalist road and the socialist road, we find formulated, undialectically, the contrast between the law of value and the "planning principle," between private economy and state economy. *The extension of the latter is somehow expected automatically to inhibit commodity, money, and capitalist relations,* and engender an entirely new reality, analysis of which is no longer to be a matter for political economy (or for historical materialism), but for "a different science which is itself transitional between political economy and social technology,"[83] one which replaces analysis and treatment of contradictions with handling of problems of "organization."

The ideas expressed by Preobrazhensky were formally rejected by the Bolshevik Party, but, in fact, the conception employed in *The New Economics* influenced the Party to an increasing extent. There developed toward the end of the 1920s *an ideology which regarded the plan as a "form of organization" that was capable by itself of "transcending" social contradictions.* This ideology helped to "subordinate" the treatment of class contradictions to the "fulfillment" of the objectives of economic plans, and brought in its train some profoundly negative social and economic consequences, especially in strengthening the influence of the "technicians," "organizers," and "planners."

In an apparently paradoxical way, the myth of a plan capable of "transcending" social contradictions helped to strengthen *the monetary and financial illusions* which had already developed at the beginning of the NEP.[84] An ideological element thus took shape which was utterly alien to Marxism, even in its most superficial forms.

The strengthening of monetary and financial illusions was manifested vigorously in 1927–1928. It led to the idea that the problems of industrialization would be "solved" as soon as the financial resources needed for industrialization had been obtained. This "monetary illusion" caused the higher political authorities to fail to reckon with the indications provided by the forecasts of material balances—to regard it as unimportant that these forecasts revealed the prospect of a series of shortages and bottlenecks making materially impracticable some of the projects which it was possible to "finance." From the spring of 1927, under pressure from increasingly acute contradictions and the "state-of-emergency" atmosphere which was developing, the monetary illusion became more and more dominant: money now being *formally* "subordinated" to the "plan," the power to "deal with contradictions" which was attributed to the latter seemed to reinforce the illusory "power" of money. Hence the surprising result that, through the combination of planning with money, *exchange value came to predominate over use value.* In this way a component of the Bolshevik ideological formation appeared which encouraged the Party leaders to set targets that were materially unrealizable. Part of the planning apparatus, more directly at grips with the material problems involved, tried to oppose this tendency—but less and less vigorously, because such opposition was soon labeled "anti-Soviet activity."

In 1930 the role of the monetary illusion was such that the Gosplan journal published an article in which this appeared: "The planning of investments is based on costs expressed in money terms. The elements of material and technological concretisation are almost entirely absent. The plan presents exclusively the money credits assigned for building and equipment: as for *what* equipment will be needed, and *when* such-and-such machinery will be required, that will become clear only in the course of the execution of the plan."[85]

Closely linked with the ideological factor mentioned was the slogan which appeared at that time: "tempos decide everything." According to this formula, the higher the growth rates, the better the situation. This slogan complemented the monetary illusion. It expressed the ruling preoccupation with "quantity": quantitative growth was more important than the changing of social relations, and the latter was appreciated essentially for the "quantitative" effects which were expected to follow from it.[86]

In reality, the stress upon "quantity" is also, in another form, a feature of the "technicist" ideology. That these ideological forms could play so important a role in the system of ideas and in the practice of the Bolshevism of the late 1920s testifies to the depth of the political and ideological crisis resulting from the breakdown of the worker-peasant alliance which was beginning to happen at that time. This crisis incited to a "flight forward," bound up with the illusion that, thanks to technology, organization, planning, and money "subordinated" to planning, a whole series of objectives would become attainable.

And so the internal contradictions of the Bolshevik ideological formation were deepened, and positions were strengthened that were in conflict with revolutionary Marxism—with the Marxism-Leninism which was the theoretical basis of Bolshevism.

At the end of the 1920s and the beginning of the 1930s, the existence of the contradictions in the Bolshevik ideological formation which have been discussed above *contributed* to the strengthening of other ideological and political elements that were also alien to revolutionary Marxism. These were the *ideological and political effects* of the contradictions mentioned, and it is these that we must now examine.

II. The ideological and political effects of the development of the internal contradictions of the Bolshevik ideological formation

What is covered by the expression "ideological and political effects" must be explained through two preliminary observations:

(1) I here call "ideological effects" a certain number of changes in the Bolshevik ideological formation which were connected with the previous ones, in that they were "necessary" in order to maintain a certain coherence among the increasingly dominant ideological forms and between these and the Party's practices. These effects concerned mainly the status and structure of *dialectical materialism*.

(2) I here call "political effects" the consequences entailed,

on the political plane, by the growing role which the changes already examined assigned to certain ideological notions such as that of the Party's "monolithic" character. More broadly, this expression refers to the *political role* of the Bolshevik ideological formation in its *changed* form.

Essentially, the changes in the Bolshevik ideological formation tended to inhibit some of the teachings of Marxism-Leninism, to *reduce Bolshevism's ability to use revolutionary Marxism as an instrument for analyzing reality*. Under these conditions, the Bolshevik ideological formation in its changed form served, with ever greater frequency, to *"justify" after the act the adoption of political lines which were no longer based on a rigorous concrete analysis of reality*. It then functioned as a "system of legitimation," as a grid of ideological notions which one "applied" to reality, and not as a set of concepts to be used in a living analysis. This was one of the consequences of the appearance in the Soviet Union of a "simplified" or "congealed" form of Marxism,[87] which departed from revolutionary Marxism.

In the last analysis, of course, the changes in the Bolshevik ideological formation and its role resulted from objective contradictions, and from class contradictions first and foremost. In their turn, however, through not having been subjected to critical analysis, these changes reacted upon the Soviet social formation by impoverishing the Marxism upon which the Bolshevik Party relied, and favoring both a mechanistic view of reality and interventions which had effects other than those the Party expected—effects of major political importance.

We must stress here an essential point, namely, that these "political effects" did not apply only in the USSR, but also tended to operate *on the international plane*: for the Bolshevik ideological formation, with the changes that it underwent, was the ideological form through which the Comintern and its various sections defined, as a rule, their political line. The changes in the Bolshevik ideological formation nevertheless played such a role internationally only in so far as they corresponded, at bottom, to the types of relations which the Comintern's sections maintained with the realities of their own countries, and to the practices to which these sections were committed. The best proof (*a contrario*) of this is offered by the fact that the changes in the Bolshevik ideological formation and in the ideology of the Comintern failed to produce the same effects (development of sectarianism and of *ouvriériste* and ultraleft attitudes) in the Chinese Communist Party (which was linked increasingly with the peasantry and engaged in revolutionary war) as it did in the Communist Parties of Europe and America. That became quite clear after 1935, when the Chinese Communists developed their revolutionary line on a broad front, under the leadership of Mao Tse-tung.

(a) Organic totality, interdependence, and contradictions

Among the various changes in the Bolshevik ideological formation which ensured a certain degree of coherence among the ideological notions which tended to become dominant from the late 1920s, the most important was the affirmation of a *principle of totality*. This was, indeed, the *first principle* affirmed by Stalin in his exposition of "the Marxist dialectical method."[88]

According to this principle, dialectics regards nature as "a connected and integral whole, in which things, phenomena, are organically connected with, dependent on and determined by each other."[89]

"Nature" is thus presented as an organic totality in which coherence and unity take precedence over contradiction. This being so, one cannot understand any of the changes undergone by the objects and phenomena which make up nature if these changes are "isolated from surrounding phenomena."

Correlatively with the idea of an *organic totality* there is thus affirmed an *interdependence* of phenomena, presented through the concept of an *environment* which is supposed to condition every phenomenon.[90] External causes of change take precedence of internal causes. When, *only at the end* of his exposition of the "principal features" of Marxist dialectics,

Stalin says that "internal contradictions are inherent in all things and phenomena of nature," and that the conflict of opposites "constitutes the internal content of the process of development,"[91] this appears as *a mere supplement to a body of principles already set forth*, and is not articulated with them. It serves as a mode of "observation" and not as a *principle of explanation*.

The fundamental question of the *unity of opposites* is thus not raised, so that the propositions put forward in Stalin's essay are remote from those which Lenin formulates in his *Philosophical Notebooks*, especially when he says: "In brief, dialectics can be defined as the doctrine of the unity of opposites."[92]

The political consequences of the conception of dialectical materialism expressed by Stalin are all the more important because, after describing "the Marxist dialectical method" in relation to "nature" in the way we have seen, he proceeds to "the extension of the principles of dialectical method to the study of social life."[93] The ways in which this extension is effected are not very explicit, but Stalin's formulations, including those devoted to historical materialism, show that "society," too, is to be seen as an organic whole, the development of which is due to external causes operating as an environment.

The "development of society" thus appears to depend mainly upon the changing of its relations with nature, these relations consisting above all in the productive forces, so that the development of the latter is seen as the driving force of social changes.[94]

(1) The fight for socialism and the fight for "organization"

The notion of *organic totality* presumes that *unity* takes precedence over *contradiction*. The more this notion became dominant in Bolshevik writings of the late 1920s and the early 1930s, the more "society" appeared to be an "organization" or a "system," so that the Party's interventions in the social process tended to be thought of not in terms of dealing with contradictions but in terms of "measures of organization and planning" of the social process. Hence the slogan of the 1930s: "Organization decides everything." Along with this there appeared many formulations resembling those of Bogdanov[95] (whose theses were nevertheless formally condemned). But this "convergence" must not lead us to an idealist interpretation which would one-sidedly stress the Bogdanovist "origin" of these formulations.

To be sure, the influence of Bogdanov's ideas upon many Bolsheviks is undeniable, and it is not hard to find formulas directly borrowed (perhaps "unconsciously") from Bogdanov. Thus, in his *Dialectical and Historical Materialism,* Stalin used a typically Bogdanovist expression when he speaks of the "organising . . . value of new ideas."[96]

What is essential, however, is the set of social conditions which caused ideas resembling Bogdanov's to acquire ever greater importance from the late 1920s on. These conditions were due to a certain situation in the class struggle which accorded decisive weight to the State as the apparent "organizer" of social changes.[97]

(2) The dominance of unity over contradiction

The thesis of the dominance of unity over contradiction (inherent in the idea of "society" functioning as a "totality" whose transformations are determined by changes in its relations with the "environment") holds a central position in the altered conception of "dialectical materialism" which emerged (implicitly or explicitly) after the late 1920s. This thesis of the primacy of unity over contradiction tended to play a decisive ideological role in so far as it was "extended" or "applied" to whatever might be considered as constituting "an object." It thus tended to inhibit Lenin's thesis that "the splitting of a single whole and the cognition of its contradictory parts . . . is the *essence* (one of the 'essentials,' one of the principal, if not the principal, characteristics or features) of dialectics."[98]

The thesis of the primacy of unity over contradiction is "rightist-leftist" in character. Depending on the conjuncture of the class struggle, it functions either as a "conciliatory" thesis providing a "basis" for renunciation of struggle, especially inside the Party (in the name of *unity at any price*), or, as was the case at the end of the 1920s, as a thesis providing a "basis" for sectarianism, for "ruthless struggle" (in the name of *a unity which seems preservable only by excluding all contradiction*). The first type of effect is rightist, while the second looks as though it is "left," by virtue of the "rigorousness" of its consequences: it implies *negation of the diversity of contradictions, and of their universality.*

In the situation of extreme tension which existed at the end of the NEP period and at the beginning of the 1930s, the thesis of the primacy of unity over contradiction was accepted by the majority of the revolutionary elements in the Party and the working class, and it developed "ultraleft" effects.

A few concrete examples will serve to show what these effects were in the conjuncture of the period.

The most immediate effect (which was one of "legitimation") concerned the *conditions in which the Party worked*: it corresponded to the assertion of the *political thesis* of the necessarily *monolithic* character of the Party.

The theme of the "monolithic" character of the Bolshevik Party was actually tackled in a systematic way at the end of 1928. It played a key role in Stalin's speech of November 19.[99] In this speech he correctly pointed out the difference of principle separating the Bolshevik Party from the Social Democratic parties (in their class basis, in their ideology, and in the organizational forms resulting from these). However, when speaking about the way the Party worked, he "summed up" this difference *not by referring to the role of democratic centralism but by mentioning the necessarily "monolithic" character of the Party.*[100] But the idea of a "monolithic" party not only conflicts with the experience of Marxism-Leninism, it is illusory. The Party is inevitably traversed by contradictions, especially by those forced upon it by its role as the instrument through which the proletariat is able to *unite the broad masses under its leadership,* so that, in one way or another, the interests of the different strata making up these masses produce an effect within the Party. Divergent points of view necessarily appear when these contradictory interests have to be evaluated, and the problem is how to arrive correctly at an agreement between views reflecting the differing aspirations of masses whose support is needed if the revolution is to continue to progress. This was why Lenin wrote, in his *Letter to the Congress*: "Our Party relies on two classes and therefore its instability would be possible and its downfall inevitable if there were no agreement between these two classes."[101]

If the "monolithic principle" is carried to its logical conclusion, the Party deprives itself of the means of uniting the broad masses, because it is *led to reject, in practice, the principle of democratic centralism*. This latter principle presupposes, indeed, *that different ideas can be centralized* after being examined and critically discussed. Genuine application of this principle demands recognition of the need to ensure the *contradictory unity of centralization and democracy*, and of the fact that *the first term can possess meaning only under the domination of the second.* "Monolithism" rejects this principle in the name of a formal "unity" which is to be secured, in an always illusory way, by means of *ruthless* struggle. This struggle to obtain "perfect" unity tends to weaken the dictatorship of the proletariat, *isolate* the working class from the rest of the masses, intensify administrative coercion of the masses, and develop the machinery of repression.

In the short term, one-sided stress on unity and centralism at the expense of democracy may make it possible to win quick successes, especially in the field of industry and technology. In the long term, it produces effects which are harmful to the working class, and even to the leading role of the Party. The strengthening of the machinery of repression tends to develop its independence of the Party, and to increase its interference in Party life, especially in connection with purges. Eventually, therefore, the fight for "monolithism" becomes *a weapon in the class struggle*, a weapon which, after it has made it possible "to solve rapidly" a certain number of problems, serves the bourgeois forces in society, because it hinders consolidation of the Party's leading role and its strengthening through clear ideological struggle.

While the thesis of the primacy of unity over contradiction serves to "legitimize" a "monolithic" conception of the Party, it is obviously not what "produces" this conception. The latter develops on the basis of *objective conditions*: it is essentially a consequence of the development of class struggles which the Party is unable to direct, and which it can affect only by strengthening its unity through coercion.

This was shown by the changes which were introduced into the way the Bolshevik Party worked after the Kronstadt rebellion, the strikes at the beginning of 1921, and the peasant revolts of the winter of 1920–1921, in a period when Lenin said of the peasantry that "their dissatisfaction with the proletarian dictatorship is mounting."[102] In a period such as that was, Lenin considered that the rules which had governed the Party's functioning until then should be modified, and oppositional activity within the Party reduced.[103] It was then that measures were adopted which *restricted* this activity. Nevertheless, opposition was not *forbidden* but *regulated*, and means of expression were provided for those who disagreed with the majority.[104] There was then no question of any "monolithic" conception of the Party. However, the measures taken in the particularly difficult situation at the beginning of 1921 could serve as the starting point for practices aiming at "monolithism."

Actually, all through the NEP period, opportunities to express divergent views within the Party were being restricted more and more, so that gradually they ceased to have anything in common with what had once been normal practice. The immediate reason for this change in political relations was the Party's weakness in the rural areas. This was seen as the sign of a still dangerous situation which gave reason for seriously limiting the scope for discussion in the Party. This situation *tended to obscure the idea that it could be right to swim against the stream*. It often caused oppositionists themselves to renounce the expression of their views, and even to say that they could not be in the right "against the Party." In this way a certain practice became established, of which Trotsky gave an example when, while not repudiating his views, he nevertheless declared, before the Thirteenth Congress (in 1924): "Comrades, none of us wishes to be right, or can be right, against his Party . . . I know that one cannot be right against the Party. One can be right only with the Party and through the Party."[105] Although discussions did still take place during the NEP period, none of them was *carried through to the end*: disciplinary measures were taken before the theoretical roots of the divergences had been revealed and the Party as a whole had given its judgment on the substance of the problems involved. The main reason for this was not—at the beginning, at least—the "disciplinary" measures applied to oppositionists, or the repression to which they were subjected. What was dominant, and explains why the discussions were not carried through to the end, or were conducted in language comprehensible only to a few, was the concern common to all sides to affirm the unity of the Party, a concern dictated above all by the Party's difficult position in the countryside, and fear lest this should threaten the Soviet power.

The result was that *the unity which was achieved remained formal. It was not based on an ideological struggle which could have made for a unity that was profoundly real,* and consequently the same debates kept on starting up again. The conception of unity which was formed in this way assumed acceptance, implicitly at least, of the primacy of unity over contradiction. This was the terrain on which arose the thesis of "monolithism," an idealist thesis which denied the universality of contradictions and the need for living unity in the Party.

The principle of "monolithism" was asserted when the situation became especially dangerous, owing to the peasants' resistance to the emergency measures. During the years of extreme tension connected with the collectivization of agriculture "from above," this principle became a dogma, for the tension caused the Party to unite its forces as much as possible, not on the basis of broad discussion but in the form of obedience or constraint.[106]

(3) *The tendency to identify the Party with the State and with the proletariat*

The specific conditions under which the Soviet revolution developed caused a tendency to appear very soon which, in imagination, identified the Bolshevik Party with the proletariat. These conditions were, especially, those which Lenin described when he said in 1919 that the soviets, instead of being "organs of government *by the working people*, are in fact organs of government *for the working people* by the advanced section of the proletariat. . . ."[107]

This phrase of Lenin's reflected a real state of affairs. He was to refer to it again and again, until his very last writings, and to appeal for the situation to be changed. This appeal was still finding echoes in the NEP years, with the efforts that were made to "revitalize" the soviets.[108]

Lenin's words clearly acknowledge that there was a *difference* between "the advanced section of the proletariat" and the working people as a whole. He did not identify the one with the other, even while claiming that the Party was the *instrument* of the dictatorship of the proletariat. Many of Lenin's writings emphasize that *this instrument cannot be identified with the proletariat, and that contradictions may develop between them, contradictions which only the practice of a mass line can prevent from deepening.*

While the concrete problems raised by the relations between the Party and the class were not "solved" by the formulations of the years 1919–1922, their existence was, nevertheless, admitted, and some elements of solution (though necessarily still only provisional) were put forward. In 1923 and the following years these problems continued to be debated, but the terms in which these debates were conducted did not usually help to clarify them. Indeed, the tendency to "identify" the Party with the proletariat grew stronger and stronger. Thus, the Twelfth Party Congress adopted a resolution declaring that "the dictatorship of the working class cannot be assured otherwise than *in the form of dictatorship of its leading vanguard, i.e., the Communist Party.*"[109]

This identification implied that *recognition of the role and place of contradiction was replaced by the thesis of an abstractly presented unity,* denying the existence of differences and contradictions.

It is significant that one of the most systematic defenders of this conception was Zinoviev, who, as we know, wavered between openly rightist positions and "ultraleft" ones. One of the passages in which the *identity* between the State, the working people, and the Party was asserted most formally by Zinoviev reads as follows: "The State is the workers, the advanced section of the workers, the vanguard. We are the State!"[110]

In 1924 Zinoviev gave formal expression to the same theme when he wrote:

> The consensus of opinion about the dictatorship of the proletariat can be expressed in the following propositions. It is the dictatorship of a class if we look at the matter from the social and class point of view. It is the dictatorship of the Soviet state, a Soviet dictatorship, if we look at the matter from the point of view of *juridical* form, i.e., from the specifically state point of view. It is the dictatorship of a party if we look at the same question from the point of view of leadership, from the point of view of the internal mechanism of the whole vast machine of a transitional society.[111]

This formulation implies *identification* of the dictatorship of the proletariat with the dictatorship of the Soviet state and the dictatorship of the Party. It *obliterates,* in illusory fashion, the problems which arise from contradictions between class and Party, between class and state, and between state and Party. Such an identification can be conceived only if one's theoretical premise is the primacy of unity, and even of identity, over contradiction.

In a number of his writings of 1924 Stalin opposed this identification and reaffirmed the thesis that the Party was the "instrument of the dictatorship of the proletariat." At that time, however, the conditions necessary if the Party was to remain that "instrument" were not actually stated.[112]

At the beginning of 1926, in *Problems of Leninism,* Stalin

returned to this question, again refusing to identify the Party with the proletariat:

> Although the Party carries out the dictatorship of the proletariat, and in this sense the dictatorship of the proletariat is in essence the "dictatorship" of its Party, this does not mean that the "dictatorship of the Party" (its leading role) is identical with the dictatorship of the proletariat, that the former is equal in scope to the latter. . . . Whoever identifies the leading role of the Party with the dictatorship of the proletariat substitutes "dictatorship" of the Party for the dictatorship of the proletariat.[113]

Stalin went on to admit, explicitly, that contradictions could develop between the Party and the working class if certain conditions were not fulfilled.[114]

When, however, at the end of the NEP period, contradictions became acute between the Party and the various sections of the people, including the working class, *these contradictions were not frankly analyzed,* but passed over in silence.

This silence implicitly accepted the thesis which had been explicitly rejected, identifying the Party with the proletariat. This implicit identification gradually became dominant, providing a theoretical "basis" for the practice of "revolution from above."

The process of identifying, in imagination, the State with the Party and both with the proletariat (and later the Party with the whole people), by continuing to develop, in objective conditions which aggravated the contradictions between the Party and the masses, led increasingly to the idea that any opposition to the Party line (and even any criticism of the line) must be due to the activity of "enemies of the people."

Given these conditions, asserting the primacy of unity and denying the universality of contradiction resulted increasingly in denial also of the existence of contradictions among the people. Thereafter, all opposition seemed to originate in *external* contradictions, connected with the imperialist environment. Any divergence of view *was* opposition, and any opposition was *the act of a foreign agent.* Such conceptions were the product of objective contradictions the existence of which was denied, they were determined by practices which placed the Party above the masses, but the thesis of the primacy of unity over contradiction (presented as a "Marxist" thesis) was the *theoretical condition* thanks to which the social practices in question could be thought of as arising from the needs of a proletarian policy.

(4) *The tendency to identify the Party with Marxist theory*

The thesis of the primacy of unity over contradiction was the condition making it possible to twist Lenin's thesis on the revolutionary proletarian Party, to *change* the thesis of the *union* (always contradictory) between Marxist theory and the Party[115] into a thesis of the *unity* (without contradictions) of these two. This change tended to come about as soon as the principle was accepted that the Party was necessarily "always right,"[116] thereby withdrawing the Party from criticism by the masses—and the Party leadership from criticism by the rank and file. When this happened, as it did in the USSR in the late 1920s, the Party alone had the right to state what was or was not "theoretically correct," and, in order to eliminate any risk of "divergent interpretations," to concentrate "authority in matters of theory" in the Party leadership. This concentration reduced the possibility of genuine development of Marxism, even if the Party leadership was defending a revolutionary line, for this development calls for broad ideological class struggle and the opportunity for different analyses to be debated.[117] The tendency to equate the Party with Marxist theory (of which it is seen as the embodiment) leads, if persisted in, to the weakening of Marxism. The existence of such a tendency in the USSR had objective bases, as we know, but it did not seem "acceptable" except on the basis of the primacy of unity over contradiction.

At the same time, the identification of the Party with Marxist theory caused the Party to be less and *less alert to initiatives and ideas coming from the masses*, though such alertness is essential if theory is to be enriched and mistakes put right. A process thus began which caused the Party to act no longer as an educator itself in need of educating, but as an "authority" *giving orders*. The development of this form of action favored the use of repression against some sections of the people, so as to "bring" them to follow the Party's directives, even when they were not ready to do this.

(5) *The identification of theory with reality*

The transformation of dialectical materialism by inhibiting the primacy of contradiction over unity brought with it the possibility of another ideological effect, namely, the identification of theory with reality. The need for practice and scientific experiment tended consequently to be denied: theory was supposed to be capable, by itself, of "saying what is." When it functioned in this way, dialectical materialism in its changed form appeared to be a "science of the sciences," capable of deciding what was "science" and what was not, and seeming even to offer the possibility of "deducing" scientific knowledge from its own principles. This was the function that "dialectical materialism" tended to fulfill in and after the 1930s, when it served to "settle" scientific disputes—for example, to "legitimise" Lysenko's conceptions in the name of abstract principles.[118]

The identification of theory with reality, if taken to its logical conclusion, is equivalent to an idealist position: it eliminates the revolutionary implications of dialectical materialism and gives victory to a fundamentally conservative notion, namely: "All that is real is rational." Dialectics tends to operate no longer as an instrument for criticizing and changing "what is," but as an instrument for legitimizing it.[119] When we analyze the way "dialectical materialism" functioned in the USSR after the end of the 1920s, we see that a tendency pointing in this direction became more and more active. The objective basis for this tendency was the system of social contradictions which was developing at that time, and the place that the Bolshevik Party occupied in that system through the practices in which it engaged, especially because of the weakness of its relations with popular initiatives, starting with those of the peasant masses.

(b) The tendency to reduce Marxism to a form of "evolutionism"

Toward the end of the 1920s an "evolutionist" interpretation of Marx's theory dominated the Bolshevik Party more and more. To appreciate the change that this entailed in the Bolshevik ideological formation we need to recall that Marx's theory is something quite different from an enumeration or description of the "stages" through which every "society" *necessarily has to pass.*[120]

Marx categorically repudiated this interpretation, as when he replied, in 1877, to criticisms of his theory formulated by the Russian writer N. Mikhailovsky.[121] Speaking of this writer, Marx says:

> For him it is absolutely necessary to change my sketch of the origin of capitalism in Western Europe into an historico-philosophical theory of Universal Progress, fatally imposed on all peoples, regardless of the historical circumstances in which they find themselves, ending finally in that economic system which assures both the greatest amount of productive labour and the fullest development of man. But I must beg his pardon. This is to do me both too much honour and too much discredit. In various places in *Capital* I have alluded to the destiny which overtook the plebeians of ancient Rome. They were originally free peasants cultivating each on his own account his own parcel of land. In the course of Roman history they were expropriated. The same movement which separated them from their means of production and subsistence brought about not only the formation of the great landed estates but that of great holdings of money capital as well. Thus, one fine morning there were on the one hand free men deprived of everything except their labour power and, on the other, to exploit this labour, the holders of all acquired wealth. What happened? The Roman proletarians became, not wage-earners, but an idle *mob* . . . and beside them there developed a mode of production which was not capitalist

but based on slavery. Thus, events which were strikingly analogous, but which took place in different historical circumstances, led to entirely dissimilar results. By studying each of these evolutions separately, and by comparing them afterwards, the key to these phenomena can easily be found, but one will never succeed with the "open sesame" of an historico-philosophical theory of which the supreme virtue consists in its being *suprahistorical*.[122]

Marx here comes out categorically against any interpretation of his analyses which tends to make of them an "historicophilosophical theory" imposing on every people the necessity of passing through a determined succession of modes of production. In his correspondence with Vera Zasulich, Marx was to condemn once more, in 1881, the idea of an "historical fatalism" making every people pass through a succession of the same modes of production.[123]

Marx's theory rules out any "general theory of the evolution of human societies," because it recognizes that social reality is characterized not by the existence at each moment of *one* simple contradiction but, on the contrary, by a *real multiplicity of contradictions*.

The reduction of the movement of history to a *succession* of simple contradictions, necessarily engendering each other in a predetermined order, corresponds not to the movement of materialist dialectics but to that of Hegelian dialectics. *Though the latter does not rule out an apparent diversity of contradictions, it assumes that all the contradictions present at one time in a "society" are merely the "expression" of one fundamental contradiction.* Such a conception leads to the idea of "linear" and "irreversible" development.

The Marxist characterization of social formations by the existence of a *real multiplicity of contradictions* implies, on the contrary, that *systems of specific contradictions* may take shape, which develop under *particular conditions,* and in which this or that element may, at any given moment, play a *dominant* role.[124] The real multiplicity of contradictions conditons the *possibility of several paths of "development,"* of periods of "stagnation" or "retreat," the form and duration of

which *depend on the way in which the class struggles con-*
cretely proceed, especially on the ideological plane.

At the end of the nineteenth century and the beginning of
the twentieth, under the impact of the *reformist practices* of
the principal parties belonging to the Second International,
the influence of idealism tended to obscure the radical difference between Marx's theory and any sort of "evolutionism."
Thereafter, all reforms were conceived as being "contribu-
tions" to a fated "evolution." The influence of the evolutionist
ideas of Darwinism and Positivism obviously helped, also, to
"inhibit" the specific nature of Marx's analyses, the impossibility of reducing them to any sort of evolutionism.

Marxism-Leninism eliminates everything which, by distort-
ing Marx's theory, may reduce it to an evolutionism. But a
tendency to carry out such a "reduction" made itself felt when
the Bolshevik Party took the road of "revolution from above."
Some of Stalin's formulations encapsulate the conceptions on
this point which gradually became dominant in the Bolshevik
Party. Examples are the formulation which refers to the idea of
a succession[125] of modes of production, *presented as*
"natural" (from which follows the idea of the need, always, for
"steps forward"), and the formulation according to which a
retreat to an earlier phase would be "senseless, stupid and
unnatural."[126]

This idea makes of history *a succession of linear advances*
which take place irreversibly. It does not allow it to be seen
that *struggle between the socialist road and the capitalist*
road is inevitable. It tends to render inconceivable the possibility of a "restoration of capitalism," or to allow this to be
conceived only as a consequence of external aggression.
Thereby, the capacity of the Party and the masses to combat
the danger of capitalist restoration due to internal social forces
is gravely compromised.

To the effects of the changes in the Bolshevik ideological
formation which have just been discussed we must add those
which, while connected with those changes, resulted mainly
from the strengthening of the *"ouvriériste"* component in Bolshevism.

(c) The development of the effects of the ouvriériste *component in the Bolshevik ideological formation*[127]

In the second half of the nineteenth century a line of demarcation separated the *proletarian* positions of revolutionary Marxism from the *ouvriériste* positions of other components of the organised labor movement.[128] Revolutionary Marxism gives primacy to the *political role* which the proletariat must play in order to bring about change in the relations of production. It shows that, if it is to play this role, the proletariat must fulfill a function of *leadership,* and that it can do this because there are *other classes* which can be its *allies* in the socialist revolution. *Ouvriériste* conceptions refuse to consider the primacy of the political role of the working class. They treat as secondary the question of class alliances and emphasize *one-sidedly* the defense of the workers' immediate interests—or else they appear to assume that, *in any case,* the working class, by virtue of its place in production and its specific forms of organization, stands "spontaneously" at the head of the revolutionary processes in countries where industry plays a sufficiently considerable role.

Ouvriérisme can take on many different forms. Its existence is not necessarily obvious to members of the organizations of the working class who want to fight for socialism. From this point of view, the fight which Marx and Engels had to wage against the *ouvriérisme* of Lassalle and his supporters is highly significant. A quick survey of this fight will enable us to appreciate better the nature of the contradictions which developed within the Bolshevik ideological formation with special acuteness at the end of the 1920s.

A particularly explicit *ouvriériste* formulation is to be found in the draft program which was produced to serve as the basis, in 1875, for the formation of a socialist workers' party in Germany, and of which Marx wrote an important critique.[129] He attacked a paragraph in the draft which declared that "the emancipation of labour must be the work of the working class, relatively to which all other classes are only *one reactionary mass*."[130] To this formulation Marx counterposed that of the *Communist Manifesto*, which, while describing the proletariat as being the only "really revolutionary class" confronting the bourgeoisie, recognizes the *dual nature* of the "middle classes," including the peasantry, who are *both* reactionary in so far as they depend upon the old modes of production and revolutionary in view of their "impending transfer into the proletariat."[131]

Marx stresses the contrast between these two formulations. He shows that statements such as that which figures in the Gotha Program, presenting the proletariat as the *only* revolutionary class, entail serious consequences. One of them is the *isolating* of the working class, *depriving it of allies,* and so *preventing it from playing a leading role.* Another is the orienting of the Party towards a policy which is concerned mainly with the immediate material advantages that the working class can derive from its struggles, since it is assumed not to be concerned with relations of alliance with other classes. Under these conditions the predominant political line can easily assume a *statist* character.[132] Since the working class does not practice a policy of alliances, *it has to impose the effects of its policy on the other classes, and, for this purpose, to use state coercion*—which actually implies an unavowed "alliance" with the *agents of this coercion*. Finally, the "state framework" of the activity assigned to the working class, and the *material privileges* which it is thus called upon to win for itself, serve as the basis for a *nationalist orientation*,[133] breaking with the internationalist demands which are inherent in any revolutionary proletarian struggle.

The existence of an *ouvriériste* component in the Bolshevik ideological formation manifested itself concretely on more than one occasion. One of its material bases was the quite special integration of the Party in the working class, which was a consequence of the particular magnitude assumed, in Russia at the beginning of the twentieth century, by struggles peculiar to the working class. This *ouvriériste* component had for its theoretical condition the specific role often ascribed in the Party to the technological forms of industrial production in the formation of class consciousness.[134]

Historically, the *ouvriériste* component in the Bolshevik ideological formation was more or less influential depending on the conjuncture of the class struggle. It grew strong during "war communism," when Bukharin, Trotsky, and others spoke in a one-sided way of the working-class character of the Soviet state, gave priority to production, and underestimated the requirements of the struggle needed in order to *win the masses* for the aims of the revolution.[135] It grew weaker at the beginning of the NEP period, when the necessity of strengthening the worker-peasant alliance became vital for the Soviet power (although for many Party members this was seen as only a temporary, tactical necessity, not a strategic necessity for the whole period of transition to socialism). It grew strong again toward the end of the NEP period, owing to the sharpening of the contradictions and to the illusion (engendered by the strengthening of the *state machine*) that these contradictions could be resolved by means of rapid accumulation realized through state coercion: this accumulation, it was assumed, would strengthen the working class by increasing its numbers, and by changing the "mentality" of the peasantry and bringing about *total "unity" between them and the working class* as a result of their use of modern means of production which would put industry and agriculture *on the same technological foundation*.

The principal political and ideological effects of the strengthening of the *ouvriériste* component in the Bolshevik ideological formation must now engage our attention.[136] I shall begin by examining its effects on policy regarding recruitment to the Party.

(1) Policy on recruitment to the Party

At the time of the Thirteenth Party Congress (May 1924) *ouvriériste* conceptions wielded a certain influence, in connection with the role played at that time by the Party's organizations in the great industrial centers of Leningrad and Moscow, which were led by Zinoviev and Kamenev, respectively. That congress adopted a resolution which defined the aim of a 50 percent working-class membership of the Party. (Molotov even thought in terms of raising the working-class proportion to 90 percent.) The resolution required that the target of 50 percent be reached within twelve months.[137] It was not reached.

A temporary weakening of the *ouvriériste* component in Bolshevism was shown at the Fourteenth Congress (December 1925), being reflected in the adoption of a new line on recruitment, which gave a bigger place to the peasants. However, the ideological resistance of the middle cadres of the Party was such that recruitment of peasants remained, as we have seen, very slight.

The *ouvriériste* component in the Bolshevik ideological formation was shown also in the fact that greater significance was attributed to *class origin* than to *class position*. Consequently, there was a tendency to deny that poor and middle peasants could take up, ideologically, *revolutionary proletarian positions*, whereas these were supposed to develop "spontaneously" among workers employed in industry.

This mechanistic conception can be carried so far that in effect it is transformed into its opposite. It leads easily to the view that industrial work leaves *so deep an imprint* that it is enough for a person to have been engaged in it for a certain time for him to be "definitively" established in "proletarian positions"—hence the importance attributed to *"working-class origin,"* as against *actual occupation, that is, present integration in production relations.*

Thus, *ouvriériste* conceptions tend to identify one's ideological class position with one's original class situation. This identification was current among the supporters of Proletkult, and it became gradually accepted on a fairly wide scale, even after Proletkult had ceased to exercise any real influence. It was clearly formulated in Pletnev's article entitled "On the Ideological Front," where he said that "scholars, artists, engineers, etc.," *who have emerged from the working class will produce a "proletarian class culture and no other"*—a culture quite different from that produced by their counterparts of bourgeois origin. As Lenin remarked, this was "utter fiction."[138] Such a fiction confers upon cadres who are of working-class origin—or who have merely spent some time working in industry—a working-class "essence" which is supposed to endow them with qualities they can never lose. It is in the personal interest of these cadres to support this fiction. What the latter actually does is to contribute to abandonment of the struggle aimed at ending the separation between manual and mental work, and to underestimating the need for all cadres, even those "of working-class origin," to take part in manual work.[139]

(2) *The role assigned to technology and technicians*

In the Bolshevik ideological formation, *ouvriériste* conceptions were often combined with a conception of social development which gave a front-rank role to "technological progress," and consequently to technicians.

During the first phase of the NEP (down to 1925) the ideological elements which accorded this role to technology and technicians were not specially influential. In that period the problem of technological change was not yet on the agenda: the essential task was to get the existing factories working. Nevertheless, even then, these ideological elements produced certain political effects. This was the case with the *order of priority* followed in the reactivation of the factories which had ceased to function in 1920–1921. The dominant tendency was to try and get back into operation, first and foremost, the *large-scale enterprises,* the most up-to-date—which was not always politically correct. Lenin many times directed the Party's attention to the role that should be played by *small-scale industry,* especially rural industry, which served the peasants directly. The Party's official decisions took account of this principle, but, *in practice,* these decisions were applied only reluctantly. *The pressure of the managers and technicians of the large-scale enterprises* tended to hold back their application, in the name of efficiency and of the *"technological superiority"* of large-scale industry.

Similarly, from the start of the NEP, there was the problem of the "scientific organization of work." The way that this problem was approached shows clearly the influence of *"technicist"* elements in ideology. In order to appreciate how this influence was exerted we must first recall the way in which questions of technology were dealt with after the end of 1925.

At that time the period of "restoration" was regarded as having been completed: thereafter, the problem known as "reconstruction" was to be the order of the day. Discussion of this problem was concentrated chiefly on how much was to be invested in industry, on the respective priorities of the various branches of industry and agriculture, and on the way in which investment would be financed. The question of the technology to be used in the new factories was, however, hardly touched on. It was, in a sense, decided in advance, for it seemed *"self-evident"* that this technology must be the most "advanced," the most "highly mechanized" possible, and that the model of the very large enterprise must be preferred to any other. (In those days they spoke of "giant factories," just as, later, they were to speak of "giant *kolkhozes*"). It was implicitly accepted that this technology and these factories were most likely to "produce" a revolutionary proletariat devoted to the cause of socialism. The presence of *"ouvriériste-*technicist" conceptions is all the more obvious here[140] because the implicit "choice" made *considerably increased the amount of investment needed* in order to obtain a certain volume of production, and also necessitated *massive imports*. The Soviet Union was, in fact, not then in a position to produce for itself all the "up-to-date" equipment which this orientation made it necessary to acquire. This was to have obvious effects on the policy followed in relation to the peasantry, entailing, first, restriction of the supply of goods to them, and then increased exactions from agriculture without any counterpart, *so as to increase the exports needed in order to pay for foreign equipment.*

Other political and social effects also require our attention, namely, those which developed at the level of the production process, and concerned the bigger place taken in social life by the *technicians, specialists, and "experts."* These effects followed from the special role which assertion of the primacy of the most "up-to-date" technology assigned to dead labor (embodied in machinery) and technical knowledge (historically "concentrated" in the engineers and technicians), to the disadvantage of the living labor contributed by the immediate producers, by the workers themselves.

We can now look back at the way in which, in the first years of the NEP, the problem of the "scientific organization of work" was taken up, and show the contradictions which developed in this connection. It is significant that the persons who were, in the first place, responsible for this "organization" were former activists of Proletkult[141] and that their efforts produced two apparently contradictory tendencies[142] which, moreover, ended by *merging under the direction of the technicians,* at a conference of NOT held on March 10, 1924.

This conference adopted the theses put before it by Kuibyshev,[143] condemning as anti-Marxist the identification of NOT with "a complete system of the organisation of work" and emphasizing, together, *mechanization, rationalization of production,* and *intensification* of labor. NOT became thereafter more and more a matter for specialists—though this did not, of course, prevent the holding of workers' production conferences, at which problems of increasing productivity were also discussed. Those specialists took charge of the organization of work and "improved" the wage system by developing the system of payment of bonuses—but also of the imposition of penalties and fines. In this way the obvious "rightist" effects of the *ouvriériste*-technicist conceptions emerged.

After 1926, power in the domain of the organization of labor was practically taken away from the trade unions and concentrated more and more in the hands of managements and specialists. Emphasis was now laid much more on technology than on liberating the initiative of the workers. A social and political consequence of this line was that technicians and

experts were made privileged persons, both as regards remuneration[144] and as regards authority.[145]

(3) Distrust of, or disdain for the peasantry

What was characteristic of the NEP was the will to consolidate the worker-peasant alliance, but this will was obstructed
where many Party members were concerned by a profound
distrust of the peasantry. This distrust was due, in part, to the
tension which developed between the Soviet power and the
peasants during "war communism." Stalin warned Party
members working in the rural areas against this when he
stressed, in 1924, the need for Party members to show confidence in the non-Party peasant and to treat him as an
equal.[146]

But distrust of the peasantry had its roots also in the *ouvriériste* conceptions which were present in the Bolshevik
ideological formation. This was not expressed only in an "ultraleft" form. It even assumed, quite often, an openly "rightist" form, implying disdain for the peasantry and a sort of
appeal for unity between workers and intellectuals against the
peasantry. There are some writings by Maxim Gorky which
express this tendency very clearly. They are worthy of particular attention because Gorky, who at first showed reserve toward the October Revolution, later came to support the Soviet
power. In the early 1930s this writer enjoyed great prestige
among most Party members, and especially among the leaders.

It is therefore to be recalled how Gorky thought of the
Russian peasantry, and how he contrasted the peasant with the
"townsman," whom he described (regardless of the social
class to which this person belonged) as alone capable of
"progress" and "reason." In a work entitled *The Russian
Peasant*, which he wrote in 1922, Gorky said: "The
townsman's labour is varied, stable and enduring. . . . He has
subordinated the forces of nature to his high aims, and they
serve him like the jinns of the Eastern fables served King
Solomon. . . . He has created around him an atmosphere of
reason. . . ."[147]

With this "townsman" Gorky contrasts the peasants, about whom, he says "my thoughts weigh very heavily upon me."[148] In his eyes, it is generally true that "the people want to eat as much as possible and work as little as possible, they want to have all rights and no obligations."[149] He considers that these characteristics are especially applicable to the Russian peasants, who, moreover, he says, are opposed to all progress: "The village greets with distrust and hostility those who attempt to introduce into its life something of themselves, something new, and it rapidly expels them from its midst."[150]

In the pages that follow, expressions of disdain accumulate. For Gorky, the "psychology" of the Russian peasant is concentrated in the saying: "Don't run away from anything, but don't do anything."[151] He quotes a Russian historian who says, describing the peasants: " 'a multitude of superstitions and no ideas.' This sad judgment is confirmed by the whole of Russian folklore."[152] As he sees it, the Russian peasantry has no historical memory of its own revolts. It has forgotten those who led them—Bolotnikov, Stephan Razin, Pugachev: "All this left no trace either on the Russian peasant's daily life or on his memory."[153]

So far as the peasant masses are concerned, the Russian people seem to him incapable of change, and he adds: "I think that a feeling of particular cruelty, cold-blooded . . . is exclusively peculiar to the Russian people."[154]

There is no point in going on: all the clichés of the bourgeoisie and landowners terrified of peasant revolts are to be found in Gorky's writings.

Subsequently, though he did not repeat such crude formulations, disdain and fear of the peasantry continued to be a feature of his thinking. And it was this same disdain and fear of the peasantry which influenced some Party members who passed easily from an anti-kulak policy to a policy of repression against the peasantry as a whole.

True, from 1928 on this "slippage" took place under pressure of the accumulated difficulties arising in relations between the peasantry and the Soviet power, especially when the interests of the peasant masses were sacrificed to the aim of achieving the maximum tempo of industrialization. But what made this slippage possible, that is to say, acceptable to the majority of Party members, was the reactivation of ideological elements which led them to conclude that "civilization" had to be imposed on the peasants by means of a "revolution from above" and the application of measures aimed at checking on the peasants' activity by surrounding them with cadres who, so far as possible, were of urban origin. In fact, even the machines which were supposed to be capable of changing the peasants' "mentality" were not entrusted *to them*, but were concentrated in "machine-and-tractor stations," and operated by technicians and workers, not by the collective farmers themselves.

The ideological elements of distrust in relation to the peasantry which were reactivated in 1928–1929, and which had a decisive influence at that time, were already at work, though in a minor key, during the first years of the NEP, and obstructed the creation of a genuine *political alliance* with the peasants. They contributed to making the worker-peasant alliance seem a mere *tactical* necessity, essentially temporary, and not a fundamental *strategic* necessity.

The interpretation of the NEP as a mere tactical necessity is to be found in many writings produced long before the "great change," and even in Stalin's writings, although, as we know, he called upon Party members at that time to show confidence in the peasants. Thus, in the speech he made at the Thirteenth Conference of the Moscow Region, on January 27, 1925, he said: "The peasantry is the only ally that can be of direct assistance to our revolution *at this very moment*. It is a question of direct assistance just now, at the present moment."[155]

And he added, a little later:

As you yourselves are aware, this ally is not a very staunch one; the peasantry is not as reliable an ally as the proletariat in the developed capitalist countries. But, for all that, it is an ally. . . . That is why, *particularly at the present moment*, when the course of development of revolutionary and all other crises has slowed down somewhat, the question of the peasantry acquires exceptional importance.[156]

About a year later, on February 9, 1926, Stalin returned to this question, in replying to three correspondents. In this reply, he made explicit what he had implied in January 1925, so expressing political distrust toward the peasantry as a whole:

> It seems to me that you are somewhat offended at my calling the peasantry a not very firm ally, an ally not as reliable as the proletariat of the capitalistically developed countries. . . . Must I not tell the truth bluntly? Is it not true that, at the time of the Kolchak and Denikin invasions, the peasantry quite often vacillated, siding now with the workers, now with the generals? And were there not plenty of peasant volunteers in Denikin's and Kolchak's armies?[157]

These formulations clearly show principled distrust toward the peasantry, who were seen as an ally neither firm nor reliable. They suggest the possibility of a split in the worker-peasant alliance, which might occur if a situation of international revolutionary crisis were to develop to a sufficient degree in the "capitalistically developed countries" (as the Bolshevik Party and the Comintern expected in 1929), making "unnecessary" the political line of active alliance with the peasant masses.

(4) The alliance between workers and intellectuals and the "rallying" of the old intelligentsia

The conception which ascribed a revolutionary role to the proletariat not because of the nature of the class contradictions in which it is integrated but because of its connection with "modern technology," with "town life" and, indirectly, with "science," easily led to putting "on the same plane" the working class and those who were seen as working "to develop science." More generally, this conception helped to make the intellectuals appear as a political "vanguard." In a minor form, this conception was present in the Bolshevik ideological formation. It appeared in a major form in some of Gorky's writings. Some extracts from these deserve to be quoted, as they enable us to define an ideological trend which played a significant role in the Soviet Union.

In his essay on *The Russian Peasant,* Gorky did not shrink from writing, in defiance of all historical truth, that "the *whole* of the *Russian* intelligentsia . . . for almost a whole century has manfully attempted to set on its feet the ponderous Russian people, lying lazily, negligently and lucklessly on its soil. . . ."[158]

According to Gorky, the *Russian* intelligentsia carried out in this way a task of decisive importance, starting to awaken "common sense" among the peasants. The political implication of this conception of the historical role played by the intellectuals was clearly expressed by Gorky in a later work of his, written in 1924, when he said:

> The fundamental obstacle on the path of Russia's progress towards Europeanisation and culture is the fact of the overwhelming predominance of the illiterate countryside over the town, the zoological individualism of the peasantry, and its almost complete lack of social feelings. The dictatorship of the politically literate workers *in close alliance with the intelligentsia* was in my view the only possible escape from a difficult situation, especially complicated by the war which brought still further anarchy into the countryside. . . . *The Russian intelligentsia*—the educated people and the workers—was, is, and will long remain, the only cart-horse that can be harnessed to the heavy load of Russian history.[159]

Here Gorky opposed to Lenin's conception of an alliance between the workers and the peasants a quite different conception, that of an alliance between the working class and the Russian intelligentsia.

The Bolshevik Party never formally accepted this view, but, in the contradictory whole which constituted the Bolshevik ideological formation, ideas close to those formulated crudely by Gorky were present and were *manifested on the plane of practice.*

One of the first expressions of this ideology is to be found in a resolution adopted by the Thirteenth Party Congress, in May 1924, after Lenin's death.[160] The principal aspect of this resolution is its *ouvriérisme.* It calls, in a one-sided way, for massive recruitment to the Party from among the working class.[161] On the other hand, it says practically nothing about the need to recruit members from among the poorest sections of the peasantry.

However, there was another aspect to this resolution which was later to assume great importance because it corresponded to the new situation which a section of the intelligentsia was soon to occupy in the Party. This second aspect appears in the paragraphs dealing with Party members of nonworker origin. The resolution says that they must be removed from the Party "if they have not shown themselves to be Communists by improving the work of some organisation of the state, the economy etc., and have not had direct contact with the worker and peasant masses."[162]

In this document, being a "Communist" has nothing to do with taking up a class position, with adhesion to the principles of Marxism-Leninism, or with a way of living and acting which follows from this position and these principles, since it is possible to show oneself a "Communist" by improving the work of organizations of the State, the economy, etc. This criterion opens the Party's doors to intellectuals, administrators, and specialists who carry out "correctly" their tasks in the state machine, regardless of their class position and whether or not they adhere to the revolutionary ideology of the proletariat. This was an "opening" toward the intelligentsia which echoed Gorky's preoccupations (without explicitly coinciding with them).

The same Thirteenth Congress passed another resolution[163] certain passages of which pointed the same way. This was the appeal which the Congress addressed "to the advanced rural intelligentsia, and especially to the rural schoolteachers and the agrarian specialists," as the "vehicle in the countryside of the policy of the Party and the Soviet power."[164] This appeal was issued not to the poor and middle peasants, but to a section of the intelligentsia, which, until then, had shown itself mainly anti-Communist.

Nine months after the Thirteenth Party Congress, in January 1925, Zinoviev spoke at the first congress of schoolteachers held under Soviet rule. After recalling the hostile attitude maintained until shortly before this time by the school-teachers, Zinoviev said: "We can now say to the working class of our country that the schoolteachers and the working class have understood each other and finally come to an agreement, that the teachers of the U.S.S.R. and the Communist Party have concluded an unbreakable alliance."[165]

These sentences did not describe reality, but they set forth a program which closely resembled Gorky's thesis. This program set the aim of "winning" the peasants through the schoolteachers, who were called upon to be "the vanguard of the countryside"—which presupposed according to Zinoviev, that they did not become the "spokesmen" of the peasants (not, at any rate, of the peasants as "traders").[166]

In the months that followed, various strata of the intelligentsia "rallied" to the Soviet power. In March 1925, the VTsIK, meeting, by way of exception, at Tiflis, received a delegation of doctors who presented a declaration of loyalty. One of the members of the VTsIK, Petrovsky, greeted this event as a manifestation of the alliance between "labour and science." In May 1925 the Third Congress of Soviets received a delegation of university rectors, an event which was also seen as a "rallying" by a section of the intelligentsia. Finally, in September 1925, when the two-hundredth anniversary of Russia's Academy of Sciences was celebrated, the "reconciliation" of the world of learning with the Soviet power was made the theme of many articles and speeches, including a speech by Zinoviev to the Academy itself.[167]

Actually, these "rallyings" did not mean in the least that the intelligentsia as a whole accepted the prospect of socialism. What was happening was, in the main, a rallying to an established political authority, the recognition of an accomplished fact. That this fact was recognized was certainly a great victory for the Bolshevik Party, but it was of an ambiguous nature. Most of the members of the intelligentsia who "rallied" in this way aimed either at ensuring their survival in material conditions which were on the upgrade, or at installing themselves in the machinery of state. And, in so far as this installation took place without the intelligentsia having been ideologically transformed, and without this machinery having been revolutionized, the overwhelming majority of the intellectuals functioned as agents of bourgeois practices, both on the plane of management of enterprises and on that of teaching, scientific and technological research, art, and literature.

The maintenance of these practices affected at the same time the *new* intelligentsia, the new cadres of proletarian origin, and thus constituted a factor, in the reproduction of bourgeois social relations, the existence of which was one of the objective bases of a bourgeois path of development. The latter did not necessarily coincide with an extension of the "private" enterprises, but could fit in quite well with the rise of large-scale state-owned industry.

(5) The accelerated and one-sided development of large-scale industry, and Great-Russian chauvinism

From 1928–1929 the "maximum" (actually one-sided) development of large-scale state-owned industry, to be equipped with the "most up-to-date" technology, created an objective situation that was still more favorable to penetration by many members of the old intelligentsia into the economic and administrative apparatuses of the Soviet state. True, this penetration had its ups and downs, for the vigilance of the Bolshevik Party regarding bourgeois intellectuals remained acute. Nevertheless, the decisive problem, that of ideological influence of the old intelligentsia upon the "new Soviet intellectuals," could not be dealt with by vigilance alone.

What was needed here was a struggle to transform the ideological apparatuses and *against the separation between mental and manual work*—and this struggle was not undertaken. It was all the less undertaken because the numerical growth of the new intelligentsia gave rise to the illusion that this stratum, being partly of working-class origin, did not run the risk of falling under the influence of bourgeois ideology—

their class origin serving, somehow, to "safeguard" their class position.

In fact, this was not so, and the new intelligentsia—integrated in apparatuses which reproduced the essentials of the social relations characteristic of the old university, scientific, technological, and even administrative apparatuses—was largely dominated by the ideology of the old intelligentsia. One of the components of that ideology was Russian nationalism. It was this that determined many of the "rallyings" which took place when the great industrial projects of the First Five-Year Plan were drawn up and put into effect. The emphasis placed on these projects and on the role of "vanguard technology" revived the bourgeois nationalism of the old intelligentsia. In their view, the priority realization of these projects was not destined to strengthen the dictatorship of the proletariat but to turn Russia into a "modern great power," a "Europeanised" country, as Gorky put it.

The bourgeois nationalism of the old intelligentsia which rallied to the Soviet power at that time, and the influence it exercised upon Soviet scientists, researchers, and technicians, and, through them, upon many cadres, favored the reactivation of that "Great-Russian chauvinism" which was already present in the Bolshevik Party, as Lenin had pointed out in 1922.[168]

Thus, the series of changes which took place after 1928 in the Soviet social formation entailed very important changes in the Bolshevik ideological formation. Some of the political consequences of these changes made their appearance comparatively soon. These were the ones I have mentioned. Others took some years to make themselves felt, and will have to be analyzed later.

Notes

1. The problem of these contradictions was discussed in volume I of this work, especially pp. 469–475.
2. Lenin, *CW*, vol. 4, pp. 211–212.

3. The presence of ideological notions in every science accounts for the need for rectifications. It means that the pair of concepts, "science and ideology," does not describe two contrasting poles which are mutually exclusive, but two opposites which interpenetrate. A system of scientific knowledge is what it is insofar as the elements of science in it predominate over the elements of ideology. The non-exclusive character of science and ideology explains why Lenin was able to speak of Marxism as "the ideology of the revolutionary proletariat" (*CW*, vol. 31, p. 317), and why Marx could say that the proletarian ideology is that which the proletariat has to recognize as correct because it *corresponds* to the place occupied by the working class in the production relations.

4. A problem arises here: may not the process of the impoverishment and obscuring of the principles and ideas of revolutionary Marxism, which can affect Marxism (as historically constituted through its merging with the working-class movement) attain such a degree (in the case of a particular ideological and political trend) that what results has no longer anything but an illusory connection with revolutionary Marxism? Undeniably, this can happen. This process then engenders a "revisionism" which is merely a parody of Marxism. The appearance of a "revisionism" has as its corollary the appearance of a Marxism of the new epoch which joins battle with it. On this subject G. Madjarian makes an important observation: "The fight against 'revisionism' cannot be waged by conserving, or, rather, by merely reappropriating, Marxism as it existed historically in the previous period. Far from being the signal for a return to the supposed orthodoxy of the preceding epoch, the appearance of a 'revisionism' is a symptom of the need for Marxism to criticize itself" ("Marxisme, conception staliniene, révisionnisme," in *Communisme*, May–August 1976, p. 44).

5. Said by Marx in the later 1870s, and quoted by Engels in his letter of September 7, 1890, to *Der Sozialdemokrat* (Marx and Engels, *Werke*, vol. 22, p. 69).

6. Hence, for example, the critiques by Marx and Engels of the "Gotha" and "Erfurt" programs drawn up by the German labor movement.

7. This "overlooking" was sometimes conscious falsification. Thus, in the 1891 German edition of *The Civil War in France*, edited by Engels, the latter spoke plainly of "the Social-Democratic philistine," but in the versions printed at the time

the word "Social-Democratic" was replaced by "German," so as to hide from readers the divergences between Engels and the Social Democratic Party. The manuscript of this work is in the Institute of Marxism-Leninism in Moscow: the "correction" is not in Engels' handwriting (Marx and Engels, *On the Paris Commune*, pp. 34 and 301, n. 18).

8. The divergences between Marx's revolutionary theory and the Marxism of German Social Democracy were not usually "proclaimed" by Marx and Engels, but nevertheless they did not hide them. They wrote of them not only in their critiques of the Gotha and Erfurt programs but also on a number of other occasions. To make a survey of these divergences (which were not, as a rule, expressed explicitly), it is necessary to refer to several writings. Here I will mention only: Marx's interview for the *Chicago Tribune*, January 5, 1879, on "Social-Democracy, Bismarck and the Anti-Socialist Law" (published in German in *Zeitschrift für Geschichtswissenschaft*, vol. XII, no. 1 [1964]; in Russian in *Voprosy Istorii K.P.S.S.*, no. 10 [1966]; and in French in Marx and Engels, *La Social-Démocratie allemande*, Collection "10/18," Paris, 1975, p. 97); Marx's notes on Bakunin's book *Statism and Anarchy (Marx and Engels and Lenin on Anarchism and Anarcho-Syndicalism*, pp. 147–152); and some observations by Engels in his 1885 article "On the History of the Communist League" (Marx and Engels, *Selected Works in Three Volumes*, vol. 2, pp. 173 ff.).

9. See volume I of the present work, especially pp. 20–32; 113 ff.; 368 ff.; 497 ff.

10. One of these currents was, as we shall see, Bogdanovism, the ideological system worked out by Bogdanov (see below, p. 570, n. 26). In modified forms, this current was constantly present in the Bolshevik ideological formation.

11. In his foreword to D. Lecourt's book *Lyssenko*, L. Althusser makes some important points on this subject (p. 13).

12. Marx, *Capital*, vol. I, pp. 173–174.

13. See the resolution on the Five-Year Plan adopted in April 1929 by the Sixteenth Party Conference, in *K.P.S.S. v rezolyutsiyakh*, vol. 2, p. 453.

14. Stalin, *Works*, vol. 11, p. 167.

15. As we have seen, this "condemnation" had been, however, largely political and "organizational," without the thorough *analysis* which would have enabled theoretical knowledge and revolutionary Marxism to make progress. This was pointed out

by Mao Tse-tung when, speaking about the late 1920s and early 1930s, he said that "at that time the Soviet Union had won victory over the Trotskyites, though on the theoretical plane they had only defeated the Deborin school" (Mao, talk on March 10, 1958, at the Chengtu Conference of the Chinese Communist Party; in Stuart R. Schram, ed., *Mao Tse-tung Unrehearsed*, p. 97 [my emphasis—C. B.]. The "Deborin school" was a philosophical trend condemned by Stalin in 1930 for "Menshevik idealism.").

16. Some of these questions had arisen already in Lenin's lifetime, as has been shown in volume I of the present work (e.g., pp. 419 ff., 523 ff.).

17. I here discuss a theme already touched upon in volume I of the present work (pp. 23–29).

18. These are fundamental themes in the *Manifesto of the Communist Party* of Marx and Engels, developed in their principal subsequent writings.

19. Marx, letter to Weydemeyer, March 5, 1852 (*Selected Correspondence*, p. 86); see also the writings assembled by E. Balibar in his book *Sur la dictature du prolétariat*, pp. 207 ff.

20. Marx, *Contribution to the Critique of Political Economy*, p. 21.

21. It is true that not all the writings of Marx and Engels show with the same rigor the connection between the processes of social reproduction and of social transformation (e.g., certain formulations in the 1859 preface to the *Contribution to the Critique of Political Economy* are not free from ambiguity). This is why we need to consider the writings of Marx and Engels, and Marxism as it has existed historically, as a contradictory combination of formulations and analyses which are revolutionary (in their content and in the conclusions that can be drawn from them) and others which are less rigorous. The latter are, as a rule, provisional and transitional expressions of the thought of Marx and Engels, and of those who have sought to carry their analyses further, but they do not form part of revolutionary Marxism. It was historically inevitable that this should be so, and that the second category of formulations and analyses should have also played a part in Marxist writings after Marx's time, especially in periods when the development of the revolutionary movement of the masses was not itself helping to draw a line of demarcation between the different writings of Marx and Engels. I return to this question later (above, p. 514).

22. Stalin, *Leninism*, pp. 591 ff. This essay was first published in

September 1938 as part of the *History of the C.P.S.U.(B.): A Short Course.*

23. Another interesting aspect of this work is that it was written not in the heat of polemic but after the main battles fought under the theoretical banner of its theses were over, at a moment when it was not necessary to "overstress" certain formulations in order to carry more conviction—at a moment, too, when a first summing-up of what had been done under the banner of these theses could be attempted.

24. Stalin, *Leninism,* pp. 591–660.

25. Ibid., pp. 600 ff.

26. Alexander Bogdanov was born in 1873. He belonged to the Bolshevik wing of the RSDLP. At first close to Lenin, he drew away from Bolshevism after the revolution of 1905. In 1907 he formed an ultraleft faction, which published the journal *Vpered.* He was at that time an Otzovist (on this point, see volume I of the present work, p. 117) and was criticized as such by Lenin. He then broke with Bolshevism. Already before 1907 Bogdanov had published (between 1903 and 1906) a neo-Kantian book which was wholly un-Marxist: *Empiriomonism.* Lenin attacked the empiricist and idealist-fideist conceptions in this work in his *Materialism and Empiriocriticism* (1909).

The subsequent development of Bogdanov's ideas was set out synthetically in his book on "tectology," which appeared in two volumes in 1913 and 1917. It confirmed his break with Marxism and dialectics: to contradiction he counterposed "equilibrium" and "organisation."

In 1917 Bogdanov returned to Russia, where he gave the first impulse to the Proletkult ("Proletarian Culture") group: see below, note 29. In 1922–1923 he opened the New Economic Policy, leading the group called "Workers' Truth." He was arrested, but released soon afterward. In 1924 some writings of his in which he expounded his economic and social ideas were published by the State Publishing House and the Communist Academy. Subsequently he devoted himself, as a doctor, to scientific research, and died in 1928.

27. Stalin, *Leninism,* p. 600.

28. The absence, in such a work, of a critique of these "sociological" ideas of Bogdanov's is obviously not accidental (see below, pp. 572–574, n. 39).

29. *Proletkult,* a movement founded after the revolution of Feb-

ruary 1917, sought to represent "proletarian culture" and promote its progress. It was led by persons close to Bogdanov. After the October Revolution it acquired a certain importance, tending to develop its own political line, based on Bogdanov's ideas—non-Marxist conceptions presented in Marxist "terminology."

Proletkult defended mechanistic positions in ideology. It saw the development of proletarian class consciousness as based primarily on *production practice*, and not on class struggle. It systematically underestimated the effects of the capitalist division of labor on the proletariat and was inclined to deny the necessary role of theory and of the proletarian party.

After October, Lenin considered it necessary to fight Bogdanov's ideas again, especially in the form which they assumed in Proletkult, an organization which was joined by some Bolsheviks. He waged this fight on the ideological and organizational planes. His interventions against Proletkult culminated in a circular from the CC, dated December 1, 1920, placing the Proletkult movement under the direction of the Commissariat of Education, thereby reducing its importance. These interventions led also to Bukharin's writing, with Lenin's agreement, a severe ideological critique (*Pravda*, November 22, 1921) and articles published in *Pravda* on October 24–25, 1922, and January 4, 1923, over the signature of Y. Yakovlev, which were directly inspired by Lenin. The second of these articles was entitled, significantly: "Menshevism under the Mask of Proletkult." On these matters, see *Ästhetik und Kommunikation. Beiträge zur Politischen Erziehung*, nos. 5–6 (February 1972), pp. 149, 200–201; also Karl Eimermacher, *Dokumente zur Sowjetischen Literaturpolitik 1917–1932*; and Lenin's correspondence with Bukharin about Proletkult, in Lenin, *Über Kultur und Kunst* (a collection of his writings on these subjects). Some of Lenin's critical writings on these questions were published for the first time in the symposium *Voprosy kultury pri diktature proletariata*, reproduced in *Ästhetik und Kommunikation*, nos. 5–6 (February 1972), pp. 113 ff. See also Lenin, *O literature i iskusstve*, pp. 470–472; and *CW*, vol. 35, p. 554, and vol. 45, pp. 392–393.

30. Stalin, *Leninism*, p. 602.
31. See above, pp. 508 ff.
32. Marx, A *Contribution*, p. 21.

33. Stalin, *Leninism*, p. 604. It will be observed that this formulation makes use of the pair of concepts "nature" and "society," which are treated as being "external" to one another, but with the second of them presented as an "environment." In this way the formal conditions are set up for a pseudo-dialectics contrasting two "entities" between which relations are external in character (I shall come back to this question, above, pp. 536 ff.) and which can develop between them "a process of exchange." This theme is also explicitly present in Bukharin's book *Historical Materialism* (published in 1921). In this work we see clearly that if the problem of "social development" is presented like that, it *tends* to show this development as depending on changes in the relations between "society" and "nature," these changes being ascribed to the "development of the productive forces." Thus, Bukharin writes: " . . . the internal structure of the system [i.e., the internal equilibrium of a society—C. B.] . . . must change *together with the relation existing between the system and its environment. The latter relation is the decisive factor;* for the entire situation of the system, the fundamental forms of its motion . . . are determined by this relation only" (ibid., p. 79). In the chapter entitled "The Equilibrium Between Society and Nature" Bukharin adds that the productive forces determine social development because they express the interrelation between society and its environment, and that in this interrelation is to be found the "cause producing a change in the system itself" (ibid., p. 107).

    A similar pseudo-dialectics is employed in Bogdanov's *Vseobshchaya organizatsionnaya nauka (tektologiya)*, a German translation of which *(Allgemeine Organisationslehre: Tektologie)* appeared in Berlin in 1926.
34. Stalin, *Leninism*, p. 604.
35. Ibid., pp. 605–606.
36. Ibid., p. 606. According to Stalin, the "unity" of these two aspects is realized in "the process of production of material values" (ibid., p. 607)—which implies that they are, to begin with, external to each other.
37. Ibid., p. 607. It will be observed that the problem of reproduction of the production relations, a fundamental point in Marx's analyses, is never mentioned.
38. Ibid., p. 608.
39. The fundamental role here attributed to the instruments of production calls for special attention, because it has a number of

ideological and political implications (to which I shall return). We notice again the similarity between Stalin's formulations just quoted and those of Bogdanov. For the latter, indeed, the productive forces tended to be reduced to *technology*. Thus, in 1923 he wrote: "In the first place, a development takes place in the domain in which man directly confronts nature, in the domain of the technological relations between man and nature, in the domain of the productive forces" (Bogdanov, "Principles of Organization of Social Technology and Economy," in *Vestnik Kommunisticheskoy Akademii*, vol. 4 [1923], p. 272, quoted in *Geschichte der Politischen Ökonomie des Sozialismus*, by a group of Leningrad University writers, p. 59). Here, as can be seen, "productive forces" are reduced to "technological relations."

The similarity between the role ascribed in *Dialectical and Historical Materialism* to the instruments of production and some of Bogdanov's formulations brings out the contradictory relations that existed between Bolshevism and Bogdanov's ideas. These were both relations of the *presence* (albeit denied) of modified forms of Bogdanovism within the Bolshevik ideological formation, and relations of exteriority. These specific relations, and the prestige which Bogdanov continued for a long time to enjoy in the Bolshevik Party, explain the equally contradictory, and unusually "carefully expressed" judgments on Bogdanov pronounced by the Party's leaders.

Thus, in his speech of December 7, 1927, at the Fifteenth Party Congress, Stalin mentioned the names of some former members of the Party who had left it as a result of serious divergences. Among these was Bogdanov, concerning whom he uttered this appreciation, with which none of the others were honored: "He was one of the most prominent leaders of our Party" (Stalin, *Works,* vol. 10, p. 380). This formulation was remarkable when one remembers that Bogdanov had broken with the Party long before, and had gone on developing conceptions which were officially considered to be incompatible with Bolshevism.

Again, in 1928, when Bogdanov died, Bukharin published in *Pravda* (April 8) an article paying homage to the *theoretician* who had passed away, saying that he had "played an enormous role in the development of our Party and in the development of social thought in Russia."

In the same article, however, Bukharin described Bogdanov

as a "semi-Marxist," adding that his "divergence from orthodox Marxism and from Bolshevism became . . . for Bogdanov a personal tragedy" (Cohen, *Bukharin,* pp. 15, 414).

In his contribution to *Geschichte der Politischen Ökonomie des Sozialismus* (chapter 3), L. D. Shirokorad recalls the great polemic in the 1920s against Bogdanov's conception of the productive forces, but he considers it possible to state that this polemic ceased at the beginning of the 1930s because by then "the influence of non-Marxist traditions in the elaboration of this category" had been, "in the main, overcome" (p. 77). If we look closely we find that the polemic ceased, in fact, because eventually a convergence came about between the positions thereafter defended by Bolshevism and the Bogdanovist conception of the productive forces and their role. (In the Russian original of the book quoted—*Istoriya politicheskoy ekonomiki sotsializma*—the page references are 62 and 88.)

40. All that we find are "the labouring masses," who are "the chief force" only in "the process of production" (Stalin, *Leninism,* p. 608), and do not figure as the agents of social change. This is why, says Stalin, "historical science . . . must above all devote itself to the history of the producers of material values" (ibid.).

41. Ibid., pp. 608–609.

42. See above, p. 569, note 21.

43. Marx and Engels, *Collected Works,* vol. 5, pp. 19–539, and vol. 6, pp. 105–212.

44. Marx and Engels, *Selected Correspondence,* p. 40.

45. Marx, *Contribution,* p. 21.

46. Marx, *Capital* (London), vol. I, p. 493.

47. Marx, "Results of the Immediate Process of Production," appendix to *Capital* (London), vol. I, p. 1026.

48. Ibid., pp. 1064–1065.

49. Stalin, *Leninism,* p. 608 (my emphasis—C. B.).

50. The obscuring of the role of production relations was overdetermined by the increasing identification of these relations with the juridical forms of ownership (see above, pp. 527 ff.).

51. Those conditions were analyzed in volume I of the present work.

52. See above, pp. 217 ff.

53. Stalin, *Works,* vol. 12, p. 171 (my emphasis—C. B.).

54. It will be observed that Stalin attached the formulation that he put forward to an extract from Lenin's report on the tax-in-kind to the Tenth Party Congress. An essential point in that report

was Lenin's denunciation of "dreamers" who (during the period of "war communism") "thought the economics basis, the economic roots of small farming could be reshaped in three years" (Lenin, *CW*, vol. 32, p. 216). Lenin emphasized that what was decisive was the transforming of the peasants' mentality and habits, which required time, and necessitated that they learn to *organize themselves* and *administer*. True, in order to strengthen his argument against harmful haste, Lenin added that the changing of peasant mentality would have to have also a *material basis*. It is not difficult to see that this meant something quite different from changing the "mentality" of the peasants through the use of machinery and tractors.

55. We know that, in fact, the changeover to collectivization did not wait for mechanization—and that was correct. What was not correct was that the tempo at which collectivization was developed was essentially the result of harsh coercion of the peasant masses.

56. *K.P.S.S. v rezolyutsiyakh*, vol. 2, p. 391. This passage echoes strikingly the claims made by Bogdanov, who, in an article published in 1918 by *Proletarskaya Kultura*, declared that proletarian consciousness, the "working together in comradeship," would "deepen with the development of technology, . . . broaden with the increase of the proletariat in the towns, in gigantic industrial enterprises" (*Ästhetik und Kommunikation*, nos. 5–6 [February 1972], p. 81). We know that Lenin's attitude to the development of large towns was very different. In an interview with H. G. Wells he said that there was no future for them under socialist conditions (*Russia In The Shadows*, pp. 133–134).

57. We have already seen that positions such as this reproduced those of Bogdanov and, more generally, of *Proletkult*. Thus, in an article published in *Pravda* on September 27, 1922, by one of the leaders of the movement, and annotated critically by Lenin, we read:

> The class consciousness of the proletariat is formed in the process of capitalist production, that is where collective class psychology is born. . . . This "being" determines the class consciousness of the proletariat. It is alien to the peasant, the bourgeois, the intellectual. . . . The peasant depends, in the process of his individual work, upon the forces of nature. . . . The proletarian enjoys completely clear relations with the external world. . . . On these

statements Lenin merely notes, in the margin: "And what about the religion of the workers and peasants?" (*Ästhetik und Kommunikation*, nos. 5–6 [February 1972], pp. 116–117; Lenin, *O literature*, pp. 570–571).

The simplistic formulations of Bogdanovism encouraged the proletariat to *isolate* itself from the rest of the masses, in the name of a *unique "existential experience."* They led those who were influenced by these formulations to *look on the peasants with distrust*, to see in them unreliable allies for the working class and to regard the NEP as a dangerous "concession" which must be taken back as soon as possible. Conceptions akin to this were obviously at work in the second half of the 1920s.

58. This slogan appeared in Stalin's speech, on "the tasks of business executives," to the leaders of industry, on February 4, 1931 (Stalin, *Works*, vol. 13, p. 43). See the remarks of B. Fabrègues, "Staline et le matérialisme historique," in *Communisme*, nos. 22–23 (May–August 1976), p. 60.

59. The theme of a "spontaneous" disappearance of the division between manual and mental labor was not explicitly developed by the Bolshevik Party, but it was implicit in the absence of any concrete struggle to prepare for this disappearance, or even any reflection on the conditions for such a struggle.

This theme was explicitly developed by Bogdanov, who wrote, for example:

In so far as . . . the machine is improved and made more complex, and becomes more and more a mechanism functioning automatically, which requires living supervision, conscious intervention, constant active attention—the unification of the two types [of labor, manual and mental] becomes more obviously necessary. . . . Henceforth, this tendency to synthesis is manifested sufficiently to paralyze the influence of the previous separation between "spiritual" and "physical" labor in the workers' thinking (Bogdanov, *Allgemeine Organisationslehre*, p. 55, quoted in *Ästhetik und Kommunikation*, nos. 5–6 [February 1972], p. 95).

The same theme is met with in Bogdanov's work *Art and the Working Class*, where he writes: "Mechanised production 'heals,' so to speak, the basic cleavages in the nature of work." Emphasizing the role of the machine, Bogdanov adds that the worker "is in command of this mechanical slave. The more complex and perfected the machine, the more the worker's task is reduced to one of supervision, examination of all the phases and conditions of the machine's operation, and intervention in its operation when this becomes necessary."

On the basis of this conception, it is not surprising to find Bogdanov saying that "it is only in the development of labour, in the development of the forces of production, that lies the fulfilment of the socialist ideal" (quoted in F. Champarnaud, *Révolution et contre-révolution culturelle en U.R.S.S.*, pp. 429, 439).

60. *The German Ideology*, in Marx and Engels, *Collected Works*, vol. 5, p. 59.
61. Proletarian *hegemony* is necessary for the *transition* from capitalism to communism. This hegemony must be distinguished from *domination*. We know that the idea figures in Lenin's analyses (see volume I of the present work, pp. 93–94). It was developed by Gramsci: but it is not clear whether for Gramsci it had exactly the same meaning as for Lenin.
62. It is not possible to present these analyses here: that would provide the subject for a distinct piece of research. Let us merely recall the passage in which Marx notes that "the existence of revolutionary ideas in a particular period presupposes the existence of a revolutionary class" (*The German Ideology*, in Marx and Engels, *Collected Works*, vol. 5, p. 60), pointing out that what is needed for a revolution is "the formation of a revolutionary mass which revolts not only against separate conditions of the existing society but against the existing 'production of life' itself, the 'total activity' on which it was based [i.e., the totality of social relations—C. B.]" ibid., p. 54).

Marx emphasizes that, in this struggle, *the revolutionary class changes itself*, and that this change is indispensable if it is to be able to build a new society: here we are very far away from an ideological transformation resulting from the struggle for production, technological changes, and "education." To be recalled, too, in this connection, is the passage from Marx quoted in volume I of the present work, p. 177.
63. *K.P.S.S. v rezolyutsiyakh* (1954 ed.), vol. 3, p. 195, quoted in Carr and Davies, *Foundations*, vol. 2, p. 446.
64. This conception was to be reaffirmed at the Sixteenth Party Congress. It led, in 1929, to explicit revision of one of the fundamental theses of Marxism concerning the withering away

of the state—a thesis which Stalin said was "incompletely worked out and inadequate" (see volume I of the present work, p. 30). He offered no "justification" for this revision other than the fact of what had happened.

65. *History of the C.P.S.U.(B.)*, p. 305.

66. Marx used the expression "revolution from above" to describe the policy of Louis Napoleon Bonaparte in an article of 1859, "Reaction is Carrying out the Programme of the Revolution" (Marx and Engels, *Werke*, vol. 13, p. 414); and Engels, in his *Critique of the Erfurt Programme*, described the effects of Bismarck's policy in 1866 and 1870 as "revolution from above" (Marx and Engels, *Selected Works in Three Volumes*, vol. 2, p. 436). On this point, see Carr and Davies, *Foundations*, vol. 2, pp. 446 ff.

67. Lenin, *CW*, vol. 25, pp. 381–491. It is noteworthy that the *History of the C.P.S.U.(B.)*, which gives a systematic survey of Lenin's principal writings, refrains from giving any presentations of *The State and Revolution*.

68. See volume I of the present work, p. 461. The whole letter is extremely interesting (Marx and Engels, *Selected Correspondence*, pp. 352–357).

69. Marx, "First Outline of *The Civil War In France*," in Marx and Engels, *On The Paris Commune*, pp. 149–150.

70. Ibid., pp. 152, 153, 156. In these same pages Marx says that the sweeping away of the "state parasites" implies that the new form of rule means "doing away with the state hierarchy altogether and replacing the haughteous [*sic*] masters of the people by its always removable servants,. . . . paid like skilled workmen . . . doing their work publicly, acting in broad daylight, with no pretensions to infallibility, not hiding itself behind circumlocution offices . . ." (ibid., pp. 154, 155).

71. See volume I of the present work, especially pp. 329 ff. and 490 ff.

72. On Lenin's statements and on the role subsequently ascribed to juridical forms of ownership, by the Bolshevik Party, see volume I of the present work, especially pp. 20 ff. and 143 ff.

73. It is in *The Poverty of Philosophy* that Marx deals most systematically with this subject, but it constantly recurs in his major writings, as also in those of Engels, especially those produced after the Paris Commune.

74. Marx and Engels, *Selected Works in Three Volumes*, vol. I. p. 188.

75. See above, pp. 302–303.
76. Let me recall that Lenin pointed out the variety of forms of existence of capitalist relations in the Soviet state enterprises: the failure to keep the salaries of the technicians and specialists down to the level of the workers' wages; the existence of a single manager, nominated by the central bodies and solely responsible for the running of the enterprise; the "financial autonomy" which enabled the enterprise to dispose of part of its profits. See volume I of the present work, pp. 54, 54 n.; 156; 166; 509–510.
77. Enterprises controlled by this bourgeoisie of a new type are what is called in China "capitalist enterprises with a socialist signboard." What is carried on in them is "private production" pursued under cover of state ownership. The functioning of such enterprises tends to reproduce the features of enterprises belonging to big joint-stock companies (or to the capitalist state), regarding which Marx observed: "It is private production without the control of private property" (*Capital* [Moscow], vol. III, p. 429).
78. Such cooperation implies that the "plan" is worked out essentially from below upward—that it results from centralization and coordination of initiatives and proposals coming from the producers themselves.
79. I shall come back to this point in the next section of this chapter.
80. Marx, *Grundrisse*, p. 705. A longer extract from this passage will be found above, p. 49.
81. The idea of struggle between market anarchy and harmonious development through planning is presented in Preobrazhensky's *The New Economics*, pp. 55–66.
82. Ibid., p. 58. This maximum accumulation was to be obtained by charging prices which ensured a transfer of value to the state sector (ibid., pp. 147 ff.).
83. Ibid., p. 63. The idea of "social technology" is one of the key ideas in Bogdanov's book on "tectology."
84. See above, pp. 62, 64 ff.
85. Reznik in *Planovoye Khozyaistvo*, no. 1 (1931), p. 49.
86. Marx observes that bourgeois economists are interested only in the magnitude of value, not in how it is determined, for "under the coarse influence of the practical bourgeois, they give their attention, from the outset, and exclusively, to the quantitative aspect of the question" (*Capital* (London), vol. I, p. 141).

87. See volume I of the present work, pp. 19 ff.
88. Stalin, *Leninism*, p. 592. This exposition forms the first part of his essay, already quoted, on *Dialectical and Historical Materialism*.
89. Ibid.
90. Ibid.
91. Ibid., p. 595.
92. Lenin, *CW*, vol. 38, p. 223.
93. Stalin, *Leninism*, p. 595.
94. See note 33, above.
95. For Bogdanov the category of "organization," with all its organicist implications, was fundamental, and this led him to endow "society" (the more or less complete realization of the essence of organization) with the status of a *subject in history*. He wrote: "In technology *society* struggles with nature and masters it. Society organises the external world in accordance with the interests of *its* life and *its* development. In the economy, *society* organises the relations of collaboration and distribution among men . . ." (quoted in Champarnaud, *Révolution*, p. 441 [my emphasis—C. B.]).

    With Bogdanov we have an idealistic philosophy of history dominated by a "principle of organization," in the biological sense. According to this, *organization strives to realize itself* through history. Class societies are merely imperfect "realizations" of the principle of organization, owing to the contradictions that prevail in them and undermine them. But *the principle of organization must triumph in the end*. This triumph will be brought about by the socialist revolution, which *puts an end to contradiction and ensures the victory of organization*.

    The proletariat thus figures as the *agent of realization of the idea of organization*, and socialist society as *the form of realization of an essence* which has been at work since the beginning of human society and will eventually be fulfilled. This fulfillment implies, in its turn, the emergence of a new "essence of Man." The idealistic character of this ideological construction, which corresponds to a specific philosophical humanism, is perfectly plain (see Lecourt, *Lyssenko*, p. 158, n. 20).

    This idealistic construction enables Bodganov to elaborate a "model" of socialist society which is characterized by centralization, rationalization, and the planning of tasks. The role of the masses who make history is absent from this conception, while the role of the organizers and planners becomes fundamental.

96. Stalin, *Leninism*, p. 603.

97. Let us recall here that Bodganovism developed after a temporary ebbing of the revolutionary workers' movement, when, under the conditions of the Stolypin reaction and of a bourgeois agrarian policy, it was especially difficult for the labor movement to join forces with the peasant masses. In this situation a small group of former Bolsheviks, headed by Bogdanov, worked out an ideological system which "glorified" the relative isolation of the working class of Russia. They issued ultraleft slogans and declared that the Russian proletariat would be able to play a leading role not through alliance with the peasantry but through the special position as organizer with which its special relationship with modern technology was supposed to endow it.

Bogdanov's philosophical theses provided theoretical conditions (abandonment of dialectical materialism) which made it possible to give an appearance of legitimacy to the "ultraleft" conceptions of the period. See on this two articles by Lenin: "Certain Features of the Historical Development of Marxism," in *Zvezda*, December 23, 1910, and "Stolypin and the Revolution," in *Sotsial-Demokrat*, no. 24 (1911), in *CW*, vol. 17, pp. 39–44 and 247–256).

98. Lenin, *CW*, vol. 38, p. 359.

99. Stalin, *Works*, vol. 11, pp. 255 ff. ("The Industrialisation of the Country and the Right Deviation in the O.P.S.U[B]").

100. Ibid., p. 293.

101. Lenin, *CW*, vol. 36, p. 594. On this point, see also volume I of the present work, p. 323.

102. Ibid., *CW*, vol. 32, p. 178. See also volume I of the present work, especially pp. 234, 398, 402.

103. At the Tenth Party Congress Lenin said "Comrades, let's not have an opposition *just now!*" (*CW*, vol. 32, p. 200 [my emphasis—C. B.]).

104. These decisions were embodied in the "Resolution on Party Unity" adopted by the Tenth Party Congress, regarding which Lenin spoke of "an extreme measure that is being adopted specially, in view of the dangerous situation" (ibid., p. 258).

105. Quoted in Carr, *The Interregnum*, p. 363.

106. At that time open debate ceased, and there were many cases of "rallying" to the general line. The contradictions in the Party seemed to have been "eliminated." In reality, they were reproduced in new forms: but that happened in connection with the problems of a period outside the limits of the present volume.

107. Lenin, *CW*, vol. 29, p. 183. See volume I of the present work, pp. 271–272.

108. See above, p. 346.

109. Quoted in Carr, *The Bolshevik Revolution*, vol. 1, p. 237 (my emphasis—C. B.).

110. Zinoviev, *The Anti-Soviet Parties and Tendencies* (1922), quoted in Alexander Skirda, *Kronstadt 1921: Prolétariat contre bolchevisme*, pp. 26–27. Zinoviev was actually quoting Lenin's political report to the Eleventh Party Congress, on March 27, 1922 (*CW*, vol. 33, p. 278).

111. *Pravda*, August 23, 1924, quoted in Carr, *Socialism*, vol. 1, p. 104, n. 3.

112. Stalin, *Works*, vol. 6, pp. 186–188. This passage stresses the "spirit of discipline" with which the proletariat must be filled, and the Party's role as educator, but does not say anything about the role of the masses in educating the Party.

113. Stalin, *Works,* vol. 8, p. 41.

114. Ibid., pp. 46, 49, 51, 53, 56. On this question see the article by Fabrègues in *Communisme*, no. 24.

115. Meaning the thesis expounded by Lenin in 1902 in *What Is To Be Done?*, where he defended the theory of the union, through the Party, of Marxist theory with the labor movement (see Lenin, *CW*, vol. 5). This is not the place to discuss all Lenin's theses in *What Is To Be Done?* or the corrections to them which he made later on.

116. See above, p. 542.

117. Thus, Marx speaks of the need for "free scientific inquiry" (*Capital*, vol. I, p. 92), and declines to "submit" to the ideas of the German Party. Similarly, Mao Tse-tung says that "it is . . . necessary to be careful about questions of right and wrong in the arts and sciences, to encourage free discussion and avoid hasty conclusions" ("On Correct Handling of Contradictions Among the People," in *Four Essays on Philosophy*, p. 114).

118. Lecourt, *Lyssenko*, pp. 60 ff. Lecourt shows (pp. 92 ff.) the *social foundations* of Lysenkoism.

119. A. Badiou draws attention to this point when he notes that what

he calls "the promotion of the principle of totality" (resulting from nonsubordination of the "laws of dialectics" to the primacy of contradiction over identity) may well serve to facilitate infiltration by metaphysics (*Théorie de la contradiction*, p. 38).

120. This interpretation began to appear as soon as Marx's ideas became widespread. It is found in the different variants of "economism." At the beginning of the twentieth century it was generally accepted in the Second International. But it is alien to Marxism-Leninism. Thus, Lenin's formulation of the theory of the "weakest link" in the imperialist chain, which made it possible to see tsarist Russia as the "locus" of the first victory of the socialist revolution, implies rejection of an evolutionist interpretation of Marx's ideas, an interpretation which was usually linked with dominance of the problemcatic of the productive forces. (See volume I of this work, pp. 32 ff.)

121. These criticisms appeared in an article published in October 1877 in *Otechestvenniye Zapiski*. Marx's reply is known to us from a copy sent by Engels to Vera Zasulich, and which appeared in a journal published by Russian revolutionary émigrés in Geneva, *Vestnik Narodnoy Voli*, no. 5 (1886).

122. Quoted in Blackstock and Hoselitz, eds., *Marx and Engels on The Russian Menace to Europe*, pp. 217–218. Marx's reference is to his study of primitive accumulation as this took place in Europe.

123. Ibid., p. 278. See also volume I of the present work, pp. 214 ff.

124. Thus, Engels showed the specific role played in the fate of the Roman world of the later Empire, and right down to the ninth century, by the fact that it "despised work as slavish" (*The Origin of the Family, Private Property and the State*, in Marx and Engels, *Selected Works in Three Volumes*, vol. 2, p. 314).

125. Stalin, *Leninism*, p. 607.

126. Ibid., p. 596. These formulations imply the idea of *a "natural order" of succession of modes of production*, meaning that it is not men who make their own history. *History appears as a "subject" of which men are merely the instruments*. So early as in *The German Ideology* Marx condemned any turning of history into a "subject," when he wrote: "History is nothing but the succession of the separate generations, each of which uses the materials, the capital funds, the productive forces, handed down to it by all preceding generations. . . . This can be speculatively distorted so that later history is made the goal of

earlier history. . . . Thereby history receives its own special goals and becomes 'a person ranking with other persons' " (Marx and Engels, *Collected Works,* vol. 5, p. 50).

127. On the connections between *ouvriérisme* and *"technicist"* conceptions, see above, pp. 516 ff., and 518 ff.

128. Proletarian positions start from the place of the proletariat in the relations of production (and in the process of production), from its *total separation* from the means of production. *Ouvriériste* positions start from the place of the working class in the labor process, its role in relation to tools and machinery: they are thus "technicist" in character.

129. Marx's *Critique of the Gotha Programme* was written in 1875. At first, the leaders of the German Social Democrats opposed its circulation, and it was not published until 1891 by the Party journal, which even then "censored" parts of it (see Engels' letter to Kautsky, February 23, 1891, in Marx and Engels, *Selected Works in Three Volumes,* vol. 2, pp. 38–39). Subsequently Marx's original text was reconstituted on the basis of his manuscript.

130. Ibid., p. 20.

131. Ibid.

132. In the Gotha Programme the statist character of the line put forward is expressed in the formula: "The German workers' party strives . . . for the free state" (ibid., p. 22). Marx comments that this must mean a state which is "free" in relation to the workers—as it is already, he adds, in the German Empire and in tsarist Russia (ibid., p. 25).

133. Hence the formulation in the Gotha Programme stating that "the working class strives for its emancipation first of all within the framework of the present-day national state." This statement also contradicts the *Communist Manifesto,* which says that the workers' struggle is international in content and national only "in form" (ibid., p. 21).

134. See above, note 2.

135. See volume I of the present work, pp. 391–392.

136. The consequences examined here are those which directly affected the Soviet Union itself. The consequences for the international Communist movement are not considered: they would require treatment at considerable length.

137. *XIII-y Syezd RKP(b),* (1963), pp. 505, 606; quoted in Rigby, *Communist Party Membership* p. 137.

138. *Ästhetik und Kommunikation,* nos. 5–6 (February 1972), p. 119; Lenin, *O literature,* pp 572–573.
139. Owing to the mechanistic and metaphysical nature of this conception, the categories of "change" and "transformation" are pushed into the background, whereas in dialectical materialism they occupy a central position. When this "inhibition" reaches a certain stage, it favors the replacement of ideological struggle by a policy of repression.
140. This presence had, of course, social bases. The preference given to very large, "up-to-date" production units seems to correspond to the role played by the heads of the enterprises, a role the importance of which seems to have been proportionate to the size of the enterprises they controlled.
141. It is to the point to note that the role played by supporters of Proletkult in the development of "NOT" was fully in accordance with Bogdanov's ideas. Thus, in the article entitled "On the Ideological Front" (*Pravda,* September 27, 1922), written by V. Pletnev, a spokesman for Proletkult it is clear that Bogdanov's ideas about "organization" lead to the masses being treated as "material" falling within the competence of "specialists." Pletnev says that, after the October Revolution, specialists are needed not only in the domain of technology and the economy: "The age we live in assigns us the task of forming a new type of savant: the *social engineer,* the engineer specialising in organisation, who is able to cope with phenomena and tasks which are getting bigger and bigger" (*Ästhetik und Kommunikation,* nos. 5–6 [February 1972], pp. 120–121). In his annotation of this article Lenin put two query marks against this proposition (see Lenin, *O literature,* pp. 574–575).

The same ideological tendency was shown in the formulation describing the proletarian writer as an "engineer of souls." Here we see again how the ideology of technology and organization becomes transformed into the ideology of technicians and organizers.
142. See above, pp. 238 ff.
143. *Trud,* March 11 and 12, 1924, and *Byulleten II-oy Vsesoyuznoy Konferentsii po NOT,* pp. 27–36, quoted in Carr, *Socialism,* vol. I, p. 384.
144. See above, pp. 248 ff.
145. At the beginning of 1926 this authority was, nevertheless, far from firmly established. The increasing gap between the in-

comes of the workers and those of the engineers, specialists, and managers gave rise to hostility on the part of some workers. Faced with this development, the Party called for strengthening labor discipline. Stalin demanded that the workers cease to show distrust toward the cadres and managers of industry, who, he said, were performing a task which required that they be "surrounded with an atmosphere of confidence and support" and not "castigated" or "kicked" (Stalin, *Works*, vol. 8, pp. 144, 146).

These formulations show that the increasing concentration of authority in the hands of the specialists and adminstrators was coming up against a certain resistance from the workers. As we have seen, the role and authority of the specialists and administrators was challenged on a number of occasions, especially at the beginning of 1928, with the development of the production conferences (see above, pp. 222 ff.); but we have seen, also, that the role played by these conferences soon diminished.

146. "The Party's Immediate Tasks in the Countryside," in Stalin, *Works*, vol. 6 pp. 315 ff.

147. R. E. F. Smith, ed., *The Russian Peasant 1920 and 1984,* pp. 13–14.

148. Ibid., p. 12.

149. Ibid.

150. Ibid.

151. Ibid.

152. Ibid., p. 13.

153. Ibid., p. 15.

154. Ibid., p. 16.

155. Stalin, *Works*, vol. 7, p. 26.

156. Ibid., pp. 28–29 (my emphasis—C. B.).

157. Ibid., vol. 8, p. 99.

158. Smith, *The Russian Peasant*, p. 26. (I have emphasized the words "whole" and "Russian," which seem to me typical of Gorky's thinking—C. B.)

159. Gorky, in *Russky Sovremennik*, vol. I (1924), p. 235, quoted in Carr, *Socialism*, vol. I, pp. 122–123 (my emphasis—C. B.).

160. The resolution "On the Immediate Tasks of Party-Building," *K.P.S.S. v rezolyutsiyakh*, vol. 1, pp. 820 ff.

161. In this respect the resolution merely ratified the decision, taken not long before, to increase the Party's membership through a wide campaign of recruitment, known as the "Lenin enrol-

ment." Such mass-scale recruitment ran counter to Lenin's views, as expressed in a letter to Molotov in which he warned against the negative consequences of too rapid recruitment from among a mass of workers who, at that time, did not form a true proletariat, since many of the persons working in the factories were "petty-bourgeois who have become workers by chance" (Lenin, *CW*, vol. 33, p. 254). The situation described by Lenin was not basically different in early 1924.

162. *K.P.S.S. Vrezolyntsiyakh*, vol. I, p. 833.
163. "On Agitation and Propaganda Work," in ibid., pp. 871 ff.
164. Ibid., p. 875.
165. Quoted in D. Lindenberg, *L'Internationale communiste*, p. 317 (my emphasis—C. B.).
166. Ibid., pp. 326–327.
167. Carr, *Socialism*, vol. 1, pp. 121–122.
168. See volume I of the present work, pp. 420–426.

Part 5
The "great change" and the emergence of new contradictions

It would be pointless to attempt to recapitulate here the results of the foregoing analyses. It is, however, necessary to discuss, for the last time, some of the explanations which have been and are still being offered for the "final crisis of the NEP." Depending on the explanation one accepts, one appreciates differently the real content of the "great change" at the end of 1929 and its class consequences.

One of the most widely accepted interpretations of the "final crisis of the NEP" states that, after 1928, a continuation of the NEP would have doomed agricultural production (and expecially the production of grain for the market) to stagnation and even decline, thereby preventing the necessary development of industry. This is the way the situation was appreciated at the time by the Bolshevik Party. It was reaffirmed in the *History of the C.P.S.U.(B.)* which was approved by the CC in 1938 and in which we read the following:

> All the signs pointed to the danger of a further decline in the amount of marketable grain. . . . There was a crisis in grain farming which was bound to be followed by a crisis in livestock farming. The only escape from this predicament was a change to large-scale farming which would permit the use of tractors and agricultural machines . . . , to take the course of amalgamating the small peasant holdings into large *socialist* farms, collective farms, which would be able to use tractors and other modern machines for a rapid advancement of grain farming and a rapid increase in the marketable surplus of grain.[1]

This "economistic" interpretation cannot be sustained. At the end of the 1920s the potentialities of NEP farming were still considerable, and could have been quickly mobilized.

For that purpose it was necessary to isolate the kulaks politically and to give systematic aid to the poor and middle peasants, in particular by making available to them a minimum of
the instruments of labor they needed, so that they might enter
voluntarily and effectively upon the road to collective farming.
Substantial positive results could have been quickly attained
in that way, provided that there was no attempt to impose
"from above" upon the peasants tempos and forms of organization which did not yet correspond to their aspirations. Experience showed that, by acting otherwise, by coercing the peasant masses, the kulaks were not isolated, while the development of "large-scale mechanized production" failed to give
the expected stimulus to grain production and stockbreeding.
On the contrary, for several years these branches of agriculture
went down and down—which nevertheless did not prevent
industry from advancing at a fast rate.

Even today, though, we find repeated the interpretation of
the "great change" as having been an "economic necessity"
imposed by the "inevitable" stagnation and decline of agricultural production at the end of the NEP and by the contradiction which developed, as a result, between agriculture and
industry. This interpretation is put forward today by Soviet
economists and historians. Thus, in a work published in Moscow in 1964, the Soviet historian Yakovtsevsky repeated the
thesis of the "exhaustion" of the potentialities of NEP agriculture and the resulting contradiction with the needs of industrialization. He wrote:

> The lagging of agriculture behind industry . . . showed that the
> impulse to development given to agriculture by the October
> Revolution had, in the main, been exhausted. The old social
> basis—small-scale individual peasant farming—could no longer
> be the source of further development for agriculture. An urgent
> necessity had been created for agricultural production to move
> over on to the rails of large-scale collective farming.[2]

But it is one thing to assert the historical necessity, if
socialism is to be built, developing collective farming, and
quite another to assert, as this writer does, that there existed in

1927–1929 an "urgent necessity" to increase agricultural production through collectivization. This assertion is all the more
senseless in that, as has been pointed out, the actual fall in
essential agricultural production which occurred after the
"great change" of 1929 did not prevent a massive increase in
industrial production.

The foregoing "economistic" interpretation is frequently
combined with a more "political" one which presents the
problem of the necessity of the "great change" in terms of the
threat from the kulaks, which is alleged to have increased
toward the end of the NEP owing to the increased economic
role of the rich peasants. This combination of the two interpretations is used by J. Elleinstein when he writes, dealing with
the situation at the end of 1927: "Industrialisation was still
inadequate and agriculture was marking time, while the role
of the kulaks was increasing in the countryside, like that of the
Nepmen in the towns."[3]

As regards agriculture "marking time" this was due precisely to the adoption of measures which departed from the
NEP line and provoked discontent among the peasant masses.
As for the role played by the kulaks, this was a limited one,
economically, and could easily have been reduced by relying
firmly on the aspirations of the poor and middle peasants and
helping them to organize themselves. The thesis of a constant
and "inevitable" strengthening of the kulaks, to which accelerated and immediate collectivization was the only answer,
does not square with the actual situation. In 1927 the relative
weight of the kulak farms in agricultural production was far
from being decisive, and mobilization of the existing potentialities of the small- and middle-sized farms could quickly
have reduced this weight, together with the dependence of
the poor and middle peasants on the rich ones.[4] If it is possible
to speak of a "strengthening of the kulaks" in the last years of
the NEP, this is so only if we mean a certain increase in their
political influence which resulted from the mistakes made by
the Bolshevik Party in its relations with the poor and middle
peasants.

The interpretation according to which the "great change"

was due above all to a mass rallying by the middle peasants to collective farming was put forward chiefly at the end of 1929. It does not stand up to an examination of the conditions in which collectivization took place, to observation of the rapid fall in the percentage of households collectivized which followed any relaxation of administrative pressure, or to consideration of the admitted "necessity" of carrying through collectivization in the form of a "revolution from above."

In fact, the way that the turn to accelerated collectivization was effected, and the way in which collectivization was carried out (with extensive use of methods of coercion) resulted from the "demands" of *a certain form and a certain tempo of industrialization.* These "demands" compelled the establishment of forms of organization of the peasantry and of agriculture (*kolkhozes* as large as possible, giant *sovkhozes,* machine-and-tractor stations) through which the state would be better able to *obtain in "sufficient" quantity* the agricultural produce which it needed, and at *prices which did not detract from the financing of investment in industry.*

The forms of agricultural organization set up after the abandonment of the NEP were such as to offer the possibility of levying from the peasantry a "tribute" sufficiently high to enable the industrialization plan to be realized. This expectation was only partly fulfilled. Owing to the conditions in which they were established, these forms of organization did not, for several years, enable essential agricultural production to be increased: but they did integrate the peasantry in a set of relations which deprived them of the ability to decide what they would or would not deliver to the state. The latter thenceforth possessed means of coercion through which it could force the peasants to supply it with quantities of produce corresponding more or less to the forecasts laid down by the central planning organs. These quantities could be, at certain times, so large that both the peasants' subsistence and the expanded reproduction of agriculture were endangered.[5]

Thus, the "crisis of the NEP" and the "great change" to which this led were determined above all by a policy of industrialization which aimed at very rapid growth rates for industry and the introduction of the most "up-to-date" technology possible. This policy led, *in fact*, to the sacrificing of agriculture to the development of industry.[6]

This industrialization policy and the forms of collectivization which it called for were not at all dictated by the "general laws of the building of socialism" or by the "principles of Marxism." They resulted from *a complex social process in which what was most important was the relations between classes.* Here a decisive role was played by the evolution of relations between the working class, the Party, and the leaders of industry—especially after the end of 1928, when the positions of the leaders of industry were strengthened, together with bourgeois forms of labor discipline. An equally important role was played by the evolution of relations between the peasantry, the Soviet power, and the working class. These developments, with the changes that resulted from them, were directly due to class struggles. The outcome of these struggles depended partly on the past history of the contending classes and the conditions in which new social forces were emerging (in the apparatuses of the Party and the State, and also in the economic apparatuses). It depended partly, also, as we have seen, on the *ideological relations in which these classes were caught*, relations bound up with the history of these classes, and on changes in the Bolshevik ideological formation. These changes determined (in the absence of any previous experience of socialist industrialization) the way in which the Party appreciated the meaning and implications of the economic and social contradictions, and also the way of dealing with these contradictions that seemed correct, or possible. It was in this unique history, which was also that of a revolutionary ideological formation, that the "crisis of the NEP" and the solutions found for it had their roots.

The uniqueness of this history does not, of course, signify that no *universal lessons* can be derived from it. These lessons concern the effects of class struggles upon the reproduction and transformation of social relations, of the economic basis, and of the superstructure. They concern also the class consequences of these changes, the way in which Marxism and revisionism, the socialist road and the capitalist road, come into conflict, and the conditions for victory of one over the other.

In volume III of this work we shall see what were the principal long-term consequences of the changes undergone by the Soviet formation in the early 1930s. As for the more immediate consequences, which will also be examined in the next volume, it is important to emphasize at once their contradictory aspects. On the one hand there was the complete defeat of the private bourgeoisie, the numerical increase of the Soviet proletariat, the modernization of the economy, and a tremendous industrial advance, which contributed to the advance of the forces fighting for socialism throughout the world. On the other hand, the worker-peasant alliance was gravely weakened, the industrial development of the USSR became more and more one-sided, and the primacy accorded to technology tended to strengthen the role played by the technicians and by the administrative and economic apparatuses, and even by the apparatus of repression. Thus, contradictions of a new type emerged. The subsequent changes undergone by the Soviet social formation were determined by the class struggles which were to develop amid these new contradictions and by the way in which the Bolshevik Party was to reckon with these contradictions and to try and handle them.

Notes

1. *History of the C.P.S.U.(B.)*, pp. 286–287.
2. Yakovtsevsky, *Agrarnye otnosheniya*, p. 297 (also in *Recherches internationales*, no. 85 [no. 4 of 1975], p. 59).
3. Elleinstein, *Le Socialisme*, p. 88.
4. The *History of the C.P.S.U.(B.)* mentions, moreover, that at the end of the NEP period "the process of the splitting up of the large farms . . . was still going on" (pp. 286–287).
5. This was the case at the beginning of the 1930s, a point to which I shall return in volume III.
6. It is necessary to say *"in fact"* because, according to the "plans," agriculture was also supposed to develop rapidly.

Bibliography

Documents of the Bolshevik Party and of the Soviet government and administrative bodies

1. Reports of the Bolshevik Party's congresses

X-y Syezd RKP(b), stenotchet. Moscow: 1963.
XI-y Syezd RKP(b), stenotchet. Moscow: 1961.
XII-y Syezd RKP(b), stenotchet. Moscow: 1961.
XIII-y Syezd RKP(b), stenotchet. Moscow: 1924 and 1963.
XIV-y Syezd VKP(b), stenotchet. Moscow: 1926.
XV-y Syezd VKP(b), stenotchet. Moscow: 1961. Vol. 2, Moscow: 1962.
Report of the 15th Congress of the C.P.S.U. London: Communist Party of Great Britain, 1928. (Abridged.)
XVI-y Syezd VKP(b), stenotchet. Moscow and Leningrad: 1930.
XVII-y Syezd VKP(b), stenotchet. Moscow: 1934.

2. Reports of the Bolshevik Party's conferences

XV-taya Konferentsiya VKP(b), stenotchet. Moscow: 1927.
XVI-taya Konferentsiya VKP(b), stenochet. Moscow: 1962.

3. Reports of Komsomol congresses

VII-oy Syezd V.L.K.S.M. Moscow: 1926.
VIII-oy Vsesoyuzny Syezd V.L.K.S.M. Moscow: 1928.

4. Reports of Trades Union congresses

VI-oy Syezd Professionalnykh Soyuzov SSSR. Moscow: 1925.
VII-oy Syezd Professionalnykh Soyuzov SSSR. Moscow: 1927 and 1929.
Professionalnye Soyuzy SSSR, 1926–1928: Otchet k VIII Syezdu. Moscow: 1928
VIII-oy Syezd Professionalnykh Soyuzov SSSR. Moscow: 1929.

5. *Reports of congresses of soviets*

X-y Vserossiisky Syezd Sovyetov. Moscow: 1923.
SSSR: IV Syezd Sovyetov. Moscow: 1927.
XIV-y Vserossiisky Syezd Sovyetov. Moscow: 1929.

6. *Other reports and collections of documents*

Byulleten II-oy Vsesoyuznoy Konferentsii po NOT. Moscow: 1924.
Direktivy K.P.S.S. i Sovyetskogo pravitelstva po khozyaistvennym voprosam. Vols. I and II. Moscow: 1957.
Kongressy Kominterna. 6 vols. Moscow: 1929.
K.P.S.S. v rezolyutsiyakh i resheniyakh. 2 vols. Moscow: 1953.
Plenum Byudzhetnoy Komissii Ts.I.K. SSSR. Moscow: 1927.
Protokoli zasedanii presidiuma V.S.N.Kh. SSSR 1928–1929. Moscow: 1929.
Sechster Kongress der Kommunistischen Internationale. Vol. III. Hamburg: 1928.
II-ya Sessiya Ts.I.K. SSSR 4 Soyuza. n.d. (1927?).
V.K.P.(b.) v profsoyuzakh. Moscow: 1940.
V.K.P.(b.) v resolyutsiyakh. Moscow: 1941.

Collections of statistics and documents concerning the control figures and economic plans

Itogi desyatiletiya sovyetskoy v tsifrakh (1917–1927). Moscow: n.d. (1928).
Kontrolnye tsifry narodnogo khozyaistva SSSR na 1926–1927 gg. Moscow: 1927.
Kontrolnye tsifry na 1927–1928 gg. Moscow: 1928.
Kontrolnye tsifry na 1929–1930 gg. Moscow: 1930.
Kontrolnye tsifry po trudu na 1928–1929 gg. Moscow: 1929.
Materialy osobogo soveshchaniya po vosproizvodstvu osnovnogo kapitala pri prezidume V.S.N.Kh., seriya III, vypusk II: perspektivy razvitiya selskogo khozyaistva. Moscow and Leningrad: 1927.
Materialy po istorii SSSR. Vol. III. U.S.S.R. Academy of Sciences: 1959.
Narodnoye khozyaistvo SSSR: statistichesky spravochnik. Moscow: 1932.

Narodnoye khozyaistvo SSSR v 1958 g. Moscow: 1929.
Narodnoye khozyaistvo SSSR v 1961 g. Moscow: 1962.
Narodnoye khozyaistvo SSSR v 1970 g. Moscow: 1971.
Osnovniye Problemy Kontrolnykh Tsifry (1929–1930). Moscow: 1931.
Perspektivy Promyshlennosti na 1925–1926 operatsionny god. Moscow: 1925.
Pyatiletny Plan Narodno-khozyaistvennogo stroitelstva SSSR. 3 vols. Moscow: Gosplan, 1929.
Sotsialisticheskoye Stroitelstvo SSSR. Moscow: 1934, 1935, 1936.
Trud v SSSR. Moscow: Central Statistics Board, 1936.
Voprosy truda v tsifrakh i diagrammakh 1922–1926 gg. Moscow: 1927.

Books and articles

The All-Union Textile Syndicate. Moscow: VSNKh, n.d.
Althusser, L. Foreword to *Lyssenko, histoire réelle d'une science prolétarienne,* by D. Lecourt. See Lecourt, below.
Angarov, A. L. *Klassovaya borba v sovyetskoy derevne.* Moscow: 1929.
Arnold, A. Z. *Banks, Credit and Money in Soviet Russia.* New York: 1937.
Badiou, A. *Théorie de la contradiction.* Paris: Maspero, 1975.
Balibar, E. *Sur la dictature du prolétariat.* Paris: Maspero, 1976. (Available in English: *On the Dictatorship of the Proletariat.* London: New Left Books, 1977.)
Baryshev, N. "Novye zavoyevaniya derevenskoy bednoty." *Na Agrarnom Fronte,* no. 9 (1928).
Bauman. "Uroki khlebozagotovok." *Bolshevik,* nos. 13–14 (1928).
Baykov, A. *The Soviet Economic System.* Cambridge (England): Cambridge University Press, 1946.
Bettelheim, C. *Class Struggles in the USSR: First Period, 1917–1923.* New York: Monthly Review Press, 1976.
———. *Economic Calculation and Forms of Property.* London: Routledge, 1976. New York: Monthly Review Press, 1975.
———. *La Plantification soviétique.* Paris: Marcel Rivière, 1946.
Bogdanov, Alexander. *Allgemeine Organisationslehre: Tektologie.* Berlin: 1926.

————. "Principles of Organization of Social Technology and Economy" (in Russian). *Vestnik Kommunisticheskoy Akademii*, vol. 4 (1923).

Bogovoi, I. "Perevybory sovyetov v derevne i rasshirenii demokratii." *Bolshevik*, nos. 9–10 (1926).

Bolshaya Sovyetskaya Entsiklopediya. 1st ed., vol. 11. Moscow: 1930.

Braverman, Harry. *Labor and Monopoly Capital: The Degradation of Work in the Twentieth Century*. New York: Monthly Review Press, 1974.

Broué, P. *Le Parti bolchévique*. Paris: Editions de Minuit, 1963.

Bryukhanov, K. "Itogi khlebnoy kampanii 1928–1929 g." *Ekonomicheskoye Obozreniye*, XI (1929).

Bukharin, N. I. *Building Up Socialism*. London: Communist Party of Great Britain, 1926.

————. "A Critique of the Opposition's Economic Platform" (in Russian). *Bolshevik*, no. 1 (1925). (Available in French in Bukharin et al, *Le Débat soviétique sur la loi de la valeur*, cited below.)

————. *Historical Materialism*. London: Allen and Unwin, 1926.

————. "The 'Law of Socialist Accumulation,' or Why We Ought Not to Replace Lenin by Preobrazhensky" (in Russian). *Pravda*, no. 153 (1926). (Available in French in Bukharin, *Le Socialisme dans un seul pays*, cited below.)

————. "Lenin i zadachi nauki v sotsialisticheskom stroitelstve." *Pravda*, January 20, 1929.

————. "Lenin's Political Testament" (in Russian). *Pravda*, January 24, 1929.

————. "Nekotorye problemy sovremennogo kapitalizma i teoretikov burzhuazii." *Pravda*, May 26, 1929.

————. "Notes of an Economist" (in Russian). *Pravda*, September 30, 1928.

————. "O nekotorykh zadachakh nashei raboty v derevne." *Bolshevik*, nos. 7–8 (1924).

————. "O novoy ekonomicheskoy politike i nashikh zadachakh." *Bolshevik*, nos. 8 and 9–10 (1925).

————. *Politicheskoye zaveschaniye Lenina*. 2nd ed. Moscow: 1929.

————. *Le Socialisme dans un seul pays*. Paris: Collection 10/18, 1974.

————. "Teoriya 'organizovannoy bezkhozyaistvennosti' " *Pravda*, June 6, 1929.

————. *Uroki khlebozagotovok, Shakhtinskogo dela, i zadachi partii.* Leningrad: 1928.

————. *V zashchitu proletarskoy diktatury: Sbornik.* Moscow and Leningrad: 1928.

Bukharin, N., et al. *Le Débat soviétique sur la loi de la valeur.* Paris: Maspero, 1972.

————. *La Question paysanne en URSS.* Paris: Maspero, 1973.

Carr, E. H. *The Bolshevik Revolution.* London: Penguin, 1966.

————. *The Interregnum.* London: Macmillan, 1965.

————. *Socialism in One Country.* Vol I. London: Macmillan, 1964.

Carr, E. H., and Davies, R. W. *Foundations of a Planned Economy (1926–1929).* London: Macmillan, 1969.

Champernaud, F. *Révolution et contre-révolution culturelle en U.R.S.S.* Paris: Anthropos, 1976.

Chernov, M. T. "Opyt khlebozagotovitelnoy kampanii 1927–1928." *Ekonomicheskoye Obozreniye,* no. 1 (1930).

Claudín, F. *The Communist Movement: From Comintern to Cominform.* London: Penguin, 1975.

Cohen, Stephen F. *Bukharin and the Bolshevik Revolution: A Political Biography, 1888–1938.* London: Wildwood House, 1974.

Collette, J. M. *Politique des investissements et calcul économique.* Paris: Cujas, 1964.

Daniels, Robert V. *The Conscience of the Revolution: Communist Opposition in Soviet Russia.* Cambridge: Harvard University Press, 1960.

————. *A Documentary History of Communism.* New York: Random House, 1960.

Danilov, V. P., ed. *Ocherki istorii kollektivizatsii selskogo khozyaistva v soyuznykh respublikakh.* Moscow: 1963.

Deutscher, I. *The Prophet Unarmed.* London: Oxford University Press, 1959.

Dobb, M. *Soviet Economic Development since 1917.* London: Routledge, 1948.

Draper, T. "The Ghost of Social-Fascism." *Commentary* (February 1960).

Dyachenko, V. *Sovyetskie finansy v pervoy faze razvitiya sovyetskogo gosudarstva.* Moscow: 1947.

Eimermacher, Karl. *Dokumente zur Sowjetischen Literaturpolitik 1917–1932.* Stuttgart: 1972.

Elleinstein, J. *Histoire de l'URSS*. Vol. 2: *Le Socialisme dans un seul pays (1922–1939)*. Paris: Editions Sociales, 1973.

—————. *Histoire du phénomène stalinien*, Paris: Grasset, 1975.

—————. *The Stalin Phenomenon*. London: Lawrence and Wishart, 1976. (This is an abridged translation of *Histoire du phénomène stalinien*.)

Entsiklopediya russkogo eksporta. Vol. I. Moscow: 1925.

Erlich, A. *The Soviet Industrialization Debate*. Cambridge: Harvard University Press, 1967.

Etchin, A. *O yedinonachalii*. Moscow: 1930.

Fabrègues, B. "La 'Révolution permanente': une absurde théorie gauchiste." *Communisme*, no. 12 (September–October 1974).

—————. "Staline et le matérialisme historique." *Communisme*, nos. 22–23 (May–August 1976).

—————. "Staline, la lutte de classes, l'état." *Communisme*, no. 24 (September–October 1976).

Fainsod, Merle. *Smolensk Under Soviet Rule*. London: Macmillan, 1959.

Gaister, A., and Levin, A. "The Composition of the Party's Rural Organizations" (in Russian). *Bolshevik*, nos. 9–10 (1929).

Geschichte der Politischen Ökonomie des Sozialismus (by a group of Leningrad University professors). Berlin: 1973.

Goldenberg, E. "The German Problem" (in Russian). *Bolshevik*, March 15, 1928.

Gorky, Maxim. *The Russian Peasant*. See R.E.F. Smith, below.

—————. Article in *Russky Sovremennik*. Vol. I. Berlin: 1924.

Grinko, G. F. "Plan velikikh rabot." *Planovoye Khozyaistvo*, no. 2 (1929).

Grosskopf, S. *L'Alliance ouvrière et paysanne en URSS (1921–1928): Le Problème du blé*. Paris: Maspero, 1976.

History of the C.P.S.U.(B.): Short Course. Moscow: Foreign Languages Publishing House, 1939.

Hoeffding, O. *Soviet National Income and Product in 1928*. New York: Columbia University Press, 1954.

Hofmann, W. *Die Arbeitsverfassung der Sowjetunion*. Berlin: 1956.

—————. *Stalinismus und Antikommunismus*. Frankfurt-am-Main: 1967.

Industrialisation and Foreign Trade. League of Nations: 1945.

Istoriya Kommunistecheskoy Partii Sovyetskogo Soyuza. Vol. IV. Moscow: 1971.

Istoriya politicheskoy ekonomiki sotsializma. Leningrad: 1972.

Ivnitsky, N. "O nachalnom etape sploshnoy kollektivizatsii." *Voprosy Istorii KPSS*, no. 4 (1964).

Kamener, L. *Nashi dostizheniya, trudnosti i perspektivy.* Moscow: 1925.

————. *Stati i ryechi.* Moscow: 1925. Vol. XII, Moscow: 1926. Vol. I and vol. XI, Moscow: 1929.

Karez, J. F. "From Stalin to Brezhnev: Soviet Agricultural Policy in Historical Perspective." In *The Soviet Rural Community,* edited by James R. Millar. Chicago: University of Illinois Press, 1971.

Kerblay, B. *Les Marchés paysans en URSS.* Paris: Mouton, 1968.

Konyukhov, *KPSS v borbe s khlebnymi zatrudneniyami v strane (1928–1929).* Moscow: 1960.

Krzhizhanovsky, G. M. *Desyat let khozyaistvennogo stroitelstva SSSR 1917–1927.* Moscow: 1928.

Kuibysheva, G. V. et al. *V. V. Kuibyshev: Biografiya.* Moscow: 1964.

Lapidus, I., and Ostrovityanov, K. *Outline of Political Economy.* London: Martin Lawrence, 1929.

Larin, Yu. *Chastnyi Kapital v SSSR.* Moscow and Leningrad: 1927.

Lecourt, D. *Lyssenko, histoire réele d'une science prolétarienne.* Paris: Maspero, 1976. (Available in English: *Proletarian Science? The Case of Lysenko.* London: New Left Books, 1977.)

Lenin, V. I. *Collected Works.* 4th ed. in English. Moscow: Foreign Languages Publishing House, 1960–1970.

————. *O literature i iskusstve.* 2nd ed. Moscow: 1960.

————. *Über Kultur und Kunst.* Berlin: 1960.

Lenin, M. "Disappearance of Planning in the Plan." *Slavic Review* (June 1973).

Russian Peasants and Soviet Power. London: Allen and Unwin, 1968.

————. "Taking Grain: Soviet Policies of Agricultural Procurement before the War." In *Essays in Honour of E. H. Carr,* edited by C. Abramsky and Beryl G. Williams. London: Macmillan, 1974.

Lindenberg, D. *L'Internationle communiste et l'école de classe.* Paris: Maspero, 1972.

Linhart, Robert. *Lénine, les paysans, Taylor.* Paris: Editions du Seuil, 1976.

————. "La NEP, quelques caractéristiques de la transition soviétique." In *Etudes de planification socialiste.* Paris: SER, 1966.

Litoshenko, L. N. "Krestyanskoye khozyaistvo i rynok." *Ekonomicheskoye Obozreniye,* no. 5 (1925).

Lorenz, Richard *Das Ende der Neuer Ökonomischer Politik.* Marburg-am-Lahn: 1970.

————. *Sozialgeschichte der Sowjetunion 1917–1945.* Frankfurt-am-Main: 1976.

Lositsky, A. E. "Perspektivy potrebleniya prodovolstvennykh produktov v Soyuze." *Planovoye Khozyaistvo,* no. 4 (1927).

Madjarian, G. "Marxisme, conception stalinienne, révisionnisme." *Communisme,* nos. 22–23 (May–August 1976).

Magaline, A. D. *Lutte de classes et dévalorisation du capital.* Paris: Maspero, 1975.

Malafeyev, A. N. *Istoriya tsenoobrazovaniya SSSR, 1917–1963.* Moscow: 1964.

Male, D. J. *Russian Peasant Organisation before Collectivisation.* Cambridge (England): Cambridge University Press, 1971.

Mao Tse-tung. *Four Essays on Philosophy.* Peking: Foreign Languages Press, 1966.

————. *Mao Tsé-toung et la construction du socialisme.* Edited by Hu Chi-hsi. Paris: Editions du Seuil, 1974.

————. *Mao Tse-tung Unrehearsed.* Edited by Stuart R. Schram. London: Penguin, 1974.

————. *Quotations from Chairman Mao Tse-tung,* 2nd vest-pocket ed. Peking: Foreign Languages Press, 1972.

Marx, Karl. *Capital.* Vol. I. London: Penguin, 1976.

————. *Capital.* Vol. II. Moscow: Foreign Languages Publishing House, 1957.

————. *Capital.* Vol. III. Moscow: Foreign Languages Publishing House, 1959.

————. *A Contribution to the Critique of Political Economy.* London: Lawrence and Wishart, 1971.

————. *Grundrisse der Kritik der Politischen* Ökonomie (in English). London: Penguin, 1973.

Marx-Bakounine: socialisme autoritaire ou socialisme libertaire. Edited by G. Ribeill. Paris: Collection 10/18, 1976.

Marx, K., and Engels, F. *Collected Works.* London: Lawrence and Wishart, 1975.

————. *Marx and Engels on The Russian Menace to Europe.* Edited by Paul W. Blackstock and Bert J. Hoselitz. London: Allen and Unwin, 1953.

————. *On The Paris Commune.* Moscow: Progress, 1971.

————. *Selected Correspondence.* Moscow: Foreign Languages Publishing House, 1956.

————. *Selected Works in Three Volumes.* Moscow: Progress, 1969–1970.

————. *La Social-Démocraticè allemande*. Paris: Collection 10/18, 1975.

————. *Werke*. Berlin: Dietz Verlag, 1962–1969.

Marx, Engels and Lenin on Anarchism and Anarcho-Syndicalism. Moscow: Progress, 1972.

Mende, G. von. *Studien zur Kolonisation der Sowjetunion*. Breslau: Priebatsch, 1933.

Mendelson, A., ed. *Pokazateli Konyunkturi, narodnogo khozyaistva SSSR za 1923-1924–1928-1929 gg*. Moscow: 1930.

Meyer, Gert. *Studien zur Sozialökonomischen Entwicklung Sowjetrusslands 1921–1923*. Cologne: Pahl Rugenstein Verlag, 1974.

Mezhlauk, V. Speech printed in *Internationale Presse-Korrespondenz*, no. 116 (1929).

Milyutin, V. "Uroki khlebozagotovok." *Na Agrarnom Fronte*, no. 4 (1928).

Narkiewicz, O. *The Making of the Soviet State Apparatus*. Manchester, England: Manchester University Press, 1970.

————. "Soviet Administration and the Grain Crisis of 1927–1928. *Soviet Studies* (October 1968).

Nove, A. *An Economic History of the U.S.S.R.* London: Penguin, 1972.

Obzor deyatelnosti NKT SSSR za 1927–1928 gg. Moscow: 1928.

Oganovsky, N. P. "Maksimalny variant perspektivnogo plana rekonstruktsii selskogo khozyaistva." *Planovoye Khozyaistvo*, no. 7 (1927).

Ostrovityanov, K. V. et al. *Political Economy*. London: Lawrence and Wishart, 1957.

Pashukanis, ed. *15 let sovyetskogo stroitelstva*. Moscow: 1932.

Patouillet, J., ed. *Le Code pénal de la R.S.F.S.R.* Paris: Librairie générale de droit et de jurisprudence, 1935.

Penal Code of the R.S.F.S.R. (Text of 1926, with amendments up to December 1, 1932.) London: HMSO, 1934.

Pollock, Friedrich. *Die planwirtschaftlichen Versuche in der Sowjetunion 1917–1927*. 1929; Frankfurt: Archiv Sozialistischen Literatur, 1971.

Postroyeniye fundamenta sotsialisticheskoy ekonomiki v SSSR 1926–1932. Moscow: 1960.

Poulain, E. *Le Mode d'industrialisation socialiste en Chine*, Paris: Maspero, 1977.

Preobrazhensky, E. *The New Economics*. Oxford: Clarendon, 1965.

Prokopovicz, S. N. *Histoire économique de l'URSS*. Paris: Flammarion, 1952.

Rashin, A. G. *Zarabotnaya plata na vostanovitelny period khozyaistva SSSR*. Moscow: 1928.

Rezunov, M. *Selskie sovyety i zemelnye obshchestva*. Moscow: 1928.

Rigby, T. H. *Communist Party Membership in the USSR, 1917–1967*. Princeton: Princeton University Press, 1968.

Rogachevskaya, L. *Iz istorii rabochego klassa SSSR*. Moscow: 1959.

Rosnitsky, N. *Litso derevni*. Moscow and Leningrad: 1926.

Rozenfeld, Y. S. *Promyshlennaya Politika SSSR*. Moscow: 1926.

Schapiro, L. *The Communist Party of the Soviet Union*. 2nd ed. London: Methuen, 1970.

Schwarz, S. *Labor in the Soviet Union*. New York: 1953.

———. *Les Ouvriers en Union Soviétique*. Paris: Marcel Rivière, 1956. (This is a French translation of *Labor in the Soviet Union*, with additional material.)

Sdvigi v selskom khozyaistve SSSR. 2nd ed. Moscow: 1931.

Shapiro, D. "Kustarno-remeslennaya promyshlennost." *Planovoye Khozyaistvo*, no. 6 (1927).

Skirda, Alexander. *Kronstadt 1921: Prolétariat contre bolchévisme*. Paris: Editions Tête de Feuilles, 1971.

Smith, R. E. F., ed. *The Russian Peasant: 1920 and 1984*. London: Cass, 1977.

Spulber, N. *Soviet Strategy for Economic Growth*. Bloomington: Indiana University Press, 1966.

———. *The Soviet Economy*. New York: Norton, 1969.

Stalin, J. V. *Leninism*. London: Lawrence and Wishart, 1940.

———. *Works*. Moscow: Foreign Languages Publishing House, 1952–1955.

Strong, A. L. *The Soviets Conquer Wheat*. New York: 1931.

———. *The Stalin Era*. New York: Mainstream, 1956.

Strumilin, S. G. *Na khozyaistvennom fronte*. Moscow: 1925.

———. *Na novykh putyakh*. Moscow: 1923.

———. *Na planovom fronte*. Moscow: 1958.

———. *Problemy Ekonomiki Truda*. Moscow: 1964.

———. "Rassloyenie sovyetskoy derevni." *Planovoye Khozyaistvo*, no. 3 (1928). Available French: *Recherches internationales à la lumière du marxisme*, no. 85 [no. 4 of 1975].)

Taniuchi, Y. *The Village Gathering in Russia in the Mid-1920s*. Birmingham: 1968.

Timofeyev, P. G. *Ekonomicheskaya geografiya SSSR*. 6th ed. Moscow: 1929.

Trapeznikov, S. P. *Kommunisticheskaya partiya v periode nastupleniya sotsializma.* 2nd ed. Moscow: 1960.

Trotsky, L. D. *De la révolution.* Paris: Minuit, 1963.

———. *Nasha pervaya revolyutsiya.* Moscow: 1925.

———. *The New Course.* London: New Park Publications, 1956.

———. *The Third International After Lenin.* 2nd ed. New York: Pioneer, 1957.

———. *Writings 1930–1931.* New York: Pathfinder, 1973.

Ulashevich, V., ed. *Zhenshchina v kolkhozc.* Moscow: 1930.

Vaganov, F. M. *Pravy Uklon v VKP(b).* Moscow: 1970.

Valentinov, N. "De la 'NEP' à la collectivisation." *Le Contrat social* (March–April 1964).

Vareikis. "O partiinom rukovodstve kolkhoza." *Na Agrarnom Fronte,* no. 8 (1929).

Voprosy kultury pri diktature proletariata. Moscow and Leningrad: 1925.

Wells, H. G. *Russia In The Shadows.* London: Hodder and Stoughton, 1920.

Yakovlev, Ya. A. *Ob oshibkakh khlebofurazhnogo balansa TsSU i ego istolkovatelei.* Moscow: 1926.

Yakovlev, Ya. A., ed. *K voprosu o sotsialisticheskom pereustroistve selskogo khozyaistva.* Moscow and Leningrad: 1928.

Yakovtsevsky, V. *Agrarnye otnosheniya v periode stroitelstva sotsializma.* Moscow: 1964. (A French translation of chapters IX and X is available in *Recherches internationales à la lumière du marxisme,* no. 85 [no. 4 of 1975].)

Yaroslavsky, Ye. *Chistka Partii.* Moscow: 1929.

Zaleski, E. *Planning for Economic Growth in the Soviet Union, 1918–1932.* Chapel Hill: North Carolina Press, 1971.

Za Marksistsko-leninskoye ucheniye o pechati. Moscow: 1932.

Zinoviev, G. *The Anti-Soviet Parties and Tendencies.* 1922.

———. *Leninizm.* Moscow: 1925.

Principal journals and periodicals

In Russian

Bednota
Bolshevik

Byulleten Konyunkturnogo Instituta
Ekonomicheskaya Zhizn
Ekonomicheskoye Obozreniye
Istoricheskiye Zapiski
Istorichesky Arkhiv
Izvestiya
Izvestiya Tsentralnogo Komiteta VKP(b)
Leningradskaya Pravda
Moskovskiye Kommunisty
Na Agrarnom Fronte
Otechestvenniye Zapiski
Partiinaya Zhizn
Planovoye Khozyaistvo
Pravda
Predpriyatiye
Sobranie Uzakonenii
Sobranie Zakonov
Sotsialisticheskoye Khozyaistvo
Sotsialistichesky Vestnik
Torgovo-Promyshlennaya Gazeta
Trud
Vestnik Kommunisticheskoy Akademii
Voprosy Torgovli
Voprosy Truda

In English

International Press Correspondence

In German
Ästhetik und Kommunikation: Beiträge zur Politischen Erziehung
Internationale Presse-Korrespondenz

Index

Absenteeism, *see* Labor discipline

Accounting, 50

Accumulation
  characteristics of relations between classes and domination of expanded reproduction by demands of, 308–15
  decisive role to, in development of industrial production, 388
  expanded reproduction and, 306–8
  maximum, Party ideology and, 506–7
  optimum rate of, 383, 385
  planning and allocation of accumulated capital, 75–76
    See also Planning
  primitive socialist, 367, 374
    recourse to, 321–23
    Stalin support for idea of, 401
  problems of, and evolution of peasant consumption, 153–58
  process of, 305–6

Actual occupation criterion, 335

Administrative apparatus
  in collectivization drive, 464

criticized (1925), 370
  fight against bureaucratization of, 435–39
    See also Bureaucracy
  intelligentsia in, 565–66
  Party members in, 335, 339
  Right deviation and, 422, 423
  role of, in orienting production, 281
    large-scale industry favored by, 202, 203
    See also Industrialization; Planning
  and soviets, 348–49
    in rural soviets, 170–71
    See also Experts; Management

"Against Vulgarizing The Slogan of Self-Criticism" (Stalin), 230–31

Agrarian Code (1922), 87, 118, 154, 174–75

Agrarian policy, *see* Agriculture; Collectivization

Agricultural Bank, 63

Agricultural laborers (*batraki*)
  attempt to organize, 41
  composition, 97
  use of, by peasants, 154–55, 369

Agricultural machinery, 92, 378
  exchange relations and, in NEP period, 138

Agricultural machinery (*cont.*)
  expanded production with, 416
  in grain procurement crisis, 89
  and ideological changes,
    519–20
  operators of, 560
  for reconstructing agriculture,
    429–31
  See also Collectivization
Agricultural production
  crisis in (1930s), 108
  and drawing up of plans,
    384–85
  increase in, over prewar figure
    (to 1932), 448
  from individual farms, in NEP
    period, 85
  industrialization and fall in
    (1929), 110
  NEP dooming, 589–90
  1921–1922 and 1926–1927, 28
  1925–1926 gross, 103
  possible by collective means,
    455
  rich peasants and, 368
  See also Agricultural machin-
    ery; *and entries begin-
    ning with term: Grain*
Agricultural products
  conversion of, into money,
    140–42
  gold-backed currency and ex-
    ports of, 58
  See also Exports
  price rise in (1929–1930),
    68–69
Agriculture
  as basis for industrial de-
    velopment, *see* Indus-
    trialization
  collective farms, 181, 473

  aid given cooperative and,
    105–7
  See also Collectivization
  degree of restoration of pro-
    ductive forces in (1925),
    26
  disadvantageous terms of trade
    for, 74
  individual farms, 85, 86
  land and, *see* Land
  policy on
    aggravation of contradictions
      through peasant and
      (1928–1929), 107–28
    and agriculture as basis for
      development of indus-
      try, 377, 383–84, 409,
      410, 448, 477, 556
    collectivization policy and
      industrialization,
      592–93
    Party role in, 357–58
    Party fight over policy,
      398–403
    shortcomings of (1924–
      1927), 102–3
    at Sixteenth Conference,
      454–59
  prices, *see* Prices
  production relations in,
    135–62
  technology and reconstruction
    of, 415–18, 429–31
  See also Agricultural
    machinery; Collectivi-
    zation; Grain procure-
    ment; Industrialization
All-Union Central Executive
    Committee (VTsIK),
    347–48, 355
All-union trusts, 271

See also Financial autonomy
Andreyev, A., 244, 375, 402
Annenkov, Pavel, 514, 515
Appropriation, planning and
    process of, 74
Authoritarianism, as class at-
    titude, 170

Balance of payments, grain pro-
    curement and, 34
Balance of trade, 1926–1929, 114
Bank financing electrification
    (Elektrobank), 63
Bank for industry (Prombank), 63
Banking system, 62–67
  illusions connected with
    functioning of, 63–67
Barter, state-peasant, 53–54
Batraki, *see* Agricultural laborers
Bazarov, V., 279
Bebel, A., 524
Bednyaki, *see* Poor peasants
Bogdanov, A. A., 510, 538
Bolotnikov (peasant), 559
Bolshevik (journal), 65
Bolshevik Party, 312, 331–42
  and contradictions between
    state and private sector,
    197
  dictatorship of proletariat and,
    see Dictatorship of pro-
    letariat
  and financial autonomy, 272
  formation and transformation
    of ideology of, 500–87
    effects of development of
      internal contradictions,
      534–66
    internal contradictions,
      508–34

gold standard and, 58–59
in grain procurement crisis, 38,
    40–41, 90
  emergency measures, 38–42
  grain balance and, 111
  See also Grain procurement
ideological and political rela-
    tions within, 355–59
  See also Industrialization;
    Worker-peasant alliance
illusions of, on control of
    economy, 65–66
illusions of, on development of
    economy, 66–67
management and
  and experts in banking sys-
    tem, 63
  and high salaries for mana-
    gers, 211
  noninterference of, 234–35
  and relations between man-
    agers and workers, 215
and mass movement of 1928,
    228–34
membership of
  bourgeoisie in, 333, 336,
    341–42
  goal of proletarianizing,
    331–34
  percent of peasants (1927–
    1929), 165
  policy of recruitment,
    553–55
  recruitment, 562–63
  working class, 334–35
NEP and, 25–27, 49, 205
  organizing peasants within
    framework of, 99
peasantry and, *see* Peasantry
planning organs and, 79, 80
  See also Planning

610 *Charles Bettelheim*

Bolshevik Party (*cont.*)
prices and
effect of price policy on,
139–40
ideological conception of
price, wages and profit
in, 285–86, 288
price policy of, 36–37,
150–51
production relations in
"socialist sector," 212
relations with working class,
215, 334–41
piece wages and, 242–45
and role of trade unions, 343
as vanguard, 317
wage differentials, 249–50
See also Trade unions;
Working class
in Smolensk affair, 223–35
social composition of, 335–37
as new bourgeoisie, 226–27
soviets and, 346–49, 367
rural soviets and, 167–73
splitting over worker-peasant
alliance, 119
See also Worker-peasant alliance
suspicious of egalitarian notions, 179–80
and unemployment
analysis of causes of, 295–98
measures to deal with, 298–
301
weak control by, of monetary
and financial systems
(until 1925), 67–68
See also Central Committee;
Central Control Com-
mission; Political
Bureau; Secretariat

Bolshevism, 501, 504, 506
reduced ability to use Marxism
to analyze reality, 535
See also Bolshevik Party
Bonuses, financial autonomy and
wage, 270
Bourgeois functions, 310–13
See also Management
Bourgeoisie
characteristics of, 552
Chinese, 379
defeat of, 594
ideology of, 181–83
intelligentsia and, 565
intensification of class struggle
with, 427
modified forms of relations between other classes and,
317–18
monolithism serving, 540–41
and nature of Soviet state, 429
in Party membership, 333, 336,
341–42
Party as new, 226–27
proletariat and, in NEP period,
32, 33, 205–6
rural, *see* Rich peasants
state ownership and expropriation of, 527
in state-owned enterprises,
528
See also Experts; Management
Budget
control of (1925), 59
gold-backed currency and, 58
growth of expenditures,
388–89
1921–1922, 55
restoration of balanced system
of, 62
Bukharin, N. I., 364

final defeat of, 459
and kulaks, 119, 155–56, 369,
    382, 383
on light and heavy industry,
    385
and new line, 116, 371, 373,
    374, 392, 398–411,
    418–35
and united opposition, 377
view of world situation by
    (1928), 404–6
working class character of state
    and, 553
Bureau of Labor Statistics, 68
Bureaucracy
    bureaucratization, 423–24
    fight against, 191, 224–25,
        435–37, 440–42, 454
    Marx on, 525
    organization of supervision by
        masses, 437–39
    restricting, not abolishing, 526
    See also Administrative ap-
        paratus; Experts; Man-
        agement

Capital
    Lenin on, 211
    planning and allocation of ac-
        cumulated, 75–76
    rural craftsmen and private,
        144
    shortage of, 297, 373
    state ownership function as
        collective, 291
    valorization of
        industrial employment and
            unemployment and,
            293, 302
        labor power and, 304–5

maintenance of demands of
    process of, 320–21
    See also Financial autonomy
Capital (Marx), 22, 67, 237, 408,
    515, 548
Capitalism
    crisis of (late 1920s), 404–5
    evolutionist view of history
        and restoration of, 550
    exploitation under, 237–38
    industrialization to avoid,
        366–67
    main base of, smashed, 471–72
    See also Rich peasants
    producing means of produc-
        tion under, 414
    and "Right danger" in Party,
        406–7
    See also Accumulation
Capitalist character
    of plans, 289–90
    of relations of production,
        266–67
Capitalist development
    NEP as road of, 25, 26
    planning organs and, 73
    of productive forces, 314–19
Capitalist relations, 49, 50
    Marx on, 516
    planning principle and, 73,
        288–90, 529–34
    unemployment and, 301–2
    See also Accumulation
CC, *see* Central Committee
CCC, *see* Central Control Com-
    mission
Central Committee (CC), 355,
    364
    authority shifted out of, 400,
        424, 459
    on banking system (1924), 64

Central Committee (*cont.*)
  Chinese question and, 379
  CLI and, 240, 241
  condemns Trotsky, 365
  "criticism" movement of 1928, 222
  decision of, on planning (Aug. 1927), 79
  decision on collectivization (1930), 468, 470, 471
  depriving Gosbank and Narkomfin of control over budgetary policy, 59
  economic planning, banking system and (1927), 65
  and grain procurement crisis, 40
    coercive measures to meet grain quotas, 125
    and 1929 grain procurement, 123
  kulak question and (1929), 465–66
  labor discipline sought by, 234
    calls for stricter labor discipline (1929), 452–53
  and mass recruitment, 333
  membership of (1926), 372
  NEP and, 25
  and new line (1928–1929), 401, 412–413, 425–47
  1925 resolution on leasing land, and wage relations in agriculture, 154
  and one-man management, 236
  and piece wages, 213, 242–43
  and platform of the 46, 362, 363
  production conferences and (1925), 218
  resolution on economic tasks (Apr. 1925), 369
  resolution on production conferences, 217
  resolution on rationalization (1927), 214
  resolution on trade (1927), 204
  on revolution from above, 523
  rural soviets and, 167, 168
  and tribute from peasantry, 403
  Trotsky and Zinoviev removed from, 381
  and united opposition, 376, 380
Central Committee of the Woodworkers' Union, 344
Central Control Commission (CCC), 224, 364, 439
  and new line (1928–1929), 425–27
  in purge of Party, 443, 444
Central Executive Committee of the Congress of Soviets, (TsIK), 118
Central Labor Institute (CLI), 239–41
Central Statistical Board, 88, 89
Central Trades Union Council, 235–36, 239, 246, 345
  production conferences and, 218–21
  and socialist emulation, 254
Chaplin, N., 240
Chauvinism, Great-Russian, 565–66
Chervonets roubles, 57, 60
Chiang Kai-shek, 379
China, 227, 312, 416
Chinese Communist Party, 316, 379, 536
Chinese revolution, 379, 380
Circular No. 33 (March 1926; "The Organization of the Management of Industrial Establishment"), 226

Circulation, role of kulaks in, 89–91

Civil Code (1922), 270

Civil personality of enterprises, 270

Civil War in France, The (Marx), 524–25

Class relations, *see specific classes*

Class struggle, 427–28, 508–9
in Party ideology, 510
Stalin's view of, 512, 513
See also Dictatorship of proletariat; *and specific classes*

Class Struggles in France, The (Marx), 527

CLD (Council of Labor and Defense), 78, 268

CLI (Central Labor Institute), 239–41

Collective agreements, 242, 373
planning and, 245–47
trade union role in, 343

Collective farms, *see* Agriculture; Collectivization

Collective forms
building, of production and distribution, 66
peasants and craftsmen in (1924–1928), 85
of cultivation, 100–1
of labor and production, 180, 181

Collective ownership, transforming state ownership into, of means of production, 291

Collectivization, 321
area of cultivation possible under, 100–1, 455
economistic interpretation of grain crisis, 187

mechanization and, 429–31
policy on, 110–11, 383
central role of state in, 526
collectivization from above, 42, 523
developing policy on, 420–22
great change in, 46–78, 590–93
new line, 413, 415–18
Sixteenth Party Conference and, 454–59
qualitative aspects of, 472–74
quantitative aspects of, 472
rural cells of Party and, 165–66
socialist ideas and, 519–20
solving procurement problems and, 126
Stalin on, 382, 462, 464, 468–70, 472
technical superiority of, 398
as voluntary act, 403, 418, 461

Comintern, 376, 379–80, 405–6, 425, 426, 501, 535–36, 561

Commercial units, number of, 204

Commissariats, *see entries beginning with term: People's*

Commission for settling labor disputes (RKK), 344

Commodity character of production and circulation, 210

Commodity exchange, development of, 29–30

Commodity production
of grain, in NEP period, 85
reconstituting, 54

Commodity relations, 49
between enterprises, and relations in production process, 266–67

Commodity relations (*cont.*)
  financial autonomy and, 269
  Party treatment of contradic-
      tions in forms of, 529–34
  planning and, 288
Communist Manifesto (Marx and
      Engels), 552
Communist Saturdays, 252
Competition, socialist emulation
      as, 253–54
"Concerning Questions of Agra-
      rian Policy in the
      U.S.S.R." (Stalin), 519
Congress of Soviets (1922), 274
Congress of Soviets (1927), 249
Consultative Council, 276
Consumer goods
  decline in investments in in-
      dustries producing, 387
  industrial investment policy
      and, 390–91
  production of, 29
    See also Agricultural
      machinery
Contracts purchase, 148, 150
*Contribution to the Critique of
      Political Economy*
      (Marx), 510, 515
Control from below, 222–36,
      230–31
Control commissions (local Party
      organs), 440
  in purge of Party, 443, 444
  rank-and-file, 436
Convention prices, 148, 149
Cooperation, aid given to foster,
      105–7
Cooperative industry
  evolution of, 199–203
  ownership of, 199
Cooperatives (and cooperative
      societies)

  craftsmen in, 144
  credit, 63
  expulsion from, for failure to
      meet grain require-
      ments, 124
  NEP and, 24
  percent of peasants in (1927),
      107
  socialism and entire peasantry
      in, 24
  workers', 312
Cost of living, grain prices affect-
      ing, 149
Council of Labor and Defence
      (CLD), 78, 268
Council of People's Commissars
      (Sovnarkom), 234,
      452–53
  Gosplan and, 78
  introduces financial autonomy,
      268
  small-scale industry and, 201
Council of syndicates, 276
Credit
  agricultural tools and system
      of, 102
  banking system and, 64
  gold-backed currency and, 58
  policy on, and return to paper
      currency, 60
  promoting state-sector ac-
      cumulation through ex-
      pansion of, 156
    See also Loans
Cultural revolution, 222, 227,
      422
Currency, 50
  balanced budget and stabiliza-
      tion of, 62
  confidence in, 68
  conversion of agricultural pro-
      duce into, 140–42

depreciation of, 55–57
and illusions of "war communism," 54–55
inflation of, to promote state-sector accumulation, 156
issuing of, 63
return to (1926) paper, 29, 54, 60–61
under "war communism," 53
See also Monetary system; *and specific monetary units*

Darwinism, 550
Death rate, fall in (1924–1927), 32
Declaration of the Eighty-three, 380
Declaration of the Thirteen, 375, 376
Democratic centralism, 356–58, 363–64, 370, 371, 378, 476–77, 507
monolithic principle and, 539–40
Democratic Centralism (group), 443
Demonstrations, 344
Deniken, A. I., 561
Dialectical and Historical Materialism (Stalin), 509–10, 513, 516, 538
Dialectical materialism, transformed, 536–48
Dictatorship of proletariat
bourgeoisie subordinated to, 318
class struggle as leading to, 509
and disappearance of proletariat, 316–17
and intensification of class struggle (1929), 427–28
NEP as form of, 22

Party as instrument of, 32, 543
See also Bolshevik Party
peasant support to consolidate, 103
monolithism and peasant opposition to, 541
percent of peasants in Party and, 167
perfect unity weakening, 540
planning under, 289–90
planning apparatus and, 50
and question of the state, 524–25
as dictatorship of the state, 544
and relations of production, 266
and rising wages, 314
and socialization of production, 210
state capitalism under, 291
state ownership under, 528
worker-peasant alliance and, 42, 358
See also Worker-peasant alliance
Discipline
Party, 424
See also Labor discipline
Distribution, planning and process of, 74
See also Planning
Division of labor, and allocation of capital, 75
"Dizzy with Success" (Stalin), 468, 470, 472
Doctors, increase in numbers of (1913–1928), 32
Dzerzhinsky, F., 219–20, 375, 386–87

Economic organs, decisive role of, as illusion, 66

Economic organs (*cont.*)
  See also specific economic organs
Economic planning, *see* Planning
Economic policy, NEP as, 24–30
  See also New Economic Policy
Economic relations, Party role in transforming, 66
Economist-technicist conception of productive forces, 508–19
  quantity and, 533–34
Economy, *see specific aspects of economy*
Education, student population, increase in, 31
Egalitarianism
  Party suspicious of, 179–80
  wage differentials and, 249–50
18th Brumaire, The (Marx), 527
Eighth Congress of the Trade Unions (1928), 233, 235, 249–50, 344, 453
Eighth Komsomol Congress (1928), 223, 224, 249
Electrification, 62, 77, 201
Eleventh Party Conference (1921), 56
Eleventh Party Congress (1922), 23, 35, 316–18, 332
Elektrobank (bank financing electrification), 63
Elleinstein, J., 591
Employment
  percent increase in (1927), 391
  wages, profits and evolution of, 293–301
  See also Unemployment
Engels, Friedrich, 420, 514, 523, 524, 551
Equipment
  obsolete, 311–12
  See also Agricultural machinery; Technology
Evolutionism, Marxism as, 548–50
Exchange
  analyzing social conditions of, 136
  constraints on, 136–39
  effect of price policy on social conditions of, 139–40
  evolution of, of agricultural produce, 140–42
  foreign
    and gold-backed currency, 58
    grain export for, 34
  participants forced into, 141–42
  town and country, during NEP period, 29–30
Exchange rate
  currency stability and legal, 61
  maintaining rouble, gold-backed currency and, 58
  maintaining parity, 59–60
Exchange value, planning with money and predominance of, over use value, 433
Executive Committee of Comintern, 376, 379–80
Experts
  currency reform and (1924), 59
  economist-technicist conception of productive forces, 508–19
    quantity and, 533–34
  in new banking system, 63
  of Osvok, 80
  and Party suspicious of egalitarian notions, 180
  of planning organs, 78

See also Planning; *and specific planning organs*
planning principle strengthening, 532
role of, in Party ideology, 555–58
technology and importance of, 518, 519
training of, 226–28
and working-class origins, 554–55
Exploitation, 95, 99, 237–38, 288, 319, 377, 428–29
Exports
gold-backed currency and policy on, 58
grain, 111, 113–14, 205
grain production fall and (1929), 110
1926–1928, 113, 114
Extractive industry, production in, 29

Farms, *see* Agriculture
February 4, 1924, decree of, 57–58
Feldman, G., 280
Fideism, 510
Fiduciary circulation, rise in (1928–1930), 69
Fifteenth Party Conference (1926), 106, 220, 221, 301, 376–78
Fifteenth Party Congress (1927), 36, 39, 86–87, 103, 105, 106, 144, 175, 176, 192, 204, 213, 221–23, 226, 301, 336, 374–76, 378–86, 391, 392
Fifth All-Union Congress of Soviets, 448–52
Fifth Komsomol Conference, 249

Financial autonomy (business accounting; *Khozraschet*), 267–84
development of, 268–76
of enterprises, 242
restricting effects of, 320
and state planning, 277–83
unemployment and, 294
Financial illusions, planning principle and, 532–33
Financial policy, and return to paper currency, 60
Financial system, weak degree of control of, 67–69
Fines for nondelivery of grain, 124
First Five-Year Plan, 122, 235, 241, 251–52, 254, 255, 319–21, 383, 418, 566
collectivization and, 460
and labor discipline, 453
large-scale industry under, 447
and machinery of state, 436
resolution on, at Sixteenth Party Conference, 448–52
Fiscal revenue, centralization of, 30
Food supply, 228
effect of, on rupture of worker-peasant alliance, 42
after 1927, 113
peasant consumption of (1926–1927), 112
Ford, Henry, 240
Foreign concessions, 199–203
Foreign exchange
and gold-backed currency, 58
grain export for, 34
Foreign trade, *see* Exports; Imports

Fourteenth All-Russia Congress of Soviets (1929), 176
Fourteenth Congress of Soviets (1927), 175
Fourteenth Party Conference (1925), 164, 169, 217, 218, 243
Fourteenth Party Congress (1925), 243, 244, 302, 333, 338, 365–76, 528, 554
Fourth Congress of the Comintern (1922), 277
Fourth Congress of Soviets (1927), 296
Free market, 29, 473–74
Frumkin, 399–400

Gastev, A., 239, 240
General Secretary, *see* Stalin, Joseph
Geneticist conception of development, 279
German Ideology, The (Marx), 514
Gold roubles, calculations in (as of March 1922), 56
Gold standard
   abandoned, 59–60, 68
   effects of adopting, 56–60
   political implications of abandoned, 60–61
Goods famine, 68, 69, 152–53
Goods-roubles, 55, 56
Gorky, Maxim, 558–59, 561, 563, 564, 566
Gosbank (state bank), 77, 78, 269, 274
   in banking system, 63
   and gold-backed currency, 58
   and monetary reform, 56, 57, 59–60
   reopened, 55–56
Goselro (State Commission for the Electrification of Russia), 77, 78
Gosplan, *see* State Planning Commission
Gotha Program, 552
GPU (State Political Administration), 466
Grain
   class differentiation of peasantry and market supply of, 88–89
   prices of, stability as goal, 149
   supplying, to towns, 33
   total marketed, 1924–1925 compared with 1913
Grain balance, problem of, 111–13
Grain exports, *see* Exports
Grain harvest
   collectivization and fall in (after 1931), 111
   fall in (1929), 110
   1925–1926, 95
   1926–1927, 28
   1926–1928, 37, 91
   1927–1928, 93, 94
   1931 estimate, 104
Grain procurement, 66
   agricultural policy and (1927–1928), 101–7
   crisis in, 37–38, 42, 101–2, 110
      basis of, 188
      chief effects of, and emergency measures, 109
      class foundation of crisis (1927–1928), 91–94

economic imbalances and
political mistakes ex-
plaining, 403
economistic interpretation
of, 187
effect of pricing scissors, 153
effects on class relations in
countryside, 114–15
emergency measures, 38–42,
108
as error of policy, 399
as kulak strike, *see* Rich
peasants
relations between classes
and, 431–33
Stalin's view of emergency
measures, 115–16
and state of worker-peasant
alliance, 33–44
fall in (1929), 123, 124
and fall in production, 109–10
gap in, and market prices for
grain, 149–50
ideological conflict in Party
and, 386
industrialization in conflict
with, 114
lack of change in agricultural
policy and, 107–8
and means of production,
94–99
1928–1929, 120–26
resistance to measures of,
121–26
and Right deviation (1929),
426–47
and tempo of industrialization,
401
tonnage of (1926–1927), 37
Grain production
collectivization, 462

decline in (1928), and renewal
of emergency measures,
109–11
fall of, worker-peasant alliance
rupture and, 42
in NEP period, 85
price policy unfavorable to,
149, 151–52
Grain reserves
exhaustion of, 110
inadequate (1926–1928), 93, 94
Great Britain, 276
Groman, V., 279
Grosskopf, S., 88, 91, 157
Group of 15, 378–79
Grundrisse (Marx), 49, 290

Handicrafts, 143–45, 200–2
Hero of Labor (decree July 27,
1927), 252
History of the C.P.S.U.(B.), 523,
589
"How to Organize Competi-
tion?" (Lenin), 253

Idealism, philosophical, 549, 550
Imports of industrial goods,
113–14
Incentives, material, 452–54
Income
percentage increase in cash
(1926–1927), 190
See also National income
Income distribution among
peasants, 112
India, 380
Industrial accidents, labor pro-
ductivity and, 243
Industrial goods
agricultural surplus and de-
mand for, 157–58

Industrial goods (*cont.*)
  gap between rural and urban
      consumption of, 156–57
  grain crisis and available, 93
  supply of, to peasantry, 142–47
    See also Agricultural
        machinery
  unavailable to peasants, 95
Industrial production
  1921–1922 and 1926–1927,
      28–29
  1925–1928, 158
  1926–1927, 200
  percent of, under state and
      cooperative sector, 32
  planned increase in (1929–
      1930), 458
Industrial sector, capital alloca-
      tion and state-owned, 75
    See also Investment
Industrial trusts
  organization of, 271
    See also Financial autonomy
Industrialization
  to avoid capitalism, 366–67
  central role of state in, 526
  effect on, of introducing sys-
      tem of financial au-
      tonomy, 273–74
  gold standard and, 58–60
  ideological conception of, 520,
      521
  importance of, 373–74
  inflation and, 194–95
  labor discipline and acceler-
      ated, 234–37
  launching of, 113–14
  mechanization and, 431
  new line on (1928), 413–15
  and Party ideology, 357–58,
      398–499, 507–8, 565–66

clashes in early 1928, 398–
      403
contradiction between in-
    dustrial and agricultural
    policy, and the great
    change, 457–60
deepening split in summer
    1928, 403–18
great change at end of 1929,
    460–78
open split, 418–33
Sixteenth Party Conference,
    433–57
peasantry and
  emphasis on industrializa-
      tion at expense of, 362,
      399–401, 409
  great change and, 457–60
  resistance of peasantry and
      accelerated, 122–23
  tribute to finance industry,
      297, 401, 403, 421, 422,
      428–29, 477, 507, 592
    See also Agriculture, policy
        on
planning and, 320
    See also Planning
policy on (1927), 382–83
production conferences and,
    218–23
as solution to unemployment,
    301
    See also Unemployment
Taylorism and socialist emula-
    tion, 237–57
trade union role in, 345
united opposition and rapid,
    374–82
VSNKh role in, 77
worker-peasant alliance and,
    119–20

See also Worker-peasant alliance

"Industrialization of the Country and the Right Deviation in the C.P.S.U.(B)" (Stalin), 413

Industry

  categories of price, wages, and profit in, *see* Prices; Profits; Wages

  contradiction between private and state sectors in, 197–208

  evolution of, 199–203

  expenditures on (1923–1928), 62

  financial autonomy of, *see* Financial autonomy

  forms and evolution of forms of ownership in, 199–203

  growth of large-scale (1929–1932), 447

  inflation and decrease of production in, 193

  integrated in overall process of reproduction of production conditions, 266–68

  investment in, *see* Investment management forms in, 210–13

  See also Management

  NEP in conflict with planning in, 206–7

  ownership of, 199

  percent of value of production by large-scale (1926–1927), 209

  private and rural handicrafts, 143–45

  selling price and cost of production in, 189–92

  small-scale industry vs. state, 202

  wages and productivity of labor in, 192–93

Inflation

  1922, 55

  1925–1927, 63

  1926–1929, 388–89

  origins of process of, 193–95

Instruments of production, 513, 516

  See also Means of production

Intellectuals

  alliance of workers and, and rallying of old intelligentsia, 561–65

  new intelligentsia, 565–66

Investment

  changes in financial autonomy and nature of, 280

  industrial, 388, 407–11

    maximum, as policy, 413–15, 417–18, 420, 422–23

    1927 and 1929, 447

    plans for (1926–1927 on), 386–88

    total (1926), 387

  job creation and, 296, 297

  origins of inflation in, 193–94

  overall plan of, 320

  profitability and, 305, 313–14

    See also Profits

  programs of, 30

  in reconstruction period, 556

Izvestiya (magazine), 366

June 8, 1927, decree of, 78–79

Juridical forms of ownership, production relations and, 527–29

Juridico-political interventions, planning as, 73

Kaganovich, L. M., 120, 235–36, 362, 375, 402
Kalashnikov, 181–82
Kalinin, M. I., 172, 365, 372, 382
Kamenev, L. B., 64, 88–89, 96, 369
    and new line (1928–1929), 421, 424
    policy criticisms by (1925), 370, 372
    policy on recruitment to Party and, 553
    and Right deviation, 412
    Trotsky attacked by, 364–65
    in united opposition, 374–82
Kerzhentsev, 240
Kezelev, 454
Khozraschet, see Financial autonomy
Kirov, S. M., 295, 372, 375
Kolchak, 561
Kolkhoz system, 108, 111, 461–62, 464
    entry of peasants into, 42
    in NEP period, 85
    See also Collectivization
Komnezamy (poor peasants' committees), 100, 124
Komsomol, 251, 252
Komsomolskaya Pravda (newspaper), 454
Kravel, I., 453
Kronstadt rebellion, 346, 541
Krupskaya, Nadezhda, 370, 377, 420–21, 459
Krzhizhanovsky, G. M., 64, 78
Kuibyshev, V. V., 59, 65, 214, 232, 235, 312, 389

line supported by, 392
and new line (1928), 398, 407–8
on NOT, 557
on plans, 280
and unrealism of plans, 451
Kulak threat (1928–1929), 102
Kulaki, see Rich peasants
Kulaks' strike, 88–90, 96, 101
Kuomintang, 379

Labor Code, 299
Labor discipline, 213–15, 220, 221, 229
    and forecasts of plan (to 1932), 452–54
    imposed from above, 234–37
    piece work and, 244
    predominant form of, 314–15
    Stalin on (1928), 231
    and unemployment, 312–13
Labor disputes
    settling, 344
    See also Collective agreements
Labor exchange statistics, 294–95
Labor exchanges, 298, 299, 453
Labor force, and illusions of "war communism" period, 267–68
Labor market, regulating, 298, 299
Labor productivity, 221
    and discipline, 453, 454
    piece wages to increase, 242–43
    and plan forecasts, 451–52
    planned increase in (to 1932), 449
    planning organs and, 246–47

shorter work day and, 228
socialist emulation and,
251–57
wages and, 192–93, 213, 390
See also Wages
trade union role in, 343, 345
work norms and need to raise,
214
Labor time, immediate, 49
Land
area under cultivation, 462
collective forms of cultivation, 100–1, 455
sowable (1924–1925), 97
changes in possession and distribution of (1928), 118
division of, among families,
180
land shortage, 296, 297, 300–1
rural overpopulation and
colonization of new,
296, 297
leasing of, 96–97
extending rights, 368, 369
right to lease, 154, 155
nationalization of, 87, 95
Land associations, small-scale
industry under, 201
Land community, 174–76
Lapidus, I., 212, 241, 274, 286–
88, 292, 302, 307, 315
Larin, Yuri, 144, 369
Lashevich, M., 375
Lassalle, F., 22, 551
Lassallism, 503
" 'Law of Primitive Socialist Accumulation,' or Why We
Should Not Replace
Lenin by Preob-
razhensky" (Bukharin),
374

League of Time (organization),
240
Left opposition, polarization in
agriculture, theses of,
86–87
Lenin, Vladimir Ilyich, 57, 361,
459
appeal to authority of, 235
and bourgeois labor parties,
331
and bureaucratization, 303,
424
cooperation as form leading to
socialist organization of
production in view of,
105–6
and development of revolutionary ideas by masses,
522
on dialectics, 537, 538
on dictatorship of proletariat,
22–23
and disappearance of pro-
letariat, 316
on economic development,
277, 278
on economics turning into
politics, 109
on financial autonomy, 271–72,
274
Great-Russian chauvinism
and, 566
internal contradictions in development as viewed
by, 509–10
and large-sclae industry, 202
Marxism and
on Marx's theory, 22, 502
on Marxism, 505
struggles to transform Marxism, 503–4

Lenin, Vladimir Ilyich (*cont.*)
   need to return to principles of
      Commune, 526
   NEP and, 49, 99, 153
      and NEP as worker-peasant
         alliance, 22–24
      as road to socialism, 66
      on small-scale industry,
         200–1, 555
   and one-man management,
      211, 288
   Party and
      on class base of Party, 540
      Party function and, 356
      on Party membership, 332–
         33, 336, 341
      and transformation of, 331,
         332
      union between Party and
         theory in view of, 546
   peasantry and
      on abuse of middle peasants,
         125
      on aid to peasants, 98–99
      and classification of farms,
         87
      collective farming and, 420,
         422
      collectivization and, 470
      organizing peasants within
         framework of NEP, 99
      on peasant opposition
         (1920), 541
      peasant soviets and, 380
      on productivity of small
         peasants, 137
      supplying peasants with
         means of production in
         view of, 430
   plans and
      planning organs as important
         to, 73

      on plans, 206–7
      on preparing plans, 448–49
   and priority development of
      industries producing
      means of production,
      414
   on relation between culture
      and class origin, 554–55
   and revolutions in the East,
      404
   and role of trade unions,
      215–16
   and socialist technique, 315
   on soviets, 543
   and Stalin's resignation, 364
   state and, 523, 524
      and destruction of state
         machinery, 368
      on role of state economic or-
         gans, 35
      on Soviet state, 429
      and state enterprise, 249
      on state machine, 436
      and state ownership, 210
   on surpassing advanced coun-
      tries, 415
   on Taylorism, 238–39
   technology and, 312, 417
   use of quotes from, 370, 371,
      477
   work norms and, 253
   and worker-peasant alliance,
      119, 420, 562
"Lenin and the Building of Collective Farms"
   (Krupskaya), 420
Lenin enrollments, 332
Leninism (Zinoviev), 370
Lessons of October, The
   (Trotsky), 364
"Letter to the Congress" (Lenin),
   364, 540

Linhart, R., 67
Livestock, 42
  reduction in number of, 117
Loans
  constraints to pay, 137
  financial autonomy and, 269,
      280
  to peasants, 107
  sought by state, in rural areas,
      58
Local trusts, *see* Financial au-
      tonomy
Lysenko, T. D., 547

Machinery
  wage differentials and, 250–51
  See also Agricultural machin-
      ery; Technology
Management
  challenge to existing forms of,
      226–28
  class struggle and role of,
      215–17
  of collective farms, 473
  control of, from below, 222–26,
      230–31
  favoring freedom to hire, 299
  and financial autonomy, 267,
      268
    See also Financial autonomy
  financial proposals of (1921),
      56
  hostile to workers' coopera-
      tives and local industry,
      312
  intelligentsia in, 564, 565
  labor discipline and, 234–37
  and new line (1928), 417
  one-man, reaffirming, 236, 246
    Lenin and, 211, 288
  piece work, wage norms and,
      213–14, 241–47

power and relative autonomy
    of, 387
pressure by (1926–1928), for
    industrialization, 391
  role of, in accelerated indus-
      trialization (to 1932),
      452–53
    See also Industrialization
production conferences op-
    posed by, 217–22
in Shakhty affair, 223–24
socialist emulation and,
    251–57
in state factories, 210–13
strengthening of, 310
Taylorism and, 238, 239
three-shift work and, 228–39
wages of managers, 249
work norms revised by, 243
worker criticism and, 33,
    228–34
  See also Administrative ap-
      paratus; Experts
*Manifesto of the Communist
    Party*, 515, 527
Manufacturing industry, produc-
    tion in, 29
Mao Tse-tung, 316, 536
Marketing
  of agricultural produce,
      1923–1924 compared
      with prewar, 140–41
  of grain, surplus (reserve) and,
      93
  grain procurement as form of,
      34
Marx, Karl, 408
  on bureaucracy, 525
  on changing labor relations,
      452
  commodity and money rela-
      tions in view of, 531

Marx, Karl (*cont.*)
  and equal rights, 180
  on evolutionist interpretation
      of his theory, 548–50
  on his not being a Marxist, 503
  ideological changes in view of,
      521–23
  on intensification of labor,
      237–38
  and labor vouchers, 60
  Lenin on theory of, 22, 502
    See also Lenin, Vladimir
      Ilyich
  on money, 54
  and ouvrièrisme, 551–52
  on political economy, 505
  on political role of producer,
      318
  on productive power, 49
  relations analyzed by, 67
  role of state ownership in view
      of, 527
  on social production process,
      289–92
  state as viewed by, 523–26
Marxism, 501–8, 593–94
  Stalin's departure from, 510,
      511, 513–17
  tendency to identify Party
      with, 546–47
  tendency to reduce, to a form
      of evolutionism, 548–50
  worker-peasant alliance and,
      22
  See also Bolshevik Party
Marxism-Leninism, 506, 535
  as theoretical basis of Bol-
      shevism, 501
Mass movement
  ebbing of, 233–34
  rise of (1928), 228–33

Means of production
  agricultural policy and, 102
  changing forms of separation of
      working class from, 317
  expansion of industry produc-
      ing, 413–15
  financial autonomy and separa-
      tion of workers from,
      269
  growth in value of, 306–7
  joint utilization of, 99
  for peasants, 429, 430
    struggle to acquire, 94–99
    underestimation of poor and
      middle peasant farms,
      103–5
    See also Agricultural
      machinery
  value from, wage relations and,
      291
Mental-manual work, separation
      between, 565
Middle peasants (*serednyaki*), 33
  in collectives, 461–62
    See also Collectivization
  deterioration of overall situa-
      tion of (1928), 116–20
  and differentiation of peas-
      antry, 86–87
  effects of taxes in favor of,
      389–90
  exchange relations for, in NEP
      period, 136–37
  forms of struggle of, 94–101
  and goal of NEP, 189
  in grain crisis, 93–94
    agricultural policy and,
      101–7
    grain requisitioned from,
      39–41
  grain sales by, 88

increase in proportion of, 86
and Party, 337, 359
as percent of peasant population, 88
pressure on, as inadmissible, 402
productivity of, 455–56
resistance of, (1929), 121–26
and role of kulaks, 90, 359
underestimation of farms, of, 103–5
Mikhailovsky, N., 548–49
Mikoyan, A., 39, 65, 375
Mir (village), 87, 101
associated ideas of farm independence and solidarity within, 180–81
idea of autonomy of, 176–78
idea of equality within, 178–80
in peasant ideology, 174–78
small-scale industry under, 201
Mode of production, as principal form of social development, 512
Molotov, V., 99, 103, 105, 106, 218, 372, 553
on kulak question, 466
line supported by, 392
and new line (1928), 398, 402, 434
and united opposition, 377
Monetary system, 53–72
class consequences of 1924 establishment of, 58–59
post-1925 changes in, 59–60
process of reconstituting, 54–57
reform of, 57–61
weak degree of control of, 67–69

See also Currency; Gold standard
Money relations, 49, 269, 531–34
Monolithic principle in Party, 539–42
Municipal enterprises bank (Tsekombank), 63
Myasnikov supporters, 443

Na Agrarnom Fronte (journal), 467, 468
Narkomfin, *see* People's Commissariat of Finance
Narkomtorg (People's Commissariat of Trade), 39, 113, 210
National income
agricultural tools as percent of (1926–1927), 102
increase of (1926–1927), 388
percent of, under state and cooperative sector, 32
rate of increasing (1925–1929), 193
Nationalism, 552, 566
NEP, *see* New Economic Policy
New Economic Policy (NEP)
abandonment of, 21, 43–44, 69, 108
emergency measures and, 110
factors determining (from 1926), 205–7
final crisis of, 589–90
planning and, 80–81
concepts of, 66–67
financial autonomy under, 272–73
an immediate purpose of, 189
Party and, *see* Bolshevik Party
peasant demands in, 53

New Economic Policy (*cont.*)
  as policy of alliance between
      peasants and workers,
      21–27
  political interventions in, 74
  VSNKh role in, 77
      See also Supreme Council of
      the National Economy
New Economics, The (Preob-
      razhensky), 307, 374, 532
Ninth Party Congress (1920), 77
NOT (*Nauchnaya Organizatsiya
      Truda*), 239, 240, 557
"Notes of an Economist" (Bukha-
      rin), 407, 408, 411, 425

"October and Comrade Trotsky's
      Theory of Permanent
      Revolution" (Stalin),
      366
October enrollments, 332, 334
Oganovsky, N. P., 104
OGPU (Unified State Political
      Administration), 376
"On the Ideological Front"
      (Pletnev), 554
Opinions, purge of, 443–44
Ordzhonikidze, S., 365, 375
Organization, fight for, 537–38
Osinsky, V. V., 362, 402
Ostrovityanov, K., 212, 241, 244,
      286–88, 292, 302, 307,
      315
Osvok (special commission for
      the restoration of fixed
      capital), 79–81, 104
Outline of Political Economy
      (Lapidus and Os-
      trovityanov), 212, 241,
      286–89, 292–93, 307,
      315
Ouvrièrisme, 551–53, 562–63

Paris Commune, 524–26
Patriarchal family, 180
Peasant assemblies (*skhod*), 90,
      118
  grain procurement and (1929),
      123
  and idea of equality within the
      mir, 178
  in peasant ideology, 174–76
  struggle for socialist forms of
      labor within, 180
"Peasant Question in France and
      Germany" (Engels), 420
Peasant revolts
  1920–1921, 541
  1929, 126
Peasantry
  in barter system, 53–54
  and Bolshevik Party, 358–59
    aid given to cooperative and
      collective farming by,
      106
    distrust and disdain by
      Party, 121, 558–61
    division in Party and possi-
      ble resistance of, 435
    monetary system and rela-
      tions between state and
      peasantry, 61
    peasant ideology and, 173,
      178–82
    percent of peasants in
      (1927–1929), 165
    recruitment, 554
    and resistance of peasants to
      coercive measures,
      121–26
    relations of exteriority, 517
    weakness among peasants,
      107–8, 113–16, 163–67
  as class, 552
  class differentiation of, and

grain supply to the market, 88–89

contradictions in ideology of, 173–83

currency, state, and, 61

discouraged from seeking work in towns, 298–99

effects of financial autonomy system on, 278

effects of planning on, 80

and end of "war communism," 53

exchange relations for, in NEP period, 136–39

financial resources drawn from, 272–73
   See also Industrialization

in goods famine, 68, 69

Lenin and, *see* Lenin, Vladimir Ilyich

mir in ideology of, 174–78
   See also: Mir

monetary reform favored by, 58

overall view of (1928), 116–21

penetration of socialist ideas among, 519–21

polarization in, 86–87

problems in accumulation and evolution of consumption by, 153–58

social differentiation of, in NEP period, 95–91

statistics illustrating differentiation of (1927), 87–88

supply of industrial goods to, *see* Agricultural machinery; Industrial goods

in system of financial autonomy, 275

unemployment and rural overpopulation, 296
   See also Agriculture; Middle peasants; Poor peasants; Rich peasants; Worker-peasant alliance

Penal Code
   Article 61, 124–25
   Article 107, 38

People's Commissariat of Agriculture, 300

People's Commissariat of Finance (Narkomfin), 54, 55, 77, 78, 274
   and changes in peasantry, 86
   Gosbank and, 56
   monetary reform (1924) and, 59–60
   and new banking system, 63

People's Commissariat of Labor, 246

People's Commissariat of Trade (Narkomtorg), 39, 113, 210

Permanent revolution, 366–67

Peter the Great (Czar of Russia), 415

Petrovsky, G. Y., 564

Petty bourgeoisie, 202–3
   bourgeoisie vs. (1926), 206
   in Party membership, 333, 336, 341–42

Philosophical Notebooks (Lenin), 537

Piece wages (and piece work), 213, 241–47

Planning
   capitalist relations and, 73, 288–90, 529–34
   commerce subordinated to objectives of, 37, 38
   credit and, 64–65

Planning (*cont.*)
  development of, 73–81
  and direct relations of production, 266
  establishment of organs of, 50
  extension of, 319–21
  financial autonomy in system of, 276–83
  grain procurement
    as a basis for, 34
    shortfall in procurement, 37
  and increase in planning organs, 191–92
  increasing role of, 30
  industrial investment (1926–1927 on), 386–88
    See also Investment
  NEP conflict with, 206–7
  organs favoring big enterprises, 313
  piece work and, 245, 246
  plan counterposed to market, 529–34
  prices and, 148, 149
    See also Prices
  Sixteenth Conference and industrial, 446–54
  trade union role in, 343
  wages, productivity and, 246–47
Platform of the 4, 370
Platform of the 46, 362–64
Pletnev, 554
Political Bureau, 244, 355
  authority shifted out of, 400, 459
  clash within (1928), 398–402, 412
  kulak question in, 466
  membership of (1926), 372
  and new line (1928–1929), 421–27, 434–35

and platform of the 46, 362
Trotsky and, 365, 376
Zinoviev removed from, 375
Poor peasants (*bednyaki*), 33
  in collectives, 461–62
    See also Collectivization
  and differentiation of peasantry, 86–87
  effects of taxes in favor of, 389–90
  exchange relations for, in NEP period, 136–37
  forms of struggle of, in NEP period, 94–101
  and goal of NEP, 189
  in grain procurement crisis, 92–94
  grain requisitioned from, 39, 41
  grain sales by, 88
  Party implantation among, 337
  as percent of peasant population, 88
  productivity of, 455–56
  reduction in proportion of, 86
  and role of kulaks, 90
  underestimation of farms of, 103–5
Poor peasants' committees (*Komnezamy*; KNS), 100, 124
Population growth, 1913–1926, 29
Postyshev, P. P., 420
Positivism, 550
Poverty of Philosophy, The (Marx), 514
Pravda (newspaper), 120, 124, 253, 366, 379, 406, 407, 420, 424–46, 454, 459, 468
Preobrazhensky, E., 89, 97, 156–58, 362, 367, 401, 507

economic views of, 307, 374,
532
on exploiting pre-socialist
forms of economy, 377
law of value contrasted with
planning principle by,
531, 532
Prices
in Bolshevik ideology, 505
class effect of policy on,
139–40
commodity relations, 529–34
conditions governing pur-
chase, for agricultural
produce, 147–53
and consolidation of worker-
peasant alliance, 65
control of trade and, 203, 204
economic problems resolved
by, 65–66
effect on, of private sector
competition with state
and cooperative agen-
cies, 36
financial autonomy and, 271,
274
grain procurement agencies
and price policy, 34
See also Exports
high industrial, low agricultural, 89, 97, 135
cost of wages and, 192
policy on (1927), 385
retail prices (1928–1929),
190
rise in agricultural produce
(1926–1929), 389
scissors problem, 150–53,
189, 190, 390
ideological conception of role,
285–93
increases in (1923–1927), 30

loss of control over system of,
69
movement of (1924–1929), 68
and ownership of industry,
199, 200
policy on, to improve peasant
living standard, 389
policy on, set at end of 1927,
36–37
regulation of, 282
resolution on (1927), 383–84
retail, of industrial goods
(1928–1929), 190
selling, and cost of production
in industry, 189–92
state industry and, 199
supply and demand and, 29
and working class hostility toward "Nepmen," 205
Primitive accumulation, *see* Accumulation
Private sector
in agriculture, 32
contradiction between state
and, in trade and indus-
try, 197–208
elimination of, 206, 321
See also Rich peasants
evolution of, 199–203
grain in (1929), 110
grain procurement by, in NEP
period, 34, 35
ownership of, 199
peasant nondelivery of grain
and recourse to, 124
percent of wholesale and retail
trade in (1926–1927),
203
proletarian discontent and
reappearance of, 338
restoration of limited, 50
retail trade in, 36

Private sector (*cont.*)
  rise in prices in (1927–1929),
    68
  wholesale trade in, 35
Problems of Leninism (Stalin),
    544–45
Processing industry, production
    in (1927–1929), 28–29
Production, planning function in,
    73
  See also Planning
Production conferences (meet-
    ings), 217–22, 233
  Party inability to help, 518
  and Party members, 340
Production costs
  planned fall in (to 1932), 449
  unemployment and, 294
Production relations
  in agriculture, 135–62
  capitalist character of, 266–67
  class struggle and struggle to
    transform, 215–34
  commodity relations and,
    266–67
  and juridical forms of owner-
    ship, 527–29
Production targets, socialist emu-
    lation and, 254, 255
Productive forces
  development of, 314–19,
    509–13
  economist-technicist concep-
    tion of, technology and,
    508–19
  social development as effect of
    development, 513–17
  as source of development of
    society, 512
Productivity
  farm, 455–56
  See also Labor productivity

Profits
  in Bolshevik ideology, 505
  and evolution of employment
    and unemployment,
    293–301
  as goal, financial autonomy
    and, 270, 272, 274,
    277–82
  ideological conception of role
    of, 285–93
  ideological conception of sig-
    nificance of, by state en-
    terprises, 292–93
  investments and, 305
  net industrial (1924–1927), 194
  obsolete equipment and,
    305–6, 311
  in private sector, 198
  unemployment and, 312–13
Proletariat
  Bolshevik Party as vanguard
    of, 331
    See also Bolshevik Party
  bourgeoisie and, in NEP
    period, 32, 33, 205–6
  characteristics of, 551, 552
  coercion and development of,
    211
  disappearance of, 316–17
  increase of Soviet, 594
  and polarization in agriculture,
    86–87
  poor peasants entering, 86
  reproduction process and
    weakness of, 315–16
  rising wages and lowered liv-
    ing standard of, 314
    See also Wages
  and surplus value, 288
  tendency to identify Party with
    state and, 543–46
  wages and "real," 250

weakening of, 309–10
See also Dictatorship of pro-
letariat; Worker-peasant
alliance; Working class
Proletkult (group), 239, 240, 510,
554, 557
Prombank (bank for industry), 63
Public health, 32
health of Party activists, 340
Public libraries, books in (1913
and 1927), 31
Public works, unemployment
and, 300
Pugachev, 559
Punishment for nonfulfillment of
grain quotas, 124–36
Purchasing power, 55
Purges
need for, and effects of Party,
439–45
of rural cells, 165–67
Pyatakov, P. I., 80, 362

Rabkrin, 86, 97
Railroads, increasing tonnage
carried by, 30
Rationalization of production,
252–53
Razin, Stephan, 559
Reading, teaching, to the masses,
31
Reality, identification of theory
with, 547–48
Red Banner of Labor (Sept.
1928), 253
Religious ideas, peasant, 173–74
Repression and principle of un-
ity, 547
Republican trusts, 271
See also Financial autonomy
Requisitioning, end of, 53–54

Revolution, from above, idea of,
523–27, 550, 560, 592
Revolutionary Marxism, *see* Bolshevik Party
Rich peasants (*kulaki*), 33
benefit from gold-backed currency, 58
curbing, 384
and differentiation of peasantry, 86–87
dominate peasant assemblies,
175
eliminating, as a class, 464–72,
591
encouraged to prosper, 155–
56, 368–69
exchange relations for, in NEP
period, 137
and goal of NEP, 189
and grain crisis, 38, 39, 41, 94,
115, 187, 399
agricultural policy and,
101–7
and economic strenghtening
of, 431–32
first phase of grain procurement and sales by, 91–92
kulaks' strike, 88–90, 96, 101
heading the *mir*, 179
increasing influence of, 86,
108, 120, 338, 359, 418,
431–32, 591
independence from, of poor
and middle peasants,
99–101
means of production and,
94–99
in peasant assemblies, 177
as percent of peasant population, 88
purchase prices of technical
crops benefiting, 148

Rich peasants (*cont.*)
  restricting tendencies of, 382,
      402, 456, 590
  Right deviation and, 119, 424
  role of, in exchange, 142
  in rural assemblies, 170–72,
      179
  in rural cells of Party, 166
  social and political role of,
      89–91
  weakened middle peasants
      aiding, 118
  See also Collectivization
Right opposition, *see* Bukharin,
      N.
"Role and Functions of the
      Trade Unions, The"
      (Lenin), 215
Rouble
  problems of integrating in
      European financial sys-
      tem, 67–68
  as paper money, 60
  See also Currency
RKK (commission for settling
      labor disputes), 344
Rudzutak, Y. E., 375
Ruling power
  planning and class character
      of, 75
  See also Bolshevik Party
Rural bourgeoisie
  polarization in agriculture and,
      86–87
  See also Rich peasants
Rural cells (of Party), 165–67,
      172
Rural industry, 312, 378, 388, 555
Rural overpopulation, 296
Rural soviets, 124, 167–73
  and agrarian policy, 456
  funds available to (1927), 175

Party preference for working
      with, 179
  skhod and, 175–77
  skhod, mir and, 174–76
  small-scale industry under, 201
Russian Peasant, The (Gorky),
      558, 562
Rykov, A. I., 382
  clashes with (early 1928), 398
  line supported by, 392
  and new line (1928–1929), 402,
      407, 412, 421–23, 425–
      27, 434

Sales syndicates, 209, 275–76, 281
Sapronov, T. V., 362
Savings banks, 63
Schlichter, 296
Second Comintern Congress, 87
Second International, 501, 550
Secrecy of economic decisions,
      66
Secretariat, 40, 355, 459
Serednyaki, see Middle peasants
Settlement notes (*svoznaks*), 55
Seventh Congress of Komsomol
      (1926), 249
Seventh Congress of the Trade
      Unions (1926), 213–14,
      221, 249, 250
Shapiro, D., 200
Shock-brigades, 252, 253
Shockworkers, 252
Short-term loans, 56
Shvernik, N. M., 345
Sixteenth Party Conference
      (1929), 121–22, 165, 235,
      241, 422, 433–57, 523
Sixth Congress of the Comintern
      (1928), 297, 404–6
Sixth Trades Union Congress
      (1924), 217

Sknod, *see* Peasant assemblies

Small-scale industry, 200–2, 555

Social classes, 22–23, 73, 552

Social democratic parties, 404, 405

Social development, dominant Bolshevik view of, 509–17

 appraised, 513–17

Social position criterion, 334–35

Social relations, absence of dialectical analysis of system of, 302–6

 effects, 305–6

Socialism

 NEP as possible road to, 25–26

 in one country, 367

  worker-peasant alliance and, 366–68

Socialist character of planning, 289–90

Socialist emulation, 230, 237–57, 453

Sokolnikov, G. Y., 59, 274, 370, 424

Soviet government, *see* State, the

Soviet school, transformation of, 181–83

Soviet trusts (state trusts), 268–69

 See also Financial autonomy

Soviet unions (state unions or enterprises), 268–69

 See also Financial autonomy

Soviets

 Lenin on, 543

 Party and, *see* Bolshevik Party

 working class and activity of, 346–49

 See also Rural soviets; Urban soviets

Sovkhozes, 85

 See also Collectivization

Sovnarkom, *see* Council of People's Commissars

Special commission for the restoration of fixed capital (Osvok), 79–81, 104

Speculation, grain procurement crisis and, 38, 39, 41

Stalin, Joseph, 89, 112, 297

 and Chinese revolution, 379, 380

 on development of industry (1925), 373

 in grain procurement crisis, 40

 view of application of emergency measures, 115–16

 on issue of worker-peasant alliance, 366–68

 and linearity of history, 550

 on need for criticism, 222–23

 and new line (1928–1929), 392, 398–407, 421, 425–33, 447

 offers resignation, 364

 Party and, 119, 164–65, 226–27, 336, 338, 365, 375, 377–78, 380–81, 509–17, 539, 544–45, 558

 and peasantry, 118, 167–71, 382, 462, 463, 468–70, 472, 519, 520, 560–61

 permanent revolution criticized by, 366

 principle of totality affirmed by, 536–37

 on religious ideas, 174

 socialism in one country in view of, 367

 socialist character of state enterprises as viewed by, 302–3

Stalin, Joseph (*cont.*)
  on socialist emulation, 253,
    255, 256
  state capitalism as viewed by,
    371–72
  state ownership and, 528
  view of world situation by
    (1928), 404–5
  and workers, 192, 218–19, 222,
    224–26, 230–31, 438
State, the
  capital accumulation and, 76
  and collective forms of peasant
    organization, 101
    and function of Gosplan,
      77–78
  Lenin and, *see* Lenin, Vladimir
    Ilyich
  Party conception of role of,
    523–27
  policy error toward peasants,
    grain and, 96
    industrial goods for peasants
      and, 98–99
  state framework for activity of
    working class, 552
  tendency to identify Party with
    proletariat, 543–46
State bank, *see* Gosbank
State capitalism, 210–12, 291,
    293, 303, 370–72
State commercial organs, 144,
    145
State Commission for the Elec-
    trification of Russia
    (Goselro), 77, 78
State and cooperative organs
  in grain procurement crisis,
    92–93
  sale of industrial goods by, 209
  trade controlled by, 203–4

State farms in NEP period, 85
State industry, *see* Industry
State ownership, 209–65, 527–29
State Planning Commission
    (Gosplan), 64, 243, 362,
    447, 529
  formed, 76
  function of, 77–79
  and grain procurement crisis,
    93
  monetary illusion of, 533
  Osvok and, 80
  and Sixteenth Party Confer-
    ence, 448
State Political Administration
    (GUP), 466
State and Revolution, The
    (Lenin), 523, 524
State sector, 32, 197–265
Stockbreeding, 42
Strikes, 243, 344–45, 370, 541
  Apr.–June 1928, 229
  1926–1928, 344
  piece work and, 243, 244
Strong, Anna Louise, 467
Strumilin, S. G., 87, 88, 280, 296,
    389, 451
Subsistence farming, 140
Surplus labor, 49
Surplus value, 288, 293, 319
Supreme Council of the National
    Economy (VSNKh), 209,
    213, 221, 268, 276, 375,
    385, 411
  financial autonomy and, 274,
    279
  function of, 76, 77
  Gosplan and, 78
  industrial plan (1928) and, 407
  industrial trusts subordinate
    to, 271

large-scale industry plans and, 447

and new line (1928), 417

Osvok and, 79–81, 104

piece work and, 245, 246

procedure for drawing up the plan, 281

production conferences and, 219–20

in scheme of financial autonomy, 269

socialist emulation and, 251

three-shift work and, 228

workers criticized by, 230

worker criticism and, 232

Syrtsov, S. I., 121

Tardiness, *see* Labor discipline

Tax-in-kind, replacing requisitioning, 53–54

Taxes
coercion to collect (from 1928), 138–39

hard, 124–25

individual, 117, 118

by land community, 175

of poor and middle peasants
abatement of, 87
constraints to pay, 137
effects of, in favor of, 389–90

reduced agricultural, 93, 369

and reintroduction of money, 54

Taylor, 238

Taylorism, 237–57

Technicians, *see* Experts; Management

Technology, 312, 517–19
economist-technicist conception of productive forces and primacy of, 508–19

increasing role ascribed to, 477

and industrial development, 414–15

labor discipline and type of development in, 314–15

Marx on, 515, 516

planning and development of, 75

and reconstruction of agriculture, 415–18, 429–31

role of, in Party ideology, 555–58

social relations changed through, 553

See also Agricultural machinery

Teleological conception of economic development, 279–80

Third Congress of Soviets, 564

Third International, *see* Comintern

Thirteenth Party Conference (1924), 57, 215, 217, 363, 364

Thirteenth Party Congress (1924), 106, 204, 542, 553, 562–63

Time-and-motion study, 214

Tomsky, M. P., 218, 235–36, 249, 345, 372
line supported by, 392
and new line (1928–1929), 398, 402, 407, 412, 421, 423, 425–27, 453
and wage differentials, 250

Totality, principle of, 536, 538–42

Towns
disturbance of relations be-

Towns (*cont.*)
    tween country and, 41,
        110–13
    See also Grain procurement
Gorky on townsmen, 558–59
new forms of bonds between
    country and, 429–30
in peasant ideology, 174,
    177–78
peasant mistrust of, 167
poor and middle peasants pro-
    visioning, 88, 89
priority give to, in consumer
    goods, 391
procurement crisis as crisis of
    relations between coun-
    try and, 188
Trade
    contradiction between private
        and state sectors in,
        197–208
    disadvantageous terms of, for
        agriculture, 74
    1923–1924 and 1924–1927
        turnover, 30
    ownership in sphere of, 203–5
    percent of turnover, under
        state and cooperative
        sectors, 32
    retail, in industrial goods in
        rural areas, 145–47
    retail, state and cooperative
        agencies in, 36
    state and cooperative, 35–37
    wholesale, concentrated in
        state and cooperative
        sector, 35–36
    See also Exports; Imports
Trade unions, 202
    broadening mass base of, and
        independence of,
        342–46

cadres of, 343
class struggle and role of,
    215–17
collective agreements with,
    242
discouraging peasants coming
    to towns for work,
    298–99
in financial autonomy system,
    271
and labor discipline, 235
noninterference by, in man-
    agement, 234
piece wages and, 243
piece work and, 245, 246
power over organization of
    labor taken from, 557
in production conferences,
    217–22
question of, at Fourteenth
    Party Conference,
    372–74
role of, in industrialization
    (1929–1932), 452–54
socialist emulation and, 254
in strikes, 344–45
and three-shift work, 229
wage differentials and, 249–50
of Western countries, 404, 405
and work norms, 213–14, 245,
    246, 343, 344
Trades Union Council, 254
Trotsky, Leon, 46, 363–67, 372,
    374–82, 421, 435, 553
Trotsky Archives, 412
Trotskyism, 157, 365, 377, 407–9,
    412, 435, 443–44, 454,
    507
Trotskyist-Zinovievist opposi-
    tion, 90
Tsekombank (municipal enter-
    prises bank), 63

Twelfth Party Conference (1922), 105
Twelfth Party Congress (1923), 288, 543

Ulyanova, Maria, 459
Unemployment, 293–306, 311–14, 449
Unified State Political Administration (OGPU), 376
United opposition, 374–82
United States, 276
Unity, primacy of, over contradiction, 543–47
Unity of opposites, 537
Urban soviets, 201, 347–48
Use value, 267–68, 307, 433

Value, 49
  in Bolshevik ideology, 505
  crop, paid in relation to farm implements and animals, 98
  exchange, 433
  law of, contrasted with planning principle, 531–32
  price, wages and, 286, 290–91
  relating to wages, 242
  transfer of, to industry, 74
  use, 267–68, 307, 433
Varga, Eugène, 297
Village, *see: Mir*
Voluntarist illusions, 389, 526–27
Voroshilov, K. Y., 365, 372
VSNKh, *see* Supreme Council of the National Economy
VTsIK (All-Union Central Executive Committee), 347–48, 355
Wages
  in Bolshevik ideology, 505

commodity relations and, 529–34
contradictions in policy on, 390–92
and evolution of employment and unemployment, 293–301
in financial autonomy system, 272
grain prices affecting real, 149
ideological conception of role of, 285–93
increasing, 193, 213, 243–44
industrialization and lowering of real, 235
labor productivity and, 192–93
level of, unemployment and, 313–14
piece, 241–47
planned rise in (to 1932), 449
shortened work day and same, 228
sliding scale of, 55
splits in working groups and inequality of, 247–51
work norms and raised, 243
See also Collective agreements
Work day
  shortened, 228
  three-shift, 228–29
Work norms, 235, 241–47
  CLI and, 241
  fixed from above, 213–15, 228
  socialist emulation and, 254–56
  trade union role in, 213–14, 245, 246, 343, 344
Worker-peasant alliance, 361–97
  collectivization and, 126, 468, 472
  See also Collectivization
  contradictory forms of, 30–33

Worker-peasant alliance (*cont.*)
  cost of wages of workers and,
      192
  distrust of peasantry and,
      558–61
  effect on, of retreat from NEP in
      trade and industry, 205
  effect of monopolistic compe-
      tition on, 276
  emergency measures and, 108
  exchange conditions influence
      on, 136
  financial autonomy and, 278
  and forecasts of plans (to 1932),
      450, 451
  and grain crisis, 33–34, 114, 116,
      188
    See also Grain procurement
  growing deterioration of (1929),
      458
  and imperialist attack on Soviet
      Union, 419–20
  and industrialization at expense
      of peasantry, 408
  and means of production, 98–99
  NEP as policy of, 21–27, 189
  1923–1924, 361–64
  1924–1925, 364–74
  1925–1927, 374–92
  and Party, 24, 31, 32, 119, 164,
      357, 358, 456, 507
  price stability and, 149
  and resistance of peasants
      (1929), 122
  scissors effect of price policy on,
      150–51
  as tactical rather than strategic
      necessity, 560
  weakened (1939s), 594

Workers' control, 221
Working class
  mass movement (1928)
      ebbing, 233–34
      rise of, 228–33
  and Marxism, 501–8
  organizational forms of,
      330–54
  Party and, relations of exterior-
      ity, 517
    See also Bolshevik Party
  in private industry, 200
  role of, in economic develop-
      ment toward socialism,
      66
  role of, in management,
      216–22
  socialist ideas among, technol-
      ogy and, 520, 521
  soviets and, *see* Soviets
World market, gold standard and,
      58–59

Yakovtsevsky, 590
Yaroslavsky, Y. M., 440, 444
"Year of Great Change, A" (Sta-
      lin), 462

Zasulich, Vera, 549
Zinoviev, G., 364
  policy criticisms by (1925),
      369–72
  policy on recruitment to Party
      and, 553
  rallying intelligentsia, 563–64
  on the state, 544
  Trotsky and, 364
  in united opposition, 374–82